D1201364

PLATE I

THE ANCIENT OF DAYS
(*Daniel vii*)

William Blake

Here the Grand Geometrician of the Universe—the Supreme Geometer to Milton and other seventeenth-century writers (see Chapter XVII)—is describing with his compasses the "world's destined orb."

By courtesy of the Whitworth Art Gallery, Manchester

FREEMASONS' GUIDE AND COMPENDIUM

FREEMASONS' GUIDE AND COMPENDIUM

BERNARD E. JONES
P.A.G.D.C.
LATE MEMBER OF QUATUOR CORONATI LODGE

WITH THIRTY-ONE PLATES IN HALF-TONE AND
MANY LINE ILLUSTRATIONS IN THE TEXT

WITH A FOREWORD BY
J. HERON LEPPER
LIBRARIAN AND CURATOR FREEMASONS' HALL 1943-52

NEW AND REVISED EDITION

CUMBERLAND HOUSE
NASHVILLE, TENNESSEE

Dedicated in affection
to my Mother Lodge,
The Pen and Brush No. 2909

FREEMASON'S GUIDE AND COMPENDIUM
NEW AND REVISED EDITION
First published in Great Britain 1950 by George G. Harrap & Co.
New and revised edition published in Great Britain in 1994 by Eric Dobby Publishing Ltd.
4 The Old School
South Street, Barming
Kent ME16 9EY

Reprinted 1950, 1951, 1952, 1953
New and Revised Edition 1956
Reprinted 1957, 1959, 1961, 1963, 1967, 1970, 1973, 1975, 1977, 1979, 1980, 1982

The new and revised edition published in 1994 by Eric Dobby Publishing Ltd.
Reprinted 2001, 2005

First Cumberland House edition published in 2006
Cumberland House Publishing, Inc.
431 Harding Industrial Drive
Nashville, Tennessee 37211

This edition for sale in North America only.

© Copyright Eric Dobby Publishing Ltd.

All rights reserved. No part of this book may be reproduced or transmitted in any form or by
means, electronic or mechanical, including photocopying and recording, or by any informati
storage and retrieval system, without permission in writing from the publisher, except for bri
quotations in critical reviews and articles.

ISBN-13: 967-1-58182-560-2
ISBN-10: 1-58182-560-9

Library of Congress Control Number: 2006927657

Printed by Gopsons Papers Ltd., India

Foreword
by the late

JOHN HERON LEPPER, P.G.D.

LIBRARIAN AND CURATOR TO THE
UNITED GRAND LODGE OF ENGLAND 1943–52

It gives me great pleasure to introduce Brother Bernard Jones to what I am confident will prove an ever-increasing circle of those interested in the history and antiquities of the Craft of freemasonry.

The aim of this book is to make available in a convenient form and size all those advances in our knowledge due to masonic historians and students of research during the past sixty years. That knowledge is scattered through a great variety of books and pamphlets, and no small amount of time and trouble has gone to the making of what might justly be termed a handbook of masonic lore.

The book is unique in that it provides the man who has small leisure for extensive reading with the essence and marrow of what has been accomplished in two generations of masonic scholarship—generations, moreover, that have produced the greatest names in this field of study.

While the contents of this book consist in the main of hard fact supported by appropriate evidence, the author in pursuing his design has had to refer to various theories, sometimes conflicting, that have at different times enjoyed popular support. To my mind he has approached this phase of his subject with admirable discretion, setting forth the hypotheses and then leaving the reader, after examination of the pros and cons, to form his own judgment about their credibility. He acts as an expositor, not as an iconoclast or partisan.

That being the scheme of the book, it will be patent to every reader of intelligence that the writer of this foreword is in no sense responsible for any of the opinions to be found in it. I must, however, express the gratification I feel that Bernard Jones has joined the band of those who are trying with proper discretion and caution to spread more light among the collective members of the masonic Order.

AUTHOR'S NOTE
TO
NEW EDITION

ALTHOUGH an individual preface to this revised edition is hardly called for, I am availing myself of the opportunity of expressing my gratitude for the generous reception so widely given to the first edition of my book by readers everywhere and in particular by masonic students whose kindly criticisms and suggestions I have found most helpful. This edition contains some minor corrections, certain revisions made in the light of recent research, and, in addition, numerous notes mostly devoted to useful points suggested in readers' letters.

I record with sorrow the deaths, since the publication of my first edition, of the Rev. Herbert Poole and of a much older friend, J. Heron Lepper, both of them masons of fine quality, Past Masters of the Quatuor Coronati Lodge, and of such high esteem in masonic authorship that the whole fraternity will long be under obligation to them; as for my own debt, I have no words in which to acknowledge all that their help has meant to me.

This new edition goes forth accompanied by my sincere wish that it will be of real help not only to many of my old readers but to an ever-widening circle of new ones.

B.E.J.

PREFACE

THE addition of one more book on freemasonry to the many thousands already in existence must invite a very proper question. Is it wanted? If not, there can be no excuse for publishing it. Let the reader judge when I say that my real object in writing it has been to provide the young mason with a concise, simply worded, and comprehensive guide to the Craft, an explanation of everything in the growth and present practice of freemasonry that (with masonic propriety) can be discussed in print. This book is intended for the ordinary member of the ordinary lodge, who usually has neither time nor facilities for making a regular study of freemasonry yet feels a definite need of instruction, but I hope that the serious student will find in it a few things new to him and possibly some ideas that will provoke his thought.

The lack of a book on the lines of this present one must have been felt by every young mason who wishes, for example, to assure himself as to the exact nature of freemasonry's claim to be an ancient system and who seeks a clear view of the rise and emergence of speculative masonry, a view not rose-coloured by romantic fictions or overlaid with hoary fallacies; who wants to know how the system of masonic government developed, how the appointments of his lodge were derived, how the rituals came to assume their form, and whence came the many curious masonic customs and how they have been influenced in the course of history.

Robert Freke Gould, still the greatest name in masonic literature, said in 1885, "The few students of our [masonic] antiquities address themselves, not so much to the Craft at large, as to each other. They are sure of a select and appreciative audience, and they make no real effort to popularize truths. . . ." His words apply with nearly as much force to-day as when he wrote them, and the need to do what the older students have largely left undone is no small part of the inspiration that led me to my task and maintained me in the doing of it.

Every mason has received the injunction to make a daily advancement in masonic knowledge, but he seldom or never has an easy means of doing so. I trust this book will provide that means, that it will serve to enlarge or even open up the young mason's interest and give him a

7

new joy in masonry, and that in hundreds of lodges lecturers will find in my pages material upon which they can base modest and plainly worded talks of a kind which I know, from my own personal experience, the brethren welcome and appreciate.

I did not decide to write this book until I had assured myself that what I had in mind was what my brethren in the lodges did in fact need, and that I either had or could acquire the necessary qualifications for the task. Although I had been long aware that such a book was wanted, it was not until I had had heart-to-heart talks with Brother J. Heron Lepper that I determined to devote a few of my remaining years to the task of writing it. Brother Lepper did two things. He finally convinced me of the need for the book. As Librarian and Curator at Freemasons' Hall, as the Treasurer of Quatuor Coronati Lodge, as a masonic authority and historian, and as one to whom freemasons all over the world go for information, he had a unique qualification to advise as to the kind of book I should write. Of his rich store of advice he gave freely and gladly, and I well know that the thanks I now tender him must inevitably be inadequate. I particularly appreciate his kindness in writing a foreword to this book. The second thing he did was to assure me, from a personal knowledge based upon an editorial association a score of years back, that he believed I was the man to attempt what both of us, as book craftsmen, knew to be a considerable task—one calling for hard work, steady application, wide yet critical reading, a flair for explanation, and ever a clear vision of the purpose that inspired the original intention.

As to my qualifications, I was initiated in 1905 in a lodge consisting almost entirely of authors, journalists, and artists, and in due course passed to the chair and to the Royal Arch and Mark Degrees. I have had thirty years as Secretary of my mother lodge, a particularly rich and useful experience. As it so happens that I have spent fifty years in the editorial production of books and journals dealing with a variety of practical subjects, including architecture and building, all written from the one point of view of instructing the uninformed reader, it should follow that I ought to have some acquaintance with the art of teaching by the printed word. May it prove that my craftsmanship is equal to my high purpose!

The point may fairly be stressed that this book presents in general an essentially modern treatment. The old-fashioned masonic books so often tell a story that is more romantic than factual, and repeat fallacies that should long ago have died a natural death. They have a way of mixing up fact and fiction so that only a well-versed student can safely pick his way through them, and they tend to give new life to unreliable stories and ideas that were either invented or put into new dress by Anderson in his *Constitutions* of 1723. Fallacies die hard, very hard indeed.

This book, being based as far as possible on modern research, is believed to be as authentic as the present state of knowledge permits, and the fact that it has been read in manuscript by Brother the Rev. Herbert Poole and one chapter of it ("Initiation") in proof by Brother Fred L. Pick is in itself an assurance on this point. Both of these brethren are well-known authorities and Past Masters of Quatuor Coronati Lodge. Brother Poole is the editor of its *Transactions*, and the author of many contributions to masonic literature; while Brother Pick is editor of the *Transactions of the Manchester Association for Masonic Research*, and is also an experienced masonic author. My warm thanks are due to both of them.

Failing the explanation I am now about to make, Brother Herbert Poole might be fathered with certain opinions for which he may have no use. It so happens that in one or two matters relating to the emergence and early history of speculative masonry, particularly Scottish, I have been led to take views with which Brother Poole is not always in sympathy. Where I have failed, in spite of all his patience, to see eye to eye with him, I have tried fairly to present both sides of the question, but my readers will understand that in no case should Brother Poole be saddled with opinions here given other than those to which his name is attached.

The scope of this book is believed to be far wider than that of any explanatory work yet offered to the English-speaking mason, a claim which a glance at the List of Contents—or even at the Index, containing more than seven thousand items—will, I think, confirm. Obviously the book includes a considerable amount of historical matter, but I offer it to the Craft as an explanatory rather than as an historical work. While I have written chiefly for my brethren in the lodges, I have addressed two long and special chapters to Royal Arch and Mark Masons; in them and in many earlier chapters they will find much to help them to understand the rise and development of the degrees in which they are specially interested. With regard to the many additional degrees, lack of space has forced me to content myself with no more than a brief introduction and list.

In immediate preparation for the writing of this book I spent more than a year in reading and in the making of notes. Boswell told Dr Johnson "that the greatest part of a writer's time is spent in reading, in order to write; a man will turn over half a library to make one book." That certainly is true in my case, for I found it necessary to read, or at any rate to consult, many hundreds of books, and to digest whatever in them offered itself to my purpose.

Some readers may object to the length of the book. I wish it were smaller, and I tried hard to make it so but failed, although I could easily, time permitting, have made it many times larger. My problem was to decide what I dare omit, and in this regard I worked to one criterion: would the information in question help the young mason to a better understanding of his Craft? If the answer was yes, then I did my best to include it. I may be asked why the reader is expected to plough through sections telling the story of architecture, medieval operative masonry, and the medieval guilds, a question I might evade by saying that he can easily skip them if he so wishes, although I am convinced that later he will turn to them as he comes to realize that in the Gothic period of English building and in the life of the guilds and other fraternities that flourished in its day the roots of modern speculative masonry have many a tenacious hold. But let any impatient reader make a start, if he so wishes, with the chapter on the London Company and the Acception, or with the following one on the emergence of speculative masonry, thus beginning the story in the seventeenth century; I feel sure that, in time, he will feel obliged to turn back to the earlier pages.

The foundation of my masonic reading was Gould's three-volume *History of Freemasonry* (1884-1887), in the production of which the author had the help of many fine masonic scholars who later came together to found the world's premier lodge of masonic research (Quatuor Coronati). The young mason generally finds Gould hard going, but his work is undoubtedly, and always has been, the outstanding history of freemasonry, and I gratefully acknowledge my indebtedness to it. On Gould I founded my masonic education. On *Ars Quatuor Coronatorum*, the Transactions of Quatuor Coronati Lodge, No. 2076, I carried it further. Since the 1880's members of that Lodge have been patiently collecting and sifting masonic evidence and communicating the results in the form of papers read to the Lodge and afterwards printed in the annual transactions. I made myself acquainted with the contents of well over fifty volumes of those transactions before I wrote a word, and I frankly confess that so very much of what is authentic in my book was originally communicated to the Quatuor Coronati Lodge. In common with all other masonic writers, I was remarkably fortunate in having such a source of information to my hand, and in being able, at will, to pick the best brains in English-speaking freemasonry—and to pick them, in my particular case, on behalf of younger brethren seldom if ever able to find time for such a lengthy task.

Next comes my heavy indebtedness to *Miscellanea Latomorum*—the masonic 'Notes and Queries'—a most valuable little print which unfortunately has found the difficulties of the times too much for it and has now temporarily closed down to await easier conditions. I have also found useful the transactions of some of the societies for masonic research in particular those of the Merseyside Association. I have referred to many Lodge histories and have consulted and abstracted a considerable number of books on freemasonry, as well as a host of books not specifically masonic. The bibliography at the end of the book includes at best only a selection from the many works to which I have gone for help.

My method in writing this book has been to elucidate the facts of masonic history, tradition, and lore where I could do so, rather than indulge in imaginative conjecture. Facts are better than guesses, better than imagination; but all three have their place when we come to consider matters in which knowledge of some of the facts died long ago with the brethren concerned in them—brethren who did not make records or, at any rate, refused to keep them. Every masonic author must have a proper regard for tradition, for in it is "a nucleus of truth to be sought diligently." The story of freemasonry is not a simple catalogue such as one may read of the names and personalities of the kings and queens of England. Parts of the story are missing where they are most needed, just where we have the keenest desire to know what happened. Obviously there is no finality in a great many of the subjects discussed. Learned authors have been arguing over them for a century or more, and will go on arguing, so we must ever be on our guard against pronouncing what pretends to be a final verdict. There is yet so much to learn.

While I have naturally had first in my mind my brethren of the English lodges, I have taken great care to see that the book contains much of direct appeal and usefulness to the Irish and Scots freemason, to the freemasons of the Dominions overseas, as well as those of the many thousands of lodges in the U.S.A. It must never be forgotten that the story of English and Scottish freemasonry in the sixteenth and seventeenth centuries is actually the story of the emergence of *World* freemasonry, and that every one of the scores of thousands of speculative lodges throughout the world is a daughter—though perhaps many places removed—of the handful of English, Irish, and Scottish lodges working in those same centuries.

It has been a source of great happiness to me that I have been writing a book designed to help my brother masons. The Right Hon. Winston Churchill has said that

> writing a long and substantial book is like having a friend and companion at your side, to whom you can always turn for comfort and amusement, and whose society becomes more attractive as a new and widening field of interest is lighted in the mind.

He clothes in eloquent words an experience which in great good fortune came to me. My book was a friend and companion all through the period of its production, every chapter a new pleasure, a welcome endeavour.

A word now on one or two practical matters that require explanation. Reference in much later pages to the *Constitutions* means the 1940 edition of the *Constitutions* of the United Grand Lodge of England. *A.Q.C.* means *Ars Quatuor Coronatorum*, the Transactions of the Quatuor Coronati Lodge, No. 2076. A bare reference to "Gould" means Gould's original three-volume *History of Freemasonry*. I make hundreds of references to 'Antients' and 'Moderns.' I spell the ordinary word 'ancient,' carrying the ordinary meaning, always with a 'c,' even when I quote the word from sources in which the word is spelt with a 't.' But I allude to the opponents of the Premier Grand Lodge of England as 'Antients,' and never by any chance as 'Ancients,' quite regardless of how the word is spelt in any source from which I may be quoting. Similarly, the ordinary word 'modern' carries the ordinary meaning, but the appellations 'Antient' and 'Modern' are always given with capital letters and in single quotation marks, as in this present sentence.

Much of my four years of work in producing this book has been done in the Library and Museum at Freemasons' Hall, London, where Brother J. Heron Lepper and his staff patiently and generously afforded me many facilities. To the Assistant Librarian, Brother W. Ivor Grantham, and the assistant Curator, Brother Henry F. D. Chilton, I am deeply obliged for all their help and for all the trouble taken on my behalf (and very much on my readers' behalf) so readily and courteously.

For permission to use the photographs, prints, etc., comprising the thirty-one full-page plates, I am under a chief obligation to the Grand Lodge of England and to the Quatuor Coronati Lodge, and I have also to acknowledge my indebtedness to the Grand Lodge of Scotland; the Britannic Lodge, No. 33; Brothers H. Hiram Hallett and Bruce W. Oliver; and the Whitworth Art Gallery, Manchester. With regard to the line illustrations in the text, I wish to thank an architectural student, Herbert F. Day, for going to the trouble of making a number of special drawings to meet my needs.

I must confess that, in spite of all the care taken to avoid blemish and error, it is quite unlikely that a book of this particular kind could be immune from the perils that beset the printed word, and it would be idle to suppose that it does not present many opportunities for criticism. Well, Dr Johnson thought it was advantageous to an author that his book should be attacked as well as praised! I can only repeat that I have done my best to produce a plainly worded but authentic book of wide scope to meet the needs of young and intelligent brethren anxious to make a daily advancement in masonic knowledge—and, for the rest, let me beg the never failing indulgence of the Craft.

BOLNEY   B. E. J.
SUSSEX

CONTENTS

BOOK ONE

OPERATIVE MASONRY AND THE LONDON COMPANY

BOOK TWO

SPECULATIVE MASONRY

BOOK THREE

THE GRAND LODGES (1717–1813)

BOOK FOUR
THE CRAFT DEGREES AND OTHER MATTERS

BOOK FIVE
THE LODGE AND MANY RELATED SUBJECTS

BOOK SIX
THE ROYAL ARCH, MARK MASONRY, AND ADDITIONAL DEGREES

ILLUSTRATIONS

PLATES IN HALF-TONE

15

ILLUSTRATIONS IN THE TEXT

BOOK ONE

Operative Masonry, and the London Company

Chapter One

THE FREEMASON'S
SHORT OUTLINE OF ARCHITECTURAL MASONRY

THE allegories that veil freemasonry, as also the symbols that illustrate it, are, as readers of this book well know, drawn from the lore of architecture and building. Freemasonry has two histories—the one, legendary and traditional, going back almost to the dawn of architecture; the other, authentic, covering a period of a few hundred years and deriving in some part from the ancient craft guilds and fraternities whose fortunes rose and fell in England with the Gothic period; in that particular period are believed to lie the main roots of world freemasonry.

The freemason can well afford to spare a few minutes in which to acquaint himself with a mere outline of architectural development and see for himself how 'English Gothic' came into being.[1]

When the draughty hovels of prehistoric man, roughly built of stones or thrown together with boughs and mud, began in the course of ages to assume some vestige of form and proportion, then was architecture born, and civilization started on its long journey. "The perception of beauty and deformity is the first thing which influences man to attempt to escape from a grovelling, brutish character."

Old-fashioned writers used to say that the Egyptians learnt architecture from the cavern, the Chinese from a bamboo-framed tent, the Greeks from a flat-roofed hut, and the Gothics from a grove of trees. This is no more than plausible, even if it be that, but it can be shown that architecture soon outdistanced any mere copying of natural and other simple forms, and grew, through six thousand years or so, to become the world's supreme art, comprising in its ultimate development a whole group of

[1] Many authorities have been consulted for the detailed information presented in this chapter, and mention must particularly be made of the 1909 edition of Professor F. M. Simpson's three-volume *History of Architectural Development* (Longmans Green), a brilliant and valuable treatise.

subsidiary arts. Masonry, which is associated chiefly with building in stone, is one of the chief of those arts.

An extremely brief glance at prehistoric masonry suffices to show that from the very dawn of the mechanical arts thousands of years ago the mason was active.

Remains of a few of the more massive examples of his work have come down to us. The monoliths are upright stones, one of which in Brittany is 63 feet high and weighs about 250 tons; sometimes they support table stones, or cromlechs, weighing up to 10 tons. In the ancient cities of Tiryns and Mycenæ are stone walls 25 feet thick and 60 feet high, built with blocks 9 feet long and surfaced in such a way as to make very tight, thin joints, even without the help of mortar. We call the unknown builders of these great walls giants, or Cyclops. There was much mighty building in Mexico and Peru thousands of years ago. The great temple at Palenque was 230 feet long and 180 feet wide; some retaining walls discovered in Peru are said to be no less than 225 feet thick and 108 feet high, and in walls elsewhere are found built-in stones as long as 27 feet, 14 feet deep, and 12 feet high, weighing about 28 tons, cut, shaped, and placed in position with extreme accuracy.

Eastern Architecture

So far as we know, Babylonia and Assyria were among the first of all the Eastern builders, but, unfortunately, in their very early days they built in brick of poor quality which returned in the course of centuries to the clay from which it had been made. When at a later stage they used more permanent materials we know from the remains brought to light by excavation that, as builders, these early people were of considerable worth. The proportions of their narrow, rectangular buildings, their handsome columns and lintels—all these are regarded as the real inspiration of Greek architecture.

In Babylon there was a great temple with alabaster floor-slabs measuring nearly 20 feet by 12 feet. The ancient Persians built in timber, but when their descendants built in stone they produced some massive work; the palace Chehil Minare, for example, had retaining walls over 1400 feet long, built of immense stones and supporting a raised platform, approached by what is regarded as the finest double staircase in the world.

Egypt. Building in Egypt must have been among the earliest in the world, and is the first of which we have written record. As builders, the Egyptians had both material and labour in their favour. Unlimited material—if not in their own country, then in bordering countries, such as Arabia, from which came, or so we are told, the great blocks of stone

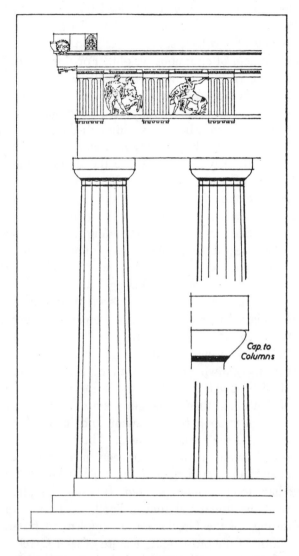

COLUMNS, SINGLE-BLOCK CAPITALS, AND FRIEZE
OF THE DORIC ORDER, THE MOST MASSIVE AND
DIGNIFIED OF THE THREE ORDERS

Drawn by Albert Lakeman

with which the Pyramids were built. Unlimited labour—slaves and serfs
compelled by brute force to do work at considerable risk to life and
limb. Overseers and artificers were well trained and highly skilled; the
rest was simply the organized and ruthless direction of slave labour. In

honour of the dead whom they worshipped the Egyptians built great tombs, the Pyramids, the largest of which has a base 768 feet square and a height originally of 490 feet, some of the stones of which it is built being 30 feet long and of enormous weight. For this one pyramid, it is said, it took twenty years to bring the stones from Arabia.

Long before written history the Egyptians were building temples in each of which a forest of columns supported a flat stone roof, the arch not then being used in great buildings, although the Egyptians did have arches, elliptical ones of brick, probably restricted to use in minor buildings. All architecture may be divided into the styles of the entablature (the joist and flat roof) and that of the arch, and we shall see later that it was the clever development and use of the arch that led to the Gothic construction with which the medieval working freemason was familiar.

Palestine. The Semitic countries, including Palestine, learnt architecture from their neighbours, chiefly the Egyptians, but it is unfortunate that circumstances compelled Solomon to build his historic temple —the most famous in the world, although far from being the most magnificent—very largely of cedar wood, so that little or nothing now remains of the original fabric. His ornate temple could not vie in size and cost with the temples of rich Egypt.

Greece. The Greeks were a nation of merchants and mariners doing business with all the known world over a long period of time, and they must at an early date have learnt from Assyria, Egypt, and other countries of the East all that could then be taught them of architecture, an art in which they themselves soon became adept, and in which they are acknowledged to-day as the greatest masters. Their judgment with regard to proportion and symmetry has never been questioned. Of the early Greek temples and other buildings nothing much is known, as they were of timber and have long since disappeared. It is supposed, but sometimes questioned, that the horizontal timber lintel, or beam supported by posts (constituting for the Greeks a rude emblem of fraternal unity), was the inspiration of the outstanding feature of later Greek architecture —the pillars of exquisite design and beautiful workmanship supporting the entablature (the horizontal architrave, the frieze, and the cornice). It will be understood that the two parts of the sloping timber roof, meeting at the ridge, produced a triangular space back and front, and this had to be filled by what is known as the pediment, another Greek characteristic.

Although the arch was not used by the Greeks in the grand manner, they were well aware of its purpose, but were content to use it in a minor way; for example, over a lintel, itself supported by columns, they would place what we now know as a discharging arch, its purpose being to prevent the weight of the masonry above bearing direct upon the lintel.

Half Front Elevation
of Cap.

COLUMNS, SCROLL CAPITALS, AND FRIEZE OF
THE IONIC ORDER; OF GREAT BEAUTY AND
LIGHTER THAN DORIC

Drawn by J. Gordon Allan

It is the Greeks who originated or developed the orders of architecture
to which the attention of the freemason is often directed. By 'orders'
are known certain arrangements of construction and ornament as applied
to columns and the lintels over them; the three greatest of them—the

Doric, Ionic, and Corinthian—are illustrated. The idea of the Doric came from Egypt, and that of the Ionic from Assyria, but the Greeks so largely redesigned these two orders as to be regarded as their originators. The order which the Greeks most loved was the Doric, the most massive of the three, but more delicate, more refined, and more dignified; generally it had a fluted shaft standing on a series of steps and having no base of its own, and the tapering of that shaft, together with the slight convexing of the horizontal lines of the lintel above, was intended to correct an optical illusion. Its capital, where the shaft supports the lintel, is moulded.

The Ionic shaft, on the other hand, had a base, and on the capital were carved scrolls or volutes; this shaft was lighter than the Doric. In the Corinthian order the shaft was lighter still, and a bell-shaped capital was deeply carved with foliage; very occasionally a scroll or volute was added.

Rome. Rome's contribution to architecture was its study and general employment of the arch and its adoption of the Greek orders in modified designs. Rome had no real architecture of its own when it conquered Greece about 146 B.C., but the Romans were quick students, and were not long in becoming great architects and mighty builders. Professor Simpson remarks that the Romans, if they had had the artistic sense of the Greeks, would have been the greatest architects the world has ever seen, for their work is vast and strong, grand and lavishly decorated, but not refined, often incomplete and carelessly finished.

There are only two ways of spanning an opening: one is to put a beam across it, the other to build an arch into it. The Greeks did not use the arch in their principal buildings; instead they used columns, but had to place them close together, because the length of the beam or lintel that spanned them was limited by its own weight and the maximum load it would bear. The Romans in using the arch could space their columns farther apart. They made their buildings many storeys in height, and designed them as a combination of column, arch, and lintel; but it is the arch, and not the lintel, that as a rule gives quality to the design.

The Romans built great show palaces, fine baths, great triumphal arches, enormous amphitheatres. They built them not only in Rome and Italy, but in the colonies which they established in many parts of the known world. The Colosseum at Rome, built in the first century A.D., was $6\frac{1}{2}$ acres in extent.

The five orders of architecture familiar to the freemason were completed by the Romans. They took the three Greek orders, the Doric, Ionic, and Corinthian, and very slightly modified them, without adding to their refinement. They thickened the shaft or column of the Doric and made it into the Roman Tuscan order. They mingled the ornaments

COLUMNS, ACANTHUS-LEAF CAPITALS, AND
PLAIN FRIEZE OF THE CORINTHIAN ORDER;
THE SHAFT STILL LIGHTER THAN IN THE IONIC

Drawn by J. Gordon Allan

of the Ionic and Corinthian by replacing with small scrolls a part of the
foliage carved on the Corinthian cap, and in this way formed the
Composite.

So now we have the Doric, dignified and simple, with tapered, fluted shafts; the Ionic, with its scrolls on the capital; the Corinthian, with its carved deep foliage; the Tuscan, hardly to be distinguished from the Doric, except by its thicker shaft; and the Composite, combining the scrolls of the Ionic with the foliage of the Corinthian. There are other differences, but these are the outstanding ones.

Early Christian Architecture

The Roman Emperor Constantine the Great legalized Christianity in the year 313, and founded Constantinople in 330, but not until two hundred years later did there emerge a style of architecture peculiar to the Roman-occupied Eastern lands. In 532 the Emperor Justinian began the building of the many-domed church of St Sophia in Constantinople and dedicated it to Eternal Wisdom. St Sophia marked a new style, to which was given the name Byzantine, from the ancient Byzantium, the site on which Constantinople was built; this combined Roman and Moham-medan traditions with the beauty of Greek architecture, the East pro-viding the domes, the rich colour, and material, and the West the large scale, the bold construction, and the perfect proportion. The Byzantine style spread quickly in the East, and strongly influenced architecture in the West.

Roman and Saxon Architecture in England

The Romans gave architecture to Britain, but it did not survive. We knew little or nothing about the art before they came. At one time we thought that we knew little of anything British in pre-Roman days, but the archæologists have taught us that the Romans did not come to an entirely barbarous country. Glyn Daniel, in a B.B.C. broadcast address published in *The Listener*, says:

> We know now that the first inhabitants of Britain lived over half a million years ago, that the first farmers and stockbreeders came to our shores about 2000 B.C. We know, too, that by the time Cæsar came to Kent some of the Britons were exporting to the Continent metal, slaves, and fat stock, leather, corn, and hunting-dogs, and in return were importing wine, bronzes, and Gaulish pottery. They were using a minted coinage as well as currency bars, and maintaining artists in metal and pottery. You can see some of their splendid and complicated patterns on the Battersea Shield, for example, the Witham Sword, or the Desborough Mirror on view in the British Museum. . . . We can see now that Cæsar and the Romans do not begin the drama of British history.

The Romans built magnificent villas and many public buildings in

England, but little more remains of them to-day than a few mosaic floors, some fragments of walls, and the broken systems of piping forming part of their bath installations; their upper storeys were usually of wood.

The Roman basilica, or hall, is the original type of the Christian church. The *domus*, also known as a basilica, was the large room of the house. Any Christian churches in England when the Romans went were soon pulled to pieces by the Saxon hordes.

The Saxons, on becoming Christians, built some churches, usually if not always of wood, but the Venerable Bede tells of the building of stone churches in the county of Durham about 680, this being regarded as the starting-point of the history of architecture in England. There were stone churches at York, Ripon, and Hexham late in the seventh century.

Saxon church-builders went back to the Temple of King Solomon for some of their ideas, the buildings being preserved and ornamented by the use of plates of precious metals, and in particular of bronze. (Centuries later Glastonbury had its church of wood covered inside with plates of gold and silver, and outside with plates of lead.)

Until late in the seventh century there were few English buildings that were not of wood and thatch, and not until about the year 1000 did English architecture evolve into anything very definite—a sturdy form of Romanesque, having over-thick walls and columns and semicircular arches—but something better was to develop before the Conquest.

Alfred the Great, late in the ninth century, and Canute, a few generations later, visited Rome, and it is more than likely that they were influential in bringing to England foreign craftsmen; masons may have come from Germany, Burgundy, and France, and carvers from Italy. Says one writer with great truth, "The world was surprisingly small in those days, notwithstanding the difficulty of travelling."

The work of the builder suffered a setback in the tenth century owing to a general belief among Christians of the day that the world was to come to an end in the year 1000.

Before the Conquest there was in England a style which we may call the Anglo-Saxon or pre-Conquest-Romanesque, and even after the Conquest, for some years, churches were being built in that style.

Norman masons occasionally worked on English churches during the pre-Conquest period, and it should be remembered that it was probably easier to travel from Normandy to England than to make any long journey by road in England itself.

Following the year 1000 an enormous number of churches and monasteries began to be built in Italy, France, and England. Canute, coming to the throne in 1017, restored the monasteries and built churches, his work being carried on by Edward the Confessor, who started the building of Westminster Abbey, not completed until after the Conquest.

The Norman masons were more skilled than the Saxons, but had no thorough grasp of constructional principles. The thickness of the masonry joint tells the story of one age or style succeeding another. In England and Northern France the joint is wide and badly made in eleventh-century work, but there is a great improvement in the following century. The early Norman masons apparently knew very little of the use of the sculptor's chisel, and did their decorative cutting with an axe; as the cutting grew deeper the chisel was used.

The coming of William the Conqueror, and with him of great numbers of Norman churchmen and skilled operatives, led to a most astonishing increase in the building of churches, unparalleled in number in any similar period in any other country. The existing Saxon churches were rebuilt under the auspices of Norman ecclesiastics. For example, Canterbury Cathedral, started by a Saxon king, had much of the work razed to the ground and rebuilt in the period 1096–1110. The use of the freestone of Caen, Normandy, was one of the causes of Normandy's leading the revival of building in the eleventh century, it being easier to send stone from France to riverside towns in England than to send it by road through France, and often easier to get sea-borne Caen stone at English cathedral sites than horse-drawn stone from English quarries. When we call ourselves freemasons we may be harking back over all the centuries to the importation and use of French freestone.

English Gothic Architecture

The twelfth century had opened up the way for the coming of the Gothic style, but there is no sharp and precise date at which one style succeeded another. A change of style took half a century or more to establish itself. In general, the Romanesque or Norman style changed in the second half of the twelfth century to the Early English or Gothic style, of which the Decorated period was from the second half of the thirteenth century until late in the fourteenth century. The Perpendicular style of Gothic came from the Decorated style in the fourteenth century, went right through the fifteenth century with some changes, and continued into the sixteenth.

Evidence as to how England achieved its Gothic style is conflicting. Some people think that Gothic was but the maturing of the English Romanesque style, but obviously it was something much more than that. It is safer to regard English Gothic as the strongly Anglicized rendering of a great architectural movement which swept over Western Europe and reached England via the western and northern provinces of France. It was architecture with pointed arches, and succeeded the architecture of round arches, the chief influence leading to the introduction of the pointed arch being undoubtedly the discovery of a method of building vaulting over wide and often uneven spaces.

"The architecture of every people is an essential part of its history," it has been said. English Gothic is a thoroughly national style despite the fact that it was inspired from abroad, and has been labelled "more perfect, more pure, more systematic, better proportioned, more consistent, than the Gothic of any other country."

The Norman Conquest, by bringing about the mingling of two different peoples, was the great historic fact influencing the development of English Gothic. It must be remembered that by about 1150 roughly one-third of what now constitutes France was under English rule, and that Normandy was architecturally part of England from soon after the Conquest until late in the twelfth century. From the Continent came a deep sense of religion, a higher culture, a far greater skill in architectural construction, than the Saxons had enjoyed; by the end of the twelfth century this fact and the still greater one that the Saxons and Normans were in course of becoming one people—the *English* people—must have made inevitable a more individual growth from the old Norman-Romanesque. But G. M. Trevelyan makes clear that "the birth and general acceptance" of the English language and the happy blending of Saxon and French words into "English tongue" which "all under-standen" did not come until Chaucer's lifetime (1340–1400). It was then that "the English people first clearly appear as a racial and cultural unit."

The Crusades at the end of the eleventh century appear to have contributed something to the architecture of France and England, for in their long and tedious travels through Europe the Crusaders must have stored up many impressions to be remembered and applied on their return home.

By the turn of the twelfth century we see the early stage of Gothic in the simple lancet arch, to which were added, as the style evolved, clustered pillars, window mullions, and tracery, which, in the opinion of many architects, produced "a degree of perfection and refinement never before dreamt of." (See the illustration at p. 31.)

The Gothic columns, "with their simple moulded capitals, carried the mind back from our provincial cathedrals to the Parthenon at Athens," says Professor Banister Fletcher. Gothic had those beautifully proportioned columns, with their dignified capitals; it had in particular the pointed arch and the ribbed vaulting of the roof; and often externally the flying buttress to give strength to the walls and carry the weight and thrust of the roof.

The Gothic arch was a great step forward in technical design. The reduction of side-thrust on pillars and walls meant that the pillars could be slighter and the walls thinner, less expensive, and much better built, for the old thick walls had often been mere casings of good masonry filled in with rubble and mortar. Externally the style could be distinguished not only by its narrow lancet-shape pointed windows, but by the bold buttresses to take some of the thrust, the light pinnacles and spires, the acute pitch of the roof.

Improvement in technical design making for the growing use of vaulting over large and often unusual spaces helped the introduction of the pointed arch. Vaulting is the great pride of the Gothic masons, as in Norwich and Durham Cathedrals—the rib vaulting of worked stone as distinct from the rough barrel vaults of earlier days. True, the Normans had invented the vaulting, but their knowledge of construction was not always sufficient to provide properly for the outward (destructive) thrusts, and as a result many examples must have disappeared. Gothic architecture of the later (Perpendicular) period glories in its open timber roofs, many fine examples of which are to be found in the old Norfolk churches.

The Gothic period was remarkable for its building activity; cathedrals, castles, churches, were built in numbers, and no other period in English history can vie with it. Of all countries, says Professor Simpson, England is the most remarkable for the number, variety, and beauty of its parish churches. The whole of England was dotted with villages, and each had its own church, whereas in France, Germany, and other countries villages were few and far apart, and the people, for safety, were forced within walled cities.

It was in this great period that freemasonry had its true foundation. Gould, a conservative assessor of masonic history, believes that "in all lodge constituent elements and appointments, the track is broad and direct to a Gothic origin."

Another historic fact was to play its part, an unfortunate one. In 1349 came the Black Death, the terrible plague that destroyed nearly half the population and had its serious consequences in every phase of national and domestic life; the shortage of labour and high prices of food led to the operatives trying to get higher wages, but legislation kept wages within very restricted limits. Much building work was still proceeding —in the seventy years following 1450 some of the finest of England's churches were built—but by the middle of the sixteenth century the Gothic style of architecture was dying. It is true that even to the end

AN EXAMPLE OF GOTHIC ARCHITECTURE—PILLAR, ARCHES,
VAULTING, ETC.—BASED ON THE CHAPTER HOUSE,
SALISBURY CATHEDRAL

Drawn by H. F.

of that century we get here and there a Gothic building and many Gothic details, but by 1600 the great medieval period known as Gothic had reached its close.

The marked similarity in style in the Gothic architecture of all the Western European countries, including England, has prompted the idea that the masons in all the countries concerned must have been guided by a secret principle handed down from one generation to another. It is this similarity that has lent plausibility to the legend of the organized bands of travelling masons, armed with Papal authority, passing from one country to another, building churches here, there, and everywhere, and into all of them pouring their own spirit of design and introducing their own exclusive secrets of construction. In later pages will be shown how much this legend is worth, but in the meantime it will merely be pointed out that some architectural writers have advanced the attractive theory that the monastic schools of masonry founded in Normandy sent forth, at the behest of kings, nobles, and great churchmen, many clever Master Masons, who took charge, artistic and practical, of the erection of a number of the most notable buildings in England, and that, inevitably, these graduates, all of the same school, produced buildings having strong family likenesses. The English, perhaps more than any other people in the world, had and have a genius for absorbing any new and foreign influence reaching their shores. Thus all over Western Europe buildings were conforming to a 'Gothic' style; here, in this country, there was Gothic with a difference—an English difference.

The Successor to English Gothic

The Reformation in the sixteenth century strongly influenced Gothic and ensured its death, but the style had lost some of its purity following the reign of Henry VII when it started to introduce Italian features. In course of time Gothic developed into the Elizabethan style of mixed Gothic and Italian, and then into what we know now as the Renaissance: a style less natural, or, rather, less national, than the Gothic, but extremely graceful, reproducing something of the old classic spirit of the Greek and Roman architecture; a style of much interest to the architectural but less to the masonic student. The work of England's great architect Sir Christopher Wren was largely based on the Gothic, to which, however, he added from his own genius the classic lightness and elegance which transformed it into a style which can best be described as—Wren.

Chapter Two

THE MEDIEVAL OPERATIVE MASON

The period following the Norman Conquest gave great impetus to building. The land of England passed into the hands of kings, nobles, and a Church all able and eager to build. They introduced from Normandy, and probably elsewhere, a few skilled craftsmen, who found the Saxons extremely apt pupils. Building became the great industry of the age.

Although the position of the country craftsman of the period was that of a serf tied to his employer and to his home locality, and although the coming of the Norman brought new restrictions on his liberty, yet slowly and quietly the English craftsman progressed through the next two centuries towards a measure of greater liberty, and by the thirteenth century we find that the city craftsman had already travelled some way along the road to personal freedom and was assuming civic obligations and privileges. Many a serf of the countryside had found sanctuary in the towns, and his children, more probably grandchildren, had entered into the guild life of the period, while the great estate-owners—the king, his nobles, and the Church—had discovered the economy of giving their serfs nominal freedom, between which and the old bondage was little more than a legal distinction. But that in itself was something. England was importing from and exporting to the Continent. The country was growing richer, with some betterment of the conditions of the artisan and labourer. The population was increasing, the two millions at a date soon after the Conquest having doubled itself by the time just before the Black Death in 1348–49, which pestilence wiped out three-eighths or more of the population, and by so doing markedly influenced the condition of the labouring classes. By the 1600's, when speculative masonry began to emerge, the population of the country was between five and six millions.

Operative masonry as a real trade had its rise, we may assume, in the early years of the eleventh century, when the Saxons began to build a number of churches in the pre-Conquest style. What we know as the operative freemason came into being during the centuries following the Norman Conquest, centuries of intense building activity, in which there grew up mason customs resulting, we can well suppose, from such conditions—Douglas Knoop and his collaborators make full reference to them

—as the congregation of masons in a lodge at quarry or building site; the mingling of masons from various parts of the country, brought together at the behest of all-powerful authorities; the very small number of possible employers—that is, of employers rich enough and economically powerful enough to erect great buildings—and the system by which leading Master Masons, the King's Master Masons, and others, controlled every item of the job from the inception of the design and lay-out to the completion of the last internal fitting. All these conditions made for the growth and regularizing of masons' customs, which in time would be mentioned in the fabric rolls of the great buildings in course of construction at the end of the fourteenth century, find themselves the subject of Acts of Parliament, and be recorded or referred to in the early manuscripts which we now know as the "Old Charges." The earliest of the known manuscripts, the Regius (or Halliwell) Manuscript, is a poem written some time late in the fourteenth century giving a legendary or traditional history of the mason trade, containing an account of the seven liberal arts, and laying down for the working mason a code of manners; possibly it was written for the special purpose of being read or recited to mason gatherings.

The Quarry Mason

Masons worked in quarries, where not only did they 'get' the stone, but roughly hewed and scappled it, sometimes, no doubt, carrying the shaping and dressing through all its stages, so that the stones could be taken to the site and there built in without further tooling. The hewers used axes of cunning shape suggested by local experience. These axes were made and maintained by the blacksmith, and quite a good finish could be obtained by their use—even shallow ornament was cut with them—but in course of time there developed a higher grade of craftsman who used finer tools, chisels and the like, with which to produce the deeper and more elaborate carved and moulded work in freestone found in the churches, etc. Another class of mason was the layer or setter, who worked, of course, on the building site, and at an early period was regarded by the cutter and shaper as having a status quite inferior to his own, but that idea gave way as the centuries passed, although evidence of it was to remain in the old Constitutions, and is possibly reflected even to-day in the speculative freemason's ritual, in which the trowel, the layer's chief tool, has quite a subsidiary place.

Apprenticeship among masons must have existed in early medieval times, but there is no record of it earlier than 1356 in the London Masons' Regulations. In 1430, in the reign of Henry VI, was passed an ordinance confirming the ancient form and custom of putting and taking of apprentices, used and contained in the City of London. About 1530 a seven-years apprenticeship was fixed for the whole kingdom, a regulation not always observed, because we find the rough masons of Norwich complaining in 1512 that apprentices were redeeming their bonds at four years and even less, and that other masons were not being apprenticed at all. An apprentice out of his time and fully accepted as a craftsman was a fellow or a master in English practice, but it does not follow that the apprentice always came into the enjoyment and freedom of his fraternity, for sometimes it did not suit the masters' interest to add to the number of masons qualified to act on their own account. Unwin's *Guilds* records that masters often took apprentices without registering them, and neglected to present them for the freedom when they came out of their time, an irregularity which must have added to the semi-skilled and cheaper labour, as was exactly the case in parts of Scotland in the seventeenth and eighteenth centuries.

The Mason's Lodge

Both at quarry and attached to the building site was a lodge for the working masons. The English mason took the word 'lodge' from the French language, and we assume that the Scots took it from the English. In early mason records the word is spelt the French way, *loge*, not in any Saxon or Teutonic form. It used to be thought that the word came from the Italian word *loggia*, familiar to everybody as an open arcade or gallery, but it is not thought that the Italian word indicated either a shop or a workshop. The French *loge* is related to the Teutonic word *Laube*, an arbour, having some possible connexion with the word 'leaf,' from which we easily build up the familiar mental picture of the countryman's lodge, a rustic building in a wooded district. In many parts of England a workshop, shed, or outhouse is still called a lodge. The word occurs in England as early as 1278, where it is used in a record of Vale Royal Abbey, but lodges must have existed for hundreds of years before then. Obviously, when a building of any importance was started, the first thing to do was to erect a shed in which the workmen could dress stone, keep their tools in order, take their meals, and spend some part of their rest time.

Just a few of the many old references to the masons' lodge may be mentioned. In 1320 a man was paid to clean out the lodge at St Stephen's Chapel, Westminster. In 1321, 2s. 6d. was paid for straw to cover the lodge at Caernarvon Castle. In 1335 the workmen at York Cathedral were to take their meals within their lodge. In 1370 at York all masons were to be each day at noon "in the lodge that is ordained to the masons at work in the close beside the church." In 1369–71 there was provided a lodge for the masons at the building of Windsor Castle. Many other instances of like nature could be given. The Regius MS., dating back to about 1400, has a reference to the secrets of the mason's calling in these two lines:

The prevetyse of the chamber telle he no mon,
Ny yn the logge whatsever they done.

It is to be assumed that in most cases the lodge was a rough-and-ready affair, with possibly a boarded or thatched roof, but where the work was expected to last a man's lifetime, then a substantial lodge was built, as we infer from the records relating to the building of King Edward's Gateway, Trinity College, Cambridge, where in the first year (1426–27) the only thing done was to erect the mason's lodge or work-shop. In 1428 a record of the work at Canterbury mentions some *lathomie de la loygge*, by which is meant the freemasons—that is, the skilled masons, the cutters and shapers of stone, who used the lodge as their headquarters. In 1541 Thomas Phillips, freemason, and another contracted "to prepare, find and make a lodge or house for masons to work in during the time of making" the Coventry Cross.

In Scotland the word was not used at such an early date as it was in England. One of the earliest uses was in 1483, when six "masons of the luge" are mentioned as engaged on work at Aberdeen. In connexion with Dundee in 1536 were used the words "the ancient consuetude of the Lady luge," the name for the workroom having thus become trans-ferred to the body of masons using it. In Scotland there was a definite development of trade custom based on the lodge. Douglas Knoop and his collaborators have written much on the subject, and have been at pains to trace the growth of the lodge—that is, the body of masons in the lodge building—from being merely a body of men engaged at work on a building, to an organized body of masons (what the authors mentioned call a Territorial Lodge) charged with the oversight of masons' trade customs in a particular town or district.

Masons' Conditions after the Black Death

After the Black Death masons' customs became more firmly estab-lished, and the division into grades or classes, of which the freemason was the superior, became more apparent. Gould has pointed out that the great employers saw themselves "threatened with ruin," but quickly Parliament fixed the wages at a low mark. According to the law, whether observed or not it is difficult to say, a worker's legal wage did not vary between the years 1350 and 1370, although during that period the price of wheat varied from 2s. to £1 6s. 8d. per quarter. The Ordinance of Labourers in 1349 was confirmed and made harsher by the Statute of Labourers, in 1350, the latter providing that a master carpenter shall not take by the day for his work more than 3d., a master freestone mason more than 4d., other masons 3d. and their servants 1d., tilers 3d., and their knaves 1d.

Ten years later, in 1360, another Statute of Labourers confirmed the wages laid down in the earlier Statute, and made "void and wholly annulled" all

> alliances and covines of masons and carpenters and congregations, chapters, ordinances and oaths, betwixt them made or to be made . . . so that every mason and carpenter . . . shall be compelled by his master . . . to do every work that to him pertaining to do, or of free stone, or of rough stone.

By this Statute the artificer was obliged to work for the Statute wage, under a penalty which had been fine and ransom, but was now made imprisonment for fifteen days. A hundred and forty years later masons were earning 8d. a day; this was doubled by 1600—that is, a century later—and by 1700 the 8d. had become 32d. But this quadrupled wage bought only about 60 per cent. as much food as the mason had bought two hundred years before!

The Master Mason

The customs and conditions of medieval masonry cannot be understood without some appreciation of the duties and importance of the Master Mason, who in early days designed the building, arranged for the supply of every scrap of material, and personally directed the whole of the work. It can easily be understood that there was little important building for private purposes before the Norman Conquest. The houses of even well-to-do people were built by carpenters and plasterers rather than by stonemasons, as they were mere timber frames filled in with local material; much time elapsed before there was a chimney of stone and brick. It is only with the building of the stone churches, castles, palaces, bridges, etc., that we associate the work of the medieval freemason. The little builder, whose work provided the domestic houses, was largely dependent on local material, which he might have to buy to resell to the building owner, but the Master Mason was not a buyer and seller: he was architect, surveyor, builder, and always the employer's agent in ordering supplies of every possible kind. He was not a principal: he was a servant, a man who had a great flair for his work and naturally stood out from his fellows. He was known *at times* by a variety of names —overseer, keeper of the works, director, clerk of the works, devizor, surveyor, supervisor, magister, etc. He was the most important man in the building craft for two or three centuries, his job finally disappearing with the coming into general use of the contract system. In early medieval days no mason was well enough founded to finance the erection of an important building, and only a king, a rich church, or a great landowner could meet an outgoing which might last for a generation.

The Master Mason had a status corresponding with that of a professional man of good standing to-day. He was treated with marked respect. For example, at Bury St Edmunds the master of the masons received "board for himself in the Convent Hall as a gentleman and for his servant as a Yeoman, the gentleman's livery for himself and the yeoman's for his servant." It was quite usual to provide the Master Mason with house and clothes.

Martin S. Briggs throws much new light upon him in his excellent book *The Architect in History*.[1] Freemasons have been too ready to assume that the Gothic building was not designed by a master mind, but just grew under the hands of workmen who did more or less as they liked, or with an ecclesiastic, a sort of gifted amateur, in charge. Martin S. Briggs explains how wrong that idea is, but agrees that "the history of any great Gothic church shows that its growth was gradual, that its design was modified or altered during erection, and that to the masons employed upon it the 'slow setting of stone upon stone' was slow indeed." It is easy to see why, in the Middle Ages, the building director was a mason, for, as Martin S. Briggs reminds us, the

> medieval building of any size consisted chiefly of masons' work. Plumbing, slating, glazing, and even carpentry were only accessory to the main structure. . . . Every important structural problem involved in the building—the thrust of the vault, the counterpoise of the buttresses, the design of the tracery, the interpenetration of the mouldings—was a masonry problem.

The King's Master Masons

Great masons served the medieval kings in the capacity of Master Mason. They were architects, overseers of every detail of construction, managers in charge of supplies and of all payments, labour supervisors, etc., etc. There may have been a King's Master Mason before the Conquest, but not so called. Edward Conder includes in his well-known book[2] an illustration that has been taken from the Cottonian MS. in the British Museum, in which there figures King "Offa" of Mercia (757–795), who built the dyke extending at one time from the mouth of the river Dee to east of the river Wye at Chepstow; in the illustration are a

[1] Clarendon Press, 1927.   [2] *Records of the Hole Crafte and Fellowship of Masons.*

monk-architect and (? the King's) Master Mason, the last-named carrying a square and a large pair of callipers or compasses. It is supposed that this group of three relates to the building of a church or abbey at what is now St Albans, antedating the present Cathedral or Abbey by 300 to 400 years.

Following the Conquest there is a long line of important craftsmen holding the regular appointment of King's Master Mason, one of the earliest being Henry, known also as Master Henry or Henry of Reyns, who was King's Master Mason from 1243 to 1253. He served Henry III at the building of Westminster Abbey, of which he is regarded as the architect. He was followed by John of Gloucester, also under Henry III, who was King's Master Mason until 1261, and responsible for work at Woodstock, Gloucester, and Westminster: he died a poor man, owing the King eighty marks. Then came Robert of Beverley, under Henry III and Edward I, who worked at Westminster and on the Tower of London. Mention should be made too of Roger Alomaly, who was King's Master Mason from 1324 to 1327, chiefly at the Palace of Westminster; he met his death by violence in some obscure way, and there is reason to suggest that William de Kurtlynton, Abbot of Westminster, had harboured those accused of aiding and abetting the murder.

The King's Master Masons had the rank and standing of an absolutely first-class architect of to-day, as is made quite clear from the marks of dignity offered them from time to time. Henry III gave Master Henry a gown of office; John of Gloucester was granted the annual provision for life of two robes with furs of good squirrels, of the quality issued to the Knights of the Household. Robert of Beverley received the royal gift of a tun of wine. And so forth.

There has been much discussion as to whether the King's Master Mason was an architect as well as a mason. We have already said that Master Henry was regarded as the architect of Westminster, and it is reasonable to assume that others holding his great office were the imaginative creators of the work which they saw growing under the hands of their workmen. The Regius MS. (date about 1390), in saying that the Master Mason is not to work at night except in study, rather suggests that when the practical work of the day was done the more theoretical work yet lay before him.

The difficult question is: Who were the architects of those days if the Master Masons were not?

It may well be that the actual design of a building was a co-operative task; that men of culture, educated and travelled monks, and the Master Mason pooled their ideas, and depended on the last-named to give them form and substance.

Such authorities as Wyatt Papworth, Martin S. Briggs, and others are in agreement that the names of many laymen responsible for the buildings of the Middle Ages are known. The names of three hundred officials connected with the English buildings are on record, and five hundred connected with French buildings, and one author says that it is possible to name, and in some degree to visualize, the whole line of the men who presided over the building of Westminster Abbey from its inception. Nevertheless the real architects of many medieval buildings had no option but to remain anonymous.

Did the Medieval Masons work from Drawn Plans?

Freemasons of to-day and many other people are tempted to believe that the buildings of the Middle Ages grew tier by tier in accordance with the whim of the Master Mason, and were not erected in accordance with plans and elevations prepared before the building was started. While we readily suppose that the Master Mason when acting as architect had powers, during the course of actual building, far greater than those of the architect of to-day, we must yet reasonably assume that practical considerations compelled the preparation of a drawing before the work started. Martin S. Briggs tells us that such drawings are mentioned in documentary records; indeed, there are reproduced in his book drawings dating back to the thirteenth century, which in their conception and execution are extremely effective and highly technical. It is obvious, though, that the old Master Mason must have possessed considerable discretion, and within certain limits could please himself as to the details of the work. The considerable diversity of design as between one pillar and another in many of the medieval churches does not suggest that the masons were always held down rigidly to a set of detailed drawings, even though they probably worked to a master plan. It is thought, too—as in all probability in the case of the contract for Catterick Church in the North Riding of Yorkshire, in the year 1412—that it sometimes happened that the written directions were so explicit as to render anything except possibly rough plans and elevations unnecessary to the craftsman of the day accustomed to an amount of freedom in interpreting instructions, and even these might have been dispensed with under very favourable conditions.

The power of the Master Mason waned with the coming into more extensive use of the contract system, known in the thirteenth century as 'task work.' Under this system the Master Mason was no longer an employer's agent: he was a builder working to a price or remunerated on a basis of measured-up completed work. Some of the work at Westminster Abbey in the thirteenth century and at Windsor Castle in the preceding century had been done on the task system, and after the Black Death, labour then being scarce, the system came into more general use for the smaller building work. It was a system that naturally adapted itself to changed conditions. Where there had been in the old days a few great employers there was in later centuries an increasing number of much smaller ones, not kings and nobles, but members of a trade. By the sixteenth century all kinds of work, large and small, was being done by contract. Douglas Knoop tells us that the contract system was adopted at Windsor and Cambridge, and that in the latter place King's College Chapel, begun on the old system in one century, was finished by contract in the next.

Under the old system the Master Mason ran no financial risk. He simply earned a wage, but under the task or contract system he stood to make either a profit or a loss, often the latter, if we may judge from an instance at the end of the medieval period—that is, in 1631–33—when three freemasons petitioned the Archbishop of Canterbury to give them £100 towards their losses, "wch will be a great comfort to you in this theyre extremity, and as meane to keep yem from prison." These losses had been incurred in "ye beautifying and enlargement of St John's Colledge, in Oxford." The Archbishop granted their prayer, and allowed an extra seventy pounds or so.

The King's Master Masons at the end of the medieval period were themselves contractors, if we may judge from one of them, Benjamin Jackson, who did work at Chatsworth, Derbyshire, for the Duke of Devonshire to the value of £12,000, and as the result of a dispute had to bring an action against the Duke to get his money.

Were Monks the Medieval Architects?

We are all familiar with the statement that the great buildings of the Middle Ages were the work of monks, who alone, it is said, possessed any knowledge of geometry and architecture. It is claimed that all masons, both artisans and overseers, worked under the orders of monks, who alone had the culture and technical knowledge necessary to the designing and execution of a fine building. Some writers have gone so far as to claim that the builder-monks were themselves freemasons—that is, members of an esoteric masonic body—and that the bishops and other dignitaries of the Church held high masonic office! It is recorded that Godfrey de Lucy, Bishop of Winchester, formed a fraternity for repairing his church during the five years following 1202, and perhaps that is the basis for the claim that the monk architects were freemasons. Edward

Conder suggests that the craftsmen at work on the early London Bridge were monks of the Society of Masons, a secret and symbolical fraternity "whose secret signs and symbols . . . had descended to them doubtless from a remote antiquity," but he does so on little or no foundation.

There can be no argument that, at any rate, the beginnings of medieval architecture were with the monks. Certainly in England, and probably in France, there was a time earlier than the year 1000 when the knowledge of building among ordinary people must have been very limited, and in most cases quite inadequate to the problems met in erecting an important building.

After the Conquest the ecclesiastics, growing vastly in every way as the years went by, and intent on building churches wherever they could, would be obliged to interest themselves in the building art. Their education—hardly anybody else had any—would allow of their mastering the mechanical and geometrical problems involved in the erection of simple buildings. Some of the monks would discover they had an aptitude for the work, and would be encouraged by their superiors to specialize and be given preferment to devote themselves exclusively to building. Then, as these privileged monks travelled, and history tells us monks of the better class travelled a great deal, they would find themselves compelled, if they wished to build churches, to take in hand the labour that offered itself and to teach and train it to the special purpose in view.

Quite early in medieval days there can be no doubt that ecclesiastics worked with their own hands in the building of churches, etc. At Hirschau, in Württemberg, monks worked as practical masons alongside their lay brethren, and in recent years we have seen mason-monks working at Buckfast Abbey, Devonshire, which in 1882 was taken over as the ruin of an ancient Cistercian monastery by French monks of the Benedictine Order. They sent one or two of their number back to France to learn the art of masonry there, that they might on their return instruct their brethren, so that in due course they might rebuild the abbey under the guidance of a professional architect. This ambitious work was more or less completed in 1932.

It is difficult nowadays to appreciate that the medieval Church was the great power in the Western world, the richest, the most co-ordinated. It requires some imagination to see the picture presented by Sir Walter Besant when he tells us that, at a time when the monastic houses formed a chain within and without the wall of London City, the Church employed perhaps one-fifth of the whole population of the City, including masons and other building craftsmen, lawyers, brewers, gardeners, and the makers of vestments, altar-cloths, candlesticks, etc., etc., all working for the Church.

There is a strong presumption that in the case of many of the great buildings of the Middle Ages Master Masons built them, but ecclesiastics took the credit. There is the case of William of Wykeham (1324–1404), who was Chancellor to Edward III and Richard II, and who is claimed to have built parts of Windsor Castle, the Cathedral and College at Winchester, and to have founded New College, Oxford. His predecessor in the See of Winchester was William of Edington, who is said to have discovered and trained William of Wykeham to be his successor. Now, Professor Hamilton Thompson has pointed out that:

> There is absolutely nothing which essentially connects Edington, a busy clerk, . . . Treasurer of the Exchequer, with architectural work beyond the fact that the priory church founded by him at his native place in Wiltshire and the remodelling of Winchester Cathedral began under his auspices. . . . The work at Edington and Winchester is obviously due to trained masons with a surpassing knowledge of their craft, not to amateurs who could only spare time for architecture from their proper business.

It by no means follows that a man in a position of apparent authority on a medieval building in course of erection possessed practical knowledge. Here is a remarkable instance: Chaucer the poet, who was not, of course, an ecclesiastic, nor could have had any real knowledge of building, held for twenty months the appointment of Clerk of the Works at Westminster, the Tower of London, and many places outside London. He received the appointment from the King "as a gift for services rendered," and part of his duty was to issue commissions under the Great Seal to empower individuals to purvey stone, timber, etc., and to take masons, carpenters, and others for the works at Westminster, etc.

When a monkish scribe of the Middle Ages records that an ecclesiastic 'built' (*fecit*) a church it means that he on behalf of his church ordered it and paid for it, reasonably suggests Martin S. Briggs, and that he preferred to commemorate the abbot or bishop, who corresponded to a modern "Chairman of the Building Committee," his concern being with the glorification of his church or order, rather than the perpetuation of a lay artist's name. The real architects, the real designers, did not conceal their names from an excess of piety: it was because they were overborne or overridden by the ecclesiastics.

Enlart, in a French manual on the architecture of France, gives the names of many of the men who in turn superintended the building of Gothic cathedrals. Some of these names are commemorated in the excellent French fashion of naming streets. Thus at Amiens, facing the south transept of the cathedral, is the rue Robert de Luzarches, and at Rheims, on the north side of the cathedral, the rue Robert de Coucy.

Surprising as it may appear to those who have not read the early history of the Church, there was a time when the fact that a man was called by the name of monk did not mean necessarily that he was an ecclesiastic. Guizot's *History of Civilization in France* says that the impression that "monks were not only ecclesiastics but, so to speak, the most ecclesiastical of all ecclesiastics" is full of error.

At their origin the monks were not ecclesiastical at all. They were laymen with a common religious object but altogether apart from the clergy. Some were ordained to make them priests or even bishops, and yet they were still laity, contracting no kind of religious engagement, often even purposely separating themselves from clergy and always distinct from it.

Of course, in time the monks ceased to be laymen and became priests, yet Dr W. F. Hook, the well-known Church historian, writing of them at a much later date, uses this phrase with regard to monks, "whether of Holy Orders or not." It is likely, then, that many men regarded historically as ecclesiastic masons were really laymen who had had plenty of opportunity to perfect themselves in the building craft.

Were the Master Masons Architects?

We must not be misled by the names or titles given either to the ecclesiastics or to the mason craftsmen of the Middle Ages. It stands to reason that many of the Master Masons *must* have been architects of fine quality. Wyatt Papworth and Hamilton Thompson are in agreement as to this. The latter states that architecture was an art that required special training and exclusive devotion on the part of those who practised it, and he refutes the claim that bishops and abbots, with certain exceptions, were the architects of their churches; he believes that they hired masters of craft and gave them directions for their work, but did not take technical control.

A common-sense view of the matter is that put forward by Professor F. M. Simpson in his *History of Architectural Development*. He says the monks themselves were the architects of the French cathedrals until the middle of the twelfth century. Their monasteries were then the centres of intellectual and artistic life; in the schools attached to them were trained priests and laymen alike, who worked on the church and buildings of the monastery in which they had learned their craft, or, as in the case of Villard de Honnecourt, who went to Hungary, were sent out to superintend building work in other countries, sometimes far distant. Gradually the teaching of apprentices passed from the monks to the lay Master Masons, many of whom had received the best education the times could provide and were as well read as the majority of clerics and nobles, and they probably took good care that the education of their apprentices was as sound as their own. Skilled craftsmen trained in this way became Master Masons, and in course of time dictated the plan and general ordinance, drawing them on parchment or paper sufficiently well to make their meaning clear to the workman. The full-size details of mouldings were drawn on the spot, probably on boards, much in the same way as the full-size heads of traceried windows are set out now. Whether the men who did this work should be termed 'architects' or 'masons' or 'masters of the work' is an academic question. The laymen who in France in the thirteenth century took the place of the monks of the earlier centuries were men of substance, held in high repute by their patrons and townsfolk, and were artists in the true sense of the word. The post of Master Mason to a town or to a cathedral was a high and responsible one, and descended in some cases from father to son, as, for example, at Amiens Cathedral and at Strassburg.

We may reasonably conclude that many of the architects borrowed by England from Normandy in the early Middle Ages were men of the type described by Professor Simpson.

The 'Travelling Masons' and the Question of the Papal Bull

In the minds of a great number of Brethren is the fixed belief that the secret modes of recognition practised by freemasons took their rise in medieval days when skilled masons, it is said, travelled from place to place on the Continent and in England seeking work and using their membership of the fraternity as an introduction and recommendation to would-be employers. The story has many elaborations, which will be explored in the course of this section. The tradition of the travelling mason reaches back to times separated from the present by as much as a thousand years, and it has been the subject of considerable controversy during the past century. Gould in his *History* devotes much space to a discussion of the tradition, and papers by J. Walter Hobbs, Douglas Knoop, and many other authors are to be found in *A.Q.C.* It is not only masonic writers who have dealt with the tradition, for there are countless references to it in general literature. Macaulay, for example, believed "that all the cathedrals of Europe came into existence nearly contemporaneously and were built by travelling companies of masons under the direction of a systematic organization."

It may surprise some Brethren to learn that there is no reference to the tradition in literature earlier than the seventeenth century. Aubrey, who is quoting Sir William Dugdale, refers to it in his *Natural History of Wiltshire*, written in 1680–90. The story, as he relates it, is that "about Henry the Third's time, the Pope gave a Bull or Diploma to a company of Italian Architects to travell up and downe over all Europe to build Churches." Almost the same story is *credited* to both Elias Ashmole and to Sir Christopher Wren, but in each case this fact is to be noted: the information is given at second-hand, although Gould believes it to be almost certain that all the references could be traced to one single source. We must emphasize that medieval writers are silent on the subject, and that we have nothing better than the statements attributed to the three worthies just mentioned and not going back further than the seventeenth century.

Briefly, the tradition has grown up on these lines: organized companies of masons, not only highly skilled, but exclusively informed in the higher branches of masonry design and construction, obtained from the Pope an authority under which they travelled all over Europe and into England. They built churches and other fine buildings and lived as best they could in lodges on the building sites, conforming all of them to the same rules of obedience and enjoying the protection of the Pope under his 'Bull' (from Latin *bulla,* a bill). These bands of highly organized and exceptionally well-skilled masons possessed esoteric knowledge, including secret modes of recognition.

This is the story which is so frequently confused with a much simpler one, a more natural one, a story easy of acceptance, which is that in the days of medieval building activity there were never enough masons in any one neighbourhood to build a great church or castle, and that therefore craftsmen from other districts had to be called upon. It is quite obvious that the medieval mason had to travel as the venue of his work shifted from time to time, but this is not the story that appeals to so many of our Brethren. They prefer to entertain the more glamorous story of the mason wandering far from his home, perhaps never to see it again until old age overtakes him, roaming from country to country as the whim takes him, and overriding by virtue of the Papal authority any objections to his entrance that might be raised by sovereign states, by guilds and other fraternities.

What are the considerations that disincline us to accept the tradition? Wyatt Papworth, whose study of building records in medieval England was of a most thorough order, could find no evidence that any such company of travelling masons had ever entered England; he refers to the search made by Governor Pownall in the Vatican Library, a few years before 1788, for the Papal rescript or document, a search which met with no success even though the then Pope himself ordered it to be most minute. "Leader Scott" (a woman, Lucy E. Baxter, who supports the story of the foreign travelling mason), writing in *The Cathedral Builders* (1899), said, "I have lately been to Rome to try and find this document, but as eight Popes reigned during the time of Henry III it is difficult to seek"—in other words, she could not find it.

Gould, who develops the matter with great industry, says that at the period in question Papal influence was dominant throughout England, and that the Pope's authority must have been constantly invoked in the small concerns of human life. His supremacy over all temporal sovereigns was unchallenged. The usage of applying for Papal sanction or confirmation was prevalent in the British Islands. Six Popes in the twelfth and thirteenth centuries confirmed the privileges and possessions of the monastery of Glastonbury. The Popes granted many privileges having reference to St Paul's Cathedral, York Cathedral, the church at Beverley, etc. In the last-named case the guild of Corpus Christi had a yearly procession of pageants acted under the particular authority of Pope Urban IV and John XXII. In the fourteenth and fifteenth centuries so great was the demand for Papal seals and letters in the City of London, Gould remarks, that their counterfeit production must have amounted to a profitable industry. It is on record that forged Bulls and other documents emanated from the Papal Chancery in Rome itself; Richard of Canterbury (1187) complained of spurious Bulls, and Pope Innocent III alluded to the forgeries, a manufactury for which was in his time discovered at Rome, and it is known that the forgeries continued to be produced long after the exposures and denunciations. England's submission to Papal authority increased after the murder of Thomas à Becket in 1170.

Thus we have to face the possibility that at some time or other a forged Bull might have been issued, and in it might have been words or phrases which, when misinterpreted or half forgotten at a great distance of time, might have been the slender basis upon which the tradition was built. It seems to be generally accepted that Pope Nicholas III in 1278 and his successors issued Letters of Indulgence to the Lodge of Masons working at Strasbourg Cathedral, and this might easily be the foundation of the tradition into which we are inquiring.

The Comacines

The tradition of the travelling masons takes its most popular form in the story of the Comacines, a story which has been accepted without question by many well-informed Brethren. It is the same story of the organized band of masons travelling under the protection of the Pope, but with a special background of its own. The Comacines are supposed to have taken their name from Como, in Lombardy, Northern Italy. The people of Como were such superior masons that they earned the name of *Magistri Comacini,* or 'Masters from Como.' Masons who passed through the different fixed stages of apprenticeship became Masters and formed a corporation of masons which built the edifices of Lombardy and then looked abroad for employment. They formed themselves into an association or fraternity, "seeking a monopoly, as it were, over the whole face of Christendom." An early edition of the *Encyclopædia Britannica* says that the Masters from Como were fraught with Papal Bulls, or diplomas, granting to them the right of holding directly and solely under the Pope alone. They acquired the power to fix the price of their labour and to regulate their own internal government, exclusively in their own general chapters,

> prohibiting all native artists not admitted into their Society from entering with it into any sort of competition. . . . Wherever they came, they appeared headed by a chief surveyor, who governed the whole troop, and named one man out of every ten, under the name of warden, to overlook the nine others. The architects of all the sacred edifices of the Latin Church . . . north, south, east or west—thus derived their science from the same central school; obeyed in their designs the dictates of the same hierarchy, and rendered every minute improvement the property of the whole body.

It is claimed that from this company of travelling masons is derived "the fraternity of adopted masons, accepted masons or free masons."

Now, as this is one of the most popular legends in freemasonry and passes in the minds of some Brethren the world over as real history, it is worth while to look into the story. The Comacine legend has been investigated by many critical writers, among them Professor Hamilton Thompson, who in *The Somersetshire Archæological Transactions,* 1920, says:

> It is unquestionable that the term *comacinus* occurs in the early Lombard laws, with reference to masons, and that Como and Comacina are in the district to which those laws refer. But *comacinus* is not a word which can be derived from either place; an inhabitant of Como is *Comensis* or *Comanus.*

Professor Thompson believes that the Comacinus was simply a mason working at a job with others, and not a term for a member of any mysterious travelling guild.

"Not a scrap of record evidence has been found to establish the existence of this migrant fraternity," says Douglas Knoop, "and the basis seems to be mainly a mistaken etymology; for *comacinus* probably meant 'fellow mason' (as *comonachus* meant 'fellow monk'), without reference to Como or any other place."

The story of the Comacines might possibly have taken its rise from the fact that in the sixth century the Lombards, a barbarous race, overran North Italy, but when their power waned two centuries later there ensued a very considerable revival of building, under the influence of the Popes, assisted by the more settled state of the country under Charlemagne.

The 'Travelling Masons' in France

In France the tradition of the travelling mason had its vogue, and also had grafted upon it a peculiar story of its own—namely, that about the year 1145 great companies of Norman masons, under a chief named Prince, emigrated to Chartres, where they helped to build the Cathedral, and on their return built and repaired churches in Rouen and its province. The slight historical basis for the story is that at the building of the Cathedral of Chartres great numbers of lords and ladies, knights, priests, and peasants harnessed themselves to the wagons on which the stone was being drawn to the site of the cathedral. Gould quotes Levasseur in saying that miracles are now associated with the story, and that the event was "a grand and remarkable demonstration of the all-consuming religious zeal of the Middle Ages—a manifestation of the same spirit which underlay the pilgrimages and the Crusades."

Still another version of the 'travelling mason' tradition must be alluded to—probably one of the earliest versions. A brotherhood, "Les Fratres Pontis," is said to have been founded in France for the express purpose of travelling anywhere and everywhere to build bridges. Apparently the only foundation for it is that companies of masons were formed to build the bridges at Avignon and Saint-Esprit in the twelfth and fourteenth centuries. Otherwise it is devoid of truth, and, as regards England, does not appear ever to have had a shadow of substance.

It is almost amusing to note how many incidents in the history of medieval architecture have been seized upon to provide a foundation for a legend of 'travelling masons.' There is reason to suppose that the sending forth of the Franciscans and the Dominicans from Italy on their missionary work throughout Europe, carrying with them the blessing of the Pope, and probably his letters of authority, is yet another basis of the legend.

The 'Travelling Masons' : Some Conclusions

An argument against the acceptance of the tradition is the great difficulty in believing that if any such organized body of masons came into England, history could have been silent on the subject. The first mention of the tradition is not until the *seventeenth century*. Further, it is not easy to see how masons in sufficient number to do all the work with which the tradition credits them could, in the Middle Ages, have travelled thousands of miles; but perhaps that is a moot point.

The churches and other notable buildings of the Middle Ages were built under the direction of men whose names are known, and no opportunity could have existed for the intrusion of foreign bands of workmen, although, as previously shown, highly skilled Master Masons from Normandy are known to have been brought to England on a number of occasions to take charge of important work. But that is a very different matter.

We cannot easily accept the picture of the medieval church mason as a sort of wandering Jubelum, sojourning here for a few months and there for a year or two, ever moving on, utterly cut off from his kith and kin in his birthplace, and unlikely in many cases ever to return to them. Such a picture, as we see it, is altogether too fanciful and unnatural, too divorced from the ordinary way of life to be accepted as a portrayal of any medieval craftsman.

Surely a truer picture of English conditions comes into our mind when we think of men being brought up to the mason's craft among town and country communities of ordinary people, among their own tribes and families, in places where there was need of their labour and where there was a long-standing mason tradition. From time to time, as work in their own neighbourhood became scarce, they would find it necessary to travel into adjoining districts, and sometimes even farther afield, and in due course they would return to their homes or, in exceptional cases, send for their families and settle down in the district in which a lifetime of activity awaited them.

The popular idea that the medieval mason was just a poor wandering soul is lent some colour, of course, by the regulations contained in the old manuscript Charges relating to the treatment of strange craftsmen; but *all* masons were not strange craftsmen, and it must be remembered that other trades, particularly the carpenters, had similar regulations.

Nowadays the great majority of masonic writers regard the 'travelling mason' as a fiction, but it would be unfair not to mention that a few well-known students withhold judgment, as, for example, G. W. Bullamore, who says that until the fabulous nature of the story or tradition is actually proved the story is entitled to consideration.

The Migratory Masons

The medieval mason was certainly at times a migratory being. Obviously, when there was no work in his home district he had to go where there was work, but we have very little insight into his family life, and are left to conjecture much. Writers like Edward Conder make a great deal of this migration, and assert that medieval workmen in many trades had tokens, or passes, which facilitated their transfer from one master to another, and that masons out of their apprenticeship and now free of their guild were entrusted with secret signs and passwords to ensure their being employed by any body of masons to whom in their travels they might apply for work. It is easy, however, to form from Conder's words a mental picture which is not warranted, it being highly unlikely that masons *normally* wandered about the countryside seeking employment, and it being quite certain that membership of any mason guilds, if such there were—purely city fraternities—was actually and relatively small, and could not have embraced the bulk of the country craftsmen. Towns were small in those days, and the area jurisdiction of any of the guilds very limited.

Bands of masons there must have been at times. Masons impressed by King's agents must have tramped in companies to the site where they were wanted. Then, too, masons finishing at one big job might voluntarily travel together for the sake of their own protection, especially if the road lay through forests in which outlaws might easily attack. Serious students, however, tend to limit the distance to which masons would travel in search of employment. It must always be remembered that any legal 'freedom' enjoyed by operatives in early medieval days was hardly one of solid fact, and few men of the labouring classes could travel as they pleased from one district to another. The working people of the countryside were at one time all the property of great lords, and even when in the fourteenth century they ceased legally to be serfs they still had no liberty of movement. The men of the towns had more apparent freedom, but even they were largely controlled by their trade fraternities. In the light of these considerations it is very doubtful whether the mason was migratory as a class, although undoubtedly there was a certain amount of movement away from the home district at times of building pressure, especially when the King or the Church impressed labour. On the other hand, it can well be argued that from the earliest days his trade made it absolutely necessary for the mason to travel, but, as, for example, in the fifteenth century, when hardly a church escaped enlargement or alteration, he might possibly have spent a lifetime without needing to extend his search for work beyond the limits of a two-day journey. The Rev. Herbert Poole gives point to this statement when he says that he has traced the path, by means of masons' marks, of a small party engaged in church work in the late fifteenth century, whose most westerly point was near Carnforth, in Lancashire, and whose most easterly (and, he believes, the last) was Kirkby Malhamdale, in the West Riding—say, a total distance as the crow flies of roughly thirty miles.

Impressment of Masons

When the King issued a written authority to his agents for the impressment of masons to work on some big building no mason could say him nay unless in the authority it was made quite clear that masons within the fee of the Church were exempt. When no such clause was included the church mason, as any other mason, had to join the band of impressed men and tramp off to where their services were awaited. Others of the great employers—the Church and nobles—sometimes impressed masons to work at a distance.

We believe that the earliest-known writ of impressment is dated 1333, and for the next 300 years or so the system was used from time to time. Here are a few examples: In 1360 thirteen sheriffs were ordered by the Crown to send 568 masons to Windsor; in 1361 seventeen sheriffs were ordered to send 1360 masons. Many more were wanted in following years, says Douglas Knoop, "either because the masons at Windsor had been attracted elsewhere by higher wages or had died of plague." (It is difficult to see how the King's impressed men could have been attracted elsewhere.)

A year or two later Thomas de Musgrave, Sheriff of York, who had been directed to send more masons to Windsor Castle, submitted a statement of expenses in which 50s. was charged for thirty red caps "with other liveries of dyed ffrustyan," lest the thirty masons chosen and taken "should escape from the custody of the conductor." But the Crown refused to pay it! (It does not look as though the masons enjoyed impressment.)

In 1370 Master Henry de Yevele, thought to be of Yeovil, and Master William de Wynford were each ordered by the Crown to take fifty hewers of stone, the one in London and the near-by counties and the other in Somerset, Dorset, etc., and bring them to Orwell. The masons had to be ready by the 1st of May to set out at the King's wages, and "all contrariants" were to be arrested and committed to prison.

In 1377 Henry de Yevele was appointed to take masons wherever found for work at the Palace of Westminster and the Tower of London, with power to imprison the disobedient, but he was not to take masons in the fee of the Church. Many such instances could be quoted.

Not always, however, were masons in the fee of the Church excepted, and not always were town masons (possibly guild masons) excepted, either. Special patents of protection were occasionally granted; thus a mason working for the Archbishop of Canterbury on the city wall of Canterbury was granted protection by patent for one year from May 1381.

'Cathedral' Masons

Arising, perhaps, from a special interpretation of the old manuscript Constitutions, and to some extent echoing the old legend of the travelling masons with their Papal Bull, many students have been inclined to believe that in early medieval days there was a class of masons who devoted themselves exclusively to the building of great churches and monasteries ('cathedrals'); that these masons did not work with the town masons who built the great castles; and that the two bodies, the cathedral-builders on the one hand and the guild builders of the town on the other, were separate and distinct. Further, it has been thought that the cathedral-builders were not subject to impressment, and were free of any constraint which the guilds might have been able to apply to the work of unorganized craftsmen. It may seem a matter of small importance, but it has evoked much argument in the past, many of the best-known authorities taking opposite sides in the matter.

We have just shown that, on occasion, the King's Patent did not exempt masons employed on church work, who, when the Crown so wished, were impressed just as every other mason was. Undoubtedly, however, they often were exempted, but this is to be taken as evidence of the great power wielded by highly placed ecclesiastics who had opportunity of urging upon the King or upon his Master Masons the priority of the work dearest to their own hearts.

Master Masons employed by Crown and Church did not work exclusively on buildings of one kind: they did whatever their great employers directed them to do, and at one time they would build a church and at another they would build a castle, and later might be building both at once. Walter of Hereford worked on the Vale Royal Abbey and also on Caernarvon Castle; Henry de Yevele on Westminster Abbey and on Westminster Palace and the Tower of London; Richard Beke on Canterbury Cathedral and London Bridge; Robert Stowell on Westminster Abbey and on Windsor Castle and the Tower of London, Robert Spillesby on York Minster and on Eton College. William Wynford rebuilt the nave of Winchester Cathedral, and also worked on Winchester College and Windsor Castle. Here we have outstanding Master Masons doing church work and secular work, in some instances at the same time.

The case against the existence of separate bodies has been well stated by J. W. Hobbs (*A.Q.C.*, vol. xl). He says that the cathedral-builders as a separate entity of specially skilled craftsmen cannot be regarded as having had any existence in England, whatever may have been the case on the Continent. Students support him in saying that the term 'cathedral-builders' for any class of person is a misnomer. Douglas Knoop and his collaborators say that the evidence, so far as it goes, is against any difference between the town or guild mason on the one hand and the church or cathedral mason on the other, and that "nothing is clearer than that the generality of masons could be used for either the Gothic work of churches or colleges or for the building of castles, town walls or bridges."

Architectural Resemblances

Resemblances, sometimes very marked, between the architecture of two countries or of two districts of one country are often relied upon to support the theory that in early medieval times the chief buildings were the work of organized bands of masons all sharing one culture and one identical training. While it is a fact that resemblances are common, it is just as true that many of these resemblances are superficial, that there are distinctions between the Gothic styles of the various Continental countries, and even that in so small a country as England almost every district had its own variety of Gothic.

Here and there, however, the similarities are such as to indicate that masons of one identical school have been at work in different places. Édouard Herriot, once Prime Minister of France, in his book *Amid the Forests of Normandy* (translated by J. Heron Lepper), in alluding to the French architect William de Sens (William de Seno), who was summoned to Canterbury to supervise construction there in the twelfth century, remarks that

> at Canterbury I cannot but feel the tie which unites this English Capital of the faith to the celebrated abbey whose ruins remain in Bec Hellouin. Once again Normandy forces us to look in turn towards England and towards France, so as to recall to the two countries the community of ideas which binds them together,

a statement which J. Heron Lepper explains by saying that when the Norman ecclesiastic with a taste for building was translated from his own country to England he would bring his architect and probably some of his skilled workmen with him.

A considerable factor in bringing about resemblances was the intercommunication and exchange of interests resulting from the coming into England of many religious orders and houses. Thus, for one example, quoting J. W. Hobbs, the Cistercian Order came to England in 1128 and settled at Waverley, Surrey, extending its locations to Rievaulx, Fountains, Tintern, Kirkstall, Furness, Buckfastleigh, Melrose, and elsewhere.

There can be little doubt, he suggests, that an ecclesiastic builder, setting to work in his new sphere, would not improbably have the help of masons with whom he had formerly been associated.

A considerable influence was exercised in England by the Black Friars of St Dominic who arrived in 1221 and the Grey Friars of St Francis of Assisi in 1224. Within thirty years the Grey Friars had forty-nine convents, and by the time of the Reformation sixty-six, at which period the Black Friars—the Dominicans—had fifty-eight. Gould notes the coincidence that the friars of both these Orders were Italians, commingled with French, German, Flemish, and others, and among them were many architects. Such an amazing influx of Continentals intent upon establishing their Houses, inspired by a great zeal for building, and able to attract to themselves the necessary money for their enterprises, must have provided the key to many of the resemblances between the monastic architecture of England and that of the Continent.

Finally, it is frequently overlooked that the English masons in their turn, but to a much smaller extent, travelled into France and other parts of the Continent. As one of a number of instances, in 1381 English masons were sent to Brittany by order of the King. English noblemen and men of substance and influence travelled from England to and from Rome, the Holy Land, etc., and would in due course bring back architectural ideas which they had gained during their travels. Bristol freemasons went across to Ireland to assist in the rebuilding of Christ Church Cathedral, Dublin, in the twelfth century. Right through the medieval period, it can be taken for granted, representative artists and leading operatives went from one European country to another.

Chapter Three

THE ENGLISH GUILDS

EDWARD CONDER and other writers have stated their belief that symbolic freemasonry is in the direct line of descent from the old Collegia which were a feature of Roman industrial life. These colleges were brought to England by the Romans, and their influence is thought by some to have survived here and there through the dark centuries, and to have led, in or about the tenth century, to the inception of the guilds, which in due course bequeathed to freemasonry much of their form and language. Students of the calibre of Gould find difficulty in accepting this belief, but do not rule out the possibility of direct descent from the Roman Collegia to the French guilds.

The Roman Colleges

The Romans in their own country brought into existence societies to foster their practical crafts, the members being brothers one of another. That concerned with building was the Collegium Fabrorum, which was governed by a *Magister* and *Decuriones* (freely translated 'Master' and 'Wardens'), the rank and file of the members being known as *sodaies*—that is, 'companions.' Some of the so-called colleges were religious; others were more of a social character, and in time developed a political aspect frowned upon by the authorities. Still others were associations of poor people, even slaves, having more the character of a benefit club.

The colleges had a common treasury and a common table. Many of them practised religious rites, candidates took an oath on admission, the members contributed to the expenses, which included helping their poor and burying their dead. The bodies of members were buried in a common sepulchre, the *columbarium,* so named because the niches containing the urns gave it the appearance of a pigeon-house, the name for pigeon being *columba.*

There is no record of colleges of masons, but it is extremely likely that the Collegium Fabrorum assisted a number of different crafts. The younger Pliny, when writing to the Emperor Trajan to inform him of a destructive fire at Nicomedia, Asia Minor, asked permission to establish a Collegium Fabrorum for the rebuilding of the city.

In the provincial colleges—a point stressed by Gould—the son succeeded to the occupation of his father, his trade being his best estate and inheritance, and the guilds and companies inherited this fundamental principle, which probably originated in distant Eastern countries long before the Romans.

When the Romans introduced architecture and other crafts to England they are believed to have brought with them their colleges. Edward Conder states confidently that the discovery of the foundation of "a temple dedicated by a Company of Roman Artificers to Neptune and Minerva in honour of the Imperial family of Claudius" fully confirms the conjecture that the Roman Collegia founded an association at Chichester. The evidence is a marble slab, discovered in that city in 1723, bearing an inscription which has been literally translated as follows: "The College or Company of Artificers [Masons], and they who preside over sacred rites by the authority of King Cogidubnus, the Legate of Tiberius Claudius Augustus, in Britain, dedicated this temple to Neptune and Minerva for the welfare of the Imperial family, Pudens, the son of Pudentius, having given the site." (There is some slight doubt, however, as to whether the inscription does actually refer to builders or masons.)

A difficult question is whether, after the Romans departed, the influence of their colleges survived right through those dark centuries until the new civilization, that of the later Saxon kings, asserted itself, a century or more before the Norman Conquest. There are writers who assert that the Collegia were the prototypes of the medieval trade guilds, and that the Collegium Fabrorum in particular was the parent of the mason guilds; but more cautious students look doubtfully at the long, blank period following the Roman occupation, and, while disposed to accept the possibility that the guilds may have owed some part of their inspiration to a survival of a Roman idea, fail to see evidence of an unbroken line between Collegia and guild. Other historians compromise by saying that if the guilds did not receive their tradition direct from the ancient Roman townsmen, then they obtained it through the new introduction of Roman principles associated with the missionary zeal of St Augustine, who brought Christianity for a second time to England. Gould argues that all knowledge of the art of the Roman style of building and, with it, of the Roman building corporations, had long been lost, and could not have been handed down to the guild period, and he thinks that organized bodies of masons did not arise until long after the appearance of guilds among the other trades—a point which will be referred to shortly.

Are there any guilds in any country for which a reasonable case for their straight descent from the Roman colleges can be made? The answer is undoubtedly "Yes." The story of the French succession from Roman

Collegia to trade guild and fraternity will be briefly told at the end of the present section.

The English Medieval Guilds

Guild, gild, geld, comes from a Saxon word *guildan*, meaning simply 'to pay'; thus when we say that a city 'guilded' we mean that it paid its taxes. The word 'guildable' meant 'liability to pay tax.'

The very first guild is believed to have been an association of tribes and families, gathered together for mutual protection and to shoulder mutual liabilities, but in the course of time the word 'guild' grew to have many meanings—a ward of the City of London, for example. At Preston, which has a long and important guild history, guild is a fraternity, an assembly or meeting, and, curiously, also the period of time separating one guild assembly from the next. The most important use of the word is to denote an associated body or brotherhood, even a town or minor incorporation, every member of which was *gildar*—that is, liable to pay (to be taxed) towards the upkeep of the body. The Guildhall was at one time both the fraternity itself and the official house in which it met. In the West Riding of Yorkshire is an ancient town Gildersome, whose name in 1181 was Gildehusum, meaning 'at the guild house,' and by 1226 Gildhus, the house or hall in which the guild met.

The freemason will find so much of special interest in the history, usages, and customs of the old guilds that he can be well advised to read the chief reference books on the subject mentioned at the end of the present book.

A curious point needing to be stressed is that, although our Craft owes much to the customs of guilds in general and of the London Company of Freemasons in particular, and although masonic authors—the present one included—often speak of freemasonry having derived this or that from the guilds, yet it appears to be quite unlikely that there ever was in Britain an ancient craft or trade guild of masons. There was a Company of Masons and Freemasons which, coming into existence somewhere about the fourteenth century, naturally modelled itself in many respects on the existing guilds, and borrowed from them much of its organization and system of government. The guilds that survived the Reformation had all developed into or become Livery Companies, as we find them in the City of London to-day, and the remodelled Guilds, now companies, and the London Company of Freemasons, which had never been a guild, enjoyed more or less a common pattern of existence in the close of the Medieval Age; accordingly, we find all of them, the Masons' Company included, referred to and regarded as guilds in the reference books of the present day. Thus freemasonry has drawn inspiration and some of its customs from the ancient guilds; from the ancient London Company of Freemasons; and, finally, from the post-Reformation Livery Companies, in whose numbers are included what remained of the guilds and of the Masons' Company.

We can see why the freemasons did not, and could not, come together in the earliest medieval times in guilds, as did the mercers, ironmongers, fishmongers, clockmakers, dyers, stationers, etc., etc. In the early medieval period no small town could find work in support of a sufficient number of masons to make a guild possible, but there was a still greater difficulty. Masons were not small masters with servant craftsmen and workpeople doing local business and easily comprehended by a local organization; on the contrary, taken as a whole, they were men of a scattered trade, and this trade could arrive at maturity only after the other trades had become prosperous and produced the riches which the King, his nobles, and the Church could spend on building in stone, chiefly by the direct employment of the masons, who worked for wages and only exceptionally for profit. In course of time the masons had their own London organization, as already stated, but it is doubtful whether any other town in England owned a closely corresponding body, although a few of them had social and religious bodies to which the name of guild was sometimes applied (see p. 70).

So it will be understood that when in this book 'guilds' are mentioned, reference is being made to the many general guilds in whose customs and usages all freemasons must be profoundly interested, and more particularly the London Company of Masons and Freemasons.

Freemasonry is fortunate in the fact that there grew up in England, instead of small guilds of purely local authority, a nation wide fraternity of operative masons, as to which the earliest of the old manuscript Charges bears witness.

Development of the Guilds

It is not easy to present an agreed sequence of guild development. The chief works of reference contradict one another, and at times seriously. The outline story now presented may be regarded as somewhere near the truth, but not as being free from the possibility of argument.

The very foundation of the guild idea is the association of tribes and families helping and protecting one another, mutually bearing the burden of taxation, and supporting one another when accused of offences against the law. By about the tenth century the guild had assumed more definite shape and had acquired more importance. It passed under strong monkish influence, its constitution being shaped more and more by the Church, until it came to be an entirely religious association. Without exception, every one of the considerable number of guilds was, at some period in its early history, of a religious character, and when the guild developed into an association of merchants and employers and later became a public body or something like it, and when, later still, it became an association of craftsmen, every one of its members continued to observe closely rules and regulations which owed their inception to men of the Church.

There were frith guilds in London by the middle of the tenth century, and at least as early as the time of Edward the Confessor, who died in 1066, there is believed to have been a merchant guild at Dover and a burgess guild at Canterbury, while soon after the Conquest weaver guilds are known to have existed. The Guild of Knights (see later) is claimed to have originated about the middle of the tenth century, but the first-known mention of a merchant guild is in 1093.

In Germany the guild appears to have been first known in the eleventh century, and is claimed to have been organized in old German drinking meetings, or to have been a direct descendant of the Roman college, claims which historians do not admit. Charlemagne issued in 779 a decree forbidding anyone to bind himself by mutual oaths in a guild (*Gelaonia*). In France the guild, probably a descendant of the Roman Collegia, was definitely known in the eighth century, and there is evidence that in the ninth clergy of Rheims were superintending the formation of religious guilds.

The guilds maintained their early purpose of "devotion and alms-deeds" for hundreds of years, whether or not they split into two classes, the one purely religious, the other economic. It is wrong to suppose that the mason fraternities were different from those of other trades because they moralized on their work and were carefully nurtured in religious ideals. As has been said, it is doubtful whether there was any English guild that was not in its early days a religious association. Bodmin Church in the fifteenth century had forty guilds connected with it and helping to support it, and at about the same time there might have been found in each bay of the nave of any great church a little chapel dedicated to the patron saint of a local trade guild, lighted with the guild's candles, and maintained by its contributions. The object of one particular guild was: "Firstly to the honour of God and all his Saints and to stir up the Commons of the people to do well and to have perseverance in well doing." The words are taken from the regulations of the Guild of Barbers of London, 1390. Members of the old Guild of Palmers in the town of Ludlow had their attention forcibly directed in the ordinances to the contemplation of the inevitable end of this mortal existence.

Frith Guilds

The frith guild, about the period 950, was undoubtedly one of the earliest forms of guild. It may have been a voluntary association, or the authorities may have brought it into existence and compelled the serf-like people to join it. In its smallest unit it could have been just a family or two, ten members or so (a tithing), having its own leader; ten groups joined to make a larger unit, the ten leaders meeting, says Unwin, "for business every month and feasting together, giving the remains to the poor." This appears to be the form of guild which preceded the ecclesiastical guild, which, in turn, made way for the economic guild. It is possible, and, indeed, probable, that the whole of the members met from time to time for feasting, and that the proceedings were so turbulent that in course of time the authorities had to interfere; but we see in this feasting of the grouped families the beginning, or possibly the survival, of a custom that persisted through the centuries in the guilds and livery companies, and is to-day represented by such functions as the Lord Mayor's banquet on the one hand and the lodge dinner on the other.

The term frithgild, or fribourg, connotes the idea of the members of the family guilds offering themselves as sureties for peace and good behaviour, represented after the Conquest by the word *frankpledge,* which persisted for a few centuries, and in which the word *frank* means 'free of constraint,' leading to the supposition that those early guilds were groups of persons who 'freely,' or allegedly freely, gave the authorities the necessary pledge of good behaviour. Every freeman at the age of fourteen (religious, clerks, knights, and their sons excepted) had to give a pledge of good deportment towards his king and country; otherwise he was imprisoned. This, however, seldom happened, for neighbours were mutually bound for one another, and, in the event of trouble, either surrendered the offender or commuted for his offences by paying a joint fine.

It would not be surprising to learn that the division of serfs into tithings of ten members came to be related to the system by which a man gave for the support of the Church one-tenth of the annual produce of his industry.

Knighten Guild, or Knights' Guild

Apparently at some time in the tenth century or earlier there were guilds governed by a council of thirteen members, including a presiding officer, the number being based upon Christ and the twelve Apostles. It is believed that one such guild was governed by twelve men, plus a woman president who represented the Virgin Mary. The story of the knights' guild, or young men's guild, is told in many ways, the version given here being due to Herbert and also Stow. The knighten (also Cnuighton, or Cnighten) guild was governed by thirteen, and may originally have been a secular guild, the tradition being that King Edgar gave a portion of land on the east part of the City of London to thirteen knights who had "gloriously performed" certain combat prescribed by him, and that this land is the Portsoken Ward of the City of London ('Portsoken' meaning 'franchise at the gate'), the subject of a written charter granted by Edward the Confessor to the knighten guild. Early in the twelfth century the land and the franchise went to the Canons of Holy Trinity, London, the guild becoming extinct.

The Merchant Guild and the Craft Guild

It is reasonable to assume that the great increase in foreign commerce following the Norman Conquest, with its stimulus to trade and industry, led to the development of the first of the two main types of guild that played so great a part in medieval civic history. It is not easy to get a clear idea of the merchant guild (or guild merchant), there being contra-diction and confusion between the terms used by the various historians, but we may take the merchant guild to be a body of influential traders into whose hands came in course of time either the direct or indirect government of the town or city. It is difficult to say where the guild ceased and the town or government began. It is even possible that the alderman of a city was originally the alderman of the guild. Obviously merchant guilds grew to great strength, and out of their strength grew their weakness—their overriding of the elementary rights of the working people.

So in time we find another type of guild arising, the craft guild, a body or fraternity of skilled craftsmen, and sometimes craftswomen, which in the end absorbed the merchant guild, for as the latter declined so the craft guild prospered. It is more than likely that the chief representatives of a trade found themselves prominent members of both of the guilds, and that as time passed the two types of guilds would find themselves doing the same work and serving the same objects, and so would naturally come together. It is thought that the first mention of the craft guilds is in the reign of Henry I—somewhere before 1135—and if this is so the merchant guild could have had only a relatively short life before its top-heaviness presaged its fall.

The craft guild came into being to watch the interests of the skilled workpeople, but it was also a religious fraternity whose members had to make frequent attendance at church. It is clear that the craft guild did not long remain purely craft; either some of its members climbed into the employers' class or the two guilds began to combine elements common to both. It is even possible, as F. L. Pick, who has made a close study of the subject, believes, that the guild merchant (the merchant guild) was sometimes an aggregation of craft guilds, and if this was so the employer element would grow side by side with the craft and worker element.

The word 'craft,' largely synonymous with the words 'art' and 'mystery,' signified a trade or calling, and the typical member of the craft guild might be—not at first, but in the course of a century or so—a well-to-do tradesman, often or always an ex-apprentice. The craft guild was largely monopolistic in its effect, on the one hand making it none too easy for apprentices to enter the ranks of the masters, and seeing to it, on the other hand, that no craftsman who had learnt his trade by irregular means, and no man born in bondage, should get much chance of earning a skilled craftsman's living in its town or city. It is thought that many of the families represented in the craft guilds had climbed all the way from serfdom to employership in the course of a few generations, and might accordingly prove a somewhat difficult and unyielding type.

The craft guild continued its successful career until some time before the Reformation, but was already on the decline when Henry VIII—by no means the first of the kings to fear its competition and to covet its wealth—confiscated its moneys and other possessions, and dissolved its membership, but at the same time made it possible for the livery company to grow from its ruin. In the first year of the reign of his son Edward VI (1547) the Crown deprived the guilds of most of the funds dedicated by them to religious usages.

The Guild and the Civic Government

There is much difference of opinion as to whether the guilds grew to be the actual government of the town or city. It approximates to the truth to say that here and there they did actually grow into identity with the city government, and that elsewhere their leading members would be so influential as to have the government of the town, if not directly, then indirectly, in their hands. It can hardly be doubted that in France the civic government of many cities was the "direct development of the ancient guild or that the free cities in the lowlands North of France came into existence in much the same way." In every city in which the guild was powerful nobody could carry on a business or work as a craftsman without its permission, and the only way to civic honours was through its membership. In Preston, Lancashire, for instance, it proves extremely difficult to distinguish between the mayor of the guild and the mayor of the town, or even between the guild and the assembly or council that governed the town, and we can be sure that few men ever had a chance of becoming aldermen and mayors who were not in good standing in their guilds. In at least two cities, Bristol and Worcester, it is known that the election of the master of the craft guild had to be confirmed by the mayor of the city, a fact suggesting a very close connexion indeed between guild and municipality.

The names of many of the old streets and lanes of London and of more than one Continental city tell of the influence of the trade guilds. In London alone we have, for example, Bread Street, Mercer Street, Milk Street, Wood Street, Ironmonger Lane, Fish Street Hill, Goldsmith Row, Mason Lane, etc., to tell us where the trades of many centuries ago and their guilds and companies were localized.

The French Guilds and the Compagnonnage

With regard to French traditions and usages, a French author, J. C. Besuchet, has reported the opinion, in relation to the year 1729, that England had restored to France only what she had already borrowed, inasmuch as freemasonry in its three first, or symbolic, degrees was of French origin; but there is no agreement, outside of France, with that opinion to-day.

It is recorded that French cities on the departure of their Roman governors in the fifth century formed a kind of Republican Government, the executive authority being placed in the hands of those who had already exercised it as the lieutenants of the Roman governor. The successors to the Roman colleges split up into their various trades, whose elected officers formed, with the priests and bishops, municipal councils which policed the town and levied taxes. There appears to be a probability of a virtual and direct descent from the Roman colleges and municipalities to the French trades, guilds, and communes of the early Middle Ages. In those parts of France protected from the incursions of the barbarians many Roman edifices still exist in a complete state of preservation, not, as elsewhere, in mere ruins. In the north of France the guild system from Germany may have influenced both craft and municipal development, but by the thirteenth century the craft guilds of the whole country were alike, and already very different from those of Germany.

In Paris the city government became vested in the offices of one great guild, the Parisian Hanse, which in course of time came to include all the well-to-do citizens. The Hanse is first met with under the name of the Marchands de l'Eau de Paris, which completely controlled, even monopolized, the commerce of Paris and the surrounding district. This guild is claimed to be of Roman origin, and to be a direct successor of the Nautæ Parisiaci, but the evidence is not entirely convincing.

The six guilds of Paris, known as the Marchands or Six Corps de Paris, included the cloth-workers, grocers, mercers, hatters, furriers, and goldsmiths; these constituted the municipality of Paris in the twelfth century, each corps electing biennially a Master and Wardens (*gardes*); each master became successively juge, consul, and finally Échevin de la Ville de Paris (sheriff or alderman of the city), and automatically became ennobled, with the title of *écuyer* ('esquire'), while the Provost of the city became *chevalier*. In 1305 the Six Corps were so strong that under their Provost they were able to dictate the impeachment of Ministers, the liberation of the King of Navarre, etc., etc., and although in 1383 Charles VI did his best to abolish the municipality, the guilds did not disband, and in 1411 the municipality itself was restored. Ultimately the Provost recovered his former authority, which he retained until the great French Revolution at the end of the eighteenth century.

The chapter on the craft guilds of France is one of the most fascinating in Gould's three-volume *History*, and has the advantage of quoting many French authors for its facts; from this source has been drawn the bare outline here presented.

In the French craft guilds the intention seems to have been to ensure good workmen by insisting on apprenticeship, able masters by providing for a masterpiece as a test of skill, good work by appointing officers to make periodical visits to the workshops and by forbidding workshops to be otherwise than open to the street, or the work to be carried on by candlelight (the work of the coffin-maker excepted). A Master had one apprentice at a time, other than members of his family. The apprentice was required to be of legitimate birth and a Catholic; apprenticeship was from two to twelve years, seven being customary. The ex-apprentice was brought before the Master of the craft and sworn on the saints to keep the craft and all points thereof. Assistants and servants not instructed in the mystery (in the trade usages and secrets) did the unskilled work. The apprentice out of his time became a journeyman, who customarily worked for short periods for the various Masters in the towns he visited in the course of making, as he called it, his "tour de France." Gould says that to assist him in this object, and for certain other reasons, the very curious organization of the Compagnonnage was instituted.

The workman, or *compagnon*, was required to produce a masterpiece. Its achievement was the crowning-point of the Master's career, and the precautions to obviate fraud were severe. The nature of the test was decided by the craft authorities. A workman unable to stand the ordeal —its expense was often considerable to apprentices unrelated to the Masters—was allowed to make a less onerous masterpiece, and received the title of *perpetual companion*, but had no power to open a shop of his own or employ other workmen. In some trades—the butchers, for example—no journeyman could obtain the mastership, not even by marrying the daughter of a Master, because it was strictly hereditary in the male line. Anyone persistently opposing the rules of the craft, at least in Paris, had his tools seized.

An institution closely allied with the craft guilds was that of the fraternity known as the Confrairie and many similar names. Each craft guild belonged as a body to fraternity, maintained an altar in a church, and decorated it with candles, the supply of which was ensured by the members' fines and fees, which were paid in wax. From this wax candle the fraternity was sometimes spoken of as Le Cierge (The Candle). A newly received Master was expected to provide the members with a banquet. The fraternities sustained and relieved their aged widows and orphans and companions in their troubles; hence the name La Charité.

An apprentice on his admission gave a pound of wax for the candle. By 'candle' was meant the fraternity. To belong to the candle was a phrase meaning that the member paid his share of the upkeep of the fraternity, all members being required to make regular contributions to the treasury chest, on which there were many calls. The French Revolution cleared away the trade guilds and fraternities, which by that time had outlived their usefulness.

The Craft 'Mystery'

The word 'mystery' is met with in many ancient documents and records relating to masonry and other crafts, and particularly in connexion with the guilds, but readers must not suppose that it always implies secrecy. In olden days any trade was an 'art and mistery,' not because its craft secrets were jealously guarded, as, indeed, they always were, nor because its members may possibly have had communicated to them any secret mode of recognition, but merely because in the language brought over to England by William the Conqueror any trade or calling was a 'métière,' or 'mestière,' words which the Saxon soon adapted in his own way to 'mystery.' Thus when, in the ancient writings, masonry is termed a 'mystery' it does not mean that masons of that day were possessed of any particular secrets, but it certainly does mean that masonry was a trade and craft. As, for example, when, in 1508, a dispute was referred to the "maisters of the mister[y] or craft of masons."

Any work of skill was, in common language, a mystery. In the Constitutions of the Fellowship of Freemasons, 1481, occurs the phrase "Craft, Mistery or Science." A sentence in a book by Robert Green (1592) is conclusive: "I would title myself with the name of a fencer, and make gentlemen believe that I picked a living out of that mystery...." The mystery in this case was the art of fencing. Any such art had its 'secrets,' of course, but they were matters of craft theory or practice or technique; they were not esoteric mysteries.

Living Members of the Lodge No. 361 ... Their Titles Mysteries or Trade is the title of a list published in 1768. Perhaps the "Revd," the "Esqr," and possibly the "Colonel" in the list were the 'titles'; all the rest—the "M.D.," the "Surgeon," the "Linnendraper," and the "Inn Keepe," were the 'mysteries' and 'trades.'

Naturally there was a strong tendency for the 'mistery' to become a trade secret, a tendency fostered through the centuries, and even to-day attributed, in spite of the great advance in scientific and technical knowledge, to some of the more old-fashioned trades.

It is easy to see, therefore, how a word originally implying nothing more than a craft came to mean a *secret* craft, and, just as a trade kept its secrets from the public gaze, so the senior workers in that trade would tend to keep their secrets from their juniors, until such time as it was thought expedient to communicate them. So it came about, in the course of time, that many a craft that had been a 'mistery' to start with had become in fact a code or a system of mysteries and secrets, which everybody seeking to join it had solemnly to swear to keep inviolate.

This was true of practically all the crafts, and not of the masons' craft in particular, as may be seen from an ordinance of the Fraternity of the Tailors, 1768, according to which:

> It is striclie statute an ordained ... that whatever entring freeman of the Craft, or any other freeman thereof, shall anyways reveal or divulge to the Magistrate or any Burgess of Guild, directly or indirectly, any of the Craft's secrets, especially anent their procedue when entring freeman of the traid, anent the composition or other expenses, etc., shall never carry public charge amongst the said traid as deacon, maister, or box master, until they give all satisfaction anent the said misdemeanour.

This quotation demonstrates another fact that freemasons should remember: fraternities besides the masons had Deacons and Masters (convertible terms at one time) and Box Masters, these last being the keepers of the money-chest, or, as we call them to-day, the treasurers. And the mason's mystery was not alone in veiling its moralizings in allegory and illustrating them with symbols drawn from its own craft.

Truth is rarely quite simple, however, and there is reason to believe that hidden away within some of the craft 'misteries' was sometimes a religious mystery, a secret cell, in which case the word might earn a double meaning. Now the dictionaries agree that so far as the Church is concerned, the word 'mystery' was derived from a Greek word meaning 'to close the lips or eyes' (see a particular reference on p. 281), and gained particular force from the custom in the Early Church of administering the sacraments in secret fashion. The ancient Fathers of the Church spoke of the "sacred" and "tremendous mysteries" of the sacrament of the Holy Communion. While, then, it is quite certain that our masonic word 'mystery' is derived originally from a word meaning trade or calling, we cannot entirely rule out just the possibility that it may at some time or other have united two distinct ideas—that of the skilled craft or trade and that of something hidden from ordinary comprehension.

Disputes

Old lodge minutes, threatening with penalties any members refusing to submit (outside) disputes to the lodge or grand lodge, may have been inspired by guild enactments of the fourteenth century imposing a fine of a pound of wax on any member hastily starting litigation while the guild was still trying to compose the quarrel.

Chapter Four

THE LONDON COMPANY OF FREEMASONS

THE records and antiquities of that unique set of survivals, the Livery Companies of London, have a value for English social history that can scarcely be overestimated, says George Unwin in his *Gilds and Companies of London*. It may be added that their value to masonic history is also considerable. Another authority, Carew Hazlitt, speaking particularly of the Mason Company of London in existence in the fourteenth century, says that the freemasons

> represent in a modified form the Society which once rose to exceptional eminence and acquired even formidable power. They enjoy the unique distinction of having laid the basis of a social cult which has immeasurably outstripped its founders.

Still another of the guild historians, Robert J. Blackham, says that the

> Masons Company . . . has not only preserved its own identity from the Middle Ages, but played a considerable part in the early development of a world-wide and esoteric organisation which has adopted an ancient title. . . . The London Livery Company of Masons may proudly claim that it is the principal connecting link in the chain of evidence which indicates that the modern social cult known as "Free and Accepted Masons" is lineally descended from the old fraternity of masons which, in association with the monastic orders, built the stately Gothic buildings of the Middle Ages.

The Origin of Masons' Fraternities

The old manuscript poem known as the Regius (or Halliwell) MS., date about 1390, makes what is probably a mythical claim that King Athelstan gave a charter to a Mason Fellowship of a national character. Equally legendary, we expect, is the story that Godfrey de Lucy, Bishop of Winchester, who rebuilt part of his cathedral, founded in 1202 a Mason Fraternity which was the origin of the Society of Freemasons. Nor can we credit Anderson's statement (1738) that William Molart, Prior of Canterbury Cathedral, in 1429 founded a Mason Fraternity under the patronage of Archbishop Chichele. None of these fraternities, if any of them ever existed, is likely to have been the association in which the mason companies had their origin. Such companies were brought into existence by the same causes as produced the trade guilds, but, while most craftsmen found their work at their door, the mason soon exhausted local requirements (except, of course, in rich, prosperous, and growing cities), and had to be prepared to go forth and seek his living. In this one fact is undoubtedly the cause of the paucity of mason companies throughout England. Whereas every great city had its variety of craft guilds, only a few had a mason guild-like company, and there is reason to believe that only that of London grew to power and influence. Masons living in small towns or scattered through a largely undeveloped country-side could neither maintain a guild nor be easily controlled by one, and we can therefore well understand that the masons of England were not organized into guilds in the early medieval days when already the trade guilds were immensely strong.

London had a strong Freemason and Mason Company. There is evidence of it before 1376, but for how long it had been in existence we do not know. There was a guild founded in Lincoln in 1313, and in the Record Office is a certificate relating to it dated 1389, the only known certificate of its kind. Fred L. Pick (*A.Q.C.*, vol. lvi) tells us that both brothers and sisters were admitted to the guild, which was a religious fraternity with a social side, and not a trade guild; the candle of the guild was set up, and one of its objects was to help members in custody, excepting those guilty of murder and theft. At Norwich in 1375 there was another guild of much the same kind. There may have been mason guilds at York, Beverley, Coventry, Chester, and Oxford, but we have no evidence that they were concerned with the regulation of the trade, although some of them might well have been. A mason guild at Exeter incorporated in 1586 had probably had a long pre-existence, and in 1684 was granted a charter incorporating it as a body of freemasons, masons, and bricklayers, glaziers, and painters. It may be, then, that the London Company was either the only true trade or craft guild-like body known to the English mason, or one of the very few; but, whatever may be the truth as to that, the freemason is comforted by the thought that at any rate the existence of the London Company is fully authenticated, and that through it he is enabled to trace the path that leads him directly back to the mason of medieval days.

A curious mistake in writing out the returns to the Common Council of the City of London in 1376 led to Herbert in his *History of the Twelve Great Livery Companies* drawing a wrong conclusion and stating that at the date mentioned there were *two* London Mason Companies, one of freemasons returning two members to the Common Council of the City of London and one of masons returning four members, and that shortly after that date the two were amalgamated into one. The Clerk, in preparing his list of names, had started by writing the word 'ffreemasons, followed by two names; evidently this was in error, so he struck it out,' and later in the record made a corrected entry, but in a misleading manner. There was one London Company of Masons and Freemasons, not two.

There is a charming reference in John Stow's well-known *Survey of London* (1633 edition) to the company of the 1410–11 period. His words are:

> The Company of Masons being otherwise termed Free Masons of ancient standing and good reconing, by means of affable and kind meetings at divers times; and as a loving brotherhood should use to do; did frequent this mutual assembly in the time of King Henry the fourth in the twelfth year of his most gracious reign.

In due course (in 1481) the members of the Company assumed or were granted a livery, which, as the word originally implied, was a sign or badge taking the form of clothing of peculiar cut and colour, designed or chosen by the Masters and Wardens of each individual company. The movement towards liveries came late in the thirteenth century. Not only members of guilds or companies, but the servants of the nobles and rich men, began to wear livery, much to the alarm of the Crown, which, about a century later, while allowing the guilds and companies of the cities and boroughs to continue to wear livery, forbade anyone else to do so if of less estate than a knight.

We suspect that the livery company in general was nothing more than the old guild brought into harmony with the spirit of the times; its powers were considerable; it had complete jurisdiction over its members, certainly as craftsmen, and even largely as private citizens. Unwin says that:

> By its judgments unruly apprentices were whipped, journeymen on strike were imprisoned and masters offending against regulations were fined. Members were forbidden to carry trade disputes before any other court, unless the court of their Companies had first been appealed to in vain.

The livery company in general was governed by a Master, Wardens, a Court of Assistants, and a livery, below whom came the general body of freemen, and below them again the apprentices. The chief officer of some companies was called a Warden, not Master. The Warden himself was a guardian of the company, and the Master of some companies might be called the Upper Warden, a term still used by some City companies, together with the term Prime Warden or First Warden. Originally co-operating with the Master and Wardens was a number of the senior livery men or freemen, who became known as the assistants. The Mason Company as a livery company was governed by its Master and two Wardens in association with the livery. The Constitutions of 1481, in which year the Company was enfranchised, which were "granted to the Fellowship of the Free Masons enfranchised within this Honourable City of London," laid down particulars of the right to a livery, and prescribed that once in every three years the persons of the Fellowship be "cladd in one clothing convenient to their powers and degrees, to be ordained for by the Wardens of the same Craft, Mistery or Science for the time being"; and, further, if anyone refuse to take the clothing and wear it, who is, by reason of his craft, entitled to it, he is "to forfeit as often as he doth so and be duly convict thereof, Six shillings and eight pence. . . ."

A constitution of the Company refers to the members officially attending Mass once every two years, and afterwards holding a dinner to which their wives could be invited. The price of the meal deserves a comment: 12d. in the year 1481 might have been two or three days' wages, and ought to have bought a good meal with wine. Edward Conder suggests that the menu was elaborate, and that masons would not be behind other citizens in respect of their table manners—but is that saying much? He holds (and who shall contradict him?) that the masons were well acquainted with certain lines in their own poem (the Regius or Halliwell MS.):

> To the mete when thow art y-sette
> Fayre and onestelyche thow ete hytte
> Fyrst loke that thyn honden be clene
> And that thy knyf be scharpe and kene
> Ny at the mete thy tothe thow pyke
> To depe yn Copp thou myght not synke
> Loke yn thy mowth there be no mete
> When thow begynnyst to drynke or speke.

We hope that Conder's authority is good for his statement that although the water-bowl, or basin, was handed round after the repast the drinking of water at such a feast was unheard of. He says the "wines were classed as red or white—either claret or Gascoigne, with sometimes Malvoisey and Alicante. The loving-cup was a mixture and generally spiced; in the winter it was served hot." We can all agree with Conder that at this very early example of a Ladies' Night held at midday "a right merry afternoon was doubtlessly spent."

Perhaps our best comment on the manners of the company is that the diners did not use forks, and the knives were those they brought with them! Five hundred years or so before, the families gathered at the homely feasts of the frith guilds had attacked the communal joint or pot with their own knives; and nearly two hundred years later, at the Lord Mayor's Feast of 1663, the guests, except a few of great distinction for whom knives were provided, still had to use their own knives or none at all. We can rely on one of the guests, Samuel Pepys, telling us the truth in such a matter.

There were four ways of obtaining the freedom of a livery company. The most regular was by apprenticeship, the terms of which had to be submitted to the City authorities for their approval. Apprenticeship involved two brief ceremonies: the Master took the lad to the Hall of his company to be bound according to the *Constitutions*, and when he was out of his time, at the end generally of seven years, and providing the Master and company were fully satisfied as to his skill and behaviour, he was 'presented' in the Hall and admitted to the full freedom. He would pay a fee on both occasions. The freeman might become a liveryman, and in due course a Warden or Master of his company.

An ancient practice of the guilds and livery companies was to admit persons by the rule of patrimony. The sons and daughters of freemen could claim the freedom of the company, whether or not they were engaged in the trade of their father, and through this door of patrimony could accordingly enter many persons of a purely non-operative character. There may have been such members in the Mason Company in the seventeenth century, in those years in which freemasonry as we know it to-day began to emerge. Certain privileges of membership of a livery company were worth having, possibly the greatest of them being that freedom of a company was a passport to civic honours.

Freedom of a company could be bought, and it could also be had from the company as a gift, and in each case we assume the persons concerned must have been of distinction or influence. It is easy to see, then, that there was, at the discretion of the Master and Wardens, an open door through which persons unconnected with the trade could enter into the freedom of the guild. There seems to have been a custom, too, of transferring from guild to guild or company to company, probably in the pursuit of some social ambition.

The Reformation Period, 1530–60

"We have got our open Bible, we have got faith and love, we can preach the Gospel of the grace of God." In this way Martin Luther summed up the blessings which the Reformation had given to many peoples. The Reformation brought to an end the Bishop of Rome's "jurisdiction in this realm of England," was the turning-point in the middle centuries of England's history, and had vast political, religious, and social effects. It is often credited with having brought to a sudden stop the great Gothic period of building, but historical evidence does not support this. Changing social and economic conditions brought the Gothic period to its close, but the movement was given impetus by the events of the Reformation. Naturally the looting and destruction of the monasteries discouraged ecclesiastical building, but it is wrong to ascribe to that event the change in the fortunes of England's building industry in general or the London Company of Freemasons in particular. The economic structure of the country was undergoing great change. One employing class was making room for another. The kings, the Church, and the nobles had built the great stone buildings of the Gothic age; hardly anybody else would have had the means to ensure a supply of material and labour; but in the sixteenth century the power of the traditional employers was waning, while that of the gentry and rich merchants was growing. The Crown did not cease to build, but it ceased to occupy the same relative position as a building employer. With their acquired riches the universities began to build, but not on the old direct-labour system, which was, after all, only possible on a large scale to employers who could force craftsmen to work for them.

From this time, and even before this time, the direct-labour system was becoming out of date. Certain mason families must have prospered and found themselves in a position in which they could command money and act as contractors; so from roughly this period we find great buildings being erected on the contract system, in which the contractor as a rule found everything, both materials and labour, at his own cost and own endeavour, and charged the building owner a price accordingly. Under the old direct-labour system the chief mason, or Master Mason, had been the servant or agent of his employer and was rewarded with a wage and emoluments, certainly not with a profit. Not only the Master Mason was affected: the wage of the working mason steadily increased from that time forward, but whether it was greatly to his advantage is a question, for, as already stated, in the year 1700 his wage bought him about 60 units of food, whereas in 1500 it had bought him 100 units.

The Crown took the opportunity afforded by the unsettled conditions of the Reformation period to deal the guilds, now livery companies, a shrewd blow, having always feared their power and coveted their wealth. The London guilds lost their possessions, but were allowed later to repurchase them on conditions very favourable to the Crown!

Unwin's *Gilds* shows that while considerable changes were, of course, effected in the disposition of guild property, and while the cessation of time-honoured customs must have been felt as a sore deprivation, "the main current of the companies' activities flowed on. . . . Their social gatherings, the administration of their charities, their regulation of industry and trade, were not disturbed."

Of all the guilds and companies affected that of the masons was one of the worst hit, but at least a century was to pass before the Mason Company came to realize "that its future was behind it."

Until some time early in the 1500's London's Mason Company had been known as the "Fellowship of Masons" or "The Company of ffree masons." A change in title was made in 1655–56. Before this date the Company had been styled in its own accounts "The Company of ffremasons of the City of London," but from that date it is "The Company of Masons." The significance of this alteration is referred to in later pages under the emergence of speculative freemasonry. It is not, however, to be assumed that from this date all operative freemasons were called masons, the former term continuing in use for a century or more, although becoming less and less used as time went by.

Curiously the Company was strong enough to obtain a Royal Charter of Incorporation from Charles II in 1677, but the key to the problem is probably, as Edward Conder puts it, that "the Privy Purse of a merry Monarch required assistance." Students may care to know that the full text of the charter can be found in *A.Q.C.*, vol. xliii, and that there is a facsimile reproduction in Edward Conder's well-known book. This is the only charter the Company has had, whereas some of the London companies have had quite a number—the Mercers ten or more, the Grocers, Fishmongers, Goldsmiths, Merchant Taylors, at least twelve each.

The charter declares the existing constituency a body politic with perpetual succession ... an unlimited licence in mortmain, ... and the power of search and control within seven miles of the Cities of London and Westminster, wherever any stones to be used in masonry should be brought, in order to see that such be of proper measure and truly wraught.

We have shown that part of the Company's duty was to watch the quality of materials and workmanship in the London neighbourhood. We find in its accounts many instances of masons being fined for bad work, and on one occasion that the Company entered an action against the Plasterers' Company to restrain them from mending church windows with mortar, it being the masons' duty to mend them with stone.

The Company's Decline

With the coming of the seventeenth century the London Company of Freemasons went into its final period of decline. The Company's surviving books and documents are not earlier than 1620, but fortunately there are City of London letter-books and other records extending from late in the thirteenth century to the middle of the seventeenth, and from these we learn that in 1607 the Company was in difficulties and its Wardens had "byn founde to be verie remisse in ye execucion of theire offices." At the Company's own petition its rules were altered and the livery obliged to assemble each year on or near the Feast of Holy Trinity and there choose among themselves a Master for the ensuing year "whoe maie be a direccion to ye wardens for the better government" of the Company, and also to choose "twoe honest hable and discreete persons" to be Wardens for one year, these officers to be presented in the Chamber of the Guild Hall and there sworn and charged.

The position of the Company was weakened in the second half of the seventeenth century by a growing custom of members of the mason trade achieving their freedom of the City otherwise than by membership of the Company, a practice which hurt the Company's revenues as well as its future membership, and which was a big factor in bringing about the fall of the Company from any position of trade government. Another trouble was the position of 'foreigners'—that is, non-members who had been attracted to London by prospects of work—not a new problem, but one that had now to be faced under great disadvantages. The Company would have liked to have seen every London mason forced into its membership, but the interest of the authorities was to get work done, not to worry over-duly about the strength of the companies associated with the various sections of the building trade. This trouble became extremely acute following the Fire of London, when, frankly, the membership of the Company was quite inadequate to deal with the tremendous amount of rebuilding suddenly forced upon the community. In spite of the livery companies concerned, it was made lawful for members of the building trade not freemen of the City to work in London until the rebuilding was completed, such foreigners being regarded at the end of seven years as having earned the right to continue to work there. The Company failed to rope in many of the foreigners; probably it could not persuade them to pay the heavy fees of admission, and therefore reverted to the old custom of imposing, or trying to impose, a quarterage at 6d. a head, a practice which must have been in the mind of the new Grand Lodge when it brought its own system of quarterages into effect, the self-same system (although with different amounts) as that under which the fraternity works to-day.

Obviously the Company was fast losing any hold upon the mason trade. There was a reluctance to enter apprentices, and in 1694 the Company presented to the Lord Mayor and Aldermen a humble petition stating that it was facing "almost utter ruin" and asking for an Act of

Common Council that all apprentices of masons free of other companies and masons bringing up their sons in the same trade, henceforth be presented bound and made free of the Masons' Company; those already bound and not made free, to be made free of the Masons.

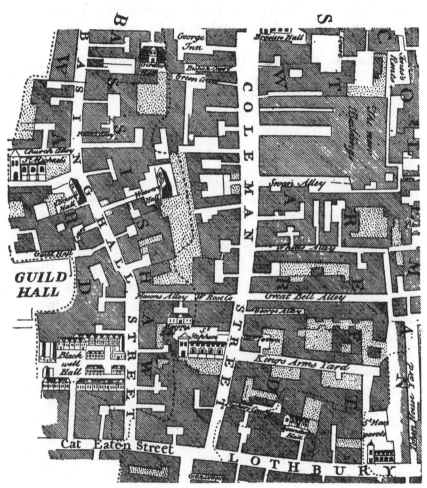

OLD CITY MAP SHOWING MASONS' HALL

This is a portion of a map in William Maitland's *History and Survey of London* (1756) and includes a tiny elevation of Masons' Hall, in Masons Alley, in which the London Company's Lodge or 'acception' was held.

There is evidence of non-operative membership in 1663, even of women being among the members. Margaret Wild, widow, was a member in the year mentioned. As late as 1713–14 we find the remarkable instance of Mary Banister, the daughter of a barber of Barking, being apprenticed to a mason for the term of seven years, the fee of 5s. being duly paid to the Company. In 1696 the Mason's Court Book gives the names of two widows, this same Court Book containing evidence that the Company no longer occupied a commanding position in the building trade. Forty members were made free *by redemption* in the period 1670–79, an indication of the considerable adulteration of the operative element.

Prominent members of the Masons' Company took part in the building of St Paul's (1675–1707), but, says Douglas Knoop, about four-fifths of all the masonry contracting work at the cathedral was carried out by contractors of country origin and training.

Masons' Hall

If the old Hall of the Worshipful Company of Masons of the City of London still existed it would be the Mecca of freemasons not only of England, but of the world, for that Company is apparently the chief link between the old-time operative freemasons and the modern Fraternity of Speculative Freemasons. The Company's first hall, built about 1463 in Hazelwood Alley, within the Ward of Bassishaw, in the City of London, was destroyed in the Great Fire, and rebuilt on the same site about 1668 at a cost of only £800 or so, equal, of course, to many thousands of pounds to-day. This second hall, which is believed to have housed a Speculative Lodge, also stood for a period of 200 years, the Company selling it in 1865 and the hall ceasing to exist soon after. Its site is indicated by Masons Alley (so named from the hall), which connects Basyags Hall (Basinghall) Street with Colmon (Coleman) Street, only a few yards to the east of London's Guildhall. Maitland's *History and Survey of London* (1756) speaks of the Masons Hall as being small but convenient, well built of stone, and as being bounded on the west by Coleman Street Churchyard. One of the maps in that book gives a tiny front elevation of the hall, a reproduction of which is given on the preceding page.

Chapter Five

THE OLD MANUSCRIPT CHARGES

FREEMASONS possess many old manuscript writings, some dating to about the fourteenth century, which throw much light upon the traditions, usages, and customs of the medieval operative masons. These Old Charges are not identical with the Charges addressed to the Initiate and (rarely) to the Fellow Craft and Master Mason in the speculative lodges of to-day, which, however, together with "The Charges of a Free-mason," printed as a preface to the General Laws and Regulations of the United Grand Lodge of England, have been largely based upon the Old Charges, and happily preserve many of their more important 'Articles' and 'Points.'

The intelligent freemason should know something of the Old Charges, but only the Brethren who can give time for a close study and comparison of the various versions can hope to become really acquainted with them. To the mason who looks upon them with a somewhat casual eye they might appear as "tombs without an epitaph," to quote the understanding Gould.

It is quite impossible in the present volume to attempt detailed treatment of the Old Charges. Any close examination of them would have to be largely technical, and, to all but the serious student, would prove rather tedious. Further, space cannot be afforded to reproduce any of them at length, but indication is given in due course where copies of the early Charges have been published, and sprinkled through these pages are many quotations of the old texts. Fortunately the reader wishing to study the matter closely has many available sources of information—namely, the writings of Dr Wilhelm Begeman, W. J. Hughan, Lionel Vibert, Douglas Knoop and his associates, the Rev. Herbert Poole, and others.

A very few of the Old Charges are mentioned by name in this section, but there actually exist more than one hundred versions, no two of them identical. The oldest of them are the Regius and the Cooke, the former being in rhymed verse, the latter in prose.

Speaking generally, most or all of the Old Charges have descended from earlier writings, any differences between them being due apparently to the mistakes, to the whims, and to the intentional deviations of the copyists, editors, and compilers through whose hands the writings have come down to us. Important work in their analysis by the method of comparison has been done, much of it by Wilhelm Begeman, in conjunction with W. J. Hughan, with later revisions by the Rev. Herbert Poole They have divided the Old Charges into six groups as follow:

I. The Regius Poem.
II. The Cooke family (3 copies).
III. The Plot family (5).
IV. The Grand Lodge (46), Tew (7), and Sloane (20) families.
V. The Roberts family (6).
VI. The Spencer family (6).

The Regius Poem dates back to about 1389, the Cooke MS. to the early fifteenth century; the Plot MS. is actually the printed part of one version of the Old Charges, and is dated 1686. The Grand Lodge No. 1 MS. is the earliest known of the Old Charges to bear its own definite date—namely, December 25, 1583. The Roberts pamphlet goes back to 1722. But the classification of the manuscripts is not based so much upon the dates at which they are believed to have been written as upon the relationship disclosed by the internal analysis.

Although we do not easily recognize in the Old Charges anything of an esoteric nature, we may regard them as a link between operative and speculative masonry. That does not mean that they contain a working basis for to-day's ritual; they do not, but undoubtedly our present traditions and ritual reflect many of the ideas and perpetuate many of the words and phrases of the old writings.

Many of the old manuscripts were parchment rolls having a length of many feet and a width of a few inches. The Regius Poem is a small manuscript book about 5 inches by 4 inches on vellum bound in Russian leather. The Cooke MS. is smaller. The Lansdowne MS. of the sixteenth century is on stout paper 11 inches by 15 inches, but the Grand Lodge MS. of about 1583 is a roll of parchment 9 feet long and 5 inches wide, and the York No. 1 MS., of the next century, is a parchment roll in three slips. One manuscript of about 1725 is of folio size, and has a frontispiece showing masons at work with the words "Inigo Jones, delin." This beautiful manuscript contains many ornaments, but there is no possibility that it is the work of Inigo Jones (1573–1652), inasmuch as it quotes text printed after the famous artist died. The Buchanan MS. is a parchment roll.

Both the Regius and the Cooke MSS. can be seen in the British Museum; facsimiles of them have been published by Q. C. Lodge, and a recent print of the text is in *The Two Earliest Masonic MSS.*, by Douglas Knoop and G. P. Jones. Lithographed facsimiles of the Grand

Lodge No. 2, the Scarborough, and the Buchanan MSS. are published by Q.C. Lodge.

Descent and Common Origin of the Old Charges

Of the Old Charges in general we can say that there must have been some early original or originals yet unknown to us, parts of which have descended through the series. This can be illustrated most simply by saying that the matter contained in the Regius and Cooke MSS. may well have existed for a considerable period before it was incorporated into those writings. Perhaps the original matter was in trade ordinances or in some statement prepared by a learned monk well acquainted with the usages and conditions of the mason trade. The two manuscripts were not drawn from exactly the same originals. The Regius Poem contains more information on trade usages, but the Cooke MS. tells us more of the traditional or legendary history.

The Old Charges have been much studied with a view to classification by the method of close comparison, which has gone a long way towards revealing their parentage or line of descent, although much has yet to be learnt. It is obvious that the long series of copyists and editors—the former by accident and error and the latter chiefly by intention—have between them produced from the earliest manuscripts many different versions, which in turn have become the raw material for other copyists and editors. Every fresh hand has introduced variation, accidental or otherwise, trivial or serious; he has omitted or he has added or he has done both, and the reader will at once recognize that much painstaking comparative analysis has been called for in tracing back the parentage of any particular manuscript.

It is certain that there have been many valuable manuscripts lost or destroyed. It is known, for example, that the London Company had in its records of 1676 the item *Book of the Constitutions of the Accepted Masons,* which book has disappeared. Anderson in his first *Constitutions* of Grand Lodge stated that valuable manuscripts had been burned by (over) scrupulous Brothers to prevent their falling into strange hands, and one or two masonic commentators have expressed their belief that on this occasion Anderson was reciting a simple fact.

The Authors of the Old Charges

The English mason craft is almost alone in having a legendary history. The reason for this has been ascribed to its association with the Church, but, without exception, all medieval crafts had such an association, although less intimate. We may well conclude that it was the old monkish scribe full of church lore and well acquainted with the building fraternity who gave us the earliest manuscripts—the Regius, the Cooke, and others—and that to some extent, large or small, he was writing for the operative mason of his day, who, not actually in himself any more religious than men of later days, had at any rate a greater regard for religious observances. He was unlettered, as were the workers in all the other crafts, and as, indeed, were a proportion of his priests as well. He was superstitious and of vast credulity, and he accepted, probably without question, the highly imaginative craft history written for him by the learned priests and undoubtedly coloured to suit the ideas and purpose of the Church. The priestly historian, when facts failed him, drew upon legend and sheer invention, but fortunately, too, he drew upon and preserved many noble traditions, for which, as freemasons, we must always be grateful.

The question will be asked as to why the learned priests wrote for men who could not read! The priests wrote, we may take it, more likely for those with ears than eyes. On suitable occasion, when masons met together in assemblies or even in small gatherings in their lodges, these manuscripts may have been read to them by a priest or by an educated Master Mason, probably not to entertain them so much as to impress upon them the dignity of their calling and their duty to God, to their Masters, to one another, and to the world about them.

It is a curious fact, but one of which we must remind ourselves, that any such composition as the Regius Poem or Cooke MS. could hardly have been written in England at a much earlier date. Certainly the English language was mature early in the fourteenth century, but "as an instrument of abstract speculation or of precise, practical instruction" it did not reach perfection for several generations, which bring us more or less to the accepted date (about 1390) of the Regius Poem. Prof. William Spalding says that books, multiplied by manuscript copies only, were rare and costly and the accomplishment of reading was unusual, except among the clergy. There followed the result that a large proportion of the literary compositions of the Middle Ages were produced in the distinct expectation that they would be heard and not read by the public to which they appealed. Many, many of them have peculiarities which cannot otherwise be explained.

The Regius Poem in Outline

This manuscript on thirty-three vellum sheets (the Regius or Halliwell MS., No. 23,198 in the British Museum) is in the beautiful Gothic writing of a priest of the period 1388–1445. It tells us that Athelstan (King of the English from 925 until his death in 940) "loved thys craft ful well" and sought to hold congregations of masons for the examination of Master Masons respecting their knowledge of the craft. The manuscript loses none of its authority, whatever that may be, because it is in verse, for did not, says an old writer, "the Ancients wrap up their Chiefest Mystries" in the "Parabolical and Allusive part of Poetry, as the most *Sacred*, and Venerable in their Esteeme, and the securest from Prophane and Vulgar Wits?" Note in the following quotation (modernized) that we have (as far back as about 1390) the title Master (Mason) and the foundation of the term Worshipful (that is, worthy, honoured) Master:

> Furthermore yet that ordained he,
> Master called so should he be;
> So that he were most worshipped,
> Then should he be so called.

The manuscript declares that "Thys craft com ynto Englond . . . Yn time of good Kynge Adelstonus day," recites thirty articles and points, and offers the mason much good advice as to his manners, morals, and religious duties.

The Regius Poem[1] speaks well of geometry, directs that masons should call another "neither subject nor servant" but "my dear brother," and includes fifteen articles and fifteen points. Article 1 is that the Master Mason be steadfast, trusty, and true; 2. that every Master Mason attend the assembly, sickness being the only excuse; 3. the master take "no 'prentice unless he have good assurance to dwell seven years with him . . . his craft to learn"; 4. that the master "he no bondman 'prentice make"; 5. that the 'prentice be of lawful blood; 6. "that the master do the lord no prejudice" by taking an unfair portion for his 'prentice; 7. that a master shall not harbour thieves, murderers, or one "that hath a feeble name"; 8. that the master may change a poor craftsman for a better; 9. that the master "no work undertake unless he can both it end and make"; 10. that no master supplant another; 11. that no mason should work by night except by "practising of wit"; 12. that a mason shall "not his fellows' work deprave"; 13 and 14. that the master does well and justly by his apprentice; 15. that the master is not to "maintain his fellows in their sin for no good that he might win; nor no false oath suffer him to make, for dread of their soul's sake."

Now as to the points. The first is that the mason "must love well God and Holy Church" and his master also; 2. that the mason work as

[1] In the preparation of the following outline sketch of the contents of the Regius Poem a modernized transcript by Roderick H. Baxter presented in 1914 before the Lodge of Research, No. 2429, Leicester, has been of great assistance.

truly as he can to deserve his hire and reward; 3. that the 'prentice "keep and close" his master's counsel, "The privities of the chamber tell he no man"; 4. that "no man to his craft be false"; 5. that the mason take his pay "full meekly" and that the master warn the mason "lawfully before noon if he will not occupy him no more"; 6. that masons should postpone their quarrels and arguments to "loveday" (a day appointed for settlement of differences); 7. the mason is enjoined to respect the chastity of his master's wife and fellow's concubine; 8. the mason to be a true mediator to his master and fellows; 9. that the masons take their turn in being stewards week after week "amiably to serve each one other, as though they were sister and brother" and do the work honestly; 10. a mason "to live without care and strife" and not to slander his fellows; 11. "A mason, if he this craft well con [know], that seeth his fellow hew on a stone, and is in point to spoil that stone," to assist by instruction to prevent the loss of the work; 12. that any decision of the assembly of Masters, Fellows, and great lords shall be maintained in the craft; 13. the mason to "swear never to be no thief"; 14. the mason to swear a "good true oath" to his Master and Fellows and to be steadfast and true to this ordinance and his liege lord, the King; 15. relates to the sheriff's duty in imprisoning the disobedient mason and confiscating his "goods and cattle."

The next part of the poem relates to *Ars Quatuor Coronatorum* (the Art of the Four Crowned Martyrs), after which are references to Noah's Flood, the Tower of Babylon, King Nebuchadnezzar, and to "the good clerk Euclid" teaching the "craft of geometry full wonder wide." The seven liberal arts and sciences are then listed—grammar, dialect, rhetoric, music, astronomy, arithmetic, geometry. Next the mason is reminded in great detail of his religious duties, given a form of prayer to "Jesu Lord," taught humility to his lord (employer), and told how to behave himself "in hall, in bower or at the board"; "good manners make a man." He is taught his table manners and instructed that if he is sitting by a worthier man to

> Suffer him first to touch the meat,
> Ere thyself to it reach.
> To the fairest morsel thou might not strike,
> Though that thou do it well like.

He is told to keep his hands fair and well, not to blow his nose on his towel, not to pick his teeth at meat, not to sink too deep in cup, and not to drink or speak when there is food in his mouth. He receives instruction with regard to his behaviour "in chamber, among the ladies bright," where he is to "hold thy tongue and spend thy sight" nor tell "all that thou hears." The mason meeting or going with a worthier man is told how to behave himself: "what thou sayest consider thee well; but deprive thou not him his tale, neither at the wine nor at the ale." The poem closes with

> Christ then of his high grace,
> Save you both wit and space,
> Well this book to know and read,
> Heaven to have for your mede [reward]
> Amen! Amen! so mote it be!
> So say we all for charity.

It will have been noted that the Regius Poem lays great stress on the mason leading a moral life and respecting the chastity of his Master's and Fellow's wife and daughter. We know very little about the social life of the early medieval mason, and although obviously at times he must have lived a communal life it would be most unnatural to assume that in many thousands of cases he did not live the ordinary family life with wife and children. It is much to be expected that masons working on a great abbey, castle, or cathedral for years on end would quite commonly have with them their wives and families.

The Charges forbade Masters to take work which they were unable to complete, severely condemned unfair competition, and prohibited unlawful games of chance. On the question of apprenticeship they laid down that the period should not be less than seven years, that the boy must be free from bondage, come of honest parents, and be whole of limb. They enjoined the craftsman to help his less skilled fellows, and admonished all craftsmen to work hard, be obedient and faithful, and to receive their pay meekly. They placed Masters under an obligation to all strange fellows to provide them with work or to give them money that would take them to the next lodge.

All the old manuscripts had a distinctly religious character, most of them laying emphasis on the Holy Trinity; thus, the Grand Lodge No. 1 MS., a parchment roll dated 1583, starts with a solemn prayer:

> The might of the Father of Heaven and the Wisdom of the Glorious Son through the grace and the goodness of the Holy Ghost that be three persons and one God be with us at our beginning; and give us grace so to govern us here in our living that we may come to His bliss that never shall have ending. Amen.

Assemblies

The early manuscripts contemplated a system of mason congregations or assemblies. Wyatt Papworth is of opinion that such assemblies were held in medieval times and that they were the gatherings sought to be prohibited by the Statutes of 15 Henry 6, in 1436–37. But the idea that there was in Athelstan's day—the tenth century—a powerful assembly in control of the mason craft must surely be ruled out, for, in an age when roads were nearly non-existent, when buildings were of wood, and when the mason trade was necessarily small and unorganized, anything approaching a national assembly of masons would appear to have been an impossibility.

Charles Martel of France

The Old Charges, strangely, as we may think, refer to Charles Martel, who was a powerful personality in France in the eighth century. He led expeditions against the Bavarians, Saxons, and others, and by defeating the Saracens in 732, and thus saving France from the fate of Spain, came to be regarded as "the saviour of Christendom." He had helped to set a king on the throne of the united Frankish kingdom, but, as Duke of France, was himself the real ruler of the Franks, besides being the founder of a great dynasty, his famous grandson being Charlemagne. The Lansdowne MS. (c. 1600) says that he set masons

> on work and gave them Charges and Manners and good pay as he had learned of other Masons, and confirmed them a Charter from yeare to yeare to hold their Assembly when they would, and Cherished them right well, and thus came this Noble Craft into France.

As the French word 'martel' means 'hammer,' and is known also in connexion with a chisel used by marble workers, there is a temptation to suppose that the Martel tradition so far as masonry, not general history, is concerned is nothing more than a story that has grown up in folk-lore style, having its roots in some simple fact of the stonemason's craft. But masonic writers appear to scorn that idea, while Gould regards the community of tradition in the French and the English legends as being "remarkable."

The Old Charges and the Early Speculative Lodges

Just as the Old Charges had been read in operative lodges, etc., so they continued, it is thought, to be read in the early speculative lodges, to be replaced in due course with the newer versions of those Charges compiled by Anderson and included in the *Constitutions* of 1723. With the coming into existence of the many new lodges in the 1720's, copies of the old manuscript Charges continued to be made, a fact suggesting that even if they were not being read in lodge there was still a belief that the possession of a copy confirmed, shall we say, the regularity of the lodge constitution. The early speculatives evidently cherished the Old

Charges and regarded them as a link between the old operatives and themselves.

The use of the old manuscript Charges was not limited to the English lodges, for we have certain information that a version of them was read in the year 1670 to every candidate admitted as Entered Apprentice to the Lodge of Aberdeen, and probably the procedure in some other Scottish lodges was much the same. Scottish masons did not find their legendary history until the 1600's, and it was in the old English manuscript Charges that they found it.

Chapter Six

THE 'ACCEPTION' IN THE MASONS' COMPANY

WE shall see in this short section that symbolic or speculative masonry owes much to what was the Worshipful Company of Freemasons of the City of London. Not only does our Craft derive from it almost certainly its name and much of its principle of government; it also gets from it or from general guild practice the titles of its chief officers, and it finances itself in much the same way, its system of admission fees and quarterages having originated in the Company. Far more important than these is the great likelihood that our Craft inherited *through* the Company some large part of its esoteric system. So conservative an assessor as Gould favours the idea that at the heart of the Company was a Society of Freemasons—that is, an inner fraternity of speculative or symbolic masons, which may have existed from some far earlier date, an idea which is developed in the next chapter.

The difficulty is to say how much or how little our Craft has been inherited in this way, for not everything bequeathed to us has come down through the Masons' Company, as we shall discuss in due course.

Edward Conder, junior, Master of the Masons' Company in 1894, produced in that year his most valuable and very readable *Records of the Hole Crafte and Fellowship of Masons,* which includes a "Chronicle of the History of the Mason Company," and from that book and from the same author's papers in *A.Q.C.*, vols.ix and xxvii, most subsequent writers on freemasonry have quoted. The present writer is no exception, and now in discussing the part played by the Company in the emergence of symbolic masonry in the seventeenth century, Conder's writings must gratefully be referred to again. We must not shut our eyes, however, to the author's optimism, and we must be prepared to place a somewhat conservative valuation on some of his main conclusions.

The Dual Condition of the Mason Company

Conder is strongly of opinion that the Company had a dual condition in the latter part of the seventeenth century, there being on the one hand operative members, who were skilled masons, and on the other non-operatives, who were made up of two classes: (*a*) those who had joined for social and similar reasons, and (*b*) those who had become 'accepted' or speculative or symbolic masons. There is no absolute evidence of this, but a very strong presumption.

We have seen in an earlier chapter that by the middle of the seventeenth century the Company had fallen away from any position of commanding importance and was failing to attract the membership of the mason trade. The ensuing half-century was one long fight to keep its head above water, and the question certainly does arise as to what inducement there was for anybody not connected with the building trade to join the Company at that time, as obviously a livery company markedly on the decline could not offer much to a man consumed with social ambition.

It is reasonable to assume, therefore, that quite a number of the non-operatives came into the Company not for social advantage but merely that they might enter upon the 'acception,' the name by which the inner fraternity appears to have been known. Conder goes so far as to express his belief that with regard to persons who had become members by patrimony, etc., their only hope of becoming liverymen was that they should first of all become accepted masons—in other words, that they should be initiated in the lodge held in the Company's Hall; but this, it seems, is mere conjecture. We are on safer ground when we say that as the number of trade members fell away and consequently fewer of them entered upon the acception, so the proportion of non-operatives 'accepted' tended to increase. We must suppose that this process was at work for some time before 1655, in which year the Company saw fit to drop from its title the one word that linked it with its ancient past. From the moment when the mason operatives became officially 'Mason' the word 'Freemason' passed as a precious asset into the possession of the speculatives.

But why did the Company in 1655 drop the prefix 'free'? What had it to gain by so doing? We know that the designation of 'freemason' as applied to the skilled operative mason was becoming obsolete, although it was still to remain in use, but always declining use, for another century or so, and we can readily suppose that the younger minds within the counsels of the Company might have insisted on the title being brought 'up to date.' Further, we can well imagine that if there was within the Company an esoteric society growing into strength and claiming the word 'freemason' for its own it was rather in the nature of things that the Company, no longer sure of its standing, would see reason for relinquishing a name which it may have thought it had outgrown and which was steadily acquiring a special meaning. For a century or so some operative masons continued to be known as freemasons.

Some Accepted Masons

We find the most definite of the indications that the Company had an 'accepted' as well as an operative membership in entries in the Company's records of 1620 and 1621. In the former year John Hince, Evan Lloyd, James ffrench, and others had been accepted into the Company's livery on payment of a gratuity. That meant, of course, that they had originally been apprentices, next members, and were then thought worthy of being made liverymen. This is emphasized to make clear that the following item from the accounts for 1621 could only mean that they were admitted into a body within the operative Company:

1621.   Att the making masons viz. John Hince, John Brown, Rowland Everett, Evan lloyd, James ffrench, John Clarke, Thomas Rose, reced of them as apereth by the Quartge book   } IX'VI'VIII

This is the most definite indication so far that the Company apparently contained within itself a fraternity only to be entered by being made a freemason.

In 1631 there were certain moneys

Paid in goeing abroad and att a meeteing att the Hall about the Masons that were to bee accepted.

In some later accounts and statements there can be no doubt whatever of the meaning of the word 'accepted.' For example, in 1648 and 1650 Thomas Moore, junior, and Richard Herneden paid in two instalments a total fine of ten pounds each "for coming on ye livery," but in 1648 Mr Andrew Mervin (a Warden at the time and necessarily a liveryman) paid one pound for "Coming on The Accepcon." It appears that it may safely be concluded that this pound was the fee for joining the society of accepted masons.

Books of Constitutions

Two Books of Constitutions are referred to, Conder tells us, in the Company's records of 1663 and 1676. One, he assumes, contained the old trade regulations and by-laws of the Company; the other was a copy of the manuscript Old Charges. The first of these was probably identical with a manuscript book of Constitutions included in the Inventory of 1722—namely, a book bound in vellum "being the Constitutions of this Company granted in the Mayoralty of John Brown the 21st year of the reign of King Edward the 4th the 15th day of Oct 1481."

The manuscript Book of Constitutions was believed to be "A Book wrote on parchment and bound or stitch in parchment containing an account of the Antiquity Rise and Progress of the Art and Mistery of Masonry."

On these and other references in the records Edward Conder bases his very reasonable belief that the use of the manuscript Constitutions at the making of masons "was no new fancy but had probably descended without a break to the Jacobean Masons from their Tudor ancestors." "In my opinion," he says,

> the Company of Masons of the City of London, in its early days, practised, and was acquainted with, ALL the traditions and moral teachings of the Fraternity, and that when the monastic guilds fell into chaos, The London Company of Masons preserved the ancient traditions of the Guild, and amongst its documents a copy of those MS. Traditions, with the object of keeping the old order of things alive; and thus assisted in handing them down to the seventeenth-century Society of Free and Accepted Masons, which revived the old order some time between 1680 and 1700.

That is how Conder sums up the connexion between the Company and the Fraternity. Two comments must be added: firstly, his use of the word "ALL" must not be taken to mean all the traditions and moral teachings familiar to the freemasons of *to-day*; secondly, more than one stream of descent has fed the flowing river of freemasonry, as the reader may well conclude after he has read the chapter devoted to the emergence of speculative masonry, but certainly we must give full value to the fact (ascertained by Herbert Strickland) that some scores of serving masons associated with the Company are known to have been members of speculative lodges up to the early 1700's.

Was there a Lodge meeting regularly in the Company's Hall?

It will always be a matter for debate whether the Lodge within the Masons' Company met at regular intervals. The books of the Company do not record any meetings of the Lodge or Fellowship. The most probable inference to be drawn from the little information available is that it was called together as and when required. There is nothing known about it after 1682, and either it had ceased to exist before the Grand Lodge came in 1717 or had by then assumed a different identity. The sanguine Conder hazards the opinion that the Lodge of Antiquity (now No. 2), one of the time-immemorial lodges that founded Grand Lodge, might have owed its origin to the Masons Hall Lodge. We first hear of No. 2 in 1717, and it was then meeting at the Goose and Gridiron, St Paul's Churchyard.

BOOK TWO

Speculative Masonry

Chapter Seven

THE EMERGENCE OF SPECULATIVE MASONRY

THIS is the first of a number of chapters on the story of the emergence of speculative freemasonry, from its first mention in the seventeenth century to the establishment of the United Grand Lodge of England in 1813. Unavoidably these chapters present the story in such a way that we must retrace our steps more than once so far as dates but not so far as matter and interest are concerned. Quiet perseverance through these few chapters, however, will help us slowly to build up a mental picture—an incomplete one; no masonic author professes to anything better—of the most fascinating but the most baffling, the formative, and therefore the most important period in speculative masonry.

It is easy to get confused between speculative masons and the gentlemen non-operative masons who found their way into masonry in medieval and later days, particularly in Scotland. In the old sense every mason who was not a practical mason was a speculative mason, but we are not using the word speculative in that old way. To readers of this book the speculative mason is the symbolic mason, a man initiated into an esoteric mystery. The first speculative known beyond question is Elias Ashmole, who was 'made' a mason in 1646 in a lodge at Warrington. How old that lodge was we do not know, nor do we know anything of its history. On the other hand, we know a great deal about the history of the operative freemasons; we know the names of a number of them, and some or many of their buildings remain for us to study. We know so much more about them than we do of many of the other crafts, because the *Constitutions* written for the old masons by learned and imaginative ecclesiastics have come down to us (or some of them have) in manuscript form, as explained on other pages of this book.

93

The Old Manuscript Charges

There is little or nothing symbolical in these old manuscript Charges. They are the rules and regulations of an organized craft, and are such as a diligent and learned priest of the Middle Ages—devout, credulous, apparently well acquainted with the mason craft and craftsmen—might have been expected to compose for the special purpose of being read at meetings of craft masons. It is obvious that they were so read, and what concerns us as speculative masons is that apparently they *continued* to be read after Lodges had lost their operative character and, indeed, in some Lodges, which, so far as we know, never had been connected with the mason trade.

We seem to miss some evidence that would more amply and definitely link up the Old Charges with our ritual, and we fall back upon the idea (about to be explored) that within the mason craft, as within most other medieval crafts, was a quasi-religious body that only just managed to survive the Reformation and the ensuing century and so provide a real but dimly perceived link between the medieval operative and the modern speculative. Straight from operative to speculative in *English* masonry might be to us a difficult journey, but from operative *via* a fraternity hidden away at the very heart of the craft and merging in the days of the Renaissance into an early form of modern symbolic masonry—yes, that is a sequence not only natural, but perfectly credible.

Is Freemasonry the One Surviving Medieval Craft Esotery?

What we mean by a fraternity within the craft will be the better understood by our posing, and trying to answer, this question: Is freemasonry the one surviving medieval craft esotery?

While some time in the 1700's there was knowledge in England of a masonic fraternity distinct from the operative masons, there does not appear to have been just a century before any awareness whatever of the existence of freemasons except members of the trade. This fact poses a problem of great perplexity. Assuming, as we must, that esoteric freemasonry was not an innovation of the early 1600's, whence was it immediately derived? What was freemasonry and *where* was it, say, in the year 1600?

In a personal discussion of this question on one occasion J. Heron Lepper offered a suggestion which, clothed in some detail, is now presented here.

It is a matter of simple history that after the Reformation the *religious* guilds and fraternities (as distinct from the purely craft guilds), having an independent existence of their own or occupying each its own special place at the spiritual core of a craft guild, were suppressed and disendowed by Henry VIII. The considerable literature relating to the English guilds will confirm this, but for the present purpose it suffices to say that George Unwin in his *Gilds and Companies of London* comments that "the cessation of time-honoured customs must have been felt as a sore deprivation by the more conservatively pious members." He points out that, although religious devotion had never supplied the primary motive of the craft guild, it may at first have been the most prominent of the subsidiary motives.

Leaving Unwin, we note that in the time of Henry VIII belief in religion of a highly miraculous nature admixed with crude superstition was common to all classes of the people, learned and unlearned, rich and poor. The religious guilds and fraternities of the day might, therefore, have comprehended many centuries-old esoteries ruled by learned chapters, whose affairs were carefully guarded from the public eye, but which must have been familiar to the privileged few of almost every craft, profession, or even class. Supported by endowments and gifts, these esoteries flourished, but from their very nature, and from the secrecy with which they were promoted, our knowledge of them to-day is but slight. Obviously, however, the very drastic and energetic suppression and confiscation by the Crown must have been inspired by a real fear that the secret fraternities—'conservative,' 'pious'—were hardly likely to be friendly disposed to the King's new religious policy. Henry, as the new head of the English Church, was now at open enmity with the Pope, and was visiting—either he or his successors—with a charge of treason all who by teaching and writing supported the Pope's authority within the King's domain.

Ostensibly, then, the old religious fraternities disappeared. Many of them must have ceased forthwith, but a number must have gone underground, there to exist as secret cells during a decade or two, and finally, in nearly all cases, to die a natural death.

Here are the significant dates. In the year 1534 Parliament declared Henry the Supreme Head on earth of the English Church. The monasteries were sacked in 1538. The Act disendowing the religious fraternities was passed in 1547. Ninety-nine years later—that is, in 1646—we get our first recorded mention of freemasonry (in the sense understood to-day) with the 'making' of Elias Ashmole a freemason at Warrington. Thus the bridge between the disendowment of the religious guilds and the 'making' of Ashmole is but one century; merely the span of four normal generations, roughly coinciding with the particular period in which the Middle Ages finally merged into a later age. Is it asking too much for us to accept the proposition that one or two cells, or Lodges, of a particular mystery kept themselves alive through those four generations, and that as a consequence we have in freemasonry the only surviving medieval craft esotery? There is, of course, a proportion of conjecture in the conceit, but we must weigh the suggestion for ourselves, and, should we find it tenable, we shall be able to account for the existence of the Lodge at Warrington in 1646 and of the Lodge in the London Company of Masons about thirty-six years later. Gould's opinion already mentioned (see p. 88) may, it is felt, be taken as giving some little support to the idea.

Speculative Masonry an English Growth

There can be little doubt that speculative freemasonry was originally wholly of English growth, and we can believe that without accepting one author's amazing contention that Shakespeare conceived and established Freemasonry and created our ritual! True, after its emergence and right through the eighteenth century, it was subject to French and German influences, but it did not derive from the Continent. Neither did it derive from Ireland. Freemasonry went out to that country probably through Bristol and other ports, and was there so well nurtured that to-day we find it in a purity of form that at times excites our envy. Nor did speculative masonry derive from the American Colonies. An early form of the system was taken to America, and, although we are inclined to regard American freemasonry as being occasionally over-dramatized, the truth remains that in much of the American working we tend to find those ancient forms which were borrowed from England in the early speculative days.

What of Scotland? The old Scots operatives are well known to have had their secret mode of recognition and their 'mason word'; history fully concedes it. We cannot prove the existence of anything similar among the English operatives, although, as Herbert Poole puts it, "the fact that such secret modes of recognition were found in the late seventeenth century among English non-operatives affords a certain measure of probability that they belong to an earlier date." There are weighty authorities who believe that English freemasonry did in fact derive a great deal from the Scottish system, and so important are their arguments that a separate and later section will treat of them. All that need be said at this point is that it is difficult to see that Scotland had any masonic system which by itself could have developed into the symbolic Craft known to the freemasons of the early 1700's.

Early Speculative Masonry

The modern history of speculative masonry starts with 1646, in which year Elias Ashmole was made a mason in a lodge at Warrington. But before we tell the story of Ashmole and of the later worthies, Randle Holme, John Aubrey, and others, we must note that there must have been English lodges in the 1640–50 period of which we know just nothing. We know a great deal about the Scottish operative lodges of the day, many of them having 'gentleman' or non-operative members in addition to the practical craftsmen; but, as to the English lodges of the mid-seventeenth century, we do not know whether they still retained operative members, or whether by that date they had become purely speculative and had completely severed any operative connexion. All we can say of the lodge at Warrington, the first speculative Lodge of which there is recorded mention, is that it existed and that Elias Ashmole was made a mason in it. We have no precise information about any lodge held in Warrington until 1755, when the 'Antients' founded one at the Cock Inn, Bridge Street, to last—or so we may conclude—no longer than a year, but in 1765 the 'Moderns' constituted at The Fleece, now unknown, the existing Lodge of Lights, No. 148.

So far as records go, we *know* of but one speculative mason up to, say, the year 1665; yet about fifty years later four Lodges of London were forming themselves into a Grand Lodge and, by inference, we know that many other Lodges must have existed. The lack of information as to what happened between 1682 and, say, 1725 or 1730 is tantalizing to a degree, particularly as concerns the development of masonic ritual and ceremony. Did Ashmole and the other learned speculatives who came into freemasonry in the 1600's hand on, as they found it, what awaited them within the lodge portals, or did they develop it almost out of all knowledge, and in fact, or in effect, create something new and different? Whence came the esoteric content of freemasonry? From a fraternity within the operative craft of two hundred years before? Or did the learned and philosophic, clever but superstitious, newcomers find in freemasonry little more than some simple mode or modes of recognition, accompanied by some small amount of moralizing, and did they 'fill out' the meagre ceremony of the day by borrowing from the ancient mysteries? What was the ritual that came into the hands of the editors and arrangers in the 1720's? How much did these men use of the material that came to them, and what did they discard? And did what they threw aside, or some of it, persist in some form or other in Lodges here and there in the countryside, and serve in due course to aggravate differences in lodge working which, in the middle of the eighteenth century, were to cause bitter discord and open a sore which would take some sixty years to heal?

It is doubtful whether there exists information by which some of these questions can be properly answered, and we can only hope that research will in time provide it. In the meantime, even if we cannot answer all the questions, we can acquire a point of view with regard to some.

A few masonic students have attempted to sidetrack some of the problems by claiming that the speculative Lodges of the 1700's had never had a connexion with operative masonry and were not the descendants of masonic fraternities, but, instead, consisted of bodies of educated gentlemen holding strong Rosicrucian and other quaint beliefs, who had deliberately chosen to call themselves 'freemasons' at a time when the old London Company of Freemasons was still so called. The claim that speculative masonry is of Rosicrucian invention—not merely that freemasonry was subject to Rosicrucian influence—has been so strongly advanced that special consideration will be devoted to it in a later section, with the intention of refuting it. In the meantime here is Lewis Edwards's excellent point that

> few, if any, institutions are *invented* off-hand. They are all creatures of growth. If we find one of them organised and in working order at a certain date, it is highly probable that, whether or not we find traces of it, it has existed for many years in a rudimentary and unorganised form; and this is obviously the case with speculative freemasonry.

Just one further matter will be referred to before we tell the story of Ashmole and the other early speculatives. There are many keen students who see in the emergence of freemasonry in the 1600's evidence of that inquiring spirit which so clearly marked the Renaissance throughout Europe. While we have good reason to believe that freemasonry takes us back to the great Gothic period, we can equally well believe in the probability that the emergence of symbolic freemasonry was possible only in a Renaissance bringing with it a remarkable 'revival of learning' and a deep interest in all historical and antiquarian matters. Masonry all through the Middle Ages had attracted fine types of learned, knowledgeable men, and in the period of operative decline and speculative ascent it continued to attract scholars of pronounced historical and antiquarian interests, who, perhaps through mere curiosity, came into masonry to *seek*, and more than likely stayed to *give*. Freemasonry carries their marks to-day. The chief evidence for the existence of speculative masonry in the eighteenth century rests on records associated with the names of Elias Ashmole, Randle Holme (the third), Sir William Dugdale, Dr Robert Plot, and John Aubrey.

Elias Ashmole

The two significant dates concerning Elias Ashmole are October 16, 1646, and March 11, 1682. The Bodleian Library at Oxford includes in its wealth of manuscripts and volumes the original manuscript of Elias Ashmole's diary entitled *Memoirs of the Life of that learned Antiquary, Elias Ashmole, Esq., Drawn up by himself by way of Diary. With an Appendix of Original Letters.* These memoirs were published in 1717 by Charles Burman, either a stepson or the son-in-law of Dr Robert Plot.

From facts drawn together by W. J. Chetwode Crawley we learn that Elias Ashmole was born at Lichfield in 1617, the son of a saddler and soldier. (He died in 1692 and is buried in St Mary's Church, Lambeth, London.) Becoming a singing boy in the choir of Lichfield Cathedral, he so profited by his education that later he went to London and in 1638 was admitted a solicitor at the age of twenty-one, and in the same year married the daughter of Peter Mainwaring, a Cheshire landowner. He saw much military service (he lived through the days of the Great Rebellion), but amid the bustle of war he found means to enter himself at Brasenose College, Oxford, where he had a successful career. In 1646 he was on a visit to his father-in-law in Cheshire. This was "a momentous visit for Freemasons," says Chetwode Crawley, "for while ensconcing himself from the Roundheads, he was made a freemason at Warrington." In London he became friendly with the three most noted astrologers of the time—Moore, Lilly, and Booker. His wife having died a few years after marriage, he took as his second wife the widow of a wealthy City knight. After the Restoration Ashmole was created Windsor Herald, elected a Fellow of the Royal Society, and given university honours. Between him, John Evelyn, and Samuel Pepys was a close community of interest, all three of them diarists, and no two of them alike in style. Evelyn, writing to Pepys, calls Ashmole "our common friend" and refers to him in his diary as "my old friend." Ashmole founded at Oxford in 1677 the well-known Ashmolean Museum, "the first public institution for the reception of Rarities in Art or Nature established in England," the building being designed by Christopher Wren.

Now let us see exactly what it is that Ashmole wrote. Here is the first extract from his diary, the date being October 16, 1646:

4.H.30.'P.M. I was made a Free Mason at Warrington in Lancashire, with Coll: Henry Mainwaring of Karnicham[1] in Cheshire. The names of those that were then of the Lodge; Mr Rich Penket Warden, Mr James Collier. Mr Rich: Sankey, Henry Littler, John Ellam, Rich: Ellam and Hugh Brewer,

---

[1] Also known as Karincham or Kerincham.

The words "Free Mason" in this extract constitute the first known use of the term carrying a speculative or symbolic meaning.

"Rich: Ellam," in his will, is a freemason, while his brother John was a husbandman; Henry Littler was probably a yeoman; the others largely country gentlemen. For the best account of all of them see Norman Rogers's paper, *A.Q.C.*, vol. lxv.

The Ashmole diary does not refer again to freemasonry until the year 1682—that is, not for nearly thirty-six years. Then appear two references, on consecutive days, March 10 and 11,

> 10. About 5ʜ:ᴘ.ᴍ. I recᵈ a Summons to appear at a Lodge to be held the next day, at Masons Hall London.
>
> 11. Accordingly I went, & about Noone were admitted into the Fellowship of Free Masons, Sʳ William Wilson Knight, Capt. Rich: Borthwick, Mʳ Will: Woodman, Mʳ Wᵐ Grey, Mʳ Samuell Taylour & Mʳ William Wise. I was the Senior Fellow among them (it being 35 yeares since I was admitted). There were present beside my selfe the Fellowes after named.
>
> Mʳ Tho: Wise Mʳ of the Masons Company this present yeare. Mʳ Thomas Shorthose, Mʳ Thomas Shadbolt,   Wainsford Esqʳ Mʳ Nich: Young. Mʳ John Shorthose, Mʳ William Hamon, Mʳ John Thompson, & Mʳ Will: Stanton.
>
> Wee all dyned at the halfe Moone Taverne in Cheapeside, at a Noble Dinner prepaired at the charge of the New-accepted Masons.

In these references of 1682 we find the names of many people of whom much is known of interest to freemasons. If Ashmole meant anything at all, he meant that he saw six men received into freemasonry: Sir William Wilson, Captain Richard Borthwick, Mr Will Woodman, Mr William Grey, Mr Samuell Taylour, and Mr William Wise. It is significant that four of these gentlemen were members of the London Company of Masons; Sir William Wilson and Captain R. Borthwick were not.

Further, the Master of the Masons Company, Mr Thomas Wise, and the following members of the Company were also present: Thomas Shorthose, Wainsford Esq., Nich Young, William Hamon (Hammon), and John Thompson, all members of the Company; and in addition two Wardens of the Company, John Shorthose and William Stanton.

In the face of such evidence it is impossible to deny the close link that must have existed between the London Company of Masons and the Lodge or Fellowship within it. At least eight of the fifteen present were prominent members of the London Company, the records of the Company showing that three of them, Wise, Thompson, and Stanton, were free of the Company in 1671–72, 1667, and 1663 respectively. Seven of them were on the Livery of the Company; four of them were on the Court of Assistants of the Company; all but two of them were, had been, or would be Wardens; and six of them had been, were, or would be Masters. Nich (Rich) Young, John Shorthose, and William Hamon were well-known contractors, whose names will be found in the records of the building of the present St Paul's Cathedral, and Hamon, in addition, was known to be the chief importer of stone into London at that period.

We see, then, that the diary entry of March 11, 1682, proves—if any diary entry can prove anything—the very close association existing at that time between the newly merging system of speculative masonry and some of the more prominent operative masters of the day.

It will be noted that the noble dinner at the Half Moon Tavern in Cheapside was paid for by the newly accepted masons, in accordance with operative practice going back, at any rate in Scotland, for hundreds of years. Further, a candidate was not then said to be 'initiated'; he was 'admitted' or 'accepted.'

The omission of all references to freemasonry in Ashmole's diary between 1646 and 1682 suggests either that he had nothing to do with freemasonry during that period, or that, in any case, his masonic association meant little to him. But how came it that about thirty-six years after his admission into freemasonry he was summoned to attend a Lodge in London? He could hardly have been *summoned* had he not maintained some connexion. There does, however, appear to be one plausible explanation. Ashmole had a great affection for Lichfield, where he was born and which he regarded with much honour and frequently visited. It so happens that Sir William Wilson, who was accepted into freemasonry on the occasion of Ashmole's visit to Masons Hall in 1682, was a well-known stonemason and the sculptor of the statue of Charles II in Lichfield Cathedral. Gould helpfully suggests that Ashmole may have been summoned or invited to be present to witness his friend's 'acception.'

Ashmole's Century

Ashmole became a freemason at a troublous time in England's history, but in one of the brightest of her intellectual periods. Shakespeare had died only thirty years and Francis Bacon about twenty years before. Ben Jonson had been dead only nine years, and one of his plays, *The Alchemist*, had been first acted in 1610, its title being an allusion to a 'philosophy' of the times, echoes of which we find in masonic history. Inigo Jones, now seventy-three years old, had designed the banqueting hall at Whitehall for James I a quarter of a century before, and Rubens had decorated it. Milton at the age of thirty-eight was writing his *Paradise Lost*. Samuel Pepys, now a boy of thirteen, would live through fourteen impressionable years before he would be starting his diary, and

John Evelyn, now twenty-six years old, was well on the way with his. Daniel Defoe and Jonathan Swift were not yet born.

Great and outstanding historical events were still fresh in the minds of the people, the Spanish Armada being easily remembered by men in their sixties, the Gunpowder Plot by those in their forties. Queen Elizabeth had died forty-three years before, and her one-time favourite, Sir Walter Raleigh, executed by James I in 1618, had a host of contemporaries still living. James I had been dead twenty-one years, and his son the first Charles, now utterly defeated, was on the road leading to his execution three years later. About forty-two years would pass before the grandson, the second James, the last of the absolute monarchs, would flee from London and leave his throne vacant, to be occupied by William of Orange, who, with his Queen, would assent to the Declaration of Rights in the following year. The "Revolution of 1688," as it was called, includes among its greatest achievements the English legal system, to which Adam Smith, the economist, attributes the prosperity of Great Britain. Means of locomotion were still much the same as, and neither much faster nor slower than, they were in the days of the Romans.

"The ashes of the last martyr-fire in Smithfield had smouldered out" as recently as 1611, only thirty-five years before, when a Unitarian was burnt "for distrust of the Athanasian and Nicene creeds." This was the very year that saw the publication of the Authorised Version of the Bible, but the poor 'witch' was still being hunted by the law and the people. Many educated men still believed not only that there were witches, but that they contracted themselves to the Devil in documents written in his 'black book' and signed maybe in blood. For another seventy years in England poor, wretched women would be accused of witchcraft and cruelly executed. The last victims were to be a mother and her nine-year-old daughter who in 1716 were "hanged at Huntingdon for selling their souls to the devil, and raising a storm by pulling off their stockings and making a lather of soap." In Scotland the evil practice was to live for six years longer.

When Ashmole was made a mason London's dreadful Plague and the cleansing Fire that followed it were still about twenty years ahead. Slavery was well-nigh universal, was recognized in England, and a form of it practised in the salt- and coal-mines of Scotland.

Randle Holme

The second of the early speculatives is Randle Holme the Third (1627–99), a contemporary of Ashmole, another remarkable man in his way, an antiquary and genealogist, enjoying at one time the distinction of being "gentleman sewer in extraordinary" to Charles II. His type of "sewer" was a 'server,' the officer who served up the King's feast, arranged the dishes, and provided water for the hands of the guests. Walter Scott, who can always be relied on for the antiquarian touch, has the lines:

> Their task the busy sewers ply
> And all is mirth and revelry.

Randle Holme was deputy for Garter King of Arms and the author of an *Academie of Armory* published in 1688, in which he writes, "I cannot but honour the Fellowship of the Masons because of its antiquity, and the more as being [myself] a member of that Society called Free-masons."

A scrap of paper in his own handwriting found bound up with Randle Holme's manuscript of the *Constitutions of the Masons* (the Harleian MS., No. 2054) was, in the opinion of British Museum authorities, written in the 1640–50 period. On it are written these significant words:

> There is seu^{r}all words & signes of a free Mason to be revailed to y^u wch as y^u will answ: before God at the Great & terrible day of Iudgm^t y^u keep Secret & not to revaile the same to any in the heares of any pson w but to the M^{rs} & fellows of the said Society of free Masons so helpe me God, xt.

Although we know Randle Holme to have been a freemason, we cannot state definitely when he was 'made.' There is good reason to believe he was made a freemason at a Lodge at Chester about 1665. Preserved among his manuscripts in the British Museum is a list, written about the year 1673, giving the names of twenty-seven persons, his own name "Ran Holme" being the fourteenth name. There can hardly be a doubt that this was a list of members of the Lodge at Chester, apparently or possibly showing in each case the number of shillings that had been paid as a fee "for to be a free Mason." It is proper to say, however, that the document is open to more than one interpretation (for example, the 'fees' *may* have been numbers of votes), the one here given being fair and reasonable. Of the twenty-seven persons, about six were masons by trade and fifteen members of other branches of the building trade.

Light is thrown on the meaning of the word 'fraternity' as used in Randle Holme's day. In his *Academie of Armory* he speaks of a

> Fraternity, or Society, or Brotherhood, or Company; are such in corpora-tion, that are of one and the same trade, or occupation, who being joyned together by oath and covenant, do follow such orders and rules, as are made, or to be made for the good order, rule, and support of such and every of their occupations. These several Fraternities are generally governed by one or

two Masters, and two Wardens, but most Companies with us by two Aldermen, and two Stewards, the later being to receive and pay what concerns
them.

A 'Divertisement' of 1676

A scurrilous sheet issued weekly in London from early 1676 to late the
following year and known as *Poor Robin's Intelligence* contained what were
called 'divertisements.' These were facetious quasi-advertisements and
burlesques. The occurrence in one of them of references to the Kaballa,
the Rosy Cross, the Hermeticks, and the Accepted Masons must give us
pause. Here is the divertisement:

> These are to give notice, that the Modern Green-ribbon'd Caball, together
> with the Ancient Brother-hood of the Rosy-Cross; the Hermetick Adepti,
> and the Company of Accepted Masons, intend all to Dine together on the
> 31 of *November* next, at the Flying-Bull in Wind-Mill-Crown-Street; having
> already given order for great store of Black-Swan Pies, Poach'd Phoenixes
> Eggs, Haunches of Unicorns, &c. . . .

Now, if the "Company" here mentioned is intended to be the London
Company of Masons, as appears to be the case, quite apart from implying
any possible association with the Rosicrucians, etc., the divertisement is
of marked interest. It shows that the London Company was in the
popular mind closely associated with *accepted* masons, although it had
for hundreds of years been operating as a trade company and was shortly
to be confirmed in that capacity by the grant of a charter from Charles II.
Whether that be so or not, this small piece of evidence goes to confirm
that the 'accepted mason' was well known as early as 1676.

Dr Robert Plot

Our next bit of evidence is from the writings of a non-mason, Dr
Robert Plot (1640–96), a 'natural philosopher'—we should call him a
naturalist—an antiquary, Secretary of the Royal Society in 1682, first
man to be appointed Reader in Chemistry at Oxford, the first keeper of
the Ashmolean Museum at Oxford, and Historiographer of James II in
1688. Dr Plot knew the learned men of his day. He was a friend of
Samuel Pepys and of John Evelyn, in whose diary he is mentioned,
and through whom he became acquainted with Elias Ashmole. Plot and
Evelyn refer to Pepys in their correspondence as "our common and
most excellent friend." He had wide knowledge and great industry, but
at the same time a most unfortunate credulity, and, further, enjoyed
giving ear to obviously impossible statements and then falling upon
them tooth and nail. He is of interest to freemasons because of what he

wrote about them and their Craft in one of his many works, *The Natural History of Staffordshire* (dated 1686), from which are reproduced the following abstracts:

85. To these add the *Customs* relating to the *County*, whereof they have one, of admitting Men into the *Society* of *Free-Masons*, that in the *moorelands* of this *County* seems to be of greater request than any where else, though I find the *Custom* spread more or less all over the *Nation*; for here I found persons of the most eminent quality, that did not disdain to be of this *Fellowship*. Nor indeed need they, were it of that *Antiquity* and *honor*, that is pretended in a large *parchment volum* they have amongst them, containing the *History* and *Rules* of the craft of *masonry*. Which is there deduced not only from *sacred writ*, but *profane story*, particularly that it was brought into *England* by St *Amphibal*, and first communicated to S. *Alban*, who set down the *Charges* of *masonry*, and was made paymaster and Governor of the *Kings* works, and gave them *charges* and *manners* as St *Amphibal* had taught him. Which were after confirmed by King *Athelstan*, whose youngest son *Edwyn* loved well masonry, took upon him the *charges*, and learned the *manners*, and obtained for them of his Father a *free-Charter*. Whereupon he caused them to assemble at *York*, and to bring all the old *Books of* their *craft*, and out of them ordained such *charges* and *manners*, as they then thought fit: which charges in the said *Schrole* or *Parchment volum*, are in part declared; and thus was the *craft* of *masonry* grounded and confirmed in *England*. It is also there declared that these *charges* and *manners* were after perused and approved by King *Hen.6*. and his *council*, both as to *Masters* and *Fellows* of this right Worshipfull *craft*.

86. Into which *Society* when any are admitted, they call a *meeting* (or *Lodg* as they term it in some places), which must consist at lest of 5 or 6 of the *Ancients* of the *Order*, whom the *candidats* present with *gloves*, and so likewise to their *wives*, and entertain with a *collation* according to the Custom of the place: This ended, they proceed to the *admission* of them, which chiefly consists in the communication of certain *secret signes*, whereby they are known to one another all over the *Nation*, by which means they have maintenance whither ever they travel: for if any man appear though altogether unknown that can shew any of these *signes* to a *Fellow* of the *Society*, whom they otherwise call an *accepted mason*, he is obliged presently to come to him, from what company or place soever he be in, nay, tho' from the top of a *Steeple* (what hazard or inconvenience soever he run), to know his pleasure, and assist him; *viz.*, if he want *work* he is bound to find him some; or if he cannot doe that, to give him *mony*, or otherwise support him till *work* can be had; which is one of their *Articles*; and it is another, that they advise the *Masters* they work for, according to the best of their *skill*, acquainting them with the goodness or badness of their *materials*; and if they be any way out in the *contrivance* of their *buildings*, modestly to rectify them in it; that *masonry* be not dishonored: and many such like that are commonly known: but some others they have (to which they are *sworn*

after their fashion), that none know but themselves, which I have reason to suspect are much worse than these, perhaps as bad as this *History* of the *craft* it self; than which there is nothing I ever met with, more false or incoherent.

Dr Plot was not a freemason, as we have said, nor was he friendly disposed towards freemasonry. He drew much of his material from an old manuscript legendary history, which he affected to regard as a factual account and criticized destructively, than which nothing could be easier. However, by repeating the statements made to him by his contemporaries (of whom, it will be remembered, Ashmole was one) he has added greatly to our knowledge of seventeenth-century freemasonry, and in spite of all his criticism, which from our point of view is wholly mis-applied, masonic history would have been much the poorer without his writings.

In brief, Dr Plot says that eminent men were masons, that freemasonry was spread over the nation, and that there was a large parchment volume containing the rules and history of the Craft. He uses the term "Lodg" for a meeting of freemasons, which he says must consist of at least five or six members; he states that candidates present the members with gloves, that the masons have secret signs, and that a fellow of the Society is called an accepted mason. His statement that a mason can be called by a sign "from the top of a steeple" has been the cause of much fun poked at the masons, and is the motif of a verse in the best-known parody of *The Entered Apprentice's Song*. He says that the Brethren find work for each other and rectify bad material and workmanship "that masonry be not dishonoured"; after which he reproduces many statements from the old legendary history, and has no difficulty in riddling them. But what he does *not* do, although he writes no later than forty years after the 'making' of Ashmole to whom he was well known, is to declare (as he would readily have done had the facts pointed that way) that freemasonry was nothing more than a Rosicrucian 'stunt.'

Sir Christopher Wren

Countless writers have ascribed to Sir Christopher Wren an important rôle in the emergence of freemasonry, but it is unlikely that he played any real part, certainly any great part, in masonic history. Anderson's *Constitutions* (1738 edition), "regarded as the basis of masonic history," credited Wren with having held the highest offices in freemasonry for a period of nearly half a century, and state that on his neglect of the Lodges a new organization with a new Grand Master was found necessary. As Anderson's account was accepted without question for a century or so, the figure of Wren has bulked large in masonic history, and he has been everywhere credited with being the genius who guided the speculatives on their road from operative masonry.

Christopher Wren was born in 1632, was a professor of astronomy in 1657 and Savilian Professor of Mathematics at Oxford in 1661, in which year Charles II appointed him as Assistant Surveyor General of the Royal Buildings. In 1663 he was commissioned to survey St Paul's Cathedral, but the great fire of London interfered with that project. He made a survey of the burnt city, proposed a plan (never adopted) for the relaying out of the whole area, built or rebuilt a great many churches and other public buildings, and, as all the world knows, was responsible for the new St Paul's Cathedral, which was begun in 1675 and completed about 1710. He was eighty-five years of age in the year of the formation of the Premier Grand Lodge (1717). He died in 1723 at the age of ninety-one, and was buried in the south-eastern corner of the crypt of his own great cathedral. A tablet bears his famous epitaph in Latin, which, translated, runs thus:

> Underneath lies buried the builder of this Church
> and City, Christopher Wren, who lived more than
> ninety years, not for himself, but for the public good.
>
> Reader, if you ask for a monument, look around.

Anderson's first edition of the *Constitutions* (dated 1723) mentions Wren just twice; once as "the ingenious Architect, Sir Christopher Wren," and secondly in a footnote, where he speaks of the Sheldonian Theatre, Oxford, "as having been designed and conducted also by Sir Christopher Wren, the King's Architect." Writing in the year in which Wren died, he has nothing more to say of the greatest architect England had produced, and does not even suggest that he was an accepted mason. Anderson published his second edition of the *Constitutions* fifteen years later (1738), by which time King George, under whose displeasure Wren had fallen, had died. He now apparently remembers not only that Wren was a member of the Craft, but that he had been Grand Warden in 1663; Deputy Grand Master in 1669 and 1673, and then onward to possibly 1685; Grand Master from 1685 (confirmed in his office by William III) until 1695, when the Duke of Richmond became Grand Master and Wren reverted to Deputy Grand Master; then three years later, in 1698, Grand Master once again. Having claimed all these honours for Wren, he continues:

> Yet still in the South the Lodges were more and more disused, firstly by the neglect of the Masters and Wardens, . . . and the annual Assembly was not duly attended. G. M. Wren .. celebrated the Capestone [of St Paul's]

... in July A.D. 1708. Some few years after this Sir Christopher Wren neglected the office of Grand Master. . . . After the Rebellion was over A.D. 1716, the few Lodges at London finding themselves neglected by Sir Christopher Wren, thought fit to cement under a new Grand Master. . . .

So, in effect, Anderson says that for a period of about fifty years Wren occupied some of the highest positions in the Craft, and finally so neglected his duties that the need for a revival arose. Wren was about eighty-four years of age when London Lodges "found themselves neglected"!

The evidence in support of the belief that Wren was actually a freemason is the entry in John Aubrey's handwriting in the Bodleian Library, under date 1691 (given in a later page of this present book in another connexion). Gould is not convinced that Wren was a freemason, and he gathers from their silence that the speculatives of 1717–23 had no reason to believe in Wren's connexion with their society. But, on the other hand, since Gould's day, many other students have studied the question; for example, Lewis Edwards, who says that Aubrey was a good and truthful reporter and that something more than the silence of contemporaries is required to invalidate his clear report.

One of Wren's sons, Christopher, was the real author of an oft-quoted work, *Parentalia—Memoirs of the Family of Wrens*. This was published in 1750, by which time, of course, the author was well aware of the high masonic rank to which Anderson had posthumously promoted his father. But Christopher says not a word about his father having been a freemason, not a word about the lofty place he is alleged to have held in the Craft!

Of all the newspaper obituaries following Wren's death, only two refer to him as a freemason. Both of them called him "that worthy freemason." Many masons of the day, however, were freemasons, but not free and accepted, or speculative, masons. It was only in 1655–56 that "The Company of ffreemasons of the City of London" had become "The Company of Masons," and the word freemason had not yet wholly earned the exclusive significance which it now carries.

Anderson's two accounts, those of 1723 and 1738, and Aubrey's diary entry of 1691 afford us material for a most revealing comparison. If Anderson was fair and just in his skimpy references of 1723, what do we make of the galaxy of masonic honours with which he invests Wren in 1738? If his second account was true, was his first unbelievably mean? What becomes of Aubrey's testimony that Wren was made a mason in 1691 if Wren was Grand Warden twenty-eight years before that date? If the Grand Lodge of 1717 was the *first* Grand Lodge—and we know of no other—how could Wren have been Deputy Grand Master in 1666?

And if Aubrey's diary entry was correct, was the whole of Anderson's second version a foolish fabrication?

Some students accept and others explain away both of Anderson's accounts and give Wren a long period of high office. Our only comment is that the *recorded* evidence upon which those students base their beliefs is exactly what we have here given.

German authors at one time credited Wren with being "the creator of the entire system of Freemasonry as it exists to-day," but their arguments have long since been brought to naught. It seems safe to conclude that Wren was almost certainly a speculative mason, but not a Grand Master of the Order, that he was neither the 'creator' of any part of the masonic system nor an important figure in the emergence of speculative masonry. As to the latter, we wish he had been!

Had Freemasonry a German Origin?

No more convenient place will occur in these pages for dealing quite briefly with the old German claim that world-wide freemasonry originated in Germany. That country's masonic writers had credited the medieval German stonemason bodies, the *Steinmetzen* and others, with having an esoteric aspect and with being so highly organized as to be a material element in the founding of stonemason fraternities in England and other countries. Side by side with this they held that speculative masonry had evolved in Germany from the old Templar Rites, but neither of these claims is now accepted—at any rate, outside Germany. It is possible that the *Steinmetzen* at some time or other possessed a grip as a means of recognition, but there is nothing in the articles of the body suggesting any esoteric content. The rules insisted on obedience and certain religious observances, did not allow a member to give instruction to an outsider but obliged him to give it unpaid to his fellows, insisted that masons must settle their debts before they departed for another building site, and that skilled fellows should not be given employment for a shorter term than two years, etc., etc.; all as might be expected from a medieval trade fraternity. As G. W. Speth has said, "The whole substructure of the *Steinmetzen* theory (that the Germans brought freemasonry to England) has been built upon surmise, false interpretation of technical terms, ill-regulated imagination and misplaced patriotism."

We have two important admissions. A German encyclopædia published as early as 1739 states that "it is certain that German freemasonry took its origin in England." The other admission comes from a prominent German mason and actor of his day, Friedrich Ludwig Schroeder (1744–1816), who was initiated in 1774, and who was a reformer of the

Continental masonic system, which had been corrupted by the invention of many additional degrees. He claimed to get back to first principles in the founding of what came to be known as Schroeder's Ritual, and based his position on his belief that freemasonry had taken its rise in England, and that for the pure unadulterated fountain of freemasonry one must look to the English *Constitutions* of 1717, etc., and to the primitive English ritual.

Many peculiar ideas were associated with the theory that the Templar Rites of the twelfth and thirteenth centuries were the real beginnings of the masonic ceremonies. Gotthold Ephraim Lessing's *Ernst und Falk* or *Gespräche für Freimaurer*[1] tells the German story in the form of a dialogue between two characters, Ernst and Falk. Lessing believed that English masonry was originally *masony*, a word deriving not from *mason*, a builder, but from *mace*, a table; thus masony was a private, intimate table-company. No court in Germany, big or small, was without one. He claimed even that the Anglo-Saxons took the idea from Germany to England, and that King Arthur's (probably fabulous) Round Table was the first and oldest masony, from which all other English masonys derived their origin. His theory includes the elevation of the masonys of the Knights Templars in the twelfth and thirteenth centuries to their very high repute. He held also that such masonys were preserved to the end of the seventeenth century in the heart of London, where they existed in great secrecy with a meeting-place near St Paul's Cathedral, which was then newly erected, Christopher Wren being of their number and, as already quoted, "creating the entire system of freemasonry as it exists to-day." The true meaning of masony was forgotten, the word being confused with masonry, particularly in connexion with the building of St Paul's Cathedral. That is the theory.

As the claims have been riddled time and time again all that need be stated here is that no claim for any German origin of the English system of freemasonry can be made good by German historians. There was no symbolic Lodge in Germany until freemasonry had emerged in England and had been transplanted to the Continent. What Germany did possess was its well-organized fraternities of operative stonemasons, including the *Steinmetzen*, whose records go back a long way, and it naturally followed that German symbolic freemasonry managed to retain many an echo of the old German operative craft. It is common knowledge that the Germans developed freemasonry into a dignified and powerful Craft which from time to time produced freemasons of great quality and masonic writers of marked ability. Under pressure of political conditions German freemasonry had closed down by May 1933; but now, writing in

[1] About 1780. Translated by the Rev. A. Cohen (Baskerville Press, 1927).

1955, it has been revived and it is hoped that it will be developed on lines allowing of fraternal recognition by the English Grand Lodge.

John Aubrey

Still another of the seventeenth-century antiquaries comes into the history of speculative masonry. John Aubrey (1626–97) was the author of a book, dated 1686, entitled *The Natural History of Wiltshire*. His manuscript of that book is in the Bodleian Library, Oxford, and on the reverse of folio 72, in the author's own handwriting, is the following ('Mdm.' is his abbreviation for memorandum):

1691.

Mdm, this day [May the 18th being Monday after Rogation Sunday] is a great convention at St Paul's church of the Fraternity of the Accepted Masons: where Sr Christopher Wren is to be adopted a Brother: and Sr Henry Goodric . . . of ye Tower, & divers others—There have been kings, that haue been of this Sodalitie.

("Accepted" in this entry was written over the word "Free," which had been crossed out.)

This reference, which has always been accepted as one of the most interesting bits of masonic history, is not, it will be noted, in the book itself, but is an endorsement on the back of one of the original folios. However, the book itself does contain a masonic reference and one upon which much false history has been built. Aubrey says on folio 73:

Sr William Dugdale told me many years since, that about Henry the third's time, the Pope gave a Bull or diploma (Patents) to a Company of Italian Architects to travell up and downe over all Europe to build Churches. From those are derived the *Fraternity of* Adopted-Masons. They are known to one another by certayn Signes & Marks and Watch-words: it continues to this day. They have Severall Lodges in severall Counties for their reception: and when any of them fall into decay, the brotherhood is to relieve him &c. The manner of their Adoption is very formall, and with an Oath of Secrecy.

("Adopted-Masons" in this entry was written over the word "Free-Masons," but the latter was not crossed out. The word "Marks" had a line drawn through it.)

It is very largely upon the strength of Aubrey's statement that there has been built up among freemasons the legend (criticized on other pages) of the Comacine masons travelling by authority of the Pope over the whole of Europe, including England, and building churches wherever they went. The reference is otherwise helpful in confirming that there were at the time Lodges in several counties, and that the acception, or adoption, of a mason was formal and accompanied by an oath of secrecy. Sir William Dugdale, Aubrey's informant, was Elias Ashmole's father-in-law through Ashmole's third wife, and, although not known to have been a freemason, was one of the many noted historians and antiquarians of his day who, whether masons or not, appear to have shared a very lively interest in matters relating to the Craft.

Lodges at Chichester, York, etc.

Another seventeenth-century reference which rather helps to build the history of that period concerns a Lodge at Chichester. In 1732 a Bro. Edward Hall, then a member of the Lodge held at the Swan, East Street, Chichester, presented a petition to Grand Lodge in the course of which he mentioned that he had been made a mason by the late Duke of Richmond at Chichester thirty-six years previously (about 1695 or 1696). The evidence gains considerably from the fact that Hall's petition was recommended by the second Duke of Richmond, son of the late Duke, and is further strengthened by the fact that in the 1725 Engraved List of Lodges the Lodge at Chichester is indicated by an emblematic swan and the words "City of Chichester, Third Fryday in every month." It is a great pity that this time-immemorial lodge ceased to exist by 1769. Originally meeting at the Swan, it had afterwards met at the Dolphin in West Street, next at the White Horse in South Street, and then again at the Dolphin.

John Theyer (1597–1673) was an antiquary of Gloucester whose library was purchased at his death by Charles II. We do not know if he was a freemason, but it may be significant that he was the owner of the Regius MS. containing the medieval poem frequently referred to in our pages and presented by George III to the British Museum with other manuscripts in 1757. It is quite impossible to say how many antiquarians and scholars were made masons in the seventeenth century, but we cannot help thinking that were the whole of the facts known we should probably find that very many of the prominent antiquarians of the day entered the fraternity.

York freemasonry is discussed elsewhere, but, to serve the present purpose of showing the existence of a number of lodges in the pre-1717 period, we may mention that in 1705–6 Sir George Tempest presided over a Lodge in York which was attracting to itself the membership of many influential men. This same Lodge met in Bradford in 1717, on which occasion eighteen gentlemen were admitted. We therefore conclude that the Lodge must have had a much earlier history, as to which there is an indication in the York No. 4 MS., dating back to 1693 and bearing the signature of the copyist, Mark Kipling, with five other names under the heading "the names of the Lodg"; but nothing is known of the Lodge or where it met.

The minutes of the Alnwick Lodge, Northumberland, are often referred to in masonic writings. It is necessary to say that this lodge was apparently wholly operative, and a speculative Lodge did not grow from it. Alnwick's first symbolic Lodge came in 1779 and met at the Beehive. The minutes of the old operative lodge as far back as 1701 were published in 1895 in book form, and have proved an extremely valuable historical record.

With these facts in our minds we shall now be prepared to appreciate that by the dawn of the eighteenth century there were scattered throughout the English counties isolated Lodges and fraternities of freemasons which, in the words of Gould, were survivors of a widespread system derived from an operative "craft that was now moribund, independent but aware of one another's existence, and still looking upon themselves as all one Society." We can instance the Lodges at Warrington, Chester, York, Chichester, and London, and in addition, we can draw useful inferences from the already quoted words of Randle Holme, Plot, and Aubrey.

Whether these Lodges, or any of them, were part of a general organization is very doubtful indeed, but their growing strength may well have suggested the advisability of setting up some central authority. And yet in this possibility we have to be cautious, particularly bearing in mind that the Grand Lodge of 1717 came into existence not apparently to create or control a national organization, but merely to cement together four Lodges—three of London and one of Westminster—as will be explained in later pages.

From allusions in general literature of the day, notably, for example, in Steele's essays in *The Tatler* (1709 and 1710), it is obvious that by that time freemasonry was already well known, and was being referred to in ordinary conversation. Speaking of certain sets of people, Steele says, "they have their Signs and Tokens like Free-Masons" and "they had some secret Intimation of each other like the Free Masons."

In 1947 a particularly valuable discovery was made in the stockroom of the Grand Lodge Library, London. It was a pamphlet printed in London in 1710 by A. Baldwin, consisting of *A Letter from a Clergy-Man in London,* and containing a reference to "the *Word, Mark,* or *Token* of a certain Company called the *Free Masons,* which is wellknown to every Member of that Sage Society, but kept a mighty Secret from all the World besides." Such references indicate that the public was very well aware, years before the advent of the first Grand Lodge, that there existed the Society of Freemasons, whose members had secret modes of recognition.

Summary of the Seventeenth-century Evidence

A writer on economic history has offered the criticism that "before the mystic year 1717" the authentic school of masonic historians "have had so little to be authentic about." Well, let us sum up the seventeenth-century evidence already given in our pages so that we may visualize just what the case is for the emergence of freemasonry following 1620. (Many seventeenth-century references to the 'Mason Word' are given in a later chapter dealing with the evolution of Scottish freemasonry and will be there considered.)

In 1621 and 1631 we learn of acceptions into the London Company of Freemasons. On a scrap of paper written by Randle Holme, himself a mason, in the 1640–50 period are words referring to the words and signs of a freemason. In 1646 Elias Ashmole is made a mason at Warrington. In 1648 a Warden of the London Company pays one pound for coming on the acception. Randle Holme, in a list written about 1673, gives the names of twenty-seven persons relating to the Lodge at Chester. In 1676 a published 'divertisement' mentions the Company of Accepted Masons. In 1682 Elias Ashmole attends a Lodge at the Masons Hall and sees six men admitted into the Fellowship of Masons, among those present being many members of the Company. In 1686 Dr Robert Plot prints many references to the Society of Free-masons, and in that same year John Aubrey refers to the Fraternity of Adopted Masons or Freemasons; on a slip of paper bearing the date 1691 Aubrey records the 'adoption' of Sir Christopher Wren and others as Brethren of the Fraternity of the Accepted Masons. In 1688 Randle Holme speaks of the 'antiquity' of the Fellowship of Masons. In 1695 or 1696 Edward Hall is made a mason at Chichester. The York No. 4 MS. (1693) gives "the names of the lodg."

One scrap of evidence not yet mentioned is a leaflet printed in London in 1698 attacking freemasonry as being a "devilish sect of men," "Anti Christ," "Evil-doers," "Corrupt people." Its author thinks it needful to warn "all godly people in the citie of London" of the "Mischiefs and Evils practised in the Sight of GOD by those called Freed Masons. I say take Care lest their Ceremonies and secret Swearings take hold of you; and be wary that none cause you to err from Godliness." Finally, we have the evidence of *The Tatler*, which in 1709 and 1710 refers to 'free-masons,' and of a pamphlet of 1710 which mentions "the certain Company called the *Free Masons.*"

The Complete Story of the Emergence still Unknown

We should be making a serious mistake if we thought that the recorded evidence includes everything that could have been included. There must have been something vital and important that all those learned speculatives discovered in the Acception. To *something* they were only too ready and willing to introduce their friends. It must obviously have been greater than anything that has come down to us in the form of a *printed or written record.* "Litera scripta manet, verbum imbelle perit." ("The written letter lives, the spoken word dies.") This explains so much of the difficulty in tracing masonic history. Hardly any records were kept until the seventeen-thirties. Where we *do* get evidence (implied, for instance, in the *exposés*, themselves a reflex of a remarkable popular interest in freemasonry) we learn of a ritual which must have had some sort of existence over a long period of years.

Everybody will agree that where there is no written record events are relatively soon forgotten. It has been said that the only families that know anything of their ancestors are those having written histories. Gould notes that in 1770 the New Zealanders had no recollection of Tasman's visit of 1642, and that the North American Indians soon lost all tradition of De Soto's expedition of 1539–42, which, with its striking incidents, might well have impressed the Indian mind. Dr Samuel Johnson well said that one generation of ignorance effaces the whole series of un-written history. "Written learning is a fixed luminary," said he, but oral tradition "is but a meteor, which, if once it falls, cannot be rekindled."

We cannot read the story of the emergence of symbolic masonry and escape the conviction that between its lines there is another story, one that we should all like to read. Is there much hope that it will ever come to light? We remember the wellnigh complete thoroughness with which our ancient Brethren concealed their Lodge business—the esoteric and important, equally with the explicit and unimportant—and there is little or nothing to encourage us in the recollection. Still we must hope, even against hope, that there will yet be discovered some record of freemasonic activity that will add substantially to our knowledge of the formative period of our Craft. Such a discovery, however unlikely, is not out of the question once we admit the possibility of such a record having at some time been reduced to writing. We remember, for example, the accidental finding in 1945–46 of the world's second copy of the "Pirate Quarto" of Shakespeare issued in 1619 and resting, lost in darkness for the time being, on the top shelf of an old library at Girsby Manor, Lincolnshire. There, through most of the years since Shakespeare's death, it waited for time or circumstance to restore it to the light. We remember, too, the discovery in 1934, in the Fellows' Library at Winchester, of Sir Thomas Malory's manuscript of *Morte d'Arthur*, from which William Caxton had printed his edition in 1485.

When we think of the pre-1700 story of the Craft, and of the fuller story that all freemasons would like to read, how we wish that Samuel Pepys, that "most excellent friend" of Dr Robert Plot, had been made a mason!

Chapter Eight

THE ROSICRUCIANS AND THE EMERGENCE

WHEN we think of Ashmole and other learned speculatives who entered freemasonry in the seventeenth century, we are reminded of the oft-made claims that he and his friends brought in with them the mysticism, the philosophies, and the Christian teaching of Rosicrucianism—the German cult that is believed to have arisen in the seventeenth century, and not the Rosicrucianism of the well-known Masonic Order, which is a later and different development.

The "Legend of the Tomb," as revered by the Rosicrucians, is to the effect that the founder, real or mythical, of the order was Christian Rosenkreuz, who had been brought up in a German monastery, and, journeying forth at perhaps twenty years of age to the Holy Land about the year 1393, is said to have made a grand tour of Palestine, Holy Land, and through the Mediterranean to Spain, seeking out and studying with learned men everywhere the mysteries of the ancient peoples. Returning to Germany in 1402 he collected many disciples, with whom he founded a secret society to study his philosophies and cast them into a "coherent form and body of doctrine," to quote Dr W. Wynn Westcott, a well-known freemason of strong Rosicrucian sympathies, whose valuable paper on the connexion between Rosicrucian and freemasonry is published in *A.Q.C.*, vol. vii. In 1484, when at least one hundred and eleven years old, he died. His embalmed body was enshrined in a vault decorated with mystical devices, and when, 120 years later, parts of the shrine were demolished the door of the vault was found intact and still bearing its original inscription, "Post centum viginti annos patebo." The Master's wishes had been observed. His shrine had not been interfered with for the specified 120 years. His embalmed body was still there. And the vault was illumined by a 'sun,' or light, in the flat heptagonal ceiling—a magical ever-burning lamp! (The superficial resemblance between the legend of the Royal Arch and the discovery of the tomb will be noted.)

The Rosicrucian Legend

The Rosicrucian legend is recited in a famous book, originally circulated in manuscript about 1610 and later published, dated Cassel, 1614, and bearing the Latin title *Fama Fraternitatis benedicti Ordinis Rosæ-Crucis* (The History of the Fraternity of the Meritorious Order of the Rosy-Cross). The *Fama*, as the work is generally called for short, together with certain tracts published in the same connexion, is the basis of the Rosicrucian belief, itself a réchauffé of Greek, Arabic, Chaldee, and Egyptian systems. The magical element in the story may owe something to old legends telling of the finding of bodies of saints whose heads were surrounded by luminous halos, and its presence can be understood in any recital made in a highly credulous age; but, apart from this, students tend to regard the whole story as a myth. An English translation of the *Fama*, published by Thomas Vaughan, a famous chemist or alchemist known also as Eugenius Philalethes, was issued in 1652, and all through the seventeenth century were published books for or against the Rosicrucian doctrines, but although there were many people who called themselves Rosicrucians it is by no means certain that they were ever members of an organized society.

As to the original doctrine of the cult, we may best quote from Dr Westcott, himself a modern Rosicrucian, and say that it was "Christian on the face of it." The members separated themselves largely from the world and each was a *Frater* (Latin for Brother), their instructor being their 'Father.' They were pledged to the relief of the suffering, to attempt the "cure of diseases and that gratis" (*Fama*), and to found hospices and retreats. They spent their lives in the "search for truth, the knowledge of man and his possibilities, and his relation to the other planes of existence beyond the material world, even up to the Divine ideal." (Michael Maier.)

By Ashmole's day—and that is the day that interests us—the original doctrines had apparently been added to or adulterated. The members were now 'scientific' dabblers, whatever else they were. As to their 'philosophy' and 'science,' it must be said frankly that much of what passed under these names in the minds of many men—even educated men—in the sixteenth and seventeenth centuries would to-day be regarded as nonsense. Chemical philosophers, alchemists, astrologers, hermetic philosophers—all at some time or other regarded themselves as Rosicrucians, and apparently any educated person with a gift for words could find a place under the Rosicrucian banner.

During the latter half of the seventeenth century the term Rosicrucian was applied to those who in the earlier half would have been called astrologers, and earlier still alchemists. The so-called alchemists sought for "the universal solvent (*alkahest*), the universal remedy (*Panacea*), and the universal transmutation of the baser metals into gold (*alchemy*)."

The name 'Rosicrucian' is believed to have been derived from *ros* ('dew'), which they held to be the most powerful solvent of gold, and *crux* (the 'cross.'), which in the chemical style signifies light, because, says Hook's *Church Dictionary*, the figure of the cross "exhibits at the same time the three letters in the word *lux*." Now light, according to this sect, is the menstruum of the red dragon—that is, the substance out of which gold is produced. "The Rosicrucians then were alchemists, who sought for the philosopher's stone by the intervention of dew and of light." The alchemists "pursued the will-o'-the-wisp of the Quinte Essence, the substance of which the heavenly bodies—the sun and the stars—were made. . . . It was confidently believed that it could be obtained by distillation."[1]

Belief in the use of the 'Philosopher's Stone,' with which to transmute base metals into gold—the predominating doctrine of alchemy—continued to hold the field for a long time, and now that the transmutation of metals by atomic energy is a scientific fact there will be, we suppose, some sort of modern revival of the old cult.

Ashmole and the Rosicrucians

The Rosicrucians rely chiefly on the personality of Elias Ashmole in their claim that their system influenced freemasonry. It so happens that a German alchemist, Michael Maier, produced a classical work on Rosicrucianism, and an English translation of it, issued in 1656, was dedicated to Ashmole, who is said to have joined a German Rosicrucian society. A few masonic writers have professed to believe whole-heartedly that Rosicrucian doctrines came into freemasonry through him and his friends. The question arises (and Gould goes into it closely) whether Ashmole was capable, either as freemason or Rosicrucian, of devising a masonic ritual or system, apart altogether from the fact that the negative evidence of his career and especially of his diary is all against the conjecture. For nearly thirty-six years, from 1646, when he was 'made,' until 1682, when he attended the Masons Hall Lodge, there is not a word in his diary about freemasonry. Is it conceivable that he could have given the necessary thought and time, either alone or in collaboration with others, to the revision or, indeed, the actual invention of a masonic ritual without some hint of such an absorbing task finding its way into his daily record?

Ashmole wrote a well-known history of the Order of the Garter, he collected and wrote learnedly on antiquities, and he was the author of books on alchemy written in his early middle life. Gould regards him as a strange being—learned, capable of writing books of "crabbed and

[1] F. Harrison.

ponderous learning," credulous, fond of litigation, and "extremely cantankerous." We know that Ashmole's otherwise cultivated mind harboured much folly and superstition. (His diary for the year 1681 tells us that he hung "three spiders about his neck to drive away his ague.") Pepys found him "a very ingenious gentleman" (was he damning him with faint praise?), while Evelyn, writing from his own unusually high standard of learning, mentions Ashmole's astrological manuscripts and believes him to be "not learned, but very industrious."

Very strongly against the suggestion that Ashmole imported Rosicrucianism into freemasonry is the fact that when he joined the Lodge at Warrington he was *not yet a mystic,* and that it was only on leaving Cheshire and returning to London that he took up with the astrologers, remaining interested in astrology, says Dr Kurt Josten, until his death, in 1692, on which point, however, possibly lesser authorities do not agree.

In opposition to the idea that a society of Rosicrucians was a factor in any new development of freemasonry it is felt that, while there may have been many writers calling themselves Rosicrucians, they were an odd lot of cranks, very unlikely to be gathered together into a society representing the considered doctrine of any real school, and quite incapable as a *body* of giving to masonry any particular moral or philosophical trend. As already hinted, some writers go so far as to suggest that the real truth is not so much that Rosicrucianism influenced freemasonry as that it actually amalgamated with freemasonry and became part of it. Gould, however, points out there is no evidence of freemasonry having ever amalgamated with any of the supposed Rosicrucian or Hermetic fraternities (which, by the way, have never been proved to have existed), for any such amalgamation would "falsify the whole of authentic masonic history, together with the admittedly genuine documents upon which it rests," while the Rev. Herbert Poole believes that Rosicrucianism came too late to exert much influence in freemasonry.

When the Rosicrucians assert "that freemasonry derived all its moral philosophy, its semi-Christian ideas and its halo of mystic secrecy" from their system, they forget that brotherly love, relief, and truth are in the foundation of most beneficent orders. It may or may not be a point in the Rosicrucians' favour to recall the fact that benevolence and the attendant virtues had small place in the avowed objects of freemasonry until well after the formation of the Premier Grand Lodge in 1717. By that time, however, Ashmole had been dead about twenty-five years. It is not to be thought that symbolism was wholly introduced by the Rosicrucian, for from the earliest times certain working tools have borne a symbolism derived from their uses; we need only note, as one example, that the Egyptians believe that all truth and justice were 'on the square.'

Count Goblet d'Alviella presents in *A.Q.C.*, vol. xxxii, a moderately worded case for the Rosicrucian theory, and concludes by saying that while he does not pretend that speculative masonry is the direct child of Rosicrucianism, he upholds that it is the legitimate offspring of a fruitful union between a professional body of medieval masons and a secret group of philosophical adepts, the first having furnished the form, and the second the spirit.

Some masonic symbols were almost certainly introduced by the alchemists, as, for instance, the all-seeing eye, a symbol of very great antiquity representing the ever-watchful and omnipresent Deity and, as a Christian symbol, supported by a host of biblical references. Even in its masonic form of an open eye within a triangle it has been used as a Church emblem, but it came to freemasonry much more probably from alchemy than from Christian symbolism.

In Vienna's permanent technical museum (approached from Maria Hilfer Strasse) has been re-erected an Austrian pharmacy or chemist's shop of the year 1720—the actual shop transported in complete detail. Surmounting the central counter is a slight wrought-iron arch in which angelic figures hold aloft a wreath within which is the familiar triangle and all-seeing eye. Bearing in mind that the chemist's art—hardly yet a science as early as 1720—had so lately grown out of alchemy, it may well be assumed that the masonic emblem is of alchemic origin and that it was brought in by the seventeenth-century mystics, who were so warmly tinged with alchemic ideas and doctrines.

It is just and proper to admit the possibility of our Craft degrees having been influenced by individual Rosicrucians, but to dismiss utterly and completely any suggestion that speculative freemasonry is largely a survival of the Rosicrucian cult or is the seventeenth-century invention of its adherents, organized or otherwise.

There are writers who take a strongly different view. One, for example, is A. E. Waite, the learned author of *The Secret Tradition in Freemasonry* and of other well-known masonic works, all written from a highly individualistic point of view. In the work mentioned, he cultivates the theory that at some period, probably in the seventeenth century, certain initiates who were Christian followers of the Kabalistic system took over the organized and crude symbolism of the mason trade guild and engrafted upon it their own richer and deeper symbolism and ritual. He believes that the Craft degrees, closely related to the old Hebrew Covenant, were intended to demonstrate the loss of a secret, the restoration of which would occur in one or more of the higher degrees, representing the new Christian Covenant. But opposing critics see in the Craft degrees only Hebraic incidents and phrasing, and they feel instinctively that these degrees are as Christian in their essence as they are Hebraic. Beneath the form of the phrases "lies the eternal teaching of all the mystic schools of the past," as well as, let us quite truthfully add, much of the moral teaching of the common-sense schools of the present.

The Kabballa

Distantly related to the cult of the Rosicrucian is the Kabballa, or Cabballa, whose "mysterious and abstruse" doctrines are claimed to have influenced freemasonry in the seventeenth century. There are many wellnigh unreadable books on the subject, but we may well be satisfied with the résumé given by Gould in his *History*.

Hook's *Church Dictionary* tells us that the word 'Kabballa' (from a Hebraic word meaning "to receive") implies a doctrine received, or handed down, by oral tradition. Many claims, extraordinary and even ridiculous, were made for the Kabballa. God himself, it is said, taught it first to a select company of angels, who, after the Fall of man, communicated it to men to supply the means of returning to the pristine state of happiness and communion with the Deity, the doctrine being handed down through Adam, Noah, Abraham, and Moses. The last-named is said to have initiated the seventy elders into its secrets, which were transmitted in line to David, Solomon, and his successors until the time of the destruction of Jerusalem. The Kabballa is thought to have been derived by the Jews from a mixture of Greek, Egyptian, and Oriental notions, and was at one time adopted by the Christian Fathers on the strength of their belief that it was of Hebrew, not pagan, origin. It has three distinct portions: the 'theoretical' teaches of the Divinity and his relations to man; the 'enigmatical' bases itself on the arrangements of words and letters in the Bible; the 'practical,' also concerned with the puerilities of word and letter arrangements, makes some profession of curing diseases.

Every now and then we find an attempt made in modern writings to answer masonic queries by means of the enigmatic 'teaching' of the Kabballa. According to this 'teaching,' says Dr Hook, every letter of a Biblical word is reduced to its numerical value, and the word is explained by means of another of the same quantity—a principle known as gematria; or, instead, every letter of a Biblical word is taken as the initial or abbreviation of a word—a system called notaricon. Two words in one sentence may be joined together to make one word, which is then evaluated in the way already noted. Whatever may or may not be said for the 'theoretic' teaching of the Kabballa, we can safely say with regard to the 'enigmatical' principle that it is a sad pity any attempt should ever have been made to explain freemasonry in terms of such appalling nonsense.

Chapter Nine

THE EVOLUTION OF SCOTTISH FREEMASONRY
AND ITS INFLUENCE ON EARLY FREEMASONRY
IN ENGLAND

THE evolution of speculative freemasonry in Scotland is a wholly different story from that of the emergence in England. Both countries have a long operative craft history, but, owing to very different economic and political conditions, the one is quite distinct from the other. In England, the known operative lodges at the time of the emergence were very few indeed; but in Scotland they were many, and the whole mason trade organization was built round them. It was long thought that Scotland had no *symbolic* masonry indigenous to the country, and that the symbolic element had wholly come from the English lodges some time early in the eighteenth century, but recent researches have introduced arguments that, in the opinion of certain eminent writers, make the belief less sure. These arguments will be examined in the course of this chapter.

Irish churchmen were building churches in Scotland in the sixth and seventh centuries, but these had disappeared by the end of the tenth and their builders forgotten. Masonry building began in Scotland probably with the immigration of English stone-workers in the twelfth century, when the Romanesque style spread north from England. The earliest churches of England and Scotland have many likenesses in style, and there are said to be evidences that a few churches in England and in Scotland were built by the same masons. The Early English style of the second half of the twelfth century reached Scotland a century later, and was in use there long after 'Gothic' had superseded it in England.

The warfare between the two countries associated with the short life and barbaric death of William Wallace (late thirteenth and early fourteenth century) brought to an end the English influence. The Scots from that time looked to the Continent for inspiration, and, as a consequence, in the fifteenth century the French influence was very marked in Scotland, as, for example, in the design and building of the famous Melrose Abbey.

In England the parish church and country mansion were representative of the national architecture, but in Scotland (as G. M. Trevelyan's *English*

Social History reminds us) the parish church, with its roof of turf or thatch, had no medieval splendours or amenities, while the lairds' stone mansions, many of them without a window on the north side, and each with its corbel-stepped gable roof, some of them adapted from the war-towers of former days, "stood up gaunt and fortresslike."

Development of the Scots Mason Craft

The economic state and the geological conditions of Scotland caused the mason craft to develop in a highly individual way. Whereas in England the medieval freemason was highly skilled in the working of the soft freestone, native or imported, and long enjoyed a status superior to that of all other mason operatives, in Scotland there was no freestone and often no money to import it. But granite and other hard stones were everywhere, so the country naturally used what it had in common supply. The effect of this, it is supposed, was to bring about a more or less general level of skill among both town and country masons, because, with good stone everywhere available, a mason could get his training almost anywhere and not just at a few quarries or on sites to which a particular class of stone could be brought cheaply by land or water. There tended, therefore, to be less sharp distinction of skill marking one *class* of mason from another; any difference was rather of regularity of training and whether, after training, masons had been accepted or recog-nized by the lodges, trade incorporations, and similar fraternities of the leading towns and cities.

It is believed that these mason trade bodies introduced a mode of recognition, lacking which any operative, whatever his skill and train-ing, was regarded merely as semi-skilled or even as a labourer. It would thus follow that the Scots country mason, a skilled mason in his own village and countryside, might be no more than a cowan in a Scots city, although were he given in lodge the secret qualification possessed by the city masons his standing would be exactly the same as theirs. In the light of these suppositions, some masonic scholars account for the institution among Scots operatives of the 'Mason Word' and for what they suppose to be the absence of any such word among the English operatives.

The term 'frie mesone' in Scots records does not imply what is meant by 'freemason' in either the early operative or early speculative sense in England. It means simply a freeman mason—that is, a member of the mason trade accepted as a freeman of his incorporation. Versions of the Old Charges revised for Scottish lodges may include the word, but only as an echo of English usage. Where the old English operative documents refer to a "freemason" the Scots documents refer to "a mason." The Lodges of Edinburgh and Kilwinning did not use the speculative term 'freemason' until a few years later than 1717.

Scots Operative Lodges and Incorporations

It is not known whether the city incorporation or the lodge came first. In Edinburgh the Incorporation of Masons and Wrights was established in 1475. The first we know of the Lodge of Edinburgh is 1491, while in Aberdeen "masons of the lodge" are spoken of in 1483.

The Schaw Statutes of 1598 and 1599 use the word 'Lodge,' which evidently referred to an organization already well known, and meant the body of masons controlling building activity in a particular town. Douglas Knoop calls such a lodge a "Territorial Lodge" to distinguish it from the meeting of operatives in a lodge, or workshop, attached to a building site.

Territorial lodges were themselves under the supervision of head lodges, such as the lodges at Kilwinning, St Andrews, Aitcheson's Haven, Edinburgh, Dundee, Perth, Dunfermline, Glasgow, Stirling, and Ayr. Not all of these important lodges were in large towns; the famous lodge at Kilwinning, for example, was in a village-town, which even at the present day, with its iron, coal, engineering, and spinning industries, has a relatively small population. Aitcheson's Haven, which gave its name to a well-known lodge whose minutes are known to date back to 1598, is not large enough for its name to find its way into the usual atlas, but a harbour was built there in 1526 under a charter granted to the monks of Newbattle, an abbey just to the south of Dalkeith, Midlothian, and approximately six miles south of the coast.

The Lodge of Kilwinning had supervisory powers over lodges in the west of Scotland; the Lodge of St Andrews over lodges in Fifeshire; and Douglas Knoop tells us that the so-called St Clair Charters of 1601 and 1628 show that five lodges united in 1601, and seven lodges in 1628 (nine lodges in all) to support the claims of an aristocratic family, the St Clairs of Roslin, to exercise jurisdiction over the masons of Scotland.

We see at a glance that the Scottish development had no parallel in England. It is true that we know something of an operative lodge at Alnwick, Northumberland, and another at Swalwell, County Durham, but nothing definitely of others in England, and even in the case of the two mentioned we must concede that their nearness to the Border probably caused them to approximate to the Scots usages. In England, there was a mason company in London and also in a few other cities, but it is quite clear that there is no history of operative lodges to be compared with that of Scotland. In that country the mason trade was closely controlled and supervised; the mason answered to his lodge, the lodge to its supervising lodge, and the masters of the supervising lodges to the King's Principal Master of Work and Warden General.

No less than twenty Scots operative lodges are recorded to have been at work before 1700, but not one of them was *known* to have had a symbolic working at that date. When the Scottish Grand Lodge was to be founded in 1736, invitations to join in the task were issued to about one hundred lodges, of whom thirty-three responded. Of the twenty pre-1700 lodges above referred to, nine became founders of the Scottish Grand Lodge, and concerning these we abstract the following particulars from Lionel Vibert's paper "The Early Freemasonry of England and Scotland," in *A.Q.C.*, vol. xliii.

Edinburgh (Mary's Chapel) No. 1. Seal of Cause of 1475 incorporates the Masons and Wrights; Statute of 1491 refers to the *common luge*. Schaw Statute of 1599 describes it as the first and principal lodge in Scotland. Minutes begin in 1599. First meeting recorded at Mary's Chapel is in 1613.

Aberdeen. Masons of the Lodge are spoken of in 1483; the Incorporation is in 1527. Patrick Copland is Warden over the masons of Aberdeen and other counties in 1590. Laws and Statutes are known to date from 1670 and may be far older.

Dundee. Old custom of the Lady Lodge of Dundee is mentioned in 1536. Minute of Mary's Chapel of 1599 records that the Master is to present himself at St Andrew's to attend a general meeting. Actually a founding lodge, its present constitution dates to 1745.

Aitcheson's Haven (Extinct). Minutes begin in 1598. Lodge had its own version of the *Old Charges* in 1666. It was a founding lodge, but within a year its name was deleted.

Kilwinning. Second head lodge of the Schaw Statutes of 1599. First Minutes are dated 1642. It had its own version of the *Old Charges* in 1665. First charter is dated 1729. At Perth in 1658 there is already a tradition in existence of lodges proceeding from Kilwinning.

Dunfermline. A founding lodge that dropped out of the lists till 1804, although its date of constitution is given as 1736.

Canongate Kilwinning, No. 2. Received authority from Kilwinning in 1677 to make masons on behalf of that Lodge. It possesses and still uses the oldest lodge-room in the world. Minutes date from 1735 and are of peculiar interest owing to the connexion of several of its members with the Rebellion of 1745.

Old Kilwinning St John, Inverness. Minutes of 1678 were known but are now lost. Existing minutes begin in 1737. The lodge was "Old Inverness Kilwinning," the St John being added in 1837.

Hamilton Kilwinning. At founding of Grand Lodge was known as

Hamilton; the Kilwinning was added in 1771. Minutes begin in 1730, the earlier ones going back to 1695 having been lost.

Honorary Members in Scots Lodges

As far back as the Reformation certain Scots lodges (not all) welcomed aristocratic neighbours as honorary members. The noble house of Montgomerie had hereditary connexions with the Lodge of Kilwinning. According to the solemn declaration of a Church court in 1652, many masons having the "word" were ministers and professors in "the purest tymes of this kirke." The Laird of Roslin and his heirs are named as patrons, protectors, and overseers to the craft in the St Clair Charters. There is the exceptional instance of Mary's Chapel Lodge of Edinburgh meeting near Newcastle in 1641 (at the time when General Hamilton's Scots army was about to invest the town of Newcastle), admitting into membership "the Right Honerabell Mr Robert Moray (Murray), General Quarter Mr to the armie off Scotlan." The admission although taking place outside Scotland was approved, the relative minute stating that "the same being approven be the hell mester off the mesone of the Log. off Edenbroth." This is claimed to be the first non-operative 'initiation' by a Scots lodge on English soil. This same Robert Murray is the Sir Robert Murray, Secretary of Scotland, who in 1673 was buried in Westminster Abbey or, as another account says, "in the Canongate Churchyard, Edinburgh."

Now, the reader will note that Murray was admitted in a lodge held on the soil of an invaded country, and we rather suspect that the whole affair was in the nature of a flourish, a gesture, by an invader. With this in mind, any suggestion that occasionally Englishmen were, or could have been, made masons in their own country in lodges under Scottish auspices is not well based, particularly as it is well known that Scottish lodges were most unlikely to condone irregular proceedings, and in any case would have recorded any exceptional 'makings' needing especial confirmation.

Mary's Chapel Lodge of Edinburgh had admitted a gentleman honorary member about forty years before the date of Murray's admission; he was John, of the famous Boswell family of Auchinleck. There were many other admissions of this nature.

A lodge charged a gentleman mason a higher fee than it did an operative. Even as late as 1740, when the speculative element in many lodges was already quite strong, the Lodge of Scoon and Perth called for a payment of ten shillings from the operative at entry but twenty shillings from the "dry-handed" mason.

There is general belief that the presence in certain Scots lodges of "gentleman masons" or "geomatic masons" was not a fact leading to any alteration in lodge character, and apparently this remained true until changing social conditions finally weakened the operative influence.

The Schaw Statutes (1598 and 1599)

Schaw was a well-known Scottish family of Sauchie, a village in Clackmannanshire, Scotland (Sir Walter Scott was one of its distant descendants). William Schaw, born in 1550, entered the Royal Household of Scotland as a young boy, and when only ten years of age went to Copenhagen as a member of a commission whose duty was to escort Ann of Denmark, the prospective bride of Scotland's James VI, to Edinburgh. The boy grew to be a man of wide culture, became Master of Works in Scotland in 1584, carried out many important works, became Chamberlain to the Queen, and will always be known for the system of trade government which he, with the approval of the Masters of the Scottish lodges, was able to achieve. He was a man of considerable authority, and in his day easily the most powerful man of his kind in Scotland. He died suddenly in 1602 when only fifty-two years of age. We have no evidence that he was a member of an inner masonic fraternity in Scotland, or that any such fraternity then existed.

In his character of Master of Works to the Crown of Scotland and General Warden of the Masons, Schaw promulgated two sets of ordinances, respectively in 1598 and 1599. The first of these regulated the mason craft in Scotland; the second, in particular, invested the Lodge of Kilwinning with supervisory powers over lodges in the West of Scotland. Of the first set, a copy is to be found in the first minute book of the Lodge of Edinburgh; of the second, no copy was known until a manuscript containing it came to light in 1861. Murray Lyon's *History of the Lodge of Edinburgh* gives the statutes in detail, while Gould in his *History* usefully summarizes them.

The First and Second Statutes

The first set of the Schaw Statutes order the Brethren to observe the ordinances and to be true to one another, to be obedient to the Wardens, Deacons, and Masters, and to be honest, diligent, and upright. No one may undertake work unless able to complete it satisfactorily, and no Master may supplant another or take an uncompleted work unless the previous Master is duly satisfied. There is to be an annual election of one Warden. No Master may have more than three Apprentices during his lifetime, and an apprentice is not to be bound for less than seven years, and is not to be made a Fellow Craft until he has served an additional seven years. Masters are forbidden to sell their Apprentices or to receive an Apprentice without informing the lodge Warden, so that his name and date of reception may be duly booked. No Master or Fellow of Craft may be received or admitted except in the presence of six Masters and two Entered Apprentices, the Warden of that lodge being one of the six, the date thereof being orderly booked, and "his name and mark insert" in the said book, together with the names of the six Masters, the Apprentices, and Intender. No one to be admitted without an assay and trial of skill. A Master is not allowed to engage in work under charge of any other craftsman, or to receive cowans to work in his society, or company, or to send any of his servants to work with them. Entered Apprentices are forbidden to undertake work beyond the value of ten pounds. Any strife among Masters, servants, or Apprentices is to be notified to the lodge within twenty-four hours, and the award accepted. Masters and others are ordered to take all needful precautions as to the erection of scaffolding, and if accidents occur through their negligence they shall not act as Masters but be subject to others. Masters may not receive runaway Apprentices. All members must attend meetings when lawfully warned, and all Masters present at any assembly or meeting are to be sworn "by their great oath" not to hide or conceal any wrong done to each other or to the owners of the work. Finally, the various penalties attaching to the foregoing were ordered to be collected and distributed by the officers of the lodge.

The second set of Statutes confirm the Edinburgh Lodge as being the first and principal lodge in Scotland, that of Kilwinning as the second, and the lodge of Stirling as the third. They make the Wardens of any lodge answerable to the presbyters (civic elders) within their sheriffdoms for the masons subject to their lodges, and regulate the election of Wardens. They also empower the Wardens of Kilwinning to test the qualifications of the Fellows within their district "of their art, craft, scyance, and *ancient memorie*," to the intent that the said Wardens shall be duly responsible for such persons as are under them. Fellow Crafts at entry and prior to admission must pay to the lodge ten pounds with ten shillings' worth of gloves, this including the expense of the banquet, and none are to be admitted without "ane sufficient essay" and "pruife of memorie and art of craft." Apprentices on admission must pay six pounds towards the common banquet, or pay for the meal. The Wardens and Deacons of Kilwinning Lodge are annually to take the oath of all the Masters and Fellows of Craft committed to their charge, and the members and their servants or apprentices may not work with cowans.

Had the Schaw Statutes an Esoteric Content?

There does not appear to be anything of esoteric interest in these statutes, but writers from time to time have tended to direct special attention or to give slight 'colour' to a phrase here and there in what may be a 'wishful' attempt to detect veiled references. The quiet, unbiased reading of the Statutes fails, however, to discover (with one *possible* exception) anything other than provisions for regulating the mason trade and for investing the lodge at Kilwinning with certain powers. That possible exception is the inclusion of the phrases "of ancient memorie" and "pruife of memorie and art of craft." These words could bear the interpretation that the craftsmen were expected to have learnt by heart something of a traditional or secret nature not expedient to name; but, since the Wardens have to answer to the civic presbyters for the masons under their charge, it reasonably follows that no such interpretation can be regarded as very likely.

It will be noted that the mason failing to satisfy the Warden is fined. A man might well be fined for not having taken sufficient notice of a series of trade customs that, at the expense of another's time and trouble, had been impressed upon him. The Schaw Statutes show those customs to be numerous, but the Mason Word, for all we know to the contrary, was simple enough, and it is wellnigh impossible to believe that there could possibly be a system of fines for forgetting it. The punishment for forgetting the Mason Word was the inability to procure a skilled job once the man had left the surroundings in which he had been trained as a mason! In fairness, however, it must be admitted that students adhering to what in later pages are called the "new school" hold that the presence of the intender at the reception of a Master or Fellow of Craft is in itself an indication that certain esoteric matters were communicated to the Candidate.

It must not be thought that the Schaw Statutes were regarded in Scotland with the veneration which appears to have been accorded to the old manuscript Charges in England. Certain Scots lodges owned for reference a copy of the Statutes, which constituted the authority under which they controlled their operative members, whereas in England, where there could be nothing resembling the Schaw Statutes, inasmuch as there was no central authority to issue them, the Old Charges appear to have been revered. No English mason assembly and, later, no speculative lodge would have considered itself as regular unless it possessed a copy of one or more of them to be read to the Brethren on occasion, and especially to Candidates on reception or initiation.

The 'Mason Word'

The subject of the Mason Word and the ceremonies thought to have accompanied its conferment has been closely studied by modern scholars at a period some fifty or sixty years after Gould presented his conclusions in the matter in his well-known *History*. In particular, Douglas Knoop and his collaborators have carried out much original and important research.

The Mason Word probably came into existence as soon as the Scots mason trade of the towns and cities was strong enough to limit the number of apprentices and to protect itself from the competition of country masons coming to town to seek their fortune. It appears to have been first used in the fourteenth or fifteenth century; it is mentioned in Henry Adamson's *The Muses Threnodie,* published at Edinburgh in 1638; and it is referred to by the English poet, Andrew Marvell, the friend of Milton, in a poem, *Rehearsal Transpros'd,* written about 1672. There are other references dating back to the late sixteen-hundreds, by which time its existence had long been a matter of common knowledge to the outside world. A minute of Mother Kilwinning Lodge of a relatively late date (1707) forbade a mason to employ a cowan—namely, "a mason without the word" (see p. 422).

There is a reference to the existence of the Mason Word in some manuscripts and letters written by the Rev. George Hickes, D.D., afterwards Dean of Worcester, at the time when he was Chaplain to John, second Earl and first Duke of Lauderdale. Among them is a letter, unfortunately not dated or signed, which is obviously from the doctor's pen, and is accompanied by a letter dated 1677. Authorities conclude that the date of this particular letter was about the late 1670's, but just possibly in the late 1690's. The letter contains this passage:

> Hence he [I] went to Halbertshire. This is a strong high tower house built by the Laird of Rosling in King James the fifth time. The Lairds of Roslin have been great architects and patrons of building for these many generations. They are obliged to receive the Mason's Word which is a secret signall masons have thro' out the world to know one another by. They alledge 'tis as old as since Babel when they could not understand one another and they conversed by signs. Others would have it no older than Solomon. However it is, he that hath it will bring his brother mason to him without calling to him or your perceiveing of the signe.

Obviously, then, late in the sixteen-hundreds, there was no secret in the public mind as to the existence of the Mason Word, however secret the word itself was kept—a point of great importance, as we shall see.

Let us refer in this connexion to the Rev. Robert Kirk, Minister of Aberfoill (or Aberfoyle), who wrote a book in 1691 (printed, or possibly reprinted, in 1815) called *Secret Commonwealth of Elves, Fauns, and Fairies*, in which he says he has found "fyve Curiosities in Scotland, not much observ'd to be elsewhere." The second of these he says is "The Mason Word . . . with ane addition of some secret signe delyvered from Hand to Hand."

Late in the sixteen-hundreds was a very superstitious time, and from what now follows it would seem that here and there were simple Scots folk who associated the Mason Word with things uncanny. In the year 1696 there was published in Edinburgh by Alexander Telfair, Minister of the Paroch of Rerrick, in the Stewarty of Kirkcudbright, a tract dealing with "apparitions" and "actings of a spirit" in the house of Andrew Mackie. "The said Andrew Mackie," says the minister, "being a meason to his employment, 'tis given out, that when he took the Meason-word, he devouted his first child to the Devil; but I am certainly informed he never took the same, and knows not what that word is." (On which we may comment that it is quite likely that a mason in a country parish would *not* know the word.)

The Mason Word has once or twice been concerned in legal discussions. Lodge Journeymen, No. 8 (originally No. 11) was an offshoot in 1707 or 1709 of the famous Mary's Chapel Lodge of Edinburgh. When it seceded, it took with it many of the journeymen members, to the sore displeasure of the mother Lodge, which, in the course of the next twenty or thirty years, became a combined speculative and operative employers' lodge, but continued to be closely bound up with the Trades Incorporation of Edinburgh, which, through Mary's Chapel, claimed the right of supervising the journeymen. Following a period of serious trouble, a "Deed of Submission" was drawn up, and the "Decreet Arbitral," as recorded in the Edinburgh Burgh Court Books, 1715, ordained that the journeymen were to be at liberty to give the Mason Word, but placed the control of the Lodge funds in the hands of Mary's Chapel.

This Lodge of Journeymen occupies a place of honour in the list of Scots lodges, and has practised benevolence in its most practical form over a period of two centuries. It has always been tenacious of old customs, and even till 1844 retained the office of "oldest entered apprentice," which was invariably held by an operative; but the speculative element has long since obtained pre-eminence. In 1794 the Journeymen proved to the satisfaction of the Scottish Grand Lodge that they were justified in their practice of holding temporary lodges at whatever place they might have any considerable work on hand, and in virtue of this prerogative opened a lodge at Biggar as late as 1858. The lodge is celebrated for its ritual of the Mark Degree, which is different in some respects from the usually accepted form; and it was largely owing to its persistent demands that its Grand Lodge, after repeated refusals, at length resolved to recognize the Mark as (in Scotland) a portion of the Fellow Craft Degree, though only to be conferred on Master Masons. This Lodge has the exclusive right to carry the 'working tools' in the metropolitan district of Edinburgh.

The Early History of Scots Esoteric Masonry

Two separate problems confront the inquirer into the early history of Scots esoteric masonry. One is whether the Mason Word, which admittedly was conferred on apprentice operatives out of their time during one or two centuries prior to 1700, was accompanied by any communication of an esoteric nature, such, for example, as might be regarded as in any sense a primitive form of our Entered Apprentice's Degree.

The above problem is closely related to a second and much more difficult one—namely, whether there were in fact *two* distinct Scots ceremonies, one for the Entered Apprentice and one for the Fellow Craft, each accompanied by the communication of secrets, and bearing some relationship to the ceremonies in use in English Lodges in, say, 1717 when the Premier Grand Lodge was founded.

Douglas Knoop and his associates and a few other writers give to the Mason Word—and consequently to the influence of early Scots masonry —an importance which Gould and many other scholars did not concede. In general, in the following pages, Gould and Murray Lyon, and the many writers who thought with them in the matter, will be referred to as the 'old school,' and Douglas Knoop, and other of to-day's writers sharing his main opinions, as the 'new school.'

The new school believe that their case is considerably strengthened, as undoubtedly it is, by the conclusion, based on the ninth item of the Schaw Statutes of 1598 (but not, in our opinion, to be accepted as being necessarily true of the whole Scots system), that when the Scots apprentices were entered to the trade they were at the *end* of their seven-year apprenticeship and not at the *beginning*. They suggest that this system points to the existence of a second degree; the first when the prentice out of his time was entered, and the second, seven years later, when the Entered Apprentice became a Fellow Craft. It is worth noting that at Alnwick, some thirty miles south of the Border, Order No. 5, made in 1701, obliges a mason "to enter" an Apprentice "and give him his Charge within one whole year after" taking him, and Order No. 9 leaves no doubt that the Apprentice "is admitted or accepted" after serving seven years. So, if the presumption as to the Scots Entered Apprentice be sound, there was a remarkable difference in practice between the north and south sides of the Border.

The old school assumed that the only secret or secrets were those communicated to the Entered Apprentice, and that when the Fellow Craft was admitted no secret was communicated to him. They argue that, although the Scottish craft declared publicly that its Mason Word was entrusted to apprentices, it never even hinted at the existence of words or secrets to be imparted at the passing of Fellow Crafts. That argument remains as strong to-day as when it was originally propounded.

Is the Mason Word alive To-day?

As to what the Mason Word was, nobody can say for certain, although if those scholars are correct who assert that it travelled south to England and was introduced to English lodges, then we might assume that the word is alive to-day. But it is not a matter on which anybody would care to be dogmatic, especially in view of some evidence, by no means of general application, that the Mason Word was actually two words.

The word might originally have travelled in an exactly opposite direction. It might have been in use among English masons of early times and by them communicated in the sixteenth century to Scottish craftsmen, who found it ready to their use when the trade incorporations discovered the need to protect their affiliated members from undue competition.

Were Scots and English Ceremonies alike in 1721?

Many masonic authorities do not agree that, simply because the earliest references to the Mason Word come from Scotland, English speculative masonry could have been derived from Scotland. The Rev. Herbert Poole has said that the Scottish versions of the Old Charges were derived from England, an indication that Scotland may have taken its speculative masonry from the same source. On the other hand, Douglas Knoop and his collaborators appear to believe that the Mason Word was the foundation of all masonic esoteric ceremony and that the Scottish and English ceremonies became combined in course of time; further, that the (admittedly meagre) ceremonial practice of the Scottish lodges had been "subject to little change" as late as 1721, and they instance in support of this statement the much-cited visit of Dr Desaguliers to Edinburgh in that year. The doctor visited Mary's Chapel Lodge, was there found to be "duly qualified in all points of masonry," and was therefore received as a Brother. But does the visit prove anything more than that Desaguliers could answer the test questions addressed to him? Could the Scots masons have answered some he could have addressed to them? Most writers have seen no reason to doubt that a few Scottish lodges at that time were slightly speculative, but most of them not speculative at all; that is the usual impression to be gained from the reading of Scots masonic history.

Now, as the new school hold firmly that 1730 and not 1717 (Premier Grand Lodge) was the crucial date in the history of English ritual, we should have to assume that most of the early ceremonial entered English freemasonry in the nine years between 1721 (the Desaguliers visit) and 1730, a belief which the great majority of masonic students would hesitate to share. Consider how impossible it would have been for the Hiramic Degree to have been separated from, or added to, any existing ritual in the middle of the 1720's unless there had been a substantial ceremonial at that time; and consider, too, the impossibility of introducing any such foundation in the altogether too brief period immediately following 1721. With all respect to the eminent scholars of the new school, it is difficult, if not impossible, to believe that masonic ceremonial south of the Border was much the same as north of it at any time in the few years immediately following the founding of the Premier Grand Lodge.

But, with the Desaguliers visit still in our minds, there is no reason to doubt that the masons of the two countries could easily share a common mode of recognition. Occasionally during the sixteenth and seventeenth centuries masons would cross the Border in either direction; Scots masons would bring their lodge customs south, and English masons would (exceptionally) settle on the other side of the Border and perhaps gain entry into Scots lodges. Influential English masons might visit Scots cities and be made honorary members of operative lodges, and we can well imagine mason fraternities in England offering hospitality to prominent Scottish masons visiting England.

In the years following the Desaguliers visit, but whether resulting from it we do not know, Scots lodges assumed a speculative complexion; in some of them, the bare ceremony was replaced, in the course of a decade or two, by the fuller and more dramatic ceremonies borrowed from the south, and within fifteen years, that is by 1736, Scotland had founded its own Grand Lodge much on the English pattern.

The old school had not the advantage of seeing and digesting *all* the evidence available to their successors, who in arriving at their conclusion attach great importance to four particular documents:

(1) Minutes of Aitcheson's Haven Lodge of 1598, indicating that a Fellow of Craft on his admission was instructed by intenders and instructors who were Fellows of Craft; similarly, when a prentice was entered his instructors were Entered Apprentices.

(2) The Edinburgh Register House MS., date believed to be 1696, discovered about 1930 in the General Register House, Edinburgh. It

is a handwritten catechism, including questions addressed to a Mason and to a Fellow Craft. Five points of fellowship are given, not necessarily all those with which readers are familiar. The catechism seems to draw a distinction between a Mason and an Entered Apprentice. The form of giving the Mason Word is described in detail, and many allusions suggest that the possible source of the manuscript is an 'exposure' designed to throw ridicule upon freemasonry. This manuscript is reproduced in *A.Q.C.*, vol. xliii, and elsewhere.

(3) The Chetwode Crawley MS., believed to be of 1730 or earlier. This again differentiates between Masters and Apprentices. This and the manuscript above mentioned at (2) are almost the same, the first portion of one being the second of the other. Apparently' they were derived from the same source—an irregular production of some kind—but what that source was is unknown. This manuscript is reproduced in a reprint issued by the Lodge of Research, Leicester.

(4) Minute of Haughfoot Lodge, 1702, containing an incomplete fragment on the manner in which the secrets are communicated, and reproducing almost word for word a sentence in the Edinburgh Register House MS. of 1696. The minute, incomplete, is as follows:

> ii   of entrie as the apprentice did Leaving out (The Common
> 22 Dec Judge)
> 1702   Then they whisper the word as before—and the Master Mason
>   grips his hand after the ordinary way.

The minute goes on to record that six persons were "duely and orderly admitted apprentices and ffellow craft." On this fragment of a minute much has been based. The phrase "as the apprentice did" is taken to mean that the whole of the words are the concluding part of a minute recording the conferment of a higher rank than that of an Apprentice. The fragment has a particular significance because it reproduces phrases to be found in MSS. 2 and 3 above, No. 2 being, say, six years earlier, and No. 3 possibly twenty-eight years later.

It is in the light of the above references that the new school hold that there were, or advance the possibility of there having been, two sets of ceremonies, each with its own particular secrets, which they say might well have been the basis of English ceremonial.

Entered Apprentices present at Fellow Craft's Reception

The thirteenth item of the Schaw Statutes of 1598 laid down that when a Master or Fellow of Craft was admitted there must be present six Masters and two Entered Apprentices, the Warden of the lodge being one of the said six; further, two attendants "shall be chosen to every person." Lyon, the Scottish masonic historian, took the view that the Masters were present to satisfy themselves that the Candidate, or applicant, was a competent craftsman, and not for the purpose of communicating secrets with which Entered Apprentices were unacquainted. He did not believe that there could be any secrets communicated to a Master or to a Fellow of Craft if at the ceremony of admission two Apprentices were required to be present. Attempts have been made to explain away this requirement in a number of ways, because, obviously, it simply must be got rid of if the theories of the new school are to be accepted. It is a crux.

If the Entered Apprentice was present at the time of the actual admission, and knew everything and saw everything that was taking place, it would be out of the question to argue that the Master or Fellow was being advanced to a degree superior to the Entered Apprentice. One suggestion made to get over the difficulty is that the Entered Apprentice retired at some point in the ceremony, but William Schaw meant nothing at all if that interpretation could be placed upon his words. Another suggestion is that the Candidate retired with the intenders, and had certain secrets communicated to him outside the lodge; which is only another way of saying that the apprentices who were required to be present were actually absent. Yet a third suggestion is that the secrets were such as could be communicated in the presence of the Entered Apprentice by the whisper of a word or the giving of a grip. That might be so, but we should have expected the extremely careful Schaw to have specifically provided for anything of the kind. Why should he insist on the Apprentices being present if they were not to hear and see? The suggested method of evasion was, however, apparently the custom a century and a half later in some Scots *speculative* Lodges.

A minute of Aitcheson's Haven Lodge, dated a fortnight before the Schaw Statutes of 1598 were issued, shows that a Fellow Craft was admitted when no Entered Apprentices were present; but this did not necessarily mean that they *could* not be present, only that they *were* not, a very different thing. It is reasonable to assume that the Schaw Statutes then coming into operation confirmed the regular practice of the Scots mason craft.

About the middle of the seventeenth century, so Murray Lyon tells us, Apprentices actually filled the offices of Deacon and Warden in the Lodge of Kilwinning. This is a strong point, and we much doubt if it is countered by his critics remarking that only two instances of the kind are known; for if, indeed, the higher officials of the Scots operative lodge had to have qualifications which were kept secret from the Entered Apprentice, we cannot imagine *one* instance of the kind quoted by Lyon, let alone *two*. The presence of an Entered Apprentice in the Deacon's or Warden's chair of a Scottish lodge is not easily accounted for by the theorists who hold that in those lodges two different esoteric ceremonies were worked. The evidence as a whole points to the Masters, the Fellows of Craft, having, of course, the higher trade status and having trading privileges not accorded to the Entered Apprentice, but that whatever were the secrets of operative masonry *at that time* they were one and the same for every class of member.

Entered Apprentices were entered at one time, Masters and Fellows admitted at another, and are separately recorded by the lodges concerned; but we find that honorary members—that is non-operative members—could be made Entered Apprentices and Fellow Crafts at one time. In the seventeenth century a gentleman mason 'entered' in another lodge became a Master Mason in the Aberdeen Lodge upon payment of two Scots dollars and a pint or more of wine. In the same lodge the duly qualified Apprentice competent to undertake work on his own account was admitted to the Fellowship, equivalent to Mastership, on his providing a dinner and a pint of wine, and we find no suggestion of his being required to pass through any second ceremony of reception. Whether there was one degree or two degrees, and whatever it was that was conferred in one session on the gentleman, or non-operative, mason, never a doubt has been raised that Entered Apprentices were present at those admissions. The Entered Apprentice shared all there was to see and hear.

Bearing on the matter, almost certainly, is the custom that has held good for two centuries or more of carrying through the larger part of the Scots ceremony of installation in the First Degree. Until comparatively recent days this ceremony was of a simple nature, and bore all the signs of having been developed at a time at which every member of the lodge was qualified to be present. This is a parallel with the English usage of carrying through the ceremony in the Second and not in the Third Degree, the indication being that the English ceremony took its rise at a time when the senior rank of Brethren was that of the Fellows.

Two Intenders Present at Fellow Craft's Reception

The Schaw Statutes insist on the presence of two Intenders at the reception of the Fellow Craft, but do not appear to convey any hint that their purpose is to instruct the Fellow in secret knowledge. They simply do not say why the Intenders should be present, and the inference is permissible that they were there to act as guides or stewards and, as older members of the trade, probably to offer words of goodwill and advice to a young man on assuming greater responsibilities and qualifying to work as his own master. It must be borne in mind that the Scots lodges were strong enough to prevent any mason in their district carrying on work unless he conformed strictly to their regulations. The new school suggest that the Fellow Craft was coached in esoteric matters by the Intenders of his new rank and afterwards examined in what they taught him, and it is claimed that support is given to these ideas by the minutes of Aitcheson's Haven Lodge of 1598. These, however, show only that a new Entered Apprentice chose Apprentices as his Intenders, and similarly a new Fellow Craft chose Fellow Crafts. A great deal would have to be read into the minute to make it appear that the Intendant's duty was to communicate secrets to the Candidate.

But let us readily admit that, as the speculative element in Scots masonry became predominant, the duty of the Intendant most likely took on a new character. We should expect it to do so. In 1745—that is, nearly one and a half centuries after the Schaw Statutes were issued—we find the Haughfoot Lodge *beginning*, so far as that lodge was concerned, the custom of appointing two Intenders charged to instruct the Initiate in all points; but by that date *Scots operative lodges had long been working a ritual largely based on that of England, or considerably influenced by it.*

What may be thought to complicate this question of the Intender is a passage in what is known as the Harris No. 1 MS. Of this manuscript the early history is unknown, but it is believed to go back to the second half of the seventeenth century. Harris No. 1 MS. resembles Harris No. 2 MS., which might have been produced quite late in the next century—that is, towards the end of the 1700's. Here is the passage:

> Then let the person which is to be a mason chose out of the lodge any one mason who is to instruct him in those secrets which must never be committed to writing . . . then let the tutor take him into another room and show him the whole mystery, that at his return he may exercise with the rest of his fellow-masons.

The Rev. Herbert Poole identifies this tutor with the Intender of the Aberdeen Lodge Statutes of 1670, which Statutes ordain that "none of our Lodge teach or instruct an Entered Apprentice until such time as he be perfected by his Intender under the faylzie (*penalty*) of being fined as the Company thinks fit." The Aberdeen statutes specially ordained that the whole of the laws and statutes, and also the Mason Charter, be read at the entering of an apprentice "that none declare ignorance." There does not seem to be any suggestion here that the Apprentices' "ignorance" refers to any esoteric matter. In any case, we are asked to believe that a member of the Lodge of Aberdeen wrongly imparting secrets to an Entered Apprentice was punished by being "fyned as the Company thinks fit." Fining is a proper punishment for infringing what is nothing but a trade rule, but it would be a ridiculous penalty for a far more serious offence.

No one can read of the masonic systems of Scotland and England in the seventeenth century without sensing the great difference between them. They were simply not the same thing. The Scots until late in the century, and in many of their lodges far later than that, was a mason trade organization. Its esoteric content comprised little more than a secret mode of recognition to qualify its members, and to protect them from the competition of stonemasons who had been irregularly trained, or who, for some reason or another, could not gain affiliation. On the other hand, the English system, its operative connexion long grown slender and in all but two or three places completely snapped, contained within itself a 'something' which the learned antiquarians and historians were eager to share, and which, by the 1720's, had enough substance to allow of its developing into two or more self-contained degrees.

Undoubtedly the whole feeling is that, whatever the Scots ceremonial was at about 1700, it was something bare and slight, with all the signs of having been nurtured in austerity but hardly in asceticism.

The very language of the ritual now shared by England and Scotland is the English of the seventeenth and eighteenth centuries, certainly not Scottish in form or inspiration, in spite of the inclusion of a few Scots terms introduced not earlier than the 1720's. Had the early masonic ceremonies derived in any marked degree from a Scottish source the early rituals would have borne an obviously Scottish likeness, which no amount of editing could have removed. Especially would this have been so with regard to the Initiation ceremony, the most likely ceremony to be closely related to the conferment of the Mason Word. But where is any Scottish influence in the English ritual apart from the names of the degrees brought in by Anderson in the 1720's?

That the Scots lodges were slow in adopting the English speculative working becomes evident when we note that the Third Degree is mentioned for the first time in Scots records in the minutes of Lodge Canongate Kilwinning, in 1735, that there were lodges that did not know this degree until the 1750's, and that even in 1760 the lodges of Aitcheson's Haven, Dunblane, Haughfoot, and Peebles did not yet work it. Many Scots lodges continued for a century after the founding of their Grand Lodge to regard any rich ceremonial with some degree of suspicion, whereas the English lodges all through the eighteenth century and in the early parts of the nineteenth developed (and even quarrelled over—a sure sign of zeal) their rites and ceremonies, ever enriching and extending them.

A significant resolution in the minutes of the Melrose Lodge in 1764 insists that the "Mason Word be administered in a simpel way and maner free of everything Sinfull and Superstitious, only word, sighn and grip and some simpel questions to distinguish a mason from a nothr man," a convincing indication indeed, if one be needed, that it was in the very nature of the eighteenth-century Scots mason to regard as superfluous anything that was not rigidly and coldly essential to the conferment of the Mason Word. The date, it must be remembered, was 1764. What support is there from this categorical evidence for the claim that as far back as 1721 the freemasonry of Scotland must have been much the same as that of England?

Douglas Knoop and his collaborators believe that the nucleus of our present First Degree and Third Degree ceremonies can *clearly* be traced back to the crude usages and phrases associated before the end of the seventeenth century with the giving of the Mason Word. Their belief, of course, is based upon years of research, but it is impossible to overlook the likelihood that any marked esoteric accompaniment of the Mason Word was an importation from England. A minute of the Lodge of Edinburgh in 1727 justifies the Initiation of several "credible citizens" (*to whom operative members had previously objected*) on the ground that "their admissions were regularly done, conformed to the knowen laws of this and all other weall Governed Lodges in Brittain," which means, briefly, that Scotland's most important lodge, till then operative and most consciously operative, was now rapidly becoming speculative. At what date was this? Ten years after England's Grand Lodge was founded and six years after the Desaguliers visit!

The Haughfoot Lodge

Much is made in masonic history of the record of the Haughfoot Lodge, whose minutes from 1702 to 1763 are available and have already been referred to. This lodge was instituted in an isolated spot, in the parish of Stow, Midlothian, just below the junction of the Lugate and Gala waters, two miles south of Stow, and why or how the lodge came to be formed there is not known. This lodge had an arrangement by which Initiates could give bills for their fees, as in the case of George Dine, who in 1749 "gave a bill for £1 10s. Scots money as his entry payable next St Johns Day." Two Fellows were ordered to instruct him in all the points of an Apprentice and Fellow Craft; they were the Intenders, whose appointment in this lodge is not earlier than 1745. In this lodge we find the term "Brethren" first used in 1747, the English custom quietly ousting the old Scots custom of referring to the members as "Fellows." The Master was known as Preses (president); the Treasurer was also the Box-master; the Secretary was also the Clerk; and the youngest Apprentice was the Messenger or Officer. We are told that "the founders of the Lodge were the neighbouring gentry, their servants [a word which might then mean anything from day-labourer to manor steward], with a sprinkling of lawyers or writers, surgeons, masons, wrights, etc." The lodge gave assistance in oatmeal to relics of two of the deceased members.

To conclude, by 1707 the Lodge was differentiating between Apprentices and Fellow Crafts since it then decided that it "would not except on speciall considerations admitt to the society both of apprentice and fellow craft at the same time, but yt ane year at least should intervene . . ." Minutes later than the early 1720's do not advance our present purpose, as it is obvious that later, some time in the 1720's, English influence was making a rapidly increasing mark on the ceremonial of some Scots lodges. So while much has been made of the Haughfoot minute of 1702, as indicating that separate secrets were communicated to Fellow Crafts, we have yet to learn that the Lodge played any part in the emergence of speculative masonry.

Seventeenth-century Scots Freemasonry : A Summing up

This short outline of the different views leads to the belief that Murray Lyon and Gould have been fairly dependable judges of Scottish conditions in the seventeenth century. It is possible that in some or in a few lodges, particularly at the end of the century, there was a separate communication of secrets to the Fellow Craft, but no general practice of the kind. But as the membership came to include a greater proportion of non-operatives it was to be expected that by the end of the seventeenth century some echoes of English esoteric masonry would be heard in the Scottish lodges, and that in a few of them the bare ceremonial was beginning to lose some of its austerity. Gould's conception of the condition of Scots masonry appears to have applied in most places and at most times in the pre-1717 era, and his critics seem to be largely relying upon isolated indications which appear to be at variance with the impression gained of Scottish masonry as a whole.

But it must be freely admitted that, in discussing in a limited space so difficult a subject and one on which members of the new school have thought and written so much, some slight element of unfairness may have been unconsciously allowed to enter. All must consult the writings of Douglas Knoop and his collaborators, of R. J. Meekren, the Rev. Herbert Poole, Murray Lyon, Gould, etc., and come to their own conclusions.

Chapter Ten

'FREE,' 'ACCEPTED,' OR 'SPECULATIVE':
HOW WE GOT THE WORD 'FREEMASON'

'FREEMASONRY' is a single word. At one time "Our rude forefathers deem'd it two," but at an early date they joined up the two words to make them one. In early medieval days the freemason was the superior of two, three, or even more grades of operative mason. In this opening section the word 'freemason' is used always as meaning an operative mason, except where the symbolic or speculative mason is quite obviously in mind. The 'mason' who is mentioned frequently in this opening section is always the operative and never the speculative.

The mason did not become a freemason until the fourteenth century, and he kept that special designation until some time late in the seventeenth or even the eighteenth century—at any rate for quite a period after the Company of ffremasons of the City of London had in 1655–56 altered its official title to "The Company of Masons." This particular Company did not always refer to its members as freemasons. Professor Knoop points out that masons' associations in Newcastle, Norwich, Kendal, Lincoln, Ludlow, and Worcester were officially known as "Companies of Masons," whereas associations in Oxford, Durham, Gateshead, Alnwick, and Bristol were called "Companies of Freemasons," and the earliest of the manuscript Charges (date of the fourteenth century) did not use the word 'freemason,' although by the fifteenth century the word seems to have come into common use side by side with the old name of 'mason.'

There are many different explanations as to how the mason originally got the prefix 'free,' but it is well to remember that during the course of the centuries this prefix did not always mean the same thing. It seems clear that, by the time the speculatives took over the term, at least two meanings, and possibly three or more, had helped to build it.

The Early Medieval Mason and Freemason

Let us first look at the word 'mason' and conjure up a mental picture of the operative in early medieval days, when there was already considerable building activity. Ignoring for a moment that Caen stone for many of England's great buildings was being imported from Normandy, let us give a moment's thought to the mason in the quarry. His job of getting and splitting the stone was rough, hard work, not free from risk to life and limb, and it fairly certainly devolved upon men of some physical strength and endurance, but as artisans reasonably well informed. They would be well acquainted with the use of tools, simple geometrical instruments, tackle, etc., and would be well experienced with regard to the cleavage planes and other natural characteristics of the stone which they quarried and worked. These men were the hewers (sometimes 'hard' hewers), the rough masons, who in addition to 'getting' the stone would do some of the preparatory dressing. The finer dressing, to fit the stones to be built in without further tooling on the building site, would be by masons of greater manual skill and a closer acquaintance with geometrical methods. These masons would be able to shape the stones to the Master Masons' requirements, shape joints and cut keys, work mouldings, and, in short, produce stones to meet any special require-ment. These same men would perform the same sort of task if their job was on the building instead of in the quarry. On an important building they would probably work on the stone that had been imported, possibly from Caen, in Normandy, or on other soft stone quarried in their native country, and in many cases they would be the skilled carvers or sculptors.

Now, it was this class of more highly skilled mason who became the freemason. On the building site was another mason—the layer, the hard layer, the rough layer, the wall builder. His job was to take the prepared stones and build them up as required, work calling for considerable skill, but which, at any rate for some long time, was regarded as inferior to that of the experienced cutter, shaper, finisher, and sculptor.

The Word 'Mason'

Firstly then, what was the mason called soon after the Norman Con-quest—say, as early as 1077? The term most frequently used for him was the Latin-like word *cementarius* or *cæmentarius*, of which the plural was *cementarii*. Sometimes this word is spelt *simentarius*, as in the Fabric Rolls of Exeter Cathedral in 1396.

Magister cementarii was the Master of the Work(s), or the Master Mason, who was assisted by his *sociis*, or fellows.

An old French word *masʒun*, the very earliest form apparently of the word 'mason,' was used in the same sense as the Latin word.

During the fourteenth century another term came into general use, *latomus* or *lathomus*, another of the Latin-like words, and some people have even supposed that this is the word from which our word 'mason' was originally formed, a suggestion not easily accepted.

In 1396 we find the phrases *Lathomos vocatos ffremaceons,* which can be translated as 'masons called freemasons,' and *Lathomos vocatos ligiers,* meaning 'masons called layers, or setters.'

The word 'mason' in its present form was known in the fourteenth century, although it was then a French word (and had been so for two centuries) and not an English one, for in 1396 Westminster Hall was built (officially) by the "Citiens et masons de Londres."

Professor W. W. Skeat, the philologist, shows that originally the mason was a man who could hew or cut stone, the Norman French *mason* coming from a Low Latin word *macio, matio,* or *mattio,* which was derived from the German. There is a German word *mezzo,* meaning 'to hew,' and associated with an older word meaning 'chisel.'

Many other derivations have been suggested; one that mason comes from a French word *maconner,* meaning "to conspire"; another that it is the same word as *maison,* a 'house' or 'mansion,' but unfortunately the early houses to which the word was applied were of wood, not of stone. Derivation from the Spanish *mazoneria* or *mazo,* meaning 'mallet,' 'mace,' or 'club,' has been put forward, or from the Spanish *masa* meaning 'mortar,' and thence 'one who worked in mortar.' Somebody has derived the word from the Latin *maceria* meaning the 'long wall,' and somebody else has thought that the word takes us back to the Saxon *maça* or *massa* meaning a 'peer,' an 'equal' or 'companion,' but this last is just a case of taking a word and finding a derivation that will fit the modern meaning. This is particularly exemplified in the attempt to derive 'mason' from *mai,* signifying 'to love,' and *son,* which is said to mean 'brother.' Thus we get 'loving brother,' which etymologically is just nonsense! All crafts had their 'loving brothers.'

Attempts have been made to derive the word *mason* from words meaning festivals and societies, but they all seem far-fetched. There is a Low Latin word *massonya* or *masonia,* signifying a 'society' or 'club,' such as that of the Round Table, and *masa* in Anglo-Saxon, meaning 'table'; masonry, therefore, is the Society of the Table! (See p. 110.) But craftsmen in *all* the guilds met round a table at their regular feasts, and if the true derivation of 'mason' is "table" how comes it that the building operatives are the only masons? It is safer and better sense to go back to Professor Skeat and agree with him that the word 'mason' means literally 'a hewer and cutter of stone.'

Early Use of the Word 'Freemason'

Postponing for a moment any inquiry into the meaning of 'free' and 'freemason,' let us glance at a few instances of early uses of the latter term. We do not meet the word until towards the end of the fourteenth century; then we find the names of Thomas Wrek and John Lesnes recorded as freemasons in the City of London, Letter Book H, dated 1376. John Wycliff (or a follower of his) in 1383 appears to have referred to "men of subtle craft, as free masons and others."[1] In a Latin document of 1396 occurs the phrase "24 masons called free masons and 24 masons called layers or setters." Of the same year is a licence for the Archbishop of Canterbury to take twenty-four masons called freemasons and twenty-four masons called ligiers for executing certain work at the college to be erected by the Archbishop of Maidstone, and from this date we find the terms 'mason' and 'freemason' commonly and rather indiscriminately used. It would be idle to mention all the references, but here is one dated 1435: "John Wode, masoun, contracted for the labour of himself and servant in building the tower of the Abbey Church of St Edmundsbury,' in all mannere of thinges that longe to free masounry.'" There are countless others.

In 1487 the word occurs for the first time in a statute of the realm, this particular statute regulating wages of masons and carpenters. Stow, the historian, writing in the sixteenth century, says that "masons were formerly called Free masons." In 1526 was printed *The Pilgrimage of Perfection*, allegorizing the freemason's work and containing what is believed to be the first use in print of the word 'freemason,' though in two separate syllables. The sentence in which it occurs is: "The free mason setteth his prentyse first longe tyme to lerne to hewe stones." The beautifully printed copy of the book, splendidly preserved, containing a manuscript note ascribing the authorship to William Boude (? William Bond), a bachelor of divinity, is in the British Museum, and attention has been especially drawn to it in *A.Q.C.*, vol. xliii, by W. J. Williams.

In 1550 Bishop Coverdale published a translation of Werdmuller's German book *A Spyrytuall and Moost Precyouse Pearle*, in which God is called the heavenly freemason. Here is the passage, as quoted by Gould:

The free mason hewyth the harde stones, and hewyth of, here one pece, & there another, tyll the stones be fytte and apte for the place where he wyll laye them. Euen so God, the heavenly free mason, buildeth a christen churche, and he frameth and polysheth us, whiche are the costlye and precyous stones, wyth the crosse and affliccyon, that all abhomynacyon & wickednes which do not agree unto thys gloryous buyldynge, myghte be remoued & taken out of the waye. *i. Petr. ii.*

We get a real insight into the difference between the freemason and the rough mason and the labourer in a record of the erection of Sir

[1] G. G. Coulton, *Social Life in Britain* (Cambridge University Press).

Thomas Tresham's Triangular Lodge at Rushton Hall, Northamptonshire (about 1593):

> [First week] Free mazons hewing coynes, rough mazons scaplinge stone and laborers digging stones at Widow Davies ...
>
> [Third week] ... making the truffle [trefoil] windowes for the lowest storie ... The roughe mazons laying all this weke brought the wall two foote from the bottom of the foundation ...
>
> [Fourth week] ... the free mazons finished the lowest truffle windows
>
> [A later week] ... All the free masons ... busied about setting of the said windows ... also in setting splayes ...
>
> [A later week] ... Free mazons squareinge and moldinge eight crockett crestes ...

It will be seen from these extracts that the freemasons did the hewing, carving, squaring, and, in the case of features such as windows, etc., the setting, while the rough masons did the rough shaping and built the walls.

In 1610, as quoted by Gould and many other authors, "a Freemason who can draw his plot, work, and set accordingly, having charge over others," is considered as worth twelve pence a day before Michaelmas and tenpence after it. A rough mason who can take charge over others was, at that time, worth tenpence and eightpence respectively.

How did the Operative Mason become a Freemason?

The word 'free' has many meanings. A man can be independent and enjoy his liberty, be free from bondage; he may have particular privileges, or may gain privileges by being 'free' of a company or of a city; he may be free of or from certain restrictions; he may be free, or generous, in the expenditure of money, time, or effort.

The word 'free' is of Germanic origin, but not so 'freemason' (a word not known in Germany until after the formation of England's Grand Lodge). Through the German we get the Anglo-Saxon *freo*, which originally meant 'loving or beloved' and was closely related to the word 'friend.' A craftsman speaks of certain materials as working in a 'free' or 'kindly' even in a 'friendly' manner.

Which of all these meanings is implied in the 'free' of 'freemason'?

Was the Mason 'Free' of Certain Liabilities and Restrictions? The suggestion has often been put forward that the mason in the early medieval days became 'free' by being freed from the operation of certain restrictive laws and rules—that is, he was not obliged to do this or that by some particular body. (This does not mean freedom from serfdom, or bondage—a matter dealt with later.) In particular, he was free, it is

said, because, having to move about as his work required, he was not
tied to the land.

The *Oxford English Dictionary* says that the term 'free' perhaps refers
to the medieval practice of "emancipating skilled artisans, in order that
they might be able to travel and render their services wherever any great
building was in process of construction." General opinion among scholars
does not favour this view, although G. W. Speth put forward years ago
the idea that (using the wording of the *Oxford English Dictionary*) the
itinerant mason was called 'free' because he claimed exemption from,
and we suppose *had* to be free from, the control of any trade bodies of the
towns in which he temporarily settled. Speth has stated his emphatic
opinion that freemasons were masons attached to monasteries and ecclesiastical orders, and therefore not under the control of mason guilds; in
other words, they were "free from" those guilds. It is to this, apparently,
that the *Oxford English Dictionary* refers. It is unlikely, however, that
there were any mason craft guilds at this period, and the suggestion begs
a very large question in taking for granted as a fact something that had
been and still is the basis of much discussion, and, further, ignores the
fact that the building of abbeys and churches was at its height at a time
when the number of town mason guilds, if indeed there were any, must
have been very few indeed and could not have even attempted to control
the masons in country districts.

A related idea is advanced by the Rev. Dr Cunningham, who thinks
that "free" men were originally free from the tolls that were levied on
those who were 'foreign'—that is, they were free from paying certain
taxes. In effect, freemasons were originally those masons, he thinks, who
were free to work in any place, without restriction or obstruction from
local bodies. By the Speth suggestion the mason was "free from interference by the guild"; by the Cunningham suggestion the mason was
"free from obstruction from the local body"—much the same thing and
subject to the same objection.

Some students, including G. W. Bullamore, believe that originally
freemasons were a guild of church and chapel builders controlled by the
Church and free of the control of the building trade. Free carpenters,
they think, would be carpenters engaged in building churches; free
fishers would supply the fish to the monasteries; free vintners would
supply the wine; and so on. But from what building-trade organization
of country-wide authority were the church-builders alleged to be free?
G. W. Bullamore, continuing his argument, thought that the Free Sewers
(sew-ers) would be engaged in the making of clerical vestments, etc.,
and would also be free from interference by the local trade guilds. But
almost everything we know of the Free Sewers is that in the fourteen-

hundreds they were licensed workpeople employed by members of the Guild of Tailors of Exeter, evidence hardly weighty enough, or even apt enough, on which to base such a special argument.

A highly fanciful account was offered as far back as 1740 by a writer in the *Gentleman's Magazine*, who has been much quoted and who succeeded in mixing together some fact and much falsehood. It purported to show that masons impressed in many parts of the country by the authority of King Edward III for work in church building and in enlarging Windsor Castle entered into a combination not to work, unless at higher wages. To achieve their end they agreed upon tokens, etc., to know one another by and to assist one another against being impressed, and they agreed further not to work unless *free* and on their own terms. Hence they called themselves 'freemasons'! History tells us of the troublous days following the Black Death when many or all the crafts sought to raise themselves from their lowly condition. It tells us also of the restrictive laws passed to hold them down in their original poverty, but it says nothing of workmen in any one trade who were so strong that they could defy the King, challenge impressment, and insist on working on their own terms! No such derivation can be accepted for a moment.

Was the Mason 'Free' by Papal Bull? Here we return to one of the hoariest morsels in the legendary history of freemasonry. Very simply, the suggestion raised in the query amounts to this. Masons—chiefly Italian, but some French, German, and Fleming—joined together to constitute a Fraternity of Architects, which, styling themselves freemasons and possessing a secret mode of recognition, travelled under the authority of Papal Bulls—that is, of documents issued by the Pope and bearing his seal, or stamp (whence the word 'bull,' from the Italian *bulla* or *bolla*). The legend is more fully dealt with on other pages. The story was set going with the *alleged* authority of Sir Christopher Wren, but nowadays is accepted by very few students. Search at the Vatican has failed to produce any documentary evidence in support of the story, which, by the way, is not the only one of its kind.

A German historian, writing on architecture, related the tradition that the Byzantine builders in the sixth and seventh centuries formed themselves into guilds and associations, travelled under the blessing and authority of the Pope, and called themselves freemasons. Now those early centuries, representing a period of almost complete architectural darkness so far as England is concerned, bridge the days of Ethelbert, King of Kent, and Edwin, King of Northumbria—a time when the Saxons buildings of England were built of wood and thatch, and when the skilled stonemason could have had no place in the craft-life of such an undeveloped country. So far as England is concerned, therefore—and it is in England alone of all the civilized countries that we look for the rise of the 'freemason'—the whole suggestion is an absurdity (see also p. 27).

Did Geometry, a Free Science, make the Mason Free? One of the strangest suggestions is put forward by W. J. Williams (*A.Q.C.*, vol. xlviii), who quotes this allusion in the "William Watson MS.": "vij sciens or craftys that ben fre in hem selfe the which vij lyuen only by Gemetry." As in all the old manuscripts of masonic interest, the word 'geometry' is a synonym for 'masonry.' W. J. Williams asks whether, if masonry was one of the seven liberal sciences, its professors were *free*-masons. The author is satisfied that geometry, one of the seven liberal sciences, is 'free' in itself; it is 'free' geometry; further, it is 'free' masonry; therefore, masters of the art or science of geometry are 'freemasons.' The theory is ingenious, but works the curious old idea of the synonymity of geometry and masonry so very hard as to be quite unconvincing.

Did Le Frère Maçon become the Freemason? The argument has been seriously advanced that the syllable 'free' is simply a corruption of the French *frère* (brother). We call a Brother a "Brother Mason" (*frère maçon*), and by a process of mispronunciation over a period of years arrive at 'freemason'! W. J. Chetwode Crawley demolished the argument as being so

> exquisitely untenable, from the philologist's point of view, that it would require an unbroken chain of historical proofs to bring it within his powers of belief. It would constitute a class all by itself. It could derive no aid from history or from analogy. It would stand without precedent, parallel or congener.

The argument is undoubtedly just one more of the attempts to explain a masonic term by taking its present-day meaning and fitting it up with a plausible and purely fanciful derivation.

Was the Mason made 'Free' by Secret Instruction? At one time it was suggested that the syllable 'free' in a compound word, such as 'freemason,' signified that the craftsman enjoyed special knowledge and skill and had received exceptional teaching and training, largely of a secret nature. Thus it was deduced that a freemason was a mason who had been taught the secret arts and hidden mysteries of his craft, artistically and theoretically as well as practically, and that he had been initiated into the theoretical and probably symbolical teachings of his art. But the theory sets the known facts at defiance and need only be mentioned to be dismissed.

Was the Mason 'Free' because he worked in Freestone? It has already been shown that the English masons of the highest operative skill worked largely in freestone (sometimes called broadstone), an even-grained, soft-cutting sandstone or limestone, highly suitable for mouldings and other special shapes. (Many old city pavements were laid of it.) We first hear of freestone in the year 1212. The Caen stone of Normandy was largely imported in medieval times into England. St Augustine's, Canterbury, was built from Caen stone, imported ready-worked. There are many English freestones (for example, those quarried at Portland), and in 1543 the townspeople of Coventry contracted with a freemason to rebuild their cross of "good, sure, seasonable free-stone of the quarries of Attilborough, or Rounton, in Warwickshire."

Probably the first-known reference (it is in the French of the period) to the mason in freestone is in a year very soon after the Black Death (1348). Half the population of England had perished, and the great shortage of manual labour had led naturally to a demand for higher wages. This demand was strongly resented by the Crown and Parliament, who in 1350 passed a statute prohibiting carpenters, masons, tilers, and "other workmen of houses" from taking "by the day for their work, but in such manner as they were wont, that is to say, a master carpenter III*d.* and another II*d.*; a master free-stone mason (*mestre mason de franche pere*) IIII*d.*" etc.

Now, this French term became in the course of a few years a definitely English one, for we find the words 'free-stone mason' on record in 1375. A moment's thought will show that this term, given time enough, would almost inevitably become shortened to a compound word—namely, 'freemason.'

Readers with preconceived notions will be reluctant to accept this evidence; but they will, surely, find it impossible to avoid the conclusion that the freemason was originally a skilled worker in freestone, although, as we shall see shortly, there came a time when the original significance was almost entirely lost, and a mason was thought to be 'free' from quite a different cause.

Let us glance at some words in Gould's *History* of 1885:

> The point indeed, for determination, is not so much the relative antiquity of the varied meanings under which this word has been passed on through successive centuries, but rather the particular *use* or *form* which has merged into the appellation by which the present Society of Freemasons is distinguished.

Study of the manner in which the mason became a freemason is indeed fascinating, but the real point at issue, as Gould has said in other words, is not (1) how he *originally* earned the appellation, but (2) what that appellation meant when the speculative freemason succeeded to it some time in the seventeenth century or perhaps earlier, and further (3) what it meant early in the eighteenth century when the ritual was beginning to take the shape we recognize to-day.

It is quite likely that the word 'freemason' represents at least three distinct meanings, each having respect to a different century. We believe it originated in the mason's use of freestone, but was its second meaning derived from the freedom of a corporation or city? Let us try to answer the question.

Did Freedom of a Corporation make a Mason 'Free'? We know that in the City of London, and possibly in one or two other big centres (not in many), a mason could become 'free' by achieving freedom—that is, membership—of his company; as could, of course, other craftsmen of their guilds. It must be remembered that the medieval masons were not necessarily congregated in towns, as most craftsmen were. They were often learning or plying their trade in remote country districts, where it is difficult to imagine the existence of an organized body powerful enough to enforce highly restrictive regulations. Consequently we must conclude—indeed, we know for certain—that the membership of the Mason Company in London was small in comparison with that of the craft guilds, and it is hardly likely in the circumstances that the mason originally became a 'freemason' because he was 'free' of a company. For, if he did, we should expect there to be Freetallowchandlers, Freedistillers, Freefeltmakers, Freepewterers, Freehatters, etc., etc., but we have none of these, although we do have, or have had, Free Sewers, Free Tylers, Free Vintners, Free Fishers and some (a very few) others.

When the word 'free' is used in connexion with other trades it is only as an adjective, and not as a part of a compound noun. Thus the Free Butchers were incorporated in 1606 as "The Art or Mistery of Butchers of the City of London." There have been Free Scriveners (writers and printers) and Free Carmen (known from as early as 1668). Free Journeymen Printers are referred to in a publication of 1666, and Free Sawyers are mentioned in the records of the Carpenters' Company in 1651. Free Vintners, established in 1437 as the Freemen of the Mistery of Vintners of the City of London incorporated in the preceding century, were free to sell wine in London and were exempt from certain financial liabilities. The Free Sewers (pronounced 'so-ers'), already mentioned, were subsidiaries of the Exeter Guild of Tailors. In this guild, by the way, there was a regulation that every Apprentice that is enrolled and "truely serveth his 'cownand' [covenanted time] shall pay a spone of selver wayying a nonsse" [an ounce] and provide a breakfast to the Master and Wardens, before he can be a freeman of the City. There were Free Watermen, or Lightermen, and Free Fishers, the last-named being 'free' to catch or obtain their fish as they could, and 'free' to sell it in their town. And, as already noted, there have been Free Tylers.

The peculiar fact is that of all the trades and crafts achieving freedom only one of them incorporates the word 'free' in a compound name—the freemason. We must assume, then, that where many crafts had the advantage of freedom of a guild to a considerably greater extent than was ever possible with the masons, it is extremely unlikely that masons became freemasons simply and only because they were made free of a livery company.

But—and here enters a somewhat baffling consideration—in spite of all we have said, there certainly does seem to be a good case for assuming that the mason, already for a couple of centuries a freemason by the then-forgotten virtue of having originally worked in freestone, was *maintained* in that designation by the fact that city masons found a new title to freedom in the membership of a company, and in so doing strengthened their hold of their former title. They were helped, no doubt, by a craft custom (of which we have already shown evidence) of regarding the freemason as superior to the ordinary mason, and allocating to him the parts of the work calling for the greater skill. So, although freedom of a company would not in itself have produced the compound designation, it did apparently serve to help to strengthen its use.

In the light of this, we can understand that, at the time of the Acception in the London Company of Masons and in the minds of some or all of the 'four old lodges' that founded the first Grand Lodge, the syllable 'free' was almost certainly associated with the freedom of a guild or company or city. Members of the lodge of the London Company of Masons were themselves largely freemen of the Company and of the City of London, while their associates and personal friends would be the freemen of other companies. Many writers, indeed, have insisted that the idea in forming the first Grand Lodge was to bring into existence a body on the lines of a City Company.[1]

The London Company had originally consisted of both freemasons and masons, but in its thriving days it preferred to call itself a Company of Freemasons, the change of name to 'Masons' not being made until 1655–56. If the freemason was at first a freestone mason, it is a question whether, in the course of centuries, he might not easily have lost his special designation but for the existence of the freemasons' Company in London.

Was the Mason 'Free' because he was born Free? It is quite idle to ignore the fact that the freedom which most of our Brethren in the lodges associate with the word 'freemasonry' is the physical freedom

[1] For further details see p. 166.

denied to the slave or serf. It is inevitably so in view of the stress laid on physical freedom in masonic ritual and lectures, and in the much earlier manuscript Charges. There must have been good reasons for this particular stress. Everybody knows that until late in the eighteenth century human slavery was a very real and ugly thing which had existed from ancient days, and was known throughout the world. Legally slavery was abolished in England in 1772, but full emancipation did not come until 1833; in France, not until 1848; in Russia, in 1861; while in the United States it was finally abolished as a result of the Civil War, which ended in 1864.

If we look at the conditions of feudal economic life we shall be able to understand why the old manuscript Charges laid such great stress on the mason being a free man and not a serf.[1] It is safe to say that in early medieval days most working people living outside the towns were serfs of one degree or another. G. M. Trevelyan tells us that the

> peasant cultivators, in relation to each other, were a self-governing community; but in relation to the lord of the manor they were serfs. They could not leave their holdings. They must grind their corn at the lord's mill. They owed him field service on certain days of the year, when they must labour not on their own land but on his, under the orders of his bailiff.

And even in the towns, apparently, in the days of William the Conqueror, labouring men were serfs, except in the City of London.

The serf could not sell or give away his own goods and cattle. He could not make contracts, could not take an office of dignity, and could not bear witness without leave of his lord. A free man marrying a woman in bondage became himself a 'bond,' and their children were born in bondage. The serf paid his lord a fee for permission, or a licence, to allow his daughter to be married. He found it well nigh impossible to apprentice his sons to any trade or craft. "All such as have been wont to labour at plough or cart, or other work or service of husbandry up to the age of twelve years" had to abide henceforward in the aforesaid labour, and any covenant of apprenticeship entered into was null and void. Any man or family not owning land producing 20s. a year at least could not set their son or daughter as apprentice to any trade or work in the cities. A statute of Henry IV says, "Let the children be set to serve at the same labour as their parents have used, or to other labours as their estates require, under pain of a year's imprisonment, and fine or ransom at the King's will."

Education was almost out of the question for children of a serf. In

---

[1] See G. M. Trevelyan, *English Social History*, and G. G. Coulton, *Social Life in England*.

1391 the Commons besought the King to prevent any serf or villein putting his children to school in order to procure their advancement by clergy, their excuse being "the maintenance and salvation of the honour of all free men in the kingdom." Fortunately the King rejected the plea.

The Church justified the condition of servitude, recognized it, and enforced it. Monks were among the richest holders of serfs, and St Anselm at an early date had no difficulty in believing that, if a man and wife were reduced through their own fault to servitude, the children born to them after their condemnation should be subject to the same servitude. Even pious people in medieval days made over their serfs to other owners. Ancient records show that a widow bequeathed to the monks of Eynsham certain land "which Roger the Palmer of Eston held of me, together with the same Roger and all his brood." To the same monks some one left "Richard Rowland of Wealde, who was my born serf, with all his brood." It looks rather as though "all his brood" was a useful technicality with which the lawyer-monk was always ready.

Any serf buying his liberty with his own money could be recalled to villeinage by his lord. There was intense feeling against any man who had been born a serf and afterwards achieved his freedom. A man could make his serf free only from his own person and his own heirs. The freed serf was not a complete freeman in the eyes of the community. He could not make suit in court against any other man if his former state of serfdom were objected to and proved against him, "even though the man thus freed from villeinage had been dubbed a Knight." A freed serf afterwards behaving 'unkynde' (not to the lord's liking) could be brought back into thraldom.

In Chaucer's century, the fourteenth, the lords of the manors found it worked better to commute, for money rents, the forced services due on their estates, and, although this did not make the serfs free men in the eyes of the law, it was in this century that the demand by the English peasant that he should be a free man was first heard in clear tones.

A serf could gain legal freedom by escaping to a chartered town and there living as a citizen for a year and a day. It was necessary that he should be in "scot and lot" for that period, which we may take to mean, either that he should duly pay any taxes demanded of him, or that he should to all intent and purposes perform the duties of a burgess. It is difficult at this long interval to guess how he was able to do those things, but we may conclude that, if the town needed the men, some way or means would be found of regularizing their presence within its boundaries. Towns and cities varied in their attitude to the matter, and it is thought that some of them gave up the serf to his lord if and when so demanded.

'Scot' was an old Anglo-Saxon word meaning 'tax' or 'payment'; persons paying 'scot and lot' were taxed according to their ability, and not uniformly. Our modern 'scot-free' perpetuates the word.

We are left in some doubt as to the attitude of the town guild to the escaped serf. There appears to be evidence that he was not accepted as an apprentice; nor, in many trades, were his children, unless born after his redemption, most of the guilds insisting that an apprentice be not only free but free-born. The freedom of the townsman himself, by the way, even of the skilled craftsman, did not amount to so very much, for, although technically he was not a serf, his life was hedged in by most rigid observances and restrictions. He had, more or less, to stay in the town he was born in, dress as he was told, and had generally to bring up his sons to his own occupation. If he dared to disobey the city authorities in these and other matters he was liable to be imprisoned. If he got his living as a mason he was liable to impressment by the King and taken to work elsewhere for months at a time.

It was once suggested that the original freemasons were country masons, serfs on a lord's estate, who had achieved their freedom by escaping to the town—in other words, that they were 'freed-masons.' But many other artisans besides masons escaped from country servitude, and it would indeed be odd if the only craft to retain evidence of this in its designation should prove to be that of the freemason! The suggestion can safely be dismissed.

An extraordinary idea, which has gained a hearing in some quarters, and which some masonic after-dinner speakers have advanced with an air of complete conviction, is to the effect that the medieval mason, when meeting a stranger purporting to be of his craft, forthwith gripped his right hand and in the course of doing so explored it to ascertain whether one of his fingers was missing. (He could not trust his eyesight!) For, if it were missing, then the stranger was a bondman and no freemason, there being, it is alleged, a custom of removing two joints of a particular finger of a serf's right hand as a permanent indication that he was of the slave class. How can anyone believe for a moment that any such custom ever did exist, or ever could have existed, in feudal England? History, silent on the matter, could not fail to provide a hint or suspicion of such a horrible barbarity. Such an idea could be put forward only by those who do not appreciate that the villeinage, or serfdom, of the early medieval worker was the natural product of economic conditions. The serf's job was to work arduously and for long hours. Even so, when in the fourteenth century the lords began the custom of taking a rent in money in the place of forced service, there was a section of the serfs who actually preferred the old system. So says G. M. Trevelyan. No estate owner in his senses would have reduced by wilful maiming the ability of a serf to render him fully efficient service. Were there the slightest truth in the story, history would afford hundreds of instances of a practice which would have left the great majority of rural workers with one finger "short."

Obviously the Old Charges were written in full consciousness of the existence of feudal serfdom. Our ritual borrowed from those Old Charges, and all through the century in which the borrowing took place the air simply echoed with discussions of the slavery question, for although feudal serfdom had long been left behind, there were other serfdoms everywhere. There was extensive slavery in the coastal districts of North Africa, fed by white captives sent there by Algerian corsairs. In many countries of the Old World and the New the slavery of the Negro was a common fact. In America that particular slavery was yet to grow into a great and terrible vested interest. In the first half of the eighteenth century British children—white children—could legally be sold into slavery in America. But the world was ceasing to be quite complacent in the matter, and, particularly in England, there arose a clear call that the whole dreadful business should be brought to an early end. This, alas, did not prevent Englishmen taking a leading part in the shipment of African Negroes across the Atlantic.

No slave could exist in England after 1772, although, as already said, complete emancipation by Act of Parliament did not come until 1833. Near the end of the eighteenth century any slave reaching the soil of Scotland was a freeman; but, as we are reminded by G. M. Trevelyan's *English Social History*, until as late as 1799 the Scottish miner, who together with his wife and children carried up the coal to cut, was transferable with the pit on any change of proprietorship. Both in the coalmines and salt-mines of Scotland at that time any worker running away from the mine could be caught and punished. Trevelyan tells us that: "The hereditary bondsmen in the mines were treated by their masters as chattels, and were spoken of by the rest of the population with a kind of pitying terror, as 'the brown yins' or 'the blackfolk.'"

It can be well understood, therefore, that not only the ecclesiastics who composed the old manuscript Charges but the editors and re-arrangers of the masonic ritual throughout the eighteenth and into the nineteenth centuries were well aware of the debasement which bondage brought to its victims, and they were absolutely determined that there was no place in freemasonry for any man who was not physically free.

The first *Constitutions*, those of 1723, make the matter clear. "The Persons admitted members of a Lodge must be good and true Men, free-born, and of mature and discreet age, no Bondmen."

In the version of the Ancient Charges prefacing the book of *Constitutions* of the United Grand Lodge of England we are told that the persons "made masons or admitted members of a lodge must be good and true men, free-born, and of mature and discreet age and sound judgement, no bond-men, no women, no immoral or scandalous men, but of good report."

Of course, it must always be remembered that all the guilds and trade fraternities, not only those of the mason, united in insisting upon the qualification of freedom from bondage. From which it will be readily understood that the word 'free' did not get into the term 'freemason' merely because the mason exclusively was a free man. The regular member of every craft was equally free. It was simply a case of our early speculative Brethren finding the word 'freemason' already made, and, ignoring what it had meant in the past, placing the current interpretation upon the first syllable.

One point still needs to be made. The early editions of the book of *Constitutions* (those of 1723, 1738, etc.) all through the eighteenth century insisted that every Candidate for freemasonry be not only a free man, but free *born*. At the Union in 1813 this qualification was confirmed, the Candidate being required to declare that he was 'free by birth.' Long after an Act of Parliament had brought to an end Negro slavery in the British Dominions it was agreed to substitute for the words 'free by birth' the words 'being a free man,' and the Candidate in English lodges declares accordingly to-day. Naturally, there have been masonic authors who have regarded the alteration as an interference with a landmark of the Order. They based their view chiefly upon the old writer, Dr George Oliver, who gave it as his opinion that "a free man born of a free woman . . . was originally considered to be an unchangeable landmark." Fortunately the question no longer arises.

And now a smile at human inconsistency! Lodge Goede Hoop, Cape Town (Nederlandic Constitution), owned two or more slaves in the 1770's, their work being to assist the Serving Brothers!

Was there an Early Scots Freemason?

Some important terms came into the Craft from Scotland, but 'freemason' does not appear to have been one of them. In that country it cannot be traced through its various meanings as it can in England and is not found earlier, apparently, than in the Melrose version of the Old Charges (dating back originally to 1581), of which the copy of 1674 alone is preserved. Gould tells us that the term 'frie mason' occurs in it frequently, that it is found also in the minutes of Mary's Chapel in 1636–37, and in the minutes of the Melrose Lodge in 1674 and 1675. But in all these references the individuals were 'frie masons,' not 'freemasons'; in other words, they were free men of their lodges, trades, or cities, and became so by virtue of having served an apprenticeship on regular lines and having thus earned their right to follow and practise their trade free of hindrance. Early Scots masonry, then, never had a 'freemason,' but when the 'frie mason' first appeared north of the Border he was the equivalent of the then 'freemason' south of it, inasmuch as the qualification for both of them was that they were free of their Craft or Fraternity. It is wise to regard the term 'frie mason' as meaning 'freeman-mason,' and to assume that the word 'freemason,' when it did come into use in Scotland, was an English form of a Scots title.

The question is gone into closely by Lionel Vibert in *A.Q.C.*, vol. xliii, and from his paper we learn that minutes of the operative lodge at Melrose for the year 1674 include the phrase "passed frie to the trade"— that is, made a freeman mason. We learn further that the point is brought out in one phrase in the so-called Charter of Lodge Scoon and Perth, year 1658: "the under subscryvers maisters, ffriemen and fellow crafts measones resident within the burgh off Perth." The same document records that King James VI of Scotland was "entered frieman measone and fellow craft," and speaks of the Lodge of Scoon as "ane ancient frie Lodge ffor entering and passing within ourselves." An ancient Seal of Cause of Chirurgeons of Edinburgh (1505) insists that "no manner of person occupy nor use any points of our said crafts of surgery, or barber craft" within the City except he be "frie-man and burgess." So there appears to be but small doubt that the Scots 'frie mason' (the description appears a number of times in old Scots records) was a mason free of his craft, in the same manner as a surgeon was a 'frie man' of his.

'Accepted'

The term 'accepted' is full of interest to the freemason. Members of the London Company of Freemasons and of the old City Companies were "accepted on the Livery." Men becoming freemasons in the lodge believed to have been held within the London Company of Freemasons were admitted to the 'acception,' as noted in the section dealing with that Company. Elias Ashmole's term was 'new-accepted.'

The English accepted or adopted mason of the seventeenth century was much more than, and essentially different from, a non-operative member. In the Mason Company there might be, on the one hand, operative masons and, on the other, men who may not have touched a tool in all their lives—'gentlemen' who had come in by patrimony or gift of membership. But the 'accepted' mason was originally a man who, in a lodge operative in origin or still partly so in character, was for all practical purposes of membership accepted as a mason. From this practice grew in course of time the use of the words 'accepted' and 'adopted' to indicate a man who had been admitted into the inner fellowship of symbolic masons.

In spite of the disjointedness and paucity of the historic references, there can be no doubt that the freemasons, more generally known in those days as accepted masons, were becoming well-known by the last quarter of the seventeenth century. How else can we explain the skit in a divertisement in the issue of *Poor Robin's Intelligence* of October 10, 1676, which has been brought to light by Lionel Vibert and is referred to on an earlier page (see p. 104). It is surprising to find the phrase 'accepted masons' apparently familiar to the public in the year 1676, at which time the Acception was still associated with the London Company of Masons. Either the Acception of the London Company was far bigger than existing evidence suggests, or the fraternity at the London Company was only one of many, and of these unfortunately we know so little—almost nothing.

'Admitted' a Common Scottish Term

The Scottish operative lodges had a practice of 'admitting' into their membership local gentry and others who had no connexion with operative masonry. Thus, in 1634 the Right Hon. the Lord Alexander was admitted into the lodge at Edinburgh; in 1640 Alexander Hamilton "Generall of the Artelerie of thes Kingdom" was admitted; in 1667 Sir Patrick Hume of Polwart was admitted a "fellow of craft"; but it is not thought that at this period there was anything esoteric in Scottish masonry other than the Mason Word.

The Alnwick Lodge, a purely operative lodge only thirty miles from the Scottish border, 'admitted' or 'accepted' its apprentices. The Lodge at Masons' Hall, London, in 1682 'admitted' its novitiates.

Free and Accepted

Although the term 'freemason' was in use in early medieval days and candidates were 'accepted' into freemasonry by the middle of the seventeenth century, we first meet the phrase 'free and accepted' in 1722, five years after the first Grand Lodge had been founded. It occurs in the title of what is known as the "Roberts Pamphlet," printed in London in 1722, *The Old Constitutions belonging to the Ancient and Honourable*

Society of Free and Accepted Masons. Officially, the phrase was used by Dr Anderson in the second edition of his *Constitutions* (1738), and in course of time it became adopted by the Grand Lodges of Ireland, Scotland, and the greater number of the Grand Lodges in the United States.

The theory is advanced that the two words came into conjunction in a simple way. Many early lodges must have had among their number members who called themselves 'accepted masons' and others who called themselves 'freemasons,' either operative or speculative or both; so, it is reasonably suggested, the name 'free and accepted' was adopted to cover two groups that were in course of rapidly fusing into one. This, at all events, is a fair explanation, in contrast with a legendary one offered in some old lectures, according to which Masons who were selected to build the Temple of Solomon were declared 'free' and were exempted, together with their descendants, from imposts, duties, and taxes. They had also the privilege of bearing arms. At the destruction of the Temple by Nebuchadnezzar the descendants of these masons were carried into captivity with the ancient Jews.

'Speculative'

The accepted mason came to be known about the middle of the eighteenth century as a speculative mason. The word 'speculative' had come by easy transition, and originally there was nothing in its meaning to suggest symbolism. There are many words in freemasonry that derive from the scholars of the seventeenth and early eighteenth centuries; 'speculative' is the most marked of them.

'To speculate' is to take a view of anything with the mind, to consider anything mentally. It comes from *specio*, meaning 'I see' or 'I look,' and there we have the basis of many words, such as spectacle, spectator, speculum, etc. In the seventeenth-century meaning of the word, anyone who was given to contemplation, to thoughtfulness, was indulging in speculation. The speculative man was the idealist, not the man of fact and practice. Literary men of the seventeenth century favoured the word, used it frequently in their text, and commonly included it in their titles. It had a 'vogue.'

Here is one of hundreds of instances. Samuel Ward, of Ipswich, wrote in 1636: "Some sciences I know, in comparison of others more operative, are termed speculative; but not one of these, whose speculation tends and ends not in some operation by which man is profited and God honoured." John Evelyn, a true representative of seventeenth-century culture, more than once uses some such phrase as "all devotion being now placed in the hearing sermons and discourses of speculative and national things.''[1] Evelyn, it must be remembered, lived and wrote at a time when what then existed of our ritual was taking an early impress. Many of the early speculatives were clever and educated, of the philosopher type—naturalists, antiquarians, historians—men of fine mental calibre; and the words and phrases introduced by them, reflecting the particular culture of the day, found an abiding place in masonic ritual.

Building and all practical processes comprised at one time considerable 'speculative work,' what would now mostly be called 'theory.' The theory of constructional design and the theory of the strength and behaviour of building materials were 'speculations' and were the province of the master-craftsman. The application of the science of geometry was 'speculation'; in a very real sense, such work was practical, but if it did not call for the use of a workman's tools it could not be practical, in the old-time language; it was just 'speculative.'

The learned men who came into freemasonry in the sixteen-hundreds would meet practical men skilled in the use of the stone-worker's tools— the masons and operative freemasons. Some of these operatives would be men of education, men of the architect and surveyor type, men who backed up their practice with theory, users of pencils and fine instruments; the newcomers would mentally dub them 'speculatives.' With the passing of many generations the word 'speculative' acquired a new meaning. As the accepted masons built up or acquired a knowledge of their symbolic Craft they fell back on their favourite word, however inadequate it was, there being none other apt enough to their purpose, and distinguished themselves from stonemasons by calling themselves 'speculative masons' or 'speculatives.' Generally, 'speculative' still means theory, contemplation; but when it is used to connote morality, philosophy, esoteric doctrines or principles it means freemasonry.

In the lodges of Scotland, which were markedly operative in character, 'gentleman' masons were often known as 'geomatics,' and although at first the word seems entirely different from the English 'speculative,' yet the train of ideas which led to its use is more or less the same. It was the men of geometry in England who were the first speculatives. 'Geomatic,' a form of 'geometric,' is suggestive of somewhat abstruse reasoning, in contrast with the word 'domatic,' by which the Scots operative mason was sometimes called, and which carried with it the idea of a great dome, or other heavy construction, in rough solid stone.

The inclusion of the word 'speculative' (in one or other of its old-fashioned spellings) in a fifteenth-century manuscript relating to medieval masonry is not, of course, evidence that speculative freemasonry, as we know it, was practised at that time. Enough has been said to make it

[1] *Diary*, September 19, 1655.

clear that the speculative mason of medieval days was a man occupied in study and with the theory and artistry of his calling, leaving to 'practical' men the skilled use of the operative's tools.

"We are not all operative, but free, accepted, or speculative masons." So we often remind ourselves, but for all practical purposes we regard ourselves to-day simply as freemasons, by which name the most highly skilled medieval masons were known. 'Accepted' and 'speculative' remind us of the formative period in masonic history and of associations which we cannot contemplate without pride; but we of to-day are *freemasons*! Our cherished inheritance is freemasonry, which has come down to us from time immemorial.

Two writers of remarkable influence in the early eighteenth century were Sir Richard Steele and Joseph Addison, both of whom were born in 1672, Addison dying in 1719 and Steele ten years later. Addison was a 'classic' of English prose, Steele a remarkable observer of his times. In *The Spectator,* their joint venture, published daily during 1711 and 1712, occurs an important passage in relation to our present subject:

> In short wherever I see a cluster of people, I always mix with them, though I never open my lips but in my own club. Thus I live in a world rather as a spectator of mankind than as one of the species, by which means I have made myself a speculative statesman, soldier, merchant, and artisan, without ever meddling with any practical part in life. I am very well versed in the theory . . . I have acted in all parts of my life as a looker on.

It is a matter of common knowledge that *The Spectator* enjoyed remarkable popularity, and we have no difficulty in seeing from this one passage the language background of the time in which our ritual was being moulded. This extract from *The Spectator* must be read, too, in the light of many statements to the effect that the founding of Grand Lodge in 1717 was part of the 'club' movement of the day, in which movement Dr Anderson himself was a personality.

A Prisoner cannot be a Candidate

Grand Lodge's decision to substitute 'free' for 'free born,' made in 1847, incidentally emphasized its declaration of 1783 that it is inconsistent with the principles of masonry to hold any regular lodge for the purpose of making, passing, or raising masons in any prison or place of confinement. This declaration followed on certain irregular happenings in the King's Bench Prison, firstly, in 1769 when John Wilkes and another prisoner were initiated, passed, and raised and, secondly, in 1783 when a military and itinerant lodge (soon afterwards erased from the list) met there more than once and initiated a number of prisoners. From this decision alone, apart from any other fact or decree, it is seen that 'lodges' held in camps of English prisoners-of-war are not regular lodges but, quoting the author's Prestonian Lecture (see p. 555), "rather meetings of Brethren for comfort and recreation in dark, distressful days."

BOOK THREE

The Grand Lodges (1717-1813)

Chapter Eleven

THE FIRST GRAND LODGE (1717)

THE first Grand Lodge—the first in the world—was founded in London in 1717, but there is a tendency among masonic scholars to hold that the real milestone of masonic history was not then, but thirteen years later —namely, in 1730, when the publication of one of the early irregular prints, Prichard's *Masonry Dissected,* clearly testified to much recent development in ceremonial and esoteric ritual. The historians take 1730 not only as the turning-point in ceremonial matters, but also in the recognition and more human understanding of the great principles which since those days have been closely associated with freemasonry. Lodge ceremonials of 1717, some historians believe, were probably more or less as they had been even before 1700, but by the year 1730 much had happened. This, so far as it concerns the pre-1700 period, is only a conjecture on their part, and in the absence of evidence either way it is just as reasonable to presume that there had been a steady development of ceremonial since the days of the Acception, and with it a growth in the number of lodges and their membership. This seems the more reasonable view, and it is possible that masonic authors are being rather too definite in making 1730 the critical year. True, the year gains importance chiefly because of Prichard's *exposé* then published, in which he was professing to reveal rituals that were then being worked by the English lodges, and which must have been worked for at least two or three years.

The importance of 1730, therefore, is not that in that year some vital change was made in masonic ritual, but that in that year there was published what was claimed to be a revelation, which was read by thousands of masons throughout the country, who, hitherto entirely dependent on a ritual handed down by word of mouth, may from that date have allowed themselves to be influenced by the contents of an irregular print.

Whether, then, the pivotal date in matters of ritual, etc., be 1730 or a year or two earlier, we may be sure that the founding of Grand Lodge in

1717 was in itself the occasion or the occasioner—the spring-head, if you will, *but not designedly so*—of much that happened in the next ten years. It was the success of the first Grand Lodge that produced Prichard's *exposé*. The quickening of masonic interest, the new breath that vitalized symbolic masonry—these could not easily have ccme, perhaps might not have come at all, to a handful of independent lodges mutually indifferent to each other's existence. The year 1717 remains the great date, and 1730 or thereabouts the unexpected sequel.

That the advent of Grand Lodge in 1717 was a 'revival' of the Quarterly Communications and Annual Assembly was Anderson's claim in his *Constitutions,* but for this to be accepted as a literal fact we should need to know for certain that there had been a national, or at least a regional, masonic authority capable of calling together such gatherings. No such evidence is available, although statements are made in the old manuscripts that annual assemblies of the old operatives were held. The Roberts print (date of 1722) mentions, for instance, that an assembly of Masons had been held in December 1663.

The first *Constitutions* tell us that the four lodges "thought fit to cement under a Grand Master as the Center of Union and Harmony." But this hardly explains what may have been in the minds of the founders. We may well suppose that the need was felt for a central authority to which the London lodges could look, as without it any considerable growth in the number of lodges and their membership might bring about chaotic conditions, but it is possible that this motive was combined with a number of others.

Some students are convinced that part of the object was to restore or strengthen something of the old guild system, and they point to the organization of freemasonry on 'livery' lines, to its system of government and the names of its officers, to its 'livery' (masonic clothing), and so forth, as evidence of such intention. The idea gains colour from the strong supposition that members of the Masons Company were members of one or more of the 'four old lodges,' and there is at once suggested an analogy between the restricted jurisdiction of the Grand Lodge and the sphere of action allowed to the London Company of Masons, which was limited to seven miles.

The Club and Benefit Society Ideas

Many masonic historians have made no secret of their belief that there was a strong connexion between the idea of the first Grand Lodge and that of the club, and they have thought it necessary to emphasize what they regard as the fact—that late in the seventeenth and early in the eighteenth centuries masonic gatherings could certainly be described as convivial affairs. G. W. Speth, for example, whose writings command respect, believed that the lodges of the accepted masons had some amount of mystic ceremony, but apart from that were convivial societies. Of course the lodges met in taverns, for there was nowhere else to go, the taverns being the customary meeting-places of the day. In them, and in the coffee-houses and chocolate-houses, clubs were born (in great numbers following 1717), and the early lodges, undoubtedly club-like in their ways, had perforce to meet there also.

The club was a product of the seventeenth century, the first known use of the word occurring in 1659. The club idea received a great fillip from the writings of Joseph Addison and Richard Steele (see p. 163), who edited their famous *Spectator* actually in a club, the members of which were of the most diverse character and represented the more intelligent and important classes of society. Addison wrote in the *Spectator* that

> Man is said to be a sociable animal, and we take all occasions and pretences of forming ourselves into those little nocturnal assemblies which are commonly known by the name of Clubs. Our modern celebrated clubs are founded upon eating and drinking, which are points wherein most men agree. . . . When men are thus knit together by a love of society, not a spirit of faction, and do not meet to censure or annoy those that are absent, but to enjoy one another . . . there may be something very useful in these little institutions and establishments.

It is obvious, then, that the Premier Grand Lodge was formed at a time when club life was just moving into great popularity, and it is easy to imagine that many a lodge of that day was, in a way, a kind of club. But to suggest that one of the chief aims in founding Grand Lodge was either to bring a club into existence, or to link masonic lodges more closely with the club movement, is fundamentally wrong. Apparently the 'knife and fork' mason who wanted a masonic club had already something of the sort in the 'convivial' assembly of his lodge, and it is difficult to see that to have added a meeting of Grand Lodge just four times a year, and one Assembly with Feast annually, would or could have done much in meeting any further desire that our early Brethren may have felt for club life. We may be quite sure that if the members of the 'four old lodges' wanted more of that life they knew exactly where to find it, or how to get it, without bringing into existence a Grand Lodge, which could do so little towards satisfying such a need.

While one of the four lodges consisted largely of well-to-do men, the three others included many artisans and craftsmen, in whose minds there might well have been another idea—that of forming a friendly society which would watch over its members and their families in time of illness or need. As a matter of fact, a private society of a strongly masonic nature, founded in 1737, was actually a friendly society, its rules and regulations consisting of sixty-six pages of skilfully drawn rules and six pages of members' names, trades, and addresses. The members were exclusively freemasons known to be ready and willing to pay their debts and under forty years of age. A member received £5 upon the death of his wife, *but only once*. The society developed into a regular lodge, and finally became the Vacation Lodge (No. 55 when it ceased to exist in 1801), all traces of the benefit society having disappeared by 1753. The benefit society idea is further alluded to on later pages (see p. 486).

The Proper Regulation of the Craft

All these ideas, and many others quite unknown and even unconjectured, may have animated some of the founders of Grand Lodge, but there seems no reason to doubt that the four lodges came together for the main purpose of doing more or less what we know they succeeded in doing—of bringing into existence a masonic centre with a Grand Master, Quarterly Communications, an Annual Assembly and Feast, and having some sort of authority, rather hazy at first, over the London lodges and their members, and finally, in all probability, to consider the preparation of a new constitution.

With the decay of the operative fraternities, the Old MS. Charges had long lost most of their usefulness, but they contained some valuable matter which it was desirable to save and make permanent in rather different form. Those old manuscript constitutions were designed for different days, different men, and wholly different conditions. We may well read into the objects of the new Grand Lodge an intention to produce a set of articles, in the light of which all matters relative to the Craft could be regulated and decided.

The Founding of Grand Lodge

"They could not escape History," a notable saying of Abraham Lincoln, applies to the decision of the 'four old lodges' to form a Grand Lodge. Their modest organization extended from St Paul's Churchyard, in the east, to Channel Row, Westminster, in the west—less than two miles as the crow flies—but from it has grown the world-wide organization of symbolic freemasonry.

We have two accounts, and two only, of the founding of Grand Lodge. One is by Dr James Anderson, who is not known to have taken any part in the event, and who published his account twenty-two years later in the second edition of his *Constitutions*. The second account is by an anonymous author, who about 1763 published *The Complete Freemason; or Multa Paucis for Lovers of Secrets*.

Anderson's account is short, and, although open to doubt in one or two details, is believed to be substantially correct. This is exactly what he says and *all* he says:

A.D. 1716, the few *Lodges* at *London* . . . thought fit to cement under a *Grand Master* as the Center of Union and Harmony, *viz*. the *Lodges* that met,

1. At the *Goose* and *Gridiron* Ale-house in *St Paul's Church-Yard*.
2. At the *Crown* Ale-house in *Parker's-Lane* near *Drury-Lane*.
3. At the *Apple Tree* Tavern in *Charles-Street, Covent-Garden*.
4. At the *Rummer* and *Grapes* Tavern in *Channel-Row,* Westminster.

They and some old Brothers met at the said *Apple-Tree,* and having put into the Chair the *oldest Master* Mason (now the *Master* of a *Lodge*) they constituted themselves a GRAND LODGE pro Tempore in *Due Form,* and forthwith revived the Quarterly *Communication* of the *Officers* of Lodges (call'd the **GRAND LODGE**) resolv'd to hold the *Annual* ASSEMBLY *and Feast,* and then to chuse a GRAND MASTER from among themselves, till they should have the Honour of a *Noble Brother* at their Head.

Accordingly

On *St John Baptist's* Day, in the 3d year of King GEORGE I., *A.D.* 1717, the ASSEMBLY and *Feast* of the *Free and accepted Masons* was held at the foresaid *Goose and Gridiron* Ale-house.

Before Dinner, the *oldest Master* Mason (Now the *Master* of a *Lodge*) in the Chair, proposed a List of proper Candidates; and the Brethren by a Majority of Hands elected

Mr ANTONY SAYER, Gentleman, *Grand Master* of *Masons,*

{Capt. Joseph Elliot,   } Grand
{Mr Jacob Lamball, Carpenter} Wardens

who being forthwith invested with the Badge of Office and Power by the said *oldest Master,* and install'd, was duly congratulated by the Assembly who pay'd him the *Homage.*

SAYER *Grand Master* commanded the *Masters* and *Wardens* of Lodges to meet the *Grand* Officers every *Quarter* in *Communication,* at the Place that he should appoint in his Summons sent by the *Tyler.*

From *Multa Paucis* we get some further details, but little of importance, although it has always been thought that its author had at his disposal information not known to or used by Anderson.

The leading facts to be derived from both accounts are that at a meeting of four lodges, with the oldest Lodge Master in the chair, Quarterly Communication known as Grand Lodge was revived, and that it was resolved to hold an Annual Assembly and Feast at which to choose the

Grand Master. At this assembly, duly held, Antony Sayer was elected Grand Master, and a Captain and a Carpenter were elected Grand Wardens. Although the idea is distinctly conveyed that the four lodges were *reviving* the Quarterly Communication, we have no record that any such quarterly communication had ever previously been held.

Multa Paucis says that the four lodges met together on St John's Day, and that the Masters and Wardens of *six* lodges assembled together. This statement has led to much argument, but most students feel that there were actually four lodges, and not six, present at the meeting.

The Four Old Lodges

A glance at the 'four old lodges' themselves will well repay the trouble.

One of them, the original No. 4—the number it still bears—meeting at the Rummer and Grapes, Westminster, appears to have been a lodge of accepted and speculative masons who had no connexion at that time with the mason trade. When, in 1723, we know something of its membership, we find the Master is the Duke of Richmond and its members are aristocrats and others of social quality. This lodge gave to freemasonry its second Grand Master (Payne) and third (Dr Desaguliers). Dr Anderson, to whom the early book of *Constitutions* is chiefly due, was also a member.

The three other lodges must have contained a fair sprinkling of artisan members or master artisans, who are likely to have provided the masons, carpenters, and blacksmith who reached the rank of Grand Wardens during the first six years of Grand Lodge; and we may well conclude that there had originally been in these lodges a strong operative element, whereas the lodge at the Rummer and Grapes (No. 4) either never had or had long forgotten any operative origin. It contributed many Grand Officers in those early days and obviously had an influential membership. In due course it became the Old Horn Lodge, later still the Somerset House Lodge (1774), and finally the Royal Somerset House and Inverness Lodge in 1828. It has met at the Freemasons' Tavern and, since 1865, at Freemasons' Hall.

The lodge at the Goose and Gridiron, St Paul's Churchyard, became in 1761 the West India and American Lodge; it was a Masters' Lodge from 1760 to 1769, and became the Lodge of Antiquity in 1770, a name it continues to bear in great honour. It is the famous No. 2, which has met at the Freemasons' Tavern and at Freemasons' Hall since 1781. The Grand Stewards' Lodge (no number), dating from 1735, and Grand Masters' Lodge, No. 1, founded in 1756, alone precede it in the list of lodges.

The lodge at the Crown, Drury Lane, expired in 1736 and was revived, unsuccessfully, in 1752.

The lodge at the Apple Tree Tavern, Covent Garden, became the Lodge of Fortitude in 1768 and the Lodge of Fortitude and Old Cumberland in 1818, having been a Masters' Lodge from 1803 to 1813. This historic lodge had the honour of providing the first Grand Master, Antony Sayer. It has met at many places in the neighbourhood of Soho, Long Acre, and Great Queen Street. Though third on the list originally, it lost its pride of place by accepting quite unnecessarily a "Constitution" from Grand Lodge in 1723, by reason of which it became No. 11 in 1729 and, after the Union, No. 12.

The Jurisdiction of the Premier Grand Lodge

There were probably two serious reasons for the new Grand Lodge restricting its jurisdiction to the lodges in London and Westminster. One was a tradition that came down to it from the London Company of Masons, whose own jurisdiction had extended only seven miles; the other was that the founding lodges were of London, and in those days of slow travel were conscious only of London. It may come as rather a shock to realize that the London represented by the jurisdiction of the Grand Lodge in 1717 did not exceed *three square miles,* and that the total area of built-up London at that time included only another two. On the north-east the houses stopped at about Shoreditch Church; in the north they fell far short of Islington, Sadler's Wells, and St Pancras; in the west the town more or less ended at Bond Street, which had open pasture as its outer neighbour. Tothill Fields adjoined Westminster on its west and south. The site of Freemasons' Hall was seven minutes' walk from the open fields, which almost touched Gray's Inn and actually surrounded Tottenham Court. From the Hall of the Masons' Company, near Guildhall, a person walking in any direction except westward would within a mile reach open fields. South of the river there was Lambeth (chiefly marsh), Southwark, the northern part of what is known as Bermondsey, and Rotherhithe. That was all.

The 'four old lodges' had Westminster as their horizon, and, having united themselves into one organization, apparently sat back content. We do not actually know whether any lodges joined them in the first three years, and possibly—it is a point on which much hinges—there was no arrangement in existence by which they could do so, or by which new lodges could be founded. The 'four old lodges' believed themselves to be of time immemorial, and it is of course possible that they may not have recognized that new lodges could have come into existence. Nevertheless, there must have been lodges, both inside and certainly outside the territory of the jurisdiction, and all the masons in them just as 'regular' in every sense as those in the 'four old lodges,' being themselves members of time-immemorial lodges having an inherent right to meet and work. Each of the unaffiliated lodges must have been a law to itself, and while it recognized as a Brother every true mason that entered through its portals, it did not dream of exercising jurisdiction over any other lodge, or of submitting itself to any jurisdiction claimed to be exercised by any other body. Obviously the new Grand Lodge had to meet from the very beginning the opposition of lodges and Brethren who regarded themselves as equals in every sense.

By finding the means whereby old lodges could come under its banner, and by which new lodges could be brought into existence, Grand Lodge quite suddenly began to grow, almost certainly at first by the addition of other London lodges, but very soon, and in spite of the original restriction of its jurisdiction, of country lodges as well.

Grand Lodge was quick to increase its area of influence so as to include lodges within ten miles of London or within the 'Bills of Mortality,' the latter a curious phrase having its origin about five hundred years before when London began to issue weekly lists of deaths. (A patent renewed by Charles I in 1636 incorporated the parishes of the City of London and of the City of Westminster and of the Borough of Southwark and fifteen adjoining parishes, others being added later. The district so impressed was known as being within the Bills of Mortality. The Bills were superseded in the 1840's.) If we look at the curious 'engraved list' of lodges of 1725, when the new Grand Lodge had existed for only eight years, we find it to include scores of lodges, of which many must have been newly constituted, and by this year Grand Lodge was actively building up the nucleus of a national organization. (See Plate IV.)

Anderson stated in his early *Constitutions*, "Now several old Brothers that had neglected the Craft, visited the Lodges; some Noblemen were also made Brothers, and more new Lodges were constituted."

Learned Men in the Craft

The new Grand Lodge had three quiet years followed by a period of great activity, in which the original four lodges appear to have grown to the considerable number of sixty-four; that is the number shown in the engraved list of 1725. Of these lodges, fifty were in London and the others were in Edgworth, Acton, Richmond (Surrey), Bath, Bristol, Norwich, Chichester, Chester (three lodges), Fulham, Greenwich, Brentford, Reading.

Freemasonry, which at its emergence in the preceding century had been so great an attraction to antiquaries and other learned men, now again attracted them in considerable numbers. Antiquarianism was a vogue in the early eighteenth century. The present Society of Antiquaries came into existence in the same year as Grand Lodge, and included in its early membership the brothers Roger and Samuel Gale, the Rev. Dr William Stukeley, Addison, Steele, Gay, and many other well-known men.

One of these, Dr Stukeley, the antiquary, has his own particular niche in masonic history. His diary entry for January 6, 1721, says, "I was made a Freemason at the Salutation Tavern, Tavistock Street [Covent Garden, London], with Mr Collins and Capt. Rowe, who made the famous diving engine." Then follows a most curious remark which has been much debated by masonic writers: "I was the first person made a Freemason in London for many years. We had great difficulty to find members enough to perform the ceremony. Immediately upon that it took a run and ran itself out of breath thro' the folly of the members." In the same year, on December 27, 1721, his diary records, "We met at the Fountain Tavern, Strand, and by the consent of the Grand Master present, Dr Beal (the D.G.M.) constituted a Lodge there, where I was chose Master."

Masonic writers have been tempted to take Stukeley's words far too seriously. We can easily suppose that he attended a lodge on an off-night, and it was the ignorance of the novitiate added to his natural extravagance of language that largely led him to write as he did.

From a memoir prepared by Gould we learn that William Stukeley was born in 1687, was both doctor of medicine and a clergyman, and evidently a man of gifts. He died suddenly in 1765, and we get some light upon his temperament from the words of Dr Warburton, Bishop of Gloucester, who wrote:

> There was in him such a mixture of simplicity, drollery, absurdity, ingenuity, superstition, and antiquarianism, that he often afforded me that kind of well-seasoned repast, which the French call an *Ambigu*, I suppose from a compound of things never meant to meet together. I have often heard him laughed at by fools, who had neither his sense, his knowledge, nor his honesty; though it must be confessed that in him they were all strangely travestied.

An historian has said that Dr Stukeley's "extravagancies, great as they are, must be considered as the occasionally wild colouring of that bright ray of genius." In the light of these extracts it is easy to see that in the statement that has been so often quoted he had probably rushed to a conclusion built on false premises. In his research work on place-names he brought ridicule upon himself by doing the same sort of thing.

But Stukeley does help us to understand why the antiquaries of his day came into speculative masonry, when he confesses that "his curiosities led him to be initiated into the mysterys of Masonry, suspecting it to be the remains of the mysterys of the ancients." He wrote books on those mysteries, and we can assume that he found in freemasonry much that was satisfying to him, for during his sojourn at Grantham, for some years following 1726, he "set up a lodg of freemasons, wh lasted all the time I lived there." When Stukeley's grave was accidentally discovered in 1886, his coffin, at a depth of about six feet, was found to be in good preservation, with an embossed brass plate ornamented with scroll work surmounted by a goat's head, and bearing a simple inscription in Latin. To the antiquary of the early eighteenth century and to all dabblers in medieval superstition the goat's head was a potent and often sinister symbol.

Early Organization of Grand Lodge and Some of its Personalities

Grand Lodge was in its earliest days a modest organization. Its officers were a Grand Master (elected annually) and two Wardens. Its members were the Masters and Wardens of the 'four old lodges' that had founded it and of any lodges that afterwards adhered to it (as to which we know little). These 'private' lodges each had its Right Worshipful Master, a Secretary, sometimes a Treasurer, a Tyler or somebody acting as Tyler, and Stewards or Brethren acting as Stewards. In many lodges until after 1813 the Treasurer, when there was one, was junior to the Secretary. In the lodges of the first half of the eighteenth century the period of election for the Master might be quarterly, half-yearly, or yearly.

There was nothing new in the appellation of Grand Master. The literature of the fifteenth to the seventeenth centuries frequently mentions the term, one instance being that of Wolsey, who, in the course of a great entertainment to French nobles at Hampton Court, not long before his disgrace, "desired the Grand Master, Anne de Montmorency, to pledge him cup and all, the which was worth 500 marks." There was a Grand Master of Water and Forests in France at about the same time, and probably long before. Latimer in a sermon before Edward VI in 1549 said, "God is great Grand Mayster of the Kynges house." Knolles in 1603 speaks of "Otto, grandmaster of the Templars."

The first Grand Master, Antony Sayer, was a 'gentleman,' but not a rich one, and he is believed to have been the first petitioner to Grand

Lodge for relief—not his only occasion of applying for help. He became Tyler of King's Arms Lodge, meeting at the Cannon, Charing Cross, and occupied that position at the time of his death. He was followed as Grand Master by George Payne, and then by John Theophilus Desaguliers, and then again by George Payne, these three being the only Grand Masters not of royal or noble birth.

Antony Sayer left but little mark on freemasonry; George Payne left many marks; while Desaguliers, to change the metaphor, played an important part in the early history of organized freemasonry. Desaguliers was Anglo-French (Jean Théophile Des Aguliers), born at La Rochelle, France, and brought to England when two years old. A Professor of Experimental Philosophy at Oxford, and a disciple and great admirer of Isaac Newton, he wrote a poem entitled *The Newtonian System* (1728) and *A Course of Experimental Philosophy* (1734). He was a Fellow and Curator of the Royal Society, and Chaplain to the Prince of Wales. In the 1744 two-volume edition of the second of the two works mentioned he gives a prophetic hint of the present-day atomic theory and of the possible splitting of the atom. Here are his exact words, written about two centuries before his prophecy was realized:

> As long therefore as the original Particles remain entire, there may for ever be Bodies made or Compos'd of them, which shall have the same Nature and Texture; But if these could be broken, worn away or diminished, then the Nature of corporeal Things, which is dependent on these, might be changed.

Other Grand Officers

A Deputy Grand Master was appointed in 1721. Grand Lodge had a Secretary in 1723 (W. Cowper, Clerk to the Parliaments) and a Treasurer also, but neither of these officers had the status of a Grand Officer at that time.

Past Grand Masters were given a vote in Grand Lodge in 1724, Past Deputy Grand Masters in 1726, and Past Grand Wardens in 1727. In 1741 the Treasurer, Secretary, and Swordbearer became members of every quarterly communication of Grand Lodge, but they did not in this way automatically become Grand Officers.

The first Grand Chaplain was appointed in 1775 on the occasion of laying the foundation-stone of Freemasons' Hall. There were two Grand Architects, the first of them appointed at the same time as the Grand Chaplain. An acting Grand Master, or Pro Grand Master, was appointed in 1782, when the Duke of Cumberland was elected Grand Master. (There is a Pro Grand Master only when the Grand Master is a Prince or

Blood Royal.) There was a Grand Portrait Painter in 1785—the only one. Grand Deacons were not known until after the Union in 1813.

Power passes to the Grand Master

For the first three years of Grand Lodge power of election and appointment were in the hands of the members attending that body, but in June 1720 it was agreed that for the future the new Grand Master should have the sole power of appointing his Grand Wardens and—in the event of "Noble Brothers" being Grand Masters—a Deputy Grand Master. In the following year the Grand Master Elect ordered the Grand Wardens to take some Stewards to assist at the approaching festival (for some reason it was not done), and in 1723 six Stewards were publicly thanked. In this we have the starting-point of the Grand Steward system.

The Grand Master Elect *proposed* his officers in 1723 and they were elected by ballot, but after that date the Grand Master Elect *appointed* his officers, the Brethren attending Grand Lodge having no voice in the matter.

The Grand Stewards and their Lodge

The six Stewards thanked for their services in 1723 were, it is thought, in the following year ordered to prepare a list of twelve Stewards to serve at the next feast. By 1732 each Steward was nominating his successor, and in 1735 Grand Lodge resolved that "for the future all Grand Officers (except the Grand Master) shall be selected out of that body" —that is, from among the Past Stewards. This has been called an astounding act, but Gould explains it by saying that the Grand Stewards themselves corresponded pretty closely to the Grand Officers of our own times. In the same year (1735) the Grand Stewards were granted the right to form themselves into a special lodge, which should be represented by twelve members, each having one vote, at each communication of Grand Lodge, instead of by the ordinary three members—namely, the Master and Wardens—and that Past Stewards should wear a particular jewel and the usual red ribbon.

Then, in 1736, Grand Lodge was declared to consist of the four present and all former Grand Officers; the Master and Wardens of all regular lodges; and the Master, Wardens, and nine representatives of the Stewards' Lodge. The nomination of stewards remained as a right of the Stewards' Lodge, and in 1771 an unsuccessful effort was made to transfer the nomination to the London lodges in rotation. In 1779 it was decided that of the Past Stewards only those who were members of the Stewards' Lodge and contributed to its funds should be eligible for Grand Office. In 1792 the Stewards' Lodge became the Grand Stewards' Lodge, with the right to head the list of lodges without a number—a position it still holds. It has met at Freemasons' Tavern and Freemasons' Hall since 1777. Its members wear crimson aprons and collars.

Nowadays, as prescribed in Grand Lodge Regulation 36, the Grand Master upon the Annual Installation appoints nineteen Grand Stewards, nominated respectively by nineteen separate lodges enjoying the privilege of recommendation. These lodges, known generally as the 'red apron lodges,' are: Grand Master's, No. 1; Antiquity, No. 2; Royal Somerset House and Inverness, No. 4; St George's and Corner Stone, No. 5; Friendship, No. 6; British, No. 8; Tuscan, No. 14; Emulation, No. 21; Globe, No. 23; Castle Lodge of Harmony, No. 26; Old King's Arms, No. 28; St Alban's, No. 29; Old Union, No. 46; Felicity, No. 58; Lodge of Peace and Harmony, No. 60; Regularity, No. 91; Shakespear, No. 99; Jerusalem, No. 197; Prince of Wales', No. 259.

The privilege of recommendation would pass from a 'red apron lodge' to another lodge, nominated by the Grand Master, were the lodge to neglect to make its recommendation. These Grand Stewards rank as Grand Officers during their year of office. Their duties are to regulate the grand festival under the Grand Master's direction and to assist in arranging for the Quarterly Communications and other meetings of Grand Lodge, under the direction of the Grand Director of Ceremonies.

Past or present Grand Stewards alone have the privilege of becoming members of the Grand Stewards' Lodge, which, constituted as a Master Masons' Lodge, has no power of making, passing, or raising masons.

Grand Lodge Minutes, Funds, and Fees

The earliest entries in the minute books of Grand Lodge relate to 1723, at the time when the first Secretary, not then called Grand Secretary, was appointed. There are no minutes whatever of any English speculative lodges before 1717. The minutes of the first (long extinct) Alnwick Lodge go back to 1701, but so far as is known that lodge was entirely operative. The earliest known minutes of Scottish lodges are dated 1598 and 1599, and those lodges also were operative.

How Grand Lodge financed itself in its first years is not clearly understood, but the expenses of any meetings appear to have been met by those present, while the secretarial expenses appear for the first seven years or so to have been made good by the Grand Master.

The first regular charge, a fee for constituting a lodge, went to the fund of general charity, and will be mentioned later.

The Grand Officers attending Grand Lodge in 1729 each paid 2s. 6d. towards expenses, and in 1736 the Grand Stewards did the same.

In 1753 it was ordered that a mason should not be made for less than one guinea (in addition to the Tyler's fee), the money to go to the lodge itself or to charity. In 1768 Grand Lodge imposed a fee of 5s. for every Initiation, and 2s. 6d. for registration of the Initiate, these fees providing a fund for general purposes. In 1777 the Grand Lodge fee for Initiation rose to two guineas, while the fee for constituting a lodge, which had been two guineas from 1729, rose to six guineas in London and four guineas in the country. The registration fee on Initiation was raised to half a guinea in 1788, and it is thought that fees then remained unaltered until the Union in 1813.

The old operative fraternities had their own way of meeting the needs of distressed Brethren. The Manuscript Charges enjoin Brethren to receive and cherish strange Brethren by giving them work or by helping them with money on their journey. The Scottish operative lodges in late medieval days appear to have been quite well organized in this respect, their 'box' under the charge of the Box-master (Treasurer) providing for the assistance of distressed Brethren and even for the education of the orphans of deceased members.

The speculative masons appear to have taken a leaf from their predecessors' book, if we can judge from the many public allusions to the charitable principles of our early Brethren, although it is thought that the specific idea of charity did not make itself strongly felt in the Craft until after 1717. There may be a most simple explanation of this—namely, that up to about that time the average speculative mason was not likely to be one in need of help. Judging from the few facts known to us, the *type* of speculative mason in the seventeenth century was not of the artisan class. Any Brethren who fell by the way were probably helped privately and unofficially, and it was only with the tremendous increase of membership following 1717, and with the corresponding extension of the membership to relatively poor men, that the need for organized charity within the Craft came to be definitely felt. We learn that in 1729 the first regular charge made by Grand Lodge, the one already mentioned—namely, two guineas for constituting a lodge, went to a fund for general charity which hitherto had depended entirely upon voluntary donations both of lodges and Brethren. The *Constitutions* of 1723 laid down that every Initiate was to "deposit something for the relief of indigent and decayed Brethren."

A scheme for raising a fund of general charity for distressed masons was proposed in November 1724, and at this meeting a petition for help from the first Grand Master, Antony Sayer, was read and recommended. (Another very early recipient of help was Joshua Timson, a Grand Warden in 1722. Sums of money were voted to Antony Sayer in 1730 and 1741, not long before his death.) A special committee appointed to consider the proposed charity fund presented a report which was adopted in February 1726; in the following year a committee to administer the charity was appointed, and the first contributions from private lodges were received by the fund in 1729.

Grand Lodge considerably extended the scope of the Committee of Charity in 1730 and referred all business relating to charity to the Committee, which was empowered to hear complaints and report thereon to Grand Lodge. By 1733 the Committee's powers were further enlarged by a resolution referring all business which could not be conveniently discharged by the Quarterly Communications to the Committee of Charity, at the same time deciding that all Masters of regular lodges, together with all Grand Officers, "present, former and future," should be members of that Committee. In this way we find the Committee of Charity acquiring many of the functions now discharged by the Board of General Purposes; in the course of time it became a Board of Masters which continued to operate through the eighteeth and nineteenth centuries, while the fund of general charity instituted in 1724 developed into the Board of Benevolence, to which every lodge, on behalf of all its subscribing members, now pays quarterage to Grand Lodge. This quarterage system was by no means an invention of Grand Lodge. It is taken from, or modelled on, a usage of the London Company of Masons, with whom it must go back to late medieval days, for in 1693 the Company "ordered that the quarterage henceforward be paid 6d. a quarter by every member" (by the way, the London Company must have had its share of difficult members, it being on record that Oswald Strong paid the sum of £1 10s. 6d. in the year 1709, being then over fifteen years in arrear).

With the coming into existence of lodges in various parts of the provinces it was inevitable that Provincial Grand Masters would be soon appointed, as, indeed, they were for Cheshire and for Wales by 1726. The statement that a Provincial Grand Master, the first in foreign parts, was appointed in Bengal in 1728 is subject to some little question.

Other Grand Lodges: Overseas Lodges and Military Lodges

Soon there were three other Grand Lodges. As from about 1724 the Old Lodge at York constituted itself a Grand Lodge. In 1725 (or thereabouts) and 1736, respectively, Ireland and Scotland followed the example and methods of the Grand Lodge of England, and without her assistance or intervention constituted their own Grand Lodges.

When the Duke of Wharton, a Past Grand Master, was in Madrid in

1728 he founded what is believed to be the first foreign lodge, but composed chiefly of Englishmen; he founded it on his own responsibility and therefore irregularly, a constitution to regularize it not being granted until the following year, by which time a lodge had been founded at Gibraltar and another in Bengal. All three lodges are now extinct. Tradition says that the Earl of Derwentwater formed a lodge in Paris in 1725.

During the eighteenth century a considerable number of military lodges came into existence, possessing the right to meet legally at whatever place the regiment might find itself. The first such lodge was Irish, and was founded in 1732, and was followed by others. Scotland had a military lodge in 1743; while the first English regimental lodge was that of the 8th Regiment of Foot, founded in 1755. The itinerant military lodges are believed to have exercised a strong influence on the ceremonial development of freemasonry during the eighteenth century.

The "Constitutions" of 1723

One of the most important things coming from the new Grand Lodge was the book of *Constitutions* in 1723, in itself a true lineal descendant of the Old MS. Charges of the fourteenth and perhaps still earlier centuries. Actually it appears to have come from Dr James Anderson, but it was published with a certain measure of Grand Lodge authority.

James Anderson, born about 1684 probably in Aberdeen, where he graduated Master of Arts at the Marischal College, went to London, and some time ending in 1734 was the minister of a Presbyterian chapel in Swallow Street, Piccadilly. It is not known when or where he was initiated, but he must have been familiar with the Scots terminology, usages, and historical claims. He is not known to have taken any part in the founding of Grand Lodge, or to have been present at Grand Lodge, until September 1721. After the publication of the *Constitutions* he stayed away from Grand Lodge for over seven years, during which time he was busy on his work *Royal Genealogies,* published in 1732. He wrote other books, but they were not of much consequence. He published the second edition of the *Constitutions* in 1738, and died in the following year.

It is not known whence he derived his doctor's degree, but a copy of his best-known work presented to his old College is inscribed in his own hand, "Jacobus Anderson, D.D." The title "Constitutions" was used by the London Company of Masons to describe their copies of the Old Charges. Anderson's original *Constitutions,* a book of ninety-two pages, was a private venture and his own property, as was also the second edition published in 1738. He allows the reader to infer that his books were official publications with which Grand Lodge was closely associated throughout their preparation. What is known as the "Approbation," occupying two pages, states that

> he has drawn forth the above-written new Constitutions, with the Charges and General Regulations: and the Author having submitted the whole to the Perusal and corrections of the late and present Deputy Grand Masters and of other learned Brethren; and also of the Masters and Wardens of particular Lodges at their Quarterly Communication; He did regularly deliver them to the late Grand Master himself, the said Duke of Montagu, for his Examination Correction and Approbation; and his Grace by the advice of several Brethren, order'd the same to be handsomely printed for the use of the Lodges.

We get a somewhat different idea of the whole matter from Lionel Vibert's reconstruction of what he calls the true genesis of the work in which he suggests that Anderson appears in Grand Lodge in September 1721, and asks permission to write and publish a history of the Order to be dedicated to the Grand Master. Desaguliers perhaps associates himself with the proposition and Anderson is given permission. The following March he produces his manuscript—the History and the Master's Song. Grand Lodge, it is suggested, then directs that the "Regulations" proposed by the second Grand Master, George Payne, shall be included in the book. Anderson rewrites and modernizes the Charges of the old Constitutions, and is possibly assisted by Desaguliers and other "learned Brethren." It is complete in the following November. The Approbation is then drawn up and signed (this being what is referred to in the words "having regularly approved in MS. by the Grand Lodge"), and the book is in print in January 1723.

The frontispiece represents a classical arcade, in the foreground of which stand two noble personages—Grand Masters—each with attendants, of whom one carries aprons and gloves. On the ground between the principal figures is a diagram of Euclid's forty-seventh proposition with the Greek word "Eureka," which Anderson thought at the time was an exclamation by Pythagoras when he found the forty-seventh proposition. He believed this proposition to be the "Foundation of all Masonry, sacred, civil and military"; but the exclamation is always attributed to Archimedes on solving the problem of how to test the amount of alloy in a gold crown, and Anderson appears to have confounded the two incidents. He uses the same frontispiece in the 1738 edition, but with the cunning addition of the words

> Pythagoras . . . became not only the Head of a new Religion of Patch Work but likewise of an *Academy* or *Lodge* of good *Geometricians* to whom he

communicated a Secret, viz. That amazing Proposition which is the Foundation of all Masonry, of whatever Materials or Dimensions, called by Masons his HEUREKA; because They think it was his own Invention.

The Old MS. Charges brought masonry, or geometry, from the children of Lamech to Soloman, and by various steps finally to England. But Anderson traces the art from Adam himself, who instructed his son Cain in geometry and made it possible for him to build a city. He introduces Noah and his sons and Grand Master Moses; he derives all civilized architecture from Solomon's Temple; he traces the progress of the science through Greece and Sicily to its culmination in Rome. All knowledge of the art is lost in Britain after the Romans retired, but Charles Martel of France helps England to recover the true art after the Saxon invasions. Monarchs up to Elizabeth all advanced the art to the best of their ability, while Renaissance architecture, which he claims as having been introduced into England by James I, was a return to a model from which Gothic had been merely a barbarous lapse. And so forth.

Anderson says that his history is collected from the general records of the Craft and their faithful traditions of many ages. Actually, Lionel Vibert tells us, he drew upon the Cooke and other manuscripts, and made additions of his own as seemed good to him. He did not then know of the existence of the Roberts MS. or he would have mentioned the General Assembly of 1663, but in his second edition he made good this omission. He drew also, of course, from the Bible and from ordinary sources, including Stow's historical works. No authority has yet been found for his story about Queen Elizabeth's commission, to the effect that, with intent to break up the annual communication, they

> brought a sufficient posse with them at York upon St John's Day, were once admitted into the Lodge, they made no use of arms, and returned the Queen a most honourable account of the ancient Fraternity, whereby her political Fears and Doubts were dispell'd, and she let them alone, as a People much respected by the Noble and the Wise of all the polite Nations, but neglected the Art all her Reign.

In his 1738 edition he improves the story with names and dates.

Peculiarly important are Anderson's uses of Scots terms, which undoubtedly have had a lasting influence on masonic ritual, as already frequently mentioned in these pages. He took 'Entered Apprentice' from the Scots practice of *entering* each apprentice in the records, the apprentice then being known as an 'entered 'prentice.' Similarly, he uses for the first time in an English work the term 'Fellow Craft' or 'Fellow of Craft,' a constantly recurring phrase in Scots operative masonry.

The history in the *Constitutions* is directed to be read at the admission of a new Brother, and this injunction is repeated in the edition of 1738, where the history occupies 139 pages of print, requiring some two and a half hours' steady reading to get through!

The celebrated Charge "Concerning God and Religion," included in Anderson's *Constitutions,* substituted for the direct injunction of loyalty to God and Holy Church, as given in the original Charges, the phrase: "'tis now thought more expedient only to oblige them to that Religion in which all men agree, leaving their particular opinions to themselves." Lionel Vibert quotes Gould, who said that the diverse religious views of members of Grand Lodge at the time must have shown the necessity of uniting on a platform which would divide them the least; and the language of the Sixth Charge, as to avoiding quarrels about religion, suggests that from its first inception the Grand Lodge had followed the line, taken by the Royal Society many years before, of forbidding discussion on the topic as the only means of preserving harmony among persons of different opinions. But Anderson had no use for the "irreligious libertine"— his strong expression to denote the Freethinker—and he denounces men of no religion and men to whom one religion is as good as another. He believed that no mason can ever be an atheist, and that they need not be uneasy if some of the learned among them are ignorantly so described. He goes on to say: "The next thing that I shall remember you of is to avoid Politics and Religion"; by which he means not merely the discussion of them but "any association with them as a Society, for," he says, "our Politics is merely to be honest and our Religion the Law of Nature and to love God above all things, and our Neighbour as our self; this is the true, primitive, catholic and universal Religion, agreed to be so in all Times and Ages."

Anderson tells us that in ancient times masons were charged in every country to be of the religion of that country or nation, whatever it was. For this, he found no warrant in the Old MS. Charges, but possibly got the idea from a phrase in Cotton's translation of Montaigne's *Essays.*

The General Regulations, to the number of thirty-nine, are said to have been

> Compiled first by Mr George Payne, Anno 1720, when he was Grand Master, and approv'd by the Grand Lodge on St John Baptist's Day, Anno 1721, at Stationers' Hall, London; when the most noble Prince John Duke of Montagu was unanimously chosen our Grand-Master for the Year ensuing.

The first minute recorded in the minute books of Grand Lodge is dated June 24, 1723, and recites that the *Constitutions* had been before approved in manuscript by the Grand Lodge and had already been produced in print and approved. Then occurred something which made it possible to say afterwards that the General Regulations had not obtained the consent of the Grand Lodge. The question was moved

> That the said General Regulations be confirmed, so far as they are consistent with the Ancient Rules of Masonry. The previous question was moved and put, whether the words "so far as they are consistent with the Ancient Rules of Masonry" be part of the Question. Resolved in the affirmative, But the main Question was not put.

From this we can only gather that the General Regulations were *not* confirmed, but another resolution was passed, this containing words well known to every mason, for the minutes go on to record:

> And the Question was moved That it is not in the Power of any person, or Body of men, to make any alteration, or Innovation in the Body of Masonry without the Consent first obtained of the Annual Grand Lodge. And the Question being put accordingly Resolved in the affirmative.

From which we conclude that whatever was new in the Regulations was of no effect.

In 1738 Anderson issued a new edition of the *Constitutions,* and in 1756 John Entick revised the whole, and drew up an entirely new code of regulations arranged on a different system, for all of which he had authority. It is Entick's code that has formed the basis of the *Constitutions* of later date; and it is through Entick that we can still trace a number of phrases that go back to Anderson's original, in which connexion *A.Q.C.,* vol. xlvi (p. 149), may be consulted by any reader particularly interested.

In all fairness to Anderson, and in spite of all the criticism to which he and his book have been subjected, the remarkable influence of his *Constitutions* on the course of world freemasonry must be freely acknowledged. The earliest Irish *Constitutions* (1730) were modelled on Anderson's. The Americans in 1735 reprinted his book word for word, and the English original, sometimes in pirated editions, went forth into every country of the world, there to play a part in transmitting the principles and tenets of freemasonry and in encouraging Brethren to found lodges on the English pattern.[1]

New Lodges constituted

The manner of constituting a new lodge "according to the ancient usages of masons" is given in the *Constitutions* of 1723, and in them it is made very clear that the new Master and Wardens were among the Fellow Crafts. A lodge was constituted by the personal act of the Grand

[1] For further information on the *Constitutions,* consult reprints of the original in the great masonic libraries and Lionel Vibert's paper in *A.Q.C.,* vol. xxxvi.

Master or his Deputy, apparently without the issue of any written warrant; a reference to "the Grand Master's warrant" probably meant nothing more than his sanction or authority expressed by his presence or that of his Deputy.

In all probability, the instructions as to the manner of constituting a new lodge were urgently needed by the growing fraternity. In 1721, the year of which Stukeley wrote, there were a few lodges under the Grand Lodge, and some others—how many is unknown—not affiliated with it. Four years later, in 1725, there were about fifty London lodges alone on the list. Of a number of possible explanations the most likely is that lodges existing prior to 1723 were unaware of any means of joining Grand Lodge, while new lodges could not regularly come into existence because of the lack of any means of legalizing their formation or constitution. It was when these matters had been put right at the instance of the second Grand Master, George Payne, and the necessary instructions or information had become a part of the printed *Constitutions*, that new lodges found it easy to come into existence, and old ones to regularize their position in relation to the Grand Lodge. (It must be noted that, as in 1724, six Fellows could get together in casual association and make masons.)

Of Lodges still in existence (other than the survivors of the 'four old lodges'), the Lodge of Friendship, now No. 6, was founded in January 1721; the British Lodge, No. 8, was founded in the following year, as were also the Tyrian Lodge, now the Westminster and Keystone Lodge, No. 10; the Tuscan Lodge, now No. 14; and the Ionic Lodge, now Royal Alpha, No. 16.

Many famous lodges were constituted in 1723, including the Old Dundee Lodge, No. 18; what is now the Royal Kent Lodge of Antiquity, No. 20; what is now the Lodge of Emulation, No. 21; Globe Lodge, No. 23; and others since expired. None of the lodges constituted in 1724 is now in existence, and only two of 1725—namely, the Castle Lodge of Harmony, No. 26, and Old King's Arms Lodge, No. 28. Only one other lodge founded before 1730 survives—that being St Alban's, No. 29, founded in January 1728.

It must always be remembered that, as has been said, there were undoubtedly lodges in existence not affiliated to the Grand Lodge, apart from such ancient operative lodges as those of Alnwick and Swalwell. There was also the Lodge at York, a time-immemorial lodge, which met at Merchants' Hall, in the City of York, and which in December 1725 formed itself into "the Grand Lodge of ALL England held at York", it became dormant in 1740, was revived in 1761, and we know nothing of it after 1792.

Personages in the Early Lodges (1723–39)

Freemasons mentioned in Grand Lodge Minute Books of 1723–39, and sufficiently well known to achieve notice in the *Dictionary of National Biography* (their names have been compiled by W. J. Williams, from whose work the information has been gleaned) include very many notable and colourful characters. There were twenty-eight of noble birth; eighteen painters, sculptors, engravers, etc.; seventeen authors, poets, dramatists, etc.; fifteen clergy and ministers; fifteen scientists, antiquarians, etc.; fourteen physicians and surgeons; twelve actors, musicians, singers, etc.; six architects; five printers and publishers; four lawyers; three men of fashion, dilettantes, etc.; and two public servants of high standing. Of a score or so of others, one was, possibly, a privateer, and another a pugilist. The former, George Shelvock, of the Horne Tavern Lodge in 1723 and 1725, commanded the privateer *Speedwell*, conducted an "independent cruise," sacked Payta, lost his ship and built a new one with which he captured three others, and was "acquitted on technical grounds when charged with piracy." The pugilist, James Figg, of the Lodge at the Castle Tavern, St Giles, in 1725, had an academy of boxing and swordsmanship; he fought a broadsword duel in the Haymarket Theatre to provide a spectacle for a visiting freemason, the Duc de Lorraine; and gave exhibitions of bear-baiting and tiger-fighting.

An Early Jewish Freemason

What is believed to be the first distinctive reference to a Jewish speculative mason is of the year 1732, and concerns Daniel Delvalle, or Dalvalle, "an eminent Jew Snuff Merchant," Master of the lodge at the Rose Tavern, Cheapside, in that year, and a member also of other lodges. This statement is considerably at variance with one made in *A History of Rhode Island* (U.S.A.), written in 1835 by the Rev. Edward Peterson, of Newport, R.I., who was not himself a mason. He declares in that history that in the spring of 1658 fifteen Jewish families arrived at Newport from Holland, bringing with them the three first degrees of masonry, and working them in the house of Mordecai Campannall, one of their members, and continuing to do so, they and their successors, to the year 1742. This statement, of the truth of which no proof exists, has been the subject of fierce controversy, but it is now thought that the manuscript on which the statement was based was almost illegible, and that those who interpreted it made out a reading which, had they had any knowledge of the subject, they would have known was quite untenable. It is agreed that there was no speculative masonry in Holland until the eighteenth century.

Lodge Lectures on Non-Masonic Subjects

Some early lodges encouraged lectures on various subjects quite unconnected with freemasonry, which we may take as evidence that in those particular lodges the ceremonies were not elaborate enough to occupy a major part of lodge time, or we may hazard a guess that in some lodges the masonic lectures worked on the question-and-answer method had been severely abbreviated. However that may be, and always remembering that there were considerable diversities in lodge practice in these early days, we find the Old King's Arms Lodge, meeting at the King's Arms in the Strand, London, discussing in 1733 the question "whether it is possible that a malefactor who is shot to death may be sensible of the Report of ye piece that occasioned his loss of life" and determining "in the affirmation unless the medulla oblongata where the nerves of the whole system centre, be torn to pieces by the ball." How much better we do things to-day, but *after* lodge is closed, can be judged from an advertisement in the masonic Press (February 1946) offering for the delectation of dining Brethren a unique entertainment, including "Sawing a Woman in Half and a Dancing Skeleton."

A Considerable Public Interest in Masonry

The public Press of the 1720's echoes the considerable interest which the public was taking in freemasonry. We find in it allusions of every sort, from the kindly, appreciative, and respectful on the one hand, to a great variety of vulgarity, scurrility, and downright, lying invention on the other. Skits on the freemasons were many, their 'leather aprons and gloves' being the point of many a jocular reference. The newspapers of the period go to show that the public was very much alive to the fact that there was a strong masonic movement in the land. We find one simple piece of evidence very convincing. Curiosity had been tickled by the publication in 1730 of Prichard's *Masonry Dissected*, and it is probably as a consequence of this that we find in one of the booths of the Bartholomew Fair of 1731 an opera being performed under the title of *The Generous Free-Mason: or, The Constant Lady* ("With the Humours of Squire *Noodle*, and his Man *Doodle*. A Tragi-comi-farcical Ballad Opera. In three acts. With the MUSICK prefix'd to each SONG. By the AUTHOR of the LOVER'S OPERA"). This opera had been printed for J. Roberts in Warwick Lane, and was sold by the booksellers of London and Westminster for a shilling. The opera itself is of no value from any artistic point of view, but that an astute showman should choose to make his bid for the favour of the Bartholomew Fair rabble with a play about free-masons reveals a measure of public interest and curiosity big enough to exploit.

The Authority of Grand Lodge not everywhere recognized

It must be obvious from what has already been said that the authority of Grand Lodge was not everywhere recognized, and it would not be surprising, were all the facts known, to find that there were some time-immemorial lodges that never did recognize it. All lodges believing themselves to exist by inherent right and from time immemorial might not easily be brought to see that they could make masons only in con-formity with regulations issued by an organization calling itself a Grand Lodge, and it may be suspected, too, that here and there a self-consti-tuted body of masons of recent growth strongly asserted its right to do exactly as it pleased in any masonic matter whatsoever. We may find an instance in the society of musicians (mentioned on p. 243) formed in 1725, which had a rule that its members should be freemasons. If the society wished to admit a prominent musician who was not a mason it forth-with 'initiated' him, and then admitted him to membership. So strongly did the society uphold its claim to do what it liked that, when it received a letter of protest from the Grand Master, it ordered that the letter lie on the table!

In a later chapter we shall see that, as the decades passed, Grand Lodge encountered considerable opposition and came under the fire of much angry cricitism—a condition which was allowed to develop into open warfare with the formation in due course of a new Grand Lodge calling itself 'Antient,' and calmly dubbing its rival 'Modern.'

The Jacobite Tradition

The possibility of English freemasonry having been subjected to Jacobite influence during the few decades immediately following 1717 has often been advanced. Many theories have been ventilated, with much conjecture, little fact; with much controversy, little agreement. There have been authors who have been downright in their statements that the freemasonry of the 'Antients'—the body that set up its own Grand Lodge in opposition to the Premier Grand Lodge—was the freemasonry of the Roman Catholics and the Stuarts—that is, of the Irish and Scottish followers of the Stuart cause who fled to France about 1688, whereas the founders of the first Grand Lodge were Protestant and Hanoverian. Others have pointed out that Jacobite influence was dying down at the time when the 'Antients' rose to strength, but they still appear to entertain the idea that the Jacobite party came into freemasonry, with or without the help of the Roman Catholics, with a view to using it as a mask for their efforts in the Stuart cause.

A peculiar twist is given by relating the Jacobite tradition to the so-called 'Scots Masonry,' the theory being that, while freemasonry recommended itself to the Jacobite movement as providing convenient, safe, and secret meeting-places for its adherents, it was obvious that freemasonry was open to Jacobites and Hanoverians alike. It was therefore decided to create a freemasonry apart, "to be made subservient to the cause they had so much at heart, with ceremonies and secrets peculiar to itself and jealously guarded from even the Masters of Craft masonry."[1] So, it is alleged, the Jacobites brought into existence the degrees known in England as 'Scots masonry' and in France as '*Maçon Écossois*,' '*Maitre Écossois*,' '*Maçonnerie Écossois*.'

It is true that there are references to Scots lodges and Scots masonry in the early speculative days (Chapter IX), and no one has yet been able to tell us exactly what they mean. In various Continental cities, too, these Scots lodges were founded. But there does not appear to be any ground for believing that the degree came from Scotland. Whatever 'Scots masonry' was, it was fairly certainly French, and mention of it continued to occur and recur in lodge minutes and other records through the eighteenth century. For example, when in 1777 the famous Cagliostro was initiated in the Esperance Lodge at the King's Head, in Gerrard Street, Soho, London, he is said to have passed through the four degrees of "apprentice, companion [fellow?], Master and Scotch Master." While we may conjecture that the degree was a mixture of Royal Arch and Mark, what it really was we simply do not know.

One author has spoken of "definite documentary evidence of the existence of a Jacobite Grand Lodge of London," but it is doubtful whether masonic writers in general are aware of any such evidence.

A plausible (perhaps for that reason, doubtful) suggestion is that Gaelic words meaning, or apparently meaning, 'widow's son' were brought into masonry by the Jacobites, it being especially noteworthy that both the Old and the Young Pretenders were widows' sons, but Gaelic scholars do not accept it, based, as it is, on the likeness between the sounds of quite different words. But it has been quite seriously put forward that "the untimely death of Hiram Abif" is an allusion to the execution of Charles I, and that the attempt to raise the Master's body is an allusion to an attempt to raise the young Prince Charles from the grave of exile to the throne of England. To add a 'convincing' touch it is

[1] J. E. S. Tuckett, *A.Q.C.*, vol. xxxii.

pointed out that *cas* is Gaelic for 'a branch of a tree,' and also for 'a young man, a lad,' and that until about 1745, when the Pretender's hopes were finally brought to naught, it was the cassia plant that was supposed to mark the Master's grave. Thus in Prichard's *Masonry Dissected* (1730) we have:

Q. What is a mason nam'd?
A. Cassia is my name, and from a just and perfect lodge I came.

And here are some coincidences. The sprig of cassia at the head of a grave became the sprig of acacia about 1745, the year of the Jacobite rising. 'Acacia' is a Greek word meaning 'innocence' or 'blameless-ness.' Among the score or so of names given to the assassins of the Master is that of Romvel, which is *supposed* to be a palpable hit at Cromwell, whom the Jacobites regarded as the murderer of Charles I. A warning: the more interesting and plausible the stories relating to the Jacobite legend are made, the more they must be treated with suspicion!

The fact that Jacobite allusions to the Pretenders occasionally reflected the idea of the 'widow's son' has been overstressed by masonic writers. The parallel of the 'widow's son' may have occurred as the purest accident. How, for example, does the informed reader regard the allusion in the following instance? Queen Anne had a cook, Joseph Centlivre, whose wife Susannah, a playwright, produced between the years 1700 and 1722 a score of comedies. One of them, *A Gotham Election,* contains this dialogue between a Jacobite mayor and a messenger coming from the Old Pretender:

THE MAYOR: Well, and how does all our friends on t'other side the water, ha? Well, I Hope?
MESSENGER: Oh *fort bien,* Monsieur Mayor, and Monsieur le Chevalier he varey much your humble serviteur, Begar.
THE MAYOR: I am very much his, I am sure—come Monsieur, to the Fatherless and Widow. (*Drink.*)

What is the reply to the Jacobite theory or tradition? Although the Roman Catholic Church was not always opposed to freemasonry, the Papal Bull of 1738 had as one of its effects the suppression of a lodge containing purely Jacobite members. There is no actual certainty, al-though considerable likelihood, that the so-called 'Scots lodges' were the *écossois* degrees in English dress. It is not known that Jacobites had any handins bringing those degrees into existence, although, of course, if the degree were largely the work of British people living in France, it is likely that such people would have been Jacobites; but it does not in the least follow that they invented the degrees as an instrument of their policies. Surely a lodge or degree designed to further the Jacobite cause would not deliberately label itself 'Scots.' Perhaps the nearest we shall get to the truth is the suggestion that any added degree formed in France at that time gave opportunity for men of similar interests and opinions to come together. And we may note, also, a point made by F. L. Pick, that early in the eighteenth century there existed Jacobite societies, having the appearance of jolly, convivial affairs, but at the same time inspired by a serious political purpose, and that some of them took a leaf from the freemason's book by wearing regalia and adopting a peculiar formality in their meetings. He wonders whether the Jacobite tradition is not really an echo of such mock-masonic societies?

The Papal Bulls against Freemasonry

Although the Roman Catholic opposition to freemasonry is common knowledge, it should be known also that there were originally a great many Roman Catholic freemasons in all the countries where freemasonry flourished, among them being priests and high dignitaries of the Church, a condition which held good for many years (indeed, all through the eighteenth century in some countries), even after Pope Clement XII in 1738 and Benedict XIV in 1751 had issued their Bulls denouncing free-masonry. In Liége, Belgium (to cite an instance given by Count Goblet D'Alviella), the Roman Catholic Bishop Velbrück, who ruled his ecclesi-astical Principality from 1772 to 1784, was a devoted freemason, as were many of his canons and officials. One of these, the Rev. Canon de Geloes, was founder and first Master of La Parfaite Intelligence, at Liége, which was first a French and later a Belgian lodge, while another, the Rev. Canon Nicolas Devaux, was Master of another Liége lodge, La Parfaite Égalité; other instances could be given. It is to be assumed that it was the comparative inattention paid to the Bulls in some quarters that led to a whole series of Papal edicts, beginning in 1821, confirming and renewing them.

The Roman Catholic objections to freemasonry are not difficult to understand, even though we, as freemasons, do not acknowledge their soundness. A pamphlet, *Freemasonry* (revised edition, 1935), published by the Catholic Truth Society, after describing Anglo-Saxon freemasons as "inoffensive and well-meaning people" and admitting that free-masonry is "beneficial to the country, or at any rate quite harmless," then makes quite clear that the solemn oath of secrecy is one of the "two main grounds of objection," the other and apparently more serious one being that freemasonry "tends to undermine belief in Catholic Christianity by substituting for it what is practically a rival religion based on deistic or naturalistic principles." In reply it should be said that freemasonry is not claimed to be a religion. It is a system of morality, of philosophy. A candidate for its privileges is entitled to hold what religious principles and beliefs he pleases; the Craft will not belittle them and will respect their holder as long as he brings into freemasonry just one all-essential part of his code—a belief in the "Glorious Architect of heaven and earth." Freemasonry calls upon its members to practise the sacred duties of morality, and offers itself, as the Ancient Charges tell us, as "the centre of union between good men and true, and the happy means of conciliating friendship amongst those who must otherwise have remained at a perpetual distance."

Aims and Relationships of the Craft

In this connexion we may well give extracts from (but cannot reproduce entire) *The Aims and Relations of the Craft*, first issued by the English Grand Lodge in 1938 and since fully subscribed to by the Grand Lodges of Ireland and Scotland:

> The first condition of admission into, and membership of, the Order is a belief in the Supreme Being; The Bible, the Volume of the Sacred Law, is always open in the Lodges. Every Candidate is required to take his Obligation on that book or on the Volume that is held by his particular creed to impart sanctity to an oath or promise taken upon it; While the individual freemason has the right to hold his own opinion with regard to public affairs, neither in any lodge nor in his capacity as a freemason, may he discuss or advance his views on theological or political questions; The Grand Lodge has always consistently refused to express any opinion on questions of foreign or domestic State policy either at home or abroad, and it will not allow its name to be associated with any action, however humanitarian it may appear to be, which infringes this policy; The Grand Lodge refuses to have any relations with, or to regard as freemasons, any Bodies, styling themselves Freemasons, which do not adhere to these principles.

In 1929 the Grand Lodge of England issued *Basic Principles for Grand Lodge Recognition*; this foreshadowed the greater part of the above declaration and laid down that any Grand Lodge asking to be recognized by the English jurisdiction shall strictly observe the principles of the Ancient Landmarks, customs, and usages of the Craft; its membership and that of its individual Lodges shall be composed exclusively of men; there shall be no masonic intercourse with mixed Lodges or with bodies that admit women to membership; the three Great Lights of Freemasonry (the V.S.L., the Square, and the Compasses) shall always be exhibited when it or its subordinate Lodges are at work.

Chapter Twelve

THE RIVAL GRAND LODGE OF THE 'ANTIENTS'

THE history of freemasonry in the eighteenth century is disfigured by a long and violent quarrel, in the course of which a rival Grand Lodge, once said to have existed from 1739, came into official existence in 1751. Only so much of the long and involved story will be told as is necessary to an understanding of how the quarrel arose, why a separate Grand Lodge was formed, and how ultimately the two Grand Lodges came together. To the objection that there can be little interest in a quarrel which ended early in the nineteenth century it must be explained that, had the rival Grand Lodge never been formed, English freemasonry to-day would be the poorer, and not one of our Craft degrees would be as it is. But for it, the Installation ceremony might be little more than the simple chairing of the elected Master; we might have had the Royal Arch Degree and the Mark Degree, but it is unlikely that we should have had them in so rich a form. The book of *Constitutions* would in all probability be different and almost certainly rather poorer in some respects. Finally, a short study of the quarrel that raged in eighteenth-century freemasonry tells us much of the conditions that helped to form the practices, ceremonies, and ritual that English freemasonry enjoys to-day.

At the outset it must be grasped that allusions in masonic literature and throughout this book to the 'Moderns' are allusions to the Premier Grand Lodge of England, the first Grand Lodge in the world, and to its adherents. That Grand Lodge was formed in 1717. The rival Grand Lodge was founded in 1751, and its adherents, believing that they practised a more ancient and therefore purer form of freemasonry, called themselves 'Antients'[1]; at the same time they dubbed those affiliated to the Premier Grand Lodge, formed decades before, the 'Moderns.' These epithets stuck. From the point of view of history they were most unfortunate and most misleading.

In general, there were two main causes of the trouble. One was the apathy and neglect of the Premier Grand Lodge and its apparent inability

[1] As already stated, throughout this book the descriptive title 'Antient' is without exception spelt with a 't' instead of a 'c' to obviate confusion with the ordinary word 'ancient.'

to rule the Craft. The other was the differences in ritual and ceremonial practice that existed or developed in the early part of the century.

As to the first of these, the Premier Grand Lodge was going through a difficult period from the 1730's to the early 1760's. Horace Walpole, himself a mason, wrote in 1743 that the freemasons were in low repute in England. A series of processions of mock-masons had cast ridicule on the Order. Its Grand Masters had taken but little interest in their duties; some of them had even neglected them. Freemasonry had lost its vogue, and even the initiation of Frederick, Prince of Wales, in 1737, had failed to bring it back.

A Grand Master installed in 1739 was only twenty-two years of age. After him came Scottish noblemen who already had been Grand Masters in Scotland, but they added little lustre to the office. Lord Byron (great-uncle of the poet) became Grand Master in 1747, when about twenty-five years old, and attended three meetings of Grand Lodge during his reign of five years, Grand Lodge meeting only nine times during that period. His absence, or that of his deputy, became such a scandal that some Brethren "grew so restive that they summoned by advertisement a meeting of the Craft to elect a new Grand Master," but a Past Grand Steward who attended the meeting persuaded the Brethren to be patient.

It is obvious that there was a bad patch in the history of the Premier Grand Lodge, and it was this patch that made it so easy for the malcontents to form a rival and successful Grand Lodge. Their task was so much the easier because of the weakness and inefficiency of the older organization. In the eleven years from 1742 to 1752 the Premier Grand Lodge had to strike off forty-five lodges in the London district. J. Heron Lepper computes that in the year 1755, of the 271 lodges nominally in existence only 199 were carried forward at the closing-up and alteration of the lodge numbers in 1756; so, apparently, more than a quarter of the private lodges adhering to the Premier Grand Lodge had died, though some of them, for all we know, may have changed over to the 'Antients.'

The second main cause of the trouble was an even more powerful factor. In 1723 and in 1730 two notable irregular prints, so-called *exposés*, had been published. The first of these was *A Mason's Examination*, printed in three issues of *The Flying Post or Postman* in April 1723. The second one has already been alluded to—namely, Prichard's *Masonry Dissected*, a highly successful publication which went through scores of editions in England, Ireland, America, and the Continent during the eighteenth century. These prints were a measure of the considerable interest which the outsider took in freemasonry, and an indication of the public curiosity following the fuller incorporation into the masonic ceremonies of the Hiramic legend.

Irregular 'makings' became common. It is recorded that a tavern displayed a notice "Masons made here for 2s. 6d." That the exposés were probably largely spurious hardly affected the matter, for, using them as manuals, it was possible for a few men to get together and pretend to initiate anyone willing to pay them money. The immediate effects of these exposés may have been over-emphasized, but we must remember that there were numbers of masons all over the country who had never acknowledged the Premier Grand Lodge, which came into existence merely to group together a few London lodges. Who can say how many well-founded lodges of London and the Provinces were never included in the printed lists of 'regular' lodges issued by Grand Lodge from time to time—lodges which resented the interference of any outside body, claimed to be all-sufficient in themselves, and were absolutely sure they were working a system quite as old as, or even older than, that approved by the Premier Grand Lodge?

Freemasonry had spread rapidly to France, and in Ireland and Scotland. Freemasons from these countries were drifting into England and bringing with them ideas which had grown up not on English soil, but which, nevertheless, were dear and precious to those who held them. Grand Lodge was probably very worried, somewhere about 1730, at the number of unaffiliated masons coming apparently from nowhere and claiming admission into their lodges. Every one of these unaffiliated masons was irregular from the official point of view, and to make things difficult or impossible for them the Grand Lodge decided about 1730 to take a very serious step. This was nothing less than a transposition, or inversion, of the modes of recognition in the First and Second Degrees, and was designed to act as a veritable shibboleth in preventing the admission to its lodges of any mason who, for lack of affiliation and attendance at a regular lodge, would be unaware of the change. Gould can be read in one or two places as casting doubt on whether the alteration was in fact made, but it is impossible to read masonic history to-day and refuse to give credence to the indictment.

Grand Lodge made the alteration with the best of intentions, but in doing so was guilty of, at least, a profound error of judgment, and in due course paid a heavy price for its mistake. The alteration was regarded by many of its own members, and by the whole of the masons outside its organization, as a grievous and wholly improper interference with a landmark purporting to date from time immemorial.

It must be understood that this alteration was by no means the only difference between the working of the masons inside and those outside the Grand Lodge. Considerable differences had existed for many years, and once a rival Grand Lodge was established they would naturally be accentuated. What some of these differences were will presently be explained.

For upwards of a century the formation of the rival Grand Lodge was referred to as a schism, and the men who formed it as seceders. 'Schism' is literally a 'splitting,' or 'cleavage'; a 'seceder' is one who formally withdraws from membership of a body. We have plenty of evidence now to prove that the event was not a schism, for while there may have been, and probably were, a number of Brethren who went over to the rival body, for the main part that body came into existence as the result of the determined efforts of Irish and Scottish masons residing in England, helped by English masons who for the most part had never owed allegiance to the first Grand Lodge.

The Foundation of the 'Antient' Grand Lodge

In the 1730's bad feeling was increasing between the Grand Lodges of England and Ireland. The English Grand Lodge is said to have regarded its sister Grand Lodges with an air of condescension, and was inclined to doubt the regularity of private lodges constituted by them. For their part the Grand Lodges of Ireland and Scotland sympathized warmly with the orthodox English masons opposed to the alterations that had been made in the English ritual. This did not make for good feeling between the English and its sister Grand Lodges, and quite trivial things occurred to make the feeling worse. The Irish and Scottish masons in England resented the assumption of superiority on the part of the English Grand Lodge, and undoubtedly lent themselves quite willingly to a proposal to establish a rival Grand Lodge. They had the support of some English masons, but not to an extent that would justify the use of the word 'schism' or 'secession.'

Many lodges were far removed from London, with no means of easy access, and it is doubtful whether such lodges ever made, or were inclined to make, the alterations ordered by Grand Lodge. There is the effect, too, of the military lodges moving from place to place to be borne in mind; such lodges are known to have existed from the year 1732, and whatever their constitution, and whether in later days they held a warrant from one Grand Lodge or the other, the only ritual known in those lodges would exercise a consistent influence towards 'Antient' working.

The regulations made by the Premier Grand Lodge for the better ordering of the Craft would be looked at askance by old-fashioned Brethren, who would resent any action which they regarded rightly or wrongly as autocratic. For example, processions were truly loved by the mason of the early-eighteenth century, but processions were banned by

Grand Lodge in 1747, to the annoyance of the rank and file. (The 'Antients' forebade public processions in 1799 but re-allowed them a few years later.) Such apparently simple matters as the action of Grand Lodge in prescribing minimum initiation fees and discouraging the making and passing of a Candidate on the one occasion were resented, but, whatever part they played, there can be no doubt that the differences—those introduced by Grand Lodge itself and those that had naturally grown up in lodges unaffiliated to any central authority—played a much bigger part.

So we find five lodges independent of any higher control forming themselves into a body and assuming the style of a Grand Lodge of "the old institution." The members did not number more than eighty. Many of them were Irish, and most of them were mechanics or shopkeepers, whereas at that day the average member of the lodges under the older Grand Lodge was of a higher social grade.

According to John Morgan, the first 'Antient' Grand Secretary, their title in 1751 was "The Most Ancient and Honble Society of Free and Accepted Masons." Morgan produced rules and orders, the concluding paragraph of which is worth quoting: "Lastly, this our Regulation shall be Recorded in our Registry, to show posterity how much we desire to revive the Ancient Craft upon true Masonical principles." His very first rule prescribes that Masters and Wardens do meet on the first Wednesday of every month. The 'Antient' Grand Lodge maintained this custom, and at the Union in 1813 it was taken over by the United Grand Lodge, so that to-day we find the meeting-day for the Quarterly Communications of Grand Lodge to be a survival of the 'Antient' procedure of 1751.

There appears to be good evidence that the 'Antient' Grand Lodge was constituted as a separate society on July 17, 1751, inasmuch as its rules and orders were agreed and settled by a conference appointed on that date; but so far it had no Grand Master. In the following May a minute of their Grand Committee records that this gathering "had been long held under the title of The Grand Lodge of Free and Accepted Masons of the Old Institution." In the course of twenty years the Grand Lodge of the 'Antients' was presided over by many influential masons, an early Grand Master being the Earl of Blesington, a former Grand Master of Ireland. In 1771 the third Duke of Atholl came to the chair, and in 1775 the fourth Duke of Atholl, both of whom had been Grand Masters of Scotland. The fourth Duke was succeeded by a former Grand Master of Ireland, the Earl of Antrim. It almost follows that while the Grand Lodges of Ireland and Scotland looked askance at the Premier Grand Lodge they were in close communion with the 'Antients.'

In the second year of the 'Antient' Grand Lodge's existence, the Grand Secretary, John Morgan, resumed his sea-duty, and there was elected in his place "a great perhaps even the greatest character in the Craft history of the eighteenth century"—Laurence Dermott, then thirty-two years of age, a man of remarkable quality and tremendous energy. He was a journeyman painter, born in Ireland in 1720, initiated in January 1740, in Lodge No. 26, in Dublin, of which he was Past Master and had been Secretary. He is believed to have become a Royal Arch mason in his Irish lodge in 1746, and to have come to England about 1747–48. Possibly he may have been a member of a 'Modern' lodge, but in 1752 he joined the 'Antient' lodge No. 9, which he soon left to join No. 10. Gould, who obviously lacked sympathy with the 'Antients,' nevertheless acknowledged that to the "force of character and demonstrative ability of Laurence Dermott must be attributed a success of the schism and the triumph of its principles." Dermott immediately proceeded to produce a set of bylaws for private lodges, and by 1756 had issued the first edition of what were actually the Constitutions of the 'Antient' fraternity. He gave them the extraordinary name of *Ahiman Rezon*, and in the course of a dedication to the Earl of Blesington he said that his object was "to let the young Brethren know how they ought to conduct their Actions, with Uprightness, Integrity, Morality, and Brotherly Love, still keeping the ancient Land-Marks in View."

'Antients' and 'Moderns'

He was thus very early insisting that his Grand Lodge was truly the 'Antient' one, and he was not long in suggesting that the old Grand Lodge represented the 'Moderns.' Gould, who admired but disliked him, shrewdly suggests that Dermott coined the epithets 'Antients' and 'Moderns' because he realized that there is a great deal in having a good 'cry' (a 'slogan' is what we should call it to-day). And

> tho' the titular 'Antients' were the actual 'Moderns,' most of the success which attended the great Schism was due to Dermott's unrivalled audacity . . . both in the choice of phrases, which placed the earlier Grand Lodge in a position of relative inferiority, and in ascribing to his own Grand Lodge a derivation from the Ancient Masons of York.

But we must be careful not to father too much on Laurence Dermott, for we learn from an advertisement in 1726 relating to "Ante-diluvian Masonry" that even in those days a distinction was being drawn between "Ancient Masonry" and "the Moderns." It is likely, therefore, that any freemasons of conservative tendency might have been in the habit of regarding themselves as 'antient' and all those who differed from them as 'modern.' After all, some such phrase as "Antient and Modern" must always have been popular; we are told that when *Hymns Ancient* and Modern was introduced in 1861 the very title secured speedy and lasting popularity in England! It is unfortunate that these particular appellations were ever adopted by masons, for they have led to much confusion. In the later part of the eighteenth century the 'Antient' lodges were commonly called Atholl lodges, from the fact that the Dukes of Atholl so long presided over them as Grand Masters.

The official title of the rival Grand Lodge became in the course of time "The Most Antient and Honourable Fraternity of Free and Accepted Masons (according to the old Constitutions granted by His Royal Highness Prince Edwin at York, Anno Domini Nine Hundred twenty and six . . .)."

"Ahiman Rezon"

Ahiman Rezon went through a great number of editions—at least eight by the time of the Union. Dermott had a smattering of Hebrew (or had the assistance of some one similarly qualified), but only a smattering, and in producing his curious title he did little more than take two Hebrew words and put them together, so forming an enigmatic title which has no true English equivalent. The Geneva or 'Breeches' Bible (1560), in the course of a table of names and their interpretations, gave 'Ahiman' as 'a Brother of the right hand,' and 'Rezon' as 'a Secretaire.' The Rev. Maurice Rosenbaum, a Hebrew scholar who did much fine work in masonic research, translates the name as 'faithful brother Secretary.' A Complete Christian Dictionary (8th edition, 1678) gives 'Ahiman' as 'a prepared Brother, one of the sons of Anak'; and 'Rezon' as 'small, lean, secret, a Secretary or a Prince.' So possibly Dermott, who undoubtedly took his Hebrew from one of the sources named, intended his title to represent some such idea as 'Brother, Secret,' or possibly 'the Brother's Secret Monitor'—very far from a literal translation, but a plausible suggestion of what might have been in Dermott's mind.[1] The title was always a stumbling block to the unlearned mason, and will be found in various forms in old-time minutes, etc. One Lodge Inventory of 1838 referred to it as "A. H. Iman's Reasons."

Just as the Constitutions of the Premier Grand Lodge were originally Anderson's own property, so Ahiman Rezon was Dermott's personal property. He compiled it rather than wrote it, taking whatever he wanted from Anderson and from Irish works by Dr F. Dassigny and others. His book recommends regular lodges as the "only Seminaries where Men (in the most pleasant and clearest Manner) may hear, understand, and learn their Duty to God; and also to their Neighbours." In connexion

[1] For further information see Cecil Adam's "Ahiman Rezon, the Book of Constitutions" (A.Q.C., vol. xlv).

with "A Short Charge to a New Admitted Mason" (the mason is told "not to neglect his own necessary avocations for the sake of masonry"), he gives this footnote, borrowed from a "Charge" to the Initiate printed at least sixteen years earlier:

> Here you are to understand that a Mason ought not to belong to a Number of Lodges at one Time, nor run from Lodge to Lodge; or otherwise, after Masons or Masonry, whereby his Business or Family may be neglected; but yet every Mason is subject to all the Bye-Laws of his Lodge, which he is strictly and constantly to obey;—for the Attendance and Dues of one Lodge, can never prejudice neither him nor his Family.

Reference must be made to Dermott's account of the treatment of William Carroll, an Irishman, who had applied to the Premier Grand Lodge for relief and had been told (in a letter notable in masonic history):

> Your being an Antient Mason, you are not entitled to any of our Charity. The Antient Masons have a Lodge at The Five Bells in the Strand, & their Secretary's name is Dermott. Our Society is neither Arch, Royal Arch or Antient so that you have no Right to partake of our Charity.[1]

This letter demonstrates a point stressed on other pages—namely, that the 'Moderns' had officially no place for the Royal Arch, and but for the affection felt for that degree by the 'Antients' there is at least some doubt whether the degree to-day would be a recognized part of the English system. In connexion with this, we must note that in the frontispiece to Dermott's second edition (1764) are depicted two sets of armorial bearings, in one of which, described as "The Arms of ye most Antient & Honourable Fraternity, of Free and Accepted Masons," we find the Lion, Ox, Man, and Eagle, with the Ark as crest, and the Cherubim as supporters. Companions of the Royal Arch will recognize some of these emblems (see also p. 551).

Points of Difference between 'Antients' and 'Moderns'

We shall fail to understand the controversy and its bearing upon present-day freemasonry unless we examine, however briefly, the differences that distinguished the two bodies. The transposition of the modes of recognition in the First and Second Degrees was an outstanding difference to which reference has already been made, and it was regarded with something akin to horror by a great many masons, whether owning allegiance to the Grand Lodge or not. There were many other differences, some of them probably going back to pre-Grand Lodge days, and

[1] The punctuation, etc., of this letter has been slightly amended.

in attempting to set them out it must be made quite clear that they did not distinguish *all* 'Modern' lodges from *all* 'Antient' lodges at any one time, but that they applied in general, with probably many exceptions, over a large part of the three-quarters of a century ending nominally in 1813. It must also be made clear that the matters comprehended by this question have been much debated and every masonic scholar has his individual opinion on many of them.

The Moderns were charged with having:

(a) *Transposed the modes of recognition in the First and Second Degrees.* 'Antients' regarded this as a complete innovation, an alteration of a landmark, something quite impossible to be countenanced.

(b) *Omitted prayers.* The charge is unproved and quite unlikely to be well founded.

(c) *De-Christianized the ritual, Anderson's "Constitutions" of 1723 being offered as proof.* From catechisms preserved to us in various ways, we learn that the ritual had originally (perhaps only in some lodges) a definitely Christian character. It is thought, too, that the early Royal Arch system included the Christian element, one of the reasons, it is alleged, why the 'Moderns' disliked the Royal Arch. In existence is the alleged fragment of a Craft ritual, apparently of some such date as 1800, which, if genuine, shows the persistence of Christian symbolism in some lodges.

(d) *Ignored and neglected the Saints' Days—that is, with holding their festivals on days that were not the days of St John.* These saints' days were a veritable shibboleth of the eighteenth-century mason of 'Antient' sympathies. The custom of observing these days still persists.

(e) *Omitted in some cases to prepare Candidates in the customary way.* It is not known how much truth there was in the accusation, but 'Antients' regarded the alleged omission as outrageous.

(f) *Abbreviated the ritual, in particular having neglected the so-called lectures, actually catechisms, attached to each degree.* 'Antients' regarded the lectures as essential, and their omission as being nothing less than sacrilege.

(g) *Ceased to recite the Ancient Charges at Initiations.* The Old Charges had lost much of their point, and probably their omission was justified, but the 'Antients' felt that yet another landmark was being thrown over.

(h) *Introduced austerity into the ceremonies, in particular having no place for the sword in the Initiation ceremony, except that the Tyler (and the Inner Tyler, where there was one) wore a sword.* The 'Antients' wore swords in lodge, but for what purpose it is difficult to see. The French masons developed a very colourful ceremony, in which, if we may trust old French engravings, the Initiate suddenly found himself confronted by many sword-points. This undoubtedly was adopted as sound 'Antient' working, and we find it surviving to-day in the old Bristol working and in the Irish working.

(i) *Allowed the esoteric ceremony at the installation of a Master to fall into disuse, although some of their lodges did work such a ceremony at an early date and continued unofficially to do so.* The 'Antients' insisted upon an esoteric ceremony, and would not allow a Brother who had not passed it to be exalted to the Royal Arch Degree, which degree the 'Moderns' would not accept until a late date as any part of freemasonry. The 'Moderns' had still less place for the additional degrees, the so-called higher degrees. On the other hand, the 'Antients' had a liking for the additional degrees, and particularly encouraged the Knight Templar and the Rose Croix.

(j) *Departed from the ancient method of arranging the lodge.* The Three Great Lights probably had different positions in lodges under the two constitutions; the situations of the Wardens, too, were different. The working was not the same in opening and closing the three degrees.

(k) *Ignored the Deacon.* 'Modern' lodges generally had no Deacons until about 1809, their work being done by Stewards; where 'Modern' lodges had Deacons, it was an indication of the 'Antient' influence. The Deacon was well regarded by the 'Antients' and the Irish lodges. The latter had Deacons as early as 1727. It must be said that the 'Moderns' regarded many of the particular differences in (j) and (k) as being the result of innovation by the 'Antients.'

From the above statement we can estimate for ourselves how great is the debt owed by the freemason of to-day to his 'Antient' Brethren.

Sixty Years of Strife and Rivalry

The conflict between the two bodies continued until the Union in 1813. The 'Antients' in 1761 were putting forward their Grand Master as 'Grand Master of Masons.' The 'Moderns,' who had done the same thing years before, revived the idea in 1766 in connexion with their own Grand Master, Lord Blayney, the idea behind the suggestion being that the Premier Grand Lodge should presumably become the supreme masonic authority in the world. Possibly the attempt legally to incorporate Grand Lodge, about to be referred to, was intended in support of the idea.

Between the years 1768 and 1772 a vigorous but unsuccessful attempt was made to incorporate the Premier Grand Lodge by Act of Parliament —that is, to obtain for it a Charter of Incorporation. The failure of the attempt was due largely to the opposition of the 'Antients,' who regarded the proposal as an act of war on themselves. Henry Somerset, Duke of Beaufort, elected Grand Master in 1767, introduced his scheme of incorporation by Royal Charter in the year following, and although at first it met with the approval of Grand Lodge, within a short time it evoked sharp difference of opinion, and during the four succeeding years was the subject of much controversy. A copy of the proposed Charter having been circulated, three lodges memorialized Grand Lodge adversely, while Caledonian Lodge entered a caveat against it in the office of the Attorney-General (for which its Master had publicly to plead pardon, or his lodge would have been erased). Ultimately, the original proposal was dropped, but in February 1772 a Bill was introduced into Parliament for the incorporation of the society, and given a first and second reading. On the motion for the third reading, the Deputy Grand Master, the Hon. Charles Dillon, himself moved that its consideration be postponed *sine die*, which was agreed to. Within five weeks the Duke of Beaufort had retired from the Grand Mastership and had been succeeded by Lord Petre. One hundred and sixty-eight lodges had been reported in favour of incorporation and forty-three against.[1]

The attempt at incorporation, remarks J. Heron Lepper, caused controversy and ill-will that lived on after the scheme itself had gone to the limbo of futilities. "The failure of the scheme gave cause for rejoicing and triumphant jeers in the camp of the 'Antients,' and none of these things helped the progress towards masonic unity." For example, Sarum Lodge, Salisbury, No. 37, withheld payment of dues for nine years and denounced "the late attempt of the Grand Lodge to impose a tax on the brethren at large."

Undoubtedly the 1770's were a period of steadily worsening feeling between the two bodies, although in 1774 it was made possible for members of 'Modern' lodges having 'Antient' sympathies to obtain an authority from the 'Antient' Grand Lodge. But was there any kindly intention behind the permission? A further resolution of the 'Antients'

[1] For fuller account see Ivor Grantham's paper in *A.Q.C.*, vol. xlvi.

ordered all fraternal communication to cease between themselves and lodges working under 'Modern' warrants but having an 'Antient' tendency, to which came the reply in 1777 from the 'Moderns' in the form of a special Communication held to "devise means for discouraging the irregular assemblies of persons calling themselves *antient masons.*" The 'Moderns' forbade its members to countenance 'Antients' in any way, but its censure did not extend to lodges or masons in the Scottish or Irish Constitutions, or to those under the patronage of any Grand Lodge in alliance with the Premier Grand Lodge of England.

The war between the two bodies continued in spite of certain moderating influences on both sides. Feeling was aggravated and embittered, and remained so in many places right up to the coming of the Union in 1813, and, indeed, for a generation after that.

Relations with other Grand Lodges

Anderson in his *Constitutions* of 1738 had referred to foreign lodges under the patronage of "our Grand Master of England." He spoke of the "old Lodge" at York City and the lodges of Scotland, Ireland, France, and Italy "affecting independency." It is doubtful whether his condescension was well received, and equally doubtful whether the Grand Lodge of England regarded the sister Grand Lodges as being equal with itself. Underlying Anderson's words is the implication that *all* lodges owed allegiance to the English Grand Lodge. All the sister lodges, excepting perhaps that of France, were 'Antient' in their practices, and, when in the course of time the 'Antient' Grand Lodge was founded, the Grand Lodges of Ireland and Scotland took an early opportunity, the one in 1762, and the other in 1773, of entering into an alliance with it. From that date, or from some time before that date, the sister lodges no longer regarded the Premier Grand Lodge as the legitimate governing body in England. They were in close communication with the 'Antient' half of the fraternity, and regarded that half as representing English freemasonry. Their ceremony and ritual were closely allied with those of the 'Antients' in England, as we learn from many instances, of which two may be quoted. 'Antient' Brethren on their way to Philadelphia early in the 1750's met some Brethren in Ireland and reported that: "On comparing notes we found to our no small satisfaction, that we agreed as exactly as face answers to face in the glass." The second instance is that of an Entered Apprentice, initiated in a Bristol 'Antient' lodge, being passed to the Degree of a Fellow Craft in Cork Lodge, No. 27.

The way in which the 'Moderns' lost Philadelphia makes a curious story. A lodge containing English, Irish, and Scots, with a Belfast Master, was given a warrant by the Grand Master of Pennsylvania, who, however, immediately withdrew it on learning that the Brethren were 'Antients' and would not change their ritual. The lodge applied to the rival Grand Lodge and were granted a warrant, No. 69, in June 1758. Subsequently, says J. Heron Lepper, "a Provincial Grand Master was appointed to govern the 'Antients' in Philadelphia, and in process of time the Provincial Grand Lodge there developed into the present Grand Lodge of Pennsylvania."

So far as Continental freemasons were concerned, the alterations made by the 'Moderns' led to disputes in many places, and there were arguments or quarrels in the lodges of Berlin, Vienna, Namur—to name just a few of the many where trouble must necessarily have been caused.

'Remakings'

We come now to a remarkable feature of the conflict. This was the custom of 'remaking,' in lodges of one persuasion, Brethren who had been initiated in lodges of the other. The 'Moderns' undoubtedly regarded any mason made in an 'Antient' Lodge as having been initiated in an irregular or clandestine manner, and any of their own members known to have assisted in the ceremony were liable to exclusion. Even a case of association with an 'Antient' mason could bring down severe censure upon the offender.

Here is a typical instance, illustrating the practice which in course of time became quite general. In 1754 a Brother visited the Old King's Arms Lodge, then No. 38 (now No. 28), meeting in Soho, London. He "was found to be a very good Mason, but made in a Clandestine Manner in an Unconstituted Lodge," so he was "that night made in the three degrees and paid what is customary." This cost him £1 11s. The usual visitor's fee was a shilling or so. The 'Moderns' had a custom of requiring visitors to take an oath, on the Volume of the Sacred Law, that they had been regularly 'made' in a lodge constituted by the Grand Master of England.

Remaking was known as early as the 1730's, the 'irregulars' of those days being chiefly members of Irish or other foreign constitutions. Following the rise of the 'Antient' Grand Lodge, remaking became so general as to earn in some quarters its own special name—'translating' as, for example, it was called in the ('Modern') Unity Lodge, No. 183. There was often a regular remission of some part of the customary initiation fee for remaking, lodges varying greatly in the matter. The Moira

Lodge, then No. 92, had apparently a custom in 1758 of fining "an Antient Meason the sum of 2s. before allowing him to join."

Undoubtedly remaking was often a protest against the *regularity* rather than the *validity* of the degrees to which Brethren had been admitted elsewhere.

The story of remaking contains many absurdities. A Brother joining the ('Modern') Lodge of Friendship, Oldham, now No. 277, was 're-made' *four years later*. Take the case of Milbourne West, an Irish and 'Antient' mason, who had been Provincial Grand Master of Quebec, 1761–63, and elected to that office by a Provincial Grand Lodge, which functioned by virtue of a power from the Premier Grand Lodge of England, conveyed to Canada by the famous Thomas Dunckerley. When in 1764 Milbourne West applied to join the Bear Lodge, now Royal Cumberland Lodge, No. 41, at Bath, his high rank availed him nothing; he had to be remade, but no fee was charged.

The reverse process was in full swing, perhaps by way of retaliation. Thus in the Anchor and Hope Lodge, Bolton, then No. 37, three members, the Worshipful Master and two Past Masters, of a 'Modern' lodge were "enter'd" on November 24, 1768; "crafted and raised Master Masons" on December 18; and in a Royal Arch Lodge "made R:L, A-M" on January 29 following.

There was the case of Bro. Joyce who was reinitiated in an 'Antient' lodge in 1784, and a month later joined another 'Modern' lodge. His experience must have been valuable when, many years later, he found himself a member of the Lodges of Promulgation and Reconciliation!

The minute book of Lodge No. 678, Markethill, County Armagh, relates that in July 1801:

> Lodge Met in due form the Mast[r] in the Chair twelve Members presant when M[r] Willi[m] Chapman Coming to visit the Lodge in Conversation it appeared he was and pass[d] him selfe to be a Modern Mason belonging to the Tyrian Lodge No. 379 England and he proving so agreeable he pay[d] the admitance as being no Mason and Received the Diffrent degrees to a Mast Mason.

Both sides continued the practice of remaking right up to the coming of the United Grand Lodge.

The 'Antients' as 'York Masons'

It will have been noted that the 'Antients' assumed or claimed connexion with York masonry, and there is no doubt that accordingly they gained much influence, inasmuch as York was at the time regarded (as it still is by many masons) as the home and origin of the "purest and most ancient of masonic systems." The York Rite and the York Grand Lodge are discussed on a later page, and in this place all that need be noted is a quotation from that fine masonic scholar, W. J. Hughan, who denied that the Old York working, known as the York Rite, is of great antiquity, but admitted that the 'Antient' claim to be really 'York masons' is not easy of confutation, seeing that it depends more on sentiment than fact for its survival. "York," he says, "is the Mecca of English Freemasonry and around it have crystallised some legends and fancies that have proved a source of weakness and difficulty to the Fraternity."

The Traditioners, the Masons in the Mid-way

Returning to an early cause of the trouble between the 'Antients' and 'Moderns'—the transposition of certain First Degree and Second Degree details in the 1720's—it is obvious that many lodges, especially those of London, faithfully but reluctantly in most cases observed the instructions issued to them by the Premier Grand Lodge; but it seems equally certain that others, chiefly those in the country some distance from London and even some in London itself, ignored the alterations. Communication between London and the Provinces was not easy in those days, and, with a poor organization and with no effective headquarters, Grand Lodge had been unable even to inform many of the lodges of the alterations. So, at one and the same time, there were lodges observing the older working; other lodges who abhorred the very idea of the interference; and a third body who went on as before, hardly aware that anything different was required of them. In the course of time, J. Heron Lepper is inclined to believe, it became a custom in lodges to explain to the Initiate, as soon as considerations of secrecy permitted, the differences between the two systems. A group midway between the 'Moderns' and the 'Antients' began to evolve and was ultimately to play a considerable part in bringing together the two conflicting parties.

J. Heron Lepper, who of all the scholars has made the closest study of the matter, regards the middle body as trimmers but calls them 'traditioners,' an unsatisfactory name but difficult to improve upon. He offers the name as an honourable designation for Brethren of the middle group who upheld two great traditions—loyalty to their Grand Lodge (the senior governing body in the world) and loyalty to the ancient forms of freemasonry; matters, as we are still taught, that admit of no innovation. The 'Traditioners' paid quarterages to the Premier Grand Lodge but were not compliant in matters of conscience.

The existence of a 'Traditioner' lodge is indicated in a number of ways, some of which were even then surprising, but with a strong Grand

Lodge in existence would have been quite impossible. Take the Anchor and Hope Lodge, of Bolton, for an illustration of one point. This lodge was founded in 1732 under the auspices of the Premier Grand Lodge, and at the height of the trouble between the two bodies—that is, in 1768 —it remade when necessary its joining members according to the 'Antient' forms! It has been stated that, at one time, a few lodges apparently worked either kind or both kinds of ceremony—in each of the three degrees!

A 'Traditioner' lodge would accept 'Antient' masons as visitors. Where we find a 'Modern' lodge holding a Royal Arch lodge, it is of the 'Traditioner' persuasion, the Royal Arch being the true touchstone by which to distinguish 'Modern' from 'Antient.' When there were Deacons in a 'Modern' lodge, that lodge was 'Traditioner.' That fine scholar, W. J. Songhurst, held that the spread of the additional degrees in the eighteenth century was mainly due to 'Antient' (including 'Traditioner') masons, and J. Heron Lepper says: "In every early British Knight Templar or Chevalier Rose Croix I see a probable scion of Antient Craft Masonry, whatever the allegiance of his Mother Lodge may have been. Does not the very name of the Ancient and Accepted Rite . . . contain a claim concerning its origin?" The 'Traditioner' lodge, then, was nominally 'Modern,' but in things that really mattered, 'Antient.'[1]

Grand Master Lord Blayney

It was in the 1760's, when the conflict was at its bitterest, that the fortunes of the 'Moderns' took a turn for the better. By the weakness of their Grand Masters and of their organization they had suffered severely since the formation of the rival Grand Lodge. They had had a series of Grand Masters who took but little interest in their duties, but in 1764 Cadwallader, the ninth Lord Blayney, became Grand Master at the age of about forty-four. He was a professional soldier, and had been initiated in a military lodge, by which it can be taken for granted that he was actually an 'Antient' mason, although fortune had brought him to the highest office in the Premier Grand Lodge. At a period of the greatest possible difficulty he was able, by the strength of his own personality, to extend the power of his Grand Lodge and of the private lodges under its banner.

He strove to reconcile the two warring bodies, and there is a suggestion, already hinted at, that his ambition was to erect the English Grand Lodge as the supreme masonic authority in the world. He definitely aimed to restore some details of the 'Antient' form of ritual. Evidence of this

[1] For further information see J. Heron Lepper's paper in *A.Q.C.*, vol. lvi.

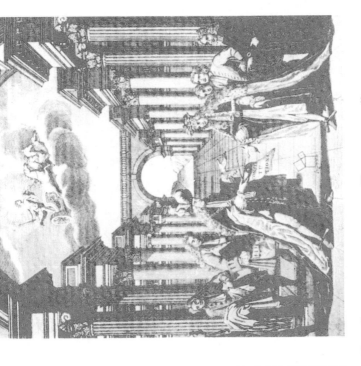

THE

CONSTITUTIONS

OF THE

FREE-MASONS.

CONTAINING THE

History, Charges, Regulations, &c.
of that most Ancient and Right
Worshipful FRATERNITY.

For the Use of the LODGES.

LONDON:

Printed by WILLIAM HUNTER, for JOHN SENEX at the Globe,
and JOHN HOOKE at the Flower-de-luce over-against St. Dunstan's
Church, in Fleet-street.

In the Year of Masonry —— 5723
Anno Domini —— 1723

TITLE-PAGE AND FRONTISPIECE OF "THE CONSTITUTIONS OF THE FREE-MASONS"

These were the first printed constitutions (1723) of any speculative masonic body—namely, the Premier Grand Lodge of England, founded in 1717. On the pavement between the Grand Masters is the proof of Euclid's 47th proposition (see Chapters XI and XXIX).

By courtesy of the United Grand Lodge of England

PLATE III

ANDREW MONTGOMERIE, "GARDER OF YE GRAND LODGE"

From a painting by A. F. V. Meulen, engraved by A. V. Haecken
(1738).

ANTONY SAYER, "GRAND MASTER OF THE MASONS,"
THE FIRST MASTER OF THE PREMIER GRAND LODGE
OF ENGLAND

The original portrait is by Joseph Highmore.

PLATE IV

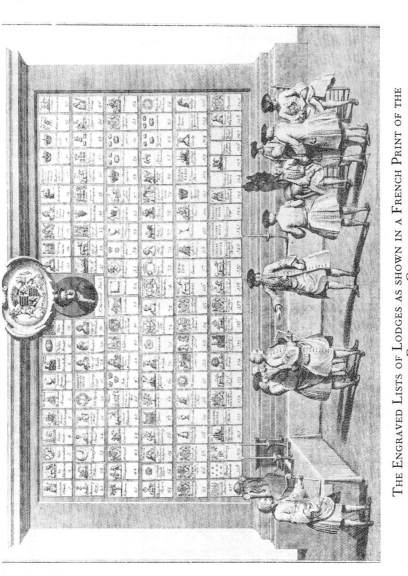

THE ENGRAVED LISTS OF LODGES AS SHOWN IN A FRENCH PRINT OF THE
EIGHTEENTH CENTURY

In the background are some only of the lists which began to be published in the 1720's and which,
from about the end of the decade, determined the seniority and numbering of English Lodges.

By courtesy of the Quatuor Coronati Lodge

PLATE V

SIR CHRISTOPHER WREN

Wren is believed to have been made a freemason in 1691 (see Chapter VII). The original painting, attributed to Sir Godfrey Kneller (1646–1723), was bought in 1788 by the Lodge of Antiquity, No. 2, with which Wren is traditionally associated.

By courtesy of the United Grand Lodge of England

GEORGE WASHINGTON

The first President of the United States of America was initiated into Freemasonry in the Fredericksburg Lodge, No. 4, Virginia, in 1752. Painted (about 1900) by R. G. Hardie, after Gilbert Stuart, a noted American portrait-painter (1755–1828).

By courtesy of the United Grand Lodge of England

PLATE VI

ENGLISH APRONS OF THE LATE EIGHTEENTH CENTURY

These richly ornamented aprons are of a type often hand-painted over a printed design.
That shown in the top illustration belonged to a member of Shakespeare Lodge, No. 516,
Stratford-on-Avon (1793–99), and is now owned by the Shakespeare Lodge, No. 284,
of Warwick.

By courtesy of the Quatuor Coronati Lodge

PLATE VII

The Moira Apron

A distinctive design printed from an engraved plate and believed to have been due originally to the painter Hobday; worn in the Moira Lodge of Honour (now No. 326), Bristol, in the years 1813–15 (see Chapter XXX).
By courtesy of the Quatuor Coronati Lodge

PLATE VIII

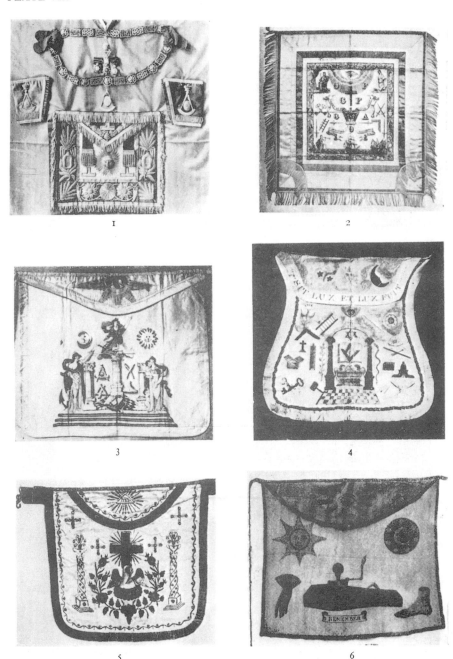

A Varied Group of Aprons

1, Regalia of the Grand Master H.R.H. the Prince of Wales, afterwards King Edward VII. 2, Square Apron with emblems of Craft and other degrees. 3, Old apron with hand-printed and gilt ornament. 4, Old apron with emblems of Craft and other degrees. 5, Apron with emblems of Allied degrees. 6, Crudely painted leather apron, possibly early American.

By courtesy of the United Grand Lodge of England

PLATE IX

Six Royal Arch Aprons

1, Apron consisting of a whole skin. 2, Printed apron by Newman. 3, Early Irish, hand-painted. 4, Early Craft and Royal Arch apron. 5 and 6, Nineteenth-century aprons with ornaments at lower corners and point of flap.

By courtesy of the United Grand Lodge of England

PLATE X

NIGHT

Painted by the great William Hogarth, freemason, and engraved by Charles Spooner.
A scene in a squand alley in which a vehicle may have been caused to break down while
carrying home members from a lodge meeting, although, if the whole intention is
burlesque or satire, the tavern may be identified as the Rummer and Grapes, Channel
Row, Westminster, the meeting-place of Lodge No. 4 from 1717 to 1723. The chief
figures wear aprons and one of them a collar with square, while the other is a tyler
carrying sword and key. On the extreme right is held aloft a mop, as to the probable
purpose of which, at the period when the picture was made (1738), see Chapter XXVI.

By courtesy of the Quatuor Coronati Lodge

PLATE XI

CHIEF OFFICERS' COLLAR BADGES IN SILVER

Top left: Square used in Phoenix Lodge, No. 173, London; probably made in Chester between 1745 and 1779.

Top right, centre, and bottom left: Badges used in a Dublin lodge at the end of the eighteenth century.

Bottom right and centre: Past Masters' badges, that on the right being commonly known as the gallows square.

By courtesy of the United Grand Lodge of England and of the Quatuor Coronati Lodge

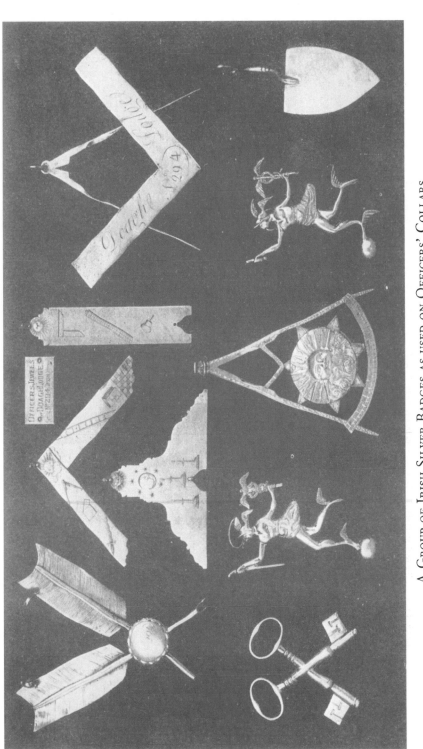

A Group of Irish Silver Badges as used on Officers' Collars
etc., in Doagh Lodge, Ireland

By courtesy of the Quatuor Coronati Lodge

PLATE XIII

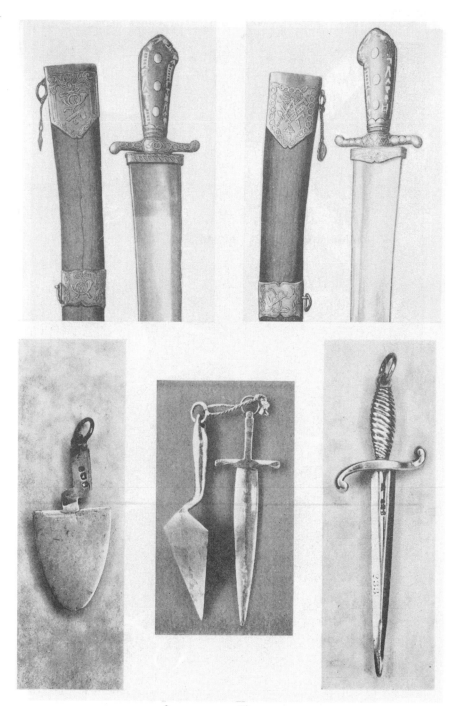

SWORDS AND TROWELS

Top: Masonic sword and sheath with emblems of lead and silver inlaid in black
mountings; from the Armeria (Royal Collection of Arms), Turin, Italy.
Bottom: Silver trowels and swords as collar badges; early nineteenth Century.

By courtesy of the United Grand Lodge of England and of the Quatuor Coronati Lodge

PLATE XIV

THE GRAND MASTER'S CHAIR

This chair has been used by all the Grand Masters of England since it was made in 1791. Its height to the top of coronet is about ten feet. It is carved and gilt and upholstered in royal blue velvet. The arms terminate in lions' heads and claws. The coronet is of the M.W. the Duke of Connaught, K.G., Grand Master.

By courtesy of the United Grand Lodge of England

PLATE XV

A Set of Four Chairs in use by the Lodge of Unanimity and Sincerity
No. 261, Taunton

Top: The Master's and Immediate Past Master's chairs, made in 1807 and 1789
respectively.
Bottom: The Wardens' chairs, made in 1858.

By courtesy of H. Hiram Hallett, Somerset Masters' Lodge

PLATE XVI

CHAIRS, PEDESTAL, AND KNEELING-
STOOLS

These were formerly used, and are still owned,
by Britannic Lodge, No. 33. They are now in
Freemasons' Hall Museum, London. Date,
about 1760. Master's chair, including emblem,
about nine feet high.

*By courtesy of the United Grand Lodge of England
and of Britannic Lodge*

intention can be seen in his visit to the Old Dundee Lodge, Wapping, where he witnessed the Initiation ceremony, and afterwards sent the lodge a message requesting the members to alter their ritual in one particular. He reappointed, as Deputy Grand Master, Colonel John Salter, a military mason and therefore an 'Antient,' who was soon to officiate at the re-constitution of a lodge (Caledonian, now No. 134), which had seceded from the rival body. This lodge changed nothing except its official allegiance, and among its members was a young freemason named William Preston (1742–1818), a printer, later Deputy Grand Secretary, and a fore-most figure in a dispute between the Grand Lodge and Lodge of Anti-quity, and in the curious sequel—namely, the foundation of the "Grand Lodge South of the river Trent" (see Chapter XIII). William Preston is called "the father of masonic history" from his authorship of *Illustrations of Masonry*, first published in 1772, and his memory is preserved in the annual Prestonian Lecture (see p. 557). He is buried in St Paul's Cathedral.

Blayney undoubtedly added greatly to the strength of the 'Moderns.' In his presence, and in that of the Duke of York who had been a mason in Germany, the Duke of Gloucester was made a mason at the Horn Tavern, Westminster—the first initiation of a royal Prince on English soil since the making of Frederick, Prince of Wales, in 1737. In the following year the Duke of Cumberland was made a mason. In 1766 Lord Blayney constituted the Lodge of Operative Masons, now Bedford Lodge, No. 157, which had existed as an operative or non-regular lodge of good repute from as early as 1739 at the least, and the early history of which, if known to us, might shed much light on the formative period of speculative freemasonry. He presided at a Grand Lodge on St John's Day in the Summer of 1766, the first time for many years that Grand Lodge had met on St John's Day, and the return to a practice which meant a great deal to the Brethren of the seventeenth century. In the following year he appointed Thomas Dunckerley as Provincial Grand Master of Hampshire. Of Dunckerley we shall hear presently.

During his Grand Mastership Lord Blayney constituted seventy-four lodges, of which nineteen are alive to-day, all bearing honoured names. Blayney was the first Grand Master of the 'Moderns' to foster the Royal Arch Degree, which until that date had not been regarded as part of the masonic system, although undoubtedly practised unofficially in many 'Modern' lodges. He himself "passed the Arch" (was exalted) during his Grand Mastership. By his Charter of Compact in 1766 he founded the Supreme Grand Royal Arch Chapter of England. J. Heron Lepper believes that Lord Blayney "set the course towards reconciliation," but that the master mind which continued the policy was that of Thomas Dunckerley, still another 'Traditioner,' "a doughty champion of the

'Modern' Grand Lodge," but himself practising the ritual observed by his opponents. Lord Blayney was succeeded in 1767 by the Duke of Beaufort, a younger man, and so much of a 'Traditioner' that Grand Lodge reverted in principle, during his Mastership, to the esoteric Chair Degree as part of the Craft working, although the official restoration did not come until 1809.

Thomas Dunckerley is a great name in eighteenth-century free-masonry. He is believed to have been a natural son of the Prince of Wales, afterwards George II, and, when he was over forty years of age, the then King, George III, grandson to the Prince of Wales just named, gave him a pension and a suite of apartments in Hampton Court Palace, and allowed him to bear the Royal Arms, to which was added the bar sinister. Dunckerley was a man of great personal charm, an educated man who was called to the Bar in 1774, but apparently hardly practised, and was admitted to high social circles. He was made a mason in 1754, held many offices in Craft and Royal Arch masonry, and also in the additional degrees. J. Heron Lepper has this to say of him:

> Experience had taught him that loyalty to the 'Antient' landmarks in ritual was not incompatible with loyalty to that Grand Lodge which had mistakenly attempted to remove them, . . . an error of judgment . . . more than outweighed . . . by the efforts to raise the status of the Craft by en-forcing a stricter discipline on the Private Lodges, decreeing a minimum fee for Initiation, and achieving the erection of a noble hall to be the head-quarters of Freemasonry in England. Dunckerley upheld the undivided authority of his Grand Lodge on English soil. His purposed end was to make his Grand Lodge supreme by wasting his rival to death. His strategy was to allow recruits from the 'Antients' to go on working as they had always worked; and he offered them a better organisation of the Degree of Royal Arch than they had known in their original *Constitution*.

What Dunckerley did for the Royal Arch is briefly told in a later section, The "noble hall" above referred to was the first Freemasons' Hall, dedicated in 1776.

Reconciliation in Sight

There can be no question that by the end of the century many of the differences existing between the ritual and practice of the two parties had in some districts become largely assimilated. It is inevitable that, in spite of all the bad feeling between them, 'Antient' and 'Modern' lodges existing side by side would imperceptibly, almost unconsciously, come in time to adopt the best points of the rival system, thus bringing about some measure, however small, of agreement. In some places the measure of agreement was quite considerable. For example, in the United States, where the conflict had waged quite bitterly, Dr Dalcho, a foremost mason personally acquainted with both systems, said, "The real difference in point of importance was no greater than it would be to dispute whether the glove should be placed first upon the right or on the left," an obvious reference to the transposition already many times referred to. We find a Duke of Atholl, Grand Master of the 'Antients,' using this simile:

> I would beg leave to ask, whether two persons standing in the Guildhall of London, the one facing the statutes of Gog and Magog, and the other with his back turned on them, could, with any degree of propriety, quarrel about their stations; as Gog must be on the right of one, and Magog on the right of the other.

These quotations leave no doubt that the transpositions had been made, but they suggest, too, that there was a tendency, as time went by, to look upon them with a more understanding eye.

Unfortunately, the mutual approach to one another of the rival parties, in Bristol and some other places, cannot be regarded as conveying a truthful impression of the general state of affairs. Assimilation there undoubtedly had been. But between the extreme 'Modern' lodge and the extreme 'Antient' lodge were still very considerable differences, as in due course the Lodge of Reconciliation was to discover.

One of the greatest factors leading to reconciliation was the undoubted preference of the majority of 'Modern' Brethren for the 'Antient' working. The seed sown by Lord Blayney and Thomas Dunckerley many years before had fallen on good ground, and was now about to yield fruit —a hundredfold. No doubt a moderate party, which has left us without known record of their names, had been at work for years trying to effect a compromise between the two sides. F. R. Radice (*A.Q.C.*, vol. lvi) well brings out the point that the bringing together of the two sides was due to the English genius for settling disputes, however violent those disputes may be. According to F. R. Radice, it is true that the original Grand Lodge had done much for the Craft: it had introduced discipline and control, but had adopted strange and revolutionary ways. The opposition, dominated by the great figure of Dermott, asserted the ancient landmarks and elicited widespread sympathy, but the fact remains that with opposing Grand Lodges in existence, disruption was inevitable. Dunckerley, the great figure of the 'Moderns,' threw overboard what could not be defended, and concentrated on what was vital—one ritual and one Grand Lodge. So we find in course of time a group of Brethren discovering the middle road, prepared to cast off the extremists on either side and to appreciate what was moderate in the views of their opponents ultimately we find this middle group effecting a balance between the two parties and imposing a settlement on them, a settlement which was a victory for neither side, but for common sense.

Very significant was a presentation to Prince Edward, later Duke of Kent, on his return from Canada in 1794, with an address signed by the Deputy Grand Masters of the rival Grand Lodges. It includes an expression of the "confident hope that under the conciliating influence of your Royal Highness, the Fraternity in general of Freemasons in His Majesty's dominions will soon be united."

Reconciliation was in sight, but still nineteen years away.

Chapter Thirteen

OTHER ENGLISH GRAND LODGES

(with a Note on 'York Masonry')

THERE have been six Grand Lodges in England, and of them four were in existence at the same time.

(1) There was first of all the Grand Lodge of 1717, the mother of all the Grand Lodges of the world. Its identity survives in the United Grand Lodge of England.

(2) In 1725 an old Lodge in the City of York formed itself into "The Grand Lodge of *ALL* England." Its influence was confined to the counties of York, Cheshire, and Lancashire. From this Grand Lodge came another one, in 1779.

(3) The third Grand Lodge was that of the 'Antients' in 1751, which, joining with the Premier Grand Lodge in 1813, survives to-day as the United Grand Lodge of England.

(4) In 1779, as the result of dissension in the time-immemorial Lodge of Antiquity on the question of an alleged "public procession of masons clothed with the badges of the Order," there was formed in London "The Grand Lodge of England, South of the River Trent," the leading spirit in the formation being William Preston, the masonic historian. It was authorized by the Grand Lodge at York, and after an uneventful existence of ten years, in which it constituted two lodges in London (one of them at the Mitre Tavern, Fleet Street), it quietly passed out.

(5) In 1813 the Premier Grand Lodge joined with the Grand Lodge of the 'Antients' to give us "The United Grand Lodge of Ancient[1] Free and Accepted Masons of England," which the English mason of to-day knows as "The Grand Lodge."

(6) After the union of 1813 there was trouble in many lodges, as a result of which four lodges erased by the United Grand Lodge formed in 1823 "The Grand Lodge of Free and Accepted Masons of England according to the Old Institutions." It was centred in Wigan. From its second year or so, it was in abeyance until 1838; an attempt to revive it in 1844 was hardly successful, as from the following year until 1858 there are no entries in the minutes, the final minute being dated 1913. During its somewhat inglorious existence it constituted six lodges of which, in

[1] Officially 'Antient.'

213

1866, only Lodge Sincerity of Wigan remained. This continued to have an independent existence until, in 1913, it was given a warrant by the United Grand Lodge, and is to-day No. 3677 in the Grand Lodge "List of Lodges." It is believed to have had its origin in the lodge originally numbered 492, which met at the Buck i' th' Vine, Wallgate, Wigan, in 1786, and afterwards at the Ring of Bells and the Royal Oak, Millgate, Wigan.

Three of the above-named Grand Lodges receive, of course, detailed attention on many other pages. They are the Premier Grand Lodge and the Grand Lodge of the 'Antients,' which together constituted the United Grand Lodge. Of the others, it is necessary to refer at length only to the Grand Lodge at York.

"The Grand Lodge of All England, held at York"

It is easy to believe that freemasonry had an early existence in York, and it may be that if we knew the facts we should find good reason for our Brethren of bygone days looking to that city as their Alma Mater. Unfortunately, however, any facts that would help us are quite unknown, and we are obliged to come to the conclusion that, although the early traditions of the Craft in York are supposed, as one writer has put it, to have given the flavour and a colouring to masonry throughout the world, many or most of the ideas relating to the old 'York rite' have small foundation.

Preston, to whom we owe so much that is sound and so much also that is doubtful in masonic history, says that Sir Thomas Sackville was sent to York in Queen Elizabeth's time to disperse the masons, but allowed himself to be initiated, and then stayed as their Grand Master to bless where he had been deputed to curse. It is very doubtful, however, whether Sackville was ever in York.

It is likely that a sixteenth-century lodge at York was purely operative, but the earliest suggestion of what may have been a speculative lodge refers to 1693, this being based upon a manuscript, copied in that year by Mark Kypling, who gave the names of five Brethren under the heading "The names of the Lodg." We do not know the character of the lodge or where it met, neither can the name of anybody mentioned in the manuscript be traced in the roll of freemen of the City of York.

Actually we know nothing definite of a purely speculative lodge at York until the year 1725, when the lodge at York constituted itself a Grand Lodge, with the title "The Grand Lodge of *All* England, held at York," as the reply of a body which regarded itself, rightly or wrongly, as being more ancient than the Grand Lodge formed eight years before in the south. The Grand Lodge at York did not warrant or authorize dependent lodges until 1761, and had no Grand Master later than 1792. It was dormant from 1740 to 1761 and only just managed to exist from that date until 1792, when it finally ceased to be. The Grand Lodge at York constituted perhaps as many as thirteen lodges and one Grand Lodge in the course of its sixty-seven years of not very active life, but a curious fact remains and must be stated (quoting Gould's typical phrasing): in foreign countries, and especially in America, even at the present day, the York rite is perhaps the most favourite expression by which the purest and most ancient of Masonic systems is implied. History fails to offer any explanation as to why this should be so.

A minute book of 1705–6 (now lost) recorded the names of certain presidents, from which it is obvious that the old lodge at York had attracted the attention of persons of distinction for some years prior to the formation of the Premier Grand Lodge. It numbered among its early presidents during that period Sir George Tempest, Bart., the Lord Mayor of York (afterwards Lord Bingley), Sir William Robinson, Bart., and Sir Walter Hawksworth, Bart. Whether the lodge was truly a speculative lodge or an operative lodge in course of translation cannot now be known, but the idea of 'president' suggests Scottish influence, and the second conjecture seems the more likely.

The earliest of the lodges at work in York to-day is the York Lodge No. 236, constituted in 1777 and originally meeting at Lockwood's Coffee House, in the Micklegate.

The 'Antients' and True York Masonry

A claim has frequently been made that the 'Antients' of the eighteenth century were the true York masons, and that they handed down to posterity an original rite which had its source at York. What are the facts? Laurence Dermott in *Ahiman Reẓon*, the *Constitutions* of the 'Antients,' says that the 'Antient' masons were called York Masons "because the first grand lodge in England was congregated at York A.D. 926 by Prince Edwin, who at the same time purchased a free charter from King Athelstan, for the use of the fraternity." But Dermott was repeating a myth, and doing so as an astute move in the 'Moderns' versus 'Antients' game. Well aware of the halo surrounding York masonry, he flagrantly borrowed an appellation which he shrewdly believed would render indelible the stamp of antiquity which he had already skilfully affixed to the 'Antients' system—a stamp whose genuineness we see no reason to question seriously, but which has not gained added authenticity by association with the white rose of York.

The Term 'York Masonry'

A valuable summing up of the York claim is to be found in a paper by Lionel Vibert, who agrees that little or nothing is known of any Craft Guild of masons in York. He tells us that the operative masons at York Minster in 1352 were agreeing with the Dean and Chapter to maintain their ancient usages, rules were made prescribing the hours of work and when the masons could break off for rest and refreshment, and that those rules mention that the masons are to be called from refreshment to labour by a knock on the door to be given by one of the Masters.

In the transition period between the decay of Gothic architecture and the revival that followed the formation of Grand Lodges, Yorkshire, perhaps more than any other locality outside London, preserved in scattered communities, remaining in touch with one another, the old traditions and usages of the Craft, until the time came when they were to be handed on to those who developed from them our freemasonry as it is to-day.

That is Lionel Vibert's conclusion. "If the phrase 'York Masonry' be understood to imply," he thinks,

not that the users of it belonged to York but merely that in common with the Brethren of that city they adhered to the ancient customs of the Order and valued its old traditions, no harm will be taken. We can still talk of "York Masonry" in that sense; we can recognise that York, in the Craft, still implies a high standard, a reverence for our time-immemorial customs, and the preservation of all that is best in freemasonry to-day.

Chapter Fourteen

THE UNITED GRAND LODGE, 1813
AND ITS EFFECT ON PRESENT-DAY CRAFT RITUAL

THE account of the quarrel between the two masonic bodies in the second half of the eighteenth century will have prepared the reader for the coming of the union. The story, to be told briefly here, is worth telling not only because of its first-class importance in the history of world-wide English freemasonry, but because of its considerable effect upon present-day ritual, firstly of the Craft and indirectly of the Royal Arch. The behind-the-scenes events leading up to the Union are not known, but the lines of the official story are clear.[1]

Towards the end of the period of strife between the 'Moderns' and 'Antients' a spirit of toleration began to manifest itself; indeed, it appears that, in a few districts, the forms of the 'Moderns' had so approximated themselves to those of the 'Antients' that there was not much difference between them, and a few lodges even took warrants from both of the opposing Grand Lodges. There was, however, much bitter feeling in many places. On both sides the moderate men realized that reconciliation and union were essential to the Fraternity, and were doing their best to bring them about both in England and its immediate neighbours, and in many countries abroad, for the quarrel had at an early date spread to every English-speaking country of the world, and the desire to end it was, late in the eighteenth century, now universally to be found in the hearts of good men and true.

Edward, Duke of Kent, on his departure from Canada for England in 1794, received a joint petition from both bodies, expressing the confident hope that the Fraternity would soon be united. That was nineteen years before union came, but when it did come the Duke of Kent and his royal brother, Augustus Frederick, Duke of Sussex, had played no inconsiderable part in bringing it about, although the greatest credit of all goes to that outstanding freemason, the Earl of Moira (afterwards first Marquis of Hastings, K.G.), Acting Grand Master 1790–1813, whose work behind

---

[1] For fuller details of the events leading to the Union see Gilbert W. Daynes' *The Birth and Growth of the Grand Lodge of England, 1771–1926*, and the papers in *A.Q.C.*, vols. xvi, xxiii, and lvi, and in *Transactions of the Merseyside Association for Masonic Research*, vols. i and ix.

the scenes, and whose influence on the royal personages mentioned, was probably the greatest of all factors in achieving peace. (In January 1814 the 'Moderns' presented him with a jewel valued at £1500, bearing an affectionate inscription in token of their admiration and gratitude.) Many fine masons must have worked to bring about the union, but the limelight falls upon the three we have named.

It must be understood that at the time of the union the 'Antient' masons in England and Ireland together greatly exceeded in number the 'Moderns' in England, while in the United States of America and Canada there were far more 'Antients' than 'Moderns.' By 1813 the 'Moderns' had enrolled 1085 lodges in England and overseas, had issued 641 warrants, and had 387 lodges remaining on the list. The 'Antients' had enrolled 521, issued 359 warrants, and had 260 lodges still on their list. Eight years before, when the numbers were only very slightly different, Ireland is said to have had 815 lodges, the Premier Grand Lodge of England 355, Scotland 284, and the 'Antients' Grand Lodge of England 258. Throughout England as a whole the 'Moderns' had three lodges for every two of the 'Antients,' but in London the difference was small enough to enable the 'Antients' to negotiate on level terms.

In 1797 the 'Antients' attempted, but without success, to appoint a committee to meet a similar committee that might be appointed by the 'Moderns.' The time was not yet ripe enough, and the chances of peace seemed to recede still farther when, in 1803, the 'Moderns' expelled Bro. Edwards Harper, who although a member of a 'Modern' lodge was an influential officer of the 'Antients.' (The resolution of expulsion was rescinded in 1810.) The turning-point came in April 1809, by which time most of the leading spirits of the 'Moderns' had become convinced that union was essential, and that their own body must take the first official step towards it. That step was nothing less than the passing of a resolution "that it is not necessary any longer to continue those measures which were resorted to, in or about the year 1739, respecting irregular Masons, and do therefore enjoin the several Lodges to revert to the Ancient Land Marks of the Society." The wording of this resolution leaves but little doubt that the alterations of which the 'Moderns' had been accused had actually been made by them, but the date 1739 is doubtful, and appears to be a mistake for an earlier one.

In the following October the 'Moderns' constituted the Lodge of Promulgation, a special lodge charged with a special duty, which will be mentioned shortly. The reply of the 'Antients' came in March 1811 in the form of a resolution "that a Masonic Union on principles equal and honourable to both Grand Lodges, and preserving inviolate the Land Marks of the Ancient Crafts, would, in the opinion of this Grand Lodge, be expedient and advantageous to both." This resolution was officially greeted by the 'Moderns' "with unfeigned cordiality."

The Lodge of Promulgation

The Lodge of Promulgation, a special lodge, was in existence from October 1809 until February 1811, and had as its special duty the task of promulgating the ancient landmarks and instructing masons of the 'Moderns' body in the alterations found necessary. (Later, its members constituted the committee that negotiated with the 'Antients.') The committee rehearsed many revised forms and ceremonies, rehearsals taking place before the Grand Master and before the Masters of many London lodges. There seems a general consensus of opinion that this committee very largely restored the 'Antient' forms and ceremonies, and in so doing considerably revised the first three degrees, either revised or remodelled the installation ceremony, and found a place in their lodge working for the Deacons, who hitherto had officially been known only in the 'Antient' lodges. Naturally the revisions affected the ceremonies of 'Modern' lodges only, but were of critical interest to the 'Antients,' who could not have considered the possibility of union until the 'Modern' ritual had been somewhat adjusted to their own. Thus, clearly, the 'Moderns' brought themselves into line with the 'Antient' practice as an essential prelude to union. They discontinued any innovations or changes introduced some seventy or eighty years before, and wholeheartedly prepared the way for a hopeful exchange of ideas with the 'Antients,' in which discussion any minor differences remaining between the workings of the two bodies would have every chance of being adjusted.

A most important resolution passed by the Lodge of Promulgation declared that "the ceremony of Installation of Masters of Lodges is one of the two Landmarks of the Craft and ought to be observed." (Let it be assumed that in this resolution the word "two" is almost certainly a copyist's error for 'true.') Without such an understanding union would have been unlikely. The 'Moderns' adopted the installation ceremony as from November 1810, at which date the phrase "The Board of Installed Masters" is believed to have taken its rise.

Examination of the minutes of the Lodge of Promulgation reveals an excellent story, but space permits only one or two bits of it here. On one occasion the Lodge had three separate Masters in one evening, this being made possible by the temporary resignation of the Master of the Lodge so that other Brethren might be installed "in due form agreeable to the ancient Constitution." It was resolved on another occasion that a member or visitor shall be admitted into the lodge "by a proof of his having ascertained the Degree in which the Lodge is opened from an inspection of the three great lights at the entrance." In some American lodges there is still a set of miniature lights in the outer room, these being changed as the lodge within passes from one degree to another; late Brethren see at a glance, on arrival, the degree which the lodge is working.

"Masonic Professor"

In the course of the report ultimately made by the Lodge of Promulgation to the Grand Master a suggestion was made for "the institution of the Office or Degree of a Masonic Professor of the Art and Mystery of Speculative Freemasonry, to be conferred by Diploma on some skilled Craftsman of distinguished requirements and general fitness. . . ." The report recommended that the Professor should select and instruct a number of assistants, after he had constructed

> a syllabus, according to the precise Forms now sanctioned . . . as a remembrance and an Aid, essentially necessary to all Lodge Officers of every class, and as a Book of reference that is indispensable on almost all occasions. . . . But above all things he should be required to prepare for preservation a Pandect [*compendium*] of the Science of Speculative Freemasonry, comprising a clear and comprehensive digest of everything relating to the Art, save and except those particulars which are forbidden to be committed to writing . . . that in cases of future occasion to ascertain points concerning which doubts, uncertainty, or differences of opinion may exist, a reference to this duly Sanctioned authority may conclusively decide the question and effectually govern the practice ever after. This Pandect should be written in Masonic cipher.

The suggestion unfortunately came to nothing, but it will never be too late for it to take effect.

The Articles of Union

The Prince of Wales, afterwards George IV, was Grand Master of the 'Moderns' from 1790 to 1813. In May of the latter year he was succeeded by his brother, Augustus Frederick, Duke of Sussex. Of the 'Antients' the fourth Duke of Atholl had been Grand Master from 1791; he too resigned in 1813, in his case in favour of Edward, Duke of Kent, the result being that two royal brothers now presided over the respective Grand Lodges. Matters had been eased by the Duke of Sussex appointing as his Deputy Grand Master the Duke of Kent, whose election to the Grand Mastership of the 'Antients' shortly followed.

Twenty-one articles of union were drawn up and signed in November

1813 by the two Grand Masters and other officers of both sides, and were ratified by the respective Grand Lodges a few days later. Among the many things recited by them was that there should be a full, perfect, and perpetual union of and between the two Fraternities, so that in all time hereafter they shall form and constitute one brotherhood. The articles declared that pure ancient masonry consisted of three degrees including the Holy Royal Arch; they agreed that the two first lodges under each Grand Lodge should draw a lot for priority, the loser to rank as No. 2, and all the other lodges to fall in alternately from the two lists. The articles decided that there should be a masonic festival, annually, on the Anniversary of the Feast of St John the Baptist, or of St George, or such other day as the Grand Master should appoint. They settled the constitution of a special lodge to be entitled the Lodge of Reconciliation, to consist of Master Masons or Past Masters from each body. (It was actually at work by the time the articles were ratified.) This lodge has played a decisive part in the fashioning of the Craft ritual as we know it to-day.

There has been much argument over the meaning of some of the articles. They are said to be slipshod. The chief difficulty in understanding them is the obvious one—that words written many generations ago in accordance with considerations well understood at the time have now to be interpreted by people ignorant of most circumstances which then applied.

One of the articles stated that brotherly application be made to the Grand Lodges of Scotland and Ireland to delegate two or more of their members to be present at the Grand Assembly at which the Union was to take place, and that all those present should engage to abide by the true forms and obligations, "particularly in matters which can neither be described nor written," in the presence of the Scottish and Irish delegates "that it may be declared, recognised and known, that they all are bound by the same solemn pledge and work under the same law." But unfortunately the shortness of the notice did not allow of these delegations being sent.

The Two Grand Lodges unite

The actual union took place at Freemasons' Hall on St John's Day December 27, 1813. The seating of members of the two bodies was so arranged that they were completely intermixed. A Grand Lodge of the 'Moderns' was opened in an adjoining room and a Grand Lodge of the 'Antients' in another room. Then the processions entered the hall, and the two Grand Masters took their place, one each side of the throne. The

Act of Union was read and ratified. Then came the proclamation from the Grand Chaplain:

> Be it known to all Men, That the Act of Union between the two Grand Lodges of Free and Accepted Masons of England, is solemnly signed, sealed, ratified, and confirmed, and the two Fraternities are one, to be from henceforth known and acknowledged by the style and title of THE UNITED GRAND LODGE OF ANCIENT FREEMASONS OF ENGLAND; and may the Great Architect of the Universe make their Union eternal!

The Act of Union itself was put inside the Ark of the Masonic Covenant in front of the throne. The members of the Lodge of Reconciliation, accompanied by a number of distinguished foreign Brethren, withdrew to an adjoining apartment, and all were made aware of the result of the previous conferences. On their return the Most Worshipful his Excellency Count De Lagardie, Grand Master of the First Lodge of Freemasons in the North, announced to the assembly that the "forms settled and agreed on by Lodge of Reconciliation were pure and correct," following which these forms were recognized as "the forms to be alone observed and practised in the United Grand Lodge,[1] and all the Lodges dependant thereon, until time shall be no more."

Everything was now ready for the constitution of one United Grand Lodge. The Duke of Sussex was elected Grand Master, to which office he was proposed by his brother the Duke of Kent, Grand Master of the 'Antients,' and Grand Officers were appointed. Grand Lodge having been called to refreshment, the Cup of Brotherly Love was presented to the Grand Master, who drank to "Peace, Good Will, and Brotherly Love, all over the world." Grand Lodge was recalled to labour and closed, the Brethren then dining at the Crown and Anchor Tavern, with the Grand Master in the chair.

Henceforward there would be no 'Atholl,' or 'Antient,' masons, no 'Modern' masons; there would just be freemasons owning allegiance to one ancient Fraternity under a United Grand Lodge. But, human nature being as it is, it was not until the generation of that day had been succeeded by its sons that the last bitterness of the old quarrel disappeared.

The Grand Masters of Masons in England, Ireland, and Scotland, respectively, together with many of their Grand Officers, constituted the membership of an International Conference held in London in 1814, at which the sister Grand Lodges assured themselves that the new Grand

---

[1] The United Grand Lodge has been inconsistent in printing its "style and title," as were also the 'Moderns' and 'Antients' Grand Lodges from which it came. See a lengthy note in *A.Q.C.*, vol. lxiv, by Ivor Grantham, the librarian at Freemasons Hall, London, since 1953.

Lodge conformed in matters of ritual, and were satisfied that there was a basis for admitting it "to the full fraternal reciprocity of Grand Lodges" and that the three Grand Lodges were perfectly in unison "on matters that can neither be written nor described."

Chance gave the 'Antients' the honour of making their Grand Master's lodge, founded in 1759, No. 1 on the new combined list. Consequently the Lodge of Antiquity, first on the 'Moderns' list, became No. 2, Lodge of Fidelity ('Antients') became No. 3, and the next 'Modern' lodge, the Royal Somerset House and Inverness, became No. 4, and so on, alternately. The youngest 'Antients' lodge surviving in the present-day list is the Union Lodge, No. 247, of Georgetown, Demerara, and similarly the youngest 'Modern' lodge is the Lodge of Unanimity, No. 339, of Penrith, both of them founded in 1813 and most aptly named.

It is obvious, then, that pre-1814 lodges bear numbers not always in close relation to their relative ages, among the reasons being the disproportion of 'Modern' lodges, and the arrangement by which, when certain numbers were vacant on, say, the 'Moderns' roll but were filled in on the 'Antients' roll, lodges of the 'Antients' were allotted numbers in sequence and vice versa. Lane's *Masonic Records* provides many facts relating to the numbering of the early lodges. This book was produced at an enormous cost of energy and time by John Lane in 1886, a second and more complete edition, also Lane's work, being published in 1895 by the Grand Lodge of England, to whom the author conveyed the copyright.

The Lodge of Reconciliation and the Question of an Authorized Ritual

The Lodge of Reconciliation, brought into existence by the Articles of Union, had as its members the two Grand Secretaries and nine Brethren from each body, but in the following year six had ceased to be members, and ten other Brethren were appointed. It arranged the details of the assembly at which the union was ratified, and was especially entrusted to "promulgate and enjoin the pure and unsullied system, that perfect reconciliation, unity of obligation, law, working, language and dress, may be happily restored to the English Craft." It remained in existence until 1816, and duly carried on the work which had been begun by the Lodge of Promulgation; but now, it will be understood, it was agreeing and rehearsing a set of ceremonies for the acceptance of a united body, whereas the earlier lodge had been working for the 'Moderns' only. It revised all the degrees and ceremonies in a spirit of reconciliation, and carried out a vast amount of instructional work. It decided, for example, that lodges should send a Master and Warden to attend a meeting of the Lodge of

Reconciliation, so as to learn the agreed ritual and instruct their lodge on their return. Further, the members of the Lodge of Reconciliation visited many lodges and gave instruction.

Many country lodges took their own time to bring their working into conformity, but there was nevertheless a genuine desire throughout the country lodges that they should acquaint themselves with the new forms.

How far the Lodge of Reconciliation went in settling the differences between the two workings; whether, for the greater part, it came down heavily in favour of the 'Antient' working, as has been generally assumed; and to what extent, if any, as has also been suggested, it fashioned new versions as a compromise to meet cases of especial difficulty—on all these points little or nothing is known, although some authors manage to create the impression that they are aware of all the facts. It must always be remembered that the Lodge of Reconciliation forbade its members, or anyone present, to make a note of its proceedings, and dealt promptly with any offender. There had always been objection to reducing the ceremonies to writing or print, and we find it still strong in the early decades of the nineteenth century. Furthermore, it is not in the least likely that any member of the Lodge of Reconciliation could have come away from its final meeting with a word-perfect recollection of the agreed rituals. H. Hiram Hallett points out that its Master presided over nine only of the recorded twenty rehearsals, that members were lax in their attendance, that there were intervals of many weeks between rehearsals, that detail changes were made from time to time, and that there was an interval of more than a year preceding the final rehearsal.

This must be borne in mind when any claim is made that any particular working of the masonic ceremonies is a faithful reproduction of the ceremonies approved by the Lodge of Reconciliation. It is quite inevitable that the Brethren would go from that final rehearsal back into their various lodges, where they would teach the new forms, and every one of them would have a *slightly* different idea as to the working and wording of some of the details. This readily explains how it was that, in 1819, certain Brethren brought complaints before the Board of General Purposes that lectures were being worked contrary to the stipulations of the Act of Union. The Board in its wisdom decided that the charges had not been made out, the Grand Master shortly afterwards stating that: "It was his opinion that so long as the Master of any Lodge observed exactly the Land Marks of the Craft he was at liberty to give the Lectures in the language best suited to the character of the Lodge over which he presided. . . ." That opinion, not of course to be interpreted too literally, holds good to-day.

The ritual agreed on by Grand Lodge when the Lodge of Reconciliation completed its work was not ordered to be universally adopted, but with regard to the Obligations in the First and Second Degrees and with regard, also, to the opening and closing of lodge, the resolutions were much more definite. With regard to the Obligations, it was "Resolved and Ordered that the same be recognised and taken in all time to come, as the only pure and genuine Obligations of those Degrees, and which all Lodges dependent on Grand Lodge shall practise." The ceremonies of opening and closing, as agreed by the Lodge of Reconciliation, were ordered to be used and practised. For the rest, the ceremonies were "approved and confirmed," but again let it be borne in mind that no written note, if made, of any of these ceremonies has come down to us.

Brethren are fond of repeating the statement that there is no authorized ritual. But is not this rather a technicality, something of a legal fiction, a convenient formula? Obviously it is true that, with certain small exceptions, no written or printed ritual has been authorized by the United Grand Lodge, but is it not equally true to say that Grand Lodge would soon assert itself, as it has done in the past, if the essentials of the ritual were departed from?

A simple view, and probably the correct one, is that the ritual approved by Grand Lodge in 1816 is actually an authorized ritual for the use of English lodges, any variations practised in various lodges being non-essential and limited to matters of detail. It will be objected that the usefulness of this statement is greatly discounted by the absence of any written record. There is in English lodges one essential ritual, fully approved and recognized by regular usage extending back to the early years of the nineteenth century, handed down unaltered from generation to generation, but subject to scores of trivial variations.

Certain sister Grand Lodges authorize and issue the ritual to be followed in their lodges. Under the Scottish Grand Lodge the position, it is suggested, is the same as under the English Grand Lodge, but the Irish Grand Lodge has what is known as the Grand Lodge of Instruction, consisting of its Grand Master and his Deputy, the Grand Wardens, Grand Treasurer, the Grand Registrar, the Grand Secretary, together with a number of skilled Past Masters. Its decisions on all questions of the ritual or ceremonies of ancient Craft masonry, when approved by the Grand Lodge, are binding on every lodge and every member of the Craft under the Irish jurisdiction. It has power to appoint committees to instruct any lodge in the proper working of any of the ceremonies "and such conjoint instruction shall be received . . . as the working authorised and deemed correct by the Grand Lodge of Ireland." Its Secretary ranks as a Grand Officer, and its members have the privilege of wearing on the left breast a quatrefoil jewel, returnable to the Grand Secretary on membership ceasing.

In the Supreme Grand Chapter of New South Wales, a committee on ritual has power to decide all questions of ritual practice, and the correctness of regalia and furniture of a chapter. Certain of the American Grand Lodges closely supervise the ritual practised in the lodges under their jurisdiction; one of them used to issue a copy of the Craft ritual in cipher to each lodge Master, who duly passed it on to his successor. American chapters work to an approved ritual issued to them in cipher.

Variations in the English Ritual

The variations in masonic ritual are a never-ending subject of discussion among Brethren, some few of whom occasionally may be tempted to regard their doxy as orthodoxy and the other man's doxy as heterodoxy. If one thing above all others is clear, it is that the Lodge of Reconciliation agreed on certain essentials, its compelling motive being nothing more than the necessity of adjusting differences existing between the 'Moderns' and the 'Antients,' but it did not lay down a cast-iron ritual, word by word. The members and visiting Brethren went from that lodge all over the country and taught as they remembered. There is reason to believe that much 'give and take' went on unofficially, and that the ceremonies, while retaining every essential, deviated considerably in detail during the next ten years. Consequently, it is impossible to believe that any one system of ritual derived line by line, word by word, directly, and without alteration, from the Lodge of Reconciliation. That is the conclusion arrived at by various Brethren who at different times have studied the matter. Of the many variations met in the workings of the different lodges in matters of unimportant detail it is impossible to say that some, but not others, have the authority of time-immemorial usage.

The variations in themselves have a value and provide special interest. "I should be very grieved," says one writer, "if at any time my own lodge ceased to invest its new initiate with the jewel of an Entered Apprentice, or if a certain portion of the inner working of the Installation ceremony peculiar to this Province, were to lapse." Says another:

It is unfortunate that many ancient usages in the Craft have become gradually discontinued in some of our lodges and are now practically forgotten. The Order loses with these old customs and methods some of its character. The movement to spread the use of one particular form of working makes it difficult for some of the old lodges to maintain practices which have been handed down from time immemorial. Whatever the value of uniformity may be in some phases of life, it does tend to a loss of things of interest and romance.

Various Workings

Stability. High in the estimation of the Craft are two workings—namely, Stability and Emulation. The Stability Lodge of Instruction (sanctioned by the Lodge of Stability, now No. 217, formerly an 'Antient' lodge) had among its seventeen founders sixteen Brethren of the 'Antient' body, and it was founded in 1817, a year after the Lodge of Reconciliation had finished its work. Three members of that lodge were among its founders, and are claimed to have taught the forms and ceremonies rehearsed in it. In all, eight members of the Lodge of Reconciliation joined the Stability Lodge of Instruction at various times. The detailed differences between its working and that of the Lodge of Emulation are many, but can scarcely be referred to here.

Emulation. The Emulation Lodge of Improvement was founded six years later than Stability—that is, in 1823—under the sanction of a London lodge, an old 'Antient' lodge, now the Royal York Lodge of Perseverance, No. 7; but in 1830 it passed to the sanction of the Lodge of Unions, No. 256, formerly a 'Modern' lodge, under which it still acts. Of the twenty-one founders, ten were of the 'Antient' body and eleven of the 'Moderns.' Unfortunately its early records are lost, but the lodge has had the advantage of having its history written by the late Bro. Henry Sadler. Originally this Lodge of Improvement was intended for Master Masons and for working the lectures only, but five years or more after 1825, when Peter Gilkes became its leading spirit, it began to teach the three degrees. Gilkes, who was born about 1765 and died in 1833, was a 'Modern' who had been initiated as far back as 1786, and he stands out in the history of freemasonry as a teacher of the first order. The lodge bases its claims for pre-eminence on its association with Gilkes, who, critics remind us, was not a member of the Lodge of Promulgation or the Lodge of Reconciliation, but was a visitor to the latter about ten times. Peter Gilkes as an instructor would not allow the slightest deviation from set forms, and to-day Emulation working is noted for its strict adherance to precise verbal detail, a point again subject to the criticism that it was wellnigh impossible to bring away from the Lodge of Reconciliation an infallible recollection of every line of the ceremonies. For this reason, and for the further one that there was a gap of some years between the approval of the Craft degree ritual and Emulation's starting to teach it, there may be some doubt about the claim made by Bro. Sadler, the historian of the lodge, that the Emulation standard is "fixed, unaltering and unalterable," but exactly the same criticism applies to any other standard.

Printed Rituals

One minute of the Lodge of Reconciliation tells its own story: "Bro —— having offended . . . in printing certain . . . tending to convey information on the subject of Masonic instruction, should for this offence be reprimanded. . . . The Master did express accordingly the high sense of disapprobation which the Lodge felt," and he proceeded to collect any available copies and place them in the custody of the Lodge of Reconciliation. In spite of this experience, however, manuscript and printed rituals began to appear soon after the Union, but in general were frowned on by the lodges. We have already made clear the position of the Grand Lodge of England on the question of the authorized ritual, and it naturally follows that there is no authorized printed ritual. No rule of Grand Lodge refers to the subject.

After an irregular ritual issued in 1826, or slightly later, probably the earliest regular one was *The Whole of the Lodge Ceremonies and Lectures in Craft Masonry: as taught by the late P. Gilkes, together with the Ceremony of Installation,* published about 1835, followed in 1838 by George Claret's *A Series of Masonic Illustrations, comprising all those taught by the late Bro. P. Gilkes with many others.* It follows, then, that the earliest printed rituals were Emulation.

The Text Book of Freemasonry (published by Reeves and Turner, London, 1870), contained the three Craft degrees, the Ceremony of Installation, the three Lectures, and—most surprisingly—the Ceremony of Exaltation to the Royal Arch. In the preface of the first edition the compiler expressed surprise that no authentic ritual had hitherto been published.

In 1871 "A. Lewis" published *The Perfect Ceremonies of Craft Masonry from Standard Authority, and as taught in the Unions Emulation Lodge of Improvement for Master Masons.* This ritual has gone through a great number of editions, and was the subject of an important law case which reached the Appeal Court in 1935, the Court deciding that *The Perfect Ceremonies* in its 1896 edition was a "new work for purpose of copyright," but that any copyright in it had not passed to the publisher, and that no edition between 1896 and the date of action had contained alterations sufficiently substantial to constitute it a new work for purposes of copyright.

The "West End" ritual was first published about 1882, but represents a working considerably older. It appears to have had its rise in some one or more London lodges of instruction.

The "Oxford," which probably came into general use in the Province of Oxford about 1870, is thought to be more free from grammatical errors than many others. It is associated with the name of R. G. Spiers, of the Alfred Lodge, No. 340, Oxford, but is not believed to represent the local working of the Oxford Province, but rather to reproduce the substance of *The Whole of the Lodge Ceremonies,* etc., already mentioned.

Of comparatively late revision is the *Logic* which represents an old working modernized, a new and different interpretation being given to instructions and phrases that have been the subject of difficulty in earlier rituals.

There are many other printed rituals, most of them being derived from the Stability working. *The Standard Ceremonies of the Stability Lodge* was printed about 1902.

Manuscripts are in existence of provincial and other workings that still retain many time-honoured features.

BOOK FOUR

The Craft Degrees and Other Matters

Chapter Fifteen

HOW THE MASONIC DEGREES CAME TO US

FEW things in masonic history are more perplexing than the question of how the degrees came into existence and of what they consisted and how many there were of them in the very early seventeen-hundreds. It is accepted that two degrees were worked in 1723 and almost certainly much earlier, but how the two *became* three is a matter that has been argued to and fro for the past century. Confusing the issue is the fact that the Edinburgh Register House MS. of 1696 and the Sloane MS. of 1659 both refer to two degrees; the Trinity College, Dublin, MS. of 1711 and the Graham MS. of 1726 refer to *three* degrees, and the last-named undoubtedly gives an inkling that a three-degree system may have gone back some years. What is the explanation?

At a time when lodges were few in number and the country lodges were far apart, with each lodge a separate entity and owning—so far as we can see—not the slightest allegiance to any other body, it is obvious that each did more or less as it liked. Some lodges, both inside and outside the 1717 Grand Lodge organization, might not have discovered—certainly did not adopt—the Third Degree until near the middle of the century; but it must be remembered that apparently the Grand Lodge was formed not to control the ritual of lodges throughout England but to provide a rallying-point for a few lodges of London and Westminster. It can therefore be well understood that lodges outside London, and quite likely some inside also, continued in their own sweet way to do exactly as they pleased in everything. It would not be surprising to learn, in fact, that well before 1717 there were some lodges working one comprehensive degree, others working two related degrees, and even some lodges working three degrees. We should expect the rituals worked in these lodges to vary from one another, although doubtless fairly uniform modes of recognition were taught. This is a view of the matter that may be recommended to the general inquirer.

A degree literally is a step. In II Kings xx, 9, Isaiah asks the question "Shall the shadow go forward ten degrees, or go back ten degrees?" The word comes from the Latin *de, gradus*, and means 'down a step.' 'Grade' has, in its masonic sense, exactly the same meaning as 'degree'; thus 'in the higher degrees' is the same as 'in the higher grades.'

It was an old-established custom in American lodges to open a lodge 'on a step,' just as an English lodge opens 'in a degree.' In the lodges of Maine, U.S.A., in 1769, the Master opened the lodge on whichever 'step' he pleased; the ceremony over, he closed the lodge on that step, and, if necessary, opened it again on another one; in some lodges the minutes were read on each step. The Anchor and Hope Lodge, Bolton, in the 1790's installed its Master and Wardens separately "on the 3rd stepe of Masonry." In the Rose and Crown Lodge, founded in Sheffield in 1765, and in some other lodges the custom was to open on any given step and in some lodges in the 1700's the Candidate was obligated on a step, either a real one or one indicated by lines drawn on the floor. The steps to the Master's and Wardens' chairs are closely associated with the idea of degrees; for example, St John Lodge, No. 6, Canada West, had built in 1801 a chair for the East with three steps; one for the West with two steps; and one for the South with one step.

The occurrence of the word 'degree' in the medieval manuscripts of the mason craft is not evidence that the old operative lodges, or even the earliest speculative lodges, used the word as we now understand it. True, the Regius MS. of about 1390 mentions *degre*, the then Norman-French form of the word in England, but not in a sense implying a grade or step; how could it, when this same manuscript expressly says that "alle schul swere the same ogth"? We cannot be sure that the word was generally known in its present sense even when the *Constitutions* of 1723 were prepared, but an irregular print dated 1730 uses on its title-page the word 'degree' apparently in our sense.

The London Mason's Ordinances of 1481 include the phrase "persones of the saide Craft mistere or science from hensfurthewarde ones in every iii yeres be cladde in one Clothing convenient to ther powers and degrees to be ordeigned for by the wardeynes of the same Craft mistere or science. . . ." This might hastily be read as implying the existence of a masonic degree at that early date, but in fact the word means nothing more than the class, quality, or station in life of the brother, as is the case in the Grand Lodge MS. No. 2 of 1663, which contains the words "noe person of what degree soever be accepted a Free Mason . . ."

The orders of the original Alnwick Lodge in 1701 state that "all Fellows being younger shall give his Eldr Fellows the Honour due to their degree and Standing," but here again it would be wise to read the word subject to the explanation already given; so far as is known, the original Alnwick Lodge was wholly operative in character.

Shakespeare uses the word 'degree,' but not in our masonic sense. In *Timon of Athens,* written somewhere about 1608, he has the phrase: "manners, mysteries, and trades, degrees, observances." Here the word almost certainly has reference to rank or relative condition. Elsewhere Shakespeare calls a degree, or step, a 'grise,' which is a form of the word 'gree,' derived exactly as the word 'degree' from the Latin *gradus.*

How many Degrees were there in Early Days?

In discussing the difficult and complicated question of the degrees, it will be assumed that, while it certainly looks as though there could have been either one or at most two degrees when Elias Ashmole was made a mason and for many years afterwards, by the time that the first Grand Lodge was founded (1717) two degrees were being generally worked, and some lodges apparently knew three. It would be idle to shut our eyes to the possibility that the learned speculatives who came into free-masonry in the 1600's may have been responsible for some elaboration of the ceremonies. Although without information as to any details of what they did, we may reasonably conjecture whether, in the course of many decades prior to 1717, they took the ceremonial in hand and developed it. This is not to suggest that every lodge worked two degrees, but that freemasonry by the year 1717 was in general a two-degree system. There have been weighty authorities who have thought other-wise; for example, J. G. Findel, a German scholar greatly respected by English students, who thought that there was only one degree in those early days, the initiation ceremony being the one and only ceremony that freemasonry then afforded; but his assumption was founded on a mis-reading of the evidence.

It so happens that in 1704 Governor Jonathan Belcher, who was then about twenty-three years of age, came from Boston, U.S.A., to visit England, where he was admitted a freemason. Thirty-seven years later, in the course of a speech, he used these words, ". . . it is now thirty-seven years since I was admitted into the Ancient and Honourable Society of Free and Accepted Masons. . . ." Some historians have based upon that bare statement the opinion that Governor Belcher passed through *one* ceremony only—that of initiation; but surely that is taking far too much for granted. We have equally good, probably better, evidence for assuming that the Governor's words mean just what they say, that he was 'admitted,' and for all we learn from his statement to the contrary he may have been given two degrees on the one occasion and have afterwards passed through another ceremony. Do any of us, in speaking of our own initiation, use a form of words really different from the Governor's? "I was initiated in such and such a year," we commonly say.

We shall assume, then, that in 1717, the year in which the first Grand Lodge was founded, most but not all lodges, certainly the affiliated lodges, were working at least two degrees, probably on the same evening, one degree following the other. We cannot actually prove this, but six years later all doubt in the matter is removed, for in the *Constitutions* of 1723 is a much discussed regulation—Regulation XIII. Now, this regulation called all Apprentices who wished to become Masters and Fellow Crafts to pass through the necessary ceremony at Grand Lodge itself! So when we say that in the affiliated lodges there was definitely in 1723 a two-degree system at the least, we do not expect serious contradiction.

'Regulation XIII'

Regulation XIII lays down that 'Apprentices must be admitted Masters and Fellow Craft only here [*i.e.*, in the Grand Lodge] except by dispensation.' This regulation has occasioned more trouble to the masonic historians than any other phrase in the records of the Order. It has perplexed scores of writers and, while it has illumined some conditions of the early 1700's, it has, on the other hand, clouded some matters of great importance.

Old degrees thought to have been in existence in the early 1700's will be referred to, not by numbers, but by the letters *A* and *B* respectively, in order to obviate any risk of seeming to suggest that a First Degree of that day corresponds to the First Degree of this, and so forth.

It has been assumed that in those days there were at least two degrees. The first of these, *A*—the Initiate's Degree—appears to have included much of the matter of our present Entered Apprentice and Fellow Craft Degrees, but the Candidate initiated into that degree was an Apprentice. He was not a Fellow Craft until he had been 'raised' or 'passed' to the next degree, the content of which probably varied considerably as between lodge and lodge. If Degree *A* provided the bases of our Degrees First and Second, then it would appear likely that Degree *B* would somewhat correspond to our Third Degree, a statement to be taken far from literally—in fact, to be regarded for the time being with much caution. In that early day our degrees were in the making, and readers can be quite sure that neither Degree *A* nor *B* was the equivalent of any present-day degree.

The oft-quoted regulation that apprentices must be admitted 'Masters and Fellow Craft' was taken at one time as *proof* that there must have been three degrees in 1723, the year in which the *Constitutions* were issued. But it so happens that Grand Lodge repealed the regulation in 1732, and the resolution repealing it does not mention Fellow Crafts, but says that the Master of each lodge may make Masters at his discretion—not 'Masters and Fellow Crafts,' as in the original regulation.

Now it would be ridiculous to suppose that Grand Lodge proposed to retain in its own exclusive hands the making of *Fellow Crafts* only, after insisting some years before that both Masters and Fellow Crafts must be made in Grand Lodge. It is inconceivable that it would wish to allow the private lodges to make a superior grade of Master Mason, while strictly keeping to itself the right to make the middle grade—the Fellow Craft. We are led to ask, then, whether 'Masters and Fellow Craft' in the original regulation meant one and the same thing—that is, Brethren of one grade (as it did in Scotland, from whose operative customs and practice the double description had probably been taken). We must carefully note that when the 1723 Regulation was made it is not known for certain that there were any Master Masons in English lodges—that is, any Brethren who were so called by virtue of having been raised to a Third Degree. Brethren of the only superior degree, the Second, were Fellows. Grand Lodge in referring to them as Masters and Fellow Crafts had introduced a Scotticism borrowed probably by Anderson from his early practice.

We should all doubtless like to think that so far is so clear! But is it? Grand Lodge had withdrawn from private lodges in 1723 the right of making 'Masters and Fellow Crafts,' and by an ill-drawn resolution had restored it in 1732. But in the meantime something had happened. Was that something the beginning of the recognition in general lodge practice of a Third Degree—the Master Mason's Degree, the Hiramic Degree —corresponding to and on the lines of, but not identical with, our present Third Degree? If so, this curious fact reveals itself: the word 'Masters' in the 1723 *Constitutions* and that same word in the repeal resolution of 1725 meant two different things! It was the *Fellow Craft* (Degree *B*) who in 1723 was required to be made in Grand Lodge. It was the new *Master Mason* (new Third Degree) who some years later was permitted to be made in the Lodges.

Anderson's use in the *Constitutions* of the term 'Fellow Craft' was an innovation. The old English operative freemason was a 'fellow.' The second grade in early English speculative masonry was also 'fellow,' the highest grade a Brother could reach—at any rate in the great majority of lodges—and one qualifying him for every office in freemasonry, be it Warden, Master, Grand Warden, or Grand Master.

The old qualification for mastership of a lodge being possession of the degree of a Fellow Craft, it follows, apparently, that Regulation XIII meant (while it operated) that no Brother could attain in course of time to the mastership of his lodge unless he had gone through a ceremony at Grand Lodge, which might be interpreted as really meaning that any Brother lacking the approval of Grand Lodge could not become the Master of a lodge. We cannot appreciate what this statement means until we realize what the then Grand Lodge was. It was very far indeed from being an elaborate and powerful organization. Its ordinary meetings must have been small and much the same as any other lodge meetings of the time, except that those present were Masters and Wardens of the constituent lodges.

We do not know whether Regulation XIII was ever observed, even by a single lodge, and we are left to guess why it was repealed, but we can assume that it had proved both unwelcome and unworkable. The London lodges in general must have viewed it with grave dislike. The provincial lodges, which grew in number so rapidly in those years, probably disliked it even more, because for them there was the added disadvantage of distance and difficulty.

It is unfortunate that the poor drafting of Regulation XIII, and the brevity of the resolution that repealed it, serve to conceal so much information, for in the early 1720's the Hiramic Degree (the prototype of our Third Degree) had begun to establish itself in its separate existence or, shall we say, was being increasingly worked in the lodges. We can assume that, perhaps for decades, a legend of the Hiramic Order must have been known in some or many lodges, but not until the 1730 period did it begin to come into general adoption in the lodges affiliated to the Premier Grand Lodge.

The Reason for the Regulation

We are left to guess at the reason for making the regulation. The Craft was developing at a rate and in a way completely unforeseen by the four founding lodges. Some matters undoubtedly had slipped beyond their reach, and it may be that the regulation was an attempt to gain a measure of control over difficult conditions.

Only five or six short years had passed since Grand Lodge had been founded to group together a few time-immemorial lodges, and there were now nearly fifty lodges, some of them in the outer suburbs, while many more, country lodges among them, were on the way. Grand Lodge may have been considerably worried at the ease with which new lodges came into existence—with or without their approval—and might possibly have thought that by controlling the making of Fellow Crafts, the grade from which the Masters of lodges were taken, they might be applying a very desirable brake. While originally Grand Lodge may not have given a thought to the creation of new lodges and the control or unifying of ceremony and ritual, it is a fair guess that by 1723 they were deeply concerned with both of these matters, having probably found themselves powerless to prevent the rise of new lodges or to stem the flood of Initiates, each lodge tending to accept candidates without reference to any other body or authority.

We can well believe that some of the Brethren of the 'four old lodges' must have viewed the new lodges with very mingled feelings, and might have hoped that, although the reduction in the number of Initiates was a task beyond their power, they could at any rate apply a much-needed brake in between the Initiate's Degree and that of the Fellow Crafts. In this way they might effect some little control over the number, just possibly the type, even the personality, of the Brethren who in the ordinary course would become Fellows, ultimately Masters of lodges, and the likely founders of new lodges. We are left to conjecture so much, and many different interpretations are possible.

In the interval between 1723 and 1733 there was a strong tendency for lodges to form 'Masters' Lodges'—that is, lodges that (as explained later in this present section) would be open for ceremonial business in the Third Degree only. Some students argue that the original incentive to form such lodges came from the regulation in question. Obviously, however, the Masters' Lodge at this early date was a sequel to the evolution of the Hiramic Degree, and it is difficult at this distance of time to see how observance of the regulation had much to do with it.

Another suggestion is that the regulation might have been intended solely to restrict to Grand Lodge the working of the weighty Hiramic ceremonial. But this is pure conjecture, with little on which to base it, for while in some lodges in 1723 Degree B must have contained some allusion to a legend of the Hiramic Order it is not likely that any such legend was a widely accepted part of the then masonic ceremonial. Most people will agree that if Grand Lodge had in its mind anything so clear and definite as the separation of the Hiramic Degree and a wish to work it exclusively in Grand Lodge, it would or could have worded the regulation very differently.

Why Regulation XIII was made, and why it was repealed, nobody knows. We may well suspect, however, that in some curious and unexplained way both the regulation and its repeal had important consequences in the development of masonic ceremonial in the first half of the eighteenth century, and that they played their part in the rearrangement of the degrees.

How the Early Degrees may have been formed

In what precise manner the degrees were rearranged we do not know. Possibly the original *A* Degree provided the basis of our First and Second, and the original *B* Degree (added to, edited, rearranged) was renamed the Third Degree, but we must not press the suggestion hard or apply it too literally. Whether our First and Second Degrees contain most of the original *A*, and whether our present Third contains part of the original *B*, or whether it contains, as well, some of the original *A* —these are points on which we have no information. In view of the internal evidence afforded by our present degrees, it might even be possible that at one time there was one degree in existence containing some matters which now are distributed over all three degrees.

A clear-cut view of the matter is hardly possible. All that can be said is that the truth is more or less comprised in some such alternative statement as the following, in which Nos. 1 and 2 are closely related:

(1) The whole of the
     Ancient Ritual   = Foundation of our First and Second Degrees

(2) Ancient Degree *A* = Foundation of our First Degree
     Ancient Degree *B* = Foundation of our Second Degree

(3) Ancient Degree *A* = Foundation of our First Degree
     Ancient Degree *B* = Foundation of both our Second and Third Degrees

(4) Ancient Degree *A* = Foundation of both our First and Second Degrees
     Ancient Degree *B* = Foundation of our present Third Degree

What are the chief difficulties offered by these alternatives? In the case of Nos. 1 and 2, if the whole of the content of the ancient ritual went to provide the basis of our present First and Second Degrees, it is obvious that the Third Degree had to be invented or imported some time in the late seventeenth or early eighteenth century.

On the other hand, if (as in No. 3) the ancient Degree *B* was the prototype of our Second and Third Degrees, allowing us to assume that the Hiramic story had long been·known in freemasonry, then it would appear that our present First and Second Degrees, which are so obviously part and parcel of each other, were not closely associated in ancient days, contrary to all our impressions.

It is easier to view with favour alternative No. 4—namely, that the ancient Degree *A* gave us our First and Second Degrees, and *B* gave us the Third; but some modern students of great repute consider this to be against the weight of evidence, particularly that of Regulation XIII. They believe that the Trinity College, Dublin, MS. proves that the Hiramic Degree goes back at any rate to 1711 and inferentially much further. Even as early as Ashmole's day, they feel, two degrees were given in a single session and they see no reason to suppose that Ashmole did not receive all three degrees. With regard to Regulation XIII, they believe that the only official significance of the term 'Master' was that of Master of a lodge, and consequently it was Brethren of that grade who were to be 'made' nowhere but in Grand Lodge, not Brethren who were to be made Fellow Crafts or 'token' Masters. They feel that by 1732, when the Regulation was repealed, the terminology may have altered and that it was unnecessary to say more than 'Master,' the meaning being the same as when the regulation was made, although perhaps by that time the lodge degree of Master had been officially recognized.

Perhaps we shall find some of our difficulties removed if we look at the matter in a rather different way. Let us assume that prior to 1717 many lodges had as one of their two degrees a self-contained degree which included the basis of our First and Second, or, if we prefer it so, of our Second and Third. In the early days of the eighteenth century there was apparently a spirit of innovation, but there was one of co-ordination also, for by 1730, or some such date, many lodges under the Grand Lodge had more or less settled down to the actual working of a three-degree system, acceptance of which must in some cases have called for considerable compromise on their part. In the new order of things some lodges must have seen not only innovation of arrangement but innovation of subject matter as well, while others recognized, though almost certainly in an edited or rearranged form, elements with which they had long been familiar in lodge ceremonial.

Every lodge without exception had to consider, sooner or later, its attitude to a rearrangement, a revision, and a reordering of the steps, or degrees, containing much that was different from its old practice. For example, some lodges may have replaced their old two degrees with three degrees; some may have found their new Second Degree more or less a part of their old *A* Degree, while others may have found it strongly reminiscent of their old *B* Degree. To some lodges may have been introduced a complete innovation—the Hiramic legend; while others found themselves presented with an extended and more dramatic version of a legend which had long been known to them, but which may possibly have centred around different characters. The more we meditate on the conditions in the first three decades, the more likely we are to feel that the picture here imperfectly presented is likely to be the approximately true one. Really, it is less a picture than a series of related hints, from which each of us can draw for himself a sketch in soft lines with many of its details unavoidably indistinct.

The degrees were 'in the making'—a process that continued actively for wellnigh a hundred years.

In whatever way the early degrees were rearranged, we are forced, in the words of J. Heron Lepper,

> to make a choice between two possibilities: first, that the original system of two degrees contained the skeleton of what we now possess in our tri-gradal system; or, alternatively, that the third degree, as we know it now, was a masonic novelty. . . . We can accept one or other of these twain according to taste—for I fear it is and will remain a matter of faith rather than of logical reasoning—but for my own part I cannot think that the beautiful symbolism of the Hiramic legend is what one would expect as an invention of the early eighteenth century.

We can be definite only on one point—that by 1730 the three-degree system was in course of taking practical shape. There were some lodges working only two degrees as late as the middle of the century, and perhaps those degrees did not contain any ceremonial based on the Hiramic legend, although we may safely conclude that one distinct feature of their Fellow Craft Degree can now be found in our Third Degree.

There was no official recognition of the three-degree system until the issue of the *Constitutions* of 1738.

When in 1732 a French lodge was constituted in London by the Earl of Strathmore "le Maitre, les Surveillants (the two Wardens), les Compagnons (Brethren), et les Apprentiss," were alone particularized by the Grand Master. In a lodge at Lincoln as late as 1742 only two degrees were worked, and we simply do not know whether they included most of the contents of the three degrees worked in many other lodges of the time.

In the fact that in a great many lodges all through the eighteenth century the First and Second Degrees were given to the Candidate on the same evening—that, in other words, he was initiated and passed on the one occasion—there exists a possible indication that our First and Second Degrees were originally parts of one degree.

When the contents of the old *A* Degree were distributed over the new First and Second, and probably to some slight extent over the Third, the charity test in the English ritual was left as an experience through which the Candidate should pass at a very early moment in his masonic career. But in Ireland we find the charity test coming in the Second Degree—a fair indication that the First and Second Degrees are part of the same original, the contents of which, however, were distributed differently in England from in Ireland. J. Heron Lepper, one of Ireland's masonic historians, tells us that even until the year 1858 the degrees of Apprentice and Fellow Craft were almost invariably conferred on one evening, and that, even to-day, almost the first words heard by the Initiate in an Irish lodge inform him that he is about to join a society of Brethren *and Fellows,* both the phrase and the idea surviving from days when our First and Second Degrees were one.

The reader may give a thought to the familiar phrase 'The Five Points of Fellowship.' He knows the degree in which these words occur—the Master's Degree, not the Fellow Craft's Degree, although it is in the latter that he would expect to find an explanation of points so named. Is it not apparent that when the Third Degree attained a separate existence it carried with it elements from one or both of the others?

It has been stated more than once that the old (real) qualification for a Brother in the early 1700's wishing to pass the Master's chair was that he should be a Fellow Craft. When, in the course of rearranging the degrees, the old Fellow Craft became a Master Mason, no thorough attempt was made apparently to bring the ceremony of the Master's installation into line with the altered facts. Consequently we find to-day that, so far as the rank and file of the Brethren are concerned, an essential part of the ceremony takes place in the Second Degree and not where it might be expected to be, in the Third.

Although, as late as 1777, Grand Lodge decided that the First and Second Degrees must be given to a Candidate on separate evenings, there are many lodge records pointing to the non-observance of the rule, and, curiously, there exists a combined tracing-board for these two degrees believed to be of the year 1790. It once belonged to the Old Dundee Lodge, No. 18. It exhibits all the usual emblems associated with the First and Second Degrees (not in any particular order) and includes a group of tents, and a road passing over a bridge spanning a stream (? a fall) of water, in which last emblem there is a suggestion of early Mark ritual.

We still, even to-day, observe the legal fiction of the possession of the Fellow Craft Degree qualifying a Brother for the chairs of Warden and Master. True, it is not covered by any regulation of Grand Lodge, but our *Constitutions* are prefaced by "The Charges of a Freemason" which have the sanctity of age. Charge 4, "Of Masters, Wardens, Fellows and Apprentices," states that "No brother can be a warden until he has passed the part of a fellow-craft, nor a master until he has acted as a warden, nor grand warden until he has been master of a lodge, nor grand master unless he has been a fellow-craft before his election. . . ." This Charge perpetuates in theory the principle that held good through the eighteenth century when the Master of a lodge need be only a Fellow Craft. To-day, of course, in fact only a Third Degree Mason could pass through the offices and arrive at the chair. The suggestion has been made that a reason for the persistence of the fiction is a failure of the eighteenth-century editors to bring the Charges into line with the altered conditions of the Craft, and J. Heron Lepper points out that from 1730 the Irish *Constitution*, based upon the English one, was altered to suit the new division into three degrees, the Master Mason thus officially becoming the qualifying degree and not the Fellow Craft, a change which in those days may have been a change in little more than name.

It is obvious from the wording of the old *Constitutions* that, when they were originally prepared, the lodges under the Premier Grand Lodge knew no Brother higher in grade than Fellow Craft, as witness "the most expert fellow craftsman shall be chosen or appointed the *Master*, or Overseer of the Lord's work, who is called Master by those at work under him."

That the Fellow Craft could then hold any position in lodge or Grand Lodge is not left in doubt, for in referring to the constitution of a new lodge there occurs this expression: "The Candidates, or the new Master and Wardens, being yet among the Fellow Craft . . ."

In a great many lodges, following the 1720's, a Fellow Craft could be raised to the Master Mason Degree, but whether his qualification for office was enhanced thereby is open to doubt, for occasionally through the century Brethren occupied office, and sometimes high office, who were Fellow Crafts but not Master Masons. The Right Worshipful Master John Smith, M.P., was raised to the Third Degree in 1768, actually *after* he became the Master of a well-known Bath lodge, now the Royal Cumberland Lodge, No. 41. This is particularly to be remarked inasmuch as this lodge came into existence in 1733 when the three-degree system was already in course of becoming general.

The Three-degree System: Its Age

Accepting the evidence of the Trinity College, Dublin, MS., we must believe that even as far back as 1711 three separate classes of Brethren were known—Entered Apprentices, Fellow Craftsmen, and Masters; each with its own secrets. This manuscript bears the date 1711 in an endorsement which good authority regards as accurate.

A speech made in 1726 at York by Dr Francis Drake may be assumed to have special reference to York practice, although there is no evidence to support that conjecture. This Francis Drake was a doctor of medicine, a Fellow of the Royal Society, and an antiquary. Initiated probably at York in September 1725, only three months later he became Junior Grand Warden of the Grand Lodge of *All* England—the York Grand Lodge.

A year later he delivered the address so frequently quoted in masonic writings. He became Grand Master at York in 1761. The doctor uses a phrase which is recorded in black-letter initials, so: E-P-F-C & M-M, which can only be taken to mean "Entered 'Prentices, Fellow Crafts, and Master Masons." So *some* Lodges must have been familiar with the three-degree system by 1726.

Dated 1726 is the Graham MS. (extended reference to it is made on pp. 314–316), which is believed to have been copied from an earlier document and undoubtedly supports the idea that the Third Degree legend in some form or other was known in the seventeenth century.

A musical society, boasting the high-sounding title of the Philo-Musicæ et Architecturæ Societas, met at the Queen's Head, near Temple Bar, London, in 1725, and is generally credited with having worked three degrees in that year, including that of 'passing Masters.' Of eight members of the society seven belonged to the lodge at the Queen's Head, and apparently had been made masons there. The minutes of the society say that three Brethren—Charles Cotton, Papillon Ball, and Thomas Marshall—were passed Fellow Crafts on February 1, 1725, and that on the twelfth day of May, Cotton and Ball "were regularly passed Masters." This musical society, which thus takes its place in masonic history, was charged by the Grand Master in December 1725 with having made masons irregularly, but the charge did not worry the society, which continued to make masons until the end of its short life in March 1727.

The earliest known reference to the Master Mason Degree in regular lodge minutes is that in the minutes of the lodge at the Swan and Rummer, London, of April 27, 1727. "Order'd That a Lodge of Masters be summoned for Fryday next at 6 o'clock on special affairs." Two days later there is an entry that two esquires, one 'Mr' and one Captain, were admitted masons. Two years later, March 1729, we have this entry: "at a particular Lodge for passing of Masters." At this Masters' Lodge six Brethren were admitted Masters and it was resolved that no Brother for the future be admitted (as a Master) for a less expense than ten shillings and sixpence.

It must be admitted that by 1730 the three-degree system had established itself in a number of lodges, but undoubtedly there was quite a proportion of lodges that knew only two degrees and would do so for very many years to come. For example, Lodge No. 71, meeting at the Rose, Cheapside, London, spoke in one of its bylaws dated 1732 of "The Superior Degree of Masonry" in referring to its Second Degree, and there are many similar instances in other lodges of still later date.

If we can put ourselves in the place of Fellow Crafts at about the year 1730, or at any time between then and the middle of the century, we can easily see that once the Hiramic Degree became an entity of its own many masons may have regarded it as a degree to which, at their leisure and convenience, they would one day seek to be 'passed,' but which, in the meantime, they could afford to neglect, because its possession would not improve their qualification to fill the highest offices in the lodge or even in Grand Lodge.

Masonic students do not conceal their belief that the amazing popularity of a so-called 'exposure' published in 1730 played no small part in the gradual standardizing of lodge work and ritual. This was Prichard's *Masonry Dissected*, which, unreliable as all such irregular prints must necessarily be, yet gave the public of the day some idea of the masonic ritual, and nowadays is valuable to the historian chiefly because by its use of such terms as Enter'd Prentice, Fellow Craft, and Masters' Part it indicates that speculative masonry in 1730 or before was acquainted with the Hiramic legend. Prichard's book of twenty-two pages was the publishing best-seller of its day; it ran through three editions in eleven days, was reprinted in two newspapers, separately published in Scotland, Ireland, in the Continental cities, and in America, and passed through an immense number of editions—on an average one every three years in England alone—through a period of about a century.

The three-degree system is thought to have been working in Paris in 1731, in Kirkcudbright, Scotland, in 1735; in Sweden in 1737; but it must not be thought that wherever it went it was welcomed. There were many English lodges in which it was not eagerly adopted, while in some Scottish lodges it met open hostility, as is made clear elsewhere in these pages.

Rapid Progress through the Degrees

It will be apparent from the remarks on earlier pages that it was common all through the 1700's for Candidates to be initiated and passed at one continuing ceremony. The practice continued in many cases until the coming of the United Grand Lodge in 1813, for in the Old Dundee Lodge, No. 18, of Wapping the First and Second Degrees were always given on the same evening up to the year 1809 or so, and there was a very strong feeling in the lodge against relinquishing the practice.

The Irish lodges had the illuminating phrase "entered and crafted," meaning that a Candidate had progressed through the First and Second Degrees in the one evening.

The minutes of one lodge tell us, indeed, that this system was "a practice of most of the best lodges." In 1752 an English lodge in the Province of Leeward Islands gave a confirmatory Charter to certain

Brethren of the Lodge Perfect Harmony, New Orleans, and in a letter accompanying the Charter said:

> Particularly we do strictly recommend to our Brethren of the Parfait Harmony to continue in the use of giving the two degrees of Entered Apprentice and Fellow Craft Imeditly the one after the other without any delay as is the practice of most of the best lodges, and as we do ourselves for severall reasons that cannot be exprest here has convinced of the necessity of this . . .

An irregular print of 1766 says ". . . in most Lodges at this time, they are made Enterd Apprentices and Fellow Crafts the same evening," and this is well confirmed by contemporary and later lodge records, *but it was not always the First and Second Degrees that were so given.* For instance, in the Lodge of Friendship, Oldham, now No. 277 (founded at the Ring of Bells, Goulbourne, Oldham, in 1789), it was common to confer the First and Second Degrees on one occasion, and on other occasions the Second and Third; five times in five years the Second and Third Degrees were conferred at the one time.

Occasions have been known when Candidates have gone through all three degrees on the one evening, as, for example, in the Phœnix Lodge, Portsmouth, in March 1787, when William Mason was made a mason: "Admitted passed to ye second degree—& Raised to the Sublime Degree," by no means the only instance. A Grand Lodge order of 1754 and the *Constitutions* of 1767 do not permit a lodge 'to make and raise' the same Brother at one and the same meeting without a dispensation; but was the instruction generally observed? We have already said that there existed a tracing-board of the combined First and Second Degrees believed to be of the date 1790.

In the Lodge of Antiquity, time-immemorial, the Candidate could be initiated and passed on the one occasion as late as 1777, in which year it was resolved that "no person shall be initiated into more than the first Degree of Masonry on the first night of his reception," and that other lodges be so informed; but the other lodges did not necessarily fall into line. Apparently the idea was sponsored by no less a person than the famous William Preston, member of Lodge of Antiquity, whose lectures have an important place in masonic literature, and who shortly afterwards was to find himself in serious trouble with Grand Lodge, as explained in a later section. There appears to be ground for supposing that the Lodge of Antiquity continued to confer the two first degrees on the one occasion until as late as 1792.

We have already noted an instance of one Candidate passing through all three degrees on one occasion, but it is by no means a record. In the Lodge of Friendship, Chichester (then No. 624 and since united with another lodge), John Newman, a London banker, was initiated, passed, raised, made a Past Master of 'Arts and Sciences,' and finally made a Knight of the Red Cross of Babylon—all five degrees on one occasion, September 6, 1813.

As can be expected, promotion could be remarkably rapid in the eighteenth century. In the old lodge at Bath, Howell Gwynne and Lord Ann Hamilton (the latter so named after his godmother, Queen Anne) were initiated in May 1742. In the very next month Gwynne became the Master of the Lodge, a position he held for six months, and was then succeeded by Lord Ann Hamilton.

To-day, in the lodges under the English constitution, the ordinary interval between degrees is a minimum of four weeks; under the Scottish constitutions, two weeks; under the many constitutions of the U.S.A. it varies considerably, being in general from four to five weeks. Under some of the American constitutions promotion from degree to degree is entirely a matter for the lodge, and is made to depend on the proficiency of the Candidate, who has to be wellnigh word-perfect in his replies to test-questions, it being theoretically possible in some lodges for a Candidate particularly apt at memorizing to receive the next degree at an interval of only a few days. In some South American lodges there is an interval of three months between the First and Second Degrees, and six months between the Second and Third.

'Master' often confused with 'Master Mason'

Both in England and in Scotland the term 'Master Mason' is of ancient usage, but it has not always meant the same thing. A Durham Fabric Roll going back to early medieval days says that "the Master Mason [is] to be paid by the Sacrist." The Sacrist was the Treasurer in charge of the sacred vessels. This Master Mason is not known to have been a speculative mason, except so far as he was acquainted with the theory of design and construction, which was 'speculative' rather than 'operative'; but the term certainly did not connote speculative masonry as we understand it to-day. 'Master Mason' as an operative term is nearly obsolete, but until recently a Master Mason was part of the establishment of the Corporation of the City of London. In Scotland a Master Mason is a mason working on his own account—in other words, a Master Builder, which in England is the corresponding term. A well-qualified English mason became a master in his calling; master and craftsman and fellow having the same meaning. The experienced mason who presided over a lodge of operatives was its 'Master'; his office was a measure of the confidence his fellows reposed in him and not a grade—so far as we know—acquired by submitting himself to any ceremony of an esoteric nature.

The term 'Master Mason' in its present speculative meaning is used in the *Constitutions* of 1738, by which time, of course, freemasonry had in a great many lodges comprehended three grades—the Entered Apprentice, Fellow Craft, and Master Mason.

In those early days a Brother was 'passed' to the Master Mason Degree, but within a few years it became more usual, but by no means general, to speak of 'passing' to the Second and 'raising' to the Third. One of the earliest references in support of this is a minute of the lodge at the Maid's Head, Norwich, in 1747, in which it is "agreed that Brother Jollings and Brother Ivory, be raised Masters at next St John's Night."

The 'Masters' Part' is a phrase used from the 1720's to designate the Master Mason Degree—that is, the Hiramic Degree. It did not commonly refer to the inner working of the installation ceremony (although it might possibly, much later in the century, have been used by some lodges in that way). Prichard's *Masonry Dissected* (1730) uses this term 'Masters' Part' and includes this jingle:

> A Master-Mason I was made most rare,
> With Diamond, Ashler, and the Square.

However, we find curiously contradictory things in these spurious rituals, and it is likely that the particular Master Mason referred to in the couplet is the old fellow, or Fellow Craft, and not the Third Degree mason.

There is much confusion in eighteenth-century records in references to Third Degree masons and to Brethren who are Masters of lodges. This confusion arises chiefly from the early custom of reterring to the ceremony of making the Master Mason as a 'Passing,' and then calling the Third Degree mason a 'Pass'd Master.' Usually such terms as 'Ps Master,' 'Pas Master,' and 'Past Master' indicate the Master who has passed the chair of a lodge, but often it is necessary to study the context very closely to be sure. The confusion is the greater because of the frequent practice in the 1600's and 1700's of giving the past tense of the verb 'to pass' as 'past.' In an epitaph of 1615 we have this example:

> How do I thank Thee Death and Bless thy Power
> That I have past the Guard and Scap'd the Tower.

Early Installations

In early speculative days the senior Fellow present in lodge could act as the Master of the lodge, and it somewhat naturally follows that, with the growth of the custom by which the lodge appointed one particular master for a period of a few months or of a year, the ceremony of putting him in the chair of the lodge was at first of the barest kind. There is apparently no definite knowledge of any ceremony peculiar to the occasion, or of any secrets accompanying the chairing of the Master, until the 1750's, when the 'Antients' are believed to have introduced the installation ceremony requiring for its working the presence of Past Masters of the lodge, and to have thus brought into existence the rank, or quasi-degree, of Past Master. Any ceremony in the 'Modern' lodges had possibly been restricted to some little speech of advice and congratulation, delivered by the outgoing Master or a senior Fellow Craft, and almost certainly the recital of an Old Charge. (While the ceremonial method of installing a Master does not appear therefore to be more than about two centuries old, the Charge read to the Master includes material going back very much earlier.)

In this matter of installation, however, we may easily go astray, bearing in mind the 'Antient' claim that the esoteric ceremony of chairing the Master was of old usage. Indeed, one of the points of difference between them and their opponents was that the 'Moderns,' so the 'Antients' said, had discarded that old ceremony. It might well be, therefore, that, although we are accustomed to regard the installation ceremony as dating from the middle of the eighteenth century, it may conceivably go back to a much earlier day. It is only fair to say that it is considered likely that a number of the lodges under the Grand Lodge (the 'Moderns') in those early days did use a special little ceremony when putting their Master in the chair, but apparently ceased to do so about 1736. We must remember, too, that the time-immemorial Lodge of Antiquity, the first in precedence of all the 'Modern' lodges, claims to have administered an obligation and imparted peculiar secrets to the Master at his installation from as early as 1726, and to have regarded the Immediate Past Master as an important rank by the year 1739.

What is meant by 'Installation' and 'Investiture'?

'To install' is literally to put a person in a seat or chair. A stall is a chair, or any seat of dignity, such as the seat in the choir or chancel of a church. Ordained priests were put into seats—that is, installed in their churches. For six hundred years Knights of the Garter have been installed in the Chapel of St George, at Windsor Castle.

Early speculative masons spoke more of chairing the Master than of installing him, the Installing Master being often called the Chairing Master.

Occasionally in the early lodge minutes there occurs, instead of the term 'to chair' or 'to install,' the word 'induct' or 'induction.' This was borrowed from Church practice, but is also capable of good masonic interpretation, being based on a Latin word meaning 'to lead.'

Masonically, the word 'installation' is not thought to go back earlier than 1723 when it occurs in the first edition of the *Constitutions*.

Our Board of Installed Masters, a Masters' Lodge charged with the duty of installing the Master Elect, was not known, it is thought, *by that name* earlier than 1827, in which year there was warranted a lodge, or board, of Installed Masters.

Some early minutes are at fault in using the word 'installation' when referring to the Master's investiture of officers of the lodge, and occasionally we still find this error made in masonic addresses. The only officer *installed* is the Master, when he is put into the chair. All other officers, even the Wardens, are not put into their chairs; instead, they are clothed with the insignia of their office—and there we have the literal, but far from the whole, meaning of 'to invest,' which originally signified the act of transferring a property, a title, or even a power through the presentation of a particular symbol. Accordingly, as we learn from Hook's *Church Dictionary*, when the Sovereign endowed or invested an ecclesiastic with certain rights, he made these apparent by the presentation of symbols—to a canon of a book, to an abbot of a pastoral staff, to a bishop of the staff and ring. Masonic custom perpetuates that old idea when the Master of a lodge hands the column and gavel to a Warden, the wand to a Deacon, the sword to the Tyler, and in general when he places around the neck of an officer the collar from which depends the emblem of his office. The lodge officer will therefore appreciate that his investiture is much more than merely receiving the clothing and symbol of his office; traditionally and symbolically the conferment of the symbol endows him with a particular power or authority.

The 'Antients' contended that an installing ceremony was essentially an ancient practice, and when the two great sections of freemasonry came together in 1813 after their long quarrel the Lodge of Reconciliation either recognized the 'Antients'' claim, or was faced with the fact that the installation ceremony had by this time become a much respected part of most English masonic working. Gould believed, however, that not until 1811 were Masters of lodges under the Premier Grand Lodge —even those of London—installed in the ceremonial way to which we are accustomed. G. W. Speth, too, has described that in his mother Lodge in the year 1815, following the union, the Master Elect could not be placed in the chair because no one present knew what to do, and a high official of the former rival and 'Antient' Grand Lodge attended at the next lodge-night to perform the ceremony.

Many Scots lodges were bitterly opposed to an installation ceremony, and not until the 1870's did all Scots lodges adopt it.

The Lodge of Promulgation resolved that the "ceremony of Installation of Masters of Lodges is one of the two landmarks of the Craft and ought to be observed." The occurrence of the word "two" in this statement has led to much confusion and argument, but it is now believed with good reason that it was a literal error for 'true.'

Nowadays it hardly needs to be pointed out that the 'Inner Working' by the Board of Installed Masters does not officially constitute a Fourth Degree in English lodges, whatever in fact it is. 'Step' and 'degree' having the same meaning, it is obvious that the Master Mason is given a most important fourth step in being put into the chair of his lodge. Here is a minute, dated 1839, of the United Lodge of Harmony and Friendship, Lewes, now extinct: "The W.M. then desired all the Brethren to retire from the Lodge that was below the P.Masters degree when the Lodge was opened in the Fourth or P.Masters degree." The use of the term 'Past Masters' Degree' is a loose way of referring to the ceremony of installation; officially, no such degree or ceremony as that of the 'Past Masters' is recognized to-day by the Grand Lodge of England.

The 'Extended' Ceremony of Installation

Not wholly unrelated to the question of the installing ceremony being a 'Fourth Degree' is the 'extended working' or 'extended ceremony' of installation, which some masons believe to have been the form of ceremony worked by the 'Antient' lodges in the eighteenth century. Dermott includes in *Ahiman Rezon* this footnote referring to the ceremony of installing the Grand Master: "This is a most noble and grand Ceremony, but cannot be described in Writing, nor ever known to any but Master-Masons." Possibly he had in mind what we now call the "extended working." The phrase in the *Constitutions* "the Master so elected shall be duly installed according to ancient usage" has been claimed to bear that meaning, but that was not the view held by Sir Edward Letchworth, Grand Secretary, who in a letter dated December 16, 1910, said there was

> no doubt whatever that this so-called ceremony is entirely irregular and was never recognised by, or even known to, Grand Lodge at the Union in 1813 . . . there is strong reason to believe it was imported from America. The matter was brought before the Board of General Purposes some years ago, when they ruled that it was entirely irregular and should not be practised by any English lodge.

Sir Edward's may have been a personal expression not binding on the Craft. However, in 1926 the extended ceremony was banned by Grand Lodge, which later, however, became converted to the view that the ceremony had been practised in many lodges over a long period, in particular at Bath, and accordingly agreed in December of the same year to permit it to be worked, but deprecated the use of signs, tokens, or words unrecognized by the majority of English Installed Masters. This permission was subject to the Installing Master precisely declaring to the Master Elect that the signs, etc., given in the course of any extended portion of the working, are not known to and are not to be required from Installed Masters generally, *and that no further Degree in Masonry is being conferred.*

A printed ritual by Dr H. Hopkins, published in 1868, indicates that in effect, but certainly not officially (Grand Lodge is very definite on that point) the "Board" in this particular working is a degree, corresponding, we suppose, more or less to the 'Antient' Chair Degree of the eighteenth century. In the course of the working, the Junior Warden is proved an Installed Master by the perfect ashlar or perpend ashlar, "a stone of a true die and square, fit only to be tried by the square and compasses." Towards the end of the ceremony the Installing Master gives a special explanation drawing attention to the virtues of the plumbline, after which the Board is closed in extended form—much as any lodge is closed. The instructions of Grand Lodge are carefully observed. The ceremony is believed to be in accord with much American practice, and although Sir Edward Letchworth evidently thought to the contrary, there does appear a likelihood that our American Brethren originally took the ceremony from early English or Irish lodges.

' Worshipful '

It very early became the custom for the Master of a lodge to be called the 'Worshipful,' or even the 'Right Worshipful,' Master. The second of these terms is now reserved under the English Grand Lodge for the Deputy, Assistant, Provincial, and District Grand Masters, and for the Grand Wardens. 'Worshipful' is derived from medieval custom, being a title of courtesy and honour then in common use. To be 'Worshipful' is to be honourable, worthy; indeed, one form of worship is 'worthyship.' An early translation of the New Testament uses the phrase 'worshipful seat' in referring to a seat of honour at a feast. The familiar words of the marriage service "With my body I thee worship" mean "With my body I thee *honour.*"

Wycliff's translation of the Bible says, "If any man serve Him, my

Father shall worship him"—an extraordinary statement to modern eyes, but one that simply means "If any man serve Him, my Father shall honour him."

Friends and relatives writing to one another in the fifteenth century frequently addressed one another as 'Worshipful.' John Paston writing to his elder brother, another John, addresses his letter to the "Right Worshipful Sir John Paston, Knight." John Paston's cousin, Elizabeth Brews, whom he afterwards married, addresses him as "My worshipful cousin," and after her marriage to him addresses him as "My right reverend and worshipful husband," and also as "Right Worshipful Master," another correspondent calling him "My full Worshipful special good Master." The Earl of Oxford, writing to Sir John Paston, addresses him as "the right worshipful and my right entirely well-beloved." The term 'Worshippffull Master' (of a ship) is found in a ballad, *Maudline*, in the Roxburghe collection, apparently written about 1600 or before.

The London Companies commonly used the title "Worshipful," sometimes in the form of "worthy," as in "The Worthy Companie of Masons, 1647," and the term is still used by them. The Masons Company of London styled itself the Worshipful Company of Masons in 1655–56, and it is reasonable to assume that the speculative masons inherited 'Worshipful' from that Company.

Masters' Lodges

In any consideration of the degrees in the early eighteenth century a place must be found for a discussion of the Masters' Lodge, the special purpose of which was to 'pass'—later 'raise'—Brethren to the rank of Master Mason. (In the earliest speculative days, it will be remembered, the Master Mason was the Fellow Craft, and, in somewhat later days, a Brother who had been raised to the Hiramic Degree.)

Whatever the ceremony originally worked in a Masters' Lodge, it is obvious that, with the re-coordinating of the degrees and the general establishment of the Hiramic Degree, the Masters' Lodge was reserved exclusively to Brethren who had been raised to the Third Degree, and the ceremony *at that time* worked in it was the raising of Fellow Crafts. It must be remembered, however, that while this statement generalizes the practice there were almost certainly marked divergences as between the various lodges. We can understand nothing of masonic practice in the first half of the 1700's unless we always remember that, although lodges were banded together under Grand Lodges, as a matter of fact they often just pleased themselves as to what they did and how they did it. In general, let us say, a Masters' Lodge confined itself to working a degree that made Masters, and was not concerned with the initiation of Candidates. It might be that an ordinary lodge would set aside certain days in the month to work as a Masters' Lodge (which might be tantamount to a lodge nowadays agreeing to take the Third Degree only on stated evenings), but more generally the Masters' Lodge was an independent lodge based, however, on an existing lodge, and *for the time being* exclusively working the Third Degree.

The origin of the Masters' Lodge has been sought in old operative practice, but it is doubtful whether it can be found there. It is more likely to have had some now quite unknown connexion with the Grand Lodge Regulation XIII, calling for Masters and Fellows to be made at Grand Lodge only (see earlier pages). Or, more likely still, it may have been the sequel to the more general establishment of the Hiramic Degree, inasmuch as relatively few Brethren would be able to work the ceremony, and lodges might very naturally, for purposes of their own convenience, make a custom of working this degree on a particular evening, and this evening, in the course of a year or two, would come to be regarded as set aside for the Masters' Lodge. From some such a beginning, in all probability, grew the independent Masters' Lodge, separate in every sense from the ordinary lodge, except that it would be originally based upon an ordinary lodge, from which it would draw both its officers and its Candidates.

In a true sense any lodge opened in the Third Degree is a Masters' Lodge, but nowadays there is a tendency to confine the term to a lodge whose members are installed Masters.

In earlier pages is told the extraordinary story of how another Grand Lodge arose in England (more than one, to be exact), and the first Grand Lodge came to be dubbed 'Modern,' while the later foundation gloried in its descriptive adjective of 'Antient.' It was a case of the oldest being dubbed the newest. It is thought that, in general, only the 'Modern' lodges—those under the Premier Grand Lodge—worked the Third Degree in Masters' Lodges, the so-called 'Antients' working it in their ordinary lodges. The 'Antient' worked other degrees, too, in course of time—early forms of the Royal Arch and Mark, very likely—all in their ordinary lodges. These deviations were frowned upon by the Premier Grand Lodge, as may be seen from a well-known statement made by the Grand Secretary, that his society was "neither Arch, Royal Arch, or Antient." In spite of this statement there is not the slightest doubt that many 'Modern' lodges pleased themselves in the matter, and actually worked some early forms of the Royal Arch and of the Mark ceremonies; otherwise, Grand Lodge would not have found it necessary, late in the century, either to forbid its lodges to carry on the business of the Royal

Arch Degree on their stated lodge nights, or to instruct them never to insert the transactions in their regular lodge books.

An early reference to a Masters' Lodge in actual minutes is in those of a lodge meeting at the Swan and Rummer, Finch Lane, London, in 1727: "Order'd That a Lodge of Masters be summon'd for Fryday next at 6 o'clock on special Affairs." The earliest published reference is in a list of lodges of 1733, in which Lodge No. 115, meeting at Devil Tavern, Temple Bar, is called a Scotch Masons' Lodge (see p. 189), and No. 116, meeting at the Bear and Harrow, in the Butcher Row, a Master Mason Lodge.

We get a clear indication, too, from a minute of the Old King's Arms Lodge, No. 28, dated 1733, recording that from time to time a summons "should be sent to the abodes of each of the members, both of the Fellow Craft and Masters Lodge."

Occasionally a Masters' Lodge transgressed an understanding and 'made' masons. A minute of the lodge just referred to, dated 1744–45, states that a Brother had been made a mason in a lodge of Masters only, and therefore contrary to the present constitution. It was agreed that he "be regularly initiated in this Lodge"; so nineteen days later the Brother was balloted for, duly elected, and "he put on his cloathing accordingly." From that wording we may gather that the resolution in the minute regularized the Brother's initiation, and that without passing through the initiation ceremony again he was entitled to clothe and enter the lodge.

There was no feeling against the holding of a Masters' Lodge in a private house.

By the 1740's and 1750's there would be a considerable number of Brethren closely acquainted with the Third Degree, which simple fact alone would prepare the way for the decay of the Masters' Lodge, and for the working of the Third Degree as a regular part of the ordinary lodge business. More and more, the ceremony of making a Master Mason is referred to as a 'raising.' We do not yet hear of the Sublime Degree, but in the Old King's Arms Lodge, No. 28, of 1745, we read of "the high degree of a Master."

Not all Masters' Lodges disappeared, however; some of them remained to work ceremonies that may have had no proper place in a Craft lodge. They became Royal Arch Lodges, possibly Mark Lodges, or so it has often been suggested; but it must be clearly borne in mind that no definite evidence has so far come to light.

We learn of a Masters' Lodge being attached to a Craft lodge constituted by the famous Thomas Dunckerley, by special authority of the Premier Grand Lodge, on board H.M.S. *The Prince*, at Plymouth, in

1762. The Royal Somerset House and Inverness Lodge, a time-immemorial lodge, is to-day's representative of that old lodge.

Of course we still have Masters' Lodges to-day, even apart from every lodge opened in the Third Degree, which is a true Masters' Lodge. The Plymouth and District Masters' Lodge, No. 5898, for example, while having the power to make, pass, and raise freemasons, was founded for the special purpose of interesting Brethren

> by means of Papers upon History, Antiquities, and Symbols of the Order, to cultivate a desire for Masonic Research, and to stimulate a high standard of working in Local Lodges, and generally to foster Masonic goodfellowship, and to promote the Grand Principles upon which our Order is founded.

This is but one of many, and the Somerset Masters' Lodge may be particularly mentioned. The Grand Stewards' Lodge, heading the list of English lodges, is a purely Masters' Lodge.

'Scots Mason' or 'Scots Master' Lodges

The mysterious degree known as the 'Scots Master' is mentioned in the minutes of some lodges in the 1730's and thereabouts; for example, in the minutes of an old Bath lodge we learn that "the Lodge of Masters met Extraordinary & our following worthy Broth^{rs} were made & admitted *Scots Mas^r Masons*." This minute is typical of a number. It is fairly well agreed that the word 'Scots' is no real indication that the degree was of Scottish origin, but there is a strong feeling that it might have been the creation of French masons, possibly influenced by Scots, large numbers of whom had fled from Scotland in the Jacobite troubles to take refuge in France. It is likely that the Scots Degree was a preliminary to either the Royal Arch or the Mark Degree—just possibly to both. The Scots Degree remains a mystery, and anything that can be said on the subject is nothing more than conjecture. Some students believe it to be connected with an alleged Jacobite movement (see p. 188).

"Passing the Chair"

During the second part of the eighteenth century Brethren wishing to 'pass the chair' merely to qualify them for membership of the Royal Arch were often given facilities. There are references to the matter on other pages. (To-day the qualification of being an Installed Master in the Craft is necessary in the case of the principal officers only of the Royal Arch.) The 'Antients' commonly passed Brethren to the chair for the purpose named, such Brethren often being said to have had conferred on them a Fourth Degree—that of a "Past Master of Arts and Sciences." (All

Installed Masters know a similar phrase.) We read that in 1790 the Master of the Salopian Lodge, Shrewsbury, a 'Modern' lodge constituted in 1788, but consistently working the 'Antient' ritual, resigned his chair. Bro. B. was immediately elected Master, installed, and thereupon resigned office, the old Master being then re-elected and reinstalled. In 1824 four Brethren "passed the chair" in St John the Baptist Lodge, No. 39 (founded at the New Inn, Exeter, in 1732), apparently to qualify them to attend an installation, only one of the four ever becoming Master of the lodge, and it is known that 'virtual' past masters continued to be made in one North Country lodge as late as 1840, one brother taking the degree only two months after his initiation.

John R. Rylands, in a valuable paper (*A.Q.C.*, vol. lxv), which should be read at first hand, brings to light that in the Lodge of Unanimity, Wakefield (founded 1766), the degree was at times conferred without reference to, or association with, the Royal Arch. Only two of the sixteen Brethren 'raised' to the degree in 1826 are known to have proceeded to the Royal Arch. In 1815 a brother was given the 'Constructive Degree'; in the next year he was exalted; in 1818, about four years before he was installed Master, he presided over a Regular Meeting. By 1837 the degree was undoubtedly associated with the Royal Arch, but between 1816 and 1826, says the writer just referred to, the degree was taken as an end in itself, conferred certain rights or privileges, qualified a Brother to preside in his lodge, and at that time was not essentially associated with the Royal Arch.

Ceremonial and Ritual

We may conclude this chapter with a few notes on ceremonial and ritual, a subject obviously closely associated with the degrees. The men who gave freemasonry its present formal dress were wise. They knew that in providing ordered ceremonies they were meeting a need common to most of us, and, while they were aware that ceremonies were not in themselves the whole of masonry, they surely were convinced that the most telling and effective way of impressing on the Brethren the tenets of the Craft was by means of ceremonial ritual. With this, surely, all freemasons will agree. There is an eloquent passage in the Prestonian Lecture of 1936 by Lewis Edwards, who distinguished between, on the one hand, the type of mind that feels "most in touch with things unseen when in direct and solitary communion with them and to whom rites and ceremonies seem but as obstacles to that communion," and, on the other hand, some who

see in what at first sight appear but as outward forms and ceremonies a means of strengthening the appeal of things spiritual, and who see them as "things which religion hath hallowed" and which lead and direct them. To the first class freemasonry, being "veiled in allegory and illustrated by symbols," can obviously make little appeal. The other class perceives in our ritual and ceremonial, not a religion—in spite of the suggestion so frequently and so wrongly made—but a means for enforcing and illustrating religious and ethical principles and precepts. . . . Further, there is a discipline, a working together in carrying out a common rule of life in which impulses, which might otherwise lose themselves and become vain, may be taken up and directed to the spiritual advantages of one and of all.

Fine distinctions are often drawn between ceremony, ceremonial, rite, and ritual, but the more the modern applications of these terms are considered the more their present meanings are seen to overlap one another, whatever their original derivations may have been. It might indeed be said that, while ceremonial is a ritual of forms, ritual is a ceremony of words.

Ceremony in general is an observance, a form, a formal rite, a stately usage, a religious or a masonic rite.

Ritual, on the other hand, has been defined as a prescribed order of performing a service; the book in which it is set forth is itself known as a ritual, but probably more accurately as a formulary. In the old Church practice a rite was distinct from a ceremony, for the former was the service expressed in words, and the latter the service expressed in gestures and acts, the ritual then being the outward order, such as standing to sing or kneeling to pray. A rite nowadays is so confused with form and ceremonial as to be hardly distinguishable from them. It is a usage, a custom, a solemn act, a ceremony or observance; particularly one that has been prescribed by authority. The rite has been thought literally to signify, or symbolize, a well-trodden path, an idea which lights up the meaning of the word for the freemason. Masonically, we use the word 'rite' as meaning a ritual system, as for example, the York Rite, the Scottish Rite, etc., etc., in which cases the term implies a ritual of words combined with a particular order of ceremonial acts. It must be stressed again, then, that whatever may have been the original meaning of the words under discussion they now so overlap as to be scarcely distinguishable from each other.

Chapter Sixteen

INITIATION

To initiate a man is to make him a mason, to admit him into the Craft in accordance with the ancient masonic rite, to make him a Brother among masons. The Scots happily refer to it as 'brithering' (brothering). So far as we know, the word 'initiate' was not used in its masonic sense earlier, or much earlier, than 1728, although it was common in religious writings long before it was known to masonry. In *The Wisdom of Solomon,* one of the books of the Apocrypha, translated in the sixteenth century, we read, "for she is initiated into the knowledge of God." It is more than likely that the speculative mason adopted the actual term 'initiate' from the old customs of the Church. The Church Fathers in their homilies commonly refer to the baptized brethren as 'the initiated.'

Literally, the initiate makes a 'beginning.' That is the meaning of the Latin word from which 'initiate' is derived.

'Candidate,' too, comes from the Latin and meant originally 'clothed in white,' from the custom of Roman candidates for office being obliged to wear the white robe, the *toga candida.* The masonic Candidate is a man who requests the favour of a degree, who aspires to one, or who is about to pass through or is passing through a ceremony conferring a degree upon him.

Some of the older masonic writings, particularly the French, speak of the uninitiated person as a 'profane'—that is, a heathen, a man not initiated into religious rites, one who is 'outside the temple.'

The custom of calling the uninitiated person a 'cowan' derives entirely from the use of this term in the *Constitutions* of 1723, and is dealt with at length in Chapter XXVIII.

The Candidate's Declaration

There was long ago put into neat form what should be the Candidate's correct approach to freemasonry. We find it in the Candidate's Declaration, which under the English Constitution every Candidate must sign before Initiation. This declaration is as follows:

To the Master, Wardens, Officers, and Members of the Lodge of ——, No. ——.

I, *A.B.,* being a free man, and of the full age of twenty-one years, do declare that, unbiassed by the improper solicitation of friends, and uninfluenced by mercenary or other unworthy motive, I do freely and voluntarily offer myself a candidate for the mysteries of Masonry; that I am prompted by a favourable opinion conceived of the institution, and a desire of knowledge; and that I will cheerfully conform to all the ancient usages and the established customs of the Order.

This declaration, occupying a separate page of a printed book kept by the Tyler, has the blessing of old custom, its present wording being much the same as in the eighteenth century. In American lodges Candidates make this declaration orally.

The Candidate's Qualifications

A Candidate for freemasonry must be a man of good reputation and integrity and well fitted to become a member of the Lodge in which he seeks Initiation. He must be a free man, of the full age of twenty-one years, and the tongue of good report must have been heard in his favour. He must be well and worthily recommended and have been regularly proposed and approved in open lodge. He must come of his own free will and accord, humbly soliciting to be admitted to the mysteries and privileges of freemasonry. He will be asked to make a solemn affirmation that he puts his trust in God, and he must, at the right time and in the right way, be presented to the lodge to show that he is a fit and proper person to be made a mason. The serious responsibility resting on his sponsors (his proposer and seconder) is shared by the Master, Officers, and Committee, who inquire into the Candidate's credentials. The Grand Lodge of England does not lay down any minimum period for which a Candidate must be known beforehand to his sponsors; "it is the extent of the knowledge which is important, and Lodge Committees are desired to investigate every case in full light."

At one time in the 'Antient' lodges of the eighteenth century a man could not be made a mason before he was twenty-five years of age, but as the century progressed it became usual to admit a man at the age of twenty-one. Then, at the union in 1813, it was resolved that twenty-one be the minimum age, except by dispensation of the Grand Master or those acting for him. Most of the English-speaking Grand Lodges (Ireland, Scotland, America, etc.) make twenty-one the minimum age, but in Scotland the lewis may become a mason at eighteen, whereas in an English lodge the lewis, by tradition, may be made a mason first of a number of Candidates, but has no right to be initiated at an earlier age than twenty-one. A general impression that undergraduates at English Universities have a right to be initiated when only eighteen years of age has no basis, although it is a fact that large numbers of undergraduates are initiated at that age, but in every case, without exception, it is by dispensation of the Grand Master or those acting for him.

Inasmuch as the Old MS. Charges required a prospective apprentice to be of "honest parentage" or to "come of good kindred," we must assume that young men of illegitimate birth were not generally acceptable to the guilds and trade fraternities, whether mason or otherwise. This may have been the result of priestly influence, itself a reflection of the Jewish and Early Christian refusal to admit bastards to the priesthood, based on that ruthless verse in the Book of Deuteronomy (xxiii, 2), "A bastard shall not enter into the congregation of the Lord; even to his tenth generation." And, further, it might have been occasioned by a determination of the guilds to prevent such individuals from qualifying for craft positions from which they might on occasion rise to high civic authority, there being a most marked oneness between guild and city government.

That the requirement of the English MS. Charges was common to the Continental fraternities may be inferred from a rule of the *Steinmetzen* (German stonemasons) demanding that the prospective apprentice prove himself to be of legitimate birth.

It is likely that in some quarters a bastard was not regarded as being really 'free born.'

The old *Charges of a Freemason* accompanying the *Constitutions* of the United Grand Lodge state that "no master should take an apprentice unless . . . he should be descended of honest parents," and we know that in the superstitious days of the 1700's many speculative lodges took this old direction quite literally, believing that the illegitimate child was spiritually unfit as the halt and the maimed were physically so. But that idea is quite dead, we hope, or shall we say very nearly so? Feeling in the Craft, as also in all enlightened legal systems, is now opposed to any discrimination against a man merely because of illegitimacy, and is increasingly opposed, also, to any avoidable publicity being given to the fact that any unfortunate circumstances attend his birth.

Operative freemasons in medieval days would not admit to apprentice-ship a youth that had a bodily blemish. Apparently they were prompted by priestly insistence on certain Old Testament laws and by obvious considerations of a practical nature. That the apprentice mason should have the full and proper use of his limbs is fully understandable when we remember that he would be called upon at times to do work demanding strength and agility, such as the moving of heavy blocks of stone with the use of simple tackle. Any youth physically unequal to such tasks might soon have found himself broken, and thereby have added to the risks of those with whom he worked, thereafter becoming a charge upon his Brethren or upon the lord that employed him.

But many trades besides the masons and other workers in heavy material insisted upon physical perfection in their apprentices. Is it not on record that a goldsmith, having accepted a hunchback as an apprentice, was fined by his guild and the indentures cancelled? G. W. Bullamore tells us that in 1420 the Cutlers' Guild insisted on the apprentice being "of free birth and condition, handsome in stature, having straight and proper limbs"; that the Brewers examined apprentices in the Common Hall of the Craft as to "their birth, clean-ness of their bodies," etc.; and that the Barber Surgeons were particular as to the "colour and complexion of the said man or child, if he be avexed or disposed to be 'lepur or gowty,' maimed or disfigured in any p'ties of his body whereby he shall fall in disdain or loathfulness unto the sight of the Kings liege people".

Candidates for the ancient mysteries many thousands of years ago were required to be unblemished in hand or foot, while Leviticus xxi, 7–23, should be read for a statement of the extremely strict Jewish law by which a man who had a bodily blemish could not even come nigh unto the altar, his presence in the sanctuary being a profanation. But it is difficult to see why speculative masonry took over that requirement and so punctiliously applied it. Eighteenth-century bylaws insisting on "uprightness in body and limbs" kept out of freemasonry thousands of men who ought to have been within it. That the prohibition did in fact operate is obvious from a minute recording that the Maid's Head Lodge at Norwich, in 1809, was proceeding to make a Candidate "as an Entere'd Apprentice Mason but in consequence of his not being upright in body, he could not be admitted and therefore was rejected accordingly."

During the nineteenth century the Craft began to look at the matter more sensibly and humanely, and to-day we find English lodges admitting men of good report whether they have physical blemish or not, so long as any blemish does not "render them incapable of learning the art." The Grand Secretary, in a letter dated March 15, 1902, said that the fact that a Candidate had no thumb would not bar his admittance, providing that he was a satisfactory Candidate in every other way.

We have come to see what we, as speculatives, should have seen all along, that many of the lame and the halt are capable of becoming speculative masons of outstanding quality and merit. In this connexion many Brethren will think of a well-known Brother Mason who succeeded in doing quite a remarkable work for freemasonry, one whose name, as that of an authority, is quoted on many pages of this book. He was a life-long cripple. He came into Irish masonry by special dispensation, and the application to him of the old prohibition would have robbed free-masonry of a much-valued and much-loved son.

There are some physical blemishes, but only a few, that would make it difficult for a man to benefit from freemasonry or to do his duty by it. Obviously every case must be judged on its merits, always remembering how Shakespeare sums up the matter for us: "In nature there's no blemish but the mind."

Our American Brethren still hold—at any rate, nominally—to the medieval requirement, and this is what Josiah H. Drummond, an American lawyer, public man, and writer of the nineteenth century, had to say about it:

> We may be a Masonic heretic, but we must frankly confess that we cannot master a sober face to read or listen to the judgments rendered upon the momentous issue of a defective eye or lost finger-joint. . . . These are seriously regarded as crucial tests in the selection of workmen to whom we have little or no physical work to assign, but meet them on the threshold with the information that the preparation is in the heart, that the temples we have to build are only moral edifices. Was there ever greater incongruity of practice and profession?

No question of physical blemish seems to have applied when an odd character of eighteenth-century freemasonry, the Polish dwarf, Count Boruwlaski, was made a mason at the Feathers Inn in Bridge Street, Chester, in 1783, at a meeting attended by the half-dozen lodges of the city. The dwarf did not exceed in size a child of four or so, being about thirty-nine inches high, but was perfectly proportioned. He was born in 1738, was well educated and intelligent; he married, became the father of children, and lived to the great age of ninety-eight.

Proposing a Candidate: Initiation Fees

The serious responsibility resting on the proposers of a Candidate has already been mentioned. The rules of the English Grand Lodge provide for full publicity being given to the name, age, profession, private address and business address of a Candidate, and the names of his proposer and seconder. These particulars must be provided in proper form, and at the right time will find their place in the printed summons to a meeting. There was a custom in German lodges of writing the name of a Candidate on a blackboard which was displayed on the lodge premises for a month, so as to ensure full publicity of the Candidate's intention, and give members and visiting Brethren full opportunity of lodging an objection if they thought the Candidate was not worthy. In Oldham

Lancs, and in some other places it is still customary for the names of Candidates to be circulated to all lodges in the area.

The sponsor or proposer of a Candidate is known, both in France and in Germany, as the Candidate's godfather, whereas in England the masonic father, or godfather, of a Candidate is generally regarded as the Master that initiates him.

The question of giving publicity to the name of the proposer has been looked at rather differently, notably in some German lodges, where the name of the proposer was not made known until after the ballot, in order that the Brethren of the lodge should not be influenced one way or the other by the proposer's rank and station. A comment on this is that in some English lodges, but only some and then on rare occasions, it has been felt that it might be unwise for the Master to propose a Candidate, on the score that members might be unduly influenced in the exercise of their vote.

Quite early in the eighteenth century a lodge, then No. 15, meeting in the Bedford Arms, Covent Garden, had this unusual bylaw: "That no Person shall be propos'd As & for A Member of this Lodge who is of the same Profession or Trade with any Member of this Lodge; But who shall be proposed to this Lodge by the Member of that Profession or by his permission." Nowadays this principle applies, in effect, to Candidates of so-called 'class' lodges connected with individual professions, etc.

In prescribing minimum Initiation fees for all Candidates other than 'serving brethren,' Grand Lodge does not allow any Lodge to forgo or defer the fee, and would have looked askance at some lodges of the eighteenth century which accepted the fee by instalments, and which sometimes allowed a 'gifted Brother' likely to be useful to slip into membership without paying a fee.

The 'Moderns' agreed, in 1753, not to make a mason for a fee of less than one guinea, and the 'Antients,' whose members in general were much poorer men, made the minimum fee two guineas. So long ago as 1733 a noted lodge at Bath had an Initiation fee of only half a guinea, but ten years later trebled it for a resident of Bath, and made the fee three guineas for a stranger. In some of the eighteenth-century lodges a separate fee was payable for admission to each of the degrees.

A little scandal is related by A. F. Calvert concerning a famous lodge, the Albion, now No. 9, one of the earliest of the 'Antient' lodges, and warranted in 1769. Back in its early days some of its officers were charged with having initiated many persons for the mere consideration of a leg of mutton for dinner or supper! This was rightly held to be a disgrace to the Craft, and the officers were debarred from being admitted into "any 'Antient' Lodge during their natural lives."

A 'pledge to appear' was insisted on by at least one lodge about 1800, the Candidate depositing half a guinea as a security that he would duly attend. It is known that a few lodges still follow the custom, the deposit or proposition fee being accepted as part of the Initiation fee, to be returned if the Candidate were not elected.

The Ballot

It is a general custom to ballot for Candidates, both for Initiation and joining. All grand lodges insist on a ballot being taken, and closely guard it against risks of irregularity.

A candidate rejected in the ballot is said to be 'blackballed,' the term deriving from a custom, dating to at least the days of Ovid (born 43 B.C.), of casting a white ball in favour of a Candidate and a black one against him. 'Balls,' by the way, were often pebbles.

It is a custom in lodge to use white balls only, the ballot box having two divisions, one marked 'Yes' and the other 'No.' But it is not invariable, and there are still lodges, more particularly outside the London area, that prefer the two-ball system as being less likely to lead to accidental mistakes. Voting by ballot was encouraged by the ancient Greeks, who tied it up with elaborate rules and with whom the 'balls' (pebbles, counters, copper and wooden discs, etc.) were articles of commerce.

By regulations of the English Grand Lodge the ballot goes against the Candidate if three black balls appear, but it is quite proper for the bylaws of a lodge to enact that a smaller number than three shall exclude.

In American lodges the ballot is examined and declared to the accompaniment of much ceremony. Assume that a particular ballot will prove on examination to be in favour of the Candidate, this is what happens. A junior officer presents the completed ballot to the Junior Warden, who examines it carefully, and when asked by the Master how he has found the ballot replies, "Clear in the South." The box having been inspected in the West, the question is put to the Senior Warden, who replies, "Clear in the West." Finally, the Master examines the ballot and declares that it is "Clear in the East," and that the Candidate is elected. But should one of the reports prove "Not clear," or "Cloudy," then the Master declares accordingly. This custom is not believed to be wholly American in its origin, for we find the early German speculative lodges describing a favourable ballot as 'white.'

In some jurisdictions very special care is taken to ensure that an unfavourable ballot is not due to mistake or thoughtlessness on the part of any Brother exercising his vote. In English lodges it is customary, should there be the faintest suspicion that a black ball is due to a mistake, for the

Master to order a new ballot. There is, however, no method in the English system to justify the type of ballot practised now, or in the past, in many French and German lodges, and it is doubtful whether it would commend itself to the English Craft. The French system can be best explained by taking a regulation applying in a French-speaking lodge, the Parfaite Harmonie, of New Orleans, in 1752, and brought to light by N. S. H. Sitwell. Two black balls excluded, but when there was only one black ball the ballot was taken again at the next meeting; then two black balls would again exclude, but one black ball would again defer the ballot. At the third meeting, should there be one black ball, the objector would have to reveal himself to the Master and state the reason for his objection; should this weigh with the Master, the Candidate would be rejected, but if the Master thought the objection frivolous he would repeat it aloud in open lodge without naming the objector. A fourth ballot would then be taken forthwith, the Candidate being rejected only if two black balls or more appeared.

The system of justification followed in the German Lodges was not quite on those lines. The Candidate's name having been displayed on the blackboard for four weeks, a ballot was taken. Every black ball in the ballot had to be justified, or was wholly disregarded. Four black balls or more meant the adjournment of the application for a year, but the Candidate was not rejected unless the black balls numbered one-third of the entire ballot! With three black balls or less, the Brethren who cast them were invited to reveal their identity and explain to the Master in confidence their reasons; then the Master assembled his officers and placed the objections before them, the matter being finally laid before the Brethren and a new ballot taken.

In some masonic jurisdictions it is open for the whole Lodge to see how a Brother casts his vote. There are Brethren who see a source of danger in the irresponsibility of a secret ballot, and while we agree that some small danger there may be, surely this is outweighed and offset by a Brother's ability to cast his vote without fear or favour, free from external influence.

The minutes of old lodges reveal many curiosities of the ballot, as might well be expected. P. R. James recites the case of William Purdie, who worked the ferry at Bath running between Spring Gardens and what is now Orange Grove, and who, as a visitor to the old Bath Lodge, No. 41, in January 1765, was made a Fellow Craft, and four days later was rejected as a joining member. Four days later, again, he attended as a visitor, and by October of the next year he had been elected to membership, becoming ultimately Master of the Lodge. We go to the same source for another instance in the Bath Lodge, that of William Collins, who afterwards became ale-tester to the Bath Corporation. He was rejected by two balls in October 1755, and in the following March by four balls, his election being then postponed for three months, during which time he attended six meetings as a visitor. In June he was successful in the ballot, and in the following year became secretary, and ultimately Master.

In many of the old English Lodges a Candidate had to be separately proposed and seconded and elected to each of the superior degrees. In the Druidical Lodge of Rotherham, under the York Grand Lodge, in 1779, "Bro^r. Moses & Bro^r: Thomas proposed themselves to be raised to the Degrees of M:M:."

Under the English jurisdiction a Brother (not a serving Brother) automatically becomes a subscribing member of a lodge in which he is initiated. In past days the Initiate became a member only if he expressed his wish to do so at the time of his Initiation, and even to-day in Lodge No. 41, Bath, there is a convention by which an Initiate is asked whether he wishes to become a subscribing member.

The Candidate's 'Preparation'

The physical preparation of a Candidate for Initiation is in close accord with tradition, but unfortunately it must be admitted that the meanings of some of its details are not now fully understood. The officer responsible for the preparation is the Tyler, who should be an experienced craftsman well able to ensure, both by his knowledge and his personality, that the Candidate enters upon his preparation in the right spirit.

In the ceremonies connected with the mysteries of thousands of years ago, as much care was taken with the preparation of the Candidate as with the Initiation that followed. Biblical texts can be given that tend to show that there is strong Jewish influence in the traditional preparation of a masonic candidate. Mackey quotes the Talmudic *Baracoth*, which insists that "no man shall go into the Temple with his staff, nor with shoes on his feet, nor with his outer garment, nor with money tied up in his purse," reminding us that in many but not all American lodges, as in the early English lodges, the Initiate is "neither naked nor clad" and may wear a special white garment designed to give effect to that description.

The minutes of some English Lodges between 1770 and 1809 indicate that their Candidates wore dress of an especial style. Some of these minutes have a quaintness all their own, as, for example, those of Lodge Percy of London, meeting at the Three Tuns, Cross Street, Hatton Garden, which record in 1795: "Wee order'd a pair of flannel Drawers to bee made for the use of the Lodge." In 1775, the Marquis of Granby Lodge, Durham, No. 124, had "one pair of Fustian Drawers"; in 1788 the Anchor and Hope Lodge, Bolton, No. 37, had "one pair Trowsers linen"; in 1812, the Lodge of Felicity, No. 58, had "Sundry Cloathing, *i.e.*, five flannel jackets, four pr. draws, five pr. slippers." A few English and many American lodges still provide special garments for Candidates.

The special arrangement in English lodges of the Candidate's dress, taking three particular points in their well-known order, is thought to have been designed (1) possibly to ensure that the Candidate conceals no weapon of defence or offence, a provision that may have had meaning hundreds of years ago; (2) by uncovering the heart, to reveal sex, but even more likely, in view of the wellnigh universal tradition that the heart is the seat of the soul, to suggest the Candidate's fervency and sincerity; and lastly (3) as evidence of the Candidate's humility, perhaps the greatest of all the qualities that freemasonry sets out to teach.

The Candidate is deprived of moneys, metallic substances, and of "everything valuable" before he enters the lodge, so that, emblematically, he is received into masonry poor and penniless, a symbolism which we might regard as being all-sufficient. In 1730, or earlier, the "Lectures" included the following:

> Q. And pray how much money had you in your pocket when you was made a Mason?
> A. None att all.

Tradition has attached to this item of the Candidate's preparation an allusion to the building of King Solomon's Temple, of which we read that "the house, when it was in building, was built of stone made ready before it was brought thither: so that there was neither hammer nor axe nor any tool of iron heard in the house, while it was in building." (I Kings vi, 7.) The old lectures include questions and answers based on this text.

In the Bristol working the Candidate is informed that part of the reason for his being deprived of metallic substances is to prove to the Brethren that he has brought nothing offensive or defensive into the lodge. Masonic writers have attempted to fasten other but sometimes doubtful interpretations upon the custom, these ranging from the assurance of the peace and harmony of the lodge to the preparation of the soul of man for the life hereafter.

It can be well understood that Candidates for the mysteries, all through the ages, have been required to be blindfolded, and it follows naturally that in every mystery, including freemasonry, the hoodwink is an emblem, not only of secrecy, but of the darkness that vanishes in the light of initiation. Milton's words, "What in me is dark, illumine; what is low, raise and support," should be the prayer of every Candidate, whose physical darkness symbolizes his spiritual ignorance. Plato said that "the ignorant suffered from ignorance, as the blind man from want of light."

Here is part of an old catechism of the eighteenth century:

Q. Why was you hoodwink'd?

A. That my heart might conceal or conceive, before my eyes did discover.

Q. The second reason, Brother?

A. As I was in darkness at that time, I should keep all the world in darkness.

The more we study the question of the Candidate's 'slipshodness' the more we are likely to believe that this item of the Candidate's preparation was not casually introduced, but, on the contrary, possessed originally very great significance. Unknotted garments and the unlatched shoe, or missing shoe, carried too much importance in ancient and medieval folklore for any other conclusion to be possible. In old Scottish days every knot in the clothing of the bride and bridegroom was carefully loosened before the wedding ceremony; afterwards, the couple separated, each with their attendants, to retie the knots, the whole company then walking round the church, carefully keeping the church walls always upon the right hand (that is, unconsciously following what their ancient forebears had thought to be the path of the sun). Knots were thought to mean danger, particularly in relation to the fruitfulness of the union of the young couple. Obviously, a later custom of the Scots bridegroom attending his wedding with the left shoe unlatched—a custom that is not yet entirely a matter of the past—is a rather less inconvenient survival of the older one, although probably all that the bridegroom knows about it now is that the unlatched shoe makes for 'luck' and averts 'danger.'

It is highly probable that the Candidate's slipshod shoe came into masonry chiefly, but not perhaps entirely, from folklore, and part of its original purpose was to avert danger from him. Danger of what? We must assume it to be the danger, or risk, of his violating his obligation, but we cannot entirely rule out that the risk in mind was that of the Candidate's failing to be 'born again' into a state of true enlightenment.

The slipshod condition is usually associated with two ancient Jewish traditions, the one providing the suggestion that the slipshod condition is a gesture of reverence, and the other that it is the confirmation of a covenant.

With regard to the first of these, the reference is to the well-known story of Moses and the burning bush, in which "the angel of the Lord appeared unto him in a flame of fire out of the midst of a bush": and Moses received the command: "Draw not nigh hither: put off thy shoes from off thy feet, for the place whereon thou standest is holy ground." (Exodus iii, 2, 5.) There are other and similar biblical texts.

The poet has well caught the idea in these lines:

> Earth's crammed with heaven,
> And every common bush afire with God;
> But only he who sees takes off his shoes.[1]

We are told that the nations of antiquity worshipped their gods barefooted and we know that in connexion with religious and magical rites the Romans often had their feet bare, as, for example, when noblemen of the first rank, their feet naked, gathered together the remains of the body of Augustus from the funeral pyre, and when the sorceresses, intent on the exercise of their art, went with one foot or both feet naked, as illustrated on some Roman fictile (clay) vases. People attended the worship of Isis with naked feet, and in the same condition went in procession to beg the gods to send rain in times of drought.

The idea of the bare or slipshod foot is so ancient that we cannot even guess at its age. Jason, a celebrated figure in ancient Greek legend, who led the Argonauts in quest of the Golden Fleece, came before Pelias the Usurper without a sandal on his left foot, Pelias having been warned by an oracle that a man in that condition would appear before him. We can expect that such details were pregnant with meaning.

We have to bear in mind that the Candidate's slipshod condition may conceivably be related to one or more of the many threshold superstitions to be found in the folklore of all ages, one of the commonest being that it is ominous to stumble at the threshold of a house, or (we suppose) symbolically at the threshold of any new undertaking.

The second of the Jewish traditions is to be found in Ruth iv, 7–9, where we learn that to unloose the shoe and give it to another person was a gesture of sincerity, of honest intention, a confirmation of a contract that had been made between the two parties. The inference to be drawn from this is that the Candidate's slipshod condition is in itself a token of fealty or fidelity.

A catch question in an eighteenth-century irregular print runs:

Q. What did you pay for freemasonry?
A. An old shoe, an old shoe of my mother's.

From this we may conclude that the Initiate then wore a slipper belonging to the lodge, just as he does to-day. It is to be noted that in many American lodges the third-degree Candidate is "bare-foot."

[1] E. B. Browning, *Aurora Leigh.*

The Cable Tow

On later pages in this chapter we attempt to explain some of the complicated symbolism attaching to the cable tow as a measure of length, but in the *preparation* of the Candidate we may narrow our interpretation of the cable tow and regard it merely as a noose or halter, a symbol which had a place in the ancient mysteries, but which to-day is hardly known apart from freemasonry and even there, particularly with regard to the English Craft, cannot be said to be a symbol having a well-understood meaning. Unfortunately, the explanation given to the Initiate at the Master's pedestal in English lodges is so greatly lacking that we might well suspect that, in the editing and rearrangement of the ritual, possibly following 1813, some phrases that would have assisted us to understand the true significance of the Candidate's cable tow were accidentally omitted.

The wearing of a halter by the Initiate appears to hark back to mysteries now lost in antiquity, and students say that the noose figures in the Brahminical ceremonies as a sacred emblem, and that in the Zoroastrian system, three thousand years ago, every one was thought to have had cast about his neck a noose, which at death fell from the righteous man but dragged the wicked down to hell.

It is probable that in some of the ancient mysteries the cable tow, or halter, was the means by which the Candidate was *led*, symbolically in a state of bondage, through part of the ceremony.

Everything points to the wearing of the cable tow as being an indication of the Candidate's submission to the will of the Master and his lodge. Indeed, in a ritual of the early 1800's, the Initiate refers to the cable tow as "this humbling power."

From time immemorial the halter has been the symbol of captivity, serfdom, slavery, and was so exemplified, even in the nineteenth century, by the sorry superstition then prevailing among a few poor and ignorant people that a man might lawfully sell his wife to another man, providing he deliver her over with a halter about her neck!

Conquerors in both ancient and medieval days obliged the leaders of a defeated people to come before them wearing halters. When Israel had defeated Ben-hadad and the Syrians, Ben-hadad's servants said to him, "Let us, I pray thee, put sackcloth on our loins, and ropes upon our heads, and go out to the king of Israel: peradventure he will save thy life." (I Kings xx, 31.) Some citizens of London got into trouble on what is known as Evil May Day, 1517. Many were taken prisoner and appeared before the King, Cardinal Wolsey (Lord Chancellor), and members of the Commons. The prisoners, who were bound together in their shirts and with halters about their necks, set up such a piteous cry for mercy that the King pronounced them pardoned; whereupon, giving a great shout, they threw up their halters towards the roof, crying, "God Save the King!"

In the year 1347 the people of Calais appeared before Edward III of England in their shirts, each with a cable tow round his neck, in full token that they were at his mercy. In which connexion we recall the entry in John Evelyn's *Diary* for October 1641. He is writing of the statue of Charles V standing in the market-place of Ghent, to which, as he was told, "the magistrates and burghers were wont to repair on a certain day every year with ropes about their necks, in token of submission and pennance for an old rebellion of theirs; but now the hemp is changed to a blue ribbon." From which we are led to conjecture whether the silken collar of pride and consequence was not, once upon a time, the rough halter of humility.

The wearing of the cable tow may be thought to be at variance with the fundamental tenet that the Candidate must be a free man. Although the halter in this case signifies only bondage to a state of ignorance, we feel that the Irish and the Bristol workings offer an acceptable symbolism in this regard, the Candidate wearing the sign of servitude only until he is about to take the Obligation. Then it is removed and thrown contemptuously on the floor behind him, the Conductor, in the Irish working, informing him that naught but a free man may be made a freemason.

It is possible that there is an ancient connexion between the presence of a halter, or cable tow, about the neck and the taking of a solemn oath. *The History of Dunblane*,[1] quoting from an old account, tells us that armed men, one column headed by the Earl of Argyle and another by Lord James Stewart, Prior of St Andrews, entered Dunblane Cathedral in the year 1599. Round the neck of every one of them was a halter. "We come," said the Earl, "to set forward the reformation of Religion . . . and to purify this Kirk. . . . We have banded ourselves together . . . and bound ourselves by a great oath that we are willing to part with this life as these symbols round our necks testify if we turn back or desist." They then tore down and threw into the river the altars, shrines, and images.

The Knocks

The knock or series of knocks on the outer door of a lodge is an alarm, an indication that some one seeks admittance. Much of its symbolism comes from the familiar, homely knock on the door of one's house, which

[1] A. B. Barty (Stirling, 1944).

has been a figure through the ages. Thus, "Behold, I stand at the door, and knock: if any man hear my voice, and open the door, I will come in to him, and will sup with him, and he with me." (Revelation iii, 20.) And "To him that knocketh it shall be opened." (Matthew vii, 8, and Luke xi, 10.)

Brethren have sought to see in the knocks on the door of the lodge all sorts of elaborate symbolism, some of which is of early date, as for instance:

> Q. Brother, you told me you gave Three Distinct Knocks at the Door: Pray what do they signify?
> A. A certain text in scripture.
> Q. What is that text, Brother?
> A. Ask, and you shall have; seek, and you shall find; knock, and it shall be opened unto you.
> Q. How do you apply this text in Masonry?
> A. I sought in my Mind; I asked of my Friend; I knocked, and the Door of Masonry became open unto me.

The theory is held by some students that when the Candidate reaches the outer door of the lodge, the knocks are given by his 'Friend' or proposer, on his behalf, but by proxy. Possibly the following catechism in an old ritual supports the idea:

> Q. Who brought you to be made a Freemason?
> A. A friend whom I afterwards found to be a Brother.
> Q. How did you gain admission?
> A. By three distinct knocks.

In an irregular print of 1730 it is an Entered 'Prentice who has brought the Candidate to the lodge.

According to the old author, Durandus, in the ceremony of consecrating a church in the thirteenth century, the bishop's procession made three circuits of the church, the bishop knocking on the door after each of them, but being admitted only at the third knocking. "Rightly . . . doth the bishop strike three times, because that number is most known and sacred; . . . without the invocation of the Trinity there can be no sacrament in the Church." As the Christian influence was strong in masonry for a long period, it is by no means unlikely that the triple knock originally carried with it an allusion to the Triune God. But there is a wholly masonic explanation of the necessity of giving three knocks. One writer has suggested that there are three obstructions and three doors (one door real, and two, not imaginary, but symbolical) to be negotiated by the Candidate. There are three distinct knocks to obtain admission, and three distinct knocks to pass each obstruction.

The Reception of the Candidate

The reception accorded to the Candidate at the moment of entering the lodge must be much the same as that which all candidates for initiation, not necessarily masonic, have met at any time through thousands of years. There is brought home to him the seriousness of the step which he proposes to take, and he is reminded of the responsibility that will rest on him to guard the secrets about to be entrusted to him. It emphasizes the difficulty of entrance, in more than one sense, and even its danger if admission has been improperly achieved.

In the First Lecture, as also in the First Degree ritual of the Bristol and Irish workings, the suggestion is conveyed by the Conductor, or other officer, to the Candidate that the recollection of the manner of his reception will ever be torture to his mind and conscience, should he ever be about to violate the confidence placed in him.

We may just refer to what appears to be a startling suggestion made by G. W. Bullamore—namely, that the Inner Guard's precaution is intended to prevent the impersonation of the Candidate by a malignant spirit. Bullamore naturally admits this to be a mere conjecture, and to most people it will hardly sound convincing. But it is fair to say that in medieval days the possibility of an evil spirit impersonating a human being was firmly held by all sorts of people who, however, generally believed that the infallible means of detecting the imposture and frightening off the intruder was to confront him with the sign of the cross.

The Candidate is called upon to affirm in open lodge that in all cases of difficulty and danger he puts his trust in God. So much every candidate in the old operative days had to affirm. "The Charges of a Freemason," which preface the *Constitutions* of the United Grand Lodge, and have a strong medieval background, say in their very first paragraph :

A Mason is obliged, by his tenure, to obey the moral law; and if he rightly understand the art he will never be a stupid atheist nor an irreligious libertine. He, of all men, should best understand that God seeth not as man seeth; for man looketh at the outward appearance, but God looketh to the heart. A mason is, therefore, particularly bound never to act against the dictates of his conscience. Let a man's religion or mode or worship be what it may, he is not excluded from the Order, provided he believe in the glorious architect of heaven and earth, and practise the sacred duties of morality. Masons unite with the virtuous of every persuasion in the firm and pleasing bond of fraternal love; they are taught to view the errors of mankind with compassion, and to strive, by the purity of their own conduct, to demonstrate the superior excellence of the faith they may profess. Thus masonry is the centre of union between good men and true, and the happy means of conciliating friendship amongst those who must otherwise have remained at a perpetual distance.

The Candidate's Circumambulation

By his circumambulation of the lodge the Candidate is being ceremoniously but very effectively presented to the Brethren. This long word, from the Latin, means 'walking all round,' and frequently is confused with another word from the Latin, 'perambulation,' which means 'walking through.'

Of all religious rites circumambulation is one of the most ancient, and made its mark upon popular custom probably thousands of years ago. Circumambulation always proceeded sunwise—that is, in the direction assumed to be taken by the sun. We use the term 'clockwise' to explain the same thing, and we speak of the contrary direction as being 'against the sun,' or 'counter-clockwise,' while the Scots have their own curious word for it—'withershins,' or 'widdershins.'

Thousands of years ago people became nervous of proceeding except in the sunwise direction. We read that when Plato, who lived in the fifth century B.C., gave a symposium—a dinner and drinking party—the greatest care was taken to pass the wine cups round from right to left, and even conversation and everything that took place in the entertainment was made to observe that same rule. The superstition was strongly held through the centuries and is often met to-day. For instance, who has not noticed the look of horror on a guest's face when his left-hand neighbour at table has attempted to pour him wine with his left hand? The superstition appears in simply countless guises. Here is a ludicrous example. A man of marked learning became Lord Chancellor of England in 1529. He was the famous Sir Thomas More, one of the greatest men of his day and a sombrely pious man. His receipt for curing toothache is just this—"For the toothache go thrice about a churchyard and never think on a fox's tail."

In the mysteries and religions of all ages there has been the formal procession three times around a sacred place or object, and always sunwise—that is, with the devotee's right side on the inner side of the procession. The Romans of old closely observed the custom; indeed, it was part of their ceremony of expiation and purification, and their word *lustratio* implies not only purification by sacrifice, but a moving in a circular direction. The rite prevailed in ancient Britain in the days when the stones of Stonehenge were put in place, and we are told that the old Welsh names for the cardinal points of the sky—the north being the left-hand

and the south the right—are evidence of the ancient Celtic practice of turning to the rising sun. Folklore contains numerous references to circle-magic which is assumed to have been derived from ancient sun-worship.

It was inevitable that, in the course of time, the stately rite of circum-ambulation should be adopted by the Christian Church. Everywhere the Church still observes it. We have already quoted Durandus, who des-cribed it as being practised by the bishops as far back as the thirteenth century.

Whether, therefore, freemasonry took the rite from the religion of either ancient or medieval days, we recognize in the circumambulation of the Candidate an element of most or of all the mysteries, stretching back, probably, to before the dawn of civilization.

The Obligation

An oath to keep secret what would be communicated to him has naturally been demanded of every initiate in every mystery. In medieval days the craft apprentice took an *oath*. To-day the speculative Appren-tice takes an *obligation*. The two are not quite the same. An oath is a solemn appeal to God in support of the truth of a declaration and in witness that a promise will be kept. An obligation is a binding agreement.

All craftsmen in medieval days, not only the mason operatives, took solemn oaths to conceal and keep secret what should be communicated to them. Here, for example, is the oath of the Barber and Surgeons Guild of 1606: "You shall concale, keep secrett and not disclose such councill as att any tyme hereafter shall be used or spoken of by or amongst the said company soe helpe me God and by the Holy contents of this Booke."

The manner of taking an oath has varied with time and circumstance. Frequently, in ancient days, merely the right hand was lifted up, or it was placed upon the Scriptures or other sacred object. In Hebrew 'to raise one's hand' was a common phrase for 'to swear.' It is good Scots practice to raise the right hand when taking an oath, and we learn that in 1498 a member of a Scots operative lodge took an obligation "by his hand upholden." In a purely Jewish lodge, the Obligation may be taken standing and covered.

Among the Teutonic nations many were the forms of oath devised to impress the conscience of the candidate. Gould informs us, in the course of a helpful discussion of the subject, that among some of the ancient German peoples the soldier swore on the edge or blade of his sword; the pagan Danes swore by the holy bracelet; among the Alemans (early Teutonic tribes) a widow swore by her bosom or her hair. The ancient Jews took an oath with their hands on the book of the law, a custom which we continue when we take an oath on the Bible or New Testament. Sometimes the ancient peoples swore with their hands upon an altar victim, or on the altar itself.

In general, the ancient Jews took an oath standing, and, so far as was possible, in an attitude of prayer, or with their hand upon some sacred object, the effect being to bring in as witness the Deity, by whom the oath was sworn.

Let us look at the forms of some of the old oaths and obligations of masonry, operative and speculative.

The earliest known masonic manuscript, the Regius Poem, contains these words:

> To be true to the Ordinances
> A good true oath he must there swear
> To the Masters and Fellows that be there.
> And all these points herein before
> To them thou must needs be swore,
> And all shall swear the same oath
> Of the Masons, be they willing or loath.
> . . . Amen, Amen, so mote hyt be.

The Grand Lodge MS. No. 2 (date about 1650) contains the following oath of secrecy:

> I, *A.B.*, do in the presence of Almighty God and my Fellows and Brethren here present promise and declare that I will not at any time hereafter by any act or circumstance whatsoever directly or indirectly publish, discover or reveal or make known any of the secrets, privileges or counsels of the fraternity or fellowship of Freemasonry which at any time hereafter shall be made known to me. So help me God and the holy contents of this Book.

The Harleian MS. No. 2054 (date 1650–90) has attached to it in the handwriting of Randle Holme, the well-known herald and antiquary, who was himself a freemason, a slip containing the first-known English allusion to masonic words and signs:

> There is a seurall words and signs of a free Mason to be revailed to yu wch as you will ans: before God at the great and terrible day of Judgm^t yu keep secrett & not to revail the same to any in the hears of any pson but to the M^{rs} and fellows of the said Society of free Masons so helpe me God. xt.

The Buchanan MS. (date 1660–80) contains some wording with which the Freemason of to-day will be familiar:

> These Charges that you have received you shall well and truly keep, not disclosing the secrecy of our Lodge to man woman nor child: stick nor stone: thing movable or unmovable: so God you help and his holy Doome. Amen.

The curious phrase 'holy doome' will be noted. In other of the old manuscripts it is given as 'hallydome,' 'hallidome,' 'holydoom,' etc., and we recognize in all of them the oath often used in romantic literature—"By my halidom!" The word suggests a state of holiness, and can be regarded as giving a secret or religious character to the Candidate's word of honour. The word has also been spelt 'halidam,' and has then been thought to mean the Holy or Blessed Dame, or Virgin. The lands of an abbey or other religious foundation were sometimes known as a halidome.

The Colne MS. No. 1 (date about 1685), describes the manner in which the Charge should be received (actually, the oath taken): "One of the eldest taking the Bible shall hold it forth that he or they which are to be made Masons may impose and lay their right hand upon it and then the Charge shall be read."

The Harris MS. No. 1 (date, second half of seventeenth century), contains the following:

> These charges which we now rehearse to you and all the other Charges Secrets and Mysteries belonging to Freemasonry you shall faithfully and truly keep together with the Councel of this Lodge or Chamber. You shall not for any Gift, Bribe, or Reward, favour or affection, directly or Indirectly, for any Cause whatsoever divulge or disclose to either Father or Mother, Sister or Brother, Wife, Child, friend, Relation or stranger, or any other person whatsoever. So help you God your Holy doom and the Contents of this Book.

The manuscript tells us that after taking the oath the book is "kist."

The Sloane MS. No. 3329 (date about 1700) gives an oath containing what is now a very familiar phrase:

> The mason word and every thing therein contained you shall keep secrett; you shall never put it in writing directly or indirectly; you shall keep all that we or your attenders shall bid you keep secret from Man Woman or Child Stock or Stone and never reveal it but to a brother or in a Lodge of Freemasons and truly observe the Charges in ye Constitucion; all this you promise and swere faithfully to keep and observe without any mann^r of Equivocation or mentall resarvation directly or indirectly so help you God and by the Contents of this book. (*The Candidate kisses the book.*)

The Thistle Lodge MS. (date about 1756) neatly sums up in this way: "We bind ourselfs to all the above artikls, as on the substins of which canot be writen, but as writen in the hart."

The Ordinances of the Masons of Halberstadt (date 1693) include the following clause:

> A Master shall enjoin a servant whom he has passd according to custom of the Craft, that he shall keep enclosed in his heart on peril of his soul's

salvation, that which has been entrusted to him OF WORDS and by no
means make the same known to anybody but an honest mason under pain of
losing his handicraft.

G. W. Speth believes this to be the only ordinance extant which refers to
the existence of a secret word or words in the system of the German
Steinmetzen (stonemasons).

It will be noted that some of the Old Charges required the oath to be
kept "without any manner of equivocation or mental reservation."
What exactly does this imply? Mental reservation on the part of one who
takes an obligation means simply the intentional failure to disclose something that affects the meaning of the statement made, and which, were it
disclosed, would change the import; thus, the Obligation, as the individual intends and well knows, means one thing to him that enters into
it and another to those that receive it or hear it recited. The full phrase
is found for the first time, we believe, in the Protestant Declaration or
Oath of 1678 and 1679, and *Miscellanea Latomorum*, in its very first
volume, tells us that it was the outcome of the national frenzy engen-
dered by Dr Titus Oates, who in 1678 professed to have discovered a
popish plot against the King. Since the first year of William and Mary
the phrase has formed part of the Declaration made by the English
Sovereign before taking the Coronation Oath, the actual words being:

> And I do solemnly, in the presence of God, profess, testify and declare,
> that I do make this declaration and every part thereof in the plain and
> ordinary sense of the words read unto me, as they are commonly under-
> stood by the English Protestants, without any evasion, equivocation or
> mental reservation whatsoever.

Freemasons might well ask what is the origin of the severe penalties
attached to the Obligation? Gould lights up the subject for us when he
says that in the earliest times the necessity was felt of making as conspicuous as possible, in the most varied but always telling ways, the
penalties that would be incurred by a breach of oath or promise. While
there is no historical record, he says, of their actual infliction, the retention
of the barbarous penalties of medieval days in so many local codes bears
witness to their high antiquity.

It was common in ancient days for the parties to a contract to profess
to subject themselves, in the event of their violating their engagements,
to such a death as had befallen a victim sacrificed by them in making the
contract. Thus, among the ancient Hebrews, the contracting parties killed
and cut in twain a heifer and then walked between its two portions. We
learn of this in the Book of Jeremiah where, speaking of the men that have

transgressed His covenant, and had not performed the words of the covenant which they had made before Him when they cut the calf in twain and passed between the parts thereof, the Lord said, "I will even give them into the hand of their enemies, and into the hand of them that seek their life: and their dead bodies shall be for meat unto the fowls of the heaven, and to the beasts of the earth." (xxxiv, 20.)

In the days of King Edgar, according to Gould, a thief was punished by mutilation, his body, in which there was still life, being "cast to the beasts of prey and the fowls of heaven." A murderer in old German days was punished by having his "flesh and body" thrown to the "beasts in the forest, the birds in the air, and the fishes in the sea."

Punishments of a horrible description were known to be the rule many hundreds of years ago in many parts of the world. The subject can be followed in *Old-time Punishments*, by William Andrews (1891), from which the following extract is reproduced:

> In the curious ordinances which were observed in the reign of Henry VI. for the conduct of the Court of Admiralty for the Humber, are enumerated the various offences of a maritime connection, and their punishments. In view of the character of the court, the punishment was generally to be inflicted at low-water mark, so as to be within the proper jurisdiction of the Admiralty, the chief officer of which, the Admiral of the Humber, being, from the year 1451, the Mayor of Hull. The court being met, and consisting of 'masters, merchants & mariners with all others that do enjoy the King's stream with hook, net or any engine,' were addressed as follows: 'You masters of the quest, if you, or any of you, discover or disclose anything of the King's secret counsel, or of the counsel of your fellows (for the present you are admitted to be the King's counsellors), you are to be, and shall be, had down to the low-water mark, where must be made three times, O Yes! for the King, and then and there this punishment, by the law prescribed, shall be executed upon them; that is, their hands and feet bound, their throats cut, their tongues pulled out, and their bodies thrown into the sea.'

It is on record that in 1557 six pirates were hanged at Wapping on the shore at low-water mark, where they were left until three tides had overwashed them. And from *A Dialogue between Simon and Philip*, dating back to 1730, or perhaps many years earlier (made available by Douglas Knoop and G. P. Jones), we learn of this dreadful penalty alleged to be incurred by the old mason should he break his oath:

> ... my Heart pluck'd from my Left breast, my Tongue pluck'd from the roof of my mouth, my Throat cutt, my Body to be torn to pieces by Wild Horses, to be bury'd in the Sands of the Sea where the Tide flowes in 24 Hours, taken up and burn't to Ashes and Sifted where the four winds blow that there may be no more Remembrance of me. SO HELP ME GOD.

Whether the medieval penalty clauses of a masonic obligation are in keeping with the days we now live in, and, if not, whether they should continue to be included as an essential element of the Obligation, is a question arising now and then. Brethren have asked whether, inasmuch as some penalty clauses reflect the cruelty and mental darkness of other days, Obligations including them as essentials may properly be sworn on the V.S.L., and have ventured to wonder whether any reasonable modification would leave the Craft any the poorer or constitute an 'innovation' affecting any true landmark of the Order? They have argued that the oaths taken by operative brethren in days of old did not include babarous penalties, and that nothing of the kind has been traced in connexion with the forms of obligation adopted in the Scottish operative lodges, although, as one writer puts it, "the peril to a man's soul, for the breaking of the vow, was nearly always insisted on." They have reminded us that many of the German lodges regarded the old oath as a matter of history only, and in its place put a simplified obligation incorporating a solemn vow.

On the points so raised it may be remarked that, although most English Brethren assume that the medieval penalty clause is an absolutely essential part of the Obligation as also of the ceremony of Initiation, we have to remember that even in the one country of England the penalty clause is given in different ways. In the Bristol working, for example, it concludes with these words "*or until* this horrible punishment 'shall be inflicted, the less dreadful (but to an honest mind) of being further branded as etc., etc." And in the Irish lodges, the Candidate in the course of his Obligation *bears in mind* "the ancient penalty of having etc., etc." and binds himself "under the real penalty of being deservedly branded as an etc., etc."; the ancient penalty is referred to in the Irish working as the *symbolic* penalty. Of course, that is the real position in all English-speaking lodges, and it would be all to the good if Initiates were definitely taught strictly to regard the penalty entirely in that light, clearly insisting that they should understand the real penalty to be that of being branded as a wilfully perjured individual, void of all moral worth, etc., etc. In the words of the old German oath already recorded, let the Initiate be taught to keep his masonic secrets "enclosed in his heart on peril of his soul's salvation."

The question has been raised whether a Candidate who is a member of the Society of Friends (Quakers), and consequently prevented by his religious principles from taking an oath, would be allowed to make an affirmation. There have been outstanding Quaker members of the Craft, and it so happens that the Grand Lodges of Ireland, England, and of certain American states have discussed the question of the admissibility of Quakers, some of them more than once. In 1835 the Grand Lodge of Ireland asked the Grand Lodge of England for information as to the English practice in the event of a Quaker seeking admission to the Order, and in reply received an expression of the opinion (with which the Irish Grand Lodge agreed) that the Candidate should make, in lieu of the usual Obligation, a solemn affirmation, including a statement that he had been one of the people called Quakers for the period of one entire year, following which he might be initiated. In the year 1834, in the Newcastle-on-Tyne Lodge, No. 24, a Quaker had been allowed to affirm in accordance with a dispensation from the Grand Master. A. G. Mackey, the American author, says that the whole practice of American lodges is against affirmation in lieu of the Obligation.

There are obvious difficulties in dealing in a printed book with that part of the initiation ceremony in which the secrets are conferred, but the whole world knows that the Initiate receives a grip, as to which it is to be noted with pleasure that the mere act of shaking hands, as a gesture of faith and confidence, was part of the symbolism of Roman Law, and as such has continued to be observed by all civilized peoples.

We speak of the grip as a 'token,' the use of which word has been objected to by some writers who suppose that a token must be a physical thing, such as a piece of metal doing duty as a coin, or the Past Master's breast jewel, which in many lodges represents the brethren's good-will; but there is nothing in the derivation of the word to limit its use in that way, and the word is quite correctly used as implying a means of recognition between members of a fraternity. We read in the Book of Genesis (ix, 13) of the rainbow which was the *token* of God's covenant with man. The word comes from old German, and originally meant 'to teach,' 'to point out,' 'to indicate.'

On the subject of masonic secrecy much could be written, but little that would matter. It must, however, be clearly stated that freemasonry is not a secret society. Instead, it is a society having secret modes of recognition between its members—which is a distinction with a real difference. Necessarily the Initiate is sworn to secrecy. The Obligation closes his lips, much as, but not exactly as, in the ceremony of 'making' a cardinal in the Roman Catholic Church, in which the Pope closes the new cardinal's lips to remind him of the discretion required of his office, and later opens them again to indicate the need for fearlessness in pro-claiming truth and justice.

Freemasonry makes no secrecy of the great principles it teaches. It publishes the names of its members and officials, and the times and places of its meetings. It prints its *Constitutions*. The Grand Master, the Prince of Wales, in his speech at the laying of the cornerstone of Truro Cathedral, in May 1880, said:

> We have among us secrets concealed from those who are not Masons, but they are lawful and honourable, and not opposed to the laws either of God or man. They were entrusted to Masons in ancient times, and, having been faithfully transmitted to us, it is our duty to convey them inviolate to our posterity.

An Irish clergyman once remarked (and every freemason under the English-speaking jurisdictions could do the same with equal truth) that "no secrecy of masonry obliged him to conceal anything which, as a Christian, he should divulge, and the concealing of which might prove injurious to his fellow creatures."

The design, the object, the moral and religious tenets and doctrines of freemasonry are those of an open society, "one that could meet on the highway beneath the sun of day and not within the well-guarded portals of the Lodge." But there is in freemasonry a secret, a real secret, although an open one to him whose heart inclines him towards its discovery. It slowly dawns upon the faithful Brother, who rarely shares it with anybody—for one thing, because it is difficult to put into words. Perhaps Emerson was getting near it when he said that humility is the secret of the wise. But probably, in a roundabout way, one of Disraeli's characters was getting still nearer when he said that sensible men are all of the same religion. "And pray, what is that?" inquired the prince. "Sensible men never tell," was the response.[1]

The badge, working tools, the warrant, the bylaws, and certain other things that have a place in the Initiation ceremony are separately referred to in later chapters.

The Word 'Brother'

The remainder of this chapter will be devoted to some matters about which the Initiate might expect information—explanations of one or two masonic words and phrases, of what is meant by the length of the freemason's cable tow and of the masonic customs relating to right and left.

Freemasons, in calling each other Brother, are following old guild and old operative practice, as well, of course, as basing themselves upon Biblical custom. The word 'Brother' was not by any means restricted to the mason craft in early days, for in nearly every guild the members were enjoined to call one another Brothers and Sisters. The Old MS. Charges of the English operative masons contain the injunction, "you shall call masons your Brother, or else your fellows, and no other foul

[1] Benjamin Disraeli, *Endymion*, chapter 81.

names." Then, too, the swearing of brotherhood was a mere drinking custom during the Middle Ages.

The admission of a working mason to the fellowship of his craft in Scotland was frequently known as 'brothering,' or 'brithering.' Robert Burns, freemason, had that well in mind when he wrote:

> For a' that and a' that,
> It's comin' yet, for a' that,
> That man to man, the warld o'er
> Shall brithers be for a' that.

'Brotherhood' and 'Fraternity' look different, but actually both of them have descended from the Greek *phrater* ('brother'), the one through the Saxon tongue, and the other through the Latin.

'Brother' is a common word in the language of the Bible, and, of the many classes of men there so called, the freemason is chiefly interested in those who have a community of nature, who are equals, and who have a natural affinity for one another. Freemasons are Brothers one of the other, inasmuch as they come into one or more of those categories, have all passed through the same ordeal of Initiation, have been made brothers of Hiram Abif, have been given particular modes of recognition, and have been taught the same philosophy.

"So Mote It Be"

"Amen! Amen! So Mote It Be! So say we all for Charity." The earliest of all masonic manuscripts (1390) ends in that way. "So mote it be" is known as an optative exclamation, because it expresses a wish, or desire. The 'Amen,' that at one time preceded the exclamation, means 'verily,' 'certainly,' 'truly'—in everyday phrasing, "Yes, we agree." (There is another 'Amen'; in this case a noun carrying the meaning 'the faithful one,' 'the true one,' as in the Book of Revelation (iii, 14): "These things saith the Amen, the faithful and true witness, the beginning of the creation of God.") "So mote it be" includes a part of speech of the Anglo-Saxon word *motan*, having the general meaning of 'to be allowed.' Thus "So mote it be" is simply "So may it be."

Apparently, in the early lodges the word 'Amen,' coming from the Master or from a Senior Brother, was endorsed by the Brethren's "So mote it be," but in course of time the 'Amen' has fallen from use, although it is still customary in some American lodges, as follows:

Master. May the blessing of heaven rest upon all regular masons. May Brotherly Love prevail and every moral and social virtue cement us. Amen.
Brethren. So mote it be.

The Cable Tow as a Measure of Length

The cable tow as a measure of length is not known outside free-masonry, and has given rise to much fruitless argument. The Master Mason swears to answer and obey all lawful signs and summonses sent to him from a Master Masons' lodge, "if within the length of his cable tow." Elsewhere in the ritual occurs the phrase, "a cable's length from the shore." Such allusions are symbolical of the binding covenant into which the mason has entered, and of the 'length' beyond which he should not go. In the Royal Arch Degree a cable, or cord, has other significance; it is there regarded as the cord of amity and the cord of love, special emphasis in this respect being given to the cord in the Irish Royal Arch chapter. At the Wakefield Royal Arch Lodge in 1769 a toast was drunk "to him that first shake'd his cable." In a masonic catechism, dating back to early in the eighteenth century, the 'length of the cable' was a figure of speech relating to the concealment of secrets.

What actually is a cable tow? We know that a cable is a strong rope made of cords twisted together, often around a centre cord. One defini-tion of 'tow' is the hemp or other fibre used in rope-making, but it is unlikely that this is the kind of 'tow' here meant, in spite of the use in a Bradford lodge of the phrase "a cable of hemp or tow." The cable tow, or cable rope—that is, a towing rope or tugging rope—may colloquially be called a 'tow,' and it seems very likely that the term comes from German masonry in which *kabel* means 'ship's cable' or 'rope,' and *tau,* a 'cord' or 'rope,' whilst *kabellaenge* means 'cable's length.'

The phrases 'a cable's length,' and 'the length of my cable tow,' can be regarded as having the same meaning. A cable's length is variously given at 100, 120, and 130 fathoms, equal to 200, 240, and 260 yards; but the length of an actual towing cable varies with conditions of water and wind, with the size and weight of the vessel to be towed, and with the thickness of the cable itself. A 'cable' is a measure of length at sea, and is then about 100 fathoms, or about 200 yards—more accurately, one tenth of a nautical mile, and just short of 203 yards. No such length as any of the above was in the minds of those who arranged the early rituals, but eighteenth-century ideas of the length of a cable tow, as expressed by Dr Oliver and still earlier writers, were arbitrary and un-practical. Every Brother was expected to attend his lodge if he was within the length of his cable tow, and that length is said to have been three miles—about as far, presumably, as he could be expected to walk.

An irregular print of 1766 says in a footnote: "A cable tow is three miles in length; so that if a Fellow-Craft is that distance from his lodge, he is not culpable on account of his non-attendance." It is idle to suppose that a speculative mason's cable tow has, or ever did have, any physical length, in spite of Dr Oliver and other early writers.

When a freemason is summoned to attend the duties of his lodge, the phrase "if within the length of my cable tow" can mean only "if within all reasonable possibility," or "if within the scope of my ability," pleading no excuse thereto except "sickness or the pressing emergencies of my public or private avocations."

The old catechisms had many odd references to the cable tow.

'Right' and 'Left'

Traditional masonic teaching with regard to the 'right' and the 'left' is far from clear. We all know that mankind in the main is right-handed, and that in olden days it was normally the right hand that held the weapon, while the left shielded the heart, slightly to the left of the body's centre, from the enemy's blows.

The English word 'right' is derived from an old word meaning 'straight' or 'direct,' a meaning included in such a phrase as 'the right road to take.' It is easy to see that the right hand would come to imply 'of good omen,' 'propitious,' and to be regarded as in some respects superior to the left. For example, we set a guest of honour on our right, we serve him wine with our right hand, and with our right hand shake the hand of a friend, this last idea being supported by many Biblical references.

The Latin form of the word 'right' is 'dexter,' to be contrasted with the Latin form of 'left' which is 'sinister,' a word obviously suggesting bad omen. So, if we take a long view, we may say that the invitation to the Candidate to place his right hand on the open V.S.L. is the continuation of a practice which goes back hundreds of years, for in both English and Scottish operative masonry the candidate, on taking the oath, supported the Bible on his left hand and placed his right down upon the open page.

It goes without saying that the word 'right' is entirely different from 'rite,' which in its original Latin meant a 'custom,' and now means 'a solemn ceremony.'

With regard to the 'left,' the symbolism is not so clear as with the 'right.' Generally, but not always, the 'left' has been supposed to mean 'weak,' 'worthless,' although by some old authorities the left side of the body was regarded as the sacred side. A writer of the second century A.D. speaks of a "symbol of equity, a left hand fashioned with the palm extended" and of its "being endowed with no craft and no subtlety."

In the old Pagan auguries, in which prophecies were influenced by the flight of birds, a flight in a direction against the sun—that is, in an *awkward* or *sinister* direction—was always regarded as an ill omen.

If there be any symbolism implied in the Candidate's starting off 'with the left foot,' it has now been forgotten, and it can only be supposed that the request to the Candidate is nothing more than an attempt to ensure that he and his guide proceed in step. But this is a matter in which we might easily be wrong, for the custom might have been derived from folklore. James Grant, in his *Mysteries of all Nations,* states that "it is thought lucky to step out with the left foot first."

There is always the possibility that the custom of starting off with the left foot was introduced in the military lodges of the eighteenth century. Bearing in mind that a right-handed man, in particular a soldier carrying arms at his left side, naturally tends to start off with the left foot, as otherwise he might lose balance, it is easy to see that what originally was a matter of drill might quite naturally have become a ceremonial detail in purely military lodges, which, from their migratory habits and their strongly 'Antient' sympathies, are known to have exerted marked influence on masonic ritual and custom from their institution in Ireland in 1732 and in England in 1750 right on through the 1700's. The last of the English military lodges—the Lodge of Charity, Peace, and Concord, No. 316—surrendered its military warrant in 1949 and is now a stationary lodge in London.

Perhaps it is worth while recalling, however, the extremely ancient superstition (based probably on an earlier religious idea) that a person entering another man's house on his left foot took ill luck in with him, and the apparent contradiction of this when the masonic Candidate, who is undoubtedly crossing the threshold of a mystic building, starts his perambulation in the lodge on his left foot. So strong was the superstition in ancient Rome that a rich man would station a boy at the door of his house to remind his guests to enter on the right foot. It may be conjectured as to whether the intention in instructing the Candidate to start with the left foot was that he should step *over* and not *on* the threshold of the symbolic lodge.

Undoubtedly, at one time masonic ritual testified to the supposed weakness of the left side of the body. Take, for example, this catechism from an irregular print of 1766:

> *Q.* When you was made an Apprentice, why was your Left Knee bare bent?
> *A.* Because the Left knee is the weakest Part of My Body, and an Enter'd Apprentice is the weakest Part of Masonry.

'Hele'

"I will always *hele*, conceal, and never reveal." In this phrase the Candidate may think that he meets for the first time a very unusual word. As a matter of fact, it is a delightfully simple word, and the Candidate has often met it in related forms. Although obsolete among townsmen, it is still used by countrymen, as it has been for centuries. Its origin is the Anglo-Saxon *helan*, meaning 'to cover and conceal,' and its significance to the Initiate is that, by its use in the Obligation, not only does he undertake not to reveal the secrets of freemasonry, but he undertakes to cover them up and conceal them. The use of the word prepares him for the Master's injunction cautiously to avoid all occasions which may inadvertently lead him to disclose any of those masonic secrets which have been entrusted to his keeping.

Chaucer and even much earlier writers used it, although Shakespeare, in a later day, does not appear to have done so. We find in the Matthew Cooke MS. (early fifteenth century) the first masonic reference to the word: "That he can *hele* the counsel of his fellows in lodge and in chambr and in every place where masons be."

Of about the same period is the oath (quoted by Gould) made by a burgess of Reading, who, in the time of Henry VI, swore on his admission, to the following effect:

> The comyn counsell of this said gilde, and felishipp of the same, that shall ye heele and secret kepe, and to no p'sone publice, shew, ne declare, except it be to a burgess .'. All these things shall ye observe, an truly kepe in all poynts to y'or power, so help you God, and holy dome, and by this boke.

Chaucer has a noteworthy example of the use of the word: Mordre [murder] is so wlatsome [disgusting] and abhominablé to god . . . that he ne wol nat suffre it *heled* be."

In the English countryside the word even to-day has many interesting uses. Thus, a Sussex auctioneer's announcement of 1946 speaks of a "sectional house . . . corrugated healed"—in other words, a house roofed with corrugated material. Many country people speak of 'healing' a house, where the townsman would speak of 'slating' or 'tiling' it. Countrymen 'hele' or 'heel' in a plant when they cover up its roots to await a convenient time for proper planting. They 'hele' their potatoes and other roots in clamps, when they store them protected from light and weather. In Kent, country people 'hele' a child when they cover it up in its cradle. In the old days there was undoubtedly a word 'unheale' in common use. Spenser, in *The Faerie Queene*, uses it.

'Hellier,' 'healyer,' etc., are the old names, still in occasional use, for the 'roof slater' and 'tiler'; hence we get these words as common surnames. In some country districts a cover, such as a drain cover, is a 'heler.'

'Hell' meant originally the covered, or concealed, world or place; thus, in the Apostles' Creed, occur the words, "He descended into hell" —the covered place. The helmet covers the head; 'helm' is one form of the same word. A hill whose crest is covered by cloud is said to be 'helmed.'

Some students have associated the word with the healing of a wound —that is, with the covering of the wound by the new, growing skin; but this is subject to argument. In the sixteenth century a book was 'healed' when it was bound between covers.

In early centuries, undoubtedly, 'hele' rhymed with 'mail' or 'male,' and for this reason, we suppose, some printed rituals include an instruction to pronounce the word in that way; but the matter is not quite so simple as that. When the editors of the early eighteenth century ritual brought together those three words, 'hele,' 'conceal,' 'reveal,' it is quite obvious that they meant them to form a sequence known as a rhyming assonance, and the words ought still to rhyme. A practical purpose was intended—that of making a special mark on the hearer's mind, and fixing the three words in his memory. Formerly, not only 'hele,' but also 'conceal' and 'reveal' commonly rhymed with 'mail' or 'male,' and of this we have frequent proof in the writings of the period, where sometimes the words are spelt as they were then pronounced.

Although we are told that in parts of the West Country, including Cornwall, 'hele' is still pronounced 'hale,' in most if not all other country districts where the word has survived, it is now spoken as it is spelt— 'hele.'

While every Master of a lodge will please himself, it does appear that, if the original intent of the phrase is to be maintained, as it certainly should be, then all three words must continue to rhyme, either with 'hale' or with 'hele.' That is the first point. But if they are to be intelligible, then the old pronunciation is quite out of the question. "Hale, consale and never revale" would either be meaningless, or would invite a smile at a point in the ceremony where least desired.

Of course, the *a* sounds of many other words have in the course of time become *e* sounds—even 'sealing wax' was 'sailing wax'—and here are two rhyming lines from Pope's *Rape of the Lock*, and addressed to Queen Anne:

> Here thou, great Anna! whom three realms obey,
> Dost sometimes counsel take—and sometimes tea.

From this we see that two centuries and more have robbed of its rhyme, but not of its humour, a couplet well demonstrating what has happened to the three words under discussion.

The word 'heal' ('to restore to health') has also been used masonically. A Brother was 'healed' from 'Modern' to 'Antient' masonry, or vice versa, the implication being that his Initiation, having been of doubtful regularity, his masonic condition was now healed—made good and sound—by reinitiation.

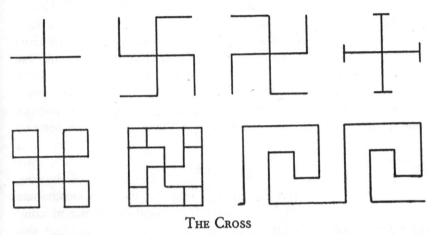

THE CROSS

These figures show the Cross and its development into various forms of the swastika (fylfot) and similar devices, most of them demonstrating the Cardinal Points.

'Cardinal'

We speak in freemasonry of cardinal virtues, cardinal points, cardinal winds. Briefly, this curious word means 'important, 'significant,' and carries with it a mental image of matters of great moment all revolving round a centre-point acting as a hinge, or pivot (Latin, *cardo*). Much ecclesiastical history is wrapped up in this word, which is associated with the red colour of the robe worn by the Roman Catholic cardinal— that is, worn by a powerful priest occupying a fundamentally important place. We go to the doors made and hung by the ancient peoples for the original idea of the meaning of the word. There were two vertical pins, or dowels, projecting from the door, one from the top and one from the bottom, each fitting into a socket, and on these pivots the door swung. The ancients took this hinged door as a figure, or symbol, and supposed that at the top of the universe was a pivot upon which the heavens revolved, while at the bottom was another pivot, corresponding to that at the bottom of the door.

In course of time, the old Roman writers applied the word 'cardinal' to the four points: east, west, north, and south, and to the winds blowing from those quarters. The east symbolizes wisdom; west, strength; north, darkness; and south, beauty. We are told that the cardinal—that is, the most important—virtues in masonry are prudence, temperance, fortitude, and justice; the first to direct, the second to chasten, and the third to support a Brother, while the fourth should be a guide to all his actions. But the Initiate is also taught the high place occupied by other excellencies of character—secrecy, fidelity, and obedience—of which the ritual offers a full explanation.

The cross is an image of the cardinal points and has been so from long before Christian days, in particular the swastika form of cross, the fylfot, commonly regarded as a good luck charm. The name swastika derives from Sanskrit words meaning 'well being.' The 'true' swastika indicates the sunwise direction or 'sacred circuit,' the 'false' one (curiously, the one debased by its adoption as a Nazi symbol) the anti-sunwise direction.

Due Guard

Still surviving in a very few English lodges, in most Irish lodges, and in lodges throughout the U.S.A. is the Due Guard, which was no doubt in use in the English lodges of the early eighteenth century, and is very likely to have been inspired by, or borrowed from, operative practice. Lodges in the American system appear to lay as much emphasis in their ceremonies on the Due Guard as they do on the sign or signs of the degree.

In general, the Due Guard relates to the attitude of the Candidate at the time of taking the Obligation in any one of the degrees. It is a sign in itself, but its real purpose can be compared with that of the keeper-ring, which serves as a protection against the loss of the wedding ring. The Due Guard is just that—a keeper, a protection against the accidental loss or betrayal of the real sign of the degree, because any invitation to give that sign is immediately countered by a demand for the Due Guard. Thus, without the Due Guard from one Brother, the sign of the degree will not be vouchsafed by another. Every separate rite in the American system appears to have its own individual Due Guard, although in the Irish system the Due Guard is only known in the First and Third of the Craft Degrees, an indication, perhaps, that both of the Due Guards belonged originally to the old First and Second Degrees before their rearrangement and the addition of the Third.

The old French term *Dieu* for 'God' was known in early English literature, and there may be a relation between the two terms, although it seems that the word 'Due' is used in a most obvious way as meaning 'correct,' 'proper,' in the sense of the term 'due form.' *The Oxford Dictionary of English Proverbs* (1935) gives a number of references. We are told, for example, that a 'beck' or 'becke' (a 'bow' or a 'nod') is as good as a 'Dieu Gard,' and that the old French *dieu vous garde* ('God keep you') was a polite salutation of the year 1538. 'Dieugard' (sometimes spelt 'Dew Guard') was Middle English for the same salutation.

Words relating to Secrecy

It is worth while to look at some of the many words meaning, or relating to, secrecy as used by freemasons.

A 'secret' is something concealed or hidden. It is 'inviolable' when the promise to keep it is not capable of being broken. Secret matters are often 'abstruse' or 'profound'—that is, hard to understand. With regard to secrets and mysteries we are 'reticent' (reserved), and we continuously avoid occasions which might inadvertently lead us to disclose them.

A 'mystery' is something hidden; literally, the lips and the eyes are closed so far as the mystery is concerned.

We sometimes call a book of ritual, or formulary, an 'esotery,' or say it is of an 'esoteric' nature—that is, it is understood by the few, or designed only for the few to understand, or has been prepared for the enlightened, and for them only.

We 'hele' our secrets—that is, we cover them up, or conceal them and do not reveal them to the common light. Things hidden from observation or common knowledge are said to be 'occult.'

Secret things, or things secret except to the few, are sometimes said to be 'cryptic'; in freemasonry, we associate the word with a crypt or vault, a hiding-place.

'Arcana' are secrets, even inner secrets, the word being sometimes used to mean also the literature of arcane subjects. 'Arcanum' is from the Latin *arca*, a chest, ark, or box, and carries the meaning of something shut in or hidden; by this word the alchemists knew the 'great secret' (the transmutation of metals), to the search for which they directed their endeavours.

In the ceiling of some of the lodge rooms in which our early Brethren met was a painted or modelled rose, the flower associated with Harpocrates, whom the Greeks and Romans (mistakenly) regarded as the god of silence, the significance being that everything said and done by the Brethren 'under the rose' was secret, a matter of strict confidence between them all. The Tudor Rose is part of the beautiful ceiling decoration of some of the lodge rooms at Freemasons' Hall, London, and of very many other places where freemasons regularly meet.

Chapter Seventeen

THE FELLOW CRAFT AND HIS DEGREE

THERE is difficulty in writing about the Fellow Craft's Degree as an entirely distinct entity. None of us can escape the consciousness that the Second Degree is very much a continuation of the First—an extension of it, in fact. We do not know what led up to the separation, or how it was made, and we know only a little more as to what happened to the Second Degree itself when, in the same decade, the Third came to be generally separated. It is obvious, however, that the interest and importance of the Second Degree considerably suffered by its separation from an inferior degree, and later by the shedding of part of its most interesting material to a superior degree.

The Second Degree, Then and Now

There is one marked difference between the old operative fellow, or fellow craft, and the speculative Fellow Craft. The operative had taken a big step as a man and as a mason when, from being an entered apprentice he became a fellow, for he was now a fully fledged member of the community and could work as a master whenever opportunity came his way, because he was already of the master's grade. And in speculative masonry, too, early in the eighteenth century, an exact parallel could be drawn, for once there were conferred upon the Apprentice the privileges of the Second Degree he had all the qualification needed to become Master of his lodge and an officer of high rank in the Order. But with the passage of the years this altered.

The 'Antients' emphasized the importance of the masonic grade of Master Mason; they insisted that the Fellow Craft must become a Master Mason before he could qualify to be the Master of a lodge, and that he could not assume that office until he had passed through an esoteric ceremony of Installation, with which qualification he could then rise to any rank in the Order.

In the lodges of the so-called 'Moderns' the Fellow Craft still remained the fully qualified mason, for Masters and Grand Officers could be drawn from his grade; but with the reconciliation between the two bodies in 1813 the Fellow Craft finally lost his earlier importance. The ceremony of the Fellow Craft Degree was probably still further depleted in the course of effecting a peaceful compromise between the two bodies, with the consequence that to-day we regard the Fellow Craft as having achieved little more than a midway position in freemasonry, superior in status to that of an Entered Apprentice, but definitely inferior to that of the Master Mason, to which he hopes shortly to attain. His ceremony has certainly carried further the ideas and philosophies to which he was introduced at his Initiation, but, apart from that, it has been little more than a stepping-stone from the experience of one Initiation to the even richer experience of another yet to come.

Evidence still remains to us of the significance attaching to the Second Degree in early days. The Fellow Craft's tools, undoubtedly the most important of all the speculative's tools, were a Master's tools, and they still provide the jewels of the Master and his two Wardens respectively, while it is to be noted that the tools now associated with the Master Mason's Degree did not come into use until after the union of 1813. The stress laid upon the five points of fellowship in the Third Degree has obviously been borrowed from the Second. The necessary preparation of the Master Elect for his high office is conducted (in English lodges) in the Fellow Craft's lodge, and not in the Master Mason's. There can be no doubt, then, that originally the Fellow Craft's Degree was one of supreme importance, and of this, fortunately, there still survive many traces.

'Craft'

'Craft,' one of the medieval words inherited by freemasonry, was originally a common Teutonic word (*kraft*) meaning 'power' and 'strength.' In England, and in England alone, it developed in the thirteenth century a second meaning, the one which freemasons associate with it—'art,' 'dexterity,' 'skill,' or 'cunning' of hand or mind. The poet Chaucer speaks of "crafty people," meaning skilful, clever, and, sometimes, merely sensible people. (The use of the word 'craft' to mean 'trickery,' 'deceit,' 'artifice,' etc., came in course of time, and we are not concerned with it.) 'Craft' came naturally in due course to mean a 'skilled trade' or 'occupation.' Our early seventeenth-century Authorized Version of the Bible, telling the story of the Apostle Paul's arrival at Corinth, says that he stayed with a certain family "because he was of the same craft, ... for by their occupation they were tent makers." (Acts xviii, 3.)

It is easy to see how 'craft' came to mean a trade mystery, a guild, and a brotherhood, or fraternity. The early merchant guilds developed in course of time into craft guilds, and the guild of this kind came to be known as a "craft,' in which sense the word came down to freemasonry, probably through the London Company of Masons. It is applied particularly to the first three degrees, known as the symbolic degrees.

'Fellow' and 'Fellow Craft'

The craftsman obviously is one who practises a craft. Among freemasons he is one who has been passed to the Second Degree. In the old days a mason was 'crafted' by being made a Fellow Craft. In the Lodge of Dunblane, in the year 1720, a Brother was said to be "duly passed from the square to the compass"—that is, from an Entered Apprentice to a Fellow of Craft. There is an old term 'crafts-master'; he was a man highly skilled in his craft, into which, in all likelihood, he was born.

We derive the word 'fellow' from an old Norse word *felage*, meaning 'partnership,' and implying equality and friendly association. The Regius Poem repeatedly speaks of a mason as a 'fellow,' and many other of the Old Charges use the term, sometimes in the form 'Masters and Fellows.' A 'fellow' in those days was a member of a fraternity, such as a guild. The fellows of a guild laid down their money and assumed obligations jointly with one another. There we have the essence of the word 'fellow.' To-day, with the meaning of 'member of a fraternity or society,' we have 'Fellow of a College.'

Often guilds were known as fellowships. Freemasonry itself was, and is, known as a fellowship. In the lodge at Alnwick the masons constituted a fellowship, its members being Masters and Fellows. Elias Ashmole in 1682 described himself as "the Senior fellow" among the masons gathered at the lodge in the London Company of Masons. It is obvious, therefore, that in the 1600's the English word for one enjoying full membership of the masonic fraternity was 'fellow.'

English masons might never have known the 'Fellow Craft' but for an importation from Scotland. It is at any rate possible that they saw it for the first time in the *Constitutions* of 1723, when, under the heading "*of Masters, Wardens, Fellows and Apprentices,*" the text speaks of an Apprentice being "made a Brother and then a Fellow-Craft in due time," and later states that no Brother can be a Warden until he has passed the part of a Fellow Craft, and that the Grand Master is to be a Fellow Craft before his election.

The *Constitutions* used three words all meaning the same thing— Fellow, Craftsman, and Fellow Craft—and by the introduction of the last of these, a Scots term, they transformed the old English 'Fellow' into a 'Fellow Craft,' for, although possibly the English freemason first met the word in 1723, it had in the course of only a couple of years or so given its name to the Second Degree. 'Fellow Craft' was the term used in the lodges of Aberdeen (Anderson's home city) and elsewhere in Scotland, and had the same, or much the same, meaning as Master Mason during the seventeenth century. The Schaw Statutes and early Scots minutes use the term 'Fellow of Craft,' and we learn from it that a Fellow Craft is simply a fellow, or equal member, of a skilled craft or companionship.

The Winding Staircase and the Middle Chamber

The lecture on the second Tracing Board tells us that in King Solomon's Temple was a winding staircase, which led to the middle chamber in which the Fellow Crafts were paid their wages. Their ascent to the middle chamber was opposed by the Junior Warden who demanded from them certain tokens. We read of this peculiar construction of the Temple in I Kings vi, 8: "The door for the middle chamber was in the right side of the house: and they went up with [by] winding stairs into the middle chamber, and out of the middle into the third." The Revised Version speaks of chambers (plural) and calls them "middle side-chambers." There has been argument as to whether the customary tracing-boards accurately depict the winding staircase, as apparently it should spring from the south, whereas they often show it as appearing to spring from the north. W. J. Songhurst throws light on the subject by saying that the stations of the three principal officers were in early Continental boards marked by three closed doors, East, West, and South, conveying the idea that behind these doors were Inner Guards empowered to admit or refuse admission. The Biblical passage quoted says that the winding staircase is on the right side of the house, and in I Kings vii, 39, the word 'right' is seen to have the meaning of 'south.' The spectator in Holy Writ is therefore considered as looking towards the East with the South on his right hand, and this is the position illustrated in so many of the Tracing Boards (but not in a new and beautiful design, which is the work of Edgar Lee, of the Royal Lancashire Lodge, No. 116, Colne, Lancashire).

The winding staircase has suggested some elaborate symbolism. Here, for instance, is what Carl H. Claudy says:

> It requires more courage to face the unknown than the known. A straight stair, a ladder, hides neither secret nor mystery at its top. But the stairs which wind hide each step from the climber; what is just around the corner is unknown. The winding stairs of life lead us to we know not what; for some of us a Middle Chamber of fame and fortune; for others, one of pain

and frustration. The Angel of Death may stand with drawn sword on the very next step for any of us. Yet man climbs.[1]

This is preferable to a symbolism based upon the letters of the Hebrew alphabet in accordance with the enigmatic teaching of the Kabballa, of which nonsense the less said the better.

Learned authors such as Donald A. Mackenzie, in *The Migration of Symbols*, believe that the cross, the swastika, the spiral, the cardinal points, and the sunwise direction of movement are all closely related in the ancient religions. Consequently, we may reasonably impute special significance to Solomon's choice of a *winding* staircase to conduct privileged worshippers from the ground floor to the middle chamber.

Lodge Furniture of the Early Nineteenth Century

In some of the American lodges the Candidate is called upon to ascend an actual winding staircase, but we do not think that this is necessarily an example of American 'extra-illustrating,' because it is quite likely that the idea came from some of the eighteenth-century English lodges. We learn something from the story of the Bath furniture and how it came to Barnstaple, unfolded by Bruce W. Oliver in *A.Q.C.* Freemasons' Hall in York Street, Bath, built by three Bath lodges and opened by H.R.H. Augustus Frederick, Duke of Sussex, in 1819, housed some magnificent masonic furniture that had been specially designed and built. For two days before the consecration of the hall upward of two thousand persons, chiefly ladies, paid for admission to view it and its contents. But the hall and equipment had cost so much that serious financial difficulties ensued, and ultimately the hall was sold by auction in 1842, and the furniture was offered "in one lot by way of chance, ... tickets 21*s.* each or five for £5," as a result of which a person who had previously become the legal owner won the prize! He soon afterwards sold the furniture to the Loyal Lodge (now No. 251), Barnstaple, for one hundred guineas. Among the handsome furniture and other articles included in the list of effects of the Loyal Lodge are two quite unique pieces—the 'winding staircase' and the 'middle chamber'—and the following descriptions of them come from Bruce W. Oliver's account in *A.Q.C.*, vol. lvii, in which volume appear many illustrations of these and other fine pieces (see Plate XXIII).

Winding Staircase. This rises five steps, in each of which is set the appropriate letter in brass. With its wreathed strings and handrails it is an excellent example of the craft of the joiner. The stairs rise to a height of 3ft. 1in.

[1] Carl H. Claudy, *Introduction to Freemasonry* (Macoy, New York, 1932).

and if used in conjunction with the 'Middle Chamber' would raise the top of that structure to the rather astonishing height of 12ft. 7in.

The Middle Chamber. This is generally accepted as having been used in connection with the "winding staircase" in the Second Degree, but the symbol in the floor and again in the ceiling suggests its possible use in the Royal Arch. It is a typical '18th century Temple,' octagonal in plan, measuring 4ft. 7in. across, the total height being 9ft. 6in. The floor, or platform, rises one step and has a chequered pavement radiating from the centre where a letter 'G' is enclosed by the 'Shield of David' within a circle. This feature is reproduced in the ceiling. The dome is constructed in canvas, supported by eight slender pillars of Doric character; the dome is painted with anthemion [honeysuckle or other flower] ornament and surmounted by a large gilt ball as a finial.

Tubal Cain

We are introduced to the tradition of Tubal Cain in the Old MS. Charges, and we learn more of that personage in the Second Degree. Tubal Cain had a place in the ritual as far back as 1743, but the interpretation put upon his name was not known in masonry until many years later. That interpretation has led to a great deal of controversy, which has revealed many facts, but ends apparently in the agreement that we do not know how the name was derived or what it properly means.

Apart from the reference in the Old Charges the ritual seems to have gone for information to the Geneva Bible (issued in 1560), where, in a marginal note, 'tubal' is explained as meaning 'borne,' 'brought,' or 'worldly' and 'cain' as 'possession.' Thus 'Tubal Cain,' by the simple process of putting the two meanings together, is interpreted as 'worldly possession.' There was a fundamental error in this interpretation, for the scholars were assuming that the primeval language was Hebrew, quite a common assumption in olden days, but one which we now know to be untenable. A simpler interpretation would be 'Tubal the Smith,' because the word 'cain' is not a part of his name, but an indication of his occupation—namely, a smith or artificer. The Authorized Version of the Bible says that Tubal Cain was an instructor of every artificer in brass and iron. Scholars to-day, however, say that a more accurate translation than 'instructor' would be 'whetter' or 'sharpener,' and the Revised Version says that he was the forger of every cutting instrument of brass and iron, and explains in a marginal reference that 'brass' may be 'copper.' Josephus, the Jewish historian, says that Tubal Cain invented brass; here, again, it is thought that 'brass' is 'bronze,' or 'a kind of copper' from which could be made cutting tools and weapons.

Briefly it may be said that Tubal Cain was a blacksmith and, in particular, an armourer, and it is not beyond possibility that there may be confusion between his name and that of Vulcan, or Vulcanus, the ancient fire-god, the protector of workers in metals, and a forger of shields and weapons. It has been hinted that Tubal Cain was identical with a primitive fire-deity known to an ancient Altaic people who apparently were among the earliest metal-workers in the world. W. W. Covey Crump has suggested that

> Jabal, Jubal, and Tubal Cain, brothers, sons of one and the same father, may have been mythical demigods, who, it is asserted, prophesied great catastrophies and recorded their prophecies on two pillars, as to which there is a tradition that once upon a time, somewhere east of the Mediterranean, certain inscriptions on stone and baked clay had been discovered, so prehistoric as to be deemed antediluvian in origin.

There is a further suggestion that there was a nomadic tribe, the Kenites, travelling tinkers or gypsies, whose name was formed from the word 'cain'; and there are those who have hazarded the opinion that Tubal Cain is not an individual, but rather a figure representing an early race living in a district south-east of the Caspian Sea many thousands of years ago, a race which might well have been concerned in the very early use of metallic iron.

We can afford to smile at an old book, Sir John Ferne's *Blazon of Gentrie* (1586), which apparently found an easy task in assigning heraldic arms to many Biblical characters, including Tubal Cain, who is fitted up with "sable, a hammer argent, crowned or." Sir John had a simple job with Tubal!

The Letter 'G'

In English lodges the letter 'G' is found in the centre of the ceiling, and is on every Second Degree Tracing Board. In American lodges it is on or near the Master's chair. In other English-speaking lodges also it usually has a place, but is there represented by a triangle containing the Hebrew name for God.

The absence of the letter 'G' in the appointments of foreign lodges is a key to much of the misunderstanding surrounding the symbol. A moment's thought will show that 'G' can be the initial letter of the word 'God' only in English and in a very few other languages—all of Saxon or Gothic origin. In no ancient language could 'G' mean 'God.'

It is reasonably certain that the letter was not used in English lodges as meaning 'God' until late in the eighteenth century, although it was a feature of lodges quite early in the eighteenth, and possibly during the seventeenth, centuries.

Dr W. Wynn Westcott has said the present masonic interpretation of the letter 'G' is foolish. Dr Oliver took the symbol without question as referring to the Great Architect of the Universe. But an earlier writer, William Hutchinson, "a man and a mason, whose head and heart went in unison, whose life was blameless, and whose memory is still fondly regarded by freemasons," says in his *Spirit of Masonry* (published in 1775 with the special sanction of Grand Lodge) that the name of God is only part of the masonic import of the letter; this significant letter, he says, "denotes Geometry, which to Artificers is the science by which all their labours are calculated and formed; and to Masons, contains the determination, definition, and proof of the order, beauty, and wonderful wisdom of the power of God in His creation."

How far back the letter 'G' was used as a symbol for geometry can only be guessed at, but we are told that Ptolemy's *Geography*, in an edition printed at Strasburg in 1525, contains an ornamental margin which includes a pillar, a small part of the spring of the arch above it, with foliage, cherub, and fluting decoration. On the base, in a panel, are the square and compasses with, in the centre, the letter 'G' "believed to stand for Geometry." In view of the date of this—1525—Mackey's statement that the letter 'G' is a *modern* symbol, which can be traced back to the word 'God,' and not to 'Geometry,' is not convincing.

The Continental masons who inscribed the name of God, or Jehovah, in Hebrew letters within the triangle, and displayed this in their lodges —as we do to-day in the Royal Arch Chapter—were harking back to an ecclesiastical custom of the sixteenth century.

The majority of masonic writers believe that the letter 'G' refers to Geometry, and the old catechisms also point that way. Here is a catechism printed in 1730:

Q. Why was you made a Fellow-Craft?
A. For the sake of the letter G.
Q. What does that G denote?
A. Geometry or the Fifth Science.

And here is another version of this same catechism:

Q. Why was you made a Mason?
A. For the sake of the Letter G.
Q. What does it signifye?
A. GEOMITRY.
Q. Why GEOMITRY?
A. Because it is the Root and foundation of all Arts and Sciences.

In the course of the eighteenth century there was much ritual-making, leading to great diversity between various workings. Take, for example, the following catechism (slight variations of it are known), printed in an *exposé* of 1766:

Q. Why was you made a Fellow-Craft?

A. For the sake of the Letter G, which is inclosed in a Great Light (the Blazing Star).

Q. What does the G denote?

A. Glory, Grandeur and Geometry, or the fifth Science—Glory for God, Grandeur for the Master of the Lodge, and Geometry for the Brothers.

In some lodges, if we are to draw conclusions from an *exposé* of 1730, the letter 'G' was given a definitely Christian significance:

Q. When you came into the middle, what did you see?

A. The Resemblance of the Letter G.

Q. Who doth that G denote?

A. One that's greater than you.

Q. Who's greater than I, that am a Free and Accepted Mason, the Master of a Lodge?

A. The Grand Architect and Contriver of the Universe, or He that was taken up to the Top of the Pinnacle of the Holy Temple.

In the days when the above was published the letter 'G' was a symbol of the Fellow Craft lodge. In May 1742 two freemasons who had got themselves into trouble with Grand Lodge organized a procession of mock-masons, and from a newspaper report of the day we learn that the letter 'G' then signified geometry, or the fifth science, for the sake of which "all Fellow-Crafts are made. This letter G is the essence of the Fellow-Craft's lodge." (So closely identified was the letter 'G' with the Fellow Craft that we find him referred to as "a letter-G man.")

The same newspaper report tells us that when the lodge was raised from the First to the Second Degree a square was placed in the centre of the blazing star, so that Brethren could tell in which degree the lodge was working. From this fact John T. Thorp draws certain conclusions in a paper contributed to the Merseyside Association for Masonic Research (1924–25). "It so happens," he remarks, "that the old 'gallows' square ⌐ is one original form of the Hebrew *ghimel*, the Hebrew character in the roof, and also of the Greek *gamma*, both of which correspond to our English letter G; this fact may thus account for the gradual substitution of the letter G for the square."

A sound old masonic writer once said that much of what has been written concerning the letter 'G' in freemasonry is far more imaginative than useful. A wise view is that God Himself and Geometry have much in common, and that to-day we may regard the symbol as standing for each and both of them. Then we shall not be far wrong when we teach the Fellow Craft that the letter 'G' denotes God who is the Grand Geometrician of the Universe. We can quote great authorities. Sir Thomas Browne in *Religio Medici* (1643) said, "God is like a skilful

geometrician." Plato, four centuries B.C., said that God is a geometer—
that is, one versed in geometry, a geometrician. Bertrand Russell, in
our own day, says that the influence of geometry upon philosophy has
been profound, and that mathematical objects, which are eternal and not
in time, can be conceived as God's thoughts.

Milton, writing in the middle of the seventeenth century, must have
seen God as the Supreme Geometer when, in his *Paradise Lost*, Book VII,
he composed these remarkables lines:

> Then stayed the fervid wheels, and in his hand
> He took the golden compasses, prepared
> In God's eternal store, to circumscribe
> This Universe, and all created things.
> One foot he centred, and the other turned
> Round through the vast profundity obscure,
> And said, 'Thus far extend, thus far thy bounds,
> This be thy just circumference, O World!'

Colloquial Words derived from Freemasonry

The fact that the word 'square' has been used symbolically for
thousands of years by many kinds of people prompts the remark that
ordinary language contains many terms strongly resembling masonic
words and phrases. The ancient Egyptians used their word 'square' as
meaning 'just' and 'proper.' To the ordinary public a thing is 'on the
square' when it is straight, and honest and above board; similarly a
thing is 'on the level' when it is free from dishonest twist. Shakespeare
says, "She's a most triumphant lady, if report be square to her"—that
is, if report be true to her. A matter presented 'squarely'—to a Committee, for example—is presented fully and honestly, without mental
reservation, every fact relevant to the matter being revealed. The Scots
'square-man' originally was a stone-squarer; the square man to-day is a
man whose deeds square and do not present a number of divergent angles
—an honest man.

We must admit that a few slang words have been derived from freemasonry, not always, to our regret, complimentary to it. 'Masonics'
and 'masonry' are colloquial words for 'secrets,' 'under cover,' 'hidden,'
'out of the way.' Men speak of a bad and dishonest action as being 'on
the cross' and of a good and honest action as being 'on the square.'
Dickens used the phrase: "I have squared it with the lad . . . and it is all
right"—that is, he has done the right thing by the lad; but often the
word 'squared' has unpleasant associations, for sometimes to 'square' a
man means to bribe him, or give him some special consideration. This
meaning of 'to square' has come quite naturally from the other: in the

first case it means to settle the matter satisfactorily and fairly, in the second to settle it by hook or by crook.

The American term 'to give the third degree,' almost certainly derived from freemasonry, means to submit a person to a gruelling and possibly brutal questioning.

In the middle of the eighteenth century—say from 1730 to 1760—freemasonry was greatly abused by dishonest men—hypocrites, worthless beggars, and the like—who carried on their evil practices under the cloak of freemasonry, which caused certain masonic names and phrases to acquire very uncomplimentary meanings in the colloquial language of the day. The horse-dealer, giving worthless notes in payment for a horse, was a 'mason' or 'masoner,' while a 'mason's maund' was a particular type of begging impostor, in whom a sham sore above the elbow was made to deceive the almsgiver into supposing that the beggar had an injured arm.

Having distorted the meaning of the honourable word 'cowan,' free-masonry presented the public in the eighteenth century with 'cowan' as a term for a sneak, eavesdropper, or paul-pry; but as a slang term it did not have a long life.

Chapter Eighteen

THE HIRAMIC LEGEND OF THE THIRD DEGREE

THERE are many different ideas with regard to the origin, or possible origin, of the Third Degree legend, and about Hiram himself—who he was and how his name or personality came to be connected with the Legend. There is considerable literature on the subject, most of which is in the form of papers read before the Q.C. Lodge and other research lodges and associations.

How did the Hiramic Legend enter Freemasonry?

Legends in which the central figure is sacrificed in the course of his duty and miraculously brought to life again are to be found in many ancient religions. It is highly probable that the story of Hiram is related to them, but how the legend got into English freemasonry, whether it was part of ancient folklore which survived in the masonic fraternity, or whether, for instance, it was imported into masonry in the seventeenth century by men tinged with Rosicrucian ideas and mindful of the Rosicrucian Legend of the Tomb (see p. 117), is not known, and perhaps never will be.

The introduction of the Hiramic legend into our ritual confronts us with a problem. We know that a necromantic legend, not necessarily centring in Hiram, was in existence in the early 1700's, but we do not *know* that in the year 1722 or 1723 there was any lodge working a dramatized version of the Hiramic story, although in all probability there was. Nevertheless, only a year or two later some lodges are known to have been working an Hiramic degree, and by 1730 many lodges must have worked one. How had this come about? Research has so far failed to reveal any history of the legend before approximately the year 1700, and what has been found is incomplete, fragmentary, and at variance in many respects with the story that became part of masonic ritual.

The personality, if not the name, of Hiram was known in the Old MS. Charges more than two centuries before, although the available references do not suggest that the medieval mason was familiar with any tragic legend associated with it. The name generally appears in a varied or corrupt form. The earliest masonic manuscript, the Regius Poem (or

Halliwell MS.), does not mention the King of Tyre or Hiram, but the Cooke MS. of the early fifteenth century, and many manuscripts founded upon it, have some such reference as this: "And ye Kyngis sone of Tyry [Tyre] was his [Solomon's] maist^r. masen." This agrees with the opinion held by some students that Hiram was the son of King Hiram. In the Grand Lodge MS. No. 1 (1583), King Hiram is referred to as Iram, and the son is called Aynone, a master of geometry and chief master of Solomon's masons—a reference which is repeated in later manuscripts, except that the name Aynone is spelt in many different ways. Early in the seventeenth century (1610) the name becomes Aman, Amon, and Aymon, and there appears to be some likelihood that this is not so much a name as the Jewish title for an organizing chief of an important work, and which even to-day could be spelt phonetically 'unam' or 'um'n.' The spelling 'Hyman' is known as early as 1610.

There appears, then, to have been material ready to hand to be interwoven with a legend, for the purpose, say, of providing it with different characters or *dramatis personæ*.

Some students hold the theory that there was originally a craft lore containing a number of legends, of which some crept into lodge-working, crystallizing, on one side, in the institution both of the Hiramic Degree and the Royal Arch, and, on the other side, in the founding of certain additional degrees. Thus, the two legends indicated would have been part of one another, and it would have followed that it was the very nature of the one legend that led Brethren to turn to the other for satisfaction in the making good of a loss. There is no general support for this theory as a whole, but it may be admitted that a person using common sense in reading between the lines of the scrappy records might believe that there may well have been in freemasonry a bare survival of a legend of the Hiramic kind. Learned Initiates of the Ashmolean type (but not Ashmole himself; that appears to be out of the question) could have taken what they found, re-dressed it in ampler and less gruesome form, and, for all that is known to the contrary, changed the identity of the characters that played their part in the story. This suggestion, in spite of objections to it, is probably as near to the truth as we are likely to get. The legend in its new dress may have been worked in a lodge here and there, or perhaps in one lodge only. This would account for the general unawareness of it at any one time, and for the fact that it was found in general adoption a few years later.

One of two conclusions is simply forced upon us.

(*a*) The legend arose in the body of English freemasonry, in which case it may well go back to the fifteenth or sixteenth century; and it became the motif of the Third Degree by a process of rearrangement of the old *A* and *B* Degrees and, undoubtedly, by the addition of new material.

(*b*) It was devised and subsequently imposed upon freemasonry early in the eighteenth century and possibly after the founding of Grand Lodge (1717). But—and a very big 'but' too—would the new Grand Lodge, only lately nothing more than the rallying-point of a small handful of London lodges, have been able, by its eighth year or so, to impose a brand-new degree upon the lodges of the country, and get them to accept it as the highest degree in freemasonry? Could it have done anything so vastly difficult in such a short time? Even supposing the answer to be "yes," what about the minority of critics inside the Grand Lodge organization and the host of critics outside, masons of the same mentality as the Brethren who, in later years, set up an 'Antient' Grand Lodge in opposition to the original but so-called 'Modern' body? Could a brand-new Third Degree have been imposed upon Brethren so obstinately opposed to change and innovation?

Association of the Legend with the 'Five Points'

In opposition to the suggestion that the Hiramic legend was nothing more than an innovation, it is argued that it could not possibly have been accepted by the lodges unless there was behind it some previous and familiar connexion. This argument is reasonable, and, as a matter of fact, we have not far to seek for some indication of the background associations. It is curious, especially having regard to the date, that in the 1678 edition of a well-known *Christian Dictionary* (associated with the names of Thomas Wilson and others) there are definitions of certain alternative Hebrew words, which we are told mean 'the smiting of his son,' 'the poverty of understanding,' or 'the smiting of the builder.'

It is known that the Craft was familiar with the 'five points' long before we have any evidence that the Hiramic Degree came into use. It appears to be certain that their original place was in the old *B* Degree— the Fellow's Degree—but that they were transferred to the Third Degree, and given a different setting and greater ritualistic import. Douglas Knoop suggests that the original purpose of the legend was to recite an act of necromancy (an attempt to obtain secrets from a dead body), but that in the course of time a new orientation was given to it, stress was laid on the unshaken fidelity of Hiram, and the 'five points' in the existing ritual were utilized to emphasize the duty and the beauty of fellowship.

It so happens that in the sixteenth and seventeenth centuries there was much public discussion in which the phrase 'five points' had a large place, its principal reference being to the five points of doctrine to which Calvinism had been reduced.

The introduction of the Hiramic Degree might well be seen as the work of some one well acquainted with the scraps of legend to be found —some here, some there—in the rituals of the various lodges or in masonic tradition. He drew them together, perhaps, with no mean skill, gave them a dramatic setting with just possibly a new central figure, and adapted the whole story to provide a background for the five points of fellowship already familiar in lodge-working. The possible and even probable truth of this suggestion will be borne in upon us increasingly as we consider the problem of how the legend found its way into masonic ritual.

'Proof' of the existence of the Hiramic legend as far back as the fourteenth century was offered in the 1880's by authors who should have known better. They said this proof had been found in an Arabic manuscript containing, incidentally, a masonic password of which each letter was the initial of a word, and that when all these words were put together they would give the message, "We have found our Lord Hiram." The manuscript was thought to have been in the nature of a preface to the Sunnah recorded as an inspired exposition of the Koran.

The question has been asked whether the Hiramic legend may have been the subject of what, in the sixteenth century, came to be known as an interlude—a shorter and simpler form of the mystery, or miracle, play of earlier days. It has been asked whether our legend is a specially adapted version of an interlude of that popular class in which murder and burial so largely figured. The little play acted by mummers and other itinerant actors may have told the story of some one, not necessarily and even improbably a mason, having been slain and raised from the dead, and it probably taught a lesson of fidelity. Some such interlude, being completely forgotten in all but one or two memories, may have been brought to life again in a version having an altogether different setting. There is nothing unlikely in the idea.

The Biblical Basis of the Hiramic Story

The story of Hiram has some basis in Biblical history, but not as much as Brethren are wont to assume. There are two accounts of Hiram. One is in I Kings v, particularly verses 2–12, and chapter vii, verses (some of them) 13–40. The other is in II Chronicles, chapter ii, particularly verses 3–16; chapter iii, verses 15–17; and chapter iv, verses 11 and 12. Here, in parallel columns, are the two accounts based on and to some extent quoting the Revised Version:

The Account in I Kings

Solomon sent to Hiram, King of Tyre, saying he purposed to build a house for the name of the Lord his God.

He requested Hiram to hew cedar trees out of Lebanon, " my servants shall be with thy servants; ... there is not among us any that can skill to hew timber like unto the Zidonians."

Hiram rejoiced and replied saying he would do all Solomon's desire; that he would send both fir and cedar in rafts by sea unto the appointed place. In return for which Solomon gives Hiram wheat and oil, the arrangement continuing " year by year." Solomon and Hiram made a league of peace together. Solomon raised a levy of 30,000 men and sends them to Lebanon " ten thousand a month by courses." Adoniram is over the levy.

"Solomon sent and fetched Hiram out of Tyre. He was the son of a widow of the tribe of Naphtali, and his father was a man of Tyre, a worker in brass; and he was filled with wisdom and understanding and cunning, to work all works in brass. And he came to king Solomon, and wrought all his work. ... fashioned two pillars of brass ... and set up the pillars in the porch of the temple ... made the molten sea ... lavers of brass. ... Hiram made an end of doing all the work that he wrought for king Solomon in the house of the Lord."

The Account in II Chronicles

Solomon sent to Huram, the King of Tyre, saying he was building an house for the name of the Lord his God. He demanded: " Send me a man cunning to work in gold, and in silver, and in brass, and in iron, and in purple, and crimson, and blue, and that can skill to grave all manner of gravings, to be with the cunning men that are with me in Judah."

He asked for cedar trees, fir trees and algum trees out of Lebanon " for I know that thy servants can skill to cut timber ... my servants shall be with thy servants." Solomon offers wheat, barley, wine, and oil.

Hurum replied saying, "I have sent a cunning man, endued with understanding, of Huram my father's, the son of a woman of the daughters of Dan, and his father was a man of Tyre, skilful to work in gold, and in silver, in brass, in iron, in stone and in timber, in purple, in blue, and in fine linen, and in crimson; also to grave any manner of graving, ... that there may be a place appointed unto him with thy cunning men, ... we will cut wood out of Lebanon, as much as thou shalt need: and we will bring it to thee in floats by sea to Joppa; and thou shalt carry it up to Jerusalem."

Solomon set 70,000 " strangers" to bear burdens, etc., etc.

And Solomon made before the house two pillars and set them up before the Temple. He made an altar of brass, the molten sea, lavers, and gold candlesticks. "And Huram made the pots, and the shovels, and the basons. So Huram made an end of doing the work that he wrought for king Solomon in the house of God: the two pillars, ... the pots also, and the shovels, ... and all the vessels thereof, did Huram his father make for king Solomon...."

What are the chief differences between the two accounts? In Chronicles Hiram the metal-worker becomes Huram; Solomon asks for a particular kind of artist or workman; the cunning man sent to Solomon is of "Huram my father's," and "Huram his father" made the vessels, etc., for Solomon. Both versions agree that Solomon asked for timber; that he was lent the services of the metal-worker—the widow's son, Hiram or Huram—whose mother, according to Kings, was of the tribe of Napthali, and, according to Chronicles, of the tribe of Dan. There is no hint in either version that Solomon asked for or borrowed the services of an *architect* or *mason* (although one of the many materials in which Huram could work was stone).

In the Kings version there are two Hirams; one is Hiram King of Tyre, and the other the Hiram who was the widow's son. In the Chronicles version there is Huram, King of Tyre, who sends the man of skill, who at first is not named, but is said in the course of the narrative to be "of Huram my father's"; near the end we learn that Huram made the pots, etc., and later still we learn that the vessels, etc., were made by "Huram his father."

The version given in Chronicles was written about seven hundred years after that of Kings, and any divergency might be due to misunderstanding of the earlier writings, to mistakes in the copies from which the writers worked, or to the writers themselves making mistakes as they prepared their narrative. But, however caused, the divergencies provide material on which to base many different interpretations and ideas, and it is not to be wondered at that some writers believe that the accounts relate the story of one man, Hiram, King of Tyre; others, that Hiram, King of Tyre, sent an artificer having the same name as himself; while still others believe that the artificer's work was supplemented by that of his father. There is general agreement that Hiram in one narrative is the same man as Huram in the other.

Whether these divergencies in the two accounts much matter is another question. They would matter a great deal if the central figure of the masonic legend were an artificer in metal, instead of being "the principal architect at the construction of King Solomon's Temple" and the one whose duty it was to provide the plans and designs needed by the builders.

This point, then, immediately arises. Is the Hiram of the Biblical narrative the Hiram of the masonic legend? Or is there a possibility that the name of the Biblical character has been affixed to a legendary figure for whom there is no Biblical authority? W. W. Covey Crump brushes the question on one side. The Hiramic tradition, he remarks, is that the master architect died before the Temple was completed; his actual identity, and when, how, or why the tradition of his death became incorporated into a legend of King Solomon's Temple, are details of a subordinate nature, and matter little. That point of view can be under-stood without one necessarily agreeing with it.

The earliest authoritative reference to the Hiramic tradition is in the second edition of the *Constitutions* (1738), where we are informed of the "sudden death of their dear Master Hiram Abbif, whom they decently interr'd in the Lodge near the Temple, according to ancient usage." In the first edition (1723) we are told merely that King Hiram sent to Solomon "his Namesake HIRAM, or *Huram,* the most accomplish'd Mason upon Earth." There is here no hint of tragedy, and it does not appear that Anderson, the chief author of the *Constitutions,* yet knew of the Hiramic story as we know it to-day; but, characteristically, he was here linking Hiram's cunning metal-worker with "the most accomplished mason upon earth," and it is obvious from his text and footnote that he is assuming that the Biblical Hiram, the metal-worker, is Solomon's principal architect. If we were to hazard a guess as to who transformed the metal-worker into the architect it might fall upon Anderson.

On the basis of the Scripture references Solomon's principal architect could not have been any of the Biblical Hirams. The Biblical text could easily be read as indicating that Hiram, King of Tyre, himself came to work for Solomon—a very unlikely occurrence. The Old Charges of the sixteenth and seventeenth century had said that Solomon's architect was named Aymon or Aynon, and a Hebrew scholar has pointed out that this is possibly a mistake for Amon, meaning 'master workman.' It may reasonably be supposed that Anderson was familiar with the references in the Old Charges to King Solomon's Temple and his architect, and that it was this individual, Aymon or Aynon, whose identity he appears to have fastened on to the Biblical Hiram.

While, as we have seen, the medieval masons knew of Aymon, Solomon's chief architect, it is necessary to point out that there is no evidence that they knew of any story relating to his sudden death. There is no masonic record or document mentioning the sudden death of Hiram until we come to Anderson's 1738 *Constitutions,* although, of course, we have evidence in Prichard's *Masonry Dissected* (1730) that, by that time, the lodges were working an Hiramic Degree in which the story of Hiram's death was unfolded in much the same way, and with much the same phrasing, as in the version now familiar to us.

Hiram Abif

So far in this chapter Hiram has just once been given the name by which freemasons know him. Hiram Abif, or Hiram Abi, is actually a mistaken form of the name, although it is now the usual one, and there is thought to be good evidence showing how the mistake was originally made. 'Abif' is a Hebrew word signifying 'his father.' It will be remembered that Chronicles gives the name as "Huram his father." In this particular case 'father' might be 'instructor,' 'adviser,' 'counsellor,' etc., but this is not certain. The learned critics think that it was used in the same sense as in the Book of Genesis, where Joseph says, "God ... hath made me a father to Pharaoh." (xlv, 8.)

Certain early translations of the Bible—Luther's, for example—take the word 'Abif' to be a title of honour, as in fact it was, and they give the name as Hiram Abif. Coverdale's Bible of 1535 does the same. Matthew's Bible of 1537, etc., and that of Taverner (1539) use the form 'Abi.' After 1551 neither 'Abif' nor 'Abi' is found in English Bibles, but all German Bibles from Luther's day to this give the name as Hiram Abif. There is now a consensus of learned opinion that 'Abif' or 'Abi' or 'Abiv' means, not a name, but 'his father.' It looks as though, when the old legend was getting its new setting early in the 1700's, those responsible went to the old Bibles for the name.

It is thought that Hiram's name is a contraction of '*A*hiram,' meaning 'Exalted Brother,' because '*A*biram' means 'Exalted Father'; but the Biblical 'Ahiram' is not Hiram, the widow's son.

Why is the Hiram of the Kings version called Huram in the Chronicles version? Critics believe that a period of 700 years separated the two writings, and that, while Hiram is Hebrew, Huram is probably the Aramaic or Phœnician form of the same name.

Medieval Names for Solomon's Architect

In the Old MS. Charges, as already mentioned, Solomon's chief architect is called Aymon, or Amon, which in Hebrew is said to mean 'artificer,' 'architect,' 'master workman,' one found 'faithful or skilful in his business.' Aman, or Omman, means 'cunning workman.' 'Aman' also means 'entrusted.' 'Emun,' or 'Aymun,' means 'faithful true one,' and 'Amen' (not the 'so be it' of our prayers) means 'true,' 'faithful.' ('So be it' or 'so mote it be,' with which we end our prayers, is not the same word, but, most curiously, it is allied with words meaning 'strength.')

We have tried to make clear that Solomon's master architect, whose name is quite unknown, has been given in masonic ritual the name Hiram, the name which belonged to Solomon's skilled metal-worker, of whose death the Scriptures tell us nothing. All that we know is that he made an end of doing all the work that he wrought for King Solomon.

As it happens, however, there is a.Hiram whose sudden death is recorded in the Scriptures. He is *Adoni*ram (son of Abda), who we learn from I Kings iv, 6, was over the levy, or tribute, and who evidently was an important public official in whom Solomon reposed confidence. In the same book we learn that, while on a duty to which he was ordered by King Rehoboam, "all Israel stoned him with stones, that he died." (xii, 18.) The 'Adon' of his name means apparently *dominus*, or 'master,' so here we have an actual case of a Biblical Master Hiram having been slain when on duty.

In certain rituals and lectures Adoniram is said to be a Chief of Staff appointed after the death of Hiram, but it is curious that one of the *exposés* (1766) substitutes for the name of Hiram that of 'Adoniram our Father,' and it will be remembered that Hiram himself is alluded to in similar fashion in the Chronicles version of the Temple story.

This does rather support the likelihood (providing, of course, that the spurious publication did not make a careless error) that there was confusion in the early working between three distinct individuals: Solomon's principal architect, whose name is not recorded in the Bible, and of whom we know nothing; Hiram, the metal-worker, promoted by Anderson and others to be Solomon's architect, and, under the name of Hiram Abif, made the central figure in a traditional tragedy; and Adoniram, King Rehoboam's public servant, who is recorded in the Bible as having been stoned to death.

That confusion has continued to this day and seems quite inseparable from the subject. In some of the added degrees in which Adoniram is a big figure, Hiram is said to have had the title Adon (exalted) conferred on him by Solomon. The Installed Master of a Craft Lodge knows the name as that of the principal architect at the time when the Temple was completed and King Solomon, attended by a numerous retinue, went to view it.

Most freemasons assume that there were two Hirams: the Hiram who was King of Tyre and the Hiram we have come to call Hiram Abif, and for all that it really matters this may be accepted. A few writers, however, have long indulged in a belief that there were two artificer Hirams, father and son, and that the father, Hiram Abif or Huram Abif, was the more accomplished of the two, but met with an accident, and his work had to be finished by his son. W. W. Covey Crump has shown that this is in error the trouble arising from the fact that the writer of Chronicles was not sufficiently critical, and also from peculiarities in the Greek translation of Chronicles made in Egypt about 180 B.C., mainly induced by the faulty condition of such manuscripts as were then available.

Covey Crump says that the record in Kings is better authenticated than the later one. It may be suggested, then, the second account being

less reliable than the first, that authors have introduced a needless com-
plexity in taking it into consideration, and that much of the argument
would have been obviated had they gone only to the narrative in Kings.
From that one narrative we should have learnt simply that Solomon
asked Hiram, King of Tyre, for timber which Hiram sent him, and that
Solomon sent and fetched Hiram, the metal-worker, out of Tyre, who,
when his job was done, apparently returned to his own country. This
would have told us of either one or two Hirams, neither of them an
architect.

The Hiramic legend, then, is an ancient legend, which, before its
adoption into freemasonry, had a rather different form, and was not
necessarily associated with the building of King Solomon's Temple.
What led somebody to make Solomon's principal architect its central
figure, and to use the Temple as the background? We have to realize
that, although King Solomon's Temple could not compare in architecture, size, or magnificence with the buildings of the Egyptians and other
rich nations, there was perhaps no other building of the ancient world
that has excited so much attention. Throughout the Middle Ages it
considerably influenced the forms of Christian churches, and W. Harry
Rylands has suggested that it seems entirely natural that the early churches
should be imitations of the Temple at Jerusalem, in its time the wonder of
the surrounding nations. The Temple, in the eyes of both the Church
and the mason Fraternity, had been built to the honour and glory of God;
indeed, it *was* the Temple of God, and the story of its building is one of
the great masonic records in the Bible. The operative masons exerted
all their talents to raise buildings that would equal or surpass the Temple
of Solomon, and the Accepted, or speculative, masons would look to
the same source for inspiration for their legend symbolizing the building
of a Temple of Living Stones.

Absent from the English ritual, but present in many others, are the
names of the three assassins. An irregular print of 1730 says that the
24-inch gauge was the first tool used as a weapon in the course of the
murder, and that the deaths of the three assassins were in accordance
with the respective penal obligations of the three degrees. Some fanciful
versions are suggested for these names. American rituals give them as
Jubela, Jubelo, and Jubelum; but, if they have any true derivation of a
masonic nature, then it is more likely to be by some roundabout road
from the word 'ghiblim' or 'giblim' ('stone-cutter' or 'mason'), which
was regarded in the early rituals as the name of a mason, and particularly
of the Fellow Craft. In the early eighteenth century a Fellow Craft was
often called Giblim, and it is not difficult to see that the fanciful names of
the assassins might very easily have been corrupted from some such word,

more particularly, as A. G. Mackey reminds us, when we realize that the French masons of the early eighteenth century turned our hard 'g' into a soft 'j,' and produced the words 'jiblime,' 'jibulum,' and 'jabulum.' Speculative masonry went from England to France, and some of it came back in curiously distorted forms, and with peculiar additions. One can suppose that the names given to the assassins are in the same category.

There is good ground for the word 'giblim' meaning 'mason.' The gebalites, or stone-squarers, are mentioned in I Kings v, 18: "And Solomon's builders and Hiram's builders and the Gebalites did fashion them, [the stones] and prepared the timber and the stones to build the house" (Revised Version). Some scholars maintain that the word 'giblim' comes from *gebul* (a 'border'), and suggest that Giblim were masons who worked the smooth border on the rough-hewn ashlar, but the idea is altogether too fanciful.

Nothing would be gained by giving lists of the names that have from time to time been given to the assassins, and of their supposed derivations; but one must be mentioned which is often referred to as bearing upon the question of possible Jacobite influence in masonry. It is the name Romvil, or Kurmavil, which is supposed to be the word Cromwell in disguise, the alleged Jacobite intention being to pour hatred and contempt upon the name of the man chiefly responsible for the execution of Charles I, but to veil the identity in that of one of Hiram's assassins. (See also p. 190.) (Cromwell was not a freemason and could not therefore have founded Irish freemasonry, an honour that has been claimed for him.)

Other Versions of the Legend

The legend familiar to the Craft is not the only one of its kind. The principal alternative version is that to be found in the Graham MS., and centres upon Noah; but there are some other stories not so closely resembling the Hiramic Legend, which, however, do mention the name of Hiram. In a well-known book, Heckethorne's *Secret Societies of All Ages,* there is a temple legend relating that through the jealousy of three workmen the casting of the brazen sea mentioned in Kings and in Chronicles is a failure, but Tubal Cain appears to Hiram and confers on him magical powers, and the casting is then successful. Balkis falls in love with Hiram, who, at the instigation of Solomon, is murdered, the story then developing on lines familiar to freemasons, and having reference to a secret vault. The story gains a little point, perhaps, when we realize that Balkis is the Mohammedan name for the Queen of Sheba, who paid the historical visit to Jerusalem. The Koran knows her as Balkis, Queen of Saba.

An astonishingly different story of Hiram Abif, but lacking all hint of tragedy, is to be found in an old pamphlet entitled *Freemason's Hewreka and Guide*. Hiram, King of Tyre, appointed the father of Hiram Abif to be Grand Architect of Tyre and Sidon. The father failing through age and infirmity, the King appointed Hiram Abif to succeed his father, but the son chose rather to return to Tyre and comfort his aged father in his illness. On his father's death the King again appointed him successor in Sidon. Several years later Hiram's mother, who was of the tribe of Naphtali, went to dwell among her own kindred, but her health became impaired and her mind affected. Thereupon Hiram sold his possessions in Tyre, relinquished his office and honours of Grand Architect, and with filial attachment returned to Jerusalem to soothe the afflictions of his aged mother. On her death the King invested Hiram with his former honours, and, as a further reward for past services, his purity of mind, and filial affection, he granted him the honours and prerogative of Grand Architect of the Kingdom of Tyre, in addition to that of Sidon. Shortly after this the King sent Hiram to Solomon, King of Israel, who, as a reward for making a discovery—his amazing Heureka—at the time of laying the foundation-stone of the Temple, appointed him Grand Architect of Jerusalem. We have in this story more a suggestion of the Royal Arch than of the theme of the Third Degree.

The Graham MS. and the Legend of Noah

All ideas as to how the Hiramic legend came into freemasonry were considerably affected by the discovery of the Graham MS., which relates the legend of Noah being raised from the grave by his sons. So far back as the thirteenth century a French Dominican monk reflected upon the character of Ham, son of Noah. Reginald Scot's sixteenth-century work on witchcraft associates Ham with 'black art,' and echoes of this are to be found in a gruesome legend that evidently was in existence in the seventeenth century, and had probably by that time passed through more than one form. We learn of it in the Graham MS., a small manuscript which came to light in York as late as 1936, and which is dated in this peculiar way:

2

1 7 6

This might reasonably read as 1726, although the authorities of the British Museum and the Public Record Office think the handwriting might be of a period fifty years earlier; the rearrangement of the figures as 1672 might or might not be pardonable, the paper and watermark being consistent with either date. The authorities consulted were confident as to the genuineness of the document, which was first exhibited by the Rev. H. I. Robinson, Rector of Londesborough, near York, when he was initiated in 1936 and was in due course sent by Bro. Brian Shaw, Librarian, of Eboracum Lodge, No. 1611, of York, to Q.C. Lodge for its diagnosis, of which the following is a summary.[1]

The Graham MS. bears a close relation to a broadsheet of 1725, entitled *The Whole Institutions of Free-masons opened*, but analysis shows that Thomas Graham copied it, not from that broadsheet, but from another document, *not* itself a copy of the broadsheet. Probably both the manuscripts and the broadsheet are fairly near descendants from a single original. We may note its mention of Noah, Bezaleel, and Solomon, the second of these being the earliest masonic reference to the Bezaleel tradition.

It had been advanced in some quarters that as (with one doubtful exception) the earliest reference to the Hiram legend is contained in a spurious print, *Masonry Dissected*, the legend had perhaps been invented by Prichard, the 'author' of that *exposé*, who tells the story of one detachment of the 'Fifteen Loving Brothers' finding the body of Hiram

> decently buried in a handsome grave six foot east, six west, and six foot perpendicular, and his covering was green moss and turf, which surprised them; whereupon they replied, *Muscus Domus Dei Gratia*, which, according to Masonry, is, 'Thanks be to God, our master has got a mossy house.' So they covered him closely, and as a further ornament placed a sprig of Cassia at the head of his grave, and went and acquainted King Solomon.

The story proceeds on the now familiar lines, and includes the statement that "When Hiram was taken up, they took him by the Fore-fingers, and the Skin came off, which is called the Slip."

Now in the Graham MS., which cannot be later than 1726—*four years before Prichard's exposé was published*—and might be as early as 1672— that is, fifty-eight years before, we find substantially the same story told of a different character, and on an entirely different occasion. The story is told round the figure of Noah, and includes many of the characteristic details with which all Master Masons are familiar. So it is possible— indeed, probable—that here is an early version of a story which might originally have centred upon Hiram, or Noah, or somebody else. That there was a Noah tradition is evident from a newspaper cutting dated 1726 (source unknown), bearing the heading "Antediluvian Masonry," and also from Anderson's *Constitutions* of 1738, which state that Noachidæ, or Sons of Noah, was "the first Name of *Masons*, according to some old Traditions." Anderson also introduces the term into the first of the Old

---

[1] The diagnosis is set forth at length by Bro. the Rev. Herbert Poole in *A.Q.C.*, vol. l.

Charges: "A MASON is obliged by his Tenure to observe the Moral Law, as a true *Noachida*." Later in the same Charge he refers to "The Three Great Articles of Noah."

Everything about the Graham MS. suggests that it reflects the actual working of a lodge or lodges; not that lodges *in general* are thought ever to have worked a Noah ceremony, but that such a ceremony was known probably long before the 1720's, and could easily have been taken as a basis for an extended and less gruesome account—linked up with masonic principles and with characters associated with building or masonry.

It is reasonable to raise the possibility of the Hiramic legend having been at one stage of its evolution a legend of Noah and his sons and that, in that or some other form, it might well go back to early medieval times, remembering always that in the course of centuries a story of this kind would be likely to get considerably twisted and altered.

There is believed to have been in London in 1726 a lodge "which made masons after the ante-diluvian manner," which would suggest that a version alternative to the Hiramic, and older than it, was being worked in London at the time when the lodges began generally to adopt the Hiramic Degree.

The legend told in the Graham MS. is painfully gruesome; so, to a less extent, is the Hiramic legend; but the fact is not there so apparent. It probably derived from ancient folklore, which is seldom very 'nice' in such matters.

While it is true that no proof has yet appeared that freemasonry had any legend connected with Noah and his son Ham earlier than about the end of the seventeenth century, it is a matter of common knowledge that 'black art' stories relating to Ham go back into early history. Herbert de Losinga, the first Bishop of Norwich, who died in 1119, is believed to have written: "The Ark was of small compass; but even yet there, Ham preserved the arts of magic and idolity." Learned writers of the fifteenth and seventeenth centuries discussed Ham, and there were works in Latin in 1677 and 1681 gravely arguing whether Zoroaster, who is alleged to be an inventor of magic, was identified with "Noah's wicked son Ham." We cannot be sure that the legends centring on Ham associated him with necromancy, but, on the principle of giving the dog a bad name, there is not much doubt that he was supposed to be guilty of working in 'black art'—a term in itself associated with necromancy, and later regarded as having the same meaning.

Noah was the central figure in a great number of legends. A. G. Mackey, in his *Encyclopædia of Freemasonry*, says that Noah is thought to have discovered "the stone of foundation" and placed it in the ark as an altar; later, in the six hundredth year of his age, he erected this stone as an altar to the Deity. He built his ark of cedars, felled for him by the Sidonians, who felled and prepared cedars for the use of King Solomon in building his temple. (In these old legends and stories time and sequence have no meaning.) Noah's dove is a masonic symbol. He sent forth a dove three separate times: the first time the dove, finding no resting-place, quickly returned; the second time, she returned with an olive-leaf, which showed that the tops of the olive-trees were now exposed; but the third time, the waters having receded, she returned no more. The dove is an emblem of peace and good fortune, and is commemorated in one of the additional degrees. Noah died at the age of 950, having instructed his children in the great truths of religion; but his sons displeased God by building the lofty tower of Babel, with regard to which there are many legends, and round which a masonic degree of foreign origin has gathered.

A. G. Mackey's *Encyclopædia of Freemasonry* refers to a Noachite degree as having interposed itself into the masonic system, and as being "an unfitting link, unsightly interruption of the chain of legendary symbolism, substituting Noah for Solomon and Peleg (builder of the tower of Babel) for Hiram Abif." From what we are now beginning to discern, however, it is possible that there is a Noah tradition of a necromantic order older than the Hiramic story, and it is quite possible that fragments of the old Noah legends have been in the minds of those who contrived the Noachite degree.

'Noachidæ,' a word used by Anderson in his *Constitutions* of 1738, is defined as meaning the immediate tribes or families descended from Shem, Ham, and Japhet, the three sons of Noah.

An eighteenth-century tradition, as extraordinary as it was foolish, was to the effect that Ham's eldest son, Nimrod (in Scripture: "a mighty hunter before the Lord"), was Grand Master of all masons and a builder of many cities in Shinaar. But its existence is one more indication that Noah and his family had masonic associations in the minds of at least some early speculatives.

With a fair amount of plausible conjecture it is possible now to reconstruct the process by which the Hiramic legend may *possibly* have found its way into freemasonry. The medieval operatives knew of King Solomon's Temple and of Solomon's architect; there is a bare possibility that some of them or their priestly scribes might have known the necromantic legend of Noah and his son Ham. Some of the Rosicrucians, and other delvers into the mystic who came into freemasonry in the 1700's, were probably aware of the Noah story, and it is not impossible that they gave it a dramatic setting. Later editors, aware of all the foregoing, would be able to introduce the name of Hiram, the Biblical character intimately concerned with Solomon's great project. Forthwith Hiram was transformed into an architect, and made the centre of a story that fitted well into the setting of King Solomon's Temple. The grisly and necromantic elements were not discarded, but they were softened, and the story was given an apt moral and closely related to the existing five points of fellowship. If this is a reasonable reconstruction the Hiramic legend might easily have its roots in three distinct places: in the Old Charges, in the 'black art' story of Noah and his son, and in the association between Hiram, the metal-worker, and King Solomon.

The Whole History of the Widow's Son killed by the Blow of a Beetle was advertised for sale in 1726, an addition to our evidence that the Hiramic tragedy was being enacted by freemasons by that time. Prichard's *Masonry Dissected* has this question and answer:

Q. What did the Ruffians kill him with?
A. A Setting Maul, Setting Tool and Setting Beadle.

This word 'beetle' (in our lodges we use the word 'maul') is an English but somewhat curious, word derived from old Teutonic words meaning literally 'to beat.' The tree-splitting, iron wedge is driven in by blows of a beetle. A well-known Thames-side inn has the sign, "The Beetle and Wedge." Apropos of 'beating,' reference may be made to the ceremony at the reception of the French medieval millstone makers, who in their day were classed as stonemasons. While the masters were feasting in their banquet-hall, their youngest member, having a stick in his belt in lieu of sword, took the candidate into a loft upstairs, from which there then came continuous cries as though some one were being beaten to death.

The Implication of the Hiramic Legend

The legend of Hiram has been classed with all the many mysteries in which a god, a superior being, or an extraordinary man suffers death in order that he may be ushered into a more glorious existence. Whatever forms the legend passed through in the years before it took its final shape, we can have but little doubt, quoting the words of Lewis Edwards, that the original myth was connected with

the primitive rituals so widely diffused which derive from the natural processes of death and resurrection. . . . While the lesson of fidelity is clearly taught, there is, in addition, from the raising of the body for the purpose of identification and with a view to a second and more decent interment, an attempt to draw the secondary lesson of immortality and to suggest what the eye of faith shall see when "this transitory life shall have passed away."

The legend has been called a philosophical drama designed to impress upon the recipient the truth that "it is not all of life to live," thereby implying a future existence.

The Candidate, invited to reflect on the peculiar objects of the Third Degree, is taught that death has no terrors equal to the stain of falsehood and dishonour. Brethren of ancient days were fond of contemplating the subject of death. It held a strong place in medieval writings. We find Francis Bacon saying:

> I have often thought upon death, and I find it the least of all evils. All that which is past is as a dream, and he that hopes or depends upon time coming, dreams waking. So much of our life as we have discovered is already dead, and all those hours which we share, even from the breasts of our mother, until we return to our grandmother the earth, are part of our dying days, whereof even this is one, and those that succeed are of the same nature, for we die daily, and as others have given place to us so we must in the end give way to others.

Viscount Samuel, in our own day, says that "poetry, sculpture, metaphors, have led us to regard death as a thing in itself. Death is not a thing in itself. It is a cessation."

It has been thought that the legend contains an esoteric reference to any one of many different people who have met with an untimely end. W. W. Covey Crump's *The Hiramic Tradition*[1] explores many possibilities of this kind and should be read at first hand. He asks whether the legend is an allusion to the murder of Thomas à Becket, a saint so often confused with Thomas the Apostle, who in medieval art held a carpenter's square. Is it an allusion to the death of some old operative master slain in the course of doing his duty? Is the tradition a romance based on the death of Jacques de Molay and the suppression of the Order of Knights Templar, or does it refer to Maître Jacques de Moler, a stonemason murdered at the instigation of a rival? Is there a Jacobite suggestion in the story? Is the tradition a veiled reference to the execution of Charles I? Was it a deliberate attempt to introduce a Jacobite influence into freemasonry, possibly using Anderson himself, an anti-Jacobite person, as the unconscious means of its introduction? Is it an echo of a Rosicrucian story? Was a member of a guild of Master Masons slain in the sixteenth or seventeenth century, and is the tragedy echoed in the tradition? Did the Crusaders discover the legend in Europe and bring it to England? Is it an allegory of the 'death of the sun' in winter and its coming to life again in the spring? Did it spring from some ancient mystery as old as, or even older than, the colleges of ancient Rome? Was it a reference to the fertility sacrifices or—more likely—to the stability sacrifices, by which ancient system it was customary to immure in the foundation of the building a human sacrifice? Or was it, after all, an allegory of the Fall of man?

Was the real Hiram Jesus Christ? asks Covey Crump. Do we see,

[1] Masonic Record, Ltd, 1934.

he asks, the tragedy of Calvary echoed in the death of Master Hiram? He, naturally, reminds us that the mode of death of Jesus was very different from that of Hiram, and that the eleven disciples do not agree with the fifteen Craftsmen; but as to that we cannot be sure as to what the original Hiramic story contained. "Was this halting symbology," continues Covey Crump, "intended for us to see behind the traditional Hiram a reference to another Master, as 'one of the brightest characters' recorded in the Volume of the Sacred Law, one who solemnly declared concerning Himself: 'I am the Resurrection and the Life'?"

The Possible Relation of the Legend to the Foundation Sacrifice

It has already been suggested that the story of Hiram might have been derived from the ancient foundation sacrifice or stability rite, in which a human being was immured in the foundation of the intended structure, and in particular the custom of making the builder, the architect, or an apprentice the victim. In the chapter on the foundation-stone this custom will be dealt with at some length. The suggestion, it must be understood, is not that any such custom was observed in the building of King Solomon's Temple, although no one can be very certain as to that, particularly in view of the following passage in I Kings xvi, 34: "In his days did Hiel the Beth-elite build Jericho: he laid the foundation thereof with the loss of Abiram his firstborn, and set up the gates thereof with the loss of his youngest son Segub." (Revised Version.) The suggestion referred to is rather that some memory or echo of an ancient custom took its shape in the Hiram legend by a process well known to those who have read deeply in the annals of folklore. It has been said that the tradition of human sacrifice in connexion with a new building was so ingrained that a hint of a tragic legend is associated with almost every important edifice in ancient days.

The Apprentice Legend and its Interpretation

On another page is mentioned the well-known apprentice legend, which generally takes the form of a highly skilled apprentice arousing the jealousy of his master and being murdered by him. G. W. Speth gives this legend an interpretation which would link it with the Hiramic tradition. He instances the apprentice who had served his time, and whose birth as a free workman was imminent. A ceremony to mark the occasion was necessary. In all initiations there is a symbolic death and a figurative resurrection or rebirth—a death to a past life, a raising to a future one. What more natural than that the young mason should die to his apprenticehood and rise a master? What more appropriate to symbolize this than the legend of Hiram? Let it be remembered how many legends we possess of apprentices losing their lives immediately after executing their masterpieces. There are the stories of the 'Prentice Pillar' of Roslin Chapel, of the apprentice window of Rouen, of the apprentice bracket of Gloucester Cathedral; of the apprentice minaret of the Mosque at Damietta, and others. The truth behind those legends is probably that the apprentice did 'die' *as an apprentice* immediately after executing his masterpiece. In each case, says Speth, it was the masterpiece that entitled him to promotion.

The Sublime Degree of a Master Mason

It is believed that the phrase "the Sublime Degree of a Master Mason" first occurs, in the year 1754, in a certificate drawn up by the Grand Lodge of Ireland, relating to a lodge at Lurgan, No. 134, Irish Constitution, and that it was used by another Irish lodge, that of the Royal Scots, No. 11, in 1762.

In England the phrase was used in 1767 by the Lodge of Friendship No. 6, but did not come into general use in lodges under the Premier Grand Lodge until near the end of the eighteenth century; but where we do find it, there we also find as a rule evidence of the 'Antients' influence. In 1760 Thomas Dunckerley, as Master of a lodge held aboard the *Vanguard,* signed a certificate (the original is in Quebec, a photograph of it in Grand Lodge Library) to the effect that a Fellow Craft "having sustain'd with Strength, Firmness, and Courage, the most Painful Works, and Severest Tryalls, we gave unto him the most Sublime Degree of Master."

In Bristol in 1768 a lodge, founded and erased all within the twelve months, gloried in the name of the Sun Lodge of Perpetual Friendship, No. 421, and in the July of its short life its minutes refer to the Sublime Degree of a Master Mason, and, in the month following, to the Sublime Degree of a Royal Arch Mason. The St John's Lodge of Henley-in-Arden, which had a few years of existence beginning in 1791, at one time called the Master Mason's Degree 'honourable,' or 'respectable.'

So far as Scotland is concerned, we learn that in the eighteenth century the Third Degree was usually denominated the "High Degree of a Master Mason," but in Lodge Holyrood House, according to R. S. Lindsay's history of the lodge, the degree had among its various designations, between 1776 and 1778, the "Honourable Degree," the "High and Honourable Degree," the "Noble and Honourable Degree," the "Stupendous Degree" (of a Master Mason).

Reference has just been made to a 'respectable' degree. More than one lodge applied to the Third Degree, as also to Master Masons, that old-fashioned adjective, so peculiarly masonic, so commonly misunderstood. The Candidate is early advised to dedicate himself to such pursuits as may enable him to be 'respectable' in life—that is, he should so comport himself as to earn the esteem and regard of those who 'look upon' him, that being the original meaning of the word 'respect' and the meaning borne by it at the time when the word 'respectable' was brought into the ritual.

'High Twelve'

From time to time masonic writers have debated whether our Master retired to the Temple to pay his adoration to the Most High at the hour of 'high twelve' or at 'high time.' 'High twelve' is obviously noon, twelve o'clock, when the sun is highest in the heavens. Our operative brethren who built York Minster arranged in 1370 to cease work on holidays at 'high noon.' It has been suggested that possibly the term 'high time' has crept into use as a result of a misunderstanding. If there is a 'high' twelve, we suppose there is a 'low' twelve, which would be midnight; in that way 'high noon' might appear preferable to 'high twelve.' A philosophical work of 1693 refers to the 'high time' of the day, or twelve o'clock. 'High time' as a Biblical reference does not help us much. St Paul writes to the Early Christians that "it is high time to awake out of sleep:"[1] but that, of course, has no reference to the time of day. But in the Book of Genesis we read, "it is yet high day,"[2] which is a reference to noontide, or, as we say in the ritual, and are told we say incorrectly, "when the sun is at its meridian." The purists talk of the sun being "*on* its meridian."

An irregular print of the early 1700's contains this catechism:

Q. What's the Day for?
A. To see in.
Q. What's the Night for?
A. To hear.
Q. How Blows the Wind?
A. Due East and West.
Q. What's o'Clock?
A. High Twelve.

[1] Romans xiii, 11.   [2] Genesis xxix, 7.

Chapter Nineteen

THE FOUNDATION-STONE

THE ceremony of laying a foundation-stone is the one remaining link between operative and speculative masonry, a link possessing the most ancient and historical traditions—noble and inspiring on the one hand, cruel and bloodthirsty on the other. The Books of Joshua, Kings, Ezra, Isaiah, and Hebrews provide us with many apt references to foundation-stones, but possibly the greatest of them from the freemason's point of view, one containing a clear indication of the emblems to be used in testing the stone, is that of Isaiah xxviii, 16, 17: "Therefore thus saith the Lord God, Behold, I lay in Zion for a foundation a stone, a tried stone, a precious corner stone, a sure foundation: . . . Judgment also will I lay to the line, and righteousness to the plummet."

We read in Hebrews xi, 10: "He looked for a city which hath foundations, whose builder and maker is God." And from Ezra iii, 10, 11, we learn of the high ceremonial significance of the laying of the foundation-stone of the Temple:

And when the builders laid the foundation of the temple of the LORD, they set the priests in their apparel with trumpets, and the Levites the sons of Asaph with cymbals, to praise the LORD, after the ordinance of David king of Israel. . . . And all the people shouted with a great shout, when they praised the LORD, because the foundation of the house of the LORD was laid.

On such great texts as these is based the symbolism of the foundation-stone in the masonic ritual, the Entered Apprentice at a very early point in his career being made figuratively to represent that stone on which all Brethren present at his Initiation hope he will raise a superstructure perfect in its parts and honourable to the builder.

Sometimes the Bible speaks of the foundation-stone as a 'corner-stone,' which it often used to be and occasionally still literally is, but the term 'corner-stone' has also the meaning of 'the stone of highest importance,' that of being an indispensable part of the substructure of a real or symbolical building; thus, we learn in Psalm cxviii, 22, of the stone which the builders refused or rejected becoming the head, or the head stone, of the corner—a text held sacred by all Mark Masons.

History tells us of many notable foundation-stones. There is a record of the ceremonious laying of the many foundation-stones of Crowland, or Croyland, Abbey, Lincolnshire, in 1114. We know of the laying of the first foundation-stone of the altar of the Blessed Virgin in the Abbey Church of La Consomme, Aujoulême, in 1171, its top surface being inscribed with a circle or wheel at each of the four corners, with another in the centre. Two foundation-stones of the altar in Vale Royal Abbey, Cheshire, were laid in 1277, and there are scores of later records, not forgetting the mention by Pepys in his entry of October 23, 1667, of the laying of the foundation-stone of the Royal Exchange, London. Lodge of Antiquity, No. 2, possesses a mallet which tradition says Charles II used when laying the foundation-stone of St Paul's Cathedral in June 1675, and we must not necessarily assume that the tradition is contradicted by recorded evidence that Thomas Strong, Wren's Master Mason, laid the foundation-stone, the first the 'actual' one and the second the ceremonial one laid by the King.

Many accounts of stone-laying refer to the foot-stone. This, occasionally, is the foundation-stone itself, but more often is the tried and well-laid stone that will ultimately bear the ceremonial stone. Anderson in his *Constitutions* of 1738 says in the course of a highly imaginative description:

> London was rebuilding apace; and the Fire having ruin'd St Paul's Cathedral, the King with Grand Master Rivers, his architects and craftsmen, Nobility and Gentry, Lord Mayor and Aldermen, Bishops and Clergy, etc., in due Form levell'd the Footstone of New St Paul's.

The use of the foot-stone, to bear and be covered by the foundation-stone, permits of a cavity being made to receive certain 'foundation deposits'—documents, etc., which can be enclosed in a glass tube, which itself can be quite easily and securely sealed off in a flame to make it absolutely proof against air and water. The cavity can be closed in with a plate or by means of the stone that will come upon it.

Foundation Deposits

Much could be said about 'foundation deposits.' Obviously it is natural and proper to leave for posterity a record of the circumstances leading to the erection of a building, possibly of the conditions of the time, perhaps of the men who founded and designed the building; and such a practice must go back for thousands of years. It is apt that there should be foundation deposits of such a character, together with coins, newspapers, and other articles which will convey to the generations yet unborn some idea of the days in which the building began to grow. W. J. Chetwode Crawley reminds us that in the foundations of a temple built about 3000 B.C.—that is, about two thousand years before King Solomon's Temple—were found two terracotta cylinders bearing inscriptions which recite the acts which led to the building being started. The cylinders were deposited in the foundations by Gudea, ruler of Lagash, in Babylonia. The inscriptions in the terracotta include a device of the storm-bird which, as the two-headed eagle, is the symbol of the Ancient and Accepted Rite to-day; found near the site of the temple was a fine statue of Gudea, a seated figure upon whose knee was a drawing-board, while near by were depicted a rule, line, and pencil.

Foundation Sacrifices: Stability Rites

Foundation deposits of a rather different kind are linked with certain ancient and cruel superstitions. In many lands of the Far East and Southeast, a foundation sacrifice or stability rite was common. Thus, in Borneo, among the Milanau Dayaks, "at the erection of their largest house a deep hole was dug to receive the first post, which was then suspended over it; a slave-girl was placed in the excavation; at a signal the lashings were cut, and the timber descended, crushing the girl to death." At the erection of a flagstaff a live chicken took the place of the slave-girl.

The palace at Mandalay, Burma, is

> literally reared above dead men's bones, as at the time of its erection over fifty persons of both sexes, and of all ages and ranks, were sacrificed, their bodies being afterwards buried under the foundations of the city and palace. Four of the victims were even buried under the throne itself.

In Polynesia the central pillar of one of the temples at Maeva was planted upon the body of a human victim. At Galam, in Africa, a boy and girl were buried alive before the great gate of the city "to make it impregnable."

Foundation sacrifices or stability rites are known to have been the custom throughout Europe. When the broken dam of the river Nogat (below the Gulf of Danzig) had to be repaired in 1463, the peasants, advised to sacrifice a living man, are said to have made a beggar drunk and then to have thrown him in. Legend says that a young girl was built into the wall of Nieder-Manderscheid Castle, in the Eifel district, Prussia, and that she was fed through an opening in the wall as long as she was able to eat. When, in 1844, the wall was broken through there was disclosed a cavity containing a human skeleton.

There is a Thuringian legend to the effect that to make the Castle of Liebenstein fast and impregnable a child was bought from its mother for money and walled in.

Tradition relates that the bridge of Arta fell in and again fell in until they walled in the master-builder's wife, whose dying curse was that the bridge should henceforth tremble like a flower-stalk!

Were the British Isles free from such horrors? Let us see. Jacquetta and Christopher Hawkes, in their delightful *Prehistoric Britain* (1947), tell the story of Skara Brae, a hamlet in the Orkneys probably some three thousand five hundred years old, which happily has survived. They describe the hamlet and one of the houses in it—a single, fair-sized living-room (with one or more side-cells) still containing much of its original furnishing, altogether nearly as well equipped and comfortable a dwelling as many people inhabited in such remote regions up to the last century. But the element of savagery was there—hidden in the foundations were the crouched bodies of two old women, buried that their spirits might hold up the walls of the house.

The Picts followed the custom of bathing their foundation-stones with human blood, and a legend says that Columba, the Irish saint, buried another saint alive under the foundations of a monastery, in order to propitiate the spirits of the soil, who were said to be demolishing by night what Columba had built during the day. And G. W. Speth tells us of the discovery in 1876 in the foundations of the old church at Brownsover, Rugby, of two skeletons, one under the north and one under the south wall, exactly opposite each other, each skeleton being covered with what appeared to be the oak top of a carpenter's bench.[1]

Completion Sacrifices

Not only were there foundation sacrifices, but, according to many stories and legends, there were completion sacrifices—that is, sacrifices when the building was finished. G. W. Speth relates the story of the Cathedral of St Basil, Moscow, in which the architect, on the completion of his work, was killed to prevent his building any better church elsewhere. He relates, too, the well-known story of the Prentice Pillar at Roslyn Chapel, in which the Master Mason is said to have murdered his apprentice who had outshone his master in working a beautiful and difficult pillar. There are many similar stories, typical of which is the one told by Speth concerning the ancient castle of Henneburg, Saxe-Meinigen, where a mason, tempted by money, walled up his own child.

When the last stone was put in, the child screamed in the wall, and the man, overwhelmed with self-reproach, lost his hold, fell from the ladder and broke his neck. This story is noteworthy because it is one of those that refer to a double sacrifice. . . . Several tales show the double victim.

[1] For fuller details of foundation sacrifices and stability rites see G. W. Speth's *Builders' Rites and Ceremonies* (1894) and contributions to *A.Q.C.* by G. W. Bullamore. David Flather, Count Goblet D'Alviella, G. W. Speth, and others.

It is possible that the bare idea of the completion sacrifice is not wholly dead even to-day, for it is related that when in the course of building a house at Hindhead, Surrey, towards the end of the nineteenth century a workman fell from a beam and was killed, his mates declared that the accident was "lucky for the house and would ensure its stability."

Is the Stability Rite reflected in the Hiramic Legend?

What is the underlying explanation of these foundation and completion sacrifices? There was an idea once upon a time that before a house was fit for people to live in it the dead must first pass through it, but that idea does not appear to explain anything. The motive for the sacrifices might go back to a much earlier day, when the felling of a tree for the building of a rough hut was thought to be an affront to some local spirit or demon, to whom, therefore, a living sacrifice was offered to propitiate him, as otherwise he might revenge himself upon the people living in the house. A more generally accepted idea is that it was thought that the ghost, or spirit, of the poor victim would protect the building from evil influences, much as the dedication of a church to a particular saint, and the placing of the body of that saint beneath the altar, might once upon a time have been expected to have had the effect of keeping evil spirits at a safe distance.

Is the completion sacrifice a now forgotten basis, or any part of the basis, of the Hiramic legend? Who can say, but who can say that it is not? Let the reader ponder the following, which is an abbreviation of a sweeping statement by G. W. Speth, one of the best-informed of all masonic writers:

> From the rude commencements of the earliest civilizations, right through the middle ages, in all countries, at all times, no important building was erected without a human sacrifice beneath the foundations of the intended structure; in a vast majority of countries, a similar sacrifice was offered up at the completion. And if you will analyse this completion sacrifice you will find that in almost a majority of cases the victim, either in truth or legend, was the builder himself. The idea seems one innate to Masonry.

In his *Builders' Rites and Ceremonies* Speth gives eight instances (occurring, according to legend or story, in Europe, including England) in which the architect, his apprentice, or the builder was the completion sacrifice, or narrowly escaped the fate.

Sacrifice more or less symbolic replaced in time the human offering. At first, no doubt, animals were substituted for human beings; thus we find a lamb buried under a Danish altar, and we find also a live horse buried in a churchyard to inaugurate the use of the site as a burying-ground. From numberless places come stories of the substitution of a cock or a lamb whose blood was allowed to flow upon the foundation-stone, and whose body was afterwards buried beneath it. We read that French peasants entering upon a new house sprinkled the blood of a freshly killed chicken in all the rooms; of an empty coffin being built into the foundations of a building; and of burying beneath the foundation a burning lamp, whose flame was the symbol of human life. Legend speaks of Naples as being 'built on an egg,' the allusion being to the placing of the egg, as representing life, under the foundations of some of the buildings. In Egypt and Assyria human images are believed to have been buried beneath the stones of the threshold, probably to prevent the entrance of evil spirits; and in some eastern European countries, such as Bulgaria and Rumania, great care was taken that the shadow of a man fell upon the site of the first stone or timber of the intended building, the shadow being superstitiously regarded as the manifestation of a man's soul or spirit. As recently as 1970 three sheep were slaughtered as foundation sacrifices at the building of a bridge over the Bosphorus.

The Number and Positions of Foundation-stones

There may be more than one ceremonial foundation-stone in a building. For Truro Cathedral in 1880 two stones were laid, one at the northeast corner by freemasons, and one at the west end. It is not always that the stone is laid in the north-east corner, although that position may be regarded as sacred in the masonic tradition. A reason, far from convincing, advanced for this position is that on St John's Day, June 24, the sun can be taken as rising in the north-east. It has been commonly argued, but hardly logically, that a mason would naturally go to the north-east corner to start his work in the morning, because that corner would be fully illumined by the rising sun. There may, of course, be a long-lost symbolism to account for the preference, but the records of stone-laying ceremonies relating to notable medieval buildings do not support any such idea, although in the year 1114 the first corner-stone of the abbey at Croyland (Crowland), Lincolnshire, was laid "on the eastern side, facing the north."

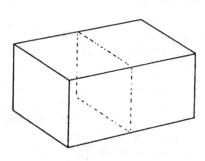

THE DOUBLE CUBE

Foundation-stones vary in their proportions with the ideas of the architect, but the double cube is very suitable.

The Ceremony of laying a Foundation-stone

There is a fund of information on the subject of foundation-stone laying in a paper by David Flather in *A.Q.C.*, vol. xlviii. Until the year 1919 the United Grand Lodge gave, with its *Constitutions*, an approved sequence of operations in the ceremonious laying of a foundation-stone, but did not closely follow it at the ceremony on July 14, 1927, at the Masonic Memorial (Freemasons' Hall, London), the procedure on that occasion being as follows:

(1) The Grand Master is requested to lay the Stone.

(2) The Stone is raised.

(3) The Phial containing the Roll and Coins is placed in the Cavity.

(4) The inscription upon the Stone is read.

(5) The Grand Master receives the Trowel and spreads the cement upon the lower Stone.

(6) The Upper Stone is lowered by three movements.

(7) The Maul is handed to the Grand Master, who strikes the Stone at each corner, "Temperance, Fortitude, Prudence, and Justice."

(8) The Plumb Rule is handed to the Grand Master, who proves the Stone Plumb.

(9) The Level is handed to the Grand Master, who proves the Stone Level.

(10) The Square is handed to the Grand Master, who proves the Stone Square.

(11) The Maul is handed to the Grand Master, who strikes the Stone three times and declares the Stone, "well and truly laid."

(12) The Stone is consecrated with Corn, Wine, Oil, and Salt.

(13) The ceremony concludes with Prayer and the Patriarchal Benediction.

David Flather criticizes the foregoing procedure, and holds that the whole ceremony can be divided into six sections, with appropriate instructions and prayers attached to each of them.

1. The preparation of the stone and the site. The stone, either square or cubical or at least having plain parallel sides and ends, is lifted and lowered by means of a lewis inserted into its top face. Any cavities for deposits should be in the foot-stone not in the stone, and should be so cut as to have a rebate, into which a steel or bronze lid plate can be dropped after the records and coins are deposited, the cement being spread right over the metal plate. The foot-stone, at least as large in area as the foundation-stone, might well be larger and form a socket into which the stone fits. No foot-stone is required when the foundation-stone can rest upon a natural rock.

2. The proving of the stone by the square. David Flather suggests, at the reference given, a simple ritual that might be adopted. The Grand Master has been handed the square and with it he tests parts of the stone that should be so tested; he declares it to be good work and square.

3. The proving of the site or foot-stone by the level. The Senior Warden then applies the level to the base upon which the stone will rest, and announces that the ground (or foot-stone) is level and suitable to receive the stone. The records, coins, etc., are deposited, any inscription on the plate is read, and the architect presents the trowel to the Grand Master.

4. The laying of the stone. The Grand Master spreads the cement over the base, and the stone is lowered with three distinct stops. The maul is handed to him, and he strikes the four corners of the stone, saying, "In Temperance, Fortitude, Prudence, and Justice may this and all our work be grounded."

5. The proving of the stone by level and plumb. The Senior Warden tries the stone with his level, and declares it to be perfect and level. The Junior Warden tries it with his plumb-rule and declares it to be perfect, true, and upright.

6. The Grand Master with the maul strikes the stone at the south side, and the west side, at the east side, and declares the stone to be well and truly laid.

7. The consecration by corn, wine, oil, and salt.

8. Prayer and patriarchal benediction.

Laying the Keystone of a Bridge

The ceremony of laying the keystone of a bridge, as worked at St Patrick's Bridge, Cork, in 1789, was naturally based on that of laying a foundation-stone. The keystone, suspended above its final position at the centre of the final arch, was lowered into place, and a Bible resting on a velvet cushion was placed upon it. The Grand Master gave the stone three distinct knocks with a mallet, and the Grand Almoner emptied a chalice of wine over the stone.

The 'Stone of Foundation'

On no account must the 'Stone of Foundation' be confused with the foundation-stone. In the legends relating to the rebuilding of the Temple we learn of one such wondrous stone discovered in a vault when preparing the ground for the building of the second Temple. It was said by some to be a perfect cube of white porphyry, bearing within a triangle certain characters, all within a circle, inscribed in precious stones. Others said it was a double cube of white marble, on the front of which were engraven the initials of exalted personages and certain mystic characters—a description much more familiar to the English Royal Arch mason. In the Jewish Talmud are many legends relating to a 'Stone of Foundation,' a stone originally taken by God from his throne in heaven and "cast into the primæval abyss to form a foundation for the world."

Chapter Twenty

THE FREEMASON'S LANDMARKS

Our masonic idea of the landmark comes from the Bible. We picture a stream, a hill, or some other natural feature by means of which a boundary-line or point can never fail to be recognized, or, in the plains where the shepherds graze their flocks, a series of massive stones—the kind of landmark that was in the mind of the writer who said: "Some remove the landmarks; they violently take away flocks, and feed thereof" (Job xxiv, 2).

In Proverbs xxii, 28, is the injunction: "Remove not the ancient landmark, which thy fathers have set," and in Deuteronomy xxvii, 17, is the malediction: "Cursed be he that removeth his neighbour's landmark. And all the people shall say, Amen." Frazer's *Folk Lore in the Old Testament* tells us that an ancient statute or custom of Rome directed that if any man ploughed up a boundary-stone both he and the oxen which had helped him commit the sacrilege should be held sacred to the God of Boundaries—that is, that both the man and his beasts should be placed outside the pale of the law, that anybody might slay them with impunity.

It is in the light of the Biblical idea—a great rock immovable, or which *should be* immovable—that we as freemasons understand the word 'landmark,' although in ordinary figurative language the landmark possesses more of the sense of an elevated mark by which the mariner can take his bearings. It is any historical event by which we estimate other events and things; it is a point outstanding in a course of advancement or development; but these are only part of what the freemason has peculiarly in mind. He goes back to the Biblical idea of the rock that cannot be moved; he sees his landmarks as a history or a tradition; as a law, a rule, or a tenet; as a rite or a custom; as a system; as a prerogative or right; as something (to him) fundamental—each and all of them in existence and coming down to him from time immemorial.

The Hebrew origin of the word 'landmark,' W. W. Covey Crump tells us, is *g'vul* (meaning 'border,' 'coast,' or 'line'), which is derived from *gabal*, meaning 'a rope.' So, conceivably, the original Hebrew idea had relation to a boundary-line determined by stretching a rope or drawing a straight line connecting point to point; and with this in mind, if the freemason needs an emblem of the landmark, he has not far to go.

Terminus was the Romans' god of territorial bounds and limits; they represented him as having neither head nor feet nor arms, perhaps to suggest fixedness. At his annual festivals in February (the *Terminalia*) the country people crowned the landmarks (*termini*) with flowers, poured over the stones milk and wine, and sacrificed a lamb or young pig. His emblem was a cubical stone, just such a stone as that which adorns the Wardens' pedestals. The beating of bounds, an old village custom in England and elsewhere, is a survival of the *Terminalia*.

The Craft ritual contains many references to landmarks. The Initiate is told that his fidelity must be exemplified by his strict observance of the constitutions of the fraternity and by adhering to the Ancient Landmarks of the Order. The Fellow Craft is told, in the course of a lecture, that he may offer his opinions under the superintendence of an experienced Master who will guard the landmarks against encroachment. The Master Mason is enjoined to preserve the landmarks sacred and inviolable. The Master Elect is required to be well-skilled in the landmarks, and has to promise that he will not permit or suffer any deviation from them. Finally, the Director of Ceremonies is informed that the preservation of the landmarks is within his province.

The first *Constitutions* (1723) state that every annual Grand Lodge has an inherent power and authority to make and alter regulations for the real benefit of this Ancient Fraternity, provided always that the Old Landmarks be carefully preserved; the 1738 *Constitutions* express the same thing but in different phrasing. The *Constitutions* to-day repeat in effect the statement in the 1723 edition when they declare that the Grand Lodge possesses the supreme superintending authority and alone has the inherent power of enacting laws and regulations for the government of the Craft, and of altering, repealing, and abrogating them, *always taking care that the ancient Landmarks of the Order be preserved*. Regulation 55 makes clear that if it shall appear to the Grand Master that any proposed resolution at the Quarterly Communication of Grand Lodge contains anything contrary to the ancient landmarks, he may refuse to permit it to be discussed. (Logically, therefore, with this as the basis, any mason is within his right in objecting to anything contrary to the ancient landmarks being raised in lodge.) The Master Elect of every lodge is required to admit: "That it is not in the power of any man or body of men to make innovation in the body of masonry."

Definition of a Masonic Landmark

Many of the best-known masonic writers have expressed themselves on the subject of the landmarks, but one of the most useful contributions is that by "A Young Mason" in volume iv of *The Transactions of the Merseyside Association for Masonic Research*. The difficulty of defining a masonic landmark is admitted by all who have given the subject serious thought. A hitherto generally accepted definition finds expression in *The Principles of Masonic Jurisprudence*, by John W. Simons:

> We assume those principles of action to be landmarks which have existed from time immemorial, whether in the written or unwritten law: which are identified with the form and essence of the Society: which, the great majority agree, cannot be changed, and which every mason is bound to maintain intact under the most solemn and inviolable sanctions.

While such a definition has been generally accepted it is not beyond criticism.

To the customs, practices, tenets, traditions, and observances that can be proved to have existed from time immemorial, some Brethren would add any customs, even if not ancient, that are universally acknowledged; but, against this, it is solidly contended that were it possible for the freemasons of the whole world to come together and agree on a new and common belief they would not and could not by so doing create a landmark! It is held that a landmark can be discovered, but not created; it cannot be changed or altered; it cannot be improved; it cannot be obliterated. Thus, a world concourse of masons, unable to create a landmark, would be equally unable to obliterate one.

William Preston's conception of a landmark was a boundary set up as a check to innovation. That looks well until you remember that the landmarks of masonry were not set up by anybody; they just were and are. A landmark has been defined as a fundamental part of freemasonry, something that cannot be altered without destroying the identity of freemasonry. Axel J. A. Poignant in *A.Q.C.*, vol. xxiv, maintains that every tenet of the Craft is a landmark, but an allegory or symbol that teaches or indicates it is not a landmark; further, that a landmark must be part and parcel of the freemason's peculiar system of morality, and not of the allegory that veils and of the symbols that illustrate it. The teaching or meaning which the allegories convey may be a landmark. His statement, fanciful in some of its details, met with criticism, but was a courageous setting out of an understandable point of view, far more in keeping with the times than the lengthy lists printed in many masonic books.

Can the Landmarks be named?

We have seen that the freemason is charged with the duty of observing the landmarks. But what are they?

Just as there is no authoritative definition, so no landmarks are named by the English Grand Lodge, which, in its wisdom, has neither defined nor specified them. It has been well said that "inferentially if the landmarks were approved by the *Constitutions* the same authority could disapprove, whereas landmarks are unchangeable." It should be impossible, therefore, for anybody to dogmatize in a matter in which Grand Lodge makes no pronouncement, and in which experienced masons cannot agree.

Unfortunately there is a tendency to use the word 'landmark' as a convenient name or description of something not having definite meaning. Thus we hear of 'the landmarks being in danger' when an attempt is made, for example, to correct a misquotation or a grammatical error in the ritual, and there is a general practice of grouping all together customs, usages, and landmarks, and assuming that they are all the same things.

Masonic writers have often quoted a list of twenty-five so-called landmarks offered by the well-known American mason, Albert G. Mackey, the original editor of *An Encyclopædia of Freemasonry* (1858), since known in many editions. They are given here greatly abbreviated:

1. Modes of recognition.

2. The division of symbolic masonry into three degrees.

3. The legend of the Third Degree constituting "the very essence and identity of masonry."

4. Government of the Fraternity by an elected Grand Master.

5–8. The prerogative of the Grand Master (*a*) to preside over every assembly of the Craft, (*b*) to grant dispensations for conferring degrees at irregular times and (*c*) for opening and holding lodges, and (*d*) to make masons at sight.

9. The necessity for masons to congregate in lodges.

10. The government of a lodge by a Master and two Wardens.

11. The necessity that every lodge should be duly tiled.

12–14. The right of every mason to (*a*) be represented in all general meetings of the Craft; (*b*) to appeal from a lodge decision to Grand Lodge; (*c*) to visit every regular lodge (known as 'the right of visitation').

15. No unknown visitor to enter a lodge without examination.

16. No lodge to interfere with the business of another lodge nor give degrees to Brethren who are members of other lodges.

17. Every mason to be amenable to the laws and regulations of the masonic jurisdiction in which he resides. "Non-affiliation, a masonic offence, does not exempt a mason from masonic jurisdiction."

18. A Candidate for Initiation to be a man—unmutilated, free-born, and of mature age. "A woman, a cripple, or a slave or one born in slavery, is disqualified."

19, 20. Belief in (*a*) the existence of God as the "Grand Architect of the Universe," and (*b*) resurrection to a future life.

21. The Book of the Law to have a place in every lodge. It is that volume

which, by the religion of the country, "is believed to contain the revealed will of the Grand Architect of the Universe."

22. The equality of all masons.

23. Secrecy. "If divested of its secret character, it would lose its identity and would cease to be freemasonry."

24. The foundation of a speculative science upon an operative art, and the symbolic use and explanation of the terms of that art, for the purposes of religious or moral teaching. "The temple of Solomon was the symbolic cradle of the Institution."

25. The crowning landmark is that these landmarks can never be changed.

Mackey's list will provide food for thought, but very little basis for agreement. Old writers used to quote the list with genuine approval, but men's minds have moved a long way from the position taken up in the middle of last century, and there are but few masons anywhere to-day who could conscientiously affirm, without mental reservation of any kind, their acceptance of it. The tendency is to reduce the list to just a few landmarks, and even then there is difficulty in finding any real measure of agreement as to which they should be. But it must be stated that Mackey's list has been officially adopted by many American Grand Lodges, one of which has increased the number to fifty-four.

To-day we realize, in the fine words of Chetwode Crawley, that the ancient landmarks of freemasonry, like all other landmarks material or symbolical, can only preserve their stability when they reach down to sure foundations. All laws, customs, and methods that obtain among free-masons and do not ultimately find footholds on this basis are conventions, in no way partaking of the nature of Ancient Landmarks.

We feel that the modern view, with which there is likely to be general but of course not universal agreement, is on the lines set forth by the American mason who said that a landmark is that without which masonry cannot exist and which determines the boundary beyond which Grand Lodge cannot go. Anything in masonry that a Grand Lodge has the right to change cannot be a landmark.

A sound statement, but possibly an unpopular one, made by the Editor of *Miscellanea Latomorum* is worthy of note. It is to the effect that when Dr Anderson used the word landmark in the 1723 *Constitutions* (the only reference to landmarks in that publication, and in effect the only reference on which the two centuries of argument has been based) he was merely using a fine-sounding phrase, as was his custom, without actually attaching to it, or intending to attach to it, any precise meaning whatever. What Anderson said was that the Regulations can be added to or altered by Grand Lodge, provided always that the old landmarks be carefully preserved. "And I fancy," says the editor of *Miscellanea Latomorum*, "that all the subsequent arguments about what Anderson had in mind, and the attempts to enumerate or define his old landmarks, are largely wasted ingenuity."

While one may have much sympathy with that point of view, we yet know that all thinking freemasons will want to make their own search for what they will regard as the landmarks, and that what one Brother finds may not exactly agree with what another may discover. With respect we offer one touchstone by which a Brother may prove his result. Would freemasonry remain essentially the same to *him* were his 'landmark' altered or removed? If the answer is Yes, then he will need to continue his search, but, successful or not, we trust he will find in the search itself its own reward.

'Making Masons at Sight'

English masons have heard vaguely of an alleged 'prerogative' of the Grand Master to 'make masons at sight.' While this phrase might possibly apply to one or two happenings in England in the eighteenth century no such 'prerogative' has been used since the Union in 1813, and no authority of the kind is given to the Grand Master by the *Constitutions* of the United Grand Lodge. In the U.S.A., however, many scores of men have been made 'masons at sight' by Grand Masters of some of the jurisdictions—noteworthy among the Brethren so made being William H. Taft, at the time President-elect of the U.S.A., whose initiation and the practice in general led to much controversy, echoes of which are still heard. The concensus of opinion in England and the trend of opinion in the U.S.A. is against the existence of any such 'prerogative.' Its inclusion in any list of so-called landmarks (see p. 335) is unfortunate. The precise meaning of the words is open to argument, for the phrase could hardly indicate the right of a Grand Master to make *any* man a mason at *any* time just as the whim seized him; the most reasonable interpretation is that the Grand Master could make a mason without causing him to be subjected to lodge scrutiny and ballot, thus dispensing with the formal preliminaries associated with lawful and regular initiation. Interested readers can see all the arguments, for and against, in Mackey's *Encyclopædia* and in a paper by H. V. B. Voorhis in the *Transactions* of the Sydney Lodge of Research for the year 1933.

Chapter Twenty-one

THE FREEMASON'S SAINTS

ALL the old crafts and guilds, both English and Continental, had their patron saints; and for hundreds of years freemasons have been holding their festivals on saints' days. Masonic writings make frequent mention of saints, and the *Masonic Year Book* shows that saints give their names to about four hundred lodges in England alone.

The saints in greatest regard among masons are St John the Baptist, St John the Evangelist, St Thomas, St Barbara, St George, and the Four Crowned Martyrs, often known by the Latin form, Quatuor Coronati.

St John the Baptist

June 24, the traditional birthday of St John the Baptist, was and is a great Church festival; but at one time it was the saint's day of martyrdom, and not his birthday, that was celebrated, a pulpit being erected in the open air and decorated with boughs and green candles, fires being lit in the open—the 'blessing fires'—and houses dressed with green boughs and flowers. The saint's birthday was at one time a day of heathen rejoicing, and how it ever came to be associated with either operative or speculative masonry is not known, for neither of the Saints John is believed to have had any special connexion with building or masonry. It is possible, however, that both of these saints have been confused with the Byzantine St John of Jerusalem, known as St John the Almoner, there being some shadowy idea that the charitable organization of St John of Jerusalem had some influence on the building craft. But freemasons have no monopoly of St John the Baptist, for it may be noted that every Master of the Merchant Taylors Company takes his oath on the day of the Saint and invokes his assistance.

Possibly going back as far as the seventeenth century, English masons have been called 'St John's Men' or 'St John's masons.' Even to-day, particularly in the North of England, the annual festival, or installation meeting, is frequently referred to as 'St John's.' Why is not known, nor is the origin of the connexion of craft masonry throughout Scotland with the name of St John.

Here is a salutation taken from an irregular publication of 1725:

Q. From whence came you?

A. I came from a right worshipful Lodge of Masters and Fellows belonging to Holy St John, who doth greet all perfect Brothers of our Holy Secret, so do I you, if you be one.

Q. I greet you well Brother, God's Greeting be at our Meeting.

From another publication of much about the same date comes the following:

Q. What Lodge are you of?

A. Of the Right Worshipful Lodge of St John's.

St John the Evangelist

Many ancient lodges had their summer festival on St John the Baptist's Day and their winter festival on St John the Evangelist's Day, December 27. This second St John was traditionally regarded as the son of Zebedee and Salome (the latter supposed to have been the sister of the Virgin Mary), and is said to have died at the age of nearly a hundred after an eventful life, but with no particular connexion with masonry or architecture.

There seems good ground for assuming that the two saints' days were originally days of heathen rejoicing, being the summer and the winter solstices, cleverly appropriated by the Early Christian Fathers and by them fastened on the two Saints John. We find that the emblem of wheel is common to both of the festivals, although chiefly associated with that of winter. A wheel used to be rolled about to signify the sun, which at the June festival occupies the highest place in the Zodiac. In some festivals it was taken to the top of the hill, straw was tied around it and set on fire, and the wheel was then set rolling down to the valley, it appearing "at a distance as if the sun had fallen from the sky. . . . The people imagine that all their ill-luck rolls away from them together with this wheel." (See also p. 407.)

The two St John days are sometimes referred to as 'The Two Great Parallels.' The phrase 'a line parallel' appears in one version of the legendary story of how the two Saints John came to be commemorated by the masonic order. In the ancient days, we are told, a general meeting of the Craft held in the city of Benjamin deputed seven members to beg St John the Evangelist to become Grand Master. He answered that

> though well stricken in years (being upwards of ninety) yet, having been in the early part of his life initiated into Masonry, he would take upon himself that office; he thereby compleated, by his learning, what the other (St John Baptist) had begun by his zeal, and drew a *line parallel*, ever since which Free Masons' Lodges have been dedicated both to St John the Baptist, and to St John the Evangelist.

Symbols of the first of these saints are a camel-hair garment, small rude cross, and a lamb at his feet; of the second, an open book, and a dragon or serpent emerging from a chalice, while in the background may be a young man with eagle. Thus the presence in a few lodges of a carved eagle may suggest that the lodge was dedicated to St John the Evangelist, as a great many lodges were, or may possibly indicate that a Royal Arch ceremonial was worked at one time.

The first Grand Master of the Premier Grand Lodge was elected and installed on St John the Baptist's Day, 1717, and for eight years afterwards his successors were installed on that day; but in most of the following years for a quarter of a century the date was altered to suit the convenience of the Grand Master, a course that offended many masons and in later days gave the 'Antients' opportunity for criticism.

St Thomas

It appears that St Thomas, who carries as his symbol the square or builder's rule or sometimes a stone, has far greater claims than the Saints John to be regarded as the patron saint of masons and architects. In the legend, Gordon Hills tells us, St Thomas, who was at Cæsarea, was sent by our Lord to Gondoforus, the King of the Indies, to build him a palace finer than that of the Emperor of Rome. The Apostle went, found the King absent, and instead of building the palace he distributed the King's accumulation of treasures to the sick and poor. The King, on his return, cast St Thomas into prison to await a fearful death, but the King was miraculously warned that St Thomas was a servant of God, and that in paradise there was a wondrous pillar of gold and silver and precious stones, which Thomas the Architect had built for the King. The saint, loosed from his bonds, told the King that his riches might prepare the way for him to such a pillar but could not follow him thither!

St Barbara

The patroness of architects and builders, St Barbara is the heroine of a romantic legend which, Gordon Hills says, was apparently brought to Western Europe by the Crusaders. Her pagan father shut her up in a high tower to prevent any possibility of her marriage. During her imprisonment she was converted to the true faith, and by directing the builders to put *three* instead of *two* windows in her chamber brought the knowledge of her conversion to her father—and led to her martyrdom at his hands. Her symbol is that tower.

St George

Although the United Grand Lodge of England had its first meeting on St John the Evangelist's Day, 1813, it has held its festivals since then on a day as near as possible to St George's Day, which is April 23. St George is symbolized by a knight on horseback transfixing a dragon, an allegory of the martyr triumphing over sin. A device of this nature forms the insignia of the Order of the Garter. There seems to be no connexion of St George with the arts of masonry.

The Four Crowned Martyrs (the Quatuor Coronati)

The Four Crowned Martyrs—actually, there were *nine*—the subjects of a legend known in many different forms, but having an historical basis, are widely recognized as patron saints of the mason's craft. The legend can be followed in its many forms in Gould's *History*, in W. J. Chetwode Crawley's learned paper in *A.Q.C.*, vol. xxvii, and in the most helpful and readable address by Gordon Hills in *A.Q.C.*, vol. xxxi, to all of which sources the student particularly interested should turn direct.

St Jerome refers to the Quatuor Coronati about A.D. 400, and there are many mentions in the later centuries; for example, Gregory the Great in the eleventh century refers to the feast day of these saints, and the famous Regius Poem (the Halliwell MS.) of about 1390 includes the following:

> Pray we now to God almyght,
> And to hys swete Moder Mary bryght,
> That we nowe keepe these Artyculus here,
> And these poynts wel al-y-fere
> As dede these holy Martyres fowre,
> That yn thys Craft were of grete honoure;
> They were as gode Masonus as on erthe schul go
> Gravers and ymage-makers they were also.

From this we see that English medieval masons regarded the Four Crowned Martyrs as their patrons, a tradition which came down through the London Guild of Masons, which in 1481 was ordering special masses for the Martyrs. The *Steinmetzen* (German masons) referred to these saints in their Regulations of 1459, and there is reason to believe that the saints were honoured also by masons in other parts of Europe.

Of the many versions of the legend, Gordon Hills provides in *A.Q.C.*, vol. xxxi, one of the neatest:

> When the Emperor Diocletian went to Pannonia to visit the stone quarries he found, among the craftsmen there employed, four skilled above all

others in the stone-squarer's art. Their names were CLAUDIUS, CAS-TORIUS, SEMPRONIANUS, and NICOSTRATUS; they were secretly Christians, and the motive of their good work was that it was all done in the Name of their LORD. To these was joined by their example a fellow craftsman, SIMPLICIUS, who also embraced their faith. By declining to make a statue of the heathen god Æsculapius they forfeited the favour of the Emperor, and eventually were done to death by being fastened up alive in leaden coffins and cast into the river. Thence a fellow Christian raised the poor remains and carried them to his own house. On his return to Rome the Emperor directed a temple to be made to Æsculapius in the Baths of Trojan, where, some time later, on its completion, the soldiers, and more especially the City Militia, were ordered to present themselves and offer incense before the image of the god. Four Christian soldiers refused to sacrifice to the idol: they were scourged to death with leaden-weighted thongs, and their bodies, thrown to the dogs, were recovered by their friends and laid to rest with other Saints. Twelve years later the Bishop founded a church on Cælian Hill, under the title of the FOUR CROWNED MAR-TYRS, dedicated to commemorate these *nine* saints all equally to be ac-counted winners of the Martyr's Crown Celestial. Later on the names of the soldiers were given as SEVERUS, SEVERIANUS, CARPOPHORUS, and VICTORINUS.

'Relics' of the martyrs were deposited in the church in the years 302 and 304.

The emblems of the Four Crowned Martyrs consist of the saw, ham-mer, mallet, compasses, and square, often or generally surmounted by a small crown. There is often, too, a dog or a wolf, to signify the animals who either refused to eat the soldiers' corpses or prevented others from eating them when exposed in the public thoroughfare. Obviously the tools represent the building craft in general (carpenters and joiners, also, regard these saints as their patrons), but why the crowns are included in the emblems is more difficult to say; but Gould in his *History* concludes that they refer to the crown of martyrdom which in process of time became peculiarly attached to them.

There was a Church of the Four Crowned Martyrs at Canterbury, possibly where St Alphege's Church now stands. An old legend relates that when, in the year 619, the greater part of the city was burnt down, the flames approached the church. Mellitus, the Archbishop, commanded his servants to carry him and set him "against the fiercest flames, which were in the place of the martyrdom of the Four Saints, where being placed, though grievously tormented with the Gout, yet by his Prayers the Wind suddenly turned, and the Fire was quenched."

The Quatuor Coronati Lodge and its Great Work

Throughout freemasonry to-day the name Quatuor Coronati is known chiefly for its association with the world's premier lodge of research, England's Quatuor Coronati Lodge, No. 2076, warranted in November 1884, and consecrated in January 1886, with Sir Charles Warren as its first Master, and Robert Freke Gould, who had just completed his *History of Freemasonry*, as the second Master. The first Secretary was G. W. Speth, who held the office until his death in 1901. The remaining founders were all men of distinction: W. H. Rylands, Sir Walter Besant, J. P. Rylands, S. C. Pratt, A. F. A. Woodford, and W. J. Hughan. The history of the lodge is reviewed by Boris Ivanoff in an address printed in *A.Q.C.*, vol. liii. In January 1887 was inaugurated the Correspondence Circle, with the object of extending to all Master Masons in good standing throughout the universe, but not necessarily possessing literary qualifications, as well as all lodges, Chapters, and other masonic corporate bodies, all the advantages of membership except the right of voting on lodge matters and holding lodge office. The *Transactions* of the lodge, the famous *Ars Quatuor Coronatorum*, contain full texts of the papers read, together with the discussions following their reading, as well as biographies, reviews, obituaries, etc. There are many other publications of the lodge, including facsimile reproductions of the Old Charges and other valuable manuscripts, etc. The lodge possesses a masonic museum which, with the library, includes over twenty thousand catalogued items.

The work of the Quatuor Coronati Lodge demands and deserves strong financial support. It can be sure of this only by the continued growth of the Correspondence Circle, and for that reason every Master Mason to whom the pages of this book make appeal should become a member of it.

It is fair and proper to say that, following the issue of Gould's famous *History* in the 1880's—at that time the greatest publishing event in the history of speculative masonry, and one that started a new fashion in masonic research—the work of the Quatuor Coronati Lodge has brought about throughout universal freemasonry a new understanding of masonic history, actual and traditional, and has led to the founding of lodges and associations of masonic research in every country where freemasonry flourishes.

BOOK FIVE

The Lodge and Many Related Subjects

Chapter Twenty-two

THE LODGE

THE *Constitutions* of our Fraternity as early as 1723 defined the lodge, and in their latest edition continue to do so in very nearly the same words. We were told in 1723 that "A Lodge is a Place where *Masons* assemble and work: Hence that assembly, or duly organiz'd Society of Masons, is call'd a LODGE, and every Brother ought to belong to one, and to be subject to its *By-laws* and the GENERAL REGULATIONS."

All Brethren know that the word 'lodge' has at least three meanings: it is the place—a building or a room—in which freemasons meet; it is the society, or body, of freemasons that meets there; it is the actual meeting of that body. When we think of the lodge all three meanings often coalesce.

In earlier pages dealing with operative masonry we noted the derivation of the word 'lodge' from *loge,* which in many and similar forms is to be found in the French and other Latin languages. The word was applied as early as about the thirteenth century to the room or building set aside for the use of the masons on any big building site. One form of old lodge was probably a workroom, which also served as the masons' 'refectory,' as beautiful a word as the modern 'canteen' is ugly, but having much the same meaning. The lodge was the masons' fraternal and social centre, and also, we expect, it was often their dormitory as well.

In general language, the word 'lodge' applies to-day to a small building, sometimes a shed, and we may note that the Incorporation of Masons, one of the fourteen trade guilds of Glasgow dating back to the eleventh century, brings its meetings to an end by 'closing the shed' with a series of knocks made by rapping with a folded rule. The word 'shed,' as meaning the masonic lodge, is known in some parts of Scotland.

In this chapter we are speaking of speculative lodges, purely and simply.

Lodge Names and Numbers

Every lodge bears a name and exclusive number. In the past lodges have tended to adopt certain popular names, with a result that, particularly as regards country lodges, there is much repetition. There are many Abbeys, Alberts, Apollos, Beacons, Benevolences, Charitys, Concords, Corinthians, Coronations, Dorics, Emulations, Felicitys, Fidelitys, Fraternitys, Freedoms, Friendships, Harmonys, Hopes, Industrys, Ionics, Loyals and Loyaltys, Minervas, Peaces, Perseverances, Priorys, Progresses, Prudences, Royals, St Georges, St Johns, St Marys, Sinceritys, Temperances, Temples, Trinitys, Tuscans, Unitys, Victorias, and Victorys.

Sometimes when, among the oldest lodges, we find an odd or curious name we can trace it to the fact that the lodge had no name in its early history, but in the course of time acquired one, perhaps taking a suggestion from the sign of the inn in which it met. Thus, the Strong Man Lodge, No. 45, in existence in 1733, had as its fifth home the Strong Man Inn, Smithfield London, where it remained roughly half a century. It left the Strong Man in 1813, in which year it officially took the name it had probably enjoyed unofficially for a long time.

The Neptune Lodge, No. 22, founded in 1757, left the Neptune Inn, Rotherhithe, eight years before receiving its name in 1831. Globe Lodge, No. 23, dating back to 1723, was at the Globe Tavern, Fleet Street, two years before it acquired its name in 1768. The Castle Lodge of Harmony, No. 26, founded in 1725, was at home from 1751 to 1763 in the Castle Tavern, Lombard Street, London, and officially named thirteen years later. The Old King's Arms Lodge, No. 28, founded in 1725, with the history of which many masons are acquainted, took its name from the King's Arms in the Strand, where it spent nine years following 1733; and so on.

The name is the property of the lodge, but can be changed only with the approval of the Grand Master.

The number of the lodge indicates its precedence (see p. 223). There is one lodge without a number—the Grand Stewards', which takes precedence of all English lodges.

Every lodge makes an annual return to Grand Lodge of its subscribing members, and remits fees accordingly; further, it returns annually to Grand Lodge the names of the Master and Wardens, and of Past Masters of and in the lodge, and, in addition, transmits to the Clerk of the Peace for the County, etc., in which the lodge is held, a list of the names, addresses, and professions of all members, this list being pursuant to an Act passed in the reign of George III.

The Consecration and Constitution of a Lodge

Since some time in the eighteenth century every new lodge must be solemnly constituted by the Grand Master or some one acting for him. A body of masons meeting to do masonic work in a lodge which had not been warranted and regularly and solemnly constituted would be meeting in a *clandestine* lodge. The warranting of a lodge is explained in a separate and later chapter.

The ceremonies of consecrating and constituting a new lodge are now combined. The Consecrating Officer, acting on behalf of the Grand Master, opens a lodge in three degrees, and, to the accompaniment of suitable prayers, scripture readings, and addresses, uncovers the lodge board and scatters corn (the symbol of plenty), pours wine (the symbol of joy and cheerfulness), pours oil (the symbol of peace and unanimity), and sprinkles salt (the symbol of fidelity and friendship). He then dedicates the lodge, and the Chaplain takes the censer three times round the lodge and offers the prayer of dedication. The Consecrating Officer then officially constitutes the lodge, and there generally follows the installation of the first Master, the election and appointment of officers, the approval of bylaws, etc., etc. In the old rites, still followed under some of the American jurisdictions, there is placed upon a table in front of the Consecrating Officer an emblem known as the 'lodge'—an oblong box of white fabric, to hold the warrant and the constitutions—and round it are three candles and the consecrating elements. The first English reference to the ceremony of consecration is probably not earlier than 1771.

Five members constitute a lodge, according to the *Constitutions* of the English Grand Lodge, which state that whenever the number of subscribing members shall be fewer than five the lodge shall cease to exist. Five members present in lodge form a quorum to transact masonic business, but one of them must be an Installed Master if a degree is to be conferred on a Candidate. A quaintly worded clause in the Grand Lodge No. 2 MS. (second half of the seventeenth century) insists that "No p'son of what degree soever be accepted a ffree Mason vnless he shall have a Lodge of five free Masons att ye least whereof one to be Master or Warden of that Limitt or division, wherein Such Lodge shall be kept and another of the Trade of ffreemasonry." We find the intention borne out by the Sloane MS. of rather later date, in which occurs this catechism:

Q. What is a just and perfect or just and lawfull Lodge?

A. A just and perfect Lodge is two Interprintices, two Fellow Craftes, and two Mast^{rs}, more and fewer, the more the merrier, the fewer the bett^r

chear, but if need require five will serve, that is two Interprintices, two Fel-low Craftes, and one Mast^r, on the Highest Hill or Lowest Valley Of the World without a crow of a Cock or the bark of a Dogg.

Place of Lodge Meeting

A regular lodge must hold its meetings at a place sanctioned by its Grand Lodge, and may not move to another venue except by dispensation or alteration of bylaws approved by Grand Lodge. This provision is of old standing—two centuries, more or less. It has long been the rule under the English Grand Lodge that a private lodge may not, except by dispensation, be held in an inn of which one of its officers is the pro-prietor or manager—to-day's version of a rule dating back to 1773 that "no master of a public house should in future be a member of any lodge holden in his house." Neither may a lodge be held in a private house, although in early days many lodges were so held. Indeed, the first English lodge, then No. 50, constituted in a foreign land by the Grand Lodge of England, was founded by the Duke of Wharton in his own apartments in Madrid in 1728, this lodge having a life of forty years and being now (or until recently) represented by the Matriteuse Lodge, No. 1, on the register of the Grand National Orient of Spain.

A statute, dated 1670, of the Lodge of Aberdeen forbids any lodge to be held within an inhabited dwelling-house, save in "ill-weather," and then only in a building "where no person shall heir or see us;" other-wise the meetings were to be held "in the open fields," which regulation, Gould comments, accords with the old tradition, already referred to, that lodges used to assemble on the "highest hills or in the lowest valleys," and that apprentices were received in "outfield lodges." Aberdeen masons were said to erect a tent for Initiation ceremonies in a hollow at Cunnigar Hill, at the Bay of Nigg, etc. Special mention is made of the "ancient outfield lodge in the mearns in the Parish of Negg, at the stonnies at the poynt of the Ness." The book of laws in a securely locked box was carried to any place where there was an Apprentice to be received, "three masters of the keys" bearing the three box keys.

The Castle Lodge of Harmony, No. 26, met in the month of June 1810, at the top of the steeple of the Church of St Nicholas Acons and St Edmund the King, Lombard Street, for the purpose of initiating a Candi-date. St Nicholas Acons, built in the days of William the Conqueror, is said to be so named because a person named Nicholas Acons, a citizen of Lycia, Asia Minor, was the first to enter the church on a certain day, and was thereupon, and for that 'reason' only, elected to be Bishop of Myræ, "in which Office his Deportment was such as to procure him a Seat in the Class of Saints." The church perished in the Fire of London and the parish was annexed to St Edmund the King, in Lombard Street.

Orientation of the Lodge

Why are lodges placed east to west, with the Master's place in the East? It is a fair question because, while freemasonry corresponds to so many ancient Jewish precedents, it apparently departs from them in orientating its lodges in a manner opposite to the example set by the Jewish tabernacle, which had its Holy Place in the west and its porchway in the east. The freemason's lodge follows the custom set for it through the centuries by the churches which, in the vast majority of cases, have their Holy of Holies in the east, the worshippers when they turn east in prayer thereby facing the altar. Many reasons have been given why Christians should face the east in this way. A thirteenth-century writer explained that "from the east Christ shall come to judge mankind; therefore we pray towards the east," while Durandus (thirteenth century) more definitely explained that "We pray towards the east because mindful of Him of Whom it is said Behold the man whose name is the east."

From remote ages it seems that men's minds have associated the east with light and life, and the west with darkness and death, an association now rooted in religious belief. We remember that learning originated in the east.

Dr Oliver said: "The principal entrance to the lodge room ought to face the east, because the east is a place of light both physical and moral; and therefore the Brethren have access to the lodge by that entrance, as a symbol of mental illumination."

Probably the whole matter is summed up by a writer of the second century who said simply that Christians pray towards the east as the place of sunrise; for that reason, too, the heathen did the same. We may fairly assume that the primitive veneration for the east sprang quite naturally from the daily recurring phenomenon and mystery of the rising of the sun following the darkness of night.

Our Craft ritual effects a happy simile when it says that as the sun rises in the east to enliven the day, so is the Worshipful Master placed in the east to open his lodge and instruct the Brethren in freemasonry.

The Form of the Lodge

There is good reason for believing that the early speculative lodges were not always rectangular. Some were almost certainly triangular, just possibly others may have been cruciform. Not, of course, that the lodge rooms were built to those shapes, but merely that the lines of the real and yet mystical lodge, the symbolic lodge, were marked out on the floor to the triangular or other shape required, or even that the furniture of the lodge was arranged to produce in effect the shape required. It is generally held that the Brethren were not truly in the lodge until they had come within the lines, as in the Canongate Kilwinning Lodge, where the Brethren pass through the porch of the lodge, but yet have not entered the real lodge until they have passed between the pillars just within the porch.

We can well imagine great diversity of lodge forms when we bear in mind that there were London lodges and country lodges, with little communication between them; that there were the lodges of the 'Moderns' and of the 'Antients'; and that there were lodges, unaffiliated and otherwise, influenced strongly by the Continental ideas of the 1730's and '40's, working degrees other than the regular Craft degrees, and inclined to allow one degree to borrow ideas and 'colour' from the others. All these influences would inevitably make for diversity in the form and working of the lodge.

Oblong-square Form of Lodge. We can take for granted that the greater number of the early lodges were oblong square in shape. To-day such a shape is thought to be more or less the ideal, but lodge rooms vary considerably, and some of them, especially in the old country inns, are almost square. 'Oblong square' is an old-time expression implying a rectangle approximately twice as long as it is wide. It was used by Sir Walter Scott (himself a freemason) in *Waverley* (1814) and in *Ivanhoe* (1819), the former in describing the Castle of Doone and the latter the lists for a tournament at Ashby, and Scott probably took the term from freemasonry and not from the general language of the time. One of the irregular masonic publications of 1762 gives the following catechism:

Q. What Form is your Lodge?
A. An Oblong Square.
Q. How long, Brother?
A. From East to West.
Q. How wide, Brother?
A. Between North and South.
Q. How high, Brother?
A. From the Earth to the Heavens.
Q. How deep, Brother?
A. From the Surface of the Earth to the Center.

The same publication included an illustration purporting to show the exact form of the drawing on the lodge floor at the making of a mason "according to the most ancient custom, and still retained in all regular lodges." The presence of Deacons suggests that the lodge was of the 'Antient' order. The illustration herewith, carefully redrawn from the original woodcut, shows the lodge to be rectangular but ending in the east in a triangle, at whose apex the Master sits. The tint lines represent, of course, the floor lines and not the walls of the room. The Brethren appear to be standing along the side walls, which is rather at variance with the accepted idea that the Brethren are not within the lodge until they have crossed the floor lines. The Wardens and Secretary are more or less in the positions in which we are accustomed to seeing them to-day. The Volume of the Sacred Law is immediately in front of the Master in the east, and there is no central altar. The original drawing states that the Senior Warden and the Junior Warden each has a "column in his hand." Three candles — in all probability supported by the traditional pillars— are arranged to form a triangle with its apex in the south, so that there is a candle immediately in front of the Junior Warden. The Senior Deacon is at the Master's right and the Junior in the southwest corner; each of them has a black rod. The Immediate Past Master is here called a Past-Master "with the Sun and Compasses, and a string of cords." The date of this illustration is approximately 1762, and it will be noted that at that time there were three steps in the west; on the first of them are the words "First Degree, or Entered Apprentice's step, Kneel with the Left Knee." On the second, "Second Degree or Fellow Craft's step, Kneel with the Right Knee." And on the third, "Third Degree or Master's step, Kneel with both Knees."

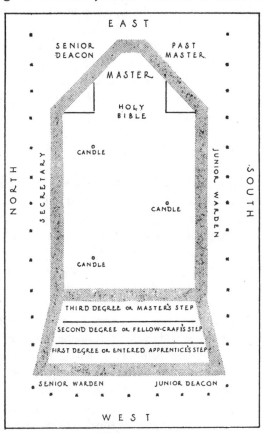

AN OLD LODGE PLAN

Redrawn from a woodcut in an irregular print issued about 1762. The shaded band represents the floor lines.

Two years before the above illustration appeared there had been published another of these irregular prints calling itself *The Three Distinct Knocks*. It is quite obvious that the illustration we have just given was borrowed from that print or that both of them borrowed from another source. The Deacons are said to have black rods in their hands, about eight feet long, at the opening and closing of lodge. The Wardens are said to have a column in their hands or by them, these columns being about twenty inches high. The candles form a triangle of which the base line is down the centre of the lodge, one candle coming apparently in front of the Volume of the Sacred Law and the other in the extreme west. Steps are represented with the same instructions as already given. Here the Immediate Past Master is called the 'Pass Master'; he "hath the Compasses and Sun, with a line of cords about his neck, viz. 60°" (a reference to a detail which has possibly been borrowed from some non-craft working).

In the eighteenth-century lodges, the presence of a table, around which the Brethren were seated, was usual. Students have suggested that it was this arrangement, or, alternatively, a floor drawing or lodge board in the centre of the lodge, that brought about the custom of 'squaring the lodge.' And it is also thought that there was a clear space at the end of the lodge in which the Obligation was taken. However, it is just as likely that the custom of squaring the lodge derived from the arrangement in which there was a central altar.

In the (old) Apollo Lodge (1811–35) there was a long table with the Master at one end in the east, the Senior Warden at the other end, and the Junior Warden half-way down in the south, the Secretary having his table immediately to the left and slightly in front of the Master. Round the table were backed benches for the Brethren. It was in this style of lodge that the old lectures were worked (by the question-and-answer method); but sometimes trestle tables were erected in the lodge after the ceremonies, and the Brethren sat round them eating, drinking, and smoking, the while the catechisms continued.

Triangle form of Lodge. We may suppose that, in some old lodges, the real lodge is indicated by the temporary floor lines (see a later chapter), or as suggested by the arrangement of the Master's and Warden's positions, took the form of a triangle, the Master sitting at the apex in the east, and both Wardens in the west. This is thought to be the arrangement at one time in the Old Dundee Lodge, Wapping, founded in 1723. In one American lodge this arrangement held good in 1924, and it is thought that it is still followed in some Continental lodges. The lodge of the Three Golden Swords, at Dresden, in 1744, is believed to have been triangular in form, and there is a suggestion that operative masons' lodges in the Middle Ages sometimes approximated to the mason's square in shape, with the Master sitting at the outer angle, or apex, of the two arms. In triangular lodges it is likely that there was often a large pillar in front of each Warden, while at the altar in the centre of the lodge most of the ceremonial work in connexion with the Candidate was performed by the Master, who left his chair for the purpose, a practice of which we get an echo in all present-day Royal Arch Chapters.

We find in some of the Scottish Craft lodges an arrangement clearly based on the triangle. The floor plan here given of the Canongate Kilwinning Lodge is redrawn from an illustration issued under the auspices of that lodge in 1903.

The room is rectangular, with the Master in the east, and both Wardens in the west, their triangular pedestals being at the points of a triangle. The Secretary is on the Master's left and the Treasurer on his right, as in many American lodges to-day. Two Standard Bearers have clearly defined positions, while near the central altar is a Bible Bearer, whose duty is to have ready the Bible for the Candidate. The Master of Ceremonies is on the Master's left, the Senior Deacon on his right. The Junior Deacon is near the Senior Warden, and the Inner Guard near the Junior Warden. Brethren enter the lodge through the porch in the west, but are not actually within the real lodge until they have passed between two large pillars which flank the entrance inside. The Brethren occupy seats along the sides of the lodge. This arrangement, believed by the Canongate

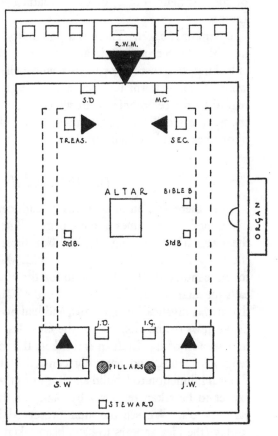

PLAN OF THE
CANONGATE KILWINNING LODGE—
A 'ST JOHN'S LODGE'

The Master's and Wardens' triangular pedestals
are at the points of a triangle.

Kilwinning Lodge to be historical, is probably followed in a few other Scottish lodges claiming to conform to the "St John's masonic lodge or chapel," a claim meaning no more, it is thought, than that the lodge is patterned on the English eighteenth-century Craft lodges, possibly those of the 'Antient' order, or even unattached at that time to any Grand Lodge.

Cruciform Lodges. There is a possibility that some of the early lodges may have been cruciform in arrangement. Reliable evidence on the point is lacking, but there are students who believe that in some cases lodges were of this pattern, impracticable though it would appear to be with regard to the ceremonies with which we are familiar. It may be that, if there were cruciform lodges, they consisted of inner lodges denoted by floor lines, within which certain parts of the ceremony were worked.

The Altar and the Ark

That there was an altar in many eighteenth-century lodges has been mentioned several times in these pages. The word 'altar' is derived from the Latin *altus* meaning 'high.' For three hundred years after Christ the Holy Board, or Table, we are told, was called the altar, but in the fourth century the familiar name for the altar was 'table.' St Augustine calls the altar *Mensa Domini,* the Lord's Table, or Holy Table, to signify that it was mystical and spiritual, and had no relation either to the sacrifice of the Jews or the idolatries of the Gentiles. It must be remembered that to a section of the Craft in early days the masonic ceremonies were of a religious nature, and naturally centred spiritually upon an altar. The Biblical injunction to "build an altar unto the Lord thy God"[1] we should expect to be taken seriously by many of the speculative masons of the early 1700's. We see the altar preserved in the Royal Arch Chapter to-day (the idea appears to have been taken from the early Craft lodges) and in the Canongate Kilwinning arrangement described earlier in this chapter. In the lodges of many masonic jurisdictions is a central altar, notably in those of the American States, and its presence undoubtedly influences the form of the ritual.

Pedestals were not always a part of the furniture of the old English lodges, and it is doubtful whether they became wholly general until English masonic ritual began to conform to a given model after the union in 1813.

The Master's pedestal, as we see it in almost any English lodge to-day, is, in a sense, a combination of altar and desk; but in some Yorkshire lodges there is a separate altar immediately in front of the Master's

[1] Deuteronomy xxvii, 5.

pedestal. In the present Alnwick Lodge, No. 1167, dating back to only 1867, there is an extra pedestal· to which the Master steps down when giving the Obligation; and in the well-known masonic temple in St Helier, Jersey, there is an altar-like pedestal many feet in front of the Master's chair, the Master advancing to it as need arises.

The Ark. Elsewhere is pointed out the possible connexion between a silk or linen box, or model, with the Ark of the Covenant. A Military lodge, before 1820, possessed an ark in the form of a wooden box which travelled with the regiment, and contained the warrant, jewels, etc., of the lodge. 'Ark' was a common old-time word for cupboard.

At one time a lodge itself was regarded as an ark, as the Ark of Noah, but to-day such an interpretation is reserved, it is believed, for certain of the additional degrees.

The Pillars

The traditional history, as reflected in the Craft ritual, attaches remarkable importance to the pillars, but only in the few lodges still preserving the old style is this importance made evident in the appointments of the lodge. In the early eighteenth-century lodge the pillars were undoubtedly the first things to strike the eye of a Brother on entering, and in the Canongate Kilwinning arrangement pillars flank the porchway, and a Brother can enter the lodge only by passing between them. Is there a survival of those pillars in the present English lodge?

We may reasonably conclude that the Wardens' miniature columns are survivals of pillars, but of *which*? Some students declare that the association of the Wardens' columns with the old pillars is 'absurd,' but it is easy to get confused in such a matter. Let us remember that in *some* of the old lodges there were two pillars and two only, undoubtedly representing those at the porchway of King Solomon's Temple. It does look as though the Warden's columns, while far from being exact miniatures of those old lodge pillars, were at one time or other intended to take their places. But the trouble is that in other of the old lodges there were *three* pillars; that in a great many lodges there were three floor candlesticks; and that sometimes the pillars themselves were the candlesticks. So we have to look in the present-day lodge for evidences of the survival of *five* pillars.

Probably, or at least possibly, we find them in the two Wardens' columns representing the porchway pillars of the Temple, and in the three tall candlesticks beside the Master's and Wardens' pedestals, and representing all that we now have of the three old pillars of Wisdom, Strength, and Beauty. These three candlesticks sometimes prove on examination to be the Ionic, Doric, and Corinthian pillars, the actual candle-holders being supported by them at the height of the adjacent pedestals; but it has been objected that, in lodges whose appointments are particularly modern, what should be classical pillars tend to be plain shafts, their designers having possibly been unaware that the pillars should answer a symbolic as well as a severely practical purpose.

In the Old MS. Charges there are two pillars mentioned—one of them would not sink nor the other burn—but these have no place in the usual Craft ritual. As all Brethren know, it is the two pillars set up at the porchway of the Temple by King Solomon on which so much of masonic ritual centres, and it is with these pillars that the Pillar of Cloud and the Pillar of Fire are sometimes associated. "And the Lord went before them [the children of Israel] by day in a pillar of a cloud, to lead them the way; and by night in a pillar of fire, to give them light."[1]

Early rituals direct attention to *three* grand pillars. These supported the masons' lodge; they are emblematical of wisdom, strength, and beauty; they were then associated with the pillars of the Doric, Ionic, and Corinthian orders respectively. They also represented Solomon, King of Israel, who built, completed, and dedicated the Temple at Jerusalem to God's service; Hiram, King of Tyre, who supported Solomon with men and materials; and Hiram Abif, whose curious and masterly workmanship beautified and adorned the Temple. Here is a part of a dialogue between Simon and Philip, taken from a manuscript of approximately the year 1730:

Q. How high was your Lodge?
A. As high as the Heavens, and as low as the Earth.
Q. How many Pillars had your Lodge?
A. Three.
Q. What did you call them?
A. Beauty, Strength, and Wisdom.
Q. What do they represent?
A. Beauty to Adorn, Strength to Support, and Wisdom to Contrive.

We now explain the pillars rather differently; the Master's, the Ionic, now represents wisdom; the Senior Warden's, the Doric, represents strength; and the Junior Warden's, the Corinthian, represents beauty. These architectural orders are illustrated on pp. 21, 23, and 25.

In many lodges of the 1700's the appropriate pillar stood before the Master and each of the Wardens, but in some lodges there was a pillar on each side of the Master's chair or behind his chair. It is obvious that each lodge had its own ideas on the subject, as have those lodges to-day which perpetuate the old style by still having pillars standing on the floor.

[1] Exodus xiii, 21.

We find the large pillars in some old lodges at Exeter, Newton Abbot, Gloucester, Cardiff, Penarth, etc., in the Danish lodges, and even in a lodge at Ottawa, Canada. In the last of these there is a central altar, between which and the Senior Warden's chair in the south are two tall wooden pillars right out on the floor.

The pillar developed in some lodges into a support for an hour-glass, a device known to the ancient peoples of the world, and symbolizing the transitory nature of human life. We are told that it was at one time a custom to bury an hour-glass with the dead. The emblem is to be found on some old Tracing Boards.

At the top of many old pillars is to be found a terrestrial globe, which appears to have been put there originally as the result of mistaking two bowls, one superimposed upon the other, for a globe. Laurence Dermott, leader of the 'Antients,' affected to believe the custom to be due to the sheer ignorance of the 'Moderns,' but the original mistake appears to have been made a century and a half before their day, for they had been led astray by the misleading woodcuts in the Geneva Bible of 1560; so now, when we glance at a Warden's column surmounted by a globe we see the surviving evidence of the 'Moderns,' and note that after nearly two centuries the globe is still where it ought not to be!

It is curious that William Preston, the old masonic writer, speaks of the *Deacon's* columns, not the Warden's. A writer of our day has sought to build upon this a suggestion that these columns were actually associated with the Deacons, and that not until some time in the last century were they transferred to the Wardens; but the idea is not supported, and there is convincing evidence that back in the eighteenth century the columns belonged to the Wardens.

The Porchway Pillars of King Solomon's Temple

Masons are familiar with descriptions of the porchway pillars of King Solomon's Temple, based upon the Biblical accounts and supported by the words of the trusty historian Josephus, who, we are reminded by J. T. Thorp, was well acquainted with Herod's temple, which was a copy of Solomon's. Josephus wrote in Greek, and the following description of the pillars is from a translation made by Professor William Whiston, Josephus tells us that Hiram

made two pillars, whose outsides were of brass. . . . There was cast with each of their chapiters lily-work, that stood upon the pillars, and it was elevated five cubits, round about which there was net-work interwoven with small palms, made of brass, and covered the lily-work. To this also were hung two hundred pomegranates, in two rows. The one of these pillars he set at the entrance of the porch, on the right hand, and called it Jachin; and the other on the left hand, and called it Boaz. . . . He also made ten large round brass vessels, which were the lavers, . . . and he set five of the lavers on the left side of the Temple, which was on that side towards the north wind, and as many on the right side, towards the south.

Professor Whiston helps us to understand which was the left and which the right pillar. Approaching the Temple from the east gates of the Courts (remembering that the Holy Place of the Temple was in the west) one would of course arrive at the east entrance to the Temple. Here were the two pillars. On the right, as the worshipper entered, was one called Boaz, and on the left the one called Jachin, the former being to the north-east of the entrance and the latter to the south-east. It thus follows that when we think of these pillars as being 'left' or 'right' we are mentally seeing them from the standpoint of the worshipper departing from the east entrance and not arriving at it.

The Jewish kings that succeeded Solomon were crowned at the foot of one of these pillars. Each pillar may possibly have borne its name inscribed on it, so that the approaching worshipper would read the name in the form of a sentence, "He in Whom strength is, may he establish [this house]." We know that two pillars that once stood at the Cathedral of Wurzburg, Germany, bore the same names.

Other commentators, among them the Rev. C. J. Ball, emphasize that the pillars were, in fact, symbols of the Deity, and corresponded to the stone pillar which Jacob set up at Bethel and poured oil upon as an offering, their names being designations of Jehovah. Others, still, have suggested that what masons regard as the left-hand pillar expresses the physical power of generation—in other words, it was a symbol of creation; whereas the right-hand one expressed the spiritual power of regeneration—in other words, salvation.

Hebrew scholars have long argued as to the precise meaning of the names given to these pillars. They agree that the name of the left-hand pillar means 'in it [Him] is strength.' According to the Rev. Morris Rosenbaum, its first syllable implies that the house of God is the embodiment of religious strength and the source of the nation's temporal power; and the second syllable that 'in God is all strength,' somewhat analogous to the Divine name denoted by the Hebrew word *shaddai*, Almighty. The pillar was named after Boaz, the great-grandfather of David, whom freemasons know as a prince and ruler in Israel; he had died a century before the days of Solomon, and was not so much a prince or ruler as a farmer of Bethel.

The above authority explains that 'Jachin,' the name given to the right-hand pillar, means 'he will establish' or 'he will make firm.' The name itself, said to be that of the Assistant High Priest, is given in the Bible, but no mention is made of a High Priest or any assistant as helping in the dedication of the Temple.

The alleged reason for casting these great pillars in hollow form— that they should serve as archives to masonry—does not carry conviction. Such massive castings could hardly have been more inconvenient for the purpose, and the whole suggestion is not of ancient origin.

Candles

The candles in the lodge are much more than a means of illumination. They are important symbols, with a long and attractive history. The candle came into the speculative lodge not only from the hall of the guild; it came from the votive offering burning before a shrine centuries ago. Its physical light is the emblem of the spiritual. The burning candle at the medieval altar and shrine carried with it the idea of consecration, of the making and keeping of vows, of gratitude for mercies which had been vouchsafed.

We have already pointed out that each of the craft guilds maintained an altar in a near-by church and kept it supplied with candles, which were paid for by fines and fees obtained from its members.

Early fourteenth-century records reveal that what was probably a religious fraternity among the masons at Lincoln "set up the candle of the Guild." By one of its rules: "Whoever is elected Graceman [*principal officer*] and refuses to take the office shall pay two pounds of wax, and whoever being elected Warden or Deacon refuses the office shall give one pound." From the custom of maintaining the candle, a guild fraternity became to be spoken of familiarly as *le cierge,* 'the candle.' Occasionally, a Master Mason taking an apprentice had to "pay 40*d.* to the maintaining of the candle."

It is easy to see that the lodge custom of burning three candles— particularly three—is originally of religious significance and has come from church and guild, whatever the modern masonic interpretation may or may not be.

The burning of candles in holy places seems to have been a heathen idea originally, and there was great opposition to it in the Early Christian Church. But Jerome (A.D. 340–420) tells us that, throughout the churches of the East when the Gospel was read, candles were lighted, even though the sun were shining, not for the purpose of driving away darkness, but as an outward sign of gladness and as symbols of that light of which we read in the Psalter, "Thy word is a lamp unto my feet, and a light unto my path." (Psalm cxix, 105.)

Men's superstitious minds in medieval days believed there was much virtue in the lighted candle. Here, for example, are some lines from sixteenth-century verse by Barnabe Googe:

> . . . a wondrous force and might
> Doth in these Candles lie, which if at any time they light
> They sure beleve that neyther storme or tempest dare abide,
> Nor thunder in the skies be heard, nor any Devils spite,
> Nor fearefull sprites that walke by night, nor hurts of frost or haile.

There were special (and beautiful although highly superstitious) prayers in the pre-Reformation Church for the hallowing of candles upon Candelmas day:

> . . . bless thou this creature of a waxen taper . . . that in what places it be lighted or set, the Divel may avoid out of those habitacions, and tremble for fear, and fly away discouraged. . . . Vouchsafe to blesse and sanctifye, and with the Candle of heavenly benediction, to lighten these tapers.

The Feast of the Purification was observed with so many lights that it came to be called Candlemas. The false or dummy candle often seen in lodges had an early counterpart, for sometimes in medieval churches a little candle was made to appear a big one by mounting it on a post painted to resemble a candle. Because of its falsity, this came to be known as a 'Judas,' the 'Judas to the Pascall' being the dummy carrying the paschal or Easter candle on or near the altar.

The candles that lit up the eighteenth-century lodges were thick and heavy, ornamented sometimes with "symbolic reliefs in white wax pressed on to the candle." If the lodges did not provide their own candles, then the innkeeper did so, and he charged so many pence per candle per hour for those kept burning during lodge time.

A freemason would hardly expect to find any association of the candle with secrecy, but the old and curious metaphor "Tace is Latin for candle," met in old-fashioned literature, means literally 'It is discreet to be silent.' The arms of the United Grand Lodge of England bear the motto, *Audi Vide Tace*—'hear, see, be silent.'

The Greater and the Lesser Lights

In the eighteenth century the 'Moderns' at first regarded their three big candles carried in high candlesticks as the three great lights, the purpose of which was "not only to shew the due course of the sun which rises in the east, has its meridian in the south and declension in the west, but also to light men to, at and from their labour" and also to represent "The Sun, Moon and the Master of the Lodge."

The 'Antients' took a less obvious view of the matter; to them the three great lights were the Volume of the Sacred Law, the Square and Compasses, while the three lesser lights were the candles of the Master and his Wardens. To the 'Moderns' the Volume of the Sacred Law, the Square and Compasses were known as the 'furniture' of the lodge; they are still often known in that way. Probably by the end of the century many of the 'Modern' lodges had come to look at the matter differently, and we find the Lodge of Reconciliation, after the union, adopting the 'Antient' practice as to the great lights, and agreeing that the three lesser lights are situated in the east, south, and west, and are meant to represent the sun, moon, and Master of the lodge.

In the old lodges the candles were arranged to form a triangle on the floor of the lodge, a position which they still occupy in a few of the older lodges, but mostly nowadays (an arrangement dating back to the early nineteenth century) the candles are at the side of the Master and the two Wardens, where the three tall candlesticks seem to do duty for the three tall pillars present in the old lodges. There does not appear to be any reason why the candlestick should be on the left or right of a pedestal, and, although the right side is the more general, the left is the more convenient so far as the work with the Candidate is concerned.

In some old French lodges there was a custom of using nine candles in the Third Degree only, in three clusters of three each, retaining the triangular arrangement. Apart from this, it is not thought that there was ever a custom of arranging the candles in different ways to indicate the degree in which the lodge was working.

In existing old lodges there must be great diversity with regard to the positions of the candles and with regard to the customs associated with them. For example, in the Lodge of Love and Honour, No. 75, Falmouth, founded in 1751, the candle in the east is lit before the Master enters the lodge. The lodge having been opened, the Wardens approach the Master's light with their candles, light them, return and place them in position, and resume their chairs. The candles stand out on the floor, the Candidate passing between them and the pedestals.

The Master of the Lodge

The early speculative lodges enjoyed great independence, much of which they have bequeathed to the lodges of to-day. In addition to electing its own Master, each lodge regulates its own proceedings, and has an undoubted right so to do providing it acts consistently with the general laws and regulations of the Craft. It frames its own bylaws (they need the approval of the Grand Master), appoints standing committees and audit committees to assist the Master in ordering the business of the lodge,

but in a number of matters—all making for uniformity and for the preven-
tion of irregularities—observes certain regulations of Grand Lodge.
Such regulations include the limitation of the number of Candidates on
any one occasion, except by dispensation; the holding of only one meeting of a lodge on any one day; the holding of an emergency meeting only
when a dispensation has been granted; the necessity of each lodge
keeping a minute book; etc.

The custom in every lodge of electing by ballot a new Master each
year is of time-immemorial, although there is evidence to show that in
many of the early eighteenth-century lodges Masters were elected to serve
for six instead of twelve months. The Master is elected from those
of the members of the lodge who have served the office of Master or
Warden, or who, in very exceptional cases, have been rendered eligible
by dispensation. The Old MS. Charges appear to indicate that the
Master, many centuries ago, was simply an experienced craftsman
presiding over the lodge, and, so far as we can see, the idea of his ruling
his lodge by virtue of his possession of peculiar secrets was not within
the comprehension of our ancient brethren; but in this matter there is
room for many different opinions. The same appears to apply to the old
Scottish operative lodges. To-day, in the speculative lodges throughout
the world, a Master is one who has been elected to the office by his
Brethren, and who has passed through a special ceremony of Installation,
in the course of which secrets peculiar to the Master's chair have been
communicated to him; but essentially the Master must always be a
Brother who is well qualified by years of service as member and officer
of the lodge to govern his Brethren in wise understanding.

The rule that a Master should first have served as a Warden is also an
old one. It was not always observed in the early speculative lodges, but
it goes right back into the history of the craft guilds from which masonry
draws its system of government by Masters and Wardens. Every Master
in the old days, as in the new, solemnly pledged himself to observe the
ancient usages and established customs, and strictly to enforce them
within his lodge. It is he who is responsible for the due observance of
the masonic laws by the lodge over which he presides.

We pay respect to the ruler of a lodge by addressing him as 'Worshipful Master.' On an earlier page it was pointed out that to be 'worshipful'
is to be 'honoured.' Thus the 'Worshipful' Master is the 'Honoured'
Master, even as the magistrate is 'Your Worship,' or, in other words,
'Your Honour.' In a great many lodges in the eighteenth century the
Master was '*Right* Worshipful,' a form of address now the exclusive
privilege of certain Grand Officers (see p. 251). The custom of calling
the Master the 'Right Worshipful Master' ceased about the time of the

union in 1813, although we find it used in a Kendal Lodge up to 1819. Outside freemasonry the use of the term 'Right Worshipful' must be of ancient standing, for in Pepys's Diary for August 4, 1661, a clergyman addresses his congregation as "Right Worshipful and Dearly Beloved." The celebrated Paul Revere, presiding as Grand Master at a Washington lodge, Massachusetts, at the end of the eighteenth century, addressed himself to the "Right Worshipful Master, Worshipful Wardens and Respected Brethren." In La Césarée Lodge, Jersey, the Master was at one time addressed as 'Venerable Master,' following an old French custom, which is still observed.

Grand Masters have always had the right of visiting a lodge within their jurisdiction, and, if they so wished, of presiding on the occasion of their visit. This right is enjoyed by the Pro Grand Master as well as by the Deputy and Assistant Grand Master and by the Provincial or District Grand Master. With a Brother of such exalted rank in the chair, the Master of the lodge sits on his immediate left, whereas when, as is sometimes the case, the Master of a lodge gives up his chair to a Past Master to work a ceremony, he sits to that Past Master's immediate *right*, or, it may be, to the right of any Grand Officer having a prior right to preside.

Scots lodges have a Depute Master, but the English Master nowadays has no deputy known by that name, although some of the eighteenth-century lodges had regular Deputy Masters, the first mention of the office being thought to occur in the minutes of the Druidical Lodge of Rotherham, Yorkshire, in the year 1779, a lodge under the York Grand Lodge. Of course, in a sense, the Senior Warden and, failing him, the Junior Warden is the Deputy Master, but neither of these Brethren, if not an Installed Master, can confer a degree in an English lodge, although (remaining in his own chair) he may preside over the lodge should the need arise. In the Master's absence a degree can be conferred on a Candidate only by an Installed Master, whether a member of the lodge or not.

The Master is assisted in carrying on the work of the lodge by his officers, two of whom—the Treasurer and the Tyler—are elected, the former by ballot; all other officers being appointed by the Master. In an English lodge his *regular* officers are two Wardens, a Treasurer, a Secretary, two Deacons, an Inner Guard, and a Tyler; *additional* officers are a Chaplain, a Director of Ceremonies and his assistant, an Almoner, an Organist, an Assistant Secretary and Stewards, but no others. A Brother can hold only one regular office at one and the same time, but may in addition be appointed by the Master to one 'additional' office. On members declining office—including Masters-elect—many old lodges imposed fines graduated in amount to the importance of the office.

The precise position of the Immediate Past Master, who is not an 'officer of the lodge,' is often a matter of debate. Grand Lodge prescribes that, as regards precedence, the Immediate Past Master comes immediately in front of the Chaplain, or, if there be no Chaplain, then immediately in front of the Treasurer; whereas, by a decision of the Board of General Purposes, the name of the Immediate Past Master in a *printed list* comes immediately after that of the Master and before the officers.

The appointment of a lodge Chaplain in 1769 is known, but could hardly have been the first of its kind.

With regard to the Almoner, the alms-chest was a box provided in church to receive contributions; in a masonic lodge it is the charity box which provides the funds with which the lodge Almoner relieves any Brother, sometimes members of a Brother's family, who need help. Originally the Almoner was an officer in a monastery. At St Paul's Cathedral, in London, he distributed the alms, had the care of the burial of the poor, and educated boys in music and literature for the service of the Church. The Almonries in the principal monasteries were often great establishments, with accommodation for the poor and infirm.

Many of the old guilds regularly relieved distressed Brethren and their families, and there are records in the fourteenth century of an amount of sevenpence per week (say, two or three days' wages) being allowed a member of the Lincoln Guild of Tailors. In the same century a London trade, the Skinners, also paid that sum from their alms-box to any member who should fall into poverty through old age or ill health. There is no doubt that the lodge charity-box, probably suggested by the alms-box of the guilds, was known far back in the eighteenth century. In a Sheffield lodge in 1764, and probably much earlier, there was a rule that

> on each Stated Lodge meeting every Mem^r shall spend and put Sixpence into the Chest for the relief of distressed Freemasons. That the Junior Warden shall keep an exact acc^t of the reckoning . . . upon his negligence or omission he shall be accountable for the deficiency.

The early lodges of the eighteenth century had their own methods of raising charity funds, for we find the Old King's Arms Lodge, No. 28, ordering in October 1733, a ticket to be bought in "the present Lottery in hopes of success as heretofore for the sake of Charity." In the following July the ticket "was reported to have come up a Blank."

Lodge Minutes

The minutes of the lodge are the responsibility of the Worshipful Master and his Secretary, but it is the latter's duty to write them. They need to be submitted for confirmation at the next regular meeting, and it is now fully understood that minutes can be refused confirmation only on the ground that they are incorrect, in which case they should be emended and afterwards confirmed. It is not now possible for something decided at one lodge meeting to be cancelled at the next merely by refusing to confirm the minute. There are other ways of overcoming any difficulty that may sometimes unfortunately arise.

There was a custom once upon a time, particularly in the Irish military lodges, of smoke-sealing instead of signing minutes on confirmation, the seal being made by coating a space with soot in a candle flame and then forcibly applying an engraved seal. The Irish Grand Lodge has from ancient days insisted that every lodge should have a seal, with which to verify lodge minutes and authenticate lodge communications to Grand Lodge. The actual device of the seal is a 'hand and trowel,' together with the number, name, and town of the lodge. The United Grand Lodge of England decided in 1819 that every lodge should have its own seal "to be affixed to all documents proper to be issued," but the rule has long been obsolete.

That old lodge minutes are frequently brimming over with unconscious humour is well exemplified by many quotations made in these pages. Secretaries in concluding their minutes are fond of the phrase, 'the lodge was closed in perfect harmony'—just a formula, but expressing the literal truth in all but one case in a thousand. But what is to be made of the minutes of a meeting of the lodge belonging to a certain regiment of Light Dragoons? It was soon after the year 1800. The meeting expelled a member for making an obnoxious threat, decided that another Brother was an improper person for admittance, erased the name of another Brother for using an unmasonic expression, and the Secretary still found it possible to bring his minutes to an end with "this night concluded with great harmony." One old London lodge in 1787 "was not open'd upon the occasion of the Landlady being sick," while another, in 1794, gave a Brother his certificate but did not transact any other business "by reason of the Landlady being in child-bed."

Behaviour in and after Lodge

The Ancient Charges which preface the General Laws and Regulations of Grand Lodge enjoin a code of behaviour upon lodges and Brethren. These charges are founded upon ancient models, and have remained much the same since Anderson took them from the old manuscripts and printed them in his *Constitutions* of 1723. Some of the injunctions hardly now apply. These are polite days, but as much can hardly be said for the eighteenth century, when it was entirely necessary to remind both lodges and Brethren of the limits to which good behaviour could go. Thus, in an old Sheffield lodge of the 1760's there was the following rule:

> If any Bro^r in this Lodge Curse, Swear, lay or offer to lay any wagers or use any reproachfull Language in Derogation of God's Name or Corruption of good manners or interupt any Officer while speaking, he shall be fined at the discretion of the Lodge.

Such rules were common in lodge bylaws of that day. We find a perfect phrase in another bylaw of about the same date:

> If any Member of the Lodge come disguis'd in liquor he shall be admonish'd (by the presiding officer) for the first Offence. For the second he shall forfeit One Shilling and for the third (or refusing to pay his fine) He shall be Excluded without any benefit from the Lodge; and reported to the Grand.

Of an earlier date, about 1746, is a bylaw of the well-known Lodge No. 41, of Bath, in which an ugly word instead of 'disguised' is used:

> If a Brother is found Distemper'd with Drink, He shall be Admonish'd to go peaceably Home; which, if he refuses, he shall be turn'd out and taken Care of with as little Disturbance as possible, and ffined Two Shillings, except the Lodge vote him excus'd from this ffine.

Erasure of Lodge

A lodge under the English jurisdiction ceases to meet should its membership drop to less than five, and the rule to this effect is more than two centuries old. A lodge failing to meet for one year is liable to be erased. Its warrant cannot be transferred (see p. 370).

Lodges of Instruction and Improvement

What are known as 'lodges of instruction' are held under the sanction of regular warranted lodges, or by the licence of the Grand Master. The lodge that gives its sanction, or the Brother to whom the licence is granted, is responsible for seeing that the proceedings are in accordance with the Ancient Charges, Landmarks, and Regulations of the Order. Each lodge of instruction makes an annual return to the Grand Secretary. Very frequently such lodges are nothing more than rehearsal lodges, serving an excellent and, indeed, essential purpose, but missing the opportunity of providing instruction for their members in such matters as those set forth in the pages of this book. Indeed, it is hoped that lodges of instruction will find this book of help to them in assisting their members to make that daily advancement in masonic knowledge so seriously enjoined by the Master on every Initiate.

Chapter Twenty-three

WARRANTS, CERTIFICATES, AND
THE MASONIC CALENDAR

THE method of bringing a new lodge into being was evidently one of the problems confronting Brethren soon after the formation of the first Grand Lodge. How the earliest of the time-immemorial lodges came into existence we do not know, but we may assume that in pre-Grand-Lodge days a new lodge formed itself much as a new colony of bees forms itself by swarming from an over-populated hive, or from a hive in which there has arisen a likelihood of rivalry to the ruling power. However that may be, we may fairly conclude that early speculative lodges founded themselves easily enough, either as offshoots from existing lodges, or by virtue of a number of Brethren meeting together for masonic business, and forthwith regarding themselves as a lodge. There is a likelihood that their proceedings were made regular by their becoming possessed of a copy of the Old MS. Charges.

It would not occur to any such naturally formed lodge that it needed the authority or warrant of any other body to regularize its existence. But the formation of the Premier Grand Lodge in 1717 brought that blissful condition more or less to an end. Brethren owning allegiance to a Grand Lodge had now to agree that new lodges could come into existence only in some regular, formal, and official manner, and it is more than likely that their recognition of this point was a cause of difference between them and the unattached lodges, who not only saw no reason to acknowledge regulations made by outside bodies, but resented any suggestion that their own lodges were not regular merely because they lacked the imprimatur, or official stamp, of the new Grand Lodge.

The Lodge Charter, or. Warrant

Of the first one hundred lodges in the official list printed in the *Masonic Year Book,* we find a number that do not owe their existence or their authority to the warrant of any Grand Lodge. The Grand Steward's Lodge, first in the list but without a number, was formed without warrant. Two time-immemorial lodges, Antiquity and Royal Somerset House and Inverness, of course have no warrant. No. 58, Felicity,

London, derives its authority from a certificate; No. 59, the Royal Naval Lodge, has no official or authentic document of origin, and it does not follow that all the others in the first hundred had warrants.

The first documents giving authority to hold lodges were simple 'deputations,' authorizing a Brother (in the absence of the Grand Master or some other qualified Grand Officer) to constitute certain Brethren, who had been meeting together, as a regular lodge, having the right to a place in the engraved list of the regular lodges, which in those days was the chief evidence that the lodge existed "according to the forms of the Order and the Laws of the Grand Lodge." We may regard the written deputation as the masonic power-of-attorney, normally issued to local, chiefly country, Brethren who wished to form or regularize a lodge. Of the first hundred lodges, six derived their authority from such deputations: No. 37, Bolton; No. 39, Exeter; No. 41, Bath; No. 42, Bury; No. 86, Prescott; and No. 88, Cambridge. The rest of the first hundred (except the time-immemorial lodges already named) have warrants, but these do not all go back to the year of their constitution, but were in some cases issued by Grand Lodge long after. Warrants of confirmation have been issued in cases where there has been some doubt as to the issue or nature of the original document of authority.

When we are talking of the early lodges the words 'constitute' and 'warrant' do not necessarily mean the same as one another, but any difference was lost as the century progressed and we get the term 'warrant of constitution.'

It has been mentioned that Lodge Felicity, No. 58, has a certificate instead of a warrant. Previous to constitution the Brethren met together as a lodge, elected a Master, and made masons (as we have reason to suppose many other lodges did at that time); but the Brethren, wishing to regularize their Lodge, sent the Grand Master (the Earl of Darnley) a petition saying that they begged

> leave to meet at the house of our Brother Joseph Parsons at the Gun Tavern in Jermain Street, and that your Lordship and your Grand Officers will be pleas'd to constitute us into a regular Lodge that we may secure the benefit & Priviledge of all our Regular Lodges.

The Grand Master granted the prayer and named August 24, 1737, at eight in the evening, for the constitution, when doubtless the appropriate ceremony was performed by the Grand Master and other Grand Officers, who then endorsed the petition with the statement that they had constituted "the before written Petitioners into a regular Lodge in full Form." Much the same happened in the case of Lodge of Peace and Harmony, now No. 60, constituted in the following year. These two lodges were both of London and therefore easily reached, but Grand

Officers would find difficulty in those days in proceeding into the country and constituting a lodge in person, and consequently there arose the practice of issuing to local Brethren a deputation or, in other words, an authority to constitute, as already explained. It was the usual method of constituting lodges beyond the sea.

Ancient Method of Constituting a Lodge

The method of constituting a new lodge is set forth in detail in a post-script of the General Regulations printed in the *Constitutions*, 1723, and then stated to be according to the Ancient Usages of Masons. The postscript states

Here follows the Manner of constituting a New Lodge, as practis'd by his Grace the Duke of Wharton, the present Right Worshipful Grand-Master, according to the ancient Usages of Masons. A New Lodge, for avoiding many Irregularities, should be solemnly constituted by the Grand-Master, with his Deputy and Wardens; or in the Grand-Master's Absence, the Deputy shall act for his Worship, and shall chuse some Master of a Lodge to assist him; or in case the Deputy is absent, the Grand-Master shall call forth some Master of a Lodge to act as Deputy pro tempore. The Candidates, or the New Master and Wardens, being yet among the Fellow-Craft, the Grand-Master shall ask his Deputy if he has examin'd them, and finds the Candidate Master well skill'd in the noble Science and the royal Art, and duly instructed in our Mysteries, etc. And the Deputy answering in the affirmative, he shall (by the Grand-Master's Order) take the Candidate from among his Fellows, and present him to the Grand-Master; saying, Right Worshipful Grand Master, the Brethren here desire to be form'd into a new Lodge; and I present this my worthy Brother to be their Master, whom I know to be of good Morals and great Skill, true and trusty, and a Lover of the whole Fraternity, wheresoever dispers'd over the Face of the Earth. Then the Grand Master, placing the Candidate on his left Hand, having ask'd and obtain'd the unanimous Consent of all the Brethren, shall say: I constitute and form these good Brethren into a new Lodge, and appoint you the Master of it, not doubting of your Capacity and Care to preserve the Cement of the Lodge, etc. with some other Expressions that are proper and usual on that Occasion, but not proper to be written.

Upon this the Deputy shall rehearse the Charges of a Master, and the Grand Master shall ask the Candidate, saying, Do you submit to these Charges, as Masters have done in all Ages? And the Candidate signifying his cordial Submission thereunto, the Grand Master shall, by certain significant Ceremonies and ancient Usages, install him, and present him with the Constitutions, the Lodge-Book, and the Instruments of his Office, not all together, but one after another; and after each of them, the Grand Master, or his Deputy, shall rehearse the short and pithy Charge that is suitable to the thing presented. After this, the Members of this new Lodge, bowing all together to the Grand-Master, shall return his Worship Thanks, and immediately do their Homage to their new Master, and signify their Promise of Subjection and Obedience to him by the usual Congratulation. The Deputy and the Grand-Wardens, and any other Brethren present, that are not Members of this new Lodge, shall next congratulate the new Master; and he shall return his becoming Acknowledgements to the Grand Master first, and to the rest in their Order. Then the Grand-Master desires the new-Master to enter immediately upon the Exercise of his Office, in chusing his Wardens; And the new Master calling forth two Fellow-Craft, presents them to the Grand-Master for his Approbation, and to the new Lodge for their Consent. And that being granted, The Senior or Junior Grand-Warden, or some Brother for him, shall rehearse the Charges of Wardens; and the Candidates being solemnly ask'd by the new Master, shall signify their Submission thereunto.   Upon which the new Master, presenting them with the Instruments of their office, shall, in due Form, install them in their proper Places; and the Brethren of that new Lodge shall signify their Obedience to the new Wardens by the usual Congratulation. And this Lodge being thus compleatly constituted, shall be register'd in the Grand-Master's Book, and by his Order notify'd to the other Lodges.

By the time the 'Antient' Grand Lodge was founded, the system of constituting lodges by warrant was well established. Irish warrants are known as early as 1731; in the year following, the Irish Grand Lodge began to issue warrants allowing military lodges to be held wherever the regiment to which they were attached was stationed.

Petitions at the Present Day

Nowadays every application for a warrant to hold a new lodge in England must be by petition to the Grand Master, signed by not less than seven Master Masons. The form of petition is given in the *Constitutions* of Grand Lodge. Every new lodge shall be solemnly constituted according to ancient usage by the Grand Master or a deputy appointed for him. The fee for a warrant is fifteen guineas in London, ten guineas in the Provinces, and five guineas elsewhere. Ordinarily, a lodge may not meet without a warrant of constitution, which is to be specially entrusted to each Master at his installation, be held by him in safe custody on behalf of the Grand Master, and to be produced by him at every meeting of the lodge. This warrant is the property of the Grand Master, and to transfer it or improperly dispose of it is a masonic offence.

There are many cases known of lodge warrants having been sold or assigned in the eighteenth century, at least seven or eight by the year 1750. After the Act of Parliament of 1799, aimed at secret societies (societies that, unlike freemasonry, seek to conceal their existence and their objects), it was for some time the practice to assign the warrant of an erased lodge to Brethren wishing to form a new one; thus the warrant of the Royal Mecklenburgh Lodge, No. 170 (London and Croydon), granted in 1763, a lodge erased in February 1809, was assigned two months later to the Moira Lodge, now the Moira Lodge of Honour, No. 326, of Bristol.

The petition to erect a new lodge must be signed by at least seven Master Masons, be recommended by two lodges in the Province or District in which it is proposed to form the lodge, and the regulations governing the matter need to be very closely observed. There was an amazing affair in the 1770's, which must have suggested to the Grand Lodges of that day many necessary safeguards. T. W. Hanson's *History of the Lodge of Probity* explains that there had been warranted in Halifax, in 1769, the Bacchus Lodge, on the recommendation of two London lodges. There was already in Halifax the Lodge of Probity, now No. 61, whose members did not take kindly to the new lodge, describing it in a letter to Grand Lodge as "a number of loose fellows." This remark led to much correspondence and inquiry, which eventually revealed that Bacchus Lodge had been formed by frequenters of the Bacchus Inn, some of whom were masons who actually used the secrecy of the lodge as cover for a society of coiners and counterfeiters. Its members were ultimately brought to justice, and the lodge itself was erased in 1783.

At one time there was a custom by which the incoming Master signed the back of the warrant, but this is not in conformity with the *Constitutions*, which say that the warrant must not bear any endorsement or other inscription except with the authority of the Grand Master. While a warrant remains lost, or if it be withheld by competent masonic authority, the lodge must suspend its meetings.

In Ireland the petition for a warrant to erect a new lodge must be signed by not less than three Master Masons and by the Brethren nominated as the first Master and Wardens, these latter being of at least five years' standing. It should be recommended by three regular lodges and, if in a Province, by the Provincial Grand Lodge or its Grand Master or Deputy. The fee is ten pounds in the metropolitan district and twenty pounds elsewhere.

The Scottish *Constitutions* provide for all lodge charters being duly recorded in the Chartulary of Grand Lodge. (Originally, a Chartulary, or Cartulary, was a register, or record, of a monastery or church.) Petitions to establish new lodges in Scotland must be signed by not fewer than seven Master Masons, and be recommended by the Masters and Wardens of at least two lodges in the provinces or district in which the new lodge is to be erected.

The term 'to erect a lodge,' meaning 'to found or constitute a lodge, will have been noted. In the sense of 'to set up' or 'to institute,' the term 'to erect' has been common for hundreds of years, and the famous Sir Walter Raleigh used it in that way. It occurs in a Charter of the Armourers of about 1453, and is still used in Scottish freemasonry.

A Brother's Certificate

The practice of issuing certificates to Brethren goes well back into the eighteenth century. The first certificates known to have been issued are Irish (1746), and we have evidence of an English one in 1748 and of an American one in 1756, but the oldest still in existence go back no further than 1761–62.

All the early certificates were written documents, as not until 1756 did the Premier Grand Lodge issue them in engraved and printed form, signed by the Grand Secretary, and then, apparently, as a move in the 'Moderns' versus 'Antients' game, as was also, apparently, the often unpopular custom in some 'Antients' lodges of obliging members to 'lodge' their certificates for the period of their membership.

It is a matter for surprise how relatively few of the old certificates have survived, but throughout the eighteenth century, and particularly in Ireland, Brethren did all they could, W. J. Chetwode Crawley tells us,

> to prevent any written information or authorisation concerned with the affairs of the Craft from passing out of fraternal keeping. The Irish freemason held it to be his plain duty to destroy any document—public or private, historical or evidential—sooner than let it pass into the hands of outsiders. Warrants, certificates, lodge registers and minute books shared the common fate. In particular, the certificate of a deceased Brother was sure to be destroyed, if his Brethren could effect its destruction. It is only an insignificant percentage that escaped. Sometimes Certificates that had been lodged as security for loans, or as evidence of identity, were preserved, for obvious reasons.

The 'Antients' issued, of course, their own form of certificate, as different as possible from that of the 'Moderns,' but in 1813 the United Grand Lodge adopted a form of certificate in some respects resembling those issued by the Grand Lodge of Ireland, but phrased in Latin as well as English; in it provision was made for the insertion of the Brother's signature in the margin where, in the English Grand Lodge certificates of to-day, we have the Latin words *Ne Varietur* to act as a warning against alteration.

To-day the English Grand Lodge issues a certificate to every regularly made Brother whose name has been returned to the Grand Lodge and with regard to whom a lodge has paid the necessary fees. Generally the certificate is issued to Master Masons only, but in special circumstances to Initiates and Fellow Crafts, who are entitled to exchange them on becoming Master Masons.

Lodges themselves are empowered to grant a certificate, free of charge, stating that a member is (if such be the case) not indebted to the lodge; they too can issue a certificate to a Brother who is no longer a member, but it must state whether he ceased to be a member by resignation or by exclusion, give the date and circumstances thereof, and whether and at what time his indebtedness was discharged. Lodges under the United Grand Lodge of England may not grant certificates of any other kind to Brethren.

There has grown up a custom of accompanying the presentation of a Brother's certificate in open lodge with a special address, but it must be clearly understood that this address, of an obvious and therefore somewhat superfluous character, is an innovation and not any part of masonic ritual. There is in some lodges the fallacious idea that the certificate can be presented only in a Master Masons' lodge, but there is no mystery about the certificate, which may be presented in a lodge open in the First or any degree, and, if not so presented, may with full Grand Lodge approval be transmitted to the owner by registered post.

The Masonic Calendar

On a Brother's certificate the date is given in two ways; one accords with the ordinary everyday calendar and the other with the masonic calendar.

The ordinary calendar year—the year of the vulgar era—is reckoned from the birth of Christ, and we speak of it as being 'A.D.,' the initials of *Anno Domini*, meaning 'In the Year of Our Lord.' Craft freemasonry officially uses that calendar and one other, the *Anno Lucis*, meaning 'In the Year of Light,' abbreviated 'A.L.,' and sometimes 'A∴L∴'

Anno Lucis is 'the Year of Masonry,' and is mentioned in the *Constitutions* of 1723 by Anderson, who arrived at it by adding to the calendar year the number 4000, representing the number of years once supposed to have elapsed since the beginning of the world. Craft masonry observes this custom to-day, and in the certificate issued by the United Grand Lodge we find the phrase, "In testimony whereof I have hereunto subscribed my Name and affixed the Seal of the Grand Lodge at London this . . . day of [let us say] A.L. 5951, A.D. 1951."

But it is confusing to find that the year 'A.L.' is sometimes found by adding 4004 to the calendar year, this being in accordance with the chronology of Archbishop Usher. It is not officially observed to-day in

Craft masonry (although one of the additional degrees, the Rite of Mis-·riam, adopts it), but it is not without the justification of eighteenth-century usage, inasmuch as a lodge constituted in 1742 used to print its summons from an old plate bearing the words "constituted A.D. 1742, A.L. 5746." Further, Grand Master Lord Blayney (who founded the Supreme Grand Royal Arch Chapter of England) was recommended "to be continued Grand Master of the G.E.C. or Fourth Degree for the year 5771"—that is, 1767 plus 4004. We may, however, assume that generally, but not universally, the conversion of *Anno Domini* to *Anno Lucis* is made by adding 4000.

The abbreviation 'A.H.' means *Anno Hebraico*, 'In the Hebrew Year,' the calendar used in the Ancient and Accepted Scottish Rite. This is found by adding 3760 to the ordinary calendar year, but after September in each year it is necessary to add one more—that is, 3761—owing to the Hebrew year beginning in September. 'A.M.' (*Anno Mundi*)—'In the year of the world'—agrees with 'A.H.' (*Anno Hebraico*).

A diploma issued by the Supreme Grand Royal Arch Chapter of Scotland was dated *Anno Domini, Anno Lucis,* and *Anno Inventionis.* The last-named means 'In the Year of the Discovery,' and alludes to the year in which Zerubbabel began to build the second temple, 530 B.C.; accordingly the year 'A.I.' is found by adding 530 to the ordinary calendar year.

The Knights Templar observe the form 'In the Year of the Order,' abbreviated 'A.O.,' the initial letters of *Anno Ordinis.* To find the year 'A.O.,' subtract 1118 from the calendar year; thus, 1950 less 1118 = 832.

Another of the additional degrees—Royal and Select Masters—speaks of 'In the Year of the Deposit,' represented by 'A.Dep.,' abbreviated from *Anno Depositionis.* To find the year 'A.Dep.' you need to add 1000 to the calendar year; thus, 1950 plus 1000 = 2950.

The year of the Strict Observance, reckoned from the destruction of the Templars in A.D. 1314, is found by subtracting 1314 from the calendar year.

The *Masonic Year Book,* already referred to, descends from the Engraved Lists of Lodges issued annually, with the authority of Grand Lodge, from (about) 1723 to 1778. A more ambitious but unofficial *Free-Mason's Calendar* was independently published for a while, beginning in 1775, to which Grand Lodge responded in 1777 with the *Masonic Calendar,* which appeared annually and became in 1814 a pocket-book and ultimately, in 1908, the *Masonic Year Book,* a pocket-size volume containing hundreds of pages giving lists of lodges, chapters, etc., etc., together with other information invaluable to all English masons. As from 1950 Grand Lodge posts a copy (prepaid) to the Secretary of every lodge under its jurisdiction.

Chapter Twenty-four

WARDENS AND DEACONS

Wardens

WE learn much of the purpose and duty of the Warden when we go back into the curious history of his designation. Some hundreds of years ago, as Canon J. W. Horsley reminds us, R. Verstegan noted in a work on history and antiquities two words which looked so different and yet actually were one and the same—'wardian' and 'guardian.' Writing in 1605, he speaks of the French, Italians, and others whose language had come from the Latin, turning the 'w' of such words as 'wardian' into a single 'u,'

> because their alphabet hath no acquaintance with the *w* at all, but then to mend the matter . . . they use before the *u* to put a *g*, and so of warden or wardian doe make *guardian,* and of ward, *guard.* . . . Hence it ariseth that we call him that waiteth at the Towre, "one of the ward" or a "warder," and he that in like livery wayteth at the Court, "one of the *Guard*" or "*Gard.*"

Thus the old writer explains that Wardian, Warden, and Guardian are all one, "a keeper or attender to the safety or conservation of that which he hath in charge."

Thus, in the Fabric Rolls of York Cathedral of 1422, John Long is named as the Master Mason, and William Waddeswyk as the Guardian or second Master Mason. In the building of the Great Hall of Hampton Court in 1531 John Molton the Master Mason was paid a shilling a day, William Reynolds the warden five shillings a week. The employment of a Warden under the Master or Master Mason was thus a common practice in the English medieval building trade, but the Warden has not always been the second-in-charge. In some lodges and associations the Warden was the principal officer.

The old guilds had and have their wardens, and it is from the guild custom that English freemasonry probably derived the office and the word. The old English guilds had their wardens of the craft and their wardens of the mystery, and it is likely that the Scots borrowed the word hundreds of years ago to apply to the chief officer of an operative lodge. The Schaw Statutes of 1599 direct that a Warden should be chosen annually to have the charge over every lodge. But this, apparently, was in some

375

slight conflict with the custom in certain of the lodges, in which the chief officer was the Deacon (a word spelt in a variety of ways). The Deacon was the actual president, and might have with him a Warden who would be more a Treasurer, or Box-master, than a ruler.

In some Scots lodges we must assume that the two offices merged into one. The operative lodge of Mary's Chapel, Edinburgh, was under the presidency at one time of a Deacon of the Masons and a Warden of the Lodge, and in other Scots lodges the Deacon was often senior to the Warden; in some, there was a Deacon but no Warden, and occasionally a Warden but no Deacon. This would relate to a period roughly the second half of the seventeenth century, in which same period there were other Scots lodges ruled by 'the Master Mason' whose deputy was a Warden. Scots operative lodges had but one Warden, and he was either the head of the lodge or the second officer. But the English guilds had Senior and Junior Wardens, or Upper and Lower Wardens, and it is from them directly, and not from Scots practice, that freemasonry appears to have derived its two Wardens.

It will be noted that one fact comes out very prominently—the close relation, and at times almost an identity between Warden and Deacon in Scots operative lodges. In English speculative masonry, the Warden came from the English guilds, as already pointed out, but the Deacon came into the English Craft from Scots practice, and he came as a close colleague of and assistant to the Warden.

There were Wardens in English speculative masonry in the seventeenth century, or so the evidence points. In the speculative lodges early in the following century each of the two Wardens had a tall, distinctive pillar standing on the lodge floor, and great was the argument throughout the century as to the position of the Wardens and their relative pillars. We hear nothing of this argument to-day, because the pillar has long ceased to be an obvious pillar as already explained.

The Warden's pedestal was not an essential part of the lodge furniture in the days when the tall pillars stood on the floor, there being much diversity in the arrangements observed by various lodges, and no general agreement as to the use of pedestals, until the coming of United Grand Lodge in 1813. Neither the Master nor Wardens had a pedestal in the very early lodges, but there was a central altar, as there still is in systems that learned their freemasonry from the English Craft early in the eighteenth century. The matter is dealt with at greater length in the chapter relating to the form of the lodge, of which again there must have been great diversity of practice right throughout the eighteenth century, and with it, quite unavoidably, some diversity in the positions of the Wardens and their pillars. (In the lodges of Denmark we find in the north-west and in the south-west a tall pillar, behind which sits the Warden almost out of sight of the Master.)

In the rectangular lodges the arrangement with which we are now familiar gradually became general—that is, with a Senior Warden in the west and a Junior Warden in the south, the pillars being replaced by the small columns on the Wardens' pedestals, although some old lodges continued and still continue to have tall pillars on the floor, in some cases one near the Master and one near each Warden.

Although the old pillars have been spoken of as having been replaced by the miniature columns, we must not overlook the fact that floor pillars remain in a great many lodges in which their presence is not even noticed or suspected. They are the floor candlesticks (one to the right of each of the three pedestals), which will often be found to be carved in representation of the three classic orders of architecture, and may be assumed to be a modification of the older and larger pillars which frequently carried candles.

The Master's gavel, or maul, and the Warden's gavels are as traditional as the pillars. In some of the Irish lodges the Masters had their hammers and the Wardens had truncheons, for a bylaw of a lodge at Tanderagee (1759–1813) declares "that there is to be a silence at the first chap [blow] of the Master's hamer, and Likeways at the first stroke of each Trenchen struck by the Senr and Junr Wardens."

The custom now followed in most English lodges of the Master when opening and closing a lodge addressing all his questions to the two Wardens is an incomplete survival from the early days, when the Master put a question personally to each officer, and obtained from each of them an acknowledgment of his place and duties. A few lodges nowadays maintain or have returned to the old custom.

There was a time in the eighteenth century when the Junior Warden himself proved the tiling of the lodge and admitted the Candidate, but only in lodges—those of the 'Moderns'—in which the office of Deacon was not yet known.

The custom by which a Warden serves a full year before he is qualified for the chair of the lodge is of old standing, although officially it may not go back earlier than 1811.

As late as 1862 it was possible in many lodges for a Warden to work the ceremonies in the absence of the Master, and we imagine in a few lodges even later. A case is on record in which a Brother was passed to the Degree of Fellow Craft by the Master Elect, who stood on the left of the Master's chair, and was not himself an Installed Master until the following day. To-day, that would be impossible. In English lodges, should the Master be absent, a Past Master may go into the chair and work the ceremonies; failing which, a Senior Warden or, in his absence, the Junior Warden, shall rule the lodge, but shall not occupy the Master's chair and shall not confer degrees. There is nothing, however, to prevent a visiting Installed Master being invited to occupy the Master's chair and work any ceremony.

The Junior Warden, on being invested, is informed in some workings that he is "the ostensible steward of the lodge"—that is, he is the officer who is the apparent, but not necessarily the real, steward of the lodge. The words quoted are now more or less an anachronism, inasmuch as in most lodges the stewards in the old sense, both real and ostensible, are the Treasurer and Secretary, and on occasion, perhaps, some other Brother especially qualified, but the Warden was the actual steward of the lodge at one time. In 1807, for example, one lodge in arranging to dine on St John's Day says "that the Wardens shall be appointed Stewards to transact all matters relating to the Feast."

Deacons

We have already seen how closely interrelated the duties of the Warden and the Deacon were in the Scots operative lodges and even in the English speculative lodges. The relationship is preserved to-day when we find the Deacon acting under the instructions of a Warden and as his personal messenger.

The English Church term 'deacon' was in use in the days of James I, but the masonic term comes to us, not through the English, but through the Scottish tradition. At one time the Church deacon was a lay officer (as he still is in some denominations), and his duties were more those of an almoner. The word is found in many Continental languages, having been derived from an ancient Greek word meaning 'servant,' and carrying with it a suggestion of 'running' and 'pursuing'; hence the idea of 'messenger.' In the Scots operative lodges, as shown, the deacon came to be in many cases the chief officer, his duties being quite different from those of a Deacon in a speculative lodge to-day. He was very much the senior, not the junior, officer. But when the Warden's colleague or assistant in the English Craft lodges came to need a designation of his own, the name deacon was borrowed from the Scottish practice; but not by our old friend Anderson, who was responsible for introducing so many Scots terms into freemasonry. It is likely that many of the early lodges of the 'Moderns' had their Deacons, who, however, since their Grand Lodge frowned upon the office, were not so called; but in the 'Antient' lodges Deacons were regular officers from the middle of the eighteenth century. It was not until the turn of the century that the

'Moderns' officially recognized the position of the Deacon, by which time he had been known for something approaching ninety or one hundred years, although the earliest known reference to him is in 1727, when he was an officer in the first lodge of Ireland, in Cork; although J. Heron Lepper thinks that the office belongs to an older freemasonry which, in his opinion, settled in Ireland long before 1717. However that may be, the Grand Lodge of Ireland knew nothing officially of the Deacon until 1811. Another early reference (the word is spelt 'Dacken') is in the minutes of a Lodge at Youghal, County Cork, in 1733.

It is believed that the first English reference relates to a lodge at Chester in 1743, where a Taster's Deacon was elected. The 'Antients' had Deacons in 1753. The Swalwell Lodge, Durham, had its Deacon in 1734, but the lodge was then operative, and one cannot help feeling that the office was a close reflection of Scottish practice.

The office of Deacon in the speculative lodge undoubtedly came into existence because there was definite need of it. The earliest Deacons were assistants and attendants on the Master and Wardens, and acted as deputies to the Wardens. They sat behind the Master and Senior Warden ready, a bylaw of 1767 reminds us, the Senior Deacon to bear the Master's messages and commands to the Senior Warden, and the Junior Deacon to carry those messages on to the Junior Warden. From this fact has arisen a question as to whether the Deacon in some lodges ever had a column of his own in his capacity as Warden's deputy.

The jewel of the Deacon clearly suggests that his duty was that of a messenger. In the eighteenth century the Deacon's jewel, or emblem, was often a figure of Mercury, with winged feet and helmet, his left foot on a globe, and his left hand holding a *caduceus*, which was the wand of the 'ancient' herald, especially that carried by Hermes, the messenger of the gods, the conductor of the dead to the lower world and the patron of travellers, orators, and (let us tell the whole truth) thieves! Since the founding of the United Grand Lodge the Deacon's jewel in England has been a dove with olive branch, an emblem believed to symbolize the messenger sent from the Ark by Noah. The Irish masons had this emblem long before it was adopted in England. The dove is said to symbolize purity, peace, and innocence, and is a Christian emblem of great importance; when represented as coming from the mouth of a saint at death it is the symbol of the soul. In Plates XII and XXVIII will be found illustrations of Deacons' badges, or jewels, in the form of the figure of Mercury with winged feet and helmet and carrying a wand, round which the serpents entwine themselves.

In the Scottish Constitution the jewel of the Grand Deacon is a maul within a circle, and that of the Junior Deacon a trowel within a circle.

Stewards

The old English guilds had their stewards, and freemasonry inherited the office from them. In the early 'Modern' lodges Stewards did some or most of the work which in the 'Antient' lodges was done by Deacons. Minutes of the Lodge of Industry, Gateshead, refer in 1734 to a Senior Deacon or Steward, or a Junior Deacon or Steward. The Steward is one of the 'additional' officers which it is in the power of a Master to appoint.

The Steward's office has suffered loss of precedence and importance, for in pre-Union days the Steward in 'Moderns' lodges commonly ranked next to the Secretary and even in a lodge in which there were Deacons he took precedence of them.

Not until the word 'steward' is closely studied do we realize its odd history, and that it includes in itself the word 'warden.' Its second syllable is 'ward' (guardian or warden). It has already been explained that the 'w' and the 'g' can be regarded in these words as identical. But the first syllable of 'steward' means 'sty,' so the 'steward' is originally the 'steward of pigs'—that is, a 'pig-ward,' or 'sty-ward'—which in due course developed into 'steward.'

The Deacon's Wand

The wand has had its place in all ceremonial rites throughout the ages and has been carried by kings and others in authority as the sign and token of office or importance, of power, strength, and government. History shows that the person's power or right to act is by virtue of his holding or carrying the wand, and from this the lodge officer—be he Director of Ceremonies, Deacon, or Steward entrusted with temporary office—learns that he, too, derives his authority from the actual carrying of a wand, which was placed in his hands by the Master of the lodge. His wand is an emblem of power, dignity, and significance deriving from ancient days.

There are numerous references to the wand in the Bible, where it is represented by the old English words 'stave' and 'rod.' We read in Exodus (xxv, 13), for example, of the Lord directing Moses to make staves of acacia (shittim-wood) and overlay them with gold, while the Revelation of St John tells us of "a man child, who was to rule all the nations with a rod of iron." (xii, 5.)

Certain high classes of Greeks and Persians had the right to bear the sceptre (one of the many forms of wand), which, in the case of the Greeks, descended from father to son, the authority which the sceptre gave passing with the sceptre. Those privileged to bear the sceptre swore by it, solemnly taking it in the right hand and raising it towards heaven. The wand was borne by Greek philosophers and by the ancient kings of Sparta. In their turn the early kings of Rome carried a wand in the form of an ivory sceptre surmounted by an eagle, and this in course of time descended to the Roman consuls.

The Romans knew the wand of authority as the *baculum* or *baculus*, literally a 'stick' or 'staff' or 'rod,' and, in particular, a 'shepherd's staff.' The lictor's staff was known as the *bacillum*—the 'little staff.' The Roman *baculum* came to be known as the *virga* or *virgula*, which was the emblem of high rank, or office, and was carried by judges, heralds, and others in authority; to-day we know it as the 'wand,' the 'rod,' the 'mace,' the 'staff,' or 'stave.' The French is *virge* or *verge*, whence is derived the name of the church officer, the verger, who carried, and often still does carry, a staff of office preceding a church dignitary. The old-time master of ceremonies (not masonic) was a verger because he carried the *verge*. In old days tenants who held their lands 'by the virge' were required, when they came to their lord to make or renew their tenancy, to approach him holding in their hands a rod as a token of their fidelity.

Sir Walter Scott in *Ivanhoe* (1819) slipped up in referring to the *baculus* as the 'abacus' (a mathematical and also an architectural term having no connexion with wand), an error which unfortunately was adopted in American freemasonry, in which, however, it has now been replaced by the word 'rod.'

We find a Roman architect, at a period soon after the Romans retired from England, carrying a golden wand as the mark of his calling.

The *caduceus* is the white wand carried by the old Roman heralds and ambassadors, and more particularly the staff carried by Hermes, whose other name is Mercury. Originally the *caduceus* is believed to have been an olive branch, and we can suppose from this that it was an emblem carried by an ambassador coming in peace or suing for peace, just as the spear or sword was an emblem of war.

The *fasces*, of which so much has been heard in modern times, consisted of a number of rods bound together to form a bundle, having an axe in the middle, and were carried by lictors (attendants) before the superior magistrates at Rome. The *fasces* were the centre of much ceremonious observation.

The wand in the form of a sceptre has always been the insignia of kings. Shakespeare talks of their "sceptred sway," and in a passage known to every schoolboy says that "his sceptre shows the force of temporal power." The dukes of old, the marshals, and others in high authority carried wands or rods on ceremonious occasions. Shakespeare causes the Duke of Gloucester to speak of his staff or wand as his "office-badge." The young prince presented in a scene of great formality to his father,

Henry VII, had a gold rod placed in his little hands. In an ancient manuscript, towards the end of the fourteenth century, a famous man of Kent, William de Say, Warden of Dover Castle, is figured in full armour and carrying in his right hand his insignia—a plain wand.

Church dignitaries carried the wand as an emblem of rank and authority; an emperor, at the moment of creating a monk as an abbot in the tenth century, placed in his hands a staff, the token of his authority; a bishop, sending to arrest a priest, gave his servant a wand which the priest would recognize as the servant's authority to arrest him. Not only abbots but abbesses carried the wand; there is, or was, proof of this in the old Convent Church of Romsey, Hampshire, where there is a gravestone covering the body of an abbess; a female hand, carved in stone and coming from under the slab, holds her wand of office, a simple stave about four feet long.

We can have no doubt that the wand carried by kings and princes and high ecclesiastics was credited by lowly people with supernatural power, to which fact can probably be related certain medieval legends telling of the wand, or staff, carried by Christ: the halt and the sick touched the wand and were made whole.

"The Middle Ages had all sorts of verge-bearing officials," says the philologist, Ernest Weekley, "some of whom still survive in royal and parliamentary ceremonies as Gold Sticks, Silver Sticks, Black Rods, White Rods, etc. The municipal officer called a Sergeant-at-Mace was formerly also known as a Sergeant of the Verge." The guilds naturally adopted the wand, and freemasonry apparently inherited it from them. For example, in the seventeenth-century celebrations of the Merchant Guild at Preston, the wardens of "all the Company's of Trades" attended in their gowns and carrying long white rods. At least one lodge, about 1786, called its Master of Ceremonies its 'Gold Stick.'

The custom of carrying a wand went down through many ranks of society in the Middle Ages. For example, we read that in a nobleman's house the porter, or janitor, carried the longest wand, the steward had a short one only eighteen inches long and as thick as a finger, while the usher carried one shorter still. In old drawings we see the doctor, or leech, holding his staff or wand while he advises his patient, and there can be little doubt that however he regarded his wand many of his patients believed much virtue to dwell in it. Messengers of the fifteenth century carried their letters in the cleft of a split wand, the presence of the wand proving their bona fides. Customs officers used to carry their written authority (and perhaps still do) contained in a short, hollow wand.

In magic and folklors the wand has always had a great place. Roman augers used the crooked wand—the *lituus*—in the course of their divining. The conjurer's and magician's wand is a descendant of the old magical wands used by the Greeks and Romans, and at one time was preferably of silver. The divining rod, still in use in many country places for detecting the presence of water and metal, has a long history and was at one time known by either of the Latin terms *virgula divina* or *baculus divinatorius*. The rod in folklore must have had many uses, and one surviving until recently was the carrying of osier wands by the bridesmen at Manx weddings.

In civic matters, as already suggested, the wand has a most important place. It is both the Lord Mayor's mace and the beadle's staff. City fathers carry it on ceremonious occasions; sheriffs bear it as a sign of their great authority; in Scottish Courts of Justice a special messenger carries a wand known as the wand of peace, while in the English law the officer of the High Court whose special duty it is to arrest persons committed by the Court carries, as the token of his authority, a staff tipped with a metal device, believed to be a bull's horn, from which fact he has from the days of Edward III been known as a tipstaff. It was originally tipped with horn, and is so referred to by Shakespeare.

We see a remarkable example of the symbolism of the wand in the staff of office carried by the Chief Gentleman Usher of the Lord Chamberlain's Department. He is also Usher to the House of Lords and to the Chapter of the Garter, and is styled in short, Gentleman Usher of the Black Rod, and, shorter still, Black Rod. He ostensibly derives his authority from his staff, which is an ebony rod surmounted by a golden lion. Among his many ceremonious duties in which the black rod plays a part is that of acting as messenger when the Lords Commissioners 'request' or the King 'commands' the attendance of the Commons in the House of Lords.

It will now be appreciated that the custom of bearing a wand is almost certainly an unbroken link with the ceremonious observances of thousands of years. It has already been suggested that the freemasons inherited it or borrowed it from the London Company of Masons, and it is possible also that it came into the lodges from Church practice.

The wand naturally lends itself to use in stately ceremony. Whether the custom of crossing the Deacons' wands at a certain point in the Initiation ceremony is ancient practice or not is not known, but it is believed to have been in use in the eighteenth century. It may have arisen from nothing more than a wish to compose an effective setting and to obviate the ragged appearance of two wands in close proximity held at awkward angles, but certainly it has now acquired a symbolism of its own—that of a gateway through which the Candidate passes to a new life—while many Brethren see in the crossed wands a suggestion of a triangle, the geometric form that has always been thought to be imbued with sacred qualities.

In some of the older lodges the bearing of a wand was not restricted to the officers responsible for the floor-work. In an early Irish lodge the Master held a black rod in his hand while the lodge was at labour, and in one old Deal lodge each of the three principal officers had a wand at his side and, in addition, a wand consisting of three separate rods bunched together. There is reason to believe that other lodge officers have at various times carried wands, the Tyler, for example.

Not only does the carrying of a wand have peculiar significance, but so does the breaking of it. When constituting St George's Lodge, Taunton (now extinct), in the year 1764, the Grand Master's proxy "pronounced the Lodge to be a regular constituted Lodge . . . and concluded the solemnity by declaring his commission at an end and breaking his white wand," in that way dramatically declaring that his authority as a Constituting Officer had ceased. This breaking of wands is thought to have been an old custom at masonic funerals, for we read that at the funeral of a Somerset tyler in 1850 the "long obsolete" custom was observed of breaking the deceased officer's wand and casting the broken pieces into the grave.

Visitors and Visiting

The Master, when investing the Junior Warden, impresses upon him his responsibility for the examination of visitors, lest through his neglect any unqualified person should gain admission to the lodge. From time immemorial that duty and responsibility have lain upon the shoulders of the Junior Warden, although in the early days he obviously was allowed to delegate part of his duties to junior Brethren, for the Senior and Junior Entered Apprentices had most definite duties with regard to the admission of visitors. In an old catechism we read:

Q. Where stands the Senior Entre'd 'Prentice?
A. In the South.
Q. What is his business?
A. To hear and receive instruction, and welcome strange Brothers.

Obviously, the Senior Entered Apprentice worked under the instructions of the Junior Warden, much as the Inner Guard does to-day.

The examination of visitors in an English lodge is lax by comparison with the custom of the eighteenth century and by comparison, also, with the custom of present-day American lodges, which inherited direct from for lodges early in that century. (The writer of these words was examined the fifteen minutes before he gained admission into a lodge at Washington, capital of the U.S.A., although he carried full credentials and at the time was a mason of twenty years' standing.)

An old Sheffield lodge had in 1764 or before, David Flather tells us, a rule that

> No Visitor be admitted after lodge hours nor at any time without the knowledge and consent of the presiding officers. And admitted into the Lodge he shall not be permitted to sit down untill he first perform a Certain Ceremony before the Brethren to the satisfaction of the Master etc. And permitted to sit down he shall pay equal with the Members.

The Right of Visit or Visiting

It is commonly believed that

> every affiliated Mason in good standing has a right to visit any other Lodge, wherever it may be, as often as it may suit his pleasure or convenience; and this is called, in masonic law, 'the right of visit.' It is one of the most important of all masonic privileges, because it is based on the principle of the identity of the masonic institution as one universal family, and is the exponent of that well-known maxim that 'in every clime a Mason may find a home, and in every land a Brother.' It has been so long and so universally admitted, that I [Mackey] have not hesitated to rank it among the landmarks of the Order . . . the admitted doctrine on this subject is, that the right of visit is one of the positive rights of every Mason, because Lodges are justly considered as only divisions for convenience of the universal Masonic family . . . but without the existence of some such good reason, masonic jurists have always decided that the right of visitation is absolute and positive, and inures to every Mason in his travels throughout the world.[1]

We must not, however, read into Mackey's words the unqualified right of *any* mason to attend *any* lodge at *any* time, and we may hesitate to say with Mackey that the "right of visit" is a landmark. A Brother's right of visitation must surely be subject to any qualifications implied in the bylaws of the lodge which he proposes to visit and in the regulations of the Grand Lodge by whose authority the lodge is held, and, further, must always be subject to the convenience of the lodge. It should also go without saying, of course, that any right to visit does not imply any right to continue in the company of the Brethren uninvited, when the labours of the lodge are ended. Every jurisdiction and its lodges have a right to exclude a mason who does not conform to the conditions laid down by them, and to exclude any Brother whose presence might disturb the harmony of a lodge, and as far back as 1765 a Taunton lodge resolved that the right of visitation should apply on one day only in each year.

[1] A. G. Mackey, *Encyclopædia of Freemasonry.*

The visiting of other lodges by Brethren is regarded with a kindly eye by the English Grand Lodge, but the injunction to the Master and Wardens of a lodge to visit other lodges as often as they conveniently can, "in order that the same usages and customs may be observed throughout the Craft and a good understanding cultivated amongst Freemasons," is no longer part of the *Constitutions*.

A Brother visiting a lodge as a stranger should take with him all his credentials, including his Grand Lodge certificate and evidence that he is in good standing in his own lodge or lodges.

The *Constitutions* of the Grand Lodge of England provide for official visits by the Grand Master and his officers, the Provincial or District Grand Master and his Officers, etc. The Grand Master may send any of his Grand Officers, present or past, to visit a lodge, and the visiting officer shall be placed on the immediate right of the Brother presiding; the same applies to the Provincial or District Grand Master. The Grand Lodge especially provides that no Brother subject to the Grand Lodge shall be admitted into a lodge unless he be personally known to, and vouched for, by one of the Brethren present, or unless he shall be well vouched for after due examination. He shall, if required, produce his Grand Lodge certificate and proof of good standing in his lodge or lodges. Every visitor during his presence in a lodge is subject to its relevant bylaws. A Brother who has ceased to be a subscribing member of every lodge of which he has at any time been a member is not permitted to visit any one lodge more than once, until he again becomes a subscribing member of a lodge; if he has been excluded from lodge membership because of non-payment of dues, or by resolution duly carried by the lodge, then he is unable to attend any lodge, or any lodge of instruction, until he again becomes a subscribing member of a lodge.

A Master of any English lodge to which an overseas visitor seeks admission must satisfy himself that the constitution from which the visitor comes is recognized by the Grand Lodge.

Early in the nineteenth century two Sussex lodges had each an officer who was known as the Examiner of Strangers, and it is to be assumed that he acted as an assistant to the Junior Warden in carrying out a particular part of his duties; but there were Examiners of Strangers working in a French craft lodge in 1752 whose duty was to visit all strangers coming to the town, sick Brethren, the hospitals, and the poor and needy. There were two of these Examiners, one of them a doctor when possible.

Chapter Twenty-five

THE TYLER AND THE INNER GUARD

"Bro. tylers should always be chosen from those who have the greatest knowledge and hold the highest rank," says a French work published in 1828. "The greatest honour a Master can confer on a Brother is to make him Tyler, because not only his own secrets but those of the whole lodge are depending on him," says in effect a manuscript of the 1750 period, in which the Tyler is compared to "the Angel Gabriel, with a flaming sword guarding the Tree of Life"! The old French lodges recognized the Tyler's office as one of the greatest importance, being convinced that as he was one of the earliest of the lodge officers to have contact with the Candidate he needed to be most carefully chosen for his task (see also p. 266). When the first Grand Lodge was formed in 1717 it put Anthony Sayer, Gentleman, into the Grand Master's chair; when he died about 1742, he was Tyler of the lodge (now No. 28) meeting at the King's Arms, Strand, London. Grand Lodge minutes first mention 'tyler' in 1732.

The Brother entrusted with the duties of the doorkeeper, probably long before a serving Brother undertook the office, was known as the Garder, or some variant of that term. (It has already been explained that the word 'garder' is identical with the word 'warder'.) From 'garder' came 'guard,' then 'outer guard' and, at a much later date, 'inner garder' or 'inner guard.' The Grand Tyler in 1738 was officially 'Garder of the Grand Lodge,' and it is in that year that we first find the term 'Tyler' in print—in Anderson's second edition of the *Constitutions*. Many lodges were slow in adopting the term; an Irish lodge, the Downpatrick, does not mention the Tyler in its bylaws until 1785, while the Eight Brothers Lodge, in the 'Antients' list and founded in 1785, first mentions the Tyler in its list of officers of 1814.

The Name 'Tyler'

How did the Tyler get his name? The simple answer 'because he tiles the lodge' would tell us nothing, because the verb 'to tile' in its masonic usage has apparently been made from the noun 'tyler,' and both of these special words have been contributed by freemasonry to the common vocabulary, not the other way about. Ordinary dictionaries, in attempting to define the words, merely refer us back to the Mason craft from which they came. Emblematically, a Tyler might be thought to 'hele,' or cover, his lodge so as to hide the interior from prying eyes, and in that sense he may 'tile'—that is, emblematically 'roof'—the lodge; but the simile is far-fetched and is based upon an impracticable idea. It is out of the question to roof and unroof a building, and then roof it again, merely to hide its interior from prying eyes. It does not seem likely that the name Tyler is derived from operative practice, although it is a point upon which we must not be dogmatic. It is also difficult to accept the Tyler as the speculative's representative of the old-time 'helier,' or 'roofer.' Then, whence comes his name?

It is worth while remembering that when we first see the name Tyler in print it is in 1738, by which time English speculative freemasonry had crossed to France and *had come back again*, bringing with it many additions, some of them strange and curious. Was one of those additions the name of the doorkeeper? The French stonemason, or stonecutter, is *le tailleur de pierre*. When the ordinary Englishman tries to pronounce the French word *tailleur* (in which the liquid 'll' is a very shibboleth) about as near as he gets to the correct pronunciation is a word sounding very much like 'tyler.' Is the name tyler, then, a variant of stonemason? Possibly, or even probably, so; but there is a missing link in the suggestion, as we are unable to say why the French should have singled out the tyler for the honour of being called a stonecutter. However, until a better derivation is forthcoming, as it may be one of these days, we may continue to question whether the tyler's name grew out of his specific duties or had any operative origin. It is worth noting that the old French lodges were said to be 'covered.' There is the bare possibility that the idea of 'tiling' the lodge comes from that idea, through a clumsy translation.

The Old-time Tyler's Duties

On other pages is explained the ancient custom of delineating the symbolic lodge with lines of chalk, tape, etc., and also that the old-time Tyler was paid a special fee for his work in preparing the lodge. We find it recorded in the minutes of Jerusalem Lodge, No. 197, that the Tyler, who received two shillings and sixpence for forming either the Fellow Craft's or a Master's Lodge, made a mistake on one occasion in the year 1772, and, having formed an Entered Apprentices' Lodge in error, a raising had to be deferred. But, apart from any work he did in forming the lodge, the old Tyler received a small payment for his duties in general. The records of the Lodge No. 41, at Bath, tell us that the Tyler was paid one shilling and sixpence for each meeting, and even for that he sometimes waited if funds were low, the amount being reduced on one occasion "because he did not do his duty in dispersing the summons." (It is recorded that forty years later the Tyler's fee was increased to half a crown.) In a few old lodges the Tyler kept the minutes.

The delivery of the summons was frequently a part of the Tyler's duties; not only did he 'disperse,' or deliver, it, but in some lodges it often fell to him to introduce into the summons itself any urgent notice. There is no record that he received any extra remuneration for relieving the Secretary of any of his work, but, truth to tell, the preparation of the summons was the Tyler's duty in some lodges. In the Twelve Brothers Lodge, of Portsea and Portsmouth, an 'Antient' lodge of short life, the Tyler received a shilling for every mason made and sixpence for every joining member. The Tyler in some of the lodges of Missouri has certain duties which in English lodges are performed by the Director of Ceremonies, matters of etiquette, in particular, being referred to him.

The Tyler was given great discretion in refusing admission when he thought there was good reason for so doing, and in the Lodge of Probity, Halifax, a lodge going back under another name into the 1730's, the Tyler was empowered "to refuse admission to any member of the lodge who is not clean and decently clad in a white neck-cloth."

In days when catechisms were popular and formed such a large part of lodge working, we may reasonably assume that the Tyler was called upon, in some lodges, to answer questions as to his place and duties, in the course of the ceremony of opening the lodge. A few lodges follow this practice to-day, and in one of them, the Lodge of Friendship, Oldham, No. 277, before the lodge is opened, the Tyler's sword lies upon the Master's pedestal. At the proper moment the Tyler is summoned into lodge, answers the questions, and the Master then hands him the sword to enable him to keep off intruders and cowans to masonry, and to suffer none to pass but such as are duly qualified.

The Tyler's 'duty' of proposing the toast named after him is referred to in another chapter.

The Tyler not necessarily a Serving Brother

It has already been pointed out that in early lodges the Tyler was not necessarily a serving Brother. In an old Bristol lodge the junior member present might be called upon to tile the lodge, or forfeit two shillings and sixpence. An unusual bylaw of the now extinct Orthes Lodge (6th Regiment of Foot) provided in the 1830's that

for preservation of Secrecy, a Brother skilled in the Master's duty shall be appointed Tyler; if more than one be required the Master has the power to nominate a Master Mason to assist in that duty for that day, but not to call on the same individual twice successively.

The principle, if not the detail, is still observed. The English *Constitutions* state that every Tyler must be a Master Mason and shall be elected by the members on the regular day of election of the Master. A lodge may resolve, however, that one of its subscribing members shall be Tyler without emolument, in which case he shall be appointed with other officers by the Master. An old bylaw of the Lodge of Loyalty, Prescot, directed that every member should act in turn as Tyler.

The Tyler, as a serving Brother, cannot be a subscribing member of the lodge which he tiles, but any member of the lodge in the absence of the Tyler may act in that capacity when invited by the Master to do so.

We learn that at a very early date the Tyler was armed. One of the old so-called *exposés* (it might be as early as 1725) says: "At the door before you are admitted stands an Entr'ed Prentice with a drawn sword to guard against droppers, as they call them, from Hearkening," which agrees with the gist of many other early catechisms.

The old Tyler's sword often had no scabbard and was wavy in form, emblematically to represent the flaming sword which "turned every way, to keep the way of the tree of life." This type of sword is only occasionally seen in lodges to-day. In a few early lodges the Tyler was armed, not with a sword, but with a pointed trowel (see page 447).

The Eighteenth-century Tyler's Dress

The dress of the eighteenth-century Tyler was intended to be impressive, but to our eyes might only succeed in being comic. We are not referring to the hat and coat with which some lodges provided their Tyler to protect him from the weather when delivering summonses to the members, but to the uniform, or costume, which he wore when carrying out his lodge duties. True, the dress of the Grand Tyler in 1736 had great dignity—a red waistcoat under a dark blue coat, trimmed with gold lace—but what can be said of the Turkish costume, complete with scimitar, always worn by the Tyler of the Lodge of Scoon and Perth when on duty? An old Tyler's coat now owned by Eaton Lodge, Congleton, No. 533, and originally belonging to the now extinct Harmony Lodge, Knutsford, is of black serge, lined, faced, and edged with red; the collar, cape, and cuffs are edged with light-blue flannel. On the front are a dozen buttons one and three-quarter inches in diameter, covered with white linen. At the back, from the waistline downward, are six more of these buttons, three on each tail.

The Lodge of St John, No. 279, of Leicester, resolved in 1791 that the Tyler be clothed at the expense of the lodge with a blue coat and waist-coat and corduroy breeches, the whole with yellow buttons, a pair of white stockings, and a three-corner'd hat. And also that he be furnished with a hairy cap to wear on public occasions, the latter to remain the property of the lodge.

There must have been many similar instances, as, for example, that of the Tyler of a Preston Lodge, in the 1790's, who was dressed in scarlet with a hairy cap.

We get an almost terrifying picture of the Tyler of the Ancient Boyne Lodge, No. 84 in the Irish Constitution, in the *History of Bandon* (1869), by George Bennett. This lodge, which was established in 1738, is one of the ten oldest lodges in Ireland, and the author must have been basing himself upon minutes and records now two centuries old. The description he gives of the redoubtable Tyler might have been inspired by the Candidate's first impression on presenting himself at the lodge for Initiation:

> A huge red cloak covered the Tyler to the very toes; the large sleeves which hung below his hands terminated in cuffs of orange velvet, on each of which was a representation of a skull and crossbones in lustrous black; the blue collar had on it moons and stars of bright yellow, and candlesticks, compasses and other cabalistic symbols of the Craft, nearly covered it with odd-looking devices. On his head was a gigantic cocked-hat, which would almost have served him for a boat, it was so large. This was surmounted with blue and red feathers, and in his hand was a flaming falchion. "Keep off!" said the terrible Dick, as the bewildered candidate moved forward a step or two, "or before you can say 'God Save Me' I'll run you through the gullet!"

It will be noted that the collars worn by this lodge are of orange velvet, yet—W. J. Chetwowde Crawley tells us—they have no political signifi-cance whatsoever, as the orange was adopted sixty years before the Orange Society was formed; and so well aware of this were the Roman Catholic Brethren that, when a deputation of two Protestants and two Roman Catholics was sent to Cork by the Ancient Boyne Lodge late in the last century, the Roman Catholics refused to wear any other colours than those of their lodge.

The 'Tyler's Oath'

We do not hear much of the 'Tyler's Oath' in England, but in the United States of America every strange visitor who is not well vouched for is taken into the Tyler's room, where he and the examining Brethren together repeat the oath that they have been regularly initiated, passed, and raised in a just and legally constituted lodge; that they do not stand suspended or expelled; and know of no reason why they should not hold masonic communication with the Brethren. Mackey's *Encyclopædia of Freemasonry* explains that each one present, the visitor as well as the members of the lodge, has a right to know that each and all the others are entitled to be present at the esoteric examination which follows, and without which, of course, the visitor is unable to gain admission to the lodge. Personal experience confirms that this examination is far from being perfunctory.

The Inner Guard

The Inner Guard developed in the eighteenth-century lodges from an Inner Tyler or Inner Garder, it being found that there was a particular need for an officer guarding the inside of the door under direct instruction of the Junior Warden, whose particular duty it was and is to see that no unqualified person gains admission. It has already been shown how the name of the officer is derived (p. 375). In effect he is the door Warden, and in some of the early lodges he was at first a serving Brother whose duties were closely concerned with those of the Tyler, who was also of course a serving Brother.

The Inner Guard has his place in Irish and Scottish lodges, but is unknown in most American lodges, in which the Junior Deacon, acting under the commands of the Junior Warden, admits Brethren, and has a special responsibility for Candidates and visitors. This responsibility he is made to feel is a very real one indeed, to be shared between him and the Tyler, whose special oath administered to every visitor has just been mentioned.

The Inner Guard existed in fact in English lodges long before he was honoured with his particular name. In 1734 the Old King's Arms Lodge, No. 28, had a 'door-keepper,' and it is likely that he was the youngest Entered Apprentice present, and that he was armed with a trowel. Not until the turn of the century did the Inner Tyler, or 'doorkeeper,' begin to be called the Guarder, or Guard, and not until about 1814 was there official recognition of the actual office of Inner Guard. In such an old lodge as the Love and Honour, No. 75, Falmouth, the first mention of Inner Guard is in the records of 1816. Grand Lodge authorized the Inner Guard's jewel—the crossed swords—in 1819. The Burlington Lodge (founded 1756), now No. 96, first mentions the Inner Guard in its minutes of 1814.

Where the Inner Guard was a serving Brother he was undoubtedly regarded as the Tyler's assistant, various old minutes making that position quite clear. In the Lodge of Honour and Friendship, Blandford, that ceased to exist in 1838 (Blandford's present lodge of that name, No. 1266, dates back to 1869), a particular Brother was allowed one shilling for each lodge night "and one shilling for every newly initiated Brother to take on himself the office of Inner Guard and to assist the Tyler . . . as he had been admitted under a dispensation of the Prov. Grand Master and initiated without fee."

The Royal Augustus Lodge of Monmouth (erased in 1830) had an Outer Tyler and a Junior Tyler.

The weapon with which the Inner Guard was armed, where tradition helps us in this respect, was the pointed trowel, and it is not apparently in keeping with oldest custom that he should be armed with a sword of any kind, for that is the emblematic weapon of the Outer Guard, or Tyler. Probably it was the serving Brother Inner Guard's position as Junior to the Tyler that led to his also being armed with a sword, albeit a sheathed one, as contrasted with the drawn sword of the Tyler. Grand Lodge in authorizing the crossed swords as the Inner Guard's jewel set its seal upon a practice which, so far as can be seen, does not accord with the earliest custom. The emblematic use of the trowel both by the Tyler and the Inner Guard in the old lodges receives special treatment on pp. 446 and 447.

Chapter Twenty-six

FLOOR-DRAWINGS, CLOTHS, CARPETS, AND TRACING-BOARDS

As long ago as 1730 there were emblems in the English lodges of three particular qualities—Freedom, Fervency, and Zeal—and those emblems were chalk, charcoal, and clay!

In the early lectures is one version of a catechism relating to them:

Q. How long should an Entered Apprentice serve his Master?
A. Seven years . . .
Q. How should he serve him?
A. With Freedom, Fervency and Zeal.
Q. Excellent qualities! What are their emblems?
A. Chalk, Charcoal and Clay.

To the modern mason the question as to why these three messy substances should be present, or should even be represented, in a speculative lodge might prove a poser, but they are the undoubted forerunners of a part of lodge equipment with which at first sight they have nothing whatever in common.

Floor Lines delineating the Lodge

From early days in the speculative lodges—so early, probably, that the custom is lost in the mists of antiquity, unless by chance it came from the French lodges quite early in the seventeen-hundreds—Brethren used to mark out on the floor the actual form of the lodge, and at the end of their meetings they effaced the marks. With the passage of time the custom gave way to the use of painted cloths on floor or on wall, which in their turn were generally discontinued in favour of the tracing-board more or less as we have it to-day.

An *exposé*, which might truly date from 1727, asks, "What's the square pavement for?" and answers it with, "For the Master Mason to draw his ground draughts on." This sufficiently indicates that our Brethren of old were draughting a symbolic building when they laid out, in temporary and easily erasable lines on the floor, the particular form of their lodge, a form which frequently varied with the degree in which they were working.

The use of chalk, charcoal, and clay, in delineating the symbolical lodge, led to some forced and rather misapplied symbolism, as already made plain. For example, Oliver tells us that these three materials

have ever been esteemed symbolically emblems of freedom, fervency, and zeal. Nothing is more free for the use of man than chalk, which seldom touches but leaves its trace behind. Nothing is more fervent than charcoal, for when well lighted, no metal is able to resist its force. Nothing is more zealous than clay, our mother earth, which will open her arms to receive us when forsaken by all our friends.

Whether the 'earthen pan' mentioned in one version of the catechism is the container in which the chalk and charcoal were kept, or whether it refers to a packed, or rammed, floor of earth (in which sense we still use the word, as, for example, 'hard pan') is hard to say, especially when we remember that the drawing of the lodge in effaceable lines might well be the survival of an ancient custom. It is extremely difficult to see why such a curious and inconvenient method should ever have been invented by our Brethren of the early eighteenth century, either French or English, meeting in the rooms of inns. There is no doubt that it was closely related to the idea of secrecy, which accounts for the great hostility offered in some quarters to the introduction of the painted floor-cloth. Maybe it was an odd survival of the age-old practice of drawing a working design with chalk on a board or stone, or scratching a design with a pointed tool in some yielding material. We can only conjecture, but we have to assist us the record of a German writer, Berlepsch, who described how the smiths of Magdeburg, Prussia, meeting as a medieval trade guild, opened their meeting by drawing on the floor a ring in chalk, the officer who drew it being responsible for rubbing it out with his hand when the meeting was over. The badge, or mark, of the guild was an incomplete circle.

For much of our information on the ancient methods of delineating the symbolic lodge we have to fall back upon the irregular prints published during the eighteenth century. One of them, dated 1766, says:

The drawing is frequently made with chalk, stone-blue and charcoal inter-mixed. . . . At the time of making [a mason], the room is very grandly illuminated; and, in some lodges, powder'd rosin, mixed with shining sand, is strewed on the floor, which (together with the extraordinary illumination of the room) has a pretty effect.

Another well-known *exposé* of the same period says that "as soon as the ceremony of Making is over, the New-made Mason (though ever so great a Gentleman) must take a Mop from a Pail of Water, and wash it out." The same publication tells us that

the candidate is also learnt the Step, or how to advance to the Master upon the Drawing on the Floor, which in some Lodges resembles the grand

Building, termed a Mosaic Palace, and is described with the utmost exactness. They also draw other Figures, one of which is called the Laced Tuft, and the other the Throne beset with Stars. There is also represented a perpendicular Line in the Form of a Mason's Instrument, commonly called the Plumb-Line; and another Figure which represents the Tomb of Hiram, the First Grand-Master, who has been dead almost Three Thousand Years. . . . The Ceremony being now ended, the new-made Member is obliged to take a Mop out of a Pail of Water brought for that Purpose, and rub out the Drawing on the Floor, if it is done with Chalk and Charcoal.

There is reason to believe that even so late as 1808 and 1811 the mop was used for erasing floor lines in the Dundee Lodge, No. 9, at Wapping. In the 1808 and 1811 accounts the Tyler was paid for tobacco, for a mop, for a pail, and for forming one lodge. In 1798 he was paid twelve shillings and sixpence for forming five lodges and one shilling for a mop. We can more readily believe the entries to indicate that the old custom was still in use when E. H. Dring tells us in a paper delivered in 1916 that he was informed that in the 1860's a Cornish lodge was still delineated by drawing lines in a sanded floor! Some customs, however inconvenient, diehard, and by becoming sacrosanct unite a body of conservative opinion in their favour.

We see in the engraving *Night* (made by the great William Hogarth in 1738 and reproduced on Plate X) what might well be evidence of the custom of using a mop for erasing the floor design. Hogarth was a freemason, one of his lodges being at the Hand and Apple Tree, Little Queen Street, London (close to the site of the present Freemasons' Hall). His scurrilous print portrays a night scene, grimly sordid, but not lacking in humour, probably set in Northumberland Street, Strand, formerly Hartshorne Lane. It is thought to contain masonic allusions, one of which is the mop carried by a figure on the right of the print. Two figures in the foreground wear leather aprons reaching to within a few inches of their buckle-shoes, and round the neck of one of them is a collar from which is suspended a square.

Some lodges evidently replaced the chalk and charcoal lines with tapes nailed to the floor. One of the *exposés* says the floor lines are of "red tape and nails . . . which prevents any mark or stain on the floor, as with chalk." The change gave rise to ridicule, for we find a mocking advertisement of 1726 (quoted by Henry Sadler, the well-known masonic historian) alluding to the "innovations . . . introduced by the Doctor [probably Desaguliers] and some other of the Moderns, with their Tape, Jacks, Moveable Letters, Blazing Stars, etc., to the great Indignity of the Mop and Pail."

The floor lines in chalk, tape, etc., delineated 'the form of the lodge,' which seems to suggest that to our ancient Brethren the lodge was not so much the room in which they met, but the space—the 'holy ground' —enclosed within the outline drawn on the floor. A Candidate took up a position relative to those lines, particularly during the Obligation, when he may have had one foot on a step indicated by certain of the lines, although, in some cases, a real step, or possibly a rough ashlar, may have been used. There is reason to suppose that at one time the circumambulation of the lodge meant merely walking round the lines drawn on the floor and, later, round a lodge board lying on the floor.

It was the custom for the old lodges to be 'prepared' by the Tyler, who was paid a small fee for his work. Many references could be quoted; in the Jerusalem Lodge, late in the eighteenth century, the Tyler was paid two shillings and sixpence for forming either a Fellow Craft or a Master's Lodge. Obviously one lodge was not the same as the other, for on one occasion, the Tyler having made the mistake of forming an Entered Apprentices' Lodge when a Master's Lodge was wanted, the raising was deferred. The Lodge of Felicity, in 1738, likewise paid the Tyler two shillings and sixpence "for drawing ye Lodge." The Grenadiers Lodge, in 1753, "agreed that Bro. Lister be a free member for Drawing the Lodges" (if there were "no making or raising them he is under obligation to pay"). In an old French lodge two members drew the lodge on the floor, leaving it to the Candidate or other junior members to erase it. A French lodge at Bordeaux had a Brother Grand Architect who was responsible for drawing the lodge "in the appointed place and with the necessary precautions"; so he evidently had to do a fresh drawing for each meeting.

The Floor-cloth

The system of drawing the lodge on the floor of the inn room must have had many inconveniences, and must have led at times, it may be imagined, to some differences of opinion between the lodge and its landlord. It was inevitable that the floor lines should be replaced sooner or later by a floor-cloth of some sort. We find reference to floor-cloths in the 1730's. In that decade the Old King's Arms Lodge, No. 28, was presented with a painted cloth representing "the severall forms of mason's Lodges"—further evidence that lodges of the three degrees were formed in different ways.

The floor-cloth was apparently a painted canvas, and in it we see an innovation which led eventually to the original purpose of the floor-drawing being quite overlooked and forgotten, for in course of time the painted cloth, which cost money and probably did not wear particularly well as a carpet, developed into a wall-cloth, or into a cloth covering a table (often a trestle table, from which it is likely that such old and curious terms as 'trasel,' 'tarsel,' etc., were corrupted). The painted cloth developed into a composite picture of symbols, and to-day in every lodge we find it in the form of the well-known tracing-board, or lodge board, in which we do not easily see the old masons' draughting-board, but from which, nevertheless, it has descended in a very roundabout way.

The floor-cloth, whether spread on the floor, covering a table, or possibly carried on a roller for display on a wall, kept its name until somewhere near the end of the eighteenth century, when the tracing-board (itself, sometimes, the old cloth framed) began to come generally into use. But more than one lodge continued to work lectures "on the floor-cloth"—actually the tracing-board.

E. H. Dring, the well-known historian of the floor-cloth and tracing-board, tells us of a cloth in the possession of the Lodge of the Marches, No. 611, Ludlow, the only one known to him in which the hand of the Master is depicted drawing on the true Tracing-Board. This cloth originally belonged to the Silurian Lodge, Kington, Herefordshire, which ceased to exist about 1801, after only ten years of life.

It must not be supposed that any such innovation as a painted cloth, whatever convenience it offered, would be received without hostility in some quarters. If the whole purpose of the temporary floor lines was secrecy, then undoubtedly that purpose was completely undone by the use of a painted cloth. There was always the risk that a lodge might have to dispose of its property, and we can well understand, without sympathizing with it, the point of view of the lodge of Edinburgh (a head lodge in operative days) when it instructed the Lodge St Andrews, in 1759, to cease the use of a "painted cloth containing the flooring of a master's lodge." Evidently a commission had been given to a painter to produce the cloth, and in his pride of achievement he had left it in his painting-shop for all to see.

Tessellated Pavement

In the absence of all the links of evidence, we are left to conclude that, with the passing of the painted floor-cloth or even much earlier, the need arose of a carpet, and that this was ultimately met by the chequered or mosaic-pattern carpet, woven with its own tessellated border, with which we are all familiar, and which traditionally, but hardly historically, represents the pavement of King Solomon's Temple. The black and white alternating squares are said to symbolize the chequered life of man. The tessellated pavement of square dies, or tesseræ, of tile or stone, was common in ancient buildings. The remains of Roman buildings provide many beautiful examples, in some of which the tesseræ were arranged to form geometric figures. Pavements of this kind were much in vogue at Damascus. We read in the Book of Esther that "the couches were of gold and silver, upon a pavement of red, and white, and yellow, and black marble." (i, 6, Revised Version.)

Tiles and stones of square shape, as commonly used in pavements for thousands of years past, naturally lent themselves to the formation of geometric designs. In a work written by William of Malmesbury about 1129–39, we are told, concerning the ancient church of Glastonbury, seventh century, that there was a floor inlaid with polished stone. "In the pavement may be remarked on every side stones designedly interlaid in triangles and squares, and figured with lead, under which if I believe some sacred enigma to be contained, I do no injustice to religion."

The Tracing-board, or Lodge Board

The tracing-board is an emblem whose history goes back indirectly to the tracing-board, or drawing-board, of the medieval mason, even though its name was reacquired in speculative times. The tracing-board of the old operative Master Mason was his draughting-board, upon which he worked out plans and details of a building. The Fabric Rolls of York Minster include in the inventory of stores for 1399, "ij tracyng bordes," the modern meaning being 'drawing-boards.' A building contract of 1436 mentions a 'trasyng on a parchement skyn.'

The board with parchment; a flat stone or slate; even the floor, on which the Master Mason designed and laid out his details for the instruction of craftsmen—any of these was his tracing-board, or drawing-board. We must not be misled by a modern application into supposing that the old-time tracing-board meant simply a piece of transparent paper laid upon a drawing attached to a board, so that a copy could be made by tracing over the lines. 'To trace' means much more than 'to copy'; fundamentally, it means 'to trace *out*,' or, in other words, 'to scheme,' 'to devise,' 'to plan,' 'to draw,' 'to sketch.' The word comes down to us from the original Latin *tractus* through the Italian, Spanish, and French languages, and in doing so has acquired all these many meanings. The beautiful 'tracery' of the Gothic windows is an application of the same word.

It would be quite wrong to conclude, as many masonic authors have been prone to, and even as the foregoing might possibly suggest, that all medieval drawings were inevitably rough and elementary. Some of them are of surprising quality. To study a working-drawing prepared in 1370, giving details of part of Prague Cathedral; to note the finished draughtsmanship, and to appreciate the knowledge of geometry essential to the production of the design—to do this will sweep away once and for always the idea that the medieval masons—at any rate, the later ones—designed as they went along, and put down in black and white only those details immediately required by the craftsmen (see pp. 40, 41).

Records show us that parchment was bought in 1377 for the making of drawings at Exeter Cathedal, and a skin was bought in 1389 on which to make the working drawings of the east window of that building. It has already been shown at the above reference that special buildings were used as drawing-offices, although not then so called.

As has been indicated, the speculatives' tracing-board is not the equivalent of those old draughting-boards, its original purpose having been lost in the course of its long and indirect descent; it is now an emblem, no longer a board on which work is done. We have seen how the lodge cloth in many eighteenth-century lodges replaced the old system of outlining the lodge in chalk or tape. It was at this point in the descent that the original idea of the tracing-board was lost. The floor-cloth of canvas, specially painted, had cost money; there was a natural objection to seeing it defaced by wear; the purpose served by the original delineation was possibly already becoming obscured; there was a tendency to drape the cloth over a table or to hang it on the wall, when of course it became purely and simply an emblem. The cloth in turn was replaced by the more convenient board—smaller, handier, and lending itself more easily to lodge procedure. But by the time the board had arrived the original purpose was completely forgotten or, to say the least, ignored. The board had become a picture representing various masonic emblems, and no longer purported to be the working drawing or the layout of a lodge or other building, however speculative.

E. H. Dring believes that probably the earliest *dated* tracing-boards in existence in Great Britain are the set belonging to Lodge Faithful, founded in 1753, at Norwich, now meeting at Harleston, Norfolk. The boards of this set are dated 1800. In the First Degree board there are in addition to the usual emblems a beehive, a sundial, a trowel, and a cornucopia. On the base of the Third Degree board is an arcade of columns, in front of which are five columns representing the five orders of architecture.

The French lodges apparently had tracing-boards long before the English lodges had them. The *planche à tracer* is known as far back as 1745. Some French lodges refer to the board as the *tracé* only, this meaning literally 'outline,' what we should in modern language call 'layout.' If we translate *planche à tracer* we get 'tracing board,' and it is reasonably certain that our term came about in that way, so reintroducing a term common in English operative lodges hundreds of years before.

It is probable that the French *planche à tracer* was an actual drawing-board, a plain board on which the Master of the lodge drew certain outlines, and it is equally probable that much earlier than the first known reference to the French *planche à tracer* some of the English boards were of this kind, and for use in one of the degrees had a 'ground plan of King Solomon's Temple' drawn upon it. So it might well be that here and there the English tracing-board did represent the true draughting-board, but that its purpose was lost during the 1700's. There is strong support for the idea in a minute of Old King's Arms Lodge (founded 1725), which in the year 1733, when meeting at the King's Arms, Strand, London, bought a copy of "de Clerc's Introduction on the Principles of Architecture," a drawing-board, and tee square for the use of the Master and his Lodge.

In some lodges in the early 1700's it was customary for Brethren to deliver lectures on subjects not strictly speculative, and in the case of the Old King's Arms Lodge it is likely that a qualified Brother gave lectures on architecture from time to time, and illustrated them on the drawing-board.

At some time in the 1700's some lodges had mosaic marble boards, or stones, but such boards were too expensive to come into general use.

Some of the old lectures agree that as the tracing-board is an immovable jewel for the Master to lay lines and draw designs on, the better to enable the Brethren to carry on the intended structure with regularity and propriety, so the Volume of the Sacred Law may justly be deemed the spiritual tracing-board of the G.A.O.T.U. How did the tracing-board come to be regarded as an 'immovable' jewel? Was it by way of contrast to the lines of chalk and tape which had to be effaced at the end of every lodge meeting? 'Immovable' had an ordinary as well as an abstract or spiritual meaning in those old lodges. The 'jewels' and the 'immovable jewels' of a lodge were loosely used terms and meant different things at different times.

In the old catechisms we find such odd terms as 'trasel board,' 'tresel board,' 'tarsel,' etc., which are just possibly corrupt forms of the term 'tracing board,' but are much more likely something quite different. Undoubtedly many old lodges supported the tracing-board on a trestle, or on a trestle table, a collapsible table being more suited to the limited conveniences of the tavern room in which the lodges met. It is extremely likely, too, that a great many lodges knew the term 'trestle board,' or some variant of it, long before they had ever heard of the tracing-board. The board was just the 'lodge board' in a great many cases.

Grand Lodge has never authorized any particular design of tracing-board, nor has it attempted to define its nature, although, of course, it countenances its use, for in the course of consecrating the lodge—a ceremony usually worked by Grand Lodge officers—the tracing-board is anointed.

Cecil Powell tells us that in the Moira Lodge of Honour, Bristol (founded in 1809 as the Moira Lodge), there is a centre table, covered with a blue cloth, on which the tracing-board of the First Degree is supported by four old brass figures, one denoting Faith, one Hope, and two of them Charity. At its western end stand two small brass columns, the one Corinthian and the other Ionic. For the other degrees, a smaller board, having the Fellow Craft design on one side and the Master Mason's on the other, is placed on that of the First Degree. On the table are also set the two ashlars with the particular working tools required during the evening, and for an Initiation three cutlasses lie on each side. For a raising there stands between the ashlars a 'triangle,' or derrick. Round the table, upon the floor, are three handsome candlesticks in the east, west, and south, with seven, five, and three steps forming the foot of each respectively. Formerly a 'pot of manna,' 'Aaron's rod,' and 'tables of stone' were used, suggestive of the 'Ark of the Covenant,' and these articles are still in existence. In the working of the lodge the 'north-east corner of the *lodge*' means the north-east corner of the *table*.

The survival of certain metal emblems in the form of templates—pillars, working tools, etc.—has given rise to the conjecture that in some of the 'Antient' lodges the actual emblems were placed on the floor or on a tracing-board.

The tracing-board used in most lodges nowadays harks back to those designed for the Emulation Lodge of Improvement about 1846, and to those published three years later by the noted designer John Harris, the miniature-painter and architectural draughtsman, who, initiated in 1818, published five years later sets of tracing-board designs. He went blind when sixty-five years of age and died about 1872, when over eighty years of age. E. H. Dring, attributing to Harris a mistake in the Hebrew lettering of the Third Degree boards, believes that Harris transcribed the Hebrew letters which he found on an earlier board designed by Bowring and converted them into cryptic letters, but overlooked that Hebrew was written from right to left. Further, says E. H. Dring, in an earlier design Harris, instead of writing ⌐ > for TC, wrote ⌐ <, an error to be found in many boards since his day.

The general practice of conferring the First and Second Degrees on the one evening during the 1700's confirms the belief that those two degrees were originally one, and the belief is given considerable support by the existence of tracing-boards which carry on the one face the emblems of both those two degrees.

In some of the American lodges the tracing-board is not used; instead, the symbols which customarily are found on it are separately projected on to a screen by an optical lantern as and when required. In lodges where this is done it is usual for illuminated signs over the Master's and Wardens' chairs to show the emblems associated with those chairs.

Not only the Royal Arch, but the Mark Degree and some of the allied degrees, occasionally use tracing-boards, more generally so in Ireland, it is thought, than in England. The Chapter of Sincerity, No. 261 (Taunton), has used a tracing-board almost all the time since it was founded in 1819.

The 'Lodge' meaning a 'Board' or 'Ark'

Old minutes provide many examples of the tracing-board being referred to as the 'Lodge.' Thus, we read of "a very handsome Lodge being presented," of the Candidate having 'the Lodge explained to him,' etc. and we have the phrase in the consecration ceremony, "I now anoint the Lodge"; and so forth. In 1771 a famous Bath lodge, No. 41, instructed Nicholas Tucker, a former Senior Warden, to "paint a Lodge," and the board that he painted has since passed into the possession of Loyal Lodge, Barnstaple; from this there can be no doubt that the 'Lodge' in old days often meant the lodge board or, as we call it to-day, the tracing-board.

But the nature of many references in old reports leads us to wonder whether the 'Lodge' sometimes took the form of an ark, chest, or box. Preston's *Illustrations of Masonry* (1772) indicates a space in the centre of the temple for the 'Lodge,' and a later edition (1781) speaks of the 'Lodge' being "covered with white satin" and "placed in the centre on a crimson velvet couch." Was this lodge an ark, or just the horizontal lodge board, here used in the sense of an altar, the white satin being in the nature of a veil to cover the face of the altar?

In one 'Antient' lodge, founded in Windsor in 1813, the working tools were displayed on a box 4 feet from east to west, 29 inches high and 28 inches wide, covered with red material, and surmounted by a white satin cloth having a gold fringe.

In the dedication of the new Grand Lodge Hall, in London, in May 1776, four Tylers carried the 'Lodge' as part of a procession which passed round the hall three times; they placed the 'Lodge' in the centre on a crimson velvet couch, and at the close of the ceremony carried it away.

In consecrating a new lodge in the United States about 1867 the 'Lodge,' consisting of an oblong box covered with white linen, was placed upon the table in front of the Grand Master, and was surrounded by three candles and vessels of corn, wine, and oil. In commenting on this and the other instances above noted, H. Hiram Hallet says there is a strong feeling, amounting almost to a conviction, that the 'Lodge' represented the ark, itself a symbolical emblem, which found a space in many earlier lodges and acted as a repository for the small and more sacred property of the lodge, such as the Volume of the Sacred Law, the warrant, etc., etc.

Such a 'Lodge,' or ark, may have had a symbolic relationship with the Ark of the Covenant, or Ark of the Testimony, the Ark of the Lord, the Ark of God's Strength—the ark used in Jewish worship which took the form of an oblong chest of acacia wood, overlaid with gold both inside and out, and carried by means of staves fastened through rings fixed to the sides. The Ark contained stone tables, the pot of manna, and Aaron's rod, and on top of it, we are told, was the mercy seat.

King Solomon's Temple

It is not beyond the bounds of possibility that the Ark did in some cases represent King Solomon's Temple, a 'model' of which was on exhibition in London in 1723 and 1730, and another one in 1759–60. W. J. Chetwode Crawley suggests that the exhibition of the first model —that of Schott—must have influenced the Craft at a time when our legends were being moulded and harmonized, and it is curious to note that the years 1723, 1730, and 1760 were severally marked by an outburst of spurious rituals called forth by the curiosity of outsiders. Our authority says that of undoubted influence, also, was an engraving, or plan, of Jerusalem, with views of the Temple, and its principal ornaments issued by John Senex, who in 1723, in which year he was Junior Grand Warden, published the first *Constitutions*. Undoubtedly, too, a stimulus was given by the publication of Sir Isaac Newton's *The Chronology of Ancient Kingdoms Amended*, a posthumous work which devotes one-fifth of its contents to a visionary description of the Temple. It was published in London in 1728, and republished in Dublin in the same year, a sure token of its popularity. Schott's model was freely advertised in 1729–30, and the following advertisement appeared in *The Daily Courant*:

To be seen at the Royal-Exchange *every Day*, The Model of the TEMPLE of SOLOMON, with all its Porches, Walls, Gates, Chambers and holy Vessels, the great Altar of the Burnt Offering, the Moulton Sea, the Lavers, the Sanctum Sanctorum; with the Ark of the Covenant, the Mercy Seat and Golden Cherubims, the Altar of Incense, the Candlestick, Tables of Shew-Bread, with the two famous Pillars, called Joachim and Boas. Within the model are 2000 Chambers and Windows, and Pillars 7000; the Model is 13 foot high and 80 foot round. Likewise the Model of the Tabernacle of

MOSES, with the Ark of the Covenant, wherein is the law of *Moses*, the Pot of Manna and the Rod of *Aaron*, the Urim and Tumin, with all the other Vessels. The printed Description of it, with 12 fine Cuts, is to be had at the same Place at 5s. a Book.

N.B. The Publick is desired to take Notice, that the Sanctum Sanctorum, with all the holy Vessels is new gilt, and appears much finer and richer than before.

Jacob's Ladder

Of the many emblems and symbols to be found on tracing-boards, that of Jacob's Ladder has always been conspicuous. It represents the ladder which Jacob saw in his dream when he beheld "a ladder set up on the earth, and the top of it reached to heaven: and behold the angels of God ascending and descending on it."[1] It is not the only ladder known as a symbol of moral, intellectual, and spiritual progress. There have been many, for the belief in the existence of a ladder leading from earth to heaven was common at one time throughout the world. Many ancient mysteries, such as the Persian, Brahmin, and Scandinavian, used this symbol. A ladder is associated with the name of St Augustine, and a ladder of perfection is known in one of the additional degrees.

Jacob's Ladder was a prominent symbol in the early days of speculative masonry, and we find it on many breast jewels of the 1760 period. The number of rungs, or steps, in the various ladders was generally seven, which has been a mystic, or sacred, number for thousands of years. Brewer's *Dictionary of Phrase and Fable* contains a list of references to the potency of this number. There were, for example, seven sacred planets; seven days in creation; seven ages in the life of man; the seventh son of a seventh son was notable; among the Hebrews every seventh year was Sabbatical; the stories of Biblical characters, such as Elijah, Pharaoh, Jacob, and Samson, often turn upon the number seven. Brewer says that from the ancient belief in the sacredness of this number "sprang the theory that man was composed of seven substances and has seven natures."

The number of steps in Jacob's Ladder in freemasonry should apparently be seven: Temperance, Fortitude, Prudence, Justice, Faith, Hope, and Charity. But often it is only three, for at some time or other an artist found he had not room enough for seven rungs on his tracing-board, so he reduced the number! In an Irish ritual of the year 1796 the ladder is shown with eleven rungs.

As might well be expected, the emblem has been found capable of varied and elaborate explanations. It was supposed to lead the thoughts of the Brethren to heaven; its rungs each represented a moral and religious

[1] Genesis xxviii, 12.

duty; if there were three rungs, then they represented Faith, Hope, and Charity, with which the whole earth could be encircled. In the Mithraic mysteries the seven-runged ladder was a symbol of the ascent of the soul to perfection, each rung being termed a gate. In certain additional degrees the seven steps represent Justice, Equity, Kindness, Good Faith, Labour, Patience, and Intelligence; in others, Justice and Charity, Innocence, Sweetness, Faith, Firmness and Truth, the Great Work, Responsibility.

On the whole, says A. F. A. Woodford, Jacob's Ladder in freemasonry seems to point to the connexion between earth and heaven, man and God, and to represent faith in God, charity towards all men, and hope in immortality.

Masonic historians of the school that believes there was considerable Jacobite influence in eighteenth-century masonry make the suggestion that Jacob's Ladder was introduced as a symbol from Continental masonry, with the object of keeping the Jacobite cause in the minds of its adherents.

The Point within a Circle

Probably many Brethren regard the symbol of the point within a circle as belonging exclusively to the Third Degree; but if we go back to the old lectures—current in the 1880's and even more recently—we find that this symbol enters into the explanation of the first tracing-board and, further, is referred to in the sixth section of the first lecture. It figured on many of the old First Degree tracing-boards, and in regard to it the lectures tell us that in

> all regular, well-formed, constituted lodges, there is a point within a circle from which a Mason cannot err; this circle is bounded between North and South by two grand parallel lines, the one representing Moses, the other King Solomon; on the upper part of the circle rests the Volume of the Sacred Law, which supports Jacob's ladder, the top of which reaches to heaven.

The point within a circle is a remarkable emblem, but let us look first at the circle itself. The circle, having neither beginning nor end, is a symbol of the Deity and of eternity, and it follows that the compasses have been valued as being a means by which that perfect figure may be drawn. Everywhere, and in every age, the circle has been credited with magical properties, and in particular has been thought to protect from external evil everything enclosed within it. Folklore contains countless instances of people, houses, places, threshed corn, etc., being protected by the simple means of describing a circle around them. The innocent child could be placed within a circle, in which it was thought to be safe from any outside malevolent influence. The virtues of the circle were also attributed to the ring, the bracelet, the anklet, and the necklace, which have been worn from earliest times, not only as ornaments, but as a means of protecting the wearer from evil influences.

The completed emblem—the point within a circle—has been borrowed, consciously or otherwise, from some of the earliest of the pagan rites, in which it represented the male and female principles, and came in time to be the symbol of the sun and the universe. Phallic worship was common throughout the ancient world, simple people being naturally inclined to adopt as the foundation of their religion so great a mystery as the generative principle. The symbol came to be regarded as the sign of the divine creative energy. Freemasonry adopted the symbol, and easily gave it a geometrical explanation:

Q. What is a centre?

A. A point within a circle from which every part of the circumference is equidistant.

Q. Why with the centre?

A. That being a point from which [not '*with* which'] a Master Mason cannot err.

The ancient peoples, in giving great religious prominence to phallic emblems, apprehended no wrong in so doing. L. M. Child has said:

> Reverence for the mystery of organized life led to the recognition of a masculine and feminine principle in all things spiritual or material. . . . The active wind was masculine, the passive mist, or inert atmosphere, was feminine. Rocks were masculine, the productive earth was feminine. . . . The sexual emblems conspicuous in the sculptures of ancient temples would seem impure in description, but no clean and thoughtful mind could so regard them. . . . The ancient worshipped the Supreme Being as the Father of men, and saw no impurity in denoting with phallic emblems the kinship of mankind to the Creator.

Some students hold that the point within the circle represented to the ancients the whole scheme of the universe, one point being the individual, or contemplator, and the circle the horizon.

In Jacob Grimm's *Teutonic Mythology* is a revealing note on the Gothic letter ⊙, representing the English letters HV. The letter, the very symbol of the sun, is plainly the shape of a wheel, and is believed to be related to the Gothic word 'HVIL,' the same as the Anglo-Saxon 'HWEOL,' from which is derived the English word 'wheel.' The sun was likened to a wheel of fire, and the "element blazing out of him" was represented in the shape of a wheel. In the twelfth and thirteenth centuries, in France and other countries, there were religious rites at midsummer in which fires were lighted and blazing wheels, representing the sun, were rolled about. This pagan wheel-symbol appears to have been adopted by the Christian Church, as evidence of which we may note

(p. 339) that a foundation-stone of an altar in a French church of 1171 carries five of these wheel devices engraven upon its top face.

There exists the possibility that the point within a circle was brought into freemasonry by the alchemists, to whom the symbol ☉ represented the sun, with which they always associated gold (see page 118).

The Beehive

On old jewels, tracing-boards, lodge furniture, banners, summonses, certificates, etc., the beehive with its flying bees is often a prominent symbol, and in at least one case is to be found in a lodge seal. Carved models of beehives, a few inches high, have a place in one or two old lodges. As far back as 1724–27, a masonic pamphlet, often attributed to Jonathan Swift (1667–1745), speaks at length of the bee and beehive as a symbol, and apparently our eighteenth-century brethren were taught that the beehive is "an emblem of industry recommending the practice of that virtue to all created things, from the highest seraph in heaven to the lowest reptile in the dust." The beehive is present in some lodge emblems and titles. Thus, it is the emblem of the Lodge of Emulation, No. 21, founded in 1723, and has been included since 1778 in the badge of the Lodge of Industry (originally the Lodge at Swalwell); the only lodges known to have used the beehive in their name are two modern ones, Nos. 2809 of London, and 6265 of Cardiff, both of them immediately deriving it from the emblem of a well-known bank, from whose staff they draw their members.

It is not known how the beehive became a masonic emblem, but there is much in the natural history of the bee and in the building of the honeycomb from which to draw inferences of a masonic nature, and we find Shakespeare speaking in *Henry V* of "the singing masons building roofs of gold." The bee has been the symbol of things other than industry; for example, it has been suggested, with what truth we do not know, that the masonic use of the emblem tended to disappear as a result of the Jacobites adopting the bee and beehive as their emblem of immortality and resurrection soon after their reverse in 1745. A convenient and inclusive store of information on the bee and beehive as symbols is G. W. Bullamore's paper on the subject in *A.Q.C.*, vol. xxxvi.

Chapter Twenty-seven

THE ASHLARS AND THE LEWIS
AND THEIR SYMBOLISM

WE are taught as freemasons that the purpose of the chisel is to smooth and prepare the stone for the hands of the more expert craftsmen, and that, as a symbol, it points out the advantages of education, by which means alone we are rendered fit members of regularly organized society William Preston, writing in the 1770's, included discipline with education

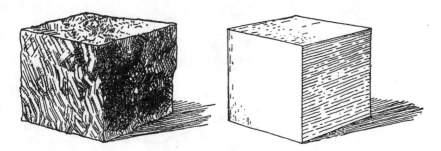

THE ROUGH AND PERFECT ASHLARS

The lessons taught by the chisel are chiefly associated with the two stones known as the rough and perfect ashlars, which have their own respective places in every Craft lodge. The Junior Warden's is the rough ashlar—the axe-trimmed, rude, roughly squared stone, more or less as it comes from the quarry, and symbolizing the natural man, uneducated and unaware of any duty to society. The Senior Warden's (now, but not always in the past, called the perfect ashlar), smooth-surfaced, die-square, and ready to be built into and form part of a sound wall, symbolizes the cultured and educated man, a man having a social conscience. The two ashlars were at one time regarded as two of the immovable jewels of the lodge.

Freemasonry is not alone in going to the true, square stone for a symbol of the fine, upright life. W. B. Hextall has drawn attention to a rare work published in 1563 (reprint, 1912) by Ihon Shute, Paynter and Archytecte, entitled *The First and Chief Grovndes of Architecture,* which offers the injunction, "Ye shall make a foure square stone like unto a dye," and then goes on to narrate the origin and rise of the architectural orders in terms so nearly approaching those of our masonic lectures as to suggest a sixteenth-century source for certain of their passages.

In 1655, in his "Commentary," William Gouge, D.D., wrote: "Unless we be quickned and made living stones fit for a spiritual building; unless we be gathered together and united to Christ the foundation, and one to another, as mutuall parts of the same building, we can never make up a Temple for God to dwell in."

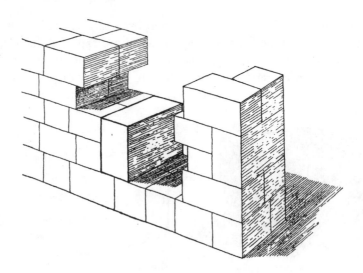

THE PERPEND ASHLAR

This sketch of stone walling indicates (in thicker lines) a true perpend Ashlar, both end faces exposed.

The stones in the walls of the church are spiritualized in a Latin work by Piere de Roissy (twelfth–thirteenth centuries), who thought that the "squared stones signify the squareness of the virtues of the saints. These are Temperance, Justice, Fortitude, and Prudence. The polished stones represent the saints polished by patience in adversity."

To the members of the Royal Order of Scotland, reputed to have been founded in 1314 by King Robert the Bruce, who had been well served by masons who had fought under him at Bannockburn, the perpend ashlar represents "the Great Architect of the Church, who called Himself the 'Rose of Sharon' and the 'Lily of the Valley'" (phrases taken from the Song of Solomon, ii, 1). Such symbolism naturally suggests itself to the thoughtful mind, and must have been attempted times without number.

An ashlar is any wall building stone whose main angles are right angles, but the speculative's ashlar is a cubical stone, although the 'perfect' ashlar originally was probably not cubical but *parpend* (literally, through the wall) or *perpend*, by which names it was known by our early Brethren, who also at times called it the 'perpent,' or 'perpin' ashlar or 'achillar,' the 'perpendester,' etc. A perpend ashlar is a stone much longer than it is wide or deep, and having its ends finished. The stone goes through the wall from *face to face* (it was sometimes called a 'through') and both of its ends are in view and 'perpend'-icular, or vertical. It follows that the perpend ashlar can very seldom be a cubical stone, because its purpose is to lie across the underneath stones and bind them, or key them, together; but, probably as a result of confusion between the terms 'perpend' and 'perfect,' the use of cubic stones has become customary in lodges, and accordingly the old idea of the perpend ashlar must disappear, which is a pity, as it taught the principle of bonding, without which any wall must fail.

The term 'boasted ashlar,' not unknown in lodge working, is but another name for the smooth, or perfect, ashlar, 'boasting' being the dressing of a stone with a broad, fine chisel. There may be confusion between this and the 'broached thurnel,' which was used or pictured in the early lodges, and is still featured on many tracing-boards, as will be described later.

In one of the old lectures the Craftsman or Fellow is entrusted with the erection of the end stones and quoins or corners of the wall, while the Entered Apprentice fills in with the stones between the ends. This happens to be regular practice in high-class walling, both of brick and stone, it being realized that if the ends and corners are not square and upright nothing else can be.

Generally, in the eighteenth-century lodges, ashlars of large size were used, the rough one on the floor in front of the Junior Warden's pedestal, and the perfect one probably, but not always, suspended near the Senior Warden. The custom survives to-day in a few old lodges. The Initiate, in some of the early lodges, is believed to have placed his right foot on the rough ashlar at one part of the ceremony, a custom which might well have reference to the old folklore beliefs associating the virtue of fidelity with certain stones. In 1821, a lodge recorded its thanks for a Brother's "elegant and useful present of a 'step' as a necessary requisite for the Candidate on his Initiation."

J. G. Frazer points out that oaths sworn upon stones in the old superstitious days had a religious character, involving an appeal to a supernatural power which visited transgressors with his anger. He gives instances of many sacred stones, and in one of them a man taking an oath stands so that his heels rest on two of seven such stones. It may be that the old lodge custom of requiring the Candidate to stand with one foot touching, or resting on, the rough ashlar might have a double significance drawn from ancient folklore; not only would the Candidate's fidelity be concerned, but the ashlar would become a symbolic touchstone to make virtue or the lack of it apparent in whoever put his foot upon it, even as the stepping-stone was thought at one time to be a test of chastity for anyone passing over it.

The ancient Danes, when proclaiming their votes in the act of choosing their king, stood on special stones, whose firmness foreshadowed the lasting nature of their deed. A boy in the course of initiation into the Brahman mysteries (J. G. Frazer tells us) put his right foot on a stone, and was exhorted to "Tread on this stone; like a stone be firm."

Why is the perfect ashlar suspended on a derrick? The use of this device, known to go back to at least 1785, and probably much earlier, indicates that the stone is a finished product about to be built into the place for which it has been prepared. Secondly, it affords an opportunity of demonstrating an emblem of strength—the lewis—a form of grapnel by which the hoisting chain is conveniently attached to the stone block, as will later be explained. (In one Australian lodge the degree being worked is indicated by regulating the height of the ashlar above the pedestal.) In old minutes the derrick is sometimes called a triangle.

The placing of the ashlars on the Wardens' pedestals is a matter of custom and convenience only. In a Manchester lodge the ashlars, of fairly large size, lie at the north-east and south-east corners respectively of the tessellated pavement. In certain of the Bristol lodges they are placed on a low table which also supports the tracing-boards, and in this position it is said that "they are used by Apprentices and Fellow-crafts for testing the accuracy of their working tools," for which use, it is suggested, there is authority in the ancient working. A perfect ashlar might lend itself as a standard for the testing of the wooden square, level, and plumb-rule, which by constant application to stone would wear away and become untrue; but there is not much in that old speculative idea, for metal squares must have been in use for thousands of years, and, in any case, every craftsman would be aware of far easier and much more satisfactory tests based on the simple reversal of the square or other implement.

The Broached Thurnel

If we look at very early French tracing-boards, and even at some English ones too, we find a picture of a pointed, cubical stone, not unlike a squat church tower, with sometimes a little axe shown as having been forced into the pointed part, or pyramid. A catechism of about the same period refers to it:

Q. What are the immoveable Jewels?
A. Trasel Board, Rough Ashlar, and Broached Thurnel.
Q. What are their uses?
A. A Trasel Board for the Master to draw his Designs upon, the Rough
Ashlar for the Fellow-Craft to try their Jewels upon, and the Broached
Thurnel for the Entr'd 'Prentice to learn to work upon.

Apparently the place taken by that old pointed stone is now occupied
by the perfect ashlar. It was a shaped stone of good surface, demonstrating the form taken by a rough ashlar once it had been broached
(worked) and finished, in this case to the form of a squat spire or some
simple form of terminal; and perhaps the reader will be surprised to know
that it has caused a considerable amount of argument, much of which
has tended to make confusion worse confounded.

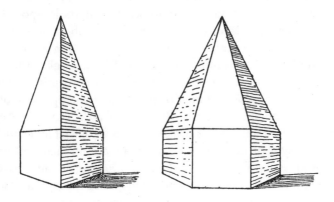

BROACHED THURNELS

The left-hand figure shows the French *pierre cubique à pointe*,
often represented with axe or hatchet driven into the pointed part.

This pointed stone had many different names—broached thurnel,
thurnal, thurmer, or turner; broached dornal or dornel; broached mal or
brohed-mal; broad ovall; etc. Minutes of a lodge in 1753 refer to it as
"the broach and trunell." Another group of names includes broached
ornel, ornell, urnell, urnall, and ovall; and there is always the possibility
that the broached, or boasted, ashlar may sometimes refer to the same
thing. It is obvious, then, that there was great confusion in the minds
of the early Brethren as to the name and the purpose of the pointed stone.
Some of the confusion is in consequence of the early French tracing-
boards depicting a little axe, like an Indian tomahawk or Roman hatchet,
driven into the stone pyramid, much as an axe could be driven into a
block of wood and there gripped in the cleft it had made. A tomahawk

would be smashed to fragments were it used with enough force to cleave the stone, and in any case no possible cleft could be made by it in which the axe would be retained. Any symbolism based upon such cleaving of the pointed stone is sheer waste of time.

Many authors have sought to show that the broached thurnel represents a stone spire; for this they go back to the ancient 'broch' or 'broach' referred to on a later page (p. 420), while they derive 'thurnel' from *tourelle*, French for 'turret;' although the French freemasons themselves knew the stone chiefly as *la pierre cubique à pointe*, 'pointed square stone.' They follow this up by stating that the stone, being a model of a broached spire, or turret, offers itself in its various outlines as a means of teaching the Apprentice the forms of the square, triangle, cube, and pyramid! They sadly underrate an Apprentice's intelligence.

Some of the old irregular prints of the eighteenth century said its purpose was for the "brother-craft to whet their tools upon it," but whoever invented that explanation knew nothing about masons' tools. The whetting, or rather sharpening, of a mason's tools might be a matter of heavy grinding, but it is often an anvil job for the blacksmith.

Then there is a suggestion that 'thurnel' is a corruption of 'ornel,' 'ornall,' 'urnall,' or 'urnell,' a kind of soft white building-stone of Kent. The word 'urnell' figures in the Rochester Castle Building Account, 1368, and there are references to ornall stone in an official letter addressed to the Lord Mayor of London in 1509–10 and also in many contracts of earlier date given in Salzman's *Building in England*; it must have been largely local, for had it been a common trade-word throughout medieval days we should surely have hundreds of references to it in books and manuscripts. But to criticize negatively does not help much. Frankly, no one knows how the pointed cubical stone got its name. We can reasonably assume that 'broached' meant 'cut' or 'shaped' or 'worked' (a pointed chisel used in cutting stone is sometimes called a broach), and the Kentish urnell may be the second word, in which case the name means simply 'worked stone.' The shape of the stone suggests that of a terminal, but we may well hesitate to say that 'broached terminal'—a worked, or shaped, terminal—is the true explanation.

The Lewis

The stonemason's lewis is a device used in raising and lowering stone blocks in the course of building, as exemplified by the smooth ashlar in the derrick on the Senior Warden's pedestal. The Romans in their day are thought to have used it in the building of the Flavian Amphitheatre, and the Saxons in the building of Whitby Abbey in the seventh century. There is ground for believing that the device was employed in putting into place some of the more massive stones of Hadrian's Wall or Roman Wall (A.D. 120–209), for what appear to have been lewis holes can still be seen in parts built by the Roman Emperor Severus, who heavily repaired the wall in A.D. 209.

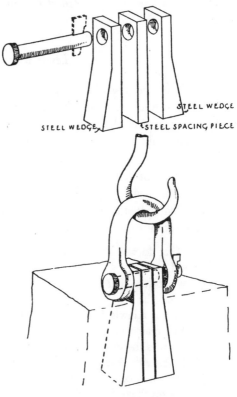

Statements that the lewis derived its name because it was used by an architect in the service of Louis XIV are wide of the mark. Documents of the years 1352, 1357, and 1368, reproduced in L. F. Salzman's book just mentioned, give the word lewis in some of its early forms (lowys, lowettis, lussis) while a six-teenth-century drawing in the same book shows a lifting-rope attached to a stone by means of the lewis.

The stonemason's lewis is a grapnel, for which a spe-cially shaped socket needs to be cut in the top face of the block of hard, strong stone that is to be lifted. (A lewis might break away in a heavy block of soft stone.) Two opposite sides or ends of the socket are undercut, *not all four* as often pictured. Two projecting wedge-shaped,

THE LEWIS

Above: the steel wedges, spacer, and bolt; *below:* a cut-away view showing the Lewis in position ready for raising or lowering the stone block.

tapered steel keys are introduced into the socket, and between them is inserted a parallel steel spacer, which spreads the wedges into the undercut parts; then a shackle-pin, or bolt, is passed through the upper extensions of all three, and provides a hold for the lifting chain. The illustration clearly shows how the device works.

The precise purpose of the lewis is to allow the hoisting chain of the derrick, or crane, to raise the stone and then lower it into its exact, final position in the wall, which could not be effected if chains or ropes passed underneath the stone. When the stone is in its exact place, the shackle-bolt is removed, thus allowing the spacing piece to be withdrawn, and then the two wedges.

Somebody has written that the lewis enables the operative "to lift the heaviest stones with a comparatively trifling expenditure of physical power," but this is a complete misconception, the lewis being nothing more than a convenient method of attaching the hoisting chain to the stone.

The Lewis as a Symbol

Obviously the lewis is an appropriate symbol of strength—a double symbol, inasmuch as its name has been given to the son of a mason, his duty being to bear the burden and heat of the day that his parents may rest in their old age, thus rendering the evening of their lives peaceful and happy. This double symbolism is mentioned in some old catechisms, but the usual Craft ritual does not refer to it, although the device has a place in Mark masonry. The American Craft system, except for the State of Pennsylvania, does not know it. From a late-eighteenth-century catechism comes the following:

Q. What do we call the son of a Freemason?
A. A Lewis.
Q. What does that denote?
A. Strength.
Q. How is a lewis depicted in a Mason's lodge?
A. As a cramp of metal (*etc.*).
Q. What is the duty of a lewis . . . to his aged parents?
A. To bear the heavy burden (*etc., etc.*) so as to render the close of their days happy and comfortable.
Q. His privilege for so doing?
A. To be made a Mason before any other person, however dignified by birth, rank, or riches, unless he, through complaisance, waives this privilege.

There is good ground for believing that the lewis originally was the first son born to a man after that man had become a freemason.

Apparently the lewis was used as a subject for moralizing in the eighteenth-century lodges, for the minutes of St Paul's Lodge, now No. 43, of Birmingham, report the offer "of a very curious and valuable triangle, perfect ashlar and luis, but it being refused as a present, it was unanimously agreed to pay £2 2 0 as a small compensation for same." We find the lewis keys depicted on a pierced silver jewel of about 1760, and they are a feature of the curious old engraving (see Plate XXII) in which the hands of the effigy are the lewis keys, while a smooth ashlar fitted with a lewis bolt rests on the square pavements.

The curious fable of how Hiram Abif attained the privilege of being a lewis is recounted in an earlier section dealing with the Hiramic tradition.

The Son of a Mason

How did 'lewis' come to mean the 'son of a mason'? It does not answer the question to say that the device supplied the name, and inevitably suggested the symbol, because the device itself appears to have gone out of use in the English operative craft, and it is difficult to find mention of the word lewis in early eighteenth-century print. In France the device was known in 1676, in which year it is to be found in an architectural work, but not by that name. Mason members of the well-known French fraternity, the Compagnonnage, used it and called it a 'louve,' possibly because a *louve* is a 'she-wolf,' and the grip of the lewis might be likened to the grip of a wolf's fangs. In course of time the device came to be known as a *louveton*, and had a plural form *louveteaux*, or, more probably, the steel wedges came to be known as *louveteaux*, the literal meaning of which is 'male wolf cubs.' The Compagnonnage, being a trade fraternity, with liabilities to its members in their days of sickness and old age, extended its charitable care to the orphan sons of its mason members; these boys came to be known as *louveteaux*—wolf cubs. Thus by this time the French masons had arrived at a ready-made symbol, which English speculative masonry adopted; but, in spite of all the learned research that has been applied to the subject, we do not know how or when the word *louveteaux* became 'lewis,' *if it ever did*.

Any readers keen enough to follow up the matter should study the later pages of *The Wilkinson Manuscript*, edited by Douglas Knoop, G. P. Jones, and Douglas Hamer, with the assistance of many skilled colleagues. This pamphlet, which contains the most serious attempt so far made to explain how the English word 'lewis' was derived, dwells upon the possibility of a natural development from the French words above given. But, with all deference to the above authorities, a digression must now be made to consider the possibility of a rather different theory.

At one time in some districts of Scotland an ex-apprentice who failed to gain admission into the fraternity was known as a 'lewis,' or 'lose,' or 'loss'; the difference between him and the cowan, if there was any at all, could hardly have been worth mentioning. The Harris MS. No. 1, dating to the second half of the seventeenth century, insists that "You shall not make any Mold, Square, or Rule for any that is but a Lewis; a Lewis is such an one as hath served an Apprenticeship to a Mason but is not admitted afterwards according to this manner and Custom of makeing Masons." Naturally, the unfortunate lewis, or cowan-lewis, might have been, and probably was, the son of a mason. Who knows? But he had ceased to be an *honoured* son, although the fault was not necessarily in him but quite possibly in the trade system.

The present writer's conjecture is that Anderson, on behalf of the English speculatives, took the emblem from the French. In his hands *louveton* and *louveteaux* became 'lewis'; the 'male wolf cub' became the 'eldest son of a mason'; but, whereas the cub had received its sustenance from the fraternity, the lewis was now expected to sustain his parents. The fact that the original lewis was not certainly a mason's son would not worry him. By uniting the French emblem with a Scottish term, and garbling both of them, Anderson was able to give the speculatives a new and attractive symbol, and ultimately to introduce—more correctly, re-introduce—to the English operatives a mechanical device whose purpose was new to most of them, and whose name may have been new to them all.

Then came a stroke of fortune! A child was about to be born to her Serene Highness Augusta, the wife of Frederick, Prince of Wales, who was initiated into masonry on November 5, 1737. There was in existence at the time "The Deputy Grand Master's Song," and on the occasion of the Prince being made a mason Bro. Gofton added this special stanza to it:

> Again let it [*the bumper*] pass to the ROYAL lov'd NAME,
> Whose glorious Admission has crown'd all our Fame:
> May a LEWIS be born, whom the World shall admire,
> Serene as his Mother, August as his Sire.

We can safely draw the inference that Gofton knew of the lewis as a masonic symbol, and was perpetrating a pun, and a particularly good one, too, bearing in mind that the Prince of Wales's second name was Lewis. Equally safely, we can conclude that the use of the word in Gofton's verse fastened itself upon the imagination of the Brethren in those rather obsequious days, and did more than anything else could have done to make the emblem popular in the Craft. Anderson, in preparing his *Constitutions* of 1738, embodied the new verse and chorus, the latter in slightly edited form.

This conjecture may contain an error which time will reveal, but meanwhile the likelihood must not be overlooked that a Scots term of reproach, applied to an unfortunate apprentice, has been promoted to be a term of honour. Cowans, loses, and lewises—all in the classes of inferiority! What an ironical position if it should prove that the speculatives' honoured lewis—the support of his father, the hoisting key that never fails to grip the stone—is only one variety of the poor old operative cowan!

A Lewis's Privileges

Although the name 'lewis' was not well known in England until late 1730's, it does not follow that there was anything new in the privileges which came to be afforded to the eldest son of a mason. In the Aberdeen operative lodge in the seventeenth century a member's eldest son, or the husband of his eldest daughter, was excused on entry from the need to make the customary gift of apron and gloves to every member, and there was a custom in the old guilds for a Master's eldest son to have his passage into the fraternity eased by the reduction or remission of fees. That benefit does not apply in English speculative masonry, where the lewis's privilege amounts to nothing more than that of being entitled by custom, and not by rule, to be initiated before any other Candidate under consideration at the time; whereas, in the Scottish system, there is a rule by which "sons of Master Masons under Grand Lodge" may be initiated at the age of eighteen, and a custom in some lodges allowing reduced fees. The English custom is not without a few exceptions, as in Anchor and Hope Lodge, Bolton, No. 37, where the lewis is admitted at a reduced fee.

Lewisa!

Readers may smile at the way in which the word 'lewis' has been bestowed on a mason's daughter. For example, the minutes of the old lodge meeting in 1739 at the Turk's Head, Fleet Street (it is now No. 20), record: "Our Brother Delarant presented the lodge with a bowl of punch on his having a Lewisa born, and her health was drunk in form." Apparently, too, in some rituals of about 1770 there was this toast: "To all our royal and loyal, great and little Lewises wherever dispersed, not forgetting the Luisas."

Chapter Twenty-eight

THE COWAN

The cowan, known in some old documents as a 'cowener,' 'kirkwan,' or 'couan,' is the most misunderstood of all the individuals mentioned in the masonic ritual. The word comes straight from Scots operative masonry of the late sixteenth century, and almost certainly was not used in England until after 1738, in which year Anderson introduced it into his *Constitutions*.

Actually there are two cowans: the real one, the old Scots operative; and the lay figure known to the speculative mason. They have but one thing in common, their place *outside* the fraternity.

Books of reference tell us that the cowan is a dry-dyker—that is, a builder of boundary walls in which the stones keep in position by their own weight, without the help of mortar. But the cowan was much more than that. Some of the books suggest that he was only half a craftsman, or no craftsman at all; but all, or almost all, they know about the cowan has been derived from masonic rituals, so that when we go to such books for enlightenment we merely end where we start.

Even if the cowan was only a builder of 'dry' walls, it does not follow that he was not possessed of considerable skill. Throughout Scotland we find the broch, a tower of native design, built twenty centuries ago of rough, square mortarless stones held together by their own weight. The walls are concentric, the inner ones being perpendicular and the outer ones bell-shaped. The broch must have been built by men of the cowan class, and those men must have been highly skilled, both as builders and as rude architects. No mere labourer could have done their work, for, as Findlay Muirhead says, "The broch is indeed a triumph of thought and skill in the art of dry-stone building, a marvel in the use of intractable material."

How is the Word derived?

There is grim humour in contemplating the fancy derivations of the word 'cowan' given in works of reference. Jamieson's *Dictionary of the Scottish Language* says that the word is derived from the French *coion*, a 'base fellow,' a 'dastardly wretch'; but this is the merest nonsense. The cowan was a humble fellow but, as a class, no more dastardly than others.

Somebody has suggested that the word comes from a Greek word meaning 'I listen'; but the cowan wasn't a 'listener,' and, if he had been, would the Scots mason have troubled the Greek tongue for an appropriate word to fit him?

Another Greek word, this time meaning 'a dog,' has been put forward many times, but the Scots have plenty of words for dogs, not all of them polite, and not until 1738, and then in England, do we get any suggestion that the cowan was of the breed. *Chaoun,* a 'screech owl'; *kajon,* a 'silly fellow'; *coglione,* a 'contemptible person'; these are but nonsense, and suggest that the dictionary-maker, puzzled by a word hardly known outside speculative masonry, had regard to its modern connotations and supplied a derivation to fit the case!

Curiously, there is a word 'cownand,' meaning 'the time covenanted for,' in which sense it is used in a very early medieval guild document relating to the Free Sewers (pronounced 'so-ers'), who were licensed workpeople employed by the Exeter Guild of Tailors. Some writers have tried to show that 'cowan' is a form of that word, but where is the connexion between the idea of covenant and the cowan, an individual who, in general, was not thought worthy of entering into a covenant, in the sense in which freemasons understand the word?

There happens to be a Scots word 'cowan' meaning 'boat'; so somebody else has been at pains to show that the word 'cowan' really means 'something different from square, that is, round or hollow,' and so he argues that a cowan is a *hollow* builder, a man who builds with unsquared stones; but such an explanation will not do. The builders of the ancient broches knew as much about square stones and square building as anybody, and the cowan of later days frequently did skilled work under licence of the mason fraternities.

We may begin to suspect that perhaps there is no proper etymological derivation of the word, but—to be in the fashion and make a suggestion —what is the matter with *quoin* (French for 'corner'), a true architectural term meaning 'corner-stone'? Admittedly it completely fails to agree with the modern conception of the cowan, but it is quite as near the mark as any other, for the corner-stones in dry dykes have to be most carefully chosen and placed.

Is it beyond all possibility that the word 'cowan' first came into the records by mistake or by accident? Is it not astonishing that, if the old-time Scots word for a dry-dyker and small country mason was really 'cowan,' we can nowhere find the history of the word, and must rely for information chiefly upon the literature of freemasonry, to which the word was wholly foreign until the end of the sixteenth century?

Who, and What, was a Cowan?

Judging from old records cowans were operatives who were permitted to do much of the less skilled work of the regular mason, who was thus left free for tasks of a higher order. The cowan was a type of workman who, in general, had learned his trade in a manner regarded by the fraternity as irregular. For example, he may have started as a labourer, or he may have been an apprentice who had failed to serve his full time. In a great many cases he was probably a country craftsman, who, when he moved to the town in search of work, was not allowed to affiliate with the fraternity, and had to be content with any class of work that fell to his portion. The stringent rules under which he was employed were designed to prevent his acquiring either the full craftsman's skill or any technological understanding of his craft.

It has often been said that a cowan is 'a mason without the word,' a definition put forward on the strength of a minute of Mother Kilwinning Lodge in 1707. Actually, that minute says: "No Meason shall employ no cowan which is to say [a Mason] without the word to work." This has been generally taken to mean that a cowan was a man who did the work of a mason, but because he has not been regularly approved or bred to the trade he had been denied a secret word—a word of recognition— the communication of which would have brought him into fellowship with the members of the Fraternity.

But the Mother Kilwinning minute is open also to the interpretation that a cowan could, on occasion, be given "the word to work." With that word we must assume that the cowan automatically and irrevocably became a mason.

The earliest record of apprenticeship in Scotland is 1466 (later than in England), and the cowan, whether so called or not, must go back to somewhere about that date. In the records of Scots operative lodges we find the word 'cowan' first mentioned in 1599. Two building accounts mention him—those for Edinburgh Castle in 1616 and 1626. The stress in Scots operative masonry laid on the economic connexion between the cowan and the Mason Word has already been explained. He was a product of peculiar trade conditions. (See p. 124.) The 'word' was communicated to the trained mason to ensure his being able to prove himself in any company of masons. Douglas Knoop thinks that the real reason for establishing that word was to prevent the cowan from doing the work of the trained regular mason.

The vocation, or calling, of the stonemason was common and wide-spread in Scotland owing to stone being almost everywhere available, but this condition was a constant menace to the craft organizations that had arisen in the towns, and which feared—and sometimes suffered—a swamping of their labour-market by an inrush of country masons. Accordingly, in course of time, those organizations introduced restrictions on the employment of outside labour, and safeguarded their restrictions with the Mason Word, either by bringing it into existence, or possibly by borrowing it from England.

The Schaw Statutes of 1598 and 1599 prohibited any Master or Fellow of Craft receiving any cowans to work in his Society or Company "nor send any of his servants to work with cowans under the pain of £20 so oft as any person offends hereuntil." Operative lodges had similar restrictions. A minute of the Lodge of Edinburgh (Mary's Chapel), 1599, remitting punishment in the case of a mason who had employed a cowan (ane cowane) to work at a chimney, provided that hereafter "the law sall stryke upon thame Indiscreta wtout exception of psonis."

The Lodge of Kilwinning allowed cowans to be employed by Master Masons for any kind of work when no regular craftsmen could be found within fifteen miles. Could there be clearer proof that the cowan's *status* was in question, not his *skill*? Much further evidence of the kind could be quoted. However, it must be said that not everywhere in Scotland was the cowan excluded from membership of a fraternity, for in 1668 John Syme (or Sim) was admitted to the Cannongate Lodge, the minute describing him as "an honest old man and cowaner." Very much later, in 1797, a stone-dyker was admitted to the Stonehaven Lodge as a regularly entered apprentice, there being in this lodge, at one and the same time, operative masons, speculative masons, and *one* cowan.

There were grades of cowans, but not always so called. When the cowan was a mason who had been irregularly apprenticed, he was in some districts called a 'lose,' a word either then or at a later date having a derogatory meaning. Loses were not allowed to know "the privilege of the compass, square, level and plumbrule."

Another type of cowan was the ex-apprentice who, for some fault, his own or his master's, was not admitted to the fraternity; he is most curiously described in Dumfries No. 3 MS. as a 'lewis,' and, as Douglas Knoop reminds us, a mason or fellow was not allowed to "make any mould, square or rule for any who is but a lewis," thus denying him all chance of learning the technical side of his calling. A 'mould' is a pattern or template by means of which an outline is transferred or checked.

What the Speculatives have made of the Cowan

The cowan's first appearance in the official literature of speculative freemasonry is in Anderson's official *Constitutions* of 1738, where it is laid down that "free and accepted Masons shall not allow cowans to work with them; nor shall they be employed by cowans without an urgent necessity, and even in that case they must not teach cowans, but must have a separate communication." Every line of this particular clause breathes the spirit of Scots operative masonry.

The speculative Craft had already seized on to the word and made it a part of lodge ritual. It is found in a manuscript prayer composed by Thomas Cooke and inserted into a copy of *Smith's Pocket Companion* (Dublin, 1735). It was probably written within a decade or so of 1738: "Direct us, O Lord by Thy most Gracious Favour, and grant that we by our lives and actions may convince all Cowans of the faith that is in us, that thereby the Craft may be more honoured."

In an early ritual not only the Entered Apprentice, but also the Fellow Craft, heard about the cowan. In reply to the question in an old catechism, "How high was the door of the middle chamber?" came the reply, "So high that a cowan could not reach to stick a pin in."

To the early speculatives the cowan was an eavesdropper. Indeed, freemasonry in the eighteenth century contributed 'cowan' to the language of slang, in which he became a 'sneak,' a 'nosy-parker'; but as a slang term it was not long-lived. Any man not a mason was a cowan in the middle of the eighteenth century (say the irregular prints of the day), and a Brother might indicate the approach of a cowan by remarking "It rains" or, in the case of a woman, "It snows." Such terms hark back to an alleged practice of punishing an eavesdropper in the manner that fitted the crime, as witness this old catechism, dated 1730:

Q. Where stands the Junior Entr'ed 'Prentice?
A. In the North.
Q. What is his business?
A. To keep off all cowans and Eves-droppers.
Q. If a Cowan (or Listner) is catched, how is he to be punished?
A. To be placed under the Eves of the House (in rainy Weather) till the water runs in at his shoulders, and out at his shoes.

The eavesdropper got his name by lurking within the 'eves-drop' (the space between the house-wall and the line where the rain-water falls from the eaves), that he might listen to the conversation inside the house, or by hiding in the 'eves-drip' (the uncultivated margin of the field, in Saxon times), that he might overhear what was said in the adjoining field or house. "Under our tents I'll play the eavesdropper."[1]

In the Preston Guild and Borough Records of 1661 is this reference to an eavesdropper, Thomas Silcocke by name:

[1] *Richard III*, Act V, Scene 3.

He is an Eve dropp, commonly called Eseing dropps, and stands undr mens windows lisoning and carrieing stories betwixt neighbour and neighbour, to the great disquietnes of neighbours an to the evell example of others therefore to pay xiijs. iiijd.

We see the cowan, then, not only as an outsider in old-time Scots masonry, but sadly libelled by the speculative to-day. We should use the word for one who is not a mason but, having regard to history, certainly not as a term of opprobrium or reproach.

Chapter Twenty-nine

SYMBOLISM—AND THE WORKING TOOLS

A SYMBOL, literally, is two things thrown together; one of them stands for or calls to mind a moral or spiritual truth. The symbol is an emblem, a figure, a type, a representation.

An emblem was originally an ornament, but it has come to mean a symbol. Learned writers speak of the confusion between the two, but one has much the meaning of the other in the language of to-day. The use of emblems under which the truths of Christianity were veiled from the heathen, but presented vividly to the minds of the faithful, is probably as old as Christianity itself.

The Initiate learns that freemasonry is a peculiar system of morality veiled in allegory and illustrated by symbols. Allegory has much the same meaning as parable. We may call it a word-figure having two meanings, one literal and the other spiritual.

The language of freemasonry is often the language of metaphor, which is a figure of speech implying a comparison; the metaphor is not a literal thing, and its meaning may border on that of the symbol.

Symbolism in Early Religious Teaching

The first learning of the world, we are told, was chiefly in symbols, and the wisdom of the ancient peoples was largely symbolic. All religious systems, right back to the dawn of history, taught their devotees by means of symbols, as witness some of the symbols associated with the Christian religion, but known still earlier to the ancient Egyptians, Assyrians, Greeks, etc. Symbols were a part of man's most primitive religious ideas, often meaning everything to the Initiate and nothing to anybody else. "In a symbol there is concealment but yet revelation," says Thomas Carlyle, "silence and speech acting together, the infinite blending with the finite."

There is much symbolism on the masonic pattern in a book by Durandus (a bishop who died in 1296), first printed in 1459 and re-printed nearly thirty times by the end of the following century. Durandus refers in the following quotation (abbreviated) to the

> winding staircases, imitated from Solomon's Temple, which wind among
> the walls and point out the hidden knowledge which they only have who

ascend to celestial things. The Faithful are the stones in the wall structure. All the stones are polished and squared, that is holy and pure, and are built by the hands of the Great Workman into an abiding place in the church. . . . Again, in the Temple of God, the foundation is Faith, which is conversant with unseen things: the roof is charity, which covereth a multitude of sins. The door is obedience. . . . The pavement is humility, of which the Psalmist saith, "My Soul cleaveth to the pavement." The four sides, walls, are the four cardinal virtues—justice, fortitude, temperance, prudence. Hence the Apocalypse saith, "The city lieth four-square."

Roughly a century after the book by Durandus was printed we have Bishop Coverdale's translation of Otto Werdmuller's *A Spiritual and Most Precious Pearl*, in which again we find some apt masonic symbolism (the inspiration of which is to be found in I Peter ii, 1–5):

> The free mason hewyth the harde stones, and hewyth off, here one pece, and there another, tyll the stones be fytte and apte for the place where he wyll laye them. Euen so God the heavenly free mason, buildeth a Christen churche, and he frameth and polyseth us, which are the costlye and precyous stones, wyth the crosse and affliccyon, that all abhomynacyon and wicked-ness which do not agree unto thys gloryous buyldynge, myghte be remoued & taken out of the waye.

Symbolism has long been closely associated with religious personages. Scores or hundreds of saints have their own symbols—ranging from a pot of ointment for St Mary Magdalene to a hive of bees for St Bernard; from shoemaker's tools for St Crispin to a builder's rule for St Thomas. A dove with olive branch in its beak is the symbol of Noah. The kingly figure standing under an arch is the symbol for King Solomon. The Early Christians are believed to have used symbols—a fish, dove, etc., engraved on their rings and seals—as a means of revealing their faith to fellow Christians without betraying themselves to their persecutors. (Both fish and dove have been used as masonic symbols.)

Masonic Symbolism

Although the medieval church taught with symbols, little of that method is echoed in the Old Charges of masonry. Douglas Knoop says:

> In a century in which allegorical interpretation of the Scriptures was com-monly practised, as is shown, for example, by the publication in 1688 of John Bunyan's *Solomon's Temple Spiritualised*, it would not be surprising to find that the use of allegory was introduced into freemasonry at that period.

But he further says that symbolism, which suffered a temporary eclipse following the Reformation but was being made use of by the Anglicans before the end of the sixteenth century, and by the Puritans somewhat later, came to be generally regarded with favour in the seventeenth century, and it is therefore easy to understand why its use might have been adopted by speculative masons in teaching the principles for which freemasonry stood.

It is a commonplace that few things are as indestructible as a symbol; that few things, too, have so many interpretations; and that, while it is difficult to destroy a symbol, it is often all too easy to alter and debase its meaning. It is unfortunate that masonic symbolism lends itself to the fertile invention of hosts of writers, who, as W. H. Rylands puts it, "guided by no sort of system and ruled only by their own sweet will, love to allow their fancies and imaginations to run wild." G. W. Speth has said it is a

> curious fact that most writers on freemasonry seem to begin with symbolism and think themselves competent to discuss its many involved problems without any historical knowledge worth speaking of. . . . Masonic symbology cannot be studied by itself; we cannot begin to understand it until we are fairly acquainted with the symbology of past and present civilisations. The books which may profitably be consulted are infinite in number and written in every tongue.

We speak of the Craft degrees of freemasonry as being the 'symbolic' degrees, a term said to be of French derivation, and certainly much used in French freemasonry in the early 1700's. A lodge opened in any one of those three degrees is a 'symbolic' lodge.

Freemasons are not the only craftsmen who have moralized over their tools and work. The cobbler and the carpenter are known to have indulged in this way, and undoubtedly many other crafts have done the same. But the masons have the advantage that they patiently build, stone by stone and in the view of all men, edifices that stand for centuries, and also that the moralizing and symbolizing so naturally inspired by such work and by the tools they use are within the comprehension of everybody. Thus, we find the compasses referred to as a symbol in the Books of Proverbs and of Isaiah, the idea of building square and true is a commonplace in the books of the Bible, and the plummet and the plumb-line are often mentioned symbolically in those ancient writings. The square, the compasses, the level, and the plumb-rule—civilized people have grown up with the symbolism attaching to these things, a symbolism which speculative masonry now preserves and teaches.

The Speculative's Working Tools

It is frequently assumed that the working tools associated with the three symbolic degrees represent the tools used respectively by Apprentices, Fellow Crafts, and Master Masons in operative work, but actually they are an arbitrary or conventional choice, for at no time could an apprentice have been limited to the use of a few simple tools, and the craftsman to one or two more. The apprentice mason learns to use a whole range of tools—axes, hammers and mauls, chisels, compasses, calipers and gauges, squares and bevels, rasps and scrapers, and all other tools that may be necessary in converting rough stones into fashioned and finished pieces. The mason who builds them up into the wall, whatever his grade, must have lines, levels, plumb-rules, trowels, hammers, etc., to enable him to work true and square on a foundation that has been meticulously set out by a master or foreman necessarily provided with all proper implements, not particularly those referred to in the ritual. It follows, then, that some of the speculative explanations must not be taken too literally.

It is possible that masonic writers have sometimes been misled by passages in the Old Charges restricting the use of certain tools to the lawful apprentice. We catch an illuminating glimpse of an old trade custom when we find these manuscripts forbidding "ye priviledge of ye compass, square, levele and ye plumrule" to unlawfully taken apprentices. This restriction was nothing more than a means of withholding what we should now call technical instruction. By keeping the geometric tools out of their hands, the labouring men and the masons who had entered the trade in some irregular way were denied any opportunity of acquiring or increasing any theoretical knowledge, thus making it very difficult for them to rise from their lowly condition. There was strong insistence on this point in the old days, and many echoes of it survive to-day in the practices of the manual trades.

It does not follow that all the working tools with which the speculative mason is now familiar have always been those recognized by the Craft. Many of the earliest breast jewels known—of the 1760 period—depict the square, level, plumb-rule, compasses, the 24-inch gauge, and heavy maul and the trowel. The square, level, and plumb-rule are mentioned in Prichard's *Masonry Dissected* (1730), and there is a veiled reference to the compasses. The ashlar is mentioned, but not the chisel, while the setting maul is referred to as the "tool with which our Master was slain." An irregular print of 1726 mentions the hammer and trowel.

The tools now associated with the three Craft degrees, and well known to every freemason, do in some purely conventional and over-simplified way associate themselves with the three grades of mason. Thus the Entered Apprentice uses the 24-inch gauge, the gavel, and the chisel; the Fellow Craft the square, level, and plumb-rule; and the Master Mason the skirret, pencil, and the compasses. Into this arrangement the trowel does not enter, but undoubtedly in the quite early symbolic or speculative lodges it had a considerable place, as will be explained later in this chapter.

The pencil, it suffices to say, teaches us, according to masonic ritual, that our words and actions are observed and recorded by the Almighty Architect, to whom we must give an account of our conduct through life. Each of the other tools demands its own special and more lengthy treatment.

The 24-inch Gauge, Gavels, Mauls, and Chisel

In Isaiah xliv, 13 (Revised Version), we read that the

carpenter stretcheth out a line; he marketh it out with a pencil; he shapeth it with planes, and he marketh it out with the compasses, and shapeth it after the figure of a man, according to the beauty of a man; to dwell in the house.

In Ezekiel xl and xlii mention is made of the 'measuring reed' (or measuring rod). Such a rod, rule, or gauge, however marked or graduated, is a tool going back into antiquity, a gauge graduated in inches being actually an old English measure. The English word 'inch' originally meant a twelfth part—that is, the twelfth part of a foot. The 24-inch gauge symbolizes the twenty-four hours of the day, and is therefore a symbol of the passage of time and, in particular, of time well spent.

The gavel, actually the iron axe, or pick, having a steel edge, or point, with which the quarryman roughly trims the stone, represents the force of conscience. The form of gavel adopted for the speculative's convenience is a wooden mallet, itself a small form of the maul (*maul-ette*). A chairman's mallet, as well as the Master's gavel, is a wooden hammer whose outline suggests that of the operative's axe, but also resembles the end-wall of a gabled house, for which latter reason it is said—but whether truthfully or not we do not know—it derives its name of gavel, a name apparently of American origin, and not known in England before the nineteenth century.

The uses of gavel and maul are frequently confused. The gavel, the implement of both the Master and his Wardens, is an emblem of power, by means of which they preserve order in the lodge; but the maul is the heavy wooden hammer with which the mason drives his chisel. Being the weapon with which the Master was traditionally slain, it is an emblem of violent death and assassination. In Proverbs xxv, 18, we find this curious figure of speech: "A man that beareth false witness against his neighbour is a maul, and a sword, and a sharp arrow." In many lodges the gavel is used by the Master at a significant point in the third ceremony where the correct implement is the heavy maul, which was used in the early English lodges and is still used in some lodges to-day.

In the Fabric Rolls of York Minster of 1360 a type of maul, or mell, is called a keevil. The word must have long continued in use, because we find it in a published description, dated 1791, of how stones for the Eddystone lighthouse were worked.

Both gavel and maul have been commonly known as a 'Hiram.' The Old Dundee Lodge bought in 1739 a set of three 'Hirams,' and we believe that in the old Bristol lodges the maul is presented under the name of the 'Hiram' to the incoming Master. The name is explained by associating Hiram's direction of the work of building the Temple with the Master's direction of the work of the lodge; but it seems more likely that the name derives from the use of the maul for its peculiar purpose in the Third Degree. The present writer has seen a particularly heavy-looking maul put to realistic work in an American lodge, and it can well be imagined that some of the old English lodges knew how to use such a tool with tremendous effect, particularly if judged from a schedule of the property of the Orthes Lodge (a military lodge moribund from about 1869) which included "a heavy maul, padded; handle, 3 feet; top, 1 foot." This was more beetle than maul.

An unusual setting maul of T shape in ceremonious use in an old Bristol lodge (it is shown in *A.Q.C.*, xlix, a plate following p. 168) has a short handle, but its double head is much longer than the total length of the handle, and each of the two striking parts is of padded leather secured by brass-headed nails to the turned-wood foundation—altogether a remarkably 'arresting' tool.

The chisel can be properly considered only in relation to the ashlars, and the reader is referred to Chapter XXIV, in which the two ashlars are discussed and their symbolism explained.

The Square

Freemasons know two squares; one is the square angle, the other the implement.

The geometric square is defined in our ritual as an angle of 90 degrees, or the fourth part of a circle. This means that, by cutting a circle into four equal parts (quadrants) by means of two lines intersecting each other at the centre, each of the four angles so formed is of 90 degrees—that is, each of them is a right angle, a square angle.

The implement known as a square has two arms of wood or metal united in the form of a right angle, and is used in setting out and testing work. The square is one of the most important tools used by creative craftsmen, notably workers in stone, wood, and metal, and its use is closely associated with that of the line, the level, and the plumb-rule. It is of great antiquity. It might be thought that the ancient peoples would not know the geometrical principles on which the square is constructed.

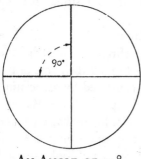

AN ANGLE OF 90°, THE FOURTH PART OF A CIRCLE

That might possibly be so, although it is most unlikely; but as a matter of fact a reasonably accurate square can be made in a minute or so by any sensible person wholly ignorant of geometrical principles. Once the craftsman had a straight-edge, whether of wood or stone, that was reasonably true, he could quickly make a square good enough for his purpose. He would first fasten the two arms together, but not quite tightly; then he would try the result by putting the square on the prepared edge and scribing a line roughly at right angles. Next he would turn the square over from right to left, or vice versa, and scribe another line starting from the same point as before. Then the variation between the two lines would indicate the amount of inaccuracy, enabling him to adjust the implement and try again.

There was nothing to prevent the early craftsman from availing himself of the square, and there is plenty of evidence to show that he did do so. Nearly 1500 B.C. there was made at Thebes (the great Egyptian city beside the Nile) a drawing in which a carpenter's square is clearly illustrated. In the tomb of Tut-ankh-amen was found a symbol made of plate gold in the form of a draughtsman's T-square.

We know that the word 'square' as meaning 'honest' and 'straightforward' goes back thousands of years, just as the compasses and the level are referred to in Chinese writings of a period reaching from the twenty-fourth to the seventh centuries before Christ. Nearly five hundred years before Christ, Confucius was using some such phrase as 'transgressing the limits of the square,' and two hundred years later a follower of his, Mencius, taught that all men must apply the square and compasses, the level and the marking-line figuratively to their lives, if they would walk in the straight and even paths of wisdom and keep themselves within the bounds of honour and virtue. Simonides, a Greek poet of the sixth century before Christ, speaks of a man being 'square as to his feet, his hands and his mind,' a comparison which is echoed by Aristotle, who lived in the fourth century before Christ. Right through the intervening literature up to the present day we find writers using the square and other geometric tools as object lessons, and it is easy to appreciate

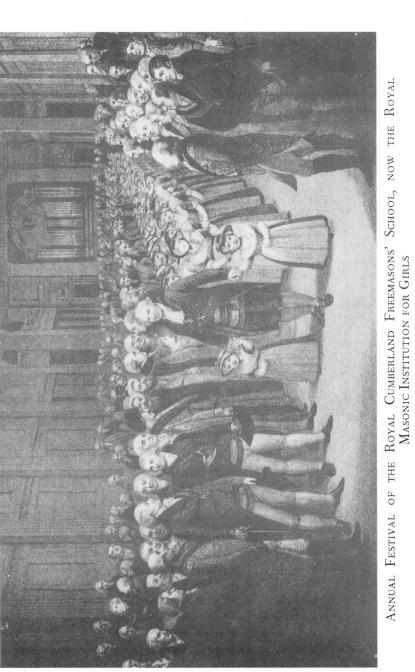

ANNUAL FESTIVAL OF THE ROYAL CUMBERLAND FREEMASONS' SCHOOL, NOW THE ROYAL MASONIC INSTITUTION FOR GIRLS

The school was established in 1788 mainly by the exertions of the brother here shown leading the procession of orphan girls—the Chevalier Bartholomew Ruspini, dentist to the Prince of Wales and founder, in 1787, of the Lodge, No. 259, named after the Prince. Painting by Thomas Stothard, published in 1802.

By courtesy of Quatuor Coronati Lodge

PLATE XVIII

"Loge Bonaparte" Membership List, 1853

Napoleon, who is portrayed here, was long thought to have been made a mason at Malta in 1798, but French opinion nowadays is against the idea. Included in one of the marble bas-reliefs at his tomb in Paris is a bold pair of compasses, one point hidden by a square. In the print reproduced above Napoleon is given the title of "Protector of Freemasonry, 1804."

By courtesy of Quatuor Coronati Lodge

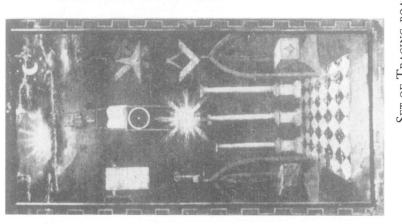

SET OF TRACING-BOARDS IN USE BY THE LODGE OF UNANIMITY AND SINCERITY,
No. 261, TAUNTON

Painted by William Dight in 1808, they were originally floor-cloths on canvas (about 3 feet by 6 feet), but are
now framed.

By courtesy of H. Hiram Haller.

PLATE XX

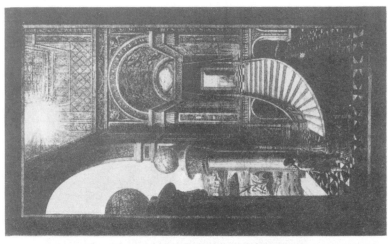

SET OF HARRIS TRACING-BOARDS

John Harris, miniature painter and architectural draughtsman, was initiated in 1818 and began work of this kind five years later.

PLATE XXI

ROYAL ARCH TRACING-BOARD

This tracing-board, in use by Sincerity Chapter, No. 261, Taunton, was originally a canvas floor-cloth, about 2 ft. 4 ins. by 5 ft. 2 ins., but is now framed. The use of the T-over-H emblem fixes its date as eighteenth-century (see Chapter XXXIV).

By courtesy of H. Hiram Hallett

PLATE XXII

AN EFFIGY COMPOSED OF A FREEMASON'S EMBLEMS

A design, dated 1754, by A. Slade, with rococo ornament typical of the period. Note the lewis keys (see Chapter XXVII) serving as hands.

By courtesy of the United Grand Lodge of England

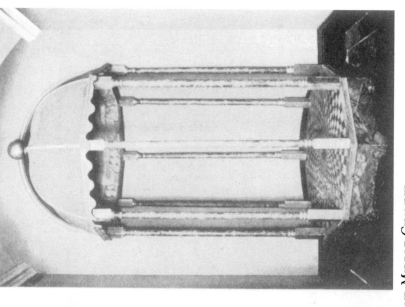

WINDING STAIRCASE AND MIDDLE CHAMBER

Part of a set of furniture built about 1819 for the use of three Bath lodges and, since about 1842, owned by
Loyal Lodge, No. 251, Barnstaple (see Chapter XVII).

By courtesy of the Quatuor Coronati Lodge and Bruce Oliver, F.R.I.B.A.

PLATE XXIV

THE INAUGURATION OF ROBERT BURNS AS POET LAUREATE OF THE CANONGATE
KILWINNING LODGE

This well-known picture by Stewart Watson is an artist's reconstruction, not a first-hand record, of a famous occasion, and incidentally provides evidence of the now obsolete custom of taking refreshment during lodge

PLATE XXV

COMPASS-AND-SECTOR JEWELS OF THE EIGHTEENTH AND EARLY NINETEENTH CENTURIES

These are Masters' Badges, in which Craft and Royal Arch emblems are often found associated.

By courtesy of the United Grand Lodge of England and of the Quatuor Coronati Lodge

PLATE XXVI

SIX SILVER JEWELS, MOSTLY EIGHTEENTH-CENTURY

1, 'Antients' pierced jewel, a Master's collar badge (about 1790). 2, Jewel giving prominence to beehive, an ancient emblem. 3, 'Antients' jewel worn by one of the 'Nine Worthies' appointed in 1792. 4, 5, and 6, Engraved jewels, about the same date as above, of a kind usually crowded with emblems—Craft and otherwise.

By courtesy of the United Grand Lodge of England

PLATE XXVII

Two Small Groups of Early Jewels

Top: Pierced and engraved silver jewels, among the earliest and most beautiful of all masonic medals.

Bottom left: Triangular jewel (Royal Arch) set in brilliant gems, an elaboration formerly much in vogue.

Bottom centre: Obverse of one of the 'Nine Worthies' jewels (see preceding plate).

Bottom right: Master's collar jewel ('Antients' Lodge of Friendship and Benevolence).

By courtesy of the United Grand Lodge of England

PLATE XXVIII

DEACONS' EMBLEMS AND ROYAL ARCH JEWELS

Top: Deacons' emblems—Mercury with winged feet.
Bottom: Pierced silver jewels of the 1790–1820 period.

By courtesy of the United Grand Lodge of England and of the Quatuor Coronati Lodge

DEDICATION STONE OF THE ROYAL MASONIC HOSPITAL, RAVENSCOURT PARK, BEING LAID BY ELECTRICAL CONNEXION IN OLYMPIA, LONDON, ON MAY 19, 1932

The ceremony was performed by H.R.H. the Duke of Connaught, K.G., Grand Master, in the presence of 11,000 brethren, including King George VI and many members of the Royal Family.

Photo Sport and General

PLATE XXX

FREEMASONS' HALL LONDON

A photographic impression of the great Peace Memorial building floodlit at night.

Photo Photochrom Co.

PLATE XXXI

THE ARMS OF THE
GRAND LODGE OF
ENGLAND

(see Appendix, p. 551).

A DECORATIVE
VERSION OF THE
ARMS OF THE GRAND
LODGE OF SCOTLAND

(see Appendix, p. 552).

how the square came to be adopted by freemasons as the symbol of morality.

Shakespeare and the Authorized Version of the English Bible (translated in the days of James I) include the word. At the rebuilding of Baal's Bridge, near Limerick, a brass square was found, inscribed with the date 1517 and bearing these words:

> I will strive to live with love and care
> Upon the level, by the square.

The tombs of the great masons and architects back to ancient days often bear symbolic representations of the square, compasses, etc. On the tomb at Rheims of Maître Hues Libergier (1263) we find the square and callipers. William Warmington, the Master Mason at Croyland Abbey in the fifteenth century, is buried in that abbey, and his tomb carries the square and compasses. Instances could be multiplied if it were necessary.

We can have no doubt about the square being very definitely a mason's tool when we read of the order of the Alnwick Operative Lodge of the year 1708 that "noe member of the lodge . . . should appear at any lodge to be kept on St John's day in church without his apron and common square fixed in the belt thereof. . . ."

The square and compasses in conjunction with each other teach us not only to square our actions, but to keep them within due bounds. The combined emblem will be considered in due course.

The Compasses

The compasses have a highly special significance, one that has been recognized for many thousands of years, and to which freemasons attach the greatest importance. The Candidate in the course of his Initiation quickly makes their acquaintance, not as the tools of a degree, but as an emblem of freemasonry itself, bringing home to him the seriousness of the obligation into which he is entering.

Not only the freemason, but the whole world has recognized the compasses as a mighty symbol. The eighth chapter of the Book of Proverbs (23–27), a taste of some of the greatest literature ever conceived by the mind of man, says:

> I was set up from everlasting, from the beginning, or ever the earth was. When there were no depths, I was brought forth; when there were no fountains abounding with water. Before the mountains were settled, before the hills was I brought forth: while as yet he had not made the earth, nor the fields, nor the highest part of the dust of the world. When he prepared the heavens, I was there: when he set a compass upon the face of the depth.

Passing to Isaiah xl (that wonderful chapter starting with "Comfort ye, comfort ye my people, saith your God"), we read in the twelfth verse: "Who hath measured the waters in the hollow of his hand, and meted out heaven with the span, and comprehended the dust of the earth in a measure, and weighed the mountains in scales, and hills in a balance?"

In an Anglo-Saxon manuscript of about the year 1000, and now in the British Museum, is a picture in which the Deity holds in his right hand a large pair of compasses and some scales, both of them being symbols of the creation of the world.[1] In the 1790's William Blake, "English mystic, poet, painter, and engraver" (1757–1827), painted his great picture, *The Ancient of Days*. It is reproduced as the frontispiece to this book. In it the 'Ancient of Days' is striking the first circle of the earth.

The truly remarkable verse in Milton's *Paradise Lost*, written in the middle years of the 1600's, at the very time when symbolic freemasonry was seeking the inspiration of word and phrase, has already been quoted (p. 301).

Freemasons are taught in the ritual that the compasses remind them of God's unerring and impartial justice, which, having defined for their instruction the limits of good and evil, will reward or punish according as they have obeyed or disregarded his divine commands. The freemason, also, is taught to 'keep within compass,' a phrase which we find in general literature as early as 1619, and probably could find much earlier.

Our Brethren in the lodges of the early 1700's held the compasses in great respect, and in one of their catechisms is a test question and answer containing an odd allusion to them:

Q. Have you seen your Master today?
A. Yes.
Q. How was he cloathed?
A. In a yeilow Jacket, and a Blue Pair of Breeches.

The explanation is that the yellow jacket was the brass legs of the compass and the blue breeches the steel points.

It is likely that mason's compasses have at times been confused with the mariner's magnetic compass, which is not unknown as a masonic emblem.

In the Irish working the compasses are regarded as an instrument for drawing the perfect figure, the circle, which teaches us to place a curb upon our passions, while the point within it denotes to us the eternal source of life. (See also pp. 406, 407.)

---

[1] An engraving of this picture is in Mrs Anna Jameson's *History of Our Lord* in *Works of Art*, vol. 1 (Longmans, 1864).

The Square and Compasses

It is when we combine the square with the compasses that we discover the most significant emblem of freemasonry. The Chinese many centuries before Christ used this emblem to suggest order, regularity, and propriety. Mencius (b. 372 B.C.) taught that men should apply the square and compasses figuratively to their lives, and the level and the marking-line besides, if they would walk in the straight and even paths of wisdom, and keep themselves within the bounds of honour and virtue. English medieval literature often refers to the compasses, and it is thought that possibly the oldest of such references is in Langland's *Vision of Piers the Plowman,* dating back to about 1377, which mentions the compasses, square, line, and level.

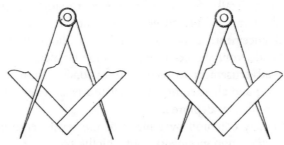

SQUARE AND COMPASSES: 'ONE
LEG OVER' AND 'BOTH LEGS UNDER'

The relative positions of the two instruments are of interest. Perhaps the most usual way of showing them is with 'one leg over'—that is, with one leg of the compass passing down in front of one arm of the square, the other leg being behind the square. In the eighteenth century there was much controversy on the matter, and this must have influenced the old English lodges and American lodges, which at one time made a custom of directing the points of the compasses lying on the V.S.L. towards the Candidate, who at the same time found himself embraced or included, as it were, in the open angle of the square; thus, the points of the compass and the ends of the square both pointed away from the Master. In most English lodges to-day the points are directed to the Candidate, but the ends of the square point away from him. An irregular print of the 1760's has this to say with regard to the position of the compasses and the places at which the V.S.L. should lie open:

The Master always sits in the East, or stands with the Bible before him and if it is the apprentice's lecture, he opens it about the second epistle of

Peter, with the compasses laid thereon, and the points of them covered with a little box square of *lignum vitae*, about 4 inches each way, and the points of the compasses point to the west, and the two points of the square point to the east. If it is the craft's lecture, the Master shows one point of the compasses, the bible being open the 12th chapter of Judges. If it is the Master's lecture, the bible is opened about the 7th chapter of the First Book of Kings, and both the points of the compasses is shewn upon the square.

Organized freemasonry has set its face against any display of masonic certificates in public places and against the association of freemasonry and masonic emblems with any matter of business development. The Board of General Purposes of the Grand Lodge of England, in keeping with all other English-speaking Grand Lodges, emphatically deprecates the exhibition in public of masonic certificates, which are often shown on business premises for what can be considered only trade purposes; and it urges Brethren generally to take every means to stop the use, in connexion with the Craft, of advertisement or appeal in any form which is for private advancement. It believes that it is in the highest degree undesirable that endeavour should be made by circular, personal solicitation, or newspaper advertisement to secure professional, commercial, or sectional advantage; and all attempts to associate freemasonry with business development are deeply deplored.

It was extremely common over much of the seventeenth century for all kinds of trade announcements, but chiefly trade cards, to exhibit masonic devices for the obvious purpose of influencing business. (There is a small collection of these cards in the Library in Freemasons' Hall, London.) The tallow chandler decorated his bill-heads with an elaborate coat of arms, from which depended the compasses, crossed pens, and crossed keys. The music-teacher, the snuff-seller, and others used the chief emblems on their cards. A fine figure, selling 'best Virginia,' held the open compasses and stands between the rough and perfect ashlars, while in a rival announcement the vendor balanced Euclid's forty-ninth proposition on his fingers. Tailors enclosed realistic drawings of codpiece breeches in rich rococo ornament supported on pillars. The undertaker and sworn appraiser, the drum-maker and cabinet-maker, mixed up their firebaskets, furniture, etc., with square and compasses. As for Benjamin Watson, chimney-sweeper and nightman of Great Portland Street, London, his offer to extinguish chimneys, when on fire, with the greatest care and expedition, was contained in a most attractive engraved plate which pictured a number of his little assistants carrying brushes, and was lent great dignity by the two pillars bearing masonic emblems. It by no means follows that all these traders were members of the Order. Far from it! Many parasites battened on freemasonry in the seventeenth century, and by their unscrupulous conduct did their worst to bring discredit to the Craft. The Grand Lodge of England was obliged to decide that, so far as their members were concerned, the association of masonic emblems with their trade advertising must cease.

It was not unusual at one time for freemasons to wear on their watch-chain a small gold compass, but the practice is now frowned upon by the English Grand Lodge, and we expect by many others. The custom is much older than might be thought, for certain divisions of the Compagnonnage (the French body of operative masons going back some hundreds of years) engaged in fights and disturbances to prove their right to bear the compass as an emblem.

Mackey's *Encyclopædia of Freemasonry* tells us of an extraordinary case that was fought out in the U.S.A. Patent Office, to which in 1873 a flour manufacturer applied for permission to adopt the square and compasses as a trade mark, the Commissioner of Patents refusing permission on the ground that the mark was a masonic emblem of peculiar character and relation to the public, and had an established mystic significance. In Massachusetts a freemason noticed a shoe-dealer wearing a masonic emblem; the dealer admitted he had no right to wear it, and that he wore it to assist trade; in a magistrate's court the dealer was fined twenty dollars under a statute enacted by the legislation of New Jersey, which made it a misdemeanour to wear, unless entitled to do so, the insignia of any incorporated fraternal organization, for the purpose of obtaining recognition or assistance.

Euclid's 47th Proposition

As freemasons we cannot properly consider the square without associating it with Euclid's 47th Proposition, the motif for the Past Master's jewel. No one knows why or when that "amazing proposition," as Anderson's *Constitutions* of 1723 call it, was adopted as the insignia of the Past Master, nor of any Craft ritual that offers any explanation of the Proposition, or any philosophical lesson it may conceivably teach.

This lack of information has led to such general ignorance among freemasons as to what the Proposition really is, that the majority of Past Masters, always excepting those of mathematical tastes, either believe the Proposition to be a mystery beyond their comprehension, or wrongly assume it to refer merely to an elementary rule comprehended by the figures 3, 4, 5. This must be the excuse for devoting some space to the subject here.

Bertrand Russell's *History of Western Philosophy* tells us that Pythagoras, the Greek philosopher (b. 580 B.C.) was "intellectually one of the most important men that ever lived, both when he was wise and when he was unwise. Mathematics begins with him." His greatest discovery, or that of his immediate disciples, was the theorem bearing his name. Bertrand Russell goes on:

> The Egyptians had known that a triangle whose sides are 3, 4, 5 contains a right angle, but apparently the Greeks were the first to observe that 3 squared plus 4 squared equals 5 squared, and, acting on this suggestion, to discover a proof of the general proposition.

Whether Pythagoras was its discoverer or not, the theorem was known to the Pythagoreans at an early date.

Euclid's 47th Proposition (which is a statement of the Pythagorean theorem) lays down a geometrical truth relating to all right-angled triangles. It does not give a simple method of constructing such triangles. Rather, practical men have deduced the simple method from the Proposition.

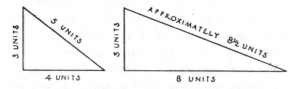

Two Right-angled Triangles

These triangles, although different in their proportions,
are closely related through Euclid's 47th Proposition.

It is essential to appreciate that the Proposition does not mention 3, 4, 5, or any other numbers; it is the craftsman who has hit upon the numbers to demonstrate the Proposition. We sometimes speak of the 3, 4, 5 'principle,' but it is not really a *principle*. It is a method.

Here are diagrams of two triangles. They are right-angled triangles —that is, one of the three angles is an angle of 90 degrees, the fourth part of a circle, in masonic language a 'square.' Although these two triangles look very different from each other they have one thing in common (other than their right angle). What is it? Not the measurements (which are given) of the lengths of the sides, for quite obviously they are very different. What then? It is the *relationship* of those lengths *when each has been squared*—that is, *multiplied by itself*, as revealed in the Proposition.

In *any* right-angled triangle the longest side, or hypotenuse (the slant line in our diagrams), equals when squared the combined squares of the two other sides. It is this relationship which gives the craftsman the simple 3, 4, 5 method of setting out an angle of 90 degrees. Thus, if we look for a moment at our two triangles arithmetically, and not geometrically, we shall learn something about them which will help us to see how the 3, 4, 5 rule was arrived at. When we construct a triangle on the method based on the Proposition, we must first have decided what the lengths of the sides containing, or including, the right angle shall be, because we are going to mark off those lengths on straight-edges, or are going to take those lengths by means of compasses or dividers.

If we were to tackle the production of the second of our triangles by the method of the Proposition we should find very great difficulty. Our base-line of 8 units would be easily marked off. Our short line of 3 units would not present difficulty. But how should we know the length of the slant line (the hypotenuse)? The square of 8 is 64. The square of 3 is 9. 64 plus 9 = 73. As we know that the hypotenuse squared is equal to the sum of the other sides, we have now to find the square root of 73. This comes to just over $8\frac{1}{2}$ units. 'Just over'! That won't do for the mason. It is not precise enough. He must work out the dimension to a few places of decimals—only to find after he has done it that he cannot transfer the dimension owing to the comparatively coarse tools which he is accustomed to use.

But it so happens that there is a simple sequence of numbers that can be used to produce a right-angled triangle, and that sequence is 3, 4, 5, which has given its name to the rule or principle. So look now at the first triangle figured. The base-line is 4 units long, and the short line 3 units.

$$4 \times 4 = 16. \quad 3 \times 3 = 9. \quad 16 + 9 = 25.$$

The square root of 25 is exactly 5 (5 times 5). Thus a triangle built up of sides representing 3, 4, and 5 units must be right-angled.

All you need do, in applying the method in a small way, is to lay down a base-line 4 units long; set your compasses to 3 units, and with one end of the base-line as centre draw an arc. Set your compasses to 5 units, and with the other end of the base-line as centre draw an arc intersecting the first one. From the intersection draw a straight line downward to join the base-line. You have now formed a right angle—the true square —and to complete the triangle you now connect the intersection with the other end of the base-line.

You have reduced the *proposition* to a practical *method*, which the craftsman finds of great use in checking an existing angle, such as the corner of a building. Indeed, it is as a testing and checking method that it offers itself, rather than as a practical method of setting out a right angle on the job, where experience shows that certain practical difficulties tend to reduce accuracy.

We are told that one of the ancient peoples used a most curious form of the method. They took a rope and marked on it 3 units, 4 units, and 5 units consecutively. They drove a rod into the ground, and two other rods in approximate positions. Then they stretched the rope round the three rods and altered the position of two of them until the marks on the rope exactly coincided with all the rods, when the rope represented a right-angled triangle. This was, one fears, a rather clumsy procedure.

In one of the additional degrees, the First Master has a rod 5 units long, the second Master has one of 4 units, and the third Master one of 3 units, the three Masters meeting and agreeing to place the three rods together to produce a right-angled triangle. Plutarch is alleged to have said that in Egypt the three rods were dedicated to Isis, Osiris, and Horus; they were coloured black, red, and blue respectively; and represented the originating, the receptive, and the product.

It is often claimed that the method based upon the Proposition was for a long period of time a mason trade secret, but this is almost certainly nothing more than a pleasant fiction. There are many other ways of arriving at a right angle, though, probably, none more suitable for the checking of the square angles of large buildings.

The Past Master's Jewel

The Past Master's Jewel (see the illustration) demonstrates the Proposition in terms of the 3, 4, 5 application, and will now be easily understood. The triangle is lying on its hypotenuse—the side 5 units long—which forms the base-line of a square containing 25 small squares ($5 \times 5 = 25$). The 'square' of the length of the side is thus demonstrated in geometry as well as in arithmetic. Both of the shorter sides are squared in the same way. The square of one contains 16 small squares (4×4), that of the other 9 (3×3). These figures agree with those already fully explained. Thus the Past Master's Jewel is an actual proof or demonstration of the construction of a right-angled triangle by the 3, 4, 5 method, based upon the 47th Proposition.

So far as is known no attempt to

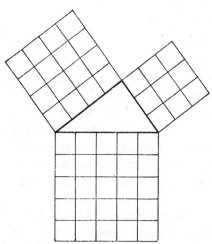

THE PAST MASTER'S JEWEL

A device demonstrating that, as proved by Euclid's 47th Proposition, any triangle whose sides measure 3, 4, and 5 contains a right (or square) angle.

offer any symbolic explanation of the 47th Proposition was made before the early eighteenth century. The Proposition figures in the frontispiece to the 1723 and 1738 editions of the *Constitutions* (see Plate II). One masonic writer has suggested that it was a symbol to Pythagoras, who is said to have made a great sacrifice for joy at its discovery. This may be taken only as an exaggerated and traditional account; yet the fact of his exultation remains, probably "because he saw a strange and striking connection between the properties of a right-angled triangle and some great important truth, probably of a theosophical character." This may be difficult for ordinary people to understand, but has not some great thinker suggested that mathematics is a source of belief in eternal truth?

Levels and Plumb-rules

Levels and plumb-rules are closely related. In each of the time-honoured patterns a line is caused to hang dead vertically by means of a weight, or bob. The bottom face, or edge, of the level is at right angles

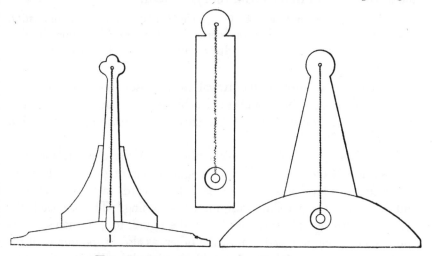

TWO LEVELS AND, CENTRE, A PLUMB-RULE

To-day regarded as conventional patterns but actually resembling the tools in use by thirteenth-century operatives.

to the line, and indicates horizontals, while the sides of the plumb-rule are parallel with the line, and indicate verticals. (Similarly, a spirit-level may be at the same time a plumb-rule.) The freemason is taught that the purpose of the level is to lay levels and prove horizontals, and that of the plumb-rule to try and adjust uprights, while fixing them on their proper bases. 'Try *and* adjust,' not 'Try *to* adjust,' for the word 'try' here is used in the old sense of testing.

Symbolically, the level teaches equality and the plumb-rule justice and uprightness of life and actions. The fifth section of the 1st Lecture explains that the level demonstrates that we have all sprung from the same stock and are partakers of the same nature and sharers in the same hope, while the plumb-rule, the criterion of rectitude and truth, teaches us to walk justly and uprightly before God and man. At Pompeii (destroyed A.D. 79) a table was discovered bearing the representation of a skull, level, and wheel, the whole being interpreted as meaning that death is the great leveller. (In the South of France levels have been found carved upon old coffins.) Both level and plumb-rule were in use by masons thousands of years ago, were figured on Roman and many other tombs, and are the subject of significant Biblical references. In the Book of Amos vii, 7–8, we are told that ". . . the Lord stood upon a wall made by a plumbline, with a plumbline in his hand. . . . Then said the Lord, Behold, I will set a plumbline in the midst of my people Israel." The second Book of Kings speaks of the Lord stretching over Jerusalem a line and a plummet. In Isaiah xxviii, 16–17, we read:

> Therefore thus saith the Lord God, Behold, I lay in Zion for a foundation a stone, a tried stone, a precious corner stone, a sure foundation: he that believeth shall not make haste. Judgment also will I lay to the line, and righteousness to the plummet.

A reference of interest to the Royal Arch mason is in the Book of Zechariah iv, 9–10: "The hands of Zerubbabel have laid a foundation of this house; . . . they shall rejoice, and shall see the plummet in the hand of Zerubbabel."

The balance is an old masonic emblem, but the close relationship between it and the level is seldom recognized, although to the Romans the craftsman's level was *libella* or *libra*, both words meaning 'balance,' and their word for 'levelling' also meant 'weighing.' The balance is the symbol of justice and impartiality, and the figure, too, of man's merits and demerits, one weighed against the other, as also of the things of the soul in one pan outweighing all the things of earth loaded into the other one.

It is worth while noting how Gwyllim in his *Heraldry*, printed in 1611, refers to the level in symbolic terms, to which in all probability the framers of our rituals had access. Speaking of the level and plumb-rule, he says:

> This instrument is the type of equity and vprightnesse in all our actions, which are to be leulled and rectified by the Rule of Reason and Iustice. For the plummet euer fals right, howsoeuer it be held, and what euer betide a vertuous man, his actions and conscience will be vncorrupt and vncontroulable.

The old Latin tag *ad amussim* ('by the plumb-line or by the rule') wil particularly interest the Royal Arch Mason, since one dictionary adds to the meaning 'correct in every particular.' The teaching of the level and plumb-rule is closely associated with the proper conduct of life. We are taught square conduct, level steps, and upright intentions. The old masonic writer William Preston spoke of "meeting on the square and parting on the level," which has been altered by our American Brethren to "meeting on the level and parting on the square," and to which they have added "and acting by the plumb."

In an eighteenth-century ceremony of Installation much was made of the symbolism of the plummet. We find it, or some part of it, surviving to-day in the 'extended ceremony' of Installation (see pp. 250, 251).

J. V. A. Andreae, a German, printed in 1623 a book in which occur the following lines (as translated by F. F. Schnitger and G. W. Speth):

> The best logician is our God
> Whom the conclusion never fails:
> He speaks—it is; He wills—it stands;
> He blows—it falls; He breathes—it lives;
> His words are true—e'en without proof,
> His counsel rules without command,
> Therefore can none foresee his end
> Unless on God is built his hope.
> And if we here below would learn
> By *Compass*, *Needle*, *Square*, and *Plumb*,
> We never must o'erlook the mete
> Wherewith our God hath measur'd us.

A verbatim translation of the eighth line would read "Unless in God he has his building." There is some suggestion that Andreae took the symbols of the working tools from the *Steinmetzen*, the German masons, and that he uses them in the sense that they were used in the early eighteenth-century rituals, which he anticipated.

The Line and the Skirret

The symbol of the line—the stretched line and the measuring line—occurs frequently in the books of the Old Testament. We read of "a man with a measuring line in his hand" (Zechariah ii, 1); that "the measuring line shall yet go forth over against it" (Jeremiah xxxi, 39); that "he marketh it out with a line" (Isaiah xliv, 13); and so forth. To the freemason the stretched line connotes the skirret, or skirrit, one of the working tools of the Third Degree; it emblematically represents the straight and undeviating line of conduct laid down for our guidance in the V.S.L., and further teaches the criterion of moral rectitude, that we should avoid dissimulation in conversation and action, and seek the path that leads to immortality.

The skirret, or some implement like it, must have been in use for thousands of years. Paintings at Thebes, Egypt, dating back to, say, 3000 B.C., show masons holding a stretched cord by means of which a line is being drawn. A limestone 'stela' ('slab' or 'tablet') set up in the capital Ur of the Chaldees more than two thousand years before

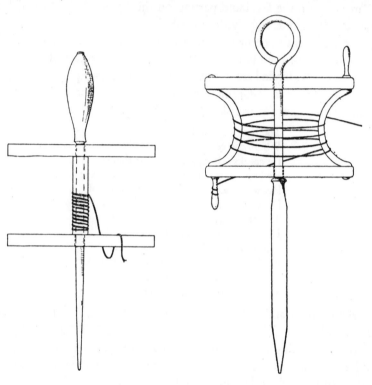

A SIMPLE FORM OF THE SKIRRET   THE EVERYDAY SKIRRET
A line-holder, rotating on a centre-pin.   The gardener's line-reel and stake.

Christ shows a measuring rod and line in use by a deity acting as architect. But, while this is so, we have no evidence of the actual existence of the implement itself earlier than a painting, *The Backgammon Players*, by the Flemish painter David Teniers the younger, who may be assumed to have produced his picture in the middle of the seventeenth century. We find no reference in print to the word 'skirret' until after the United Grand Lodge, 1813, and then as a masonic word only, and not as a word in general literature.

The skirret familiar to every freemason is a spool, or cord-holder rotating freely on a centre-pin. The loose end of the cord is attached to a second pin—a short stake—which, in use, is driven into the ground at one end of the intended line. Next, the workman walks towards the other end of the proposed line, the rotating holder giving off the cord as he moves, and he then drives the centre-pin into the ground where required, taking care to stretch the cord tightly. In this way he produces a straight line for his guidance "in marking out the ground for the foundation of an intended structure."

Some rituals speak of the skirret as being an implement from which the line "is drawn, chalked and struck"—that is, the stretched and chalked cord is 'plucked,' so as to print a white line on the surface below it. We may well believe that the use of the chalk-line has been known for thousands of years. The ancient Greeks said that the chalk-line produced a line "more exact than rectitude itself"; symbolically it was the boundary line of human life. But for use on an earth surface, the only purpose of the skirret, the chalked line would not often be suitable.

We know the implement well enough, but we know nothing of its name. General dictionaries appear to have drawn their information on the subject from masonic sources, and therefore do not help us. (It is fairly certain, by the way, that freemasonry gave this word 'skirret' to the technical vocabulary or, at any rate, rescued it from oblivion.) Some erudite and elaborate interpretations giving the word a symbolic meaning have been attempted, but can be ignored. One writer has said that the word is "genuine English although almost obsolete." Yes, genuine English for certain things botanical, but not for a rotating line-holder! Dictionaries of the present century give the word 'skirreh' as meaning a cord, but it is doubtful whether this has genuine antiquity. A few years ago an author occupied much space to explain that the word 'skirret' meant 'pure,' but this looks very much like a case of taking the masonic meaning of a word, and seeking to derive it accordingly. 'Purity' is an extremely unlikely association with the name for an operative's line-spool.

The word 'skirret' was not known, it is believed, until about 1825, and appears to have no literary history; we must conclude that if the word itself was not an invention, then it must have been derived from some fact or circumstance relating to the implement itself.

There is a bare possibility that the familiar word 'skewer'—the butcher's skewer—is allied with the word 'skirret.' One old-fashioned meaning of 'skewer' is that of a spindle fixed to a cloth-spinner's creel, and carrying a rotating bobbin from which the yarn was unwound; here we get both the sound of the word and the meaning closely allied to those of 'skirret.'

The Scots word 'skirr,' meaning 'scurry or rush,' conveys the exact mental impression caused by the sudden rotation of the cord-holder when the pull comes upon it. Then, in eighteenth-century slang, to 'skirry' was to 'run quickly' or to 'scurry.' We may suspect that 'skirret' was originally a colloquial word which owed its origin either to the 'scurry' of the line-holder or to the 'skirl,' or shrill sound, which it makes when in action.

The Trowel

Our Craft working almost ignores the trowel as a working tool, just possibly because masonic symbolism is based largely upon the art of the old freemason, who was a cutter and shaper of stone, whereas the trowel is a layer's tool; but it is quite obvious that in the eighteenth century the trowel had a much bigger place in our ceremonies than it has to-day. The fact that a lodge at Carmarthen in June 1754 paid for "5 Trowells and mending 12 others" seems to suggest that in that old lodge trowels had a considerable part to play. But what that part was we do not know.

The trowel more than comes into its own in the laying of a foundation-stone with masonic ceremonial—the only surviving link with operative masonry—the trowel used for the purpose being usually a silver emblem, of which some handsome examples are preserved in the masonic museums.

Egyptians of old are said to have regarded the trowel as an emblem typifying the profound secrecy that binds the Initiate, in which sense it is the emblem of circumspection, and is so referred to in some rituals to-day.

Early in the sixteenth century there was a Society of the Trowel, in Florence, apparently working some kind of non-masonic, and probably mock, ritual in which the trowel, hammer, square, and level were used as symbols.

The Master of the lodge refers to the trowel in his address to the Initiate, and in the Royal Arch Chapter we learn of the valour of those worthy men who, with trowel in hand and sword at side, were ever ready to defend the city and Holy Sanctuary against unprovoked attacks.

The trowel remains one of the working tools in a few old English lodges—for example, in those of Bristol and Bath, where it has a place in both the First and Third degrees, the ritual in the superior degree informing us that the "trowel is used for the noble and glorious purpose of spreading the cement of Brotherhood and affection which unites us in a sacred bond as a Society of Brethren, amongst whom no contention should ever exist." This working is observed in American Craft lodges, and there are certain additional degrees in which the trowel is known.

The Grand Lodge of Ireland resolved in 1769 that the design "for lodge seals shall consist of a Hand and a Trowel," and so the seals have remained ever since. An Irish masonic crest of 1738, showing a hand holding a pointed trowel posed as a stabbing weapon, provides a key to the use to which the tool was put in the old early speculative lodges, and even possibly in the operative lodges which preceded them; it was the Tyler's or the Inner Doorkeeper's weapon. In some Irish lodges the flat of the trowel is extended to the Candidate to receive his gift, when inviting him (in the Second Degree) to give to the cause of masonic charity. The hand and trowel are to be found on some of the earliest known jewels issued by 'Modern' lodges.

Early in the eighteenth century, and perhaps before, the trowel had become the weapon of the Junior Entered Apprentice, whose duty was to act as inner doorkeeper, a duty which later devolved upon an Inner Tyler, who later still became known as the Inner Guard. Here is an old catechism:

Q. Where stands the Senior Entre'd 'Prentice?
A. In the South.
Q. What is his Business?
A. To hear and receive instructions and welcome strange Brothers.
Q. Where stands the Junior Entre'd 'Prentice?
A. In the North.
Q. What is his Business (or Duty)?
A. To keep of all Cowans and Eves-droppers.

In some versions of this catechism the Junior Entered Apprentice (the newest Initiate) is armed with a 'sharp instrument,' which was a pointed trowel, not the poniard, or short sword, with which the mason of to-day is acquainted. When we realize that the Initiate so early in his masonic experience acted as an officer of the lodge and was armed with a trowel, we may perceive the possible, even probable, meaning of a sentence in the ancient charge delivered by the Master to the Initiate, a sentence which generally passes as a piece of somewhat vain rhetoric, but which may well be based upon the custom here alluded to. We are all familiar with it: ". . . in every age, even Monarchs themselves have been promoters of the Art, and have not thought it derogatory to their dignity to exchange the Sceptre for the Trowel."

There is support for the above idea in what we learn of the customs of a number of old lodges. For instance, the Social Lodge of Norwich still invests the Initiate with a silver trowel, with which he is exhorted "emblematically to stop up all interstices in the lodge so that not a sound shall escape from within, nor an eye pry without." In the Scientific Lodge, No. 88, Cambridge, founded in 1762, the Initiate during refreshment after the ceremony wears a small silver trowel suspended from a collar, and the

Brother proposing his health "exhorts him to the exercise of Charity which is likened to the cement which binds and perfects the building." In certain other lodges, also, the Initiate wears a silver trowel as a jewel.

In some lodges, however, a silver trowel is an emblem of either the Inner Guard or the Tyler. In the Royal Sussex Lodge, now extinct, a silver trowel was presented for the use of the Tyler as his badge of office in 1827. A trowel in the possession of a lodge thought to have ceased to exist in 1794 bore the inscription "As for me and mine house we will serve the Lord." It is recorded of the Lodge of Love and Honour, No. 75, Falmouth, in 1808, that there should be "two Tylers, Williamson to act at the door inside and Symons outside . . . Williamson should wear his badge of Office, consisting of a trowel." That trowel is still so worn by the Inner Guard of the lodge.

In one old lodge the trowel is worn as a jewel by the eldest Past Master, and in many New Zealand lodges the trowel is a working tool in the Third Degree, and is also the jewel of the Junior Deacon. In Scotland the trowel is the emblem of the Grand Junior Deacon, and in Denmark, Norway, and Sweden a tiny silver trowel is the jewel of the Initiate.

It will be understood, then, from what has been said that it is difficult to understand the almost complete exclusion of the trowel from the English Craft ceremonies. The small pointed trowel, rather than a poniard, in the hands of the Inner Guard, would appear to be more in keeping with the old tradition.

It is more than possible that the crossed sword and trowel was the Sojourner's jewel in the Royal Arch at the end of the eighteenth century. The Sojourners in Unanimity Chapter, Wakefield, each wore a crossed sword and trowel suspended from a red silk ribbon, the swords being nearly five inches long, and the trowel half an inch shorter. These really beautiful jewels were made by James Rule in 1799 at a cost of £5 15s. 6d. Rule was a watchmaker of York, and a member of the now extinct Apollo Lodge of that city.

The 'Broken Column'

The custom of members contributing to a charity-box at each lodge meeting is very ancient. The design of the box—the 'broken column'— is symbolic of death, but has no particular masonic significance, having been copied from memorial monuments of a design common to the period of its adoption, the early 1800's.

Chapter Thirty

MASONIC CLOTHING

By masonic clothing is particularly meant the apron, collar and jewels, and gloves and gauntlets—the 'regalia'—all of which have a long Craft history. In old days the hat was part of masonic clothing, and in a very few English lodges and in a great many American lodges it is so still.

Full masonic clothing, or costume, to be worn with the masonic regalia consists of evening dress, white tie, and white gloves. For 'undress' and out-of-door occasions dark clothes and black ties are usual.

The Apron

From ancient days the apron has been an emblem, a symbol, as well as part of a craftsman's working-dress. It was worn by candidates in many ancient mysteries—Egyptian, Persian, Jewish, Indian, etc.—and there is an echo of such usage in the wearing of an apron by the Church dignitary and in the freemason's custom of wearing an apron at all times in lodge. Dr O. J. Kinnamon (one of the two survivors of the group of twenty-two men who on January 3, 1924, opened the sarcophagus of King Tut-ankh-amen) relates that the unwrapping of the mummy of the King revealed an apron, but of course we have no ground for presuming that it was a *masonic* apron.

To the speculative mason the apron is first and foremost a badge, and—as he is taught in lodge—the badge of innocence and the bond of friendship. It was used as a badge by the guilds from whom English freemasonry partly derived it. To indicate their trade and grade guild members and their servants wore 'livery,' so called because the masters 'delivered' (from Old French *livrée*) the clothing to their servants. The badge itself was more particularly a device worn on the sleeve.

'Badge' was a people's word in Shakespeare's day, and the idea of the badge was still quite familiar at the time when Anderson was preparing his first *Constitutions*. Shakespeare speaks of nobility's true badge, the badge of faith, the honourable badge of service, etc.

The mason's strong, long, thick leather apron was easily recognized as the badge of his calling, and, as adopted by the speculatives, it became, as H. L. Haywood puts it, "a symbol of a profound change in the attitude

449

of society towards work, for the labour of hand and brain, once despised, is rapidly becoming the one badge of an honourable life." Sir Walter Besant, in his *London in the Eighteenth Century*, reminds us that up to about 1750 or so the craftsman's dress was often a kind of uniform by which his trade was known. "The carpenter," says Sir Walter,

> wore a white apron looped up at the side—there was a fashion in wearing aprons—and a brown paper cap neatly folded in shape; the shoemaker wore a short leathern apron; the blacksmith a long leathern apron; . . . the barber a white apron with pockets in front to hold the tackle. The butcher wore a blue coat and apron; the baker was all in white, including his cap; the waterman wore a sailor's kilt and petticoat, and a woollen jersey; the tapster was in short sleeves rolled up, with a white apron, the corner tucked into the waistband; the brewer's drayman wore a leather apron and a red cap; the printer, a stuff apron from head to foot; the shopmen, except those of the draper, all wore aprons. The apron, indeed, was the symbol of the servant and the craftsman; it belonged in varied form to every trade.

It is evident that the mason's apron was regarded at an early date as a badge and emblem of very great significance. At one time a freemason's apron was thrown into his grave at his funeral. The visit of Thomas Farncombe, the Lord Mayor of London, to the Southwold Lodge of Fidelity in 1850 was made a great occasion, to which emphasis was lent by the Master of the lodge and the Lord Mayor exchanging aprons as gifts.

The mason's working apron is pictured in paintings at Thebes, Egypt, dating back to, say, 3000 B.C. In Britain the mason's apron was commonly a sheepskin, cured or tanned, reaching well down below the knees. It had a flap, bib, or fall held up by a leather thong passing round the neck, with two other thongs holding the apron round the waist—just such an apron, in fact, as many workmen wear to-day. The leather apron of the fourteenth century was the barm-fell or barm-skin, often made of bull-hide.

As a rule the employer provided aprons; for example, York Minster in 1355 found its masons in tunics, aprons, gloves, and clogs, and a parish in Suffolk in 1430 provided each freemason working on a job with a pair of white leather gloves and a white apron. In 1433 two setters were given, as part of their remuneration, two skins for aprons, and ten pairs of gloves.

The provision of aprons was a part of the contract between master and apprentice. An indenture, dated 1685, of Symon Bond, "an apprentice with John Cooke of Harbury in the said County of Warwick ffree Mason," recites that the master will allow the apprentice "sufficient wholsome and competent Meate drinke Lodging and Aprons (all the rest of his Apparrell being to be p'vided by his said parents . . .)."

It was a practice in the Scottish operative lodges for each entered apprentice to 'clothe the lodge'—in other words, to provide every member of it with a linen apron and probably a pair of gloves, or make a money payment in lieu. This was not by any means the end of his liability; he might have to pay one rix-dollar to the officer (convener) of the lodge and also a mark-piece for his mason mark.

This practice of 'clothing the lodge' was adopted by speculative masonry. Article 7 of the first *Constitutions* (1723) provides that "every new brother at his making is decently to cloath the lodge"—that is, to give aprons and gloves to all brethren present, and to deposit something for the relief of the indigent and the decayed brethren. The rule has long been obsolete.

The curious way in which the word 'apron' has come down to us proves that not all aprons were of leather. The word comes actually from *napron*, itself derived from an old French word meaning 'cloth'; thus '*a n*apron' has become '*an* apron.' (By a similar process, a word might either lose or gain an initial letter. Thus, 'St Audrey' gave us 'tawdry,' a rustic necklace bought at a fair on St Audrey's Day in the Middle Ages.)

The stonemason's apron must have been of heavy skin or leather, for otherwise a day's hard work would have destroyed it. In 1423 we read of "two skins given to the masons to make naprons of"; in 1428 of "two napronys of leather" being provided. The early Scots lodges of a semi-operative character adopted the linen apron, probably to emphasize that it was simply an emblem.

The Speculative's Apron

When first the English speculative mason wore the apron it was his one and only badge of masonry. It was of skin, but somewhat idealized, being a white lambskin, suitably dressed. Such, essentially, is the freemason's apron of to-day, but the amount of ornament sometimes obscures that fact. A perfectly plain white apron is the Initiate's apron in English lodges. That same plain white apron is worn by all masons, in many different degrees, throughout the American system; the only added ornament—and this during the last generation or two—being a very narrow edge of blue on aprons of the symbolic degree, and of red in the Royal Arch Degree.

A well-known portrait of the first Grand Master, Anthony Sayer, shows him wearing a long leather apron with a raised flap; this was typical of its day, and represented one remove from the operative's apron. Soon the apron became much shorter. Worn as a symbol only, there was no purpose in making it of cumbersome size and heavy material.

The line illustrations showing groups of aprons clearly demonstrate how the speculative's apron has developed from the old leather apron of the operative.

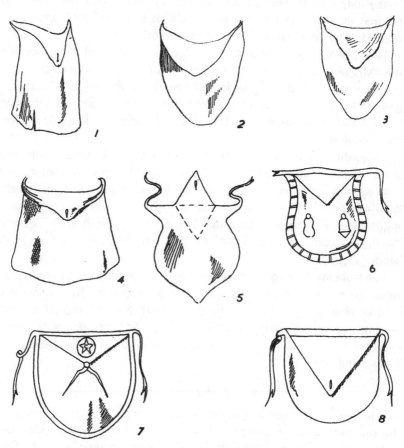

A GROUP OF EARLY APRONS

Nearly all have bibs, most of the latter with buttonholes for attachment to waistcoat

1 and 2.   English, 1738 and earlier.
      3.   French, 1747 and earlier.
      4.   English, 1754 and earlier.
5 and 6.   French, 1780's and 1790's.
      7.   French, the original being printed and hand-coloured very elaborately; probably late eighteenth century.
      8.   English, plain, simple; date about 1811.

New-made masons in the early days of the first Grand Lodge were very proud of their masonic clothing; so much we may judge from a newspaper of 1724 which, giving an account of a lodge meeting at which the Grand Master and "other noblemen" were present, states that several persons of quality accepted as masons "went home in their leather aprons and gloves."

Some time about the middle of the eighteenth century a fashion arose in the lodges of the 'Moderns' of inverting the skin so as to have the point at the bottom, as illustrated in many old prints. This gave opportunity for a burlesque printed by Laurence Dermott of the 'Antients' in *Ahiman Rezon* (1764 edition), in which he accused young gentlemen in the 'Modern' lodges of being superior to working in an apron and of agreeing to continue the practice only if the apron were turned upside down "in order to avoid appearing mechanical." The bib and strings hung down, and the 'gentlemen' in traversing the lodge often trod upon the strings and fell down. This oft-repeated but foolish story was, we hope, nothing more than an attempt by the 'Antients' to bring ridicule upon their opponents.

In Scots lodges in, say, the first half of the seventeenth century, speculatives were sitting side by side with operatives, who in their daily avocation wore a long leather apron; but, essentially, those operatives when they came to lodge were speculatives, too, and by adopting uniformly an apron of linen they demonstrated that their lodge apron was nothing more than a symbol. There is a case on record (1740–41) of a member of an English lodge being fined for wearing his working apron in lodge.

A typical regulation of lodges early in the eighteenth century was that any Brother appearing in lodge without gloves and apron should be fined, the fine varying from a few pence to one shilling. A minute of Lodge of Felicity, London, of 1737, says that "no member shall sit unclothed in the Lodge, in Lodge hours, under the penalty of one shilling, except the Landlord if he be a member." (Food and drink were commonly served in the lodge room in those days and probably the landlord did the serving.)

From the 1766 accounts of the Old Lodge at Wakefield:

Bro Nevinson for sitting down uncloath'd.	o.	o.	3.
Kilvington for sitting down uncloathed.	o.	o.	3.
Sill for Do.	o.	o.	3.
Do for Do.	o.	1.	o.

Lined and Ornamented Aprons

English and Scots lodges of the eighteenth century often bought aprons in quantity, and lent, gave, or sold them to the Brethren; thus, in the frontispiece of Anderson's *Constitutions* (1723) a Brother is shown bringing aprons and gloves into the lodge. Leather aprons then cost about one shilling each. In 1787 Canterbury freemasons bought their leather aprons from a breeches-maker at one or two shillings each. In 1812, £2 9s. was the cost of six dozen skins for making aprons for the Lodge of Relief, No. 42, Bury. Canongate Kilwinning Lodge in the year 1815 stamped its aprons "with the Iron of the Lodge." Apparently it was when this system of buying in quantity was not followed that the Brethren, individually buying their own aprons, began to introduce ornament, sometimes handsome, often elaborate, and occasionally fearsome.

PRINTED APRONS OF 1795 TO 1813 PERIOD

1. Form of simple apron as printed by William Newman (1795).
2. Apron of elaborate design (inclusive of arms of Masons' Company and Carpenters' Company) as printed by Sadthorpe (1811).
3. The Moira apron of 1813, the best known of all printed aprons (see Plate VII).

The lining of aprons (at first, it is thought, with white linen or silk) was known in 1731, and probably much earlier. Grand Lodge in that year resolved that "Masters and Wardens of particular Lodges may line their white Leather aprons with white Silk, and may hang their Jewels at white Ribbons about their Necks," and the record of this resolution, in 1738, is the first reference to the apron in the *Constitutions*. The lining of the white leather apron was possibly in some cases a matter of necessity, the dressed leather being liable to mark the clothing.

The Museum at Freemasons' Hall, London, as well as many other masonic museums, contain remarkable specimens of highly ornate aprons. For the most part, of course, the ornamentation was individually produced, but one highly popular pattern showing the figures of Faith, Hope, and Charity was printed from engraved plates.

A notable apron of the very early nineteenth century was the distinctive design said to have been copied from a painting by Hobday, and worn in the Moira Lodge of Honour (now No. 326, Bristol) from 1813 to 1815. A 'Moira' apron said to be 'designed by Bro. L. Hayes' is owned by the Loyal Lodge, No. 251, Barnstaple, Devon. It is painted on satin and has this inscription at the bottom:

If wisdom in council, eloquence in debate, valour in arms, steady patriotism and universal benevolence, be deserving of record in the pages of history and archives of Masonry, no subject in the British dominions possesses more genuine claims than the Right Honourable the

Earl of Moira A.G.M.

of England whose memory this Masonic Badge is designed to perpetuate.

This apron was purchased in 1813 and then cost twelve shillings and sixpence. At the same time one on 'jean' (a cotton cloth) was bought at six shillings, and a print on paper at five shillings and sixpence.

There is history in many of the old aprons. Of about the period 1780–90 is a highly decorative apron of the 'Antients' carrying the symbols of six or seven degrees, all of which degrees were conferred under the one Craft warrant. An Irish apron of much about the same date is of lambskin edged with three silk ribbons, the outer one blue, the middle red, and the inner one black, the three colours indicating that the owner held the Craft degrees, and was a Royal Arch mason and Knight Templar.

Tassels, Rosettes, and Levels

The earliest aprons had no decoration of any kind, not even ribbons (thongs or tapes answered their purpose), and certainly no tassels, rosettes or levels. It was the replacement of the strings by ribbons which is supposed to have suggested, more or less accidentally, the addition of the tassels in the relatively late period 1827–41. The ribbons passed under the bib, or flap, went round the body, and were tied in front where their decorated ends hung down, as clearly shown in old portraits, and in course of time led to the idea of permanent tassels.

It is not known how rosettes came to be added, but a likely suggestion is that they were adopted as a means of distinguishing the grades of Brethren. The love of ornamentation was possibly another factor. Contrary to what has been freely written on the subject, it is difficult to see how any symbolical meaning could originally have attached to them.

Perhaps the earliest reference to apron levels is in an order of the United Grand Lodge, 1814, describing how the levels are to be placed on the aprons. The levels were to be of half-inch ribbon, disposed in "perpendicular lines upon horizontal lines, thereby forming three several sets of two right angles." (This wording is still retained.) These levels were each two and a half inches wide by one inch high. The earliest aprons with rosettes in the Museum at Freemasons' Hall are of about the period 1815, and with levels about 1800.

Uniform Patterns of English Aprons

The United Grand Lodge early made a duty of simplifying the apron, which emblem had become of a bewildering number of patterns, sizes, and decorative styles. It decided, in May 1814, to insist on a uniform pattern, much the same as that in use to-day; but a generation went by before there was complete uniformity. Rule 269 of the current *Constitutions* provides details which are here abbreviated:

Entered Apprentice. A plain white lambskin, fourteen to sixteen inches wide, twelve to fourteen inches deep, rectangular, no ornament; white strings and a flap.

Fellow Craft. The same, with two sky-blue rosettes added.

Master Mason. The same, with sky-blue lining, and edging not more than two inches wide; additional rosette on the flap, silver tassels, sky-blue strings. Present Officers may have emblems of office in silver or white (surrounded by a double circle containing name and number of lodge) in centre of the apron; members of the Prince of Wales's Lodge, No. 259, may have internal half of the edging of garter-blue three-quarters of an inch wide.

Masters and Past Masters of Lodges. The same as Master Masons, but rosettes replaced by silver or sky-blue perpendicular lines upon horizontal lines, thereby forming three several sets of two right angles.

Grand Stewards' Aprons. Aprons of Grand Stewards shall have crimson lining and edging not more than three and a half inches wide, with the Master's emblems or rosettes in crimson, and with crimson strings and silver tassels; but Grand Stewards representing Prince of Wales's Lodge, No. 259, wear crimson edging two and three-quarters inches wide, and an internal border of garter-blue three-quarters of an inch wide.

Grand Officers. The aprons worn by Grand Officers have a garter-blue lining, and edging not exceeding three and a half inches wide; they are ornamented with gold lace and have garter-blue strings and gold tassels, the emblems of office being in gold or garter-blue in the centre within a wreath composed of a sprig of acacia and an ear of corn. The Grand Master's apron is ornamented with the blazing sun in gold in the centre, while on the edging are the pomegranate and lotus with the seven-eared wheat at each corner and on the fall.

Irish, Scottish, and American Aprons

Irish. The aprons of the Entered Apprentice and the Fellow Craft are similar to the English. The Master Mason's is much the same, also, but the number or badge of the lodge may be embroidered in silver, and a narrow silver braid may be worn upon the blue edging. Masters and Past Masters may add the square and compasses enclosing the letter 'G' embroidered in silver. In the apron of the Grand Officers the point of the fall is squared off, the lining and edging are of sky-blue silk, there is

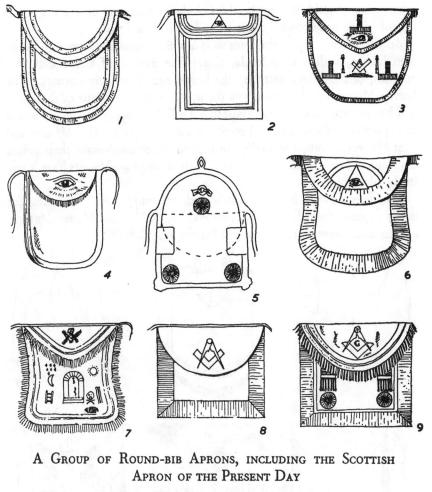

A GROUP OF ROUND-BIB APRONS, INCLUDING THE SCOTTISH
APRON OF THE PRESENT DAY

1. Apron of wash-leather, linen-lined, and edged with white silk (about 1796).
2. Heavily ornamented printed apron (about 1798).
3. Apron on which emblems have been drawn in indian ink, levels (added later) being of blue silk ribbon (about 1796).
4. An American apron (about 1820).
5. Apron of early nineteenth century, crudely painted and having rosettes (added later) of blue satin, the whole edged with red silk. Top centre rosette suggests a bow made by the tying of ribbons.
6. Apron of member of a Rotherham Lodge constituted by York Grand Lodge; it is dated 1779 and is of leather edged with silk, a rainbow (above the triangle) being of ribbon stitched on.
7. Apron (1799–1800) bearing emblems of Craft, Royal Arch, and Knight Templar masonry, originally belonging to a member of an Irish military Lodge; it is of lambskin, trimmed with blue and (outer) red silk, and fringed with black.
8 and 9. Scottish Master Masons' aprons of 1850 and the present day; in the second of these the edging, face of the flap or bib, and the rosettes are of red silk, the device and fringe being gold-coloured.

a trimming of gold lace on the sides of the edging, and on the outside is a gold fringe not exceeding one and a half inches deep.

Scottish. The Apprentice's apron is a white lambskin, sixteen by fourteen inches, with a semicircular flap. The Fellow of Craft adds two rosettes, of the colour worn by the lodge, near the lower corners. The Master Mason, in addition, edges the apron with the colour of the lodge and has an extra rosette on the lap; in his full-dress aprons the rosette may be replaced by the square and compasses and the letter 'G.' Masters and Past Masters of lodges and office-bearers wear the emblems of their offices embroidered on the lap of the apron. Masters and Past Masters have levels in the place of the rosette.

American. These, as already indicated, are simple white lambskins for every degree, there being a narrow edging of blue for Master Masons' aprons and a narrow edging of red for the Royal Arch.

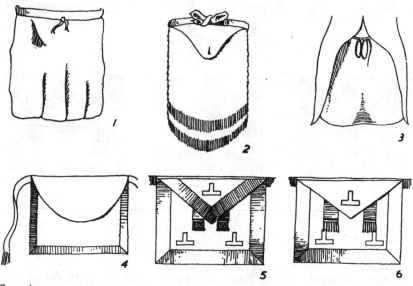

SIX APRONS DEMONSTRATING HOW THE STRINGS OR RIBBONS (SOME WITH FRINGED ENDS) TIED IN FRONT MAY HAVE LED TO THE IDEA OF TASSELS

1. Operative-style plain leather apron pictured in Hogarth's engraving *Night* (1738); note leather thong tied in front.
2. Apron tied with the bow of the ribbons in front, as pictured in the frontispiece of *Ahiman Rezon* (1778 edition), the 'Antient' Constitutions.
3. Another 'Antient' apron, believed to be of 1811.
4. An early apron, small and quite plain, showing the ribbons ending in fringes, which will come in centre of apron when tied.
5. Apron of first half of eighteenth century, the fringed ends being represented by actual tassels, while the levels are of narrow silk sewn on.
6. In this more modern apron the tassels are wider apart.

The Apron Bib, Flap, or Fall

There has been continuous argument with regard to the bib, flap, or fall of the apron, which in the operative's apron had a useful function—namely, to protect the worker's clothing, particularly when carrying heavy material—whereas in a speculative's apron the bib is only a symbol. The question is whether Entered Apprentices and Fellow Crafts should wear their aprons with the bibs up, down, or even folded inside. The 1772 edition of one of the so-called *exposés* makes the initiate say: "I tied the apron round my waist, with the flap on the inside, an apprentice not being entitled to wear it otherways." Always remembering that the apron is an emblem only, there is little purpose in the arguments in which Brethren have indulged themselves all these many years. It is, of course, possible that at one time, before the coming of rosettes, the only difference between an Entered Apprentice's and a Fellow Craft's apron was in the manner of wearing it, the former having the bib or flap turned up, on

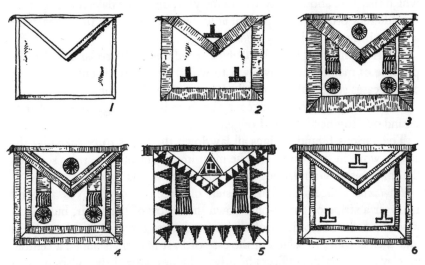

TRIANGULAR-BIB APRONS, INCLUDING THE ENGLISH AND IRISH
APRONS OF THE PRESENT DAY

1. One of the oldest patterns of English aprons of which an example still exists (date, 1731).
2. Master's apron (English) in the 1830–1850 period; no tassels.
3. Master Mason's apron (English) of the present day; white lambskin with watered-blue silk edging, etc., and silk-lined.
4. The corresponding Irish apron—of the same pattern except for a silver braid mounted on the wide silk edging.
5. English Royal Arch apron.
6. English Mark Past Master's apron.

the supposition (quite idle in an emblematical apron) that the Apprentice, doing rougher, dirtier work, needed greater protection from his apron. There is no agreement, however, as to this practice. In some American lodges the Apprentice wears his bib up, and the Fellow Craft down.

In a French lodge it was the custom for the Entered Apprentice to turn in or tuck in the flap to the back of the apron, while the Fellow Craft had his bib turned up and held in this position by fastening to a waist-coat button, which explains the purpose of a hole to be found in the bibs of many of the aprons pictured in some eighteenth-century engravings.

Collars

For hundreds of years collars, generally of gold or silver, have been known in civic life as a distinguishing mark of office or dignity. The collar has always had a considerable place in chivalry and has given its name to one of the orders—the Order of the Collar or Necklace, instituted by the Duke of Savoy in 1535. Brewer has a reference to "Collar Days," of which there are about thirty-five in the year, on which days the knights of the different orders, when present at levees or other court functions, wear all their insignia, including the collar.

Apart from being a mark of office and dignity, the collar answers the purpose of maintaining any jewel to which the wearer is entitled, and in certain cases small collars or collarettes are prescribed for the purpose. A collar of a Brother's own lodge may be worn in that lodge over a collar of Grand or Provincial Grand Lodge.

The various Grand Lodges all lay down the forms to be taken by the collars worn in their lodges. The most important of these rules so far as the three Sister Grand Lodges are concerned are as follow:

England. Officers and Past Masters of three old lodges, Nos. 2, 4, and 12, wear a stripe of garter-blue down the centre of the collar, but other-wise the collars of officers of all private lodges are of light-blue ribbon four inches wide, to which in the case of Past Masters is added a central, narrow silver braid. Officers of private lodges wear their collars only in their own lodges, or when representing their lodges as Masters or Wardens in Grand Lodge or Provincial or District Grand Lodge, or on any special occasion when ordered by the Grand Master. The plain undress collar of the Grand Officer is of garter-blue ribbon four inches wide, but the full-dress collar is heavily embroidered. In Grand Lodge and on special occasions present Grand Officers wear chains of gold or of metal gilt. Grand Stewards for the year wear collars of plain crimson ribbon four inches wide, a narrow edging of silver cord distinguishing Past rank.

Ireland. Officers of subordinate lodges wear collars of sky-blue watered ribbon about four inches wide edged with narrow silver lace; the number or badge of the lodge may be embroidered in silver on the front. In processions silver collars may be worn. Provincial Grand Officers, etc., wear collars as above, with the ends squared in front, and edged with narrow gold lace, and fringed at the ends with gold fringe similar to that worn on the aprons. Grand Officers wear gold chains of office as collars.

Scotland. Collars are not prescribed for the Masters of lodges; office-bearers wear sashes of the colour adopted by the lodge about four inches wide, embroidered with the name and number or the badge of the lodge. Master, Past Masters, and Wardens may wear gauntlets. Grand Office-bearers, etc., wear collars of thistle-green ribbon four inches wide, bound at the lower edges by narrow gold braid, and having a gold fringe. The Grand Master Mason's collar is of gold and enamel, and consists of an upper and a lower band bearing the Royal Arms of Scotland, the jewel of St Andrew, and the jewel of the Grand Master. Grand Office-bearers wear green sashes over the right shoulder and under the left arm.

Gloves

There is a time-immemorial tradition, both in masonry and outside it, of the wearing and giving of gloves. As masonic emblems, aprons and gloves are closely associated and have the same import, being emblems of innocence and of purity of heart. In some countries the Initiate has been invested, in addition to the apron, with white gloves, such gloves being the emblems of 'clean hands.' ('Hands' and 'gloves' are words coming from the same root.) "Who shall ascend into the hill of the Lord? or who shall stand in his holy place? He that hath clean hands, and a pure heart." (Psalm xxiv, 3–4.)

Remains of the ancient cave-dwellings prove that gloves were used in remote times. The Bible and Homer's *Odyssey* mention them.

There seems little doubt that freemasons inherited the custom of wearing ceremonial gloves not only from operative masonry, in which gloves were an essential protection, but from common usage, ancient and universal, in which gloves were articles of dress and also important and meaningful symbols.

Priests in the Middle Ages wore ornamental gloves of white linen to denote chastity, and metaphorically to indicate that their hands were clean and not open to a bribe. Curiously, judges did *not* wear gloves for exactly the same reason. In ancient days the judge in his court could wear gloves only when there were no cases for trial, and it is still a custom for a judge of assize to be presented with white gloves when there is an empty calendar. So long ago as 1302 a prisoner acquitted of manslaughter was required to give the Justice's Clerk a pair of gloves. A prisoner receiving pardon after condemnation made a present of gloves.

When in olden days money passed instead of gloves, it was called 'glove-money'—frequently another name for a bribe. Even to-day 'glove-money' often means a perquisite—'a little present for yourself.' Land has changed hands where part of the consideration has been a pair of gloves. In chivalry the glove was a prominent emblem, the knight-at-arms wearing his lady's glove in his helmet. A gallant gave gloves to the ladies. Gifts of gloves were common at weddings, and about the year 1500 a curate might refuse to solemnize a marriage except he be made a gift of money, hose, or gloves. Gloves were just as commonly given away at funerals as at weddings; in cases where the family was rich as many as a hundred pairs might be given away. It later became a custom for the undertaker to provide gloves for the mourners. In the eighteenth century a white glove on the door-knocker told the caller that a child had been born in the house. A girl kissing a sleeping man without waking him earned a pair of gloves. Freemasons in the eighteenth century might throw a Brother's apron and gloves into his open grave, and in so doing doubtless were only borrowing an old idea.

Among ancient customs in which gloves have a leading part is that in which a man threw down a glove or gauntlet as a challenge. "I will throw my glove to Death himself." (*Troilus and Cressida* iv, 4.) The idea is derived from the oriental custom by which the seller gave the purchaser a glove as evidence of good faith and to seal a contract, and in this connexion Ruth iv, 7 is significant: "Now this was the manner in former time in Israel concerning redeeming and concerning changing, for to confirm all things; a man plucked off his shoe, and gave it to his neighbour: and this was a testimony in Israel." In this passage the word 'shoe' is by some scholars rendered 'glove,' and apparently there is a connexion between the two words; one German word for glove is 'handschuh' ('hand-shoe').

From early medieval days employers provided masons with gloves in addition to their wages. In the Cathedral of Chartres, thirteenth century, is a picture of operative masons at work wearing gloves. The records of York Cathedral, 1355, show that masons were provided with gowns, aprons, gloves, and clogs, and there are very many similar records through the centuries.

There grew up a system by which masons, on their entry into the fraternity, were called upon to provide their fellow-members with aprons and gloves; this 'clothing the lodge,' as it was called, has already been referred to. The Schaw Statutes of 1599 direct that, at Killwinning, the Fellow of Craft shall provide at his entry a banquet and ten shillings' worth of gloves (at a later date the gloves were compounded for in money), and the same rule must have been general through the Scottish operative lodges.

Further, it was the custom throughout the eighteenth century for freemasons' lodges to present the wives of members with gloves. Here is a typical minute, dated 1756, of the Old King's Arms Lodge, No. 28, meeting in the Strand, London: "that the Lodge be cloathed with aprons once a year and at the beginning of the year gloves for the sisters." In the same lodge, twenty-two years earlier, the bill for an elegant enter-tainment includes this item: "Cloathing of 32 brethren and as many sisters at 5s. 10d. a piece . . . £9 6s. 8d. This means only that each brother had a new apron for himself and a pair of white gloves for his wife or sweetheart.

One of the irregular prints, dated 1772, says that the Master addresses an Initiate in these words:

> Put on these gloves; their whiteness is the symbol of purity, and of the innocence of a mason's manners. This other pair is for the use of the ladies; you will present them to her who holds the first place in your heart. . . . If the entrance into this respectable temple is not accessible to them, it is that we dread their beauty and the force of their charms.

Gauntlets

In early speculative days many of the plain white gloves had gauntlets, which as time went on became so elaborately ornamented with emblems that it was found more convenient to have the gauntlets detached. In an old lodge at Blandford, Dorset, white leather gloves, with extensions forming gauntlets like the modern motoring gloves, were worn by all the members, and there was in the town in 1920 a brother aged sixty who recollected seeing such a pair in his grandfather's possession. The Rural Philanthropic Lodge, No. 291, owns a set of gauntlets made of white linen, bearing the emblems of the various offices, and made to tie round the wrist with tapes.

Prior to 1883 the use of gauntlets was permissive only, but the *Constitu-tions* of the United Grand Lodge now say that garter-blue silk gauntlets gold-embroidered shall be worn by Grand Officers when wearing chains or embroidered silk collars and aprons, and by holders of London or Overseas Grand Rank and Provincial and District Grand Officers, present and past, when wearing collars and aprons having an edging of gold lace. Provincial and District Grand Stewards may wear gauntlets of red silk with silver emblems, and officers of private lodges gauntlets of light-blue silk with silver embroidery.

Wearing Hats in Lodge

An old catechism gives a clue to what must have been a general custom during the eighteenth century:

Q. Where does the Master hang his hat?
A. On nature's peg.

There is abundant evidence to show that in the early lodges the Master wore a hat—a sequel, it is thought, to the Jewish custom of remaining covered in synagogue and when taking an oath. We uncover our head as a mark of reverence and respect in a place of worship, a law court, etc., and also as a mark of courtesy to a woman, an older man, and to a superior, and it is supposed to follow from this that when one member of a company by right remains covered, while the others are uncovered, he is indicating his superiority and his authority. It has been customary for kings to wear their hats in any company, and it is related that when William Penn, the Quaker, kept his hat on in the presence of Charles II, the King removed his own hat, explaining that it was the custom in that place for only one person at a time to remain uncovered. But there was a day in which an ambassador had the right to wear a hat at court as a sign of his vicarious importance.

Usually, it was the Master of the early lodges who wore his hat during the ceremonies, but in some of the early German lodges the Brethren in general wore high silk hats, which were raised during prayer and when the name of the G.A.O.T.U. was invoked. In the Newstead Lodge, No. 47, Nottingham, the Master has long worn a top hat during ceremonies, removing it only during prayers and when administering an obligation; at his Installation he is (or was) presented with a hat, and requested to continue the custom that has long prevailed in the lodge.

In some Bristol lodges a cocked hat rests on the Master's pedestal. The Master wears it when entering and leaving lodge and for the procession of Installed Masters to and from the chapel where the actual ceremony of Installation is worked.

In the Moira Lodge of Honour, No. 326, Bristol, the outgoing Master used to wear the hat during the early part of the Installation ceremony, and at a later point it was worn by his successor to symbolize that he had become the ruler of the lodge. The custom fell into abeyance, but has since been revived. Cecil Powell informs us that the hats worn in the Bristol lodges were presented, probably in the year 1814, by the Grand Orient of France to Bro. Frederick Charles Husenbeth, a prominent mason of Bristol and three times Deputy Provincial Grand Master. Of German birth, he is said to have been made a mason at the age of seventeen by dispensation, being a lewis, in the Charles Theodore Lodge in Germany, probably in either Frankfurt or Mainz, and later reinitiated in the Beaufort Lodge, now No. 103, Bristol. He was a Roman Catholic, who late in life met with a sad reversal of fortune. The Craft subscribed funds for his support, and he died in 1848 at the age of eighty-three "with prayers upon his lips that the blessings of heaven might attend his Brethren and benefactors." Some years before his death he gave a number of books with which to start a masonic library in the Province of Bristol, among them being a set of early French rituals.

In Royal Sussex Lodge of Hospitality, No. 187, Bristol, founded in 1769, the Master carries, or did carry, his cocked hat into the lodge room, but does not wear it. Cecil Powell tells us that a cocked hat was formerly required on masonic occasions of full dress in the early years of the nineteenth century, and that when, in 1818, the Grand Master, the Duke of Sussex, visited Bath to consecrate the Freemasons' Hall there, officers of lodges and others were ordered to wear cocked hats, which apparently had to be hired for the occasion.

St George's Lodge, Exeter, No. 112, records in its minutes of the year 1830 that three dress hats for the use of W.M. and Wardens were ordered.

In lodges throughout the United States the Master invariably wears a silk hat, removing it when declaring the lodge open, and then replacing it, the Brethren of the lodge remaining uncovered. Any Past Master about to work a ceremony chooses a silk hat from a number behind the Master's chair. A visitor invited on to the dais to address the Brethren may be handed one of these hats, which he will wear while speaking. In many lodges the Master is presented with a silk hat at his Installation.

In many Continental lodges, particularly French, the Master, his Officers, and all the brethren used to wear hats. A line of ritual has come down to us confirming this; in some French lodges everybody wore a hat except the Candidate who, at the conclusion of the ceremony, was given a hat (some records say, the Master's hat) with the words "For the future, you shall be covered in a Master's Lodge." During the whole of the Third Degree funeral ceremony (which was carried out in the Master's Degree) Brethren were covered ("toujours le chapeau sur la tête"), and, apparently, the hat let down in front ("rabattu sur le devant").

In the Pilgrim Lodge (Der Pilger), No. 238, the only English lodge working since its foundation (London, 1779) a German ritual in the German language, all the Brethren wear hats, these being raised at prayers and at mention of the G.A.O.T.U. A candidate for Passing or Raising is given back his hat at the end of the ceremony—a symbol of a freedom that had been surrendered and is now restored.

Lodge Uniforms

It has been stated that with the single exception of the Grand Steward's Lodge, no English masonic body has adopted a uniform; but that is not strictly accurate, for in the Moira Lodge of Honour, Bristol, now No. 326 (founded in 1809), the wearing of a distinctive uniform, as A. F. Calvert tells us, was compulsory on all its members for at least thirty-two years prior to 1845, when it was discontinued, later attempts to restore the custom meeting with no success. This famous lodge adopted in 1813 the distinctive apron well known as the Moira apron, which was reproduced from a painting by Hobday, but under the *Constitutions* of the United Grand Lodge in 1815 it had to be discarded. The Moira uniform included a blue coat with brass buttons, these bearing the Moira badge; silk waistcoat, a white one in summer and a black one in winter; knee breeches; black silk stockings; black shoes.

Some lodges are known to have insisted on their members wearing coloured coats; for example, St Albans, No. 29 (founded 1728), whose members wore a green coat.

What has been thought to be a uniform has proved in the well-known instance of the Britannic Lodge (No. 33, founded in 1730, named in 1774 and for many years meeting at the famous old Thatched House Tavern, St James Street, London, now replaced by a modern club building) to be the rich and colourful dress affected by a gentleman of the 1780's. The centenary history of the lodge reproduces an illustration in colour of a member dressed in blue coat with frilled shirt, scarlet cape, buff waist-coat and breeches, plumed hat, buckle shoes, and white gloves.

In Isaac Newton University Lodge, No. 859, founded in Cambridge in 1861, the custom (interrupted by the Second World War) has been for officers to wear court dress (knee breeches, silk stockings, and buckle shoes) and for the other members to be encouraged to do the same; while in Apollo University Lodge, No. 357, Oxford, forty-three years older, officers have, from the early days of the lodge, worn court dress, all others present being in full evening dress with white waistcoats.

Jewels

Jewels of rank and office are customarily suspended from collars or chains and collarettes, whereas commemorative jewels are generally breast jewels. One of the earliest official references to jewels is that of June 24, 1727, when the English Grand Lodge ordered the Masters and Wardens of private lodges to wear "the jewels of Masonry hanging to a white ribbon," an instruction long since obsolete.

The *Constitutions* of the various Grand Lodges prescribe the jewels (and their collars, etc.) to be worn, and are sometimes accompanied by illustrations by which the various jewels of rank, etc., can be identified. Very briefly indeed, it may be said that the English Master's jewel is a square, to which, in the case of a Past Master, is added a diagram of the 47th Proposition; the Senior Warden's, a level; the Junior Warden's, a plumb-rule; the Chaplain's, a book on a triangle on a 'glory'; the Treasurer's, a key (in Ireland, crossed keys); the Secretary's, two pens in saltire tied by a ribbon; the Director of Ceremonies', two rods in saltire tied by a ribbon; Deacons', dove and olive branch (in Scotland, Senior's is a maul and Junior's is a trowel); Almoner's, a scrip-purse upon which is a heart (in Scotland it is a level with compasses extended thereon); Organist's, a lyre (in Ireland, an Irish harp); Inner Guard's, two swords in saltire; Steward's, a cornucopia between the legs of a pair of compasses extended; the Tyler's, a sword. ('In saltire' is a heraldic term for 'crossed.' The 'glory' above mentioned is the Blazing Star.)

The jewel of the Past Master of an Irish lodge is the square and compasses enclosing the letter 'G.' In a Scottish lodge, the Master's jewel is the compasses and square united, with arc of 90 degrees with sun; in the Past Master's jewel the sun is omitted.

Grand officers, etc., in the English system have jewels of gold or of metal gilt; officers, etc., of private lodges have silver jewels; exceptions are the officers of Lodges Nos. 2 and 8, who have jewels of gold or of metal gilt.

The earliest jewel of rank in the Grand Lodge Museum, London, is a Master's jewel, a plain silver square with the 47th Proposition in enamel hanging from the angle, and possibly dating from about 1730.

Jewels customarily presented to retiring Masters as a token of appreciation of services rendered; founders' jewels; festival jewels; etc., etc.— these are commemorative jewels fashioned to designs favoured by the lodge, Charity, etc., and generally have small relation, or none at all, to the official designs for jewels of rank, etc., prescribed by Grand Lodge. But the Charity Jewel is of a design officially approved by the United Grand Lodge, and may be worn only by Brethren who have served the office of Steward to two of the masonic charities and personally subscribed a certain minimum sum.

The jewels of rank and office date back to the 1720's and probably long before then, while the commemorative jewels, or breast jewels, may well have almost as long a history. Perhaps the earliest breast jewel known to us, a beautiful specimen, was struck in 1733 to commemorate the connexion of Charles Sackville, Earl of Middlesex (afterwards Duke of Dorset), with a lodge of freemasons at Florence, which is known to have been at work at least three years earlier. With this exception, we know little of breast jewels until the 1750's.

Commemorative jewels (from this point called simply jewels, to avoid repetition) are obviously closely connected with coins, an enormous subject on which there is a considerable literature. The earliest coins were of Lydia, Asia Minor, were of electrum (gold-silver alloy), and were issued in 716 B.C. Many of the early peoples had coins; the Romans before the days of Christ had them; even Britain before the days of the Anglo-Saxons had thick silver coins, roughly circular. Medals have been known in most European countries for many centuries. Whereas a coin is a metal token passed from hand to hand in exchange for value, the medal (the word means 'metal') commemorates an event.

A coin or medal has a face, or front, which is known as the obverse, the other side, whether decorative or plain, being the reverse; on the obverse of a penny you find the King's head, on the reverse Britannia. The reverse of a masonic jewel is generally plain, but in the eighteenth century it was frequently quite as decorative as the face. Usually, any inscription is on the reverse.

Medals have been made in quantity by striking them from engraved dies just as coins are made, but some of the most handsome medals have been produced by modelling and casting. Both these methods and many others have been used in producing masonic jewels. Most of the jewels of the 1750's and 60's are quite different from ordinary medals or coins. A few are enamelled on metal, and bear transfer designs of masonic emblems, but chiefly they are of thinnish metal seldom much thicker than a sixpenny piece. They are from one and a half to two and a quarter inches in diameter, usually circular, but sometimes elliptical, and occasionally shaped to the outline of the design. The ornament is pierced or fretted so that essentially the same design appears on each face, but there is in addition some amount of engraving, so that the obverse and reverse are not quite the same. Such jewels do not give the impression of having been made by specialist medal-makers, and perhaps an inkling as to who did make them is afforded by some watch-parts on view in the Museum of Freemasons' Hall (and probably many other museums). These parts are the watch 'cocks'—that is, the decorative plates, which, in the old watches, carry the outer bearing of the balance-wheel. These cocks are pierced or fretted and engraved, and, although only as large as a six-pence, include as many masonic emblems as many of the jewels having six times their area. These little watch-cocks are attractive and altogether most cunning examples of craftsmanship. The obvious suggestion is that many of the old masonic jewels of the type described were the work of watchmakers.

The fact that there are many thousands of jewels, many of great beauty, in the various masonic museums of the world will explain why here we are obliged to content ourselves with some details of a few of the earliest eighteenth-century designs.

We find many of the old jewels engraved with the words *Vertuti et Silentio* ('Virtue and Silence') and *Veritas est Intus*, which may be rendered as 'Truth is in the Heart.'

The emblems crowded into the early jewels included the Volume of the Sacred Law, 24-inch gauge, level, plumb-rule, square, compasses, maul, scroll with 47th Proposition, and, very frequently, the letter 'G' on which perhaps the whole design is based. In almost every jewel of the period we find Jacob's Ladder, and the sun and moon; and on many of them the flaming sword, the crossed quill-pens, a coffin, the lewis keys, the pentalpha, the all-seeing eye, clasped hands, sometimes the pair of scales and the beehive, the pillars, altar, the trowel, the triangle, the mason's pick, the façade of the Temple, Noah's Ark, a skull, the tessellated pavement, and sometimes a pedestal. It is fairly evident that in addition to the Craft degrees the owners of the jewels were working, in many cases, some degrees which nowadays are not included in the Craft working.

It is not uncommon for two jewels of the 1760 period to be of identical design, but for one of them to be pierced or fretted and for the other to be—for want of a better term—a plate jewel. Sometimes a jewel with an obverse quite different from the reverse is made by brazing or silver-soldering together two very thin stampings.

The method of production of the early thin metal jewels—pierced or fretted, incised and engraved—lent itself to the inclusion of a great number of emblems; but as the making of masonic jewels developed into a manufacturer's art, and decorative effects were increasingly to be obtained by the use of enamel (soft glass of rich colouring), and as, moreover, the Royal Arch Degree came more and more to be worked in chapters apart from lodges, it became less usual to crowd in a large number of the emblems so dear to the heart of our early Brethren. So far as is known, the first example in the Freemasons' Hall Museum, London, of an enamelled jewel is of the 1750–60 period, and handsome as the effects produced by the use of enamel came to be in later days, for sheer dignity and aptness the plain metal jewels of the early period, whether gold, silver, copper, etc., have probably never been surpassed.

The earliest R.A. jewel at present known (it can be seen in the Grand Lodge Museum, London) is dated 1766 and belonged to an exaltee in Lord Blayney's chapter of the preceding year, while the earliest mention of P.Z. jewels is in the same chapter and of the same year.

Chapter Thirty-one

MASONIC COLOURS AND THEIR SYMBOLISM

Colours have so large a place in the customs of the Craft that inevitably the question arises: Did ancient symbolism inspire the colours of masonry, or were they first chosen and the symbolism then found to fit them? Many years ago a writer who went deeply into the question came to the conclusion that the English Grand Lodge, in choosing the colours of its clothing, was guided mainly by the colours associated with the Noble Orders of the Garter and the Bath. This idea is more or less confirmed by the late Henry Sadler, an authority universally respected, who said: "Having looked at the matter from every conceivable point of view, I have failed to think of a more favourable explanation." We must conclude, therefore, that freemasonry's colours were no more derived from ancient symbolism than were the colours of the liturgical vestments of the Christian Church from those of the Jewish priests.

The clothing of three groups of degrees is related mainly to three colours: the Craft or symbolic degrees with blue; the Royal Arch with crimson; and the allied degrees with green, white, and other colours, including black. F. J. W. Crowe has suggested that the deep-blue colour —the Oxford blue—of the Grand Officers' clothing was borrowed from the ribbon of the Most Noble Order of the Garter. When the 'garter' was instituted by Edward III about 1348 (it was reconstituted in 1805 and 1831) its colour was light blue, but soon after the accession of George I, in 1714, this light blue was changed to the present deep blue to distinguish the colour of the Order from that which the Stuarts in banishment on the Continent had conferred on their adherents. As for the light blue—the Cambridge blue—of private lodge clothing, this was deliberately chosen to contrast with, and mark the difference from, the deep blue of Grand Lodge clothing.

The Grand Stewards' crimson, suggests the above author, was taken from the Most Honourable Order of the Bath, revived by George I in 1725 and enlarged in 1815 and 1847. The Scottish Grand Lodge took its green ('thistle' green) from that of the Most Ancient and Most Noble Order or the Thistle, restored by James VII and II in 1687 and re-established by Queen Anne in 1703.

The Grand Lodge of Ireland chose its light blue probably with the object of making a contrast to that of the dark blue of the English Grand Lodge, and in so doing anticipated the light blue of the Most Illustrious Order of St Patrick, founded for Ireland by George III in 1783 and revised in 1905.

Whichever came first—symbolism or colours—it is undeniable that freemasonry attaches considerable importance to colours, and it will be useful to refer briefly to those found chiefly associated with the Order.

White. Conventionally white is a colour, whatever it is technically. In the Craft and throughout the world it is the natural emblem of purity, truth, innocence, hope; a freemason's apron of white lambskin is the badge of innocence. Biblical references in support of this symbolism are many.

Blue. "Her hue she derives from the blue vault of Heaven" (J. W. Day's *The Banner Song*). The deep Oxford-blue of the English Grand Lodge clothing, and the light Cambridge-blue of private lodge clothing, have already been referred to. The light blue is the azure blue, the cerulean, or sky, blue. Universally blue denotes immortality, eternity, chastity, fidelity; pale blue, in particular, represents prudence and goodness.

The Bible mentions many liturgical uses of blue: "Where were white, green, and blue, hangings, fastened with cords of fine linen and purple" (Esther i, 6); ". . . thou shall make the robe of the ephod all of blue" (Exodus xxviii, 31); and there are many, many others.

In freemasonry blue is the emblem of universal brotherhood and friendship and "instructs us that in the mind of a mason those virtues should be as extensive as the blue arch of Heaven itself."

To the ancient Jews blue was a chief religious colour—the High Priest had a blue robe, and one of the veils of the tabernacle was of a blue colour known as tekelet (implying perfection). It is said that in ancient days the most solemn oaths were sworn on blue altars.

The question has often been asked whether the Biblical names given to colours, and particularly to blue, represent the colours known by those names to-day. Not quite, it is thought. Lewis Edwards is of the opinion that what is rendered 'blue' in the Old Testament is probably more exactly 'purple-blue' or 'violet,' the latter being twice given as a marginal alternative in the Book of Esther. He thinks, too, that the word 'purple' is more exactly rendered to-day by the term 'purple-red.' Another masonic writer has advanced the idea (which, if sound, would justify the marginal alternatives just noted) that the 'sky blue' mentioned by the ancient writers of the East must represent the 'deep blue' of the Eastern sky—"a colour approaching to black"—and not the 'light blue' of the Northern climate.

Violet and Purple. These are closely related to blue. Both the Bible and the Apocrypha have many references to ·purple, which symbolizes regal apparel and richness. The New Testament speaks of "a seller of purple" (Acts xvi, 14); the Book of Numbers says "they shall spread a purple cloth [on the altar]" (iv, 13); the Book of Judges refers to the purple raiment of the Kings of Midian (viii, 26). At the crucifixion of Christ the soldiers of Pilate, as an act of derision, "platted a crown of thorns, and put it on his head, and they put on him a purple robe" (John xix, 2). Universally violet and purple are the emblems of regal grief and death, but, in addition, violet conveys the idea of penitence, and purple the ideas of royalty, justice, and temperance. In freemasonry, but on a purely technical ground, purple has been called the emblem of union, because it is formed by the union of blue and red. Purple coloured ribands were used in the Dundee Lodge, then No. 9, at Wapping, before 1767.

Red, Crimson, and Scarlet. In freemasonry the one colour crimson represents all these three colours. Universally red is the emblem of faith, fortitude, divine love, magnanimity, and, in its suggestion of blood, martyrdom. The Bible refers to both scarlet and crimson as liturgical colours. In freemasonry scarlet is an emblem of high dignity, and has been chosen to distinguish the robe of Z in the Royal Arch.

Green. Green, always regarded as the symbol of gladness and abundance, has been directly associated with ideas of resurrection and immortality, even of victory. The Bible has but few references to it as a liturgical colour (the Book of Esther mentions the green hangings in the King's palace), but uses green to indicate the products of the good earth, in this sense associated with plenty, the reverse of famine. Green has been adopted by a number of allied masonic degrees whose teaching is closely associated with the immortality of divine truth. In the ancient mysteries green stood for the moral birth or rebirth of the Initiate. The acacia (the masonic evergreen) has been suggested as a symbol of a moral life or rebirth, and also of immortality. To the ancient Egyptians green was the symbol of hope.

The Scottish Grand Lodge has adopted thistle-green as its emblematic colour, as already noted, and a green ribbon or collar was part of the regalia of the Country Steward's Lodge, originally No. 540, which had a short life, and was constituted in 1789 for the particular association of stewards charged with making arrangements for an annual festival that met out of London. Grand Lodge permitted the members to wear a special jewel suspended from a green ribbon or collar, the colour having been chosen apparently because of its suggestion of the countryside. The members were also given the right to wear a green apron, a privilege withdrawn about 1797, although that of wearing the green collar was retained. The lodge lapsed in 1802, its number—then 449—being passed to the Lodge of Faith and Friendship, Berkeley, Gloucestershire (now No. 270), which was honoured with the prefix 'Royal.'

Black. From remote antiquity black has been the symbol of grief and sorrow and death. In heraldry it has an entirely different significance— that of prudence and wisdom—while grey symbolizes tribulation. In the allied degrees black symbolizes not only grief, but silence and secrecy. In the French rite the lodge in the Third Degree is clothed in black "strewed with tears," in token of the loss of a Principal Architect.

Yellow, Gold, and Silver. Yellow is used in freemasonry only as gold, the symbol of the sun and therefore of constancy, while silver represents the moon. Universally yellow has been held to represent jealousy, incontinence, and treachery; but in heraldry, where, as in masonry, yellow represents gold, its significance is entirely reversed.

Royal Arch Colours. In the chapters of the eighteenth century the symbolic colours were scarlet, mazarine blue, and light grey; but following the union, the scarlet robe of Z represents imperial dignity, the purple robe of H union, and the blue robe of J universal friendship and benevolence. These matters are more fully gone into in the chapter devoted to the Royal Arch.

Chapter Thirty-two

THE LODGE AT REFRESHMENT; TOASTS;
LADIES' NIGHTS

THE curious usages of the Craft in relation to refreshment appear to be echoes of the widespread convivial customs of the seventeenth or earlier centuries. The medieval operatives took their meals in their lodges on the building site, their long day, often from dawn to sunset, being a succession of periods of work separated by simple meals. Every working day consisted of little more than labour and refreshment, with often some amount of religious observance. On feast-days they went to mass, and spent the rest of the day in eating and drinking, probably in the company of their wives, and possibly of their families.

The ancient Craft tradition of refreshment and feasting was handed down by the guilds, which glories in the maintenance of medieval customs; they still do so to-day, as we see for ourselves in the cere-monious feasting of the City Corporations and Livery Companies, all of them, both corporations and companies, descendants of the earliest frith guilds. This is true of all the guilds of the European countries, and we may assume that the *Brudermahl* ('brother-meal') of the German lodges is a close relation to the old guild feast. The very inception of the guilds was a periodical meeting of a tribe or family for the purpose of feasting and the discussion of domestic matters.

Customs relating to Refreshment

Brethren well know that the use of the word 'refreshment' in the masonic ritual does not necessarily mean eating and drinking. A simple rest—a calling off in the middle of a long lodge session—is 'refreshment.' Occasionally a lodge is called from labour to actual refreshment, but generally the Brethren take their refreshment after the tiled lodge has been closed. This does not wholly reflect the early speculative usage, for undoubtedly in some, but not all, of the lodges in the early 1700's the Brethren drank, smoked, and sometimes ate during the course of the ceremonious work. At table lodges, which were then general, the Brethren sat round a table, sometimes of horseshoe pattern, and enjoyed a drink and a smoke while they worked the old 'lectures,' which actually were catechisms, questions being asked by the Master in the chair and answered by the Brethren one by one.

It is in the irregular prints, or *exposés*, giving these old catechisms that we are enabled to make any real acquaintance with the early speculative ceremonies. We cannot escape the conclusion that it was the table lodge which gave the inspiration for the dinner ritual of Royal Arch masonry. It can be well understood that in table lodges labour and refreshment were so closely intermixed that the Junior Warden's injunction to cease from refreshment and go to labour, or vice versa, was a real and intimate order. There is no difficulty, then, in comprehending the reason for the emphasis laid on the word 'refreshment' in parts of our ancient ritual.

What is in towns the general custom of holding a dinner or so-called banquet after each lodge meeting could not have applied as a fixed and general rule in the early days. Nor does it apply to-day in thousands of cases outside the capital cities of the world. Instead, we find a system by which the Brethren take light refreshment together at the end of the lodge meeting, and hold each year one big festival dinner—the Installation banquet. This is particularly so in a great many of the American lodges where the membership is so large, and the meetings so frequent, that no other course would be possible. (The present writer has a grateful recollection, one he often smiles on, of a three-and-a-half-hour visit, as a complete stranger, to Hope Lodge at Washington, No. 20, District of Columbia, and of being hospitably entertained about eleven o'clock at night with a big basin of clam chowder, followed by a slightly smaller basin of ice cream.)

The annual feast meant much to the early speculative masons. As a system it was immediately adopted by the Premier Grand Lodge of 1717, and we find to-day in the *Constitutions* of the English, Irish, Scottish, and many other Grand Lodges allusions to the custom. The English Grand Lodge normally held a Grand Festival on the Wednesday after St George's Day, to which all regular masons who had provided themselves with tickets, at a price, from the Grand Stewards for the year were admitted (United Grand Lodge, Rule 12). Ordinarily the Grand Master is installed on the day of the Grand Festival. From early in the eighteenth century the Grand Master has appointed Grand Stewards, who regulate the Grand Festival under his direction, and who possess certain privileges (see pp. 176, 177).

The Grand Lodge of Ireland meets at High Noon on the festival of St John (December 27) to proclaim and salute the Grand Officers elected for the ensuing year.

The Scottish Grand Lodge holds its festival on St Andrew's Day, when the Brethren elected or appointed as Grand Office-bearers are installed. There is traditionally a long period of feasting in Scottish lodges, the custom undoubtedly going back to remote times. Here is a typical quotation from the records of the Lodge of Aberdeen, 1698: "for ale, white bread, two legs of mutton, a pound of tobacco and pipes, and a capful of salt, £11 5s. 7d."

The world-wide custom has been to amalgamate the Annual Festival and the Installation Meeting. Our Brethren of the English speculative lodges in the 1700's were at times real 'knife and fork' masons, as evidence of which we learn from the minutes of the lodge-meeting at the Bear, Bath, in 1748, that "the Master and Wardens were properly installed and took their places accordingly, it being omitted last St John's Day on Acc^t. of the Hurry of Business." This can only mean that on the former occasion business took a little longer than had been expected, and rather than let the dinner spoil they left out some part of the Installation! This lodge must have been keen on the creature comforts, because we learn that at the festival of 1775 mine host of the White Hart, who was a member of the lodge, was expected to forfeit six bottles of wine if dinner were not on the table by three o'clock!

The old lodges made careful arrangements for the provision of food and drink. The Grand Lodge of York in 1725 said in one of its rules that "The Bowl shall be filled at the Monthly Lodge with Punch once; Ale, Bread and Cheese, and Tobacco in common; but if any more shall be called for by any Brother, either for eating or drinking, that Brother shall pay for it himself, besides his club." By 'club,' 'Yorkshire Club,' etc., is meant an arrangement by which all present equally shared the cost.

How many lodges laid down their own wine is not known, but a minute in 1736 of the Old King's Arms Lodge, No. 28, records that the landlord be desired to procure a hogshead of such wine (red port) as shall be agreeable to the committee, that it be bottled and "the corks sealed with the Master's seal and that it shall be then kept for the use of this Society and that no other Red Port be brought into the lodge." Four months later the wine was in hand and some members attended to see it bottled off; the committee having "discharged their duty to the general satisfaction of the Society, their healths were chearfully drank with thanks for their trouble and great care."

In a bylaw of the Mariners' Lodge (its members were mariners, shipbuilders, etc.) working from 1799 for only a few years at Selby, Yorkshire, is evidence of the custom of drinking in lodge. The lodge is

> to find two shillingsworth of malt liquor and one pint of gin, rum, and brandy for every lodge night only. The Lodge not to be closed for refreshment but the refreshment to be brought into the room and put on a side table and any who chooses may partake thereof paying 6d for the same, and after the

Lodge is closed those who wish to stay pay for the Liquor they call for. To have no spirits admitted into the room during the time the Lodge is open unless paid for by the person calling for it. The Bill to be paid every night.

A further bylaw of the lodge provides that: "The expence of refreshment shall not exceed one shilling per member each lodge night except on particular occasions." The lodge finances did not prosper, and in 1805 we find the Brethren entering into a weekly subscription of one shilling each for the purpose of purchasing shares of tickets in the next State lottery. The suggestion was made that tickets should be bought with funds for the 'benefit' of the lodge, but in 1811 bankruptcy overtook the lodge, at which time one Brother's refreshment bill was several months in arrear!

Old lodge minutes often refer to a closing-time for refreshment. A rule of the Grand Lodge of York, 1725, says: "The Master or Deputy shall be obliged to call for a Bill exactly at ten o'clock, if they meet in the evening, and discharge it."

Smoking in Lodge

Smoking in lodge was at one time quite usual. Smoking in the English Grand Lodge was common in its early days, but was prohibited in 1755 as being "an indecency that should never be suffered in any solemn assembly." Lodge of Antiquity (then No. 1, now No. 2) had a bylaw in 1760 permitting a member to smoke except when the "Lodge is honoured with the visit of a Brother who wears a blue apron"; then he had to get leave from the Master "unless such visitor smokes a pipe himself." In course of time the custom became unpopular, and finally was forbidden in most lodges. The next lodge on the list, Fidelity, now No. 3, prohibited smoking in lodge in the year 1802. Smoking was permissible in a number of American lodges until recently, and possibly is still allowed in some.

The Custom of Toasting

There is reason to believe that toasting got its name from a custom going back to the sixteenth century, and perhaps earlier, by which a piece of toasted bread was added to the wine or other liquor, and, when the loving-cup had made its circuit of the table and regained the host, it was his privilege to drain the cup and swallow the toast. So we are told, and for proof of the explanation we are referred to the toasted bread "which still floats in the loving-cups at the English Universities." Fable (in this case Rabelais) says that the drinking of healths was 'invented' by the giant Gabarra, but, of course, the custom was well known to the ancient peoples. Our Saxon forefathers were prodigious drinkers of healths.

It was to be expected that in an age when hard drinking was the fashion the early speculative lodges should observe many of the old drinking customs. The drinking of toasts was extremely popular throughout Europe at that time, and there is some reason to suppose that even in the course of an Initiation ceremony in some of the early eighteenth-century lodges the Brethren may have drunk a toast "to the Heart that conceals, and to the Tongue that never reveals." The *Steinmetzen*, the German stonemasons, had what they called a pledge feast, at which toasts were drunk, or pledged, with much ceremony and precision, and in so doing they were observing a custom followed in every German craft.

It has become a tradition at masonic feasts and dinners to drink a number of toasts, but there seems no good reason to suppose that all the possible toasts should be worked through on every occasion. There is a list, or calendar, on the Master's table showing the sequence, or precedence, to be observed, but it hardly dictates that every one of the toasts must be given. The matter is entirely in the Master's discretion, and he will have regard to the circumstances and the presence of any particular masonic personage.

'*The King and the Craft.*' Of all masonic toasts that of 'The King and the Craft' takes first place, and is possibly the most debated. A note on the subject by John P. Simpson, in 1910, was communicated to the lodges by Sir Edward Letchworth, a Grand Secretary of revered memory, who, in so doing, remarked that in the view of some Brethren it would be more loyal to make the first toast 'The King,' instead of coupling his Majesty's name with 'The Craft.' He pointed out, however, that it was incorrect to suppose that the health of the Sovereign was honoured in this matter only on account of his patronage of freemasonry, and just as incorrect to assume that the double toast was merely the occasion for drinking to the prosperity of the Craft simultaneously with the health of the Sovereign. He thought that the real significance of the toast was that loyalty to the King is an essential principle of freemasonry. The note claims that the toast is "the best authenticated heirloom masons have received from the remote past." It is a big claim; but, inasmuch as the Old Charges, dating back to the fifteenth century, called upon masons to be true men to God, true liegemen to the King, and true to the craft of masonry, the author may have felt justified in making it. The note informs us that in St John's Lodge, Glasgow, No. 3, is a chest which seems to have been used at great masonic functions in the seventeenth century and to contain records; on it is carved "God save the King and Mason Craft 1684." According to Anderson's *Constitutions* of 1738, this double toast was drunk by Scottish masons in the reign of James I of Scotland (about 1440), but we may well doubt his statement. In the *Constitutions* from 1738 to 1767 the toast appears as the proper one to give first after the 'Master's Song'; after 1767 neither toasts nor songs are mentioned.

Nevertheless we gather definitely that the toast was in use in the early 1700's, and probably long before. Anderson suggests that the toast was drunk at the Festival in the year 1719. A letter authorized by the Grand Master in 1757 stated that "Our Healths in Lodge are first, the King and the Craft with 3.3." Both 'Moderns' and 'Antients' agreed in this matter. The 'Antients' in 1760 and 1761 recorded the authorized toasts, and placed 'The King and the Craft' at the head of the list with full masonic honours. On the first date George II was king, on the second George III, and neither of them was a freemason.

In Dublin, in 1751, at the laying of the foundation-stone of the Parliament House exactly the same toast was drunk. It heads a list of the toasts in the *Constitutions* of the Grand Lodge of Ireland of the year 1817. At the Grand Festival (England) of 1794 the toast was 'the King and the Craft,' followed by the singing of *God Save the King*. So there can be no doubt whatever that in linking the 'King' with the 'Craft' we but follow a long and fine tradition.

Other Toasts. It would be idle to comment on every one of the toasts likely to be drunk at a masonic banquet. One of the toasts never omitted is 'The Visiting Brethren,' for which a few lodges use at table a special ritual which it is understood the Authors Lodge, No. 3456, has developed into the following form:

W.M. Brethren, we are about to honour the toast of the Visitor. Bro. S.W., what is the message from the West?

S.W. Peace—to those who enter.

W.M. What is the message from the South?

J.W. Prosperity—to those who depart.

W.M. And, Brethren, the message from the East is Blessing—to those who remain. Peace, Prosperity and Blessing—Our Visitors!

Omnes. Peace, Prosperity, Blessing—Our Visitors!

A few lodges have their own songs of greeting to visitors, or special versions of old and well-known masonic songs. In the Mariners' Lodge, No. 168, Guernsey (an 'Antient' lodge founded in 1784), the Brethren after the proposal of the Visitors' Toast, sing:

> Warm Masonic hearts to greet you,
> Hands of Mariners to greet you,
> May our welcome here to-day
> Cheer each Brother on his way.

The toast of 'Absent Brethren,' frequently observed at a given hour of the evening, was probably in use in some lodges for many years before

1914, but it was during the First World War that it came into general usage. The 'silent fire' that so often accompanies it is not an essential part of the toast, and indeed is to be deprecated as a *regular* custom.

'*Challenging.*' The drinking of healths from table to table at the sudden whim of the challengers is undoubtedly a very old custom, and a good one when not overdone. It was commonly observed at the beginning of the eighteenth century, not only by freemasons, but by club assemblies and other gatherings of that sort. The description of a meeting of the Mughouse Club, in Long Acre, London, published in 1722, lights up the subject for us (This club was one of many Mughouse gatherings fostered by the Hanoverian interest in opposition to the Jacobite cause; the Magpie and Stump, Old Bailey, is a survivor of the old inns in which the clubs met.):

> Every Wednesday and Saturday, a mixture of gentlemen, lawyers, and tradesmen, meet in a great room, and are seldom under a hundred. They have a grave old gentleman, in his own grey hairs, now within a few months of ninety years old, who is their president, and sits in an arm'd chair some steps higher than the rest of the company, to keep the whole room in order. A harp plays all the time at the lower end of the room, and every now and then one or other of the company rises and entertains the rest with a song. . . . Here is nothing drunk but ale, and every gentleman hath his separate mug, which he chalks on the table where he sits as it is brought in. . . . The room is always so diverted with songs, and drinking from one table to another to one another's healths, that there is no room for politicks, or anything that can sour conversation.

When Drinking a Masonic Toast. The holding out of a glass of wine when we drink a friend's health is said to have sprung from the old Greek custom (it seems to be a logical one) of handing the glass of wine to the person toasted, with the salutation, "This to thee!" Some such practice is the likely origin of all the expressive movements of the glass that have accompanied toast-drinking throughout the ages and which, in a form peculiar to the Craft, both with glass and without it, are part and parcel of the drinking of a masonic toast. The significant movement of hand and glass (which reminds every Entered Apprentice of a communication made to him by the Master of the Lodge soon after the light dawned upon him) was possibly suggested by the common custom at one time of making the sign of the Cross over the glass of wine, and may also have borrowed something from the Jacobites, the adherents of the banished James II (Latin, *Jacobus*), who indicated their loyalty to a king 'over the water' by expressive movements of their drinking glasses. It should clearly be stated that the signs accompanying masonic 'firing' are *not* patterned upon the characteristic movements of a trowel.

'Firing'

The custom of accompanying a toast with 'fire,' obviously of time immemorial, did not apparently originate in the bringing together of the hands, but in the crashing down on the table of a drinking vessel. Hundreds of years ago it probably had a link with other drinking customs, possibly with the intentional smashing of a glass after the drinking of a toast of more than usual importance or solemnity. 'Firing' is a custom known in many countries; in the early French lodges the drinking of a toast was called *feu* ('fire'); German students had a custom in which the drinking of the toast was done to strict order and time by the whole of the company, who then grounded their glasses in a circular path upon the table and finally crashed them on the table all at the same instant.

It is reasonable to assume that the terms 'fire' and 'firing' were derived from nothing more than the crashing down of the glasses with the double purpose of honouring a toast with noisy enthusiasm and of proving the glasses to be empty—a convivial and demonstrative way of showing that there were no heel-taps! But it is not impossible that masonic fire is a survival of the soldier's custom of firing salutes of guns after important toasts. A little support for this theory may be seen in the fact that in certain West Indian lodges the fire is called a 'battery'; but such derivation is by no means to be taken for granted, as the term 'battery' is commonly applied to regular and well-organized 'fire' throughout the American lodges. On balance, it is safer to assume that 'fire' was suggested by the sharp report caused by the crashing down of glasses.

There is definitely on record at least one instance where the drinking of toasts was followed by gunfire. Dr Richard Kuerdon, of Preston, records that in the course of solemnizing the Guild Merchant at Preston in the seventeenth century, when the Mayor's procession arrived at the "Church gate barrs," a "chief scholler" of the school made a speech, following which

> a Barrel or Hogshead of nappy Ale standing close by the Barrs is broached, and a glass offered to Mr Mayor, who begins a good prosperous health to the King, afterwards to the Queen, the Nobility and Gentry having pledged the same; at each health begun by Mr Mayor, it is attended with a volley of shot from musketiers attending.

The drinking and firing were repeated at other 'Barrs.'

'Fire,' as an image of speech, early took the imagination of the speculative mason. In a masonic 'exposure' of 1737 is the following: "The Grand Master says, 'Lay your hands to your Firelocks; then they drink the Brother's Health'." The analogy of firing was carried to a ridiculous point in some lodges if we can believe (certainly not without difficulty) a later 'exposure,' *Solomon in All his Glory* (1772), which described a tumbler or drinking glass as a 'cannon,' a bottle as a 'barrel,' wine as 'red powder,' and water as 'white powder.' "Every brother has a barrel of powder before him and charges his own cannon." After drinking a health the cannon "are brought at once upon the table at one strong stroke pretty smartly," and this action was known as firing. A minute (year 1820) of Canongate Kilwinning Lodge refers to drink as "ammunition."

'Firing Glasses'

It is easy to see how and why the wine-glass, as a firing implement, came in time to be replaced by a specially heavy glass, and finally, but not in all lodges, by the hands. The continual breaking of glasses led to the introduction of substantial ones having heavy bottoms or feet, and these 'firing glasses' were wellnigh unbreakable when crashed down on to the table. Breakage of ordinary glasses must have been rife, and it is known that fines were instituted in an attempt to lessen the amount and cost of damage. The records of the Old Lodge at Wakefield (1767) show that a Brother was fined one shilling "for a glass burst in a fire."

The especially heavy glasses came in time to be used almost exclusively for firing and not as wine-containers. Some of them were double-ended, and a number are still to be found in a few old lodges and in masonic museums.

Firing-glasses acquired the names of 'mason's glasses' or just 'masons,' and frequently were etched or engraved with the names of lodges, dates, and masonic devices. *The Cork New Evening Post* (1792) mentions

> Decanters, Rummers, Drams and Masons,
> Flutes, Hob-nobs, Crofts and Finger Baisins.

The 'rummers' are large glasses, not necessarily rum-glasses; the 'drams' are for holding nips of spirit; 'flutes' are tall, slender glasses; 'hob-nobs' are 'hob-nodding' glasses, one form being a rather squat tumbler; 'crofts' are water-bottles; and 'masons' are the firing-glasses, possibly suitably etched.

Elaborately etched firing-glasses are on view in masonic museums, but it must be remembered that ornament and dates etched or engraved upon admittedly old glassware cannot always be trusted; the collector of such objects has come to know that the ornament is not necessarily as old as the glass! It is easy to take any good, old piece of glass, and by adding date or masonic ornament to give it a false character.

The Tyler's Toast

The time-honoured toast—it was observed in 1762 or earlier—generally regarded as the Tyler's privilege may be proposed by any Brother at the wish of the Master. Curiously, in some lodges the Tyler's Toast is regularly proposed by the Senior Warden and is immediately followed by the Junior Warden proposing "To our next merry meeting." We are told that in the province of Bristol the Tyler's Toast was at one time invariably given by the Senior Warden, and that his jewel is a signal reminder of the old custom. At one time, too, in Mount Lebanon Lodge, No. 73—an 'Antient' lodge—the Master himself gave the toast, and made it the first on the list, not the last.

It is unnecessary here to give the precise wording of the toast which is so well known to every freemason, but it is interesting to note that probably the earliest form of the toast was addressed "To all charitable and distressed masons wherever dispersed," etc. That was just before the end of the eighteenth century, but forty years later it had apparently taken one or other of the few very slightly divergent forms familiar to us to-day. There is a curious twist in the last words of the toast as given in some of the country lodges. The concluding phrase "should they so desire," so often dwelt on for effect by Brother Tyler, becomes "if they desire *and deserve it.*"

One of Rudyard Kipling's many masonic poems takes as its motif the Tyler's Toast. It is *The Widow at Windsor* (Queen Victoria) beginning with:

> 'Ave you 'eard o' the Widow at Windsor
> With a hairy gold crown on 'er 'ead?

and ending with the paraphrase:

> Then 'ere's to the sons o' the Widow,
> Wherever, 'owever they roam.
> 'Ere's all they desire, an' if they require
> A speedy return to their 'ome.
> (Poor beggars!—they'll never see 'ome!)

'Silent Fire'

The 'silent fire,' well known to Brethren and frequently accompanying the Tyler's Toast, is a contradiction in terms. If indulged in on rare occasions only it adds a peculiar solemnity to a toast with which some sadness of thought or memory is associated, the effect of the 'silent fire' being heightened by contrast with the noisy fire of the preceding toasts.

As long ago as 1885 silent fire was deprecated as "an absurd innovation, for which no authority could be found." But it has its place—on rare occasions only! Provincial Grand Master Lord Euston once said it was "bad enough for our Brethren to be in distressed circumstances; we do not want to bury them."

Ladies' Nights

So far from being an innovation, as so often is thought to be the case, ladies' nights held in connexion with a masonic lodge go back many hundreds of years. Making due allowance for the fact that people in medieval days dined at noon and not in the evening, we can go back to the Ordinances of the London Masons of 1481 and find record of a custom which even then was apparently well established. In these ordinances the operative masons were ordered to go to mass every year on the Feast of Quatuor Coronati, and every two years on the Octave of Holy Trinity; after mass they were to "keep their dinner or honest recreation ... and to have their wives with them if they will." The mason's dinner cost twelve pence, the wife's dinner eightpence, and the two sums together must have represented at least about half a week's wages.

The ladies' night is a generally popular, although far from universal, annual festival nowadays. Conducted with due regard to the masonic proprieties it has much to commend it. The Brethren attending such functions may wear masonic clothing only by dispensation.

There is some question with regard to the old practice of inviting the ladies to visit the lodge room after dinner; it is frowned upon by many masons, but it is entirely a matter in the discretion of the Master and Brethren, there being in England no Grand Lodge Regulation or instruction relating to it or, indeed, any that even mentions ladies' nights. It is well known that admission of ladies to the lodge room after the banquet was a general custom at the end of the eighteenth century. "It was agreed by a majority of the Companions present," runs a minute of the Prince Edwin's Chapter (No. 128) in 1816, "that any Companion present may bring his wife up into the Room except on Arch night once but not more."

Some seventeenth-century minutes relating to ladies' nights make curious reading. The Kent Lodge, No. 15, invited 'wives' to supper in 1797, 'sisters' in the following year, and 'wives or sweethearts' in the next. The Brethren of Brixham Lodge, Devon, True Love and Unity, No. 248, met at the lodge room at nine o'clock in the morning of St John's Day in 1811, opened lodge and proceeded to church in procession. Then with their wives "or such female or friend they may chuse to bring with them" they adjourned to the lodge room for dinner. Seven years later the lodge paid nine shillings per half-gallon of rum, half a crown for two pounds of sugar; and seven shillings and sixpence per half-gallon of gin. Moving farther west to Penryn, Cornwall, we find a record of about the year 1793, when, following the lodge dinner,

> upwards of fifty ladies were introduced and received the usual plaudits of the Brethren. . . . The M.W. Grand Master called a Charge and on Bro. Turner for the Entered Apprentice's Song. . . . The M.W. Grand Master directed his Deputy to return thanks to the Ladies WITH THREE.

In 1815, at the lodge at Redruth, Cornwall, the Brethren decided unanimously that as the wine and fruit provided for the ladies had increased the expenses beyond what many of the Brethren could afford to pay,

> the same should be dispensed with at future Lodges, the Mover and Seconder being pretty Sensible that the gratifications of the Ladies consisted not in eating and drinking, but in beholding their Husbands, Sons and Brothers met together for charitable purposes in Love and Harmony.

The cost of the ladies' wine and fruit had been two pounds in a bill for sixty-three members amounting to £77 19s. 6d.!

Lodge Visits to the Theatre

As from 1725 until late in the nineteenth century there was a custom for lodges in England, Ireland, and Scotland to pay organized visits to the theatre, the earliest instance being a visit paid at the end of the first recorded meeting of the Grand Lodge of Ireland, June 24, 1725, when "they all went to the Play, with their Aprons, etc. . . ." In 1731 the same Grand Lodge bespoke the tragedy of *Cato*, all the male parts being taken by freemasons. On this and a great many similar occasions special prologues, epilogues, and songs were introduced. The newly installed Grand Master of England in 1738 "bespoke a Play" and "ordered a new Prologue and Epilogue to be made," but even this was not the first English occasion of its kind, for in 1729–30 a "bespeak" (a play especially asked for) was held at the Theatre Royal, Drury Lane. Scotland's first official theatre visit appears to have been in 1733 when Brethren marched to the Tailors' Hall in the Cowgate, Edinburgh, "in procession, with aprons and white gloves, attended with flambeaux," to see *King Henry IV*. In 1791 the Marquis of Granby Lodge, Durham, went in elaborate procession to lay the foundation stone of a new theatre. Much information on this surprisingly large subject (to which our remarks afford only the briefest introduction) is given in an address by Fred L. Pick printed in vol. xxix of *Transactions* of Manchester Association for Masonic Research.

Chapter Thirty-three

MASONIC MOURNING : THE SPRIG OF ACACIA

FUNERALS and mourning loomed large on the horizon of our Brethren early in the 1700's, and in the minds of many of them the expectation of a sickness and burial benefit was inseparable from the idea of the lodge. It was common for lodges to give regular weekly help to a Brother in sickness, and to provide his remains with a ceremonious funeral, the custom having been inherited from the English guilds and the operative bodies of both England and Scotland. Norman Rogers, who has closely studied the history of freemasonry in Bury, Lancashire, says that "the support and relief of decay'd Brothers" was one of the first principles of the Lodge of Relief, No. 42, Bury, founded in 1733. The idea of a sick and burial fund persists throughout the bylaws of this lodge for over a hundred years, during which time (in 1771) we find the sum of four shillings per week being allowed to any sick member of three years' standing, instead of leaving the amount to be fixed by the majority of the Brethren, as had been the custom; "in the event of death, a Shroud and Sheet to be provided in addition to an Oak Coffin." Members' contributions were revised more than once during the century, and in the year 1808 the age-limit for admission both to the fund and the lodge was fixed at forty.

The deep-rooted interest of a friendly-society nature lasted until 1897, when the total of £613 was calculated as belonging to the fund, and was divided among sixty-one members. The same author tells us that there was in Anchor and Hope Lodge, No. 37, Bolton, in the year 1821 a friendly society whose rules provided that a member

> rendred incapable of business, by sickness, lameness, blindness (not bringing it upon himselfe by fighting except it can be prov'd by one or more creditable witness, that such fighting was in his own defence) he shal upon demand receive eight shillings per week.

The lodge paid out the sum of five guineas on a member's funeral and three guineas on the funeral of a member's wife. The society was concerned not only with sick and death benefit, for in 1791 a Brother was paid half a guinea "towards his loss from an inundation of the sea," and in 1820 a Brother was "allowed to borrow £2 from the Lodge fund, he having lost a cow."

Funerals

In 1632, and at other dates, members of the London Company of Free-masons were fined one shilling each for failure to attend a member's funeral, and some such rule persisted for many years in speculative masonry. Some jurisdictions originally deriving from English free-masonry early in the 1700's still maintain sickness and burial funds. Here and there in England some old lodge may possibly still adhere to the custom, and in a great many United States lodges the Master Mason is entitled to a masonic funeral at the expense of his lodge.

Bands and scarves were supplied to members attending a masonic funeral in early speculative days. The service had a distinctly masonic character, and was accompanied, one authority tells us, by esoteric observances. The English Grand Lodge did not look kindly on the practice, which continued, however, in many places until more or less killed by a regulation of 1754 prohibiting a Brother from attending a funeral or any other public procession clothed as a mason, except by dispensation of the Grand Master. This, of course, holds good to-day, for although the English *Constitutions* will be searched in vain for any reference to burial or mourning, the matter is covered by the rule for-bidding any Brother clothed as a mason to appear in any place at which persons other than masons are present, without first having obtained a dispensation. Even in the early eighteenth century, one imagines, the custom of masonic observance at funerals was becoming troublesome, for a rule had to be made that no mason could be interred with masonic formalities, unless by his own special request made to the Master of the lodge of which he died a member.

Freemasons attending a Brother's funeral to-day attend in their capacity as friends of the deceased, and may drop into the open grave a sprig of acacia, which—as we all know—has a high place in masonic symbolism.

The early speculative lodges followed an operatives' custom in owning palls, known generally as mort-cloths, and lending them out on the occasion of members' funerals. An Irish lodge (Downpatrick) in 1781 let out its mort-cloth

> to all people at 2s. 8½d., except a member of the lodge, his father & mother, wife and children is to have it gratis; and if it should please God to call any two of them at one time they that apply first is to have it, and the other is to have a pall hired and paid out of the fund belonging to this Lodge that is to say, if he is a Member of this Lodge.

The lodges, in lending mort-cloths for use at members' funerals, were harking back to an ancient guild practice. George Unwin in *The Gilds and Companies of London* describes the palls, or hearse-cloths, used by the companies as being often

> magnificent specimens of the embroiderers' art, made abroad in Lucca or Pisa, consisting generally of a breadth of 'baldakin' cloth [*a rich brocade*] or cloth of gold, in the centre about 6 feet by 2 feet, to the sides and ends of which were attached embroidered velvet flaps, rectangular in shape and about 10 inches in breadth.

The pall still in the possession of the Saddlers' Company is of crimson velvet with a centre of yellow silk. Unwin describes others of these palls, and illustrates a fine example. The Fishmongers' pall, one of the Company's most treasured possessions, has a centre slip of running flower-of-gold network bordered with red on a ground of cloth-of-gold, is wrought with religious pictures, and dates from a period immediately preceding the Reformation.

The Church of St Clement Danes, Strand, London, had in 1703 six palls and cloths which it allowed out on hire, the best at twenty shillings and the worst at one shilling and fourpence, "but be it provided, that if any corps shall be interred, and none of the Parish Palls used, shall pay 10.0."

Many funeral palls in medieval times must have been worth a lot of money. Mrs J. R. Green's *Town Life in the Fifteenth Century* informs us that Sir John Paston, the owner of broad estates in Norfolk, was forced more than once to pawn his "gown of velvet and other gear," but when it occurred to him to raise money on his father's funeral pall, he found his mother had been beforehand, and had already pawned it!

Some curious ceremonies were observed at masonic funerals. A newspaper report in the year 1739 says that the pall was followed by about a dozen freemasons who lifted up their hands, sighed, and struck their aprons three times in honour of the deceased.

William Preston in his *Illustrations* (1775) gives detailed instructions on the carrying-out of a masonic funeral with full ceremonial. A few years earlier, an irregular print had described the ceremony observed at that time, the following account being an abbreviation of that description: By dispensation of the Deputy Grand Master, the Master of the lodge attended with his officers and other Brethren. The Master could invite as many lodges as he thought proper, their members "accompanying their Officers in Form." The Brethren walking in procession observed "decent Mourning, with White Stockings, Gloves and Aprons." Officers wore white sashes and hatbands. Officers of the deceased's own lodge carried white rods in addition. A procession was formed, headed by the Tyler with his sword, and ending with pall-bearers, "the Body with the Regalia placed thereon, and two swords crossed," the mourners, two Stewards, and a Tyler. Members of the lodge carried flowers or herbs in their hands. The Bible and Book of Constitutions on a cushion preceded the Master. Members of the invited lodges formed round the grave a circle which opened to receive the Brethren of the acting lodge, the mourners, etc. (It is not so stated, but the Brethren in all probability dropped herbs into the grave as, nowadays, they drop a sprig of acacia.)

Sometimes the gloves and apron of the deceased Brother were thrown into the grave, as on occasion is still done, we believe, at a ceremonious masonic funeral in America, and it is on record so late as 1850 that at the burial of a Somerset Tyler the Provincial Grand Secretary broke his own wand, and the Master of the lodge broke the wand of the deceased Tyler, the broken pieces being then cast into the open grave. Evelyn's *Diary* (February 14, 1685) records that when Charles II was buried "all the great officers broke their staves over the grave according to form."

In a few known cases, and probably in some others, the lodge itself has bought a grave. The Lodge of Harmony, now No. 220, Liverpool, buried the body of their Tyler in a grave which it had bought specially. Two of the Jersey lodges owned graves; thus Mechanic's Lodge, now the Duke of Normandy Lodge, No. 245, bought a grave in Mont à la Abbé Cemetery, in which it buried in 1863 a much-beloved Past Master, and, at a later date, his wife. And four years previously, in 1859, Lodge la Césarée (No. 590 in the English Constitution, but working in the French language) had buried the body of Dr Cuquemelle, one of the greatest names in the masonic history of the island, in a grave which it had bought in the Almorah Cemetery, in which grave the bodies of other Brethren of the lodge were later buried.

A Sprig of Acacia

The legend of the Third Degree introduces us to the sprig of acacia The Fellow Crafts had discovered the unsightly grave of the Master, and to distinguish it had stuck the sprig at its head. Some little acquaintance with this remarkable emblem will show us that the choice of the acacia for the purpose, even though it may be purely legendary, was apt and proper in every sense. Ireland's national lyrist, Thomas Moore, refers to the beauty of the acacia, which Horace Walpole years before had called "the genteelest tree of all." Sings Moore:

> Our rocks are rough, but smiling there
> Th' acacia waves her yellow hair,
> Lonely and sweet, nor loved the less
> For flow'ring in a wilderness.

Most people know the acacia as the wattle, mimosa, gum-tree, etc., many hundred varieties of which grow in Australia, Africa, India, tropical

America, etc. Of these many varieties only two have a special meaning for us:

(1) The true acacia, *Acacia vera*, the Egyptian thorn, one of the varieties of acacia from which gum arabic is obtained; it is a member of the Mimòseæ division of the Leguminòsæ.

(2) The false acacia, *Robinia pseudacacia*, of American origin and, so far as we know, not grown in the East until the seventeenth century. But it is the acacia that is frequently figured in connexion with freemasonry, and the one represented in the emblems on the clothing of Grand Officers. This false acacia is the common acacia, or locust-tree, to be found in English gardens and greenhouses, and grown for the beauty of its form and yellow flowers.

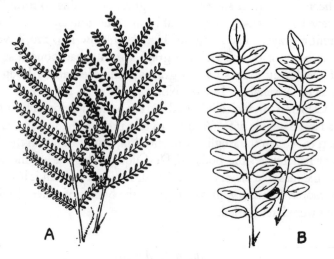

SPRIGS OF ACACIA

A, the true acacia; B, the false acacia.

The true acacia is easily distinguished from the false. In the true the leaf-stem ends in a number of leaflets, whereas in the false it ends in a single terminal leaflet.

Some people believe that the acacia of freemasonry is really the cassia, which is mentioned a few times in the Bible. *Miscellanea Latomorum* has explained that cassia is of the same botanical order as the acacia, and, so far as is known, was grown in India and not in Palestine; but it is suggested that the legend intended the use of cassia because of its marked symbolical significance. The poet Tennyson spoke of it as one of the trees of Paradise, and it is supposed to be 'the tree of knowledge of good and evil,' and 'the tree of the serpent.' An inscribed clay-tablet disinterred at Nippur, Babylonia, refers to the fall of man, saying, ". . . of the cassia he took . . . he ate . . . the plant which determined their fate there she came upon." A 'sprig of cassia' at the head of a grave is mentioned in Anderson's *Constitutions* of 1738 and a print of 1760 gives this:

> Q. What's a Master Mason named?
> A. Cassia is my Name, and from a just and perfect Lodge I come.

The Egyptians 'paid divine honour' to the acacia, one of the plants of which the ancient nations made their funeral wreaths and chaplets. It is said that the Hebrews planted a sprig of acacia at the head of a grave, but on whose authority the statement is made is not known.

The acacia is the Biblical shittah-wood (plural, shittim), a sacred wood to the Hebrews, and a symbol of immortality. The Ark and Table, the boards of the Tabernacle, and the Altar were of shittim-wood (Exodus xxv), credited with being able to resist the destructive attacks of insects.

Legend connects the acacia with the wood of the cross of Christ, and with His crown of thorns, but many other plants share that honour. Legend says also that the burning bush was the acacia.

The acacia is regarded as the symbol, or emblem, of immortality. It may also be, says Dr Wynn Westcott, the symbol of innocence, and, according to Mackey, the symbol of initiation, in the sense that initiation itself is symbolic of resurrection. It is likely that the acacias had countless associations of a symbolic nature.

It should be understood that the acacia is not the only plant associated with mourning. Branches of willow have been carried at a masonic funeral, it is said, as a symbol of the resurrection. Branches of cypress in the hall of a house indicate the house of mourning. The rosemary, myrtle, and box, being also evergreens, are all symbols of the resurrection, and in past days have been thrown into the open graves of loved ones. In old-fashioned days the mourners took their sprigs of evergreen from a bowl provided for them in the hall of the house from which the funeral started. Walter de la Mare's *Come Hither* relates that at the funeral of John Peel, the hero of the hunting song, "the old huntsmen gathered round his grave in a solid ring, each holding his dog·by the slip," and when the final 'Ashes to ashes, dust to dust' was pronounced they dropped their sprigs of rosemary upon the coffin. "That's for remembrance."

The Wearing of Masonic Mourning

In the eighteenth-century lodges much was made of the evidences of mourning, black rosettes were on aprons and collars, and sometimes the jewels worn by the officers were suspended from black ribbons. Nowadays when we as English masons wear mourning—and the custom appears to be declining—we pin crepe rosettes on the bottom corners and on the point of the flap of the apron, not obscuring the blue rosettes or levels, and put a crepe rosette on the collar at a point just above the jewel.

In all masonic mourning the tendency is always towards less display, and we may note that in 1947 on the death of the Grand Master, M.W. Brother the Earl of Harewood, Grand Lodge ordered that the Craft should go into mourning for six months, and that lodge mourning should be confined to the placing of one rosette on the collar of each officer, and to the printing of lodge summonses with a black edging or with a recognized emblem of mourning.

Sorrow Lodges

Lodges of Sorrow used commonly to be held under English and other jurisdictions. For example, in memory of Queen Victoria, Patroness of the Masonic Order, a Lodge of Sorrow was opened by the Sussex Lodge on Sunday, February 3, 1901, at St Stephen, New Brunswick, Canada. Usually these Sorrow or Mourning lodges were held on the death of a member, or at regular periods—say, once a year, or once in three years. The lodge would be draped with purple or black, Brethren would wear the signs of mourning, and a regular order of service would be strictly observed. The service authorized by the Grand Lodge of Scotland, and observed during the nineteenth century, is typical of them all. In this a solemn procession was formed, and moved off to the sound of a dirge played on the organ. On a table were displayed the insignia of the late Brother. Prayer was offered, passages from Scripture were read to which the Brethren responded, grand honours were paid to the memory of the departed, anthems were sung, more Scripture readings, more prayers, more grand honours, and the Master concluded the Sorrow Lodge with a tribute to the memory of the departed Brother.

The old lodge at Swalwell held sorrow lodges, and is believed on one occasion, at least, to have had the coffined body of the departed Brother resting in the lodge prior to burial.

BOOK SIX

The Royal Arch, Mark Masonry,
and Additional Degrees

Chapter Thirty-four

ROYAL ARCH MASONRY

THE preliminary declaration to the *Constitutions* of the Ancient Fraternity of Free and Accepted Masons, under the United Grand Lodge of England, records:

> By the solemn Act of Union between the two Grand Lodges of Free-Masons of England in December, 1813, it was "declared and pronounced that pure Ancient Masonry consists of three degrees and no more, viz., those of the Entered Apprentice, the Fellow Craft, and the Master Mason, including the Supreme Order of the Holy Royal Arch."

'Ancient' is here spelled with a 'c' to prevent confusion with the system of the 'Antients,' but we must admit forthwith that, but for our 'Antient' Brethren of the eighteenth century to whom the Royal Arch was "the root, heart and marrow of masonry," Royal Arch Masonry— even if we had it in England to-day as an officially recognized rite, a point open to some doubt—might be something less than the cope-stone of our Order.

The reader is now well aware that there were Craft degrees prior to 1717, and that by 1730 there were three such degrees, with which, however, it does not appear that our Brethren were long content. The peculiar form of the Third Degree legend *appears* to leave something to come later, and it is therefore easy to understand that the rapid rise of Royal Arch masonry might have owned much to the fact that the new degree offered Brethren what they regarded as the completion of the Third. True, there are those, like Alexander Lawrie, whose *History of Free-masonry* appeared in 1859, who believed that the Third Degree does not require to be supplemented in any way; that it is complete in itself; and that that "which was lost" can only be found "beyond the Veil of

Time, towards which the eye of the aspirant is directed." But to the majority of Master Masons the Royal Arch is all the richer and more satisfying because it "repairs a loss."

Early History of Royal Arch Masonry

There is much yet to learn about the early history of Royal Arch masonry, much that remains conjecture (although probably very reasonable conjecture), for very little is known of the degree before we suddenly find it rising in the lodges of the 1740's and 1750's as a new and separate rite. In this section we present a brief résumé of the relevant facts. Royal Arch Masons will recognize a phrase taken from St John i, 1, which occurs in the GRAND LODGE MS., No. 2, dating from the late 1600's: "In the beginning was the Word, And the Word was with God, And the Word was God." Douglas Knoop and his collaborators remind us that "the seal on the 'Deputation to Constitute,' granted by Lord Montagu, Grand Master in 1732, to St John the Baptist Lodge at Exeter, bears the motto in Greek: 'In the beginning was the Word'."

Many references may be held to indicate that coming events in Royal Arch history were 'casting their shadows before' in the 1720's and the 1730's; definitely the Royal Arch was worked in Ireland and probably in Scotland in the 1740's; minutes show the Irish and Americans to have worked the Royal Arch in the 1750's, and there are so many references to the next decade as to leave no doubt that by the 1760's rudimentary Royal Arch ceremonies were being worked throughout English, Irish, Scottish, and American freemasonry. And now, very briefly, to make good this opening statement.

In the 1720's and 1730's. It has been said that the Royal Arch was foreshadowed in the 1720's and 1730's. The instances, taken separately, may seem unimportant, but together may suggest that somewhere in freemasonry at that time there was an acquaintance with what we now recognize as the Royal Arch story.

In the 1720's there was a writer of curious books—a dreamy, credulous person—of the name of Robert Samber, who in the preface of his book *Long Livers* (1721–22) speaks of "those of you who are not far illuminated, who stand in the outward Place, and not worthy to look behind the Veil." This may be nothing more than an instance of vague, rhetorical language of no value.

Anderson, in his *Constitutions* of 1723, refers to the Royal Art being cultivated and the cement of brotherhood preserved "so that the whole Body resembles a well-built Arch." Those same *Constitutions* granted to the Master of a lodge authority to congregate the members into a chapter, and in 1733 on one occasion "the minutes of the last Chapter" of the Old King's Arms Lodge, No. 28, were read "to the satisfaction of the Society present." But whatever the word 'chapter' meant to Anderson and in the mind of the Secretary who recorded that minute, we put forward no claim that a Chapter of Royal Arch Masons was intended.

References to the 'rule of three' have been taken to indicate the existence of the Royal Arch in very early days. An irregular print of 1723 says, "If a Master Mason you would be, Observe you well the Rule of Three." In other places, too, the Master is advised to understand "the Rule of Three," but it would be unwise to find in such words any certain implication of the Royal Arch. One rule of three is impressed upon every Craft mason. Is he not taught that but for its operation the Master might not have been slain?

But perhaps it is another 'rule of three' that some masonic writers have in mind—the '3, 4, 5' rule of determining a right-angle, based upon Euclid's 47th Proposition. Nowadays this is more a matter for the Installed Master in the Craft than for the Royal Arch Mason, but nobody can say whether that was so in the 1720's.

Any claim that there were Irish Royal Arch chapters in France in 1730 is thought, says Hughan, to be based upon a typographical error.

Hughan tells us of the warrant of the Lodge of Relief, No. 42, Bury, dated July 1733, bearing a seal—namely, the arms of the Grand Lodge with a motto in Greek; not the usual motto 'Relief and Truth,' but "In the beginning was the Word."

About 1734 a Brother, in the course of a facetious letter of a private nature, referred to Richard Rawlinson, a Grand Steward, in these terms: he "makes a most Illustrious Figure . . . and he makes wonderful brags of being of the Fifth Order." But we cannot attach much importance to this, for when the Royal Arch ceremony did appear it was a fourth degree, not a fifth.

What are we to make of a reference in a letter to the Duke of Montagu in January 1735? Desaguliers had held a Sunday-evening lodge meeting at the Duke's house at Ditton, and with regard to it Mick Broughton wrote to the Duke: "On Sunday Night at a Lodge in the Library, St John, Albemarle and Russell [were] made chapters: and Bob [Webber] Admitted Apprentice." The tone of the letter suggests that everybody was having a 'good time,' and we are far from sure that there is any intended allusion to the Royal Arch.

We shall hear of the famous Chevalier Ramsay on a later page, but in the meantime we may note that at a Paris convocation of the Grand Lodge of France, 1737, he used these words in the course of an address: "This union was made after the example set by the Israelites when they erected the Second Temple, who, whilst they handled the trowel and mortar with one hand, in the other held the Sword and buckler." No Royal Arch mason will ignore this curious wording, probably the most likely of all the possible Royal Arch allusions belonging to such an early date yet brought to light.

In the 1740's. Evidence, about which there is some element of doubt, goes to show that there was in existence in Scotland in July 1743 the Stirling Rock Royal Arch Lodge. If we could remove that doubt, then the Royal Arch Lodge or Chapter at Stirling in 1743 would stand out as the oldest in the world.

Turning to Ireland, we find that in Youghal, County Cork, in 1743, Lodge No. 21 had a St John's Day in Winter procession, of which *Faulkner's Dublin Journal* reported that "The Royall Arch was carried by two Excellent Masons." Was this "Royall Arch" a mere piece of ornament (we call it 'decor' nowadays) to lend attraction and colour to the procession, or were the words a clear reference to some particular part of the lodge ceremonies? It is uncertain, but a minute of this same Youghal lodge, in 1759, recorded in its place below, may be thought to throw strong light upon the newspaper report.

Fifield Dassigny, M.D., living in Dublin, tells us, in a book (1744) claiming to treat on the decay of freemasonry in Ireland, that possibly four years prior to 1744 a Brother in Dublin had pretended to be Master of the Royal Arch, but had been detected by a Brother "who had some small space before attained that excellent part of Masonry in London." Dassigny had been informed that Royal Arch masons had assembled at York in 1744, and he uses the term "*excellent Masons.*" He stated that the Royal Arch was "an organised body of men who have passed the Chair and given undeniable proofs of their skill." Although, unfortunately, Dassigny is not regarded as reliable in all he writes, we can be fairly sure that at this date, 1744, we are entering upon an authentic period of Royal Arch history.

In Scotland's Old Lodge at Stirling, bylaws of the year 1745 provided for the payment of fees as follows: "Excelent and Super Excelent five shillings and Knights of Malta five shillings." Knowing as we do from many minutes of a later date how often the Royal Arch was called "Excellent and Super Excellent," we can reasonably accept this bylaw as a definite reference to the Royal Arch Degree, which must necessarily then have been in existence for some time. (The minutes of an English chapter record that in 1812 two Brethren "received the Degree of Exlent Super Exlent Holey Royal Arch.")

In the 1750's. Dermott says he was made a Royal Arch mason on March 4, 1752. A most conclusive minute is that of April 16, 1752 belonging to the Vernon Lodge, No. 123, of Coleraine, County Derry, a lodge which had been warranted by the Grand Lodge of Ireland in 1741, and which possesses a list of members dated 1767, there being after each name a date at which the member was made a Royal Arch mason. The earliest of such dates is March 11, 1745. Such a list is far from being 'cast-iron evidence,' although there is no reason to doubt its truth; but the minute of April 16, 1752, leaves no room for doubt: "At this Lodge Broʳ Thos. Blair propos'd Samson Moore a Master and Royal Arch Mason to be admitted a member of our Lodge." Unfortunately the minutes tell us nothing about the ceremonies of that day or of the titles borne by the officers.

A document of great historical importance is reproduced as a facsimile in *A.Q.C.* for the year 1891, and as a frontispiece in Hughan's *English Rite*. It is part of the minutes of a lodge at Fredericksburg, in the then British colony of Virginia, dated December 22, 1753, showing conclusively that the "Grand Master, Senior Warden and Junior Warden of a 'Royall Arch Lodge' " were present; that three Brethren, who were "raised to the degree of Royall Arch Masons," were actually the Master, Junior Warden, and Secretary who officiated in the Craft Lodge opened immediately following the closing of the "Royall Arch Lodge." At this Craft lodge, Entered Apprentices were present, and a Candidate "was admitted as a Member" of the lodge. The minutes, both Craft and Royal Arch, are entered on one and the same page of the minute-book, and the ceremonies (which evidently were kept most carefully distinct the one from the other) were yet merely different rites of a body of freemasons that must have regarded the Royal Arch as a fourth degree.

Dunckerley comes prominently into the early history of the Royal Arch. In a letter he says he was made a Royal Arch mason in 1754 (probably in a Royal Arch lodge attached to his mother lodge in Portsmouth). Hughan remarks that Dunckerley has wrongly been credited with being the founder of Royal Arch masonry; he was not that, but he was one of the few who helped to keep the Grand Chapter of the 'Moderns' in working order.

It has already been shown that the Royal Arch had become at home in Scotland. A lodge actually entitled "Royall Arch" was chartered in Glasgow in 1755. There is a minute of a Dumfriesshire lodge, dated 1756, which leaves no doubt that Brethren were then being 'passed' to the Royal Arch Degree.

It is possible that the oldest minutes connecting the 'Moderns' with the Royal Arch refer to meetings of a lodge at the Crown Inn, Christmas Street, Bristol, in 1758, a lodge officially 'Modern,' but probably working the 'Antient' ritual. Its minutes of August 7 and Sunday, August 13,

1758, leave us in no doubt that two Brethren were "raised to the degree of a Royal Arch."

Bristol had long had a sea connexion with Youghal, an ancient seaport on the Blackwater estuary, County Cork, and it is at Youghal that we find our next evidence of Royal Arch working. It is in a minute of which Irish masons have long been proud—the earliest minute recording the actual conferring of the degree in Ireland. The minute, dated July 30, 1759, records that two Brethren "proper Officers of this Lodge" were passed "to the dignity of Royal Arch Masons."

To sum up, the 1750's give us uncontested records of the making of Royal Arch masons in Ireland, Virginia, England, and Scotland. Royal Arch masonry had found its feet in the seven years ending 1759.

In the 1760's. There grew out of the Punch Bowl Lodge at York, constituted in 1761, one of the earliest separate Royal Arch lodges (1762). Its original members were all actors and members of the York Company of Comedians. One of them had been the first Master of the Punch Bowl Lodge. They were all men of Hull, and it is thought likely that they had been made Royal Arch masons in that city. The Punch Bowl Lodge was the centre of much masonic activity and was a factor in the revival of the York Grand Lodge. In 1768 the Royal Arch Lodge became a chapter, in due course to become a Grand Chapter. We meet the term 'Companion' in the York records in 1776, but he is still 'raised,' not exalted. The Grand Lodge of York in 1780 gave its sanction to the working of five separate degrees—the three Craft degrees, the Royal Arch, and Knight Templar.

It would be a mistake to assume that the York Grand Chapter was the first of the Grand Chapters. The one instituted by the 'Moderns' grew out of a chapter associated with the Caledonian Lodge, London, which had been an 'Antient' lodge, constituted in 1763, but in 1764 the Brethren changed their allegiance and obtained a charter from the Premier Grand Lodge as No. 325 (now No. 134). In course of time came a chapter in association with the lodge, and in this chapter Lord Blayney, Grand Master of the 'Moderns,' was exalted in 1766, many other prominent Brethren being "passed the Royal Arch" in that chapter. The Grand Chapter—the first in the world—was formed in the same year, as explained on later pages.

'Arching' is a word found originally in the records of a Bolton Lodge in 1768. Five shillings and threepence was received from each of nine Brethren "for arching."

Many Scottish chapters came into existence in the 1760's—at Edinburgh, Montrose, and Banff. Glasgow had had a chapter since 1755, and Stirling since 1759.

The reason for giving so many detail references to the early Royal Arch history is the necessity to refute the one-time prevalent but obviously inaccurate idea that the Royal Arch was invented in the last century.

Was the Royal Arch Degree Part of 'Original' Craft Masonry?

There are two main theories to account for the existence of Royal Arch masonry; one, that in its essentials or elements it was originally part of ancient, or 'original,' craft masonry; the other—and it must be put frankly —that it was invented or fabricated. Both theories have had the support of outstanding masonic writers, the earlier ones inclining to the first of the theories. Mackey, the well-known American author, believed that until the year 1740 the essential element of the Royal Arch was the concluding part of the Master's Degree, and the Rev. A. F. A. Woodford agreed with him, other writers finding support for the belief in the presence of certain words and symbols on the oldest known tracing-boards.

Count Goblet d'Alviella believed that the Hiramic legend and the Royal Arch are the surviving portions of a Craft lore that originally, or in its time, contained other similar legends. He saw no fitter theory to explain the

> spread of the speculative views, which during the first quarter of the eighteenth century, crept gradually into the Craft and finally remodelled its old aims and organisation, crystalling on one side in the institution of the Third Degree and in the adoption of the Royal Arch and on the other side in the working of the additional degrees.

Undoubtedly the Count puts into words a belief that has been widely entertained, but what does its acceptance require of us? It requires that we should agree:

(a) That the Royal Arch legend was known by freemasons before 1717, although no indication of its existence before that date has come down to us. (b) That the colourful idea, the dramatic story, of the Royal Arch ceased in some mysterious way to have a place in the craft traditions and ceremonies or, alternatively, was removed by some powerful hand. But no echo of the act of suppression has reached us, in spite of the fact that any interference with a 'completion' legend or rite must, one would have thought, have aroused turbulent opposition. (c) That there was in existence, say about 1717, an organization wide enough and strong enough' to bring about an act of suppression with ruthless finality. History, however, is completely silent about any early organization of speculative lodges prior to the Premier Grand Lodge, a body which was never strong enough to impose much of its will on the non-regular lodges, let alone to attempt the well-nigh hopeless task of extinguishing what would have been the high-light of their anceint traditions and ceremonies! (*d*) That the Royal Arch content of freemasonry fell into complete disuse and (in an age when there were no printed rituals or *aides-mémoire*) must have been soon forgotten, only to reappear most magically in the lodges of a generation or so later as a practicable degree capable of quickly gaining the respect and affection of the Craft.

In suggesting that the Royal Arch came to England from Ireland, but that Irish freemasonry itself derived from England before 1717, or possibly direct from Scotland in the seventeenth century, Douglas Knoop and his collaborators are, in effect, supporting the belief just set forth. Their theory requires us to believe that English freemasonry before 1717 possessed a particular knowledge which was passed on to the Irish, but not generally to the English craft (a difficult achievement, surely); that English masons who knew of the Royal Arch tradition kept it to themselves and on their death it died with them. This theory accordingly asks us to accept that, although a knowledge of the Royal Arch tradition (and necessarily some ceremony, however elementary) had survived right through the long, dark days, English freemasons chose to neglect it and allowed it to die—and to die stone-dead, without a word to anyone by way of funeral discourse—at the very time when freemasonry was finally emerging into the full light, and when considerable public interest and curiosity was being aroused. We are also required to believe that in Ireland, on the other hand, the newly acquired knowledge of the Royal Arch was quietly nurtured into a developed rite ready, following a generation of silence, for re-export to England, where instead of the deathly coldness it had received from an earlier generation it now enjoyed an atmosphere so warmly congenial that it rapidly grew and flourished. And we are asked to accept this in spite of the fact that the legend of the Irish Royal Arch was not that of the English!

How difficult, how impossible, to believe it! J. Heron Lepper, the Irish masonic authority, says he is unable to "accept the theory that the Royal Arch formed an integral part of the ancient masonic tradition."

It has been suggested that the 'Moderns' by dropping the Master's Part dropped the Royal Arch, whereas the 'Antients' by retaining the Master's Part retained the Royal Arch legend. Here again we are in great difficulties—those already outlined and some new ones. The 'Antient' masons were not organized until 1751, by which time Royal Arch masonry was well in course of development. Later in this chapter we shall consider how the great quarrel of the eighteenth century affected Royal Arch masonry.

W. Redfern Kelly, W. B. Hextall, William James Hughan, and others do not view with favour the idea that the Royal Arch was originally contained in the craft working and must have been removed therefrom to give it a separate entity. W. Redfern Kelly says it is hard to credit any story of a wholesale mutilation of the Third Degree ritual; any such suggestion he regards as a simple speculation quite unsupported by authentic records. Hughan says it is known that, at a critical date, there were no essential differences in the first three degrees between the French and English working; this, he suggests, is proof that no violent alterations had been made in the Third Degree for the sake of an English Royal Arch rite. Dr Joseph Robbins, the American writer, asks:

If English and American masons have the present modes of recognition, as a consequence of the alleged mutilation by which an essential portion of the Third Degree was excised and erected into the Royal Arch, *for what purpose was the Degree mutilated in Scotland or in Ireland?*

Was the Royal Arch Degree of Continental Origin?

Gould would, we may be quite sure, have made a strong case for Royal Arch masonry being an essential part of pre-1717 masonry, could he have done so on the evidence available; but he refers to the Royal Arch as a "side or bye degree," and the whole tenor of his comments is that the Royal Arch was a new degree of Continental origin. Hughan says definitely that the Royal Arch was the first of the very early ceremonies actually added to the craft degrees, although it is possible that the degree known as the Royal Order of Scotland is even older than the Royal Arch.

Dr Oliver thought that the Royal Arch Degree had been fabricated by Andrew Michael Ramsay (1686–1743), commonly known as Chevalier Ramsay, born at Ayr, Scotland, who had spent many years in Holland, France, and Italy—a clever writer and a brilliant careerist. Ramsay's Paris address in 1737, when he used phrases strongly suggestive of the Royal Arch, has already been quoted. Oliver says that Ramsay, about the year 1740, brought a number of additional degrees—so-called high grades—from Paris to London, and these included the Royal Arch. Even though this statement is not literally accepted by students (who believe that Ramsay's connexion with freemasonry had ended before that date), there seems to be a case for supposing that some of the material brought over from France to England by Ramsay, or somebody confused with him, did contain the salient features of the Royal Arch. The importation might have been fathered on Ramsay because his was a likely personality. He had, as a student, formed his own individual and peculiar theories as to the origin of freemasonry. He was a freemason of high rank—Grand Chancellor of the Grand Lodge of Paris—and he is known to have been a man of marked fertility and inventiveness.

Be Ramsay's connexion with the matter what it may, it does appear that the Royal Arch may have owed its origin to some clever Continental or other framer of degrees, by whom it was possibly evolved to harmonize or fit in with the Third Degree of our ancient craft system; and that in process of time, by further evolution, amplification, and embellishment, it became moulded into the rite we know so well. W. Redfern Kelly supposes that the degree was introduced from the Continent late in the 1730's, having been pirated from or based upon a newly fabricated Continental degree by an Englishman.

Nevertheless, as Dr Oliver insisted, the degree is very properly denominated the English Royal Arch, for it was in England that it reached its finest development. It may also be added that the early Royal Arch Degree contained only a rudimentary idea of the Degree as it was developed in the English chapters and as we know it to-day.

How came the Royal Arch to be adopted by Eighteenth-century Masons?

The reader might well ask how the Royal Arch Degree ever came to be accepted. What seems to be the most likely answer to this question is that on the introduction of the Royal Arch into England (many years before the rise of the 'Antients') it passed into the hands of some non-regular lodges, each in itself a power, and each owing no allegiance to any external body—so much so that if it wished to work in any particular way, then in that way it worked, or if it wished to embroider or prune a ceremony, all it had to consider was the feelings of its own members. To a few such lodges the newly fabricated degree was probably cunningly introduced as a part of ancient freemasonry, a part that claimed to provide the completion of the Third Degree. Its peculiar quality, its 'colour,' its religious and almost certainly its then Christian content—all these made an immediate appeal to masons, who in the main were simple, religious folk. Some of the non-regular lodges adopted the degree, worked and developed it, and presented it as an attraction to visiting Brethren, who in their turn introduced it to their own lodges under the general impression that the Royal Arch was not only the natural, but obviously the true completion of the Craft degrees. If, as many students suppose, there was some correspondence between, on the one hand, the Master's Part and any ceremony worked in the Masters' Lodges and, on the other hand, the Royal Arch—a correspondence which had grown up, perhaps, as the result of borrowings made almost unconsciously by the individual lodges—so much the easier for the new ritual to be accepted, particularly by Brethren of the 'Antient' persuasion, as the development and completion of the old.

We may assume that the independent lodges had had a Royal Arch Degree for some years; they had worked it and moulded it; their own senior members constituted its body of membership; and the ceremony was worked in their own Craft lodges, frequently on the same evenings as the Craft degrees, the one giving place to the other as the exigencies of the evening required. Thus, if this theory is anywhere near the truth, by the time that the organized body of the 'Antients' was in a position to give any thought to the matter, there would be a Royal Arch tradition, and a well-established degree ready for their official adoption at a time, be it remembered, when the 'Moderns' officially refused to acknowledge its existence.

Further, let it be made clear that the 'Antients' Grand Secretary, a shrewd man, must have recognized as a sure asset what a great majority of his Brethren regarded, sincerely but wrongly, as a part of truly ancient masonry that, most providentially, had been rescued from the dire neglect of the 'Moderns.'

This is not put forward, of course, as an account of what actually happened, but it is offered with all respect as a likely explanation of the stubborn fact that a recently devised degree became the darling of those conservative masons who delighted in dubbing their opponents 'Moderns' and 'Innovators.' We may well believe that the new degree attracted the eager attention of some Brethren in the regular lodges as well, but for many years they would have to dissemble their interest in view of the open hostility of their Grand Lodge.

How does this theory fit in with the refusal of the Irish Grand Lodge all through the eighteenth century to recognize the Royal Arch? J. Heron Lepper remarks on this "extraordinary variation from the practice" of the English 'Antients'—"to this day, Royal Arch insignia may not be worn in an Irish Craft Lodge"—and he goes on to confess that he has not yet found "the key to fit the riddle." Dare it be suggested that the key may be the fact that among the Irish lodges to which Royal Arch masonry found its way in the first place were some that were under the strict control of their own Grand Lodge, and consequently lacking the power to avail themselves of the introduction; whereas the non-regular lodges, or lodges in which the Irish Grand Lodge influence was weak, pleased themselves as to whether they adopted it or not? Be it noted that not one Grand Lodge in the British Isles countenanced the Royal Arch in its earliest years. It found a home—in all three Kingdoms —only in those lodges strong enough or weak enough to welcome it on their own account.

Was the Royal Arch originally Christian?

Some authors have held strongly that the introduction of the Royal Arch was an attempt to restore a Christian basis to freemasonry. The *Constitutions* of 1723 obliged the mason, who prior to that time apparently was expected to be a Christian, to believe in the glorious architect of heaven and earth and to practise the sacred duties of morality, whatever his religion or mode of worship might be. But there must have been many lodges working a distinctly Christian ritual at that time and for long afterwards, a conclusion that may fairly be drawn from odd scraps of ritual that have come down to us. Hughan quotes Colonel McLeod Moore, who believes that "if we could get at the earliest rituals of the Royal Arch, we should find that [Christian] doctrines were inculcated in the Chapters that were formed about the middle of the eighteenth century." Dr Oliver, declaring that he had in his possession "a genuine MS. copy of Brother Dunckerley's version of the Royal Arch," quoted from it as follows:

> The foundation-stone was a block of pure white marble, without speck or stain, and it alluded to the chief corner-stone on which the Christian Church is built, and which, though rejected by the builders, afterwards became the head of the corner. And when Jesus Christ, the grand and living representative of this stone, came in the flesh to conquer sin, death and hell, he proved himself the sublime and immaculate corner-stone of man's immortality.

On this evidence, then, we may safely conclude that there was a very strong Christian influence in early speculative freemasonry and that there must have been regular masons in the 30's and 40's of the eighteenth century who would wish to avail themselves of an added degree which restored to them an influence which they had regretfully lost in the masonic organization of the early 1720's.

How the Quarrel between the 'Moderns' and 'Antients' affected the Royal Arch

In the early years of the conflict between the 'Moderns' and 'Antients' no one thing more clearly differentiated one side from the other than the former's *official* ignorance of Royal Arch masonry and the latter's eager adoption and encouragement of it. Whereas the 'Antients' regarded it as the "Root, Heart and Marrow of Free Masonry," the Grand Secretary of the 'Moderns' in 1759, in answer to an 'Antient' Brother who had requested his charity, said, "we are neither Arch, Royal Arch, nor

Antient." In course of time, it is true, the 'Moderns' founded the Grand Chapter, the first Grand Chapter in the world, but this was an official move on the part of their Grand Master, and did not kill their natural hostility to Royal Arch masonry. Even as late as 1792 an official utterance of the Grand Lodge of England was to the effect that it had "nothing to do with proceedings of the Society of Royal Arch Masons." It is a curious anomaly that, while the 'Antients' claimed to practise only the ancient rites but encouraged the Royal Arch, the 'Moderns,' whom the masonic world at home and abroad accused of 'innovation,' officially frowned on the Royal Arch, which, so far as the consensus of opinion goes, was itself an innovation wholly or in part.

The question has often been asked whether the Royal Arch Degree actually arose out of the hostility between the two sections. The reply is quite definitely No. Royal Arch masonry was struggling to its feet actually before the 'Antients' had founded their Grand Lodge. Some writers—even including Dr Oliver, who, however, was none too careful in his statements—have said that the Royal Arch was "concocted by the 'Antients' to widen the breach, and make the line of distinction between them and the Grand Lodge broader and more indelible." But, in truth, the 'Antients' did not themselves invent or fabricate the Royal Arch Degree. They found it waiting for them, and it undoubtedly suited their purpose to encourage it for the purpose of accentuating the difference between themselves and their opponents.

We read much in masonic literature of the suggestion that the early Third Degree was 'mutilated' to provide material for the Royal Arch Degree. A curious twist has been given to this by the suggestion that the 'Moderns,' taunted with having made alterations in the modes of recognition in the First and Second Degrees, retaliated by charging the 'Antients' with having altered the Third Degree to benefit the Royal Arch. But Dr Joseph Robbins, the American writer, left little to be said on this subject of mutilation when he put the question recorded on an earlier page: *For what purpose was the Degree mutilated in Scotland or in Ireland?*" The point here is that any Royal Arch activities in Scotland and Ireland were purely unofficial, the powers-that-be frowning upon the 'innovation.'

Although the 'Moderns' officially disowned the Royal Arch—some of their official announcements on the subject were very blunt—many of their lodges worked it, and a number of their prominent members were Royal Arch masons. The 'Antients' regarded the Royal Arch as a degree for Masters in the Chair and for Past Masters. Both sides came to see the matter in that way, and availed themselves of a legal fiction to make the idea workable.

The opposite numbers in the two camps, Thomas Dunckerley in the 'Moderns' and Laurence Dermott in the 'Antients,' were Royal Arch masons, and from the remarkably interesting paper "The Traditioners," by J. Heron Lepper, in *A.Q.C.*, lvi, we learn that in Dunckerley the Royal Arch found a new and indefatigable exponent. He exalted the first Grand Master of England ever to join the Royal Arch, so far as is known, and it is most probable that by his instigation the Supreme Grand Royal Arch Chapter came into being by the Charter of Compact. Henceforward the Royal Arch would be no sure test to distinguish 'Antient' from 'Modern.' By way of reply, Dermott caused the 'Antients' to found in 1771 a nominal Grand Chapter, but it never had a separate existence, had no minutes before 1783 and was, in effect, a committee reporting to Grand Lodge. Further the 'Antients' continued to work Royal Arch ceremonies in their lodges by virtue of their Craft Warrants.

It seems likely that Royal Arch masonry began to command increased attention and regard from the time when its members began generally to meet not in a 'lodge' but in a 'chapter'—a term of early use among the medieval operatives and having a distinctly religious association. An Act of the reign of Henry VI forbade masons to meet in their 'general chapters.' The earliest *Constitutions* of the Premier Grand Lodge (1723), also included the term, but there is nothing whatever to suggest that in either case the word meant a meeting of Royal Arch Companions. The first eight chapters authorized by the 'Moderns' (1769) had double titles, thus "The —— Lodge or Chapter of ——"—a fair indication that the Royal Arch 'lodge' was in course of becoming the 'chapter' or that in that period an R.A. lodge was often known as a chapter.

The word 'chapter' has an unusual history. Ernest Weekley's *Words Ancient and Modern* tells us that it comes from the French *chapitre,* meaning 'head.' The Latin was *capitulum* (diminutive of *caput,* a 'head') and meant the 'section of a book,' a sense arising naturally from that of heading, as example, to recapitulate, meaning to run over the headings of a subject. The word

> was used especially of the divisions of the Bible. When the canons of a collegiate or cathedral church, the monks of a monastery, or the knights of an order held formal meetings, the proceedings began with the reading of a chapter from their Rule or from the Scriptures. Thus the gathering itself became known as the *Chapter,* and the room in which it was held was called the Chapter-house.

Grand Chapters

The first Grand Chapter in the world was that constituted in 1766 by Lord Blayney, Grand Master of the Premier Grand Lodge, the first

English Grand Master to be exalted (an Irish Grand Master, the Hon. Brinsley Butler, had been exalted in 1757, during his year of office). In the earlier prints of this book it is suggested that the first Grand Chapter grew from a chapter founded by members of the Caledonian Lodge, originally an 'Antients' Craft lodge and having as its second initiate the famous William Preston, at whose entrance the lodge obtained in 1764 a charter from the 'Moderns.' However, John R. Dashwood's contributions to *A.Q.C.*, vols. lxii and lxiv, have now revealed a different story. He provides transcripts of minutes (1765 to 1775) of the Excellent Grand and Royal Chapter ('Lord Blayney's Chapter') which was "in amity with, or under some obligation to," the Caledonian Lodge or its Chapter as indicated in its bylaws (see *A.Q.C.*, vol. lxii). In June, 1766, was exalted the Grand Master, Lord Blayney, who immediately became the First Principal of the Chapter and Grand Master of the Holy Royal Arch. It is believed that in the following month, July 11, 1766, the Chapter decided on the Charter of Compact (hitherto thought to have been negotiated one year *later*), so called because it recorded a compact, made by Lord Blayney, with the "Most Excellent Brethren & Companions" of the Chapter to institute and erect them "to form and be The Grand and Royal Chapter of the Royal Arch of Jerusalem." It had twenty-eight signatures.

J. Heron Lepper has said that Lord Blayney "was the first Grand Master of the 'Moderns' to foster the Royal Arch degree claimed by Laurence Dermott as an appanage of the Antients." In December, 1768, Lord Blayney was constituted, during his absence in Ireland, Grand Master of the "Most Excellent Chapter or Fourth Degree." It must be noted with what insistence our Brethren of those days regarded Royal Arch masonry as the Fourth Degree, whereas, as a result of the negotiations, arguments, and give-and-take at the Union in 1813 and later, it is now agreed (and the English Royal Arch mason is taught) that it is not the Fourth Degree, but only the Master Mason's Degree completed. In Scotland, however, but not in Ireland, the Royal Arch Degree is reckoned the Fourth Degree in freemasonry, but only from certain points of view.

In their turn the 'Antients' felt compelled some five years later to constitute their own Grand Chapter, which historians, in ignorance of the facts, have said remained in being until 1817 when it united with the 'Moderns' Grand Chapter. This is untrue as it is an established principle of English law that when an organization goes out of existence, all its subsidiary parts also disappear and as the Grand Chapter was merely a subsidiary of the 'Antients' Grand Lodge, it went out of existence when that body ceased to exist in 1813. The number of exaltations in 'Antient' lodges fell off between 1813 and 1817 and in to-day's list relatively few chapters appear to be of 'Antient' origin.

York Grand Chapter

The story of the Grand Chapter at York has often been told. The Treasurer's Book relating to that chapter takes us back to the year 1768, but the earliest minutes of Royal Arch masonry in York, which happened to be those of the Grand Chapter, are dated 1778, and it is due to a circumstance recorded in those particular minutes that the present members of the York Lodge, No. 236, constituted in 1777, print on their summonses an engraving of the Crypt of York Minster. The actual wording of the minute is: "The Royal Arch Brethren, whose names are undermentioned, assembled in the Ancient Lodge, now a sacred Recess within the Cathedral Church of York, and then and there opened a Chapter of Free and Accepted Masons in the Most Sublime Degree of Royal Arch." The York Grand Lodge in June 1780, by arrangement with the York Grand Chapter, confirmed its authority over the "Five Degrees or Orders of Masonry," the rite then consisting of (1) Entered Apprentice; (2) Fellow Craft; (3) Master Mason; (4) Knight Templar; and (5) Sublime Degree of Royal Arch. It is thought that the numerical order refers to the order in which the degrees were worked, and does not imply that the Knight Templar is the fourth Degree and the Royal Arch the fifth. The document speaks of the Initiate being "admitted," whereas the making of the Fellow Craft, Master Mason, and the Royal Arch mason is all covered by the word "raised."

Supreme Grand Chapter of Royal Arch Masons

The Supreme Grand Chapter derives from two separate pre-1813 Grand Chapters, those respectively of the 'Moderns' and the 'Antients.' The union was of course led up to by the union of the Grand Lodges. There can be no doubt that the Royal Arch was a considerable factor in the negotiations between the two Craft bodies, and any attempt, had it been made, by the Premier Grand Lodge to leave Royal Arch masonry in an unofficial or unrecognized position would have wrecked all hope of reconciliation. The Act of Union in 1813 "declared and pronounced that pure Ancient Masonry consists of three degrees and no more, viz. those of the Entered Apprentice, the Fellow Craft, and the Master Mason, including the Supreme Order of the Holy Royal Arch." Royal Arch masonry was no longer in England a fourth degree officially, whatever it was in fact; it became a complement or completion of the third.

In the year following the Act, representatives of the Grand Lodges of

England, Ireland, and Scotland met together to discuss the position of the Royal Arch. It was hoped to be able to form an International Compact but eventually each of the Grand Lodges went its own way. In England Royal Arch masonry continued to exist in a kind of limbo until 1817 when a meeting was held under the presidency of H.R.H. the Duke of Sussex, and the present Grand Chapter was born, with the happy result that the United Grand Lodge was able to pass the following resolution on September 3 of that year, a resolution that was couched in terms carefully chosen to avoid giving offence to the 'Antients'

> That the Grand Lodge having been informed that the two Grand Chapters of the Order of the Royal Arch, *existing prior to the Union of the Craft*, had formed a junction, that rank and votes in all their meetings had been given to all the Officers of Grand Lodge, and that the Laws and Regulations of that body had been, as far as possible, assimilated to those of the Craft, it was *Resolved Unanimously* That the Grand Lodge will at all times be disposed to acknowledge the proceedings of the Grand Chapter, and, so long as their arrangements do not interfere with the Regulations of the Grand Lodge, and are in conformity with the Act of Union, they will be ready to recognise, facilitate, and uphold the same.

Scottish and Irish Grand Chapters

In the same year, 1817, was formed the Grand Chapter of Royal Arch Masons for Scotland, in spite of the opposition of the Scots Grand Lodge, an opposition which seventeen years before had been so keen that the Scottish lodges had been prohibited from holding any meetings other than those of the first three degrees. The prohibition was confirmed in 1817, and it was resolved that "no person holding an official position in any Masonic Body, which sanctions higher Degrees than those of St John's Masonry, shall be entitled to sit, act, or vote in the Grand Lodge of Scotland." Naturally this was opposed by the Scots Grand Chapter, but many years were to pass before the Grand Lodge would extend any recognition to the Royal Arch. There was no Grand Chapter in Ireland until 1861.

Royal Arch Masonry in England, Ireland, and Scotland

In England a Master Mason may be exalted to the Royal Arch, the ceremony taking place in a properly constituted chapter.

In Scotland the Craft mason must take the Mark and Excellent Master Degrees before he can become a Royal Arch mason; he takes the Mark in a Craft lodge or in a chapter; he takes Excellent Master in a chapter.

In Ireland the Craft mason before he can become a Royal Arch mason must take the Mark Degree, and he can do this only in a Royal Arch chapter. Of the three countries, it is only in England that the chapters are attached to particular lodges.

It naturally followed from the way in which the Royal Arch had been introduced to the early Craft lodges and from their custom of working it on lodge evenings in the same lodge room and almost inevitably by Craft lodge officers, that in a great many lodges, particularly those of the 'Antients,' the Craft regarded the Royal Arch as part of itself. Distinction between nomenclature and officers came only with the passage of time. One Royal Arch lodge had a Master and Senior and Junior Wardens; in another a Brother was "exalted to the Third Degree"; in still another a Third Degree lodge was presided over by a Master Excellent Ruler. Quite commonly the ceremony we now call 'exaltation' was known as 'raising,' and this custom long continued, for even in 1810 in the (now extinct) Neptune Lodge of Penang, of 'Antient' persuasion, we have this minute: "2 Brethren after exclusion of M.Masons were duly raised to the High Honours of Excellent Masons."

The Constructive Degree of Past Master

It has been explained that in the 1700's the Royal Arch Degree was confined to Masters and Past Masters, an arrangement which must have proved unworkable, if only because it severely restricted the number of eligible candidates. It was apparently, but not certainly, the 'Antients' who found a way out of the difficulty, but many 'Modern' lodges managed to follow suit. The way out was to pass Brethren to the Chair for one occasion, as it were, or by instituting a Past Masters' Degree, the conferring of which duly qualified a Brother for membership of the Royal Arch. Such a degree is still worked in some American chapters, and in these only Master Masons who have passed through three preliminary (extra) degrees, including the Virtual Past Master (even though the Candidates are Installed Masters), are eligible for the Royal Arch, whereas in England ever since 1823 Master Masons have been eligible. Even as far back as 1766 the Charter of Compact establishing the 'Moderns' Grand Chapter recited, "that none but discreet and experienced Master Masons shall receive exaltation to this sublime degree in this or any other chapter. . . ."

The circumstances of the quarrel between the two sections of the Craft in the eighteenth century are full of anomalies, and here surely is one of the most curious of them—that in order merely to qualify Brethren to become Royal Arch masons the 'Moderns,' whose official organization had no love for the Royal Arch, should in fact be led to work a constructive Past Masters' degree, a degree which itself had grown or developed from an installation ceremony they themselves did not *officially* work, and the need of which they would not acknowledge. It is not known whether the Past Master ceremony was the same with 'Moderns' and 'Antients'; presumably—and almost necessarily—there was a difference, and we are led to wonder whether it consisted chiefly in the observance by the 'Antients' of ritual and signs which to-day are, to some extent at least, to be found in the extended ceremony of installation (see p. 250).

The Grand Chapter formed in 1766 issued charters to lodges authorizing them to work the Royal Arch Degree. The charter was attached to the warrant of the lodge, and in it we see the arrangement which is maintained with certain exceptions to-day—nearly two centuries later. Nowadays, however, a chapter may continue in being even if the lodge from which it sprang and to which it was attached is no longer in existence.

The Royal Arch Legend

The legend which forms a motif of the Royal Arch ritual is not everywhere the same. This rather points to the probability that, if and when the substance of the original degree came from the Continent, it arrived almost at the same time both in London and in Dublin, and in somewhat different forms. The English Royal Arch adopted as its legend the Rebuilding of the Temple, whereas the Irish based their legend on the Repairing of the Temple. The first of these legends is the narration of Ezra, the second of Josiah. In the English legend we have as the three chief officers Zerubbabel, Prince of the People; Haggai the Prophet, and Joshua the High Priest; whereas in the Irish legend the three officers, or principals, are Josiah the King, Hilkiah the Priest, and Shaphan the Scribe.

Connected with these differences is the curious fact that although Dermott, leading spirit of the 'Antients,' had learnt his Royal Arch masonry in Ireland, it was the English legend that the 'Antients' recognized. Some explanation appears to be necessary. One feels sure that Dermott did not import the degree into England; that, on the contrary, he found it already being worked there. Almost certainly many Brethren among his personal friends and colleagues were already English Royal Arch masons, and to change the legend at that date would have been beyond the powers of any one man, even if there had been a wish to make the change, and there is no record of this.

Scotland and America took the Royal Arch legend from England, bu America borrowed the names of the principals from Ireland, and is there fore working the English legend, but with principals different in name from those we know. This is not to say that the American and Scottish systems are the same as the English. They are not, particularly the American, but the basic legend is the same. In Ireland there is sequence of three grades: Excellent, Super Excellent, and Royal Arch. In America there is a sequence of four grades: Mark Mason, Past Master, Most Excellent Master, and Royal Arch. In Scotland the same system is followed as in England, where any Brother who has been raised to the Third Degree in Craft masonry is eligible for the Royal Arch.

The Temple of Zerubbabel

Whichever legend is followed, it will be the better understood after a glance at the troubled history of King Solomon's Temple. A highly informative article, presumably by Lionel Vibert, in *Miscellanea Latomorum* (1932) gives all the facts relating to the history of the Temple that here follow.

The glory of the beautiful Temple was of brief duration, for, after King Solomon's death, ten tribes under Jeroboam broke away to form the independent kingdom of Israel, which soon fell into idolatry; but Judah and Benjamin remained faithful to the line of David, and held the mountain stronghold of Jerusalem, which commanded the trade-route between two warring countries—Syria and Egypt. Palestine was ravaged by both sides for a period of four hundred years. In the fifth year of Rehoboam's reign, Shishak, King of Egypt, sacked Jerusalem and carried away all the gold from the Temple, but not the famous brasswork, the molten sea, etc. In 722 B.C. the independent kingdom of Israel became an Assyrian province, the ten tribes being removed into captivity. At Jerusalem Hezekiah secured peace by paying tribute, and he to some extent restored the Temple worship. Eighty years later Josiah repaired the Temple, and refurnished it with gold vessels. It was now that the incident occurred of Shaphan finding the lost volumes of the Sacred Law in the treasury. But Josiah was killed by the Egyptians during a war with Assyria, and in 588 B.C. we find Zedechias, the nominee of Nebuchadnezzar, as ruler of Jerusalem. He turned traitor and tried to hand over the fortress to the Egyptians. Jerusalem was thereupon sacked and the Temple vessels, both gold and brass, were carried away to Babylon, as Jeremiah, an eyewitness, relates. The two tribes were also carried into captivity, but, as Josephus says, General Nabuzaradan, who carried the people away captive, left the poorer sort and those that voluntarily yielded in the country of Judæa, commanding them to till the land.

But Assyria was now nearing its end. Cyrus, who conquered it in 538 B.C. and occupied Babylon, invited the two tribes to return and to rebuild the city and the Temple; he supplied them with treasure and materials, and promised to restore the golden vessels carried away by Nebuchadnezzar. The walls of Jerusalem, as well as those of the actual Temple, had to be rebuilt, and while the work was in progress Cyrus died, and his successor, Cambyses, influenced by the surrounding nations bitterly hostile to the Jews, stopped the work.

We now come to a picturesque incident of which the Royal Arch ceremony takes no notice, though it is familiar to members of an additional degree, and will be found in the first Book of Esdras (Apocrypha). Zerubbabel (back at Babylon, where Darius has now succeeded to Cambyses) and two other officers of the court hold an oratorical contest. One speaker says Wine is the strongest; the second, that the King is the strongest; while Zerubbabel shows that Women are strongest, but above all things "Truth beareth away the victory." Zerubbabel is adjudged the winner, the whole audience exclaiming, "Great is Truth and it shall prevail."

Darius agreed to complete the work stopped by Cambyses. Accordingly Zerubbabel, accompanied by Joshua the Priest, returned to Jerusalem to carry out the undertaking. The Sidonians sent timber by sea from Libanus, to be landed at Joppa. The Samaritans appealed to Darius to hinder the work, the Jews being comforted and encouraged by Haggai the prophet. Accordingly, as a matter of history, Zerubbabel, Joshua, and Haggai were associated only at the time of the resumption of work under Darius, and not in the days of Cyrus, perhaps a century before.

The journey back to Jerusalem from Babylon was dangerous, and Darius had need to give the treasure an armed escort. The dangers of the journey are symbolized by the Passing of the Veils—a ceremony preserved in Scotland, Ireland, Bristol, and elsewhere. In Scotland there is a preliminary degree of Excellent Master, supposed to be given at Babylon, to ensure that the volunteer is qualified to take part in the work, a privilege which Zerubbabel refused to Gentiles or half-breeds. The Veils themselves, however, are associated with Moses.

Ezra and Nehemiah figure in the English and Scottish working, but their presence is an anachronism, inasmuch as Ezra arrived in Jerusalem fifty-eight years after the completion of the Temple, Nehemiah following him fourteen years later and setting to work to rebuild the walls of the city. Josephus describes how the builders worked with their weapons by their sides in constant fear of the Samaritans. Zerubbabel ruled alone, but after his day arose the Council of Elders, from which the Great Synagogue developed, the body presumably that figures in the ceremonies as the Sanhedrin, a name belonging to a later period.

The rebuilt Temple had a tragic history. It was plundered, profaned rededicated (165 B.C.) by Judas Maccabeus, again profaned, again plundered, and finally pulled down to the very foundations by Herod the Great in order that he might rebuild it on a grander scale as a memorial to himself.

The Vault and the Book of the Law

The vaulted crypt that plays its great part in the legend is, of course, itself legendary; but it is a fact that there are several vaults on the site of King Solomon's Temple, and one of them may have been under the Sanctum Sanctorum. W. W. Covey Crump says that these crypts may be natural caves or survivals of work built by Solomon and his successors; one of them "called *Bir arruah*, that is, the Well of Souls, is said to be a place where the spirits of deceased Moslems assemble twice a week for united prayer, but originally it seems to have been a drain for carrying away the blood and offal from the altar of burnt offering."

Naturally, the vault itself has been symbolized, Mackey offering the suggestion that it becomes an "entrance through the grave into eternal life. . . . The historical relation may be true or false, . . . the lesson is still there."

The Book of the Law discovered in the vault was not the Bible, as thoughtlessly might be concluded. The scroll of sacred writings was the Torah, itself a Hebrew word for 'Law,' but used also to indicate the Pentateuch (five books), consisting exclusively of the first five books of the Old Testament: Genesis, Exodus, Leviticus, Numbers, Deuteronomy, and possibly a part of a sixth book, Joshua. It is this book, the Pentateuch, which is referred to as 'The Law of Moses,' 'The Book of Moses,' or 'The Book of the Law of the Lord.'

The Arch

The development of the masonry arch is spoken of in the first chapter of this book. Some authorities believe that it was known for at least two thousand years before Christ, others that it dates back to the very dawn of building in brick and stone. Why was it so highly thought of, and why was it introduced into early masonic ceremonies? Undoubtedly because it offered itself as a type of a peculiarly strong construction and called for considerable skill in its building—in other words, it was a symbol of strength, and the men who built it were regarded as the flower of their craft. Some writers have supposed that the masonic word 'arch' has been derived from a Greek word meaning 'chief' or 'first' (thus, Architect, Archbishop, Archdeacon, etc.), and as an indication they point to its association with the words 'excellent' and 'super excellent' in eighteenth-century masonry. The suggestion cannot be dismissed, but on the whole it seems more likely that the word has the architectural meaning, and we must recognize that although the legend goes back to days long before Christ the story itself has the architectural background of medieval days. The vaulted arch or arched roof is a Gothic idea, and the medieval masons treated the arch with a boldness, freedom, and dexterity unknown to the builders of Biblical days.

A TRUE ARCH

The illustration indicates the position and purpose of the keystone.

In the true arch, as freemasons understand the word, there is a wedge-shaped centre-stone which crowns and completes the arch and forms an absolutely essential part of it. Without this keystone the arch would collapse.

There were true arches in the first century, spanning a width of eighty-three feet and rising to a height of a hundred and twenty-one feet.

The true arch—the arch of freemasonry—derives its strength from its construction with a series of wedge-shaped stones, the first stone on each side resting on the support, or abutment. As regards the other stones, some strength is borrowed from the presence of cement or mortar in the joints; but the real strength—the capacity of the arch to sustain a great weight bearing down upon it—is due to the arch-stone or centre-stone or keystone, as it is variously called, which functions independently of any mortar or cement, and transmits a load evenly through the other stones to the vertical supports, or abutments. An arch correctly designed and built should function without the cement or mortar joints, but, of course, is better for their presence. The diagram herewith shows how the arch-stone functions.

When we call the centre-stone the 'arch-stone,' we may possibly be using the term 'arch' in the second meaning to which reference has already been made—that is, the chief, or most important, stone.

The Catenarian Arch

We are taught that the form of a Royal Arch chapter is that of a catenarian arch, that arch being a memorial of the vaulted shrine in which the sacred writings were deposited. Freemasonry knows the arch as not

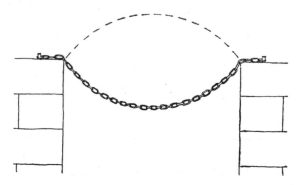

THE CATENARIAN ARCH

A chain supported horizontally assumes a natural curve
which, inverted as shown by the broken line, gives the
shape of the true catenarian arch.

only the symbol of strength but as a symbol of heaven. There is some suggestion of an arch in Job xxvi, 11: "the pillars of heaven tremble." The 'Arch or vault of heaven' is a poetic expression inspired by the fact that the sky appears to be an arch of infinite span. Thus: "What a grand and majestic dome is the sky! How is that immeasurable arch upheld?" (Hervey), and "Fanning his temples under heaven's blue arch" (Wordsworth).

What the term 'catenarian arch' really means is that the arch has a curve the same as that assumed by a chain or heavy rope suspended between two points, *catena* being the Latin for 'chain.' This little illustration gives the idea. The suspended chain assumes its own curve, and this curve *inverted* becomes an outline of an arch, a true arch, the catenarian arch. Whether this arch was known to the very ancient builders is doubtful, but the freemasons who built Henry VII's chapel and other structures of the same period knew it well.

The Triple Tau

The ritual teaches that the block of white marble wrought in the form of the altar of incense—a double cube—had certain letters on its front, and, in addition, a mark or character which we know as the triple tau. It is unnecessary to repeat the explanation of the mark taught in the ritual. It is our purpose to show quite briefly what the mark is. 'Triple tau' is literally 'three tau's,' the tau being the nineteenth letter in the Greek alphabet, and, as it happens, the twentieth letter in the English alphabet. The tau is our 'T.' Now, there is a cross known as the tau-cross; it is shaped exactly like the 'T,' and it is not only a Christian but a prehistoric religious symbol not known to Craft, Royal Arch, and Mark masonry, but finding a prominent place in certain other masonic degrees.

THE TRIPLE TAU
WITHIN TRIANGLE
AND CIRCLE
A Royal Arch jewel.

The triple tau of Royal Arch masonry, actually three T's, was in the eighteenth century 'T' over 'H.' (See diagram herewith.) It was said to be an abbreviation for *Templum Hierosolymæ*, a Latin term for the Temple of Jerusalem, and was so used by Dunckerley; but after

THE T-OVER-H AND THE TRIPLE TAU
The diagrams show how the T-over-H (*Templum Hierosolymæ*) has become the Triple Tau. Originally the letters had serifs.

the union of the Grand Chapters of the 'Moderns' and 'Antients' it ceased to be the 'T' over 'H' (1817), and became three 'T's'—the triple tau. We are told that Thomas Harper used the 'T' over 'H' on jewels made by him in 1820, but in his jewels of the following year the serifs of the letters had disappeared and the mark had become the triple tau. The Charter of Compact, 1766, includes the 'T' over 'H.'

Interlaced Triangles

Freemasonry is concerned with two or more emblems consisting of interlaced triangles. The Royal Arch to-day knows one of them only— the hexalpha, the six-pointed star—between which and another masonic emblem, the pentalpha, the five-pointed star, there has always been considerable confusion. We may note this confusion, but cannot remedy it. In the seventeenth century almost any device in a 'magic circle' was called a pentacle, one of the many names by which the pentalpha is known.

Canon Horsley once put forward a theory that these interlaced triangles were originally based on natural plant forms, as well might be the case. They are known to go back at least nineteen hundred years.

The hexalpha happens to be a device which anyone experimenting with a pair of compasses can easily and, as it were, accidentally produce. He draws a circle and steps the compasses around the circumference, thus cutting it into six parts; then, by connecting alternate points, he forms a triangle. Similarly by connecting the remaining points he forms a second triangle, the lines of which cross those of the first. He has formed two interlaced triangles, a device which, because of its ease of construction and its innate beauty, is the basis of much ornamental work.

The pentalpha is not so easily made, as it is necessary to divide the circumference of the circle into five equal divisions, a matter of trial and error.

The triangle has long been regarded as a symbol of the Trinity, but in England the interlaced-triangles device was little known until medieval times, when we find it in use as a mason's mark. Some writers are against the belief that this mark should not be associated with anything esoteric, that it was simply the mason's signature and that each mason adopted any simple combination of lines that took his fancy. G. W. Bullamore, for example, does not think that the use of these figures can be dismissed as the fancy of the workman, and he states that the interlaced triangles were a common device on the seals of medieval masons. Uncovered in 1949 in the course of rebuilding the Houses of Parliament, Westminster, are masons' marks in the crypt of St Stephen (built 1135–54) taking the form of interlaced triangles.

These two devices, the hexalpha and the pentalpha, will now be considered more closely.

The Hexalpha. According to a majority of masonic writers, the hexalpha is the Seal of Solomon and the Shield of David, but a minority give these names to the pentalpha. When Royal Arch masons speak of the interlaced triangles they mean the hexalpha. It has other names including the hexagram, a name which is applicable to any six-line or six-sided figure. It is the six-pointed star or Blazing Star. With the addition of certain characters it becomes the Ineffable Triangle. The hexalpha is not the hexagon, but it includes one—the six-sided figure described by the internal lines of the device.

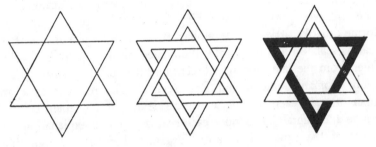

INTERLACED TRIANGLES FORMING THE HEXALPHA, THE SIX-POINTED STAR

The 'alpha' comes into each of the names with which we are dealing because Greek *alphas*—that is, 'A's'—suitably arranged, compose the device, six in one case, five in the other.

The symbolism of the hexalpha is most comprehensive. Firstly the symbol stands for the macrocosm—that is, the universe. It also represents the sun and the planets. To the Hindus it meant 'fire and water, the destroyer and the creator,' a circle containing it symbolizing the universe.

Countless works on astrology, occultism, magic, and so forth, published between the sixteenth and the eighteenth centuries, contain references to this symbol, and attribute to it many extravagant meanings. It was long regarded as a protection against fire; the Jews used it on their breweries and their houses; to-day they use it as a sign of an orthodox Jewish restaurant. Used on amulets, it was a charm against disease. Lionel Vibert, in an address to Grand Chapter in August 1936, said that it was not mentioned in Jewish literature before the twelfth century.

Solomon is supposed to have found the hexalpha a most potent talisman. There is a tradition that he confined a genie in a bottle by sealing it with the hexalpha, which is the reason for the device being known as the

Seal of Solomon; but we must always bear in mind that there is confusion with the pentalpha in this matter. The flower of the lily-plant known by the name of Solomon's Seal is roughly hexagonal. It ornaments the portico of a temple at Baalbek, ancient city of Syria, of the second or third century A.D.; Justinian's church of St Irene at Constantinople, now a mosque, has the device on its sixth-century walls; Italian craftsmen, twelfth to fourteenth centuries, used it in their mosaic ornaments. The parish church at Launton, Bicester (thirteenth-century), has a tower, one face of which is decorated with a pentangle in stone measuring eight feet across, and G. W. Bullamore says that the masons of this church are supposed to have built another Bicester church, now Ambroseden parish church, whose tower formerly was ornamented with the hexalpha.

The engraved portrait of a distinguished French physician, Charles Delorme (1630), carries the hexalpha. Both the hexalpha and pentalpha appear as seals on a curious, old illuminated manuscript roll of vellum. It dates from the late-seventeenth century; it is of German origin, and possibly Roman Catholic and Rosicrucian. The roll carries a great number of seals, each bearing a magical device, among them being the hexalpha and pentalpha. Under each seal is given an explanation. The simplest of the explanations are: "Against thunder and lightning"; "Against poisoning"; "Against sudden death"; "Against the bite of animal or snake." One is "Against despair and contrary things"; one seal is a sign for treasure, and the last of them is "When a person is imprisoned and he carry this about him he will be set at liberty."

Coming to masonic applications of the hexalpha, we find it on an eighteen-inch measure dated 1663 in possession of the York Lodge, No. 236, and on an engraved portrait of Dr Frances Drake, Grand Master of the Grand Lodge of All England in 1761. These instances go to suggest that the hexalpha had some masonic significance at an early date. The 'Moderns' Charter of Compact of 1766 has drawings of the hexalpha jewel in the margin. A white marble block dating back to 1772, formerly in Tyrian Lodge (later the Westminster and Keystone Lodge, No. 10), bears the hexalpha with other emblems.

It is not known why Royal Arch masonry adopted the interlaced triangles. The hexalpha, a Jewish symbol, does not enter into the ordinary Irish or Scottish ritual, although it is mentioned in a Scottish optional lecture (not earlier than 1820) which refers to the geometrical and mathematical explanations of the device, and links the hexalpha with the "platonic theory of the universe." But it is significant that circles interlaced, the triangles interlaced, and both of them in conjunction are regarded as Christian emblems, and are the possible basis of many things taught in chapter and at table.

GEOMETRICAL REPRESENTATIONS OF THE TRINITY
These are suggestive of Royal Arch devices and ideas.

There is evidence to show that before the union there was a strong tendency of the 'Antients' to use the pentalpha where the 'Moderns' were using the hexalpha. The earliest hexalpha jewel in the Grand Lodge Museum is dated 1775, and we seem to be on firm ground in saying that the Grand Chapter of the 'Moderns' was chiefly responsible for the adoption by Royal Arch masons of the hexalpha device.

INTERLACED TRIANGLES FORMING THE PENTALPHA,
THE FIVE-POINTED STAR

The Pentalpha. The pentalpha may not be the Royal Arch jewel of to-day, but undoubtedly in earlier days it was the jewel of the 'Antients' section of the Royal Arch, and the two devices have always been confused the one with the other. There are some writers who believe it to be the Seal of Solomon and the Shield of David. It has a great many names, including the pentacle, pentagrammaton, pentaculum, pentagram, pentageron, etc. It is the five-pointed star, not to be confused with the Blazing Star, although it is the Talisman, or Morning Star. It should not be referred to as a pentagon, by which name is known the five-sided figure described by the internal lines of the device. There are many other shapes of pentacles, less obviously pentalphas, and, as already said, the cabalistic writers were in the habit of giving the name pentacle, or some similar name, to any 'magic' device within a circle.

The pentalpha has been found on sarcophagi and ancient carvings, and has a long association with religions and with superstitions, including necromancy (but is not associated, so far as is known, with the Hiramic legend). It is a 'magic' sign in astrology, alchemy, and cabalistic law; in the last of these the five points of the pentalpha signify the spirit, air, fire, water, and earth. It has been regarded as a talisman against danger of fire, and the Pythagoreans thought it to be a symbol of health. We are told that a five-cornered linen headdress, representing the five senses, was worn as a defence against demons, and that 'magicians' themselves used it to quell the disobedience of a spirit.

The pentalpha was used as a doormark to keep out witches, but that, we may assume, is hardly the purpose of the mosaic pentalpha in certain of the thresholds of Freemasons' Hall, London!

As a Christian symbol the pentalpha with the point uppermost is supposed to be a reminder of the five wounds of Christ, and at one time possibly symbolized a full knowledge of the Christian mysteries—the "doctrine of the Trinity plus the two natures of Christ." But used *inverted*, its two points uppermost, it becomes the Witch's Foot or the Head of the Evil Goat, and then signifies the devil and black magic!

As the basis of ornament and design the interlaced triangles have had countless applications. Attempts have been made to show that they provide a principle that has been observed in architectural planning.[1] For example, while the triangle and interlaced triangles give the centres from which can be set out many architectural details, when we come to a traceried window we find that the centres of the circular window are at the intersections of lines which, continued, form diamond-shaped figures —that is, double triangles. The specially interested reader can weigh up the arguments for himself, but one criticism may be advanced here— namely, that almost every balanced example of architectural design will be found to provide the points from which equilateral triangles, as well as interlaced triangles, can be readily drawn.[2] However, Arthur Bowes (see footnote) has stated that an examination of the plans of many important Gothic buildings had satisfied him (a highly technical building man) that the equilateral triangle had been largely used as the basis of their design.

In old masonic writings a triangle formed of three points or dots is sometimes used to indicate 'degree'—thus E.A. ∴, M.M. ∴. In French writings since about 1774 the triangle of dots may mean 'lodge'—thus 'de la L ∴,' 'of the Lodge.'

---

[1] For further information on this point see *A.Q.C.*, vol. xix, for Arthur Bowes's paper on the equilateral triangle as a geometric basis for medieval stone buildings, and *A.Q.C.*, vol. viii, for W. H. Rylands' paper on the application of triangles and the pentacle in the design of important old buildings.

[2] See Sydney T. Klein's paper in *A.Q.C.*, vol. xxiii, entitled "Magister-Mathesios," which seeks to show the origin of Gothic architecture on symbolic lines.

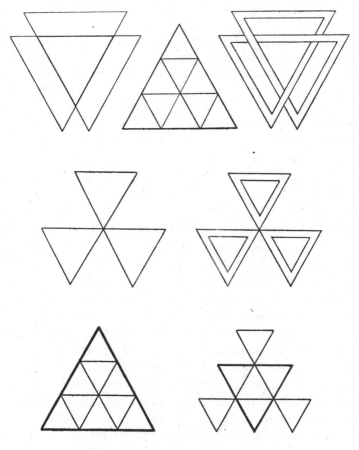

FURTHER ARRANGEMENTS OF TRIANGLES,
SOME OF THEM INTERLACED

'Passing the Veils'

The old English Royal Arch ceremony obliged the Candidate to 'pass the veils' (or 'vails') as a preliminary to his exaltation. Here and there the ceremony is still worked in England, but it is not likely to be met with in London chapters, although it was customary up to the middle of the nineteenth century, and was included in a printed ritual of 1881. It is a regular part of Royal Arch masonry in the United States of America and in some Canadian provinces. We may reasonably assume that the ceremony of the veils had a Christian significance. The veils represented certain colours—scarlet, purple, and blue—which had deep religious associations. The many Biblical references to veils are pregnant with meaning. Cruden's notes in his *Concordance* usefully sum up some of them for us:

> The Lord commanded Moses to make a vail of blue, and purple, and scarlet, and therewith to divide the holy of holies, which represented the highest heaven, from the holy place, where the church militant, or its representatives, met and served God. This vail typified the human nature of Christ, adorned with excellent gifts and graces. . . . It signified also the separation between the Jews and Gentiles, which is now removed by Christ, and therefore, at the death of Christ, this vail was rent in twain.[1]

There are references in Exodus to covering the Ark with the veil, to coming not into the holy place within the veil. References to the Veil of the Temple being rent in twain from top to bottom will be found in Matthew xxvii, 51, and elsewhere in the New Testament. We learn of the second veil in Hebrews ix, 3, and so forth. At the crucifixion the Veil of the Temple was rent. The rood screen in old churches is a symbol of that veil and the altar of the Ark of the Covenant.

An old Lancashire Craft lecture or catechism (possible date about 1800) includes very reverent interpretations of the Veil of the Temple. This leads one to hazard a guess that the catechism in question was worked in a non-regular lodge in which the Craft and Royal Arch workings had become curiously mixed and marked by strong local influences, as almost inevitably was the case in many out-of-the-way country lodges. In this catechism the Veil of the Temple "signified the Son of God, Jesus Christ, hanging upon the Altar of the Cross, as the true veil between God and us, shadowing with his wounds and precious blood, the multitude of our offences, that so we might be made acceptable to the Father." The Ark of the Covenant was a "type of Jesus Christ, Excellent and Glorious in his person, and marvellous in the Union of his Natures."

The reader may care to have some indication of the ceremony of Passing the Veils. In England the Candidate was required to pass three veils, each guarded by passwords, each passing being associated with certain Biblical instances and peculiar signs, the whole ceremony being regarded as a preparation for that of the exaltation which followed. This ceremony must have been taken from early English Royal Arch masonry to America, where essentially it remains the same, but has been elaborated and even made spectacular. The Candidate, already a Mark Mason, Past Master, and Most Excellent Master, is in the care of an officer known as the Captain of the Host. He is laid under the Living Arch formed by the Masters of the Veils; discovers the burning bush which

[1] *Cf.* Exodus xxvi, 31–33; Hebrews x, 19, 20; Ephesians ii, 14; and Matthew xxvii, 51.

was not consumed (Exodus iii and Acts vii, 30–33); is caused to travel a rough and dangerous road; passes through four veils not three, puts forth his hand to lay hold of the rod which in Exodus iv, 4, turns into a serpent, and becomes acquainted with the symbolism of the leprous hand (Exodus iv, 6–8). From this point the exaltation resembles, but is by no means the same as, the English ceremony, being a much more dramatic working. In the course of the ceremony the Captain of the Host opens the Ark of the Covenant brought by the Sojourner from the vault, and found to contain the scroll of parchment bearing the opening words of the Book of the Law. Numerous symbolic allusions occur in the ceremony, the veils having a general, and each one of them a particular, symbolism related to the colour of the veil—blue for universal friendship and benevolence, purple for union, scarlet for fervency and zeal, and white for purity.

Mackey tells us that the passage through the veils is a symbol of the trials and difficulties which are encountered and must be overcome in the search for truth and Lionel Vibert suggested that the Passing of the Veils symbolizes the dangers met by the repatriated Jews in journeying from Babylon to Jerusalem.

The Ineffable Name

We learn from the writings of the Rev. C. J. Ball, M.A., whose knowledge of Asiatic literature was profound,

> that mysterious names, which it is unlawful for a man to utter, have played a great part in the sphere of the oldest and most powerful of all influences upon the spirit and life of man. In the sphere of religion, which itself always reposes upon a basis of inexplicable mystery, we may trace the existence of such names from the earliest times of which any record is left us.[1]

Ball tells us of an inscription from *Tel-loh* in which an ancient Babylonian sovereign, who reigned more than four thousand years ago, uses these words: "The god Enzu (Lord of Knowledge), whose name man uttereth not." Enzu was a title of the moon-god. He had many names, among them being an esoteric one which was not to be spoken.

Tradition says that the forefathers of the Hebrew tribes were emigrants from Ur Casdim, or Ur of the Chaldees—the land where this and other memorials were found. Many religious ideas and customs of the Jews had their origin in Babylonia. After the return from the Babylonian exile a practice gradually prevailed of avoiding all utterance of the more 'personal' name of the God of Israel—namely, 'Jahveh' ('Jehovah'). Among the later substitutes for the name we find in the Biblical writers

[1] *A.Q.C.*, vol. v.

'Adonai' ('Lord') and 'Elohim' ('God'). In the Greek translation of the Old Testament, called the Septuagint, of which the oldest portion belongs to the third century B.C., no attempt is made to transliterate the Ineffable Name, but the Greek word for 'Lord' is always written in its place, as also in the New Testament. An early trace of this scruple may be seen in the words of Amos vi, 10: "Then shall he say, Hold thy tongue; for we may not make mention of the name of the LORD."

"The increasing awe with which the holy name was regarded naturally degenerated at last into superstition," says the Rev. C. J. Ball, "and all kinds of magical powers were attributed to the utterance of a name which men had long ceased to utter, and of which the true pronunciation was, in fact, forgotten."

We find the same superstition in Rome. Plutarch, writing in the first century, asks "what is the reason that it is forbidden to mention, inquire after, or name the chief tutelary and guardian deity of Rome, whether male or female?" He refers to the tradition that Valerius Suranus had perished miserably for expressing that name. "The Romans believed that they had their God in most safe and secure custody, he being inexpressible and unknown."

The ancient superstition was long-lived. Douglas Knoop tells us that

the idea of a Demogorgon, so dread that his name was not to be mentioned, occurs in sixteenth and seventeenth-century literature both in Scotland and England. Thus, although no specific reference in masonry to the [Royal Arch] Word has been traced before 1725, it is not unlikely that the idea is much older.

The Sanhedrin

The august Sanhedrin sat in a semicircle when in judgment. The form of the Royal Arch chapter based on the catenarian arch is thus a reminder of that ancient assembly. Actually, the assembly was not known as a Sanhedrin until the second century B.C. We learn of the Constitution of the Assembly in Numbers xi, 16, where "the Lord said unto Moses, Gather unto me seventy men of the elders of Israel, whom thou knowest to be the elders of the people, and officers over them; and bring them unto the tent of meeting, that they may stand there with thee" (Revised Version). This council met within the precincts of the Temple and its presiding officer represented the King, just as the presiding officer in a chapter also represents the King, and is correctly addressed as 'M.E.' Probably we should be more correct in saying that the presiding officers represent the King for, says W. W. Covey Crump, "the distinction which confines 'M.E.' to the First Principal is a fairly recent innovation and is symbolically wrong."

The ritual says that seventy-two is the number of members of the Sanhedrin. A helpful article in *Miscellanea Latomorum* (June 1945) suggests that this number, which, in its author's opinion, was one more than it should be as there were seventy elders in addition to the presiding High Priest, may be an allusion to the seventy-two names of God. Napoleon Bonaparte, when attempting to reconstruct a Sanhedrin from the French Jews in France by edict in 1806, fixed the number of members at seventy-one.

Royal Arch Clothing and its Colours

Masonic colours and their meanings must be understood (see pp. 470–473) before considering the significance of those that have been adopted for the robes worn by the principals of a Royal Arch chapter. The choice of colours appears to be related to certain Biblical texts, notably Exodus xxv, 3, 4, where the Israelites are required to bring offerings, among which are to be "blue, and purple, and scarlet, and fine linen." The curtains of the Tabernacle were to be made "of fine twined linen, and blue, and purple, and scarlet" (Exodus xxvi, 1). Solomon made the Veil of the Temple "of blue, and purple, and crimson, and fine linen" (II Chronicles iii, 14). Whether those colours were what to-day's terms imply is questionable.

Lewis Edwards brought together much information on the subject of Royal Arch colours in an address delivered to Grand Chapter in November 1937, when he said that the editions of the Royal Arch Regulations preceding the union of the Grand Chapters ordered the robes to be "of scarlet, mazarine blue and light gray" (Cardinal Mazarine's blue was a deep sky-blue). Present-day English rituals give Zerubbabel a robe of scarlet to denote imperial dignity; Haggai, one of purple, being an emblem of union (alleged to be based upon the technicality that blue and scarlet combined give purple); and Joshua, one of blue, signifying universal friendship and benevolence. In Irish chapters the principals do not wear robes, while in Scotland for many decades prior to 1905 the wearing of robes was optional but if worn they were respectively crimson, pale blue, and purple; after the date mentioned the First Principal wore crimson, Haggai wore purple, and Joshua pale blue. Lewis Edwards tells us further that in the United States of America the High Priest wears all four colours of his Jewish prototype—blue, purple, scarlet, and white linen; the King known to the American system wears scarlet, and the Scribe purple.

In spite of many theories advanced, it must be said that we do not know exactly what influenced the choice of colours for the Royal Arch robes, other, of course, than the Biblical instructions which in some instances are apt. Gordon P. G. Hills has put forward the suggestion that the red and blue of the Royal Arch are the colours of the livery of the Hanoverian family in contradistinction to the red and white of the Stuarts, and that these colours are worn by Royal Arch Companions in a manner similar to that in which livery colours used to be borne. Any suggestion from such a source must be treated with respect, but one would have thought that the complete rout of the Jacobites in 1745 would have removed any temptation to show political bias, especially in regard to a choice of colours that was not made until some years after the date mentioned.

The Royal Arch sash resting on the left shoulder and hanging with its device on the right side is the very reverse of the idea of supporting a sword to be drawn by the right hand while the scabbard is steadied by the left. There is evidence that the sash used to be worn on the right shoulder. In one of the earliest portraits of a Royal Arch Companion—that of Richard Linnecar, dating back to the 1770's or so—the sash is so worn, and in a painting about forty years later it is still worn in that position. (Richard Linnecar was the Secretary of Lodge then No. 361, held at the George and Crown, Wakefield, and one of the most outstanding masons of his day; he was linen-draper, wine-merchant, postmaster, playwright, poet, and coroner.) In both of the instances here concerned, the Companions were of the 'Moderns,' and the possibility exists that our present method of wearing the sash originated with the 'Antients.'

It is known that even as recently as about 1920 the principals of some few English chapters still continued to wear headdresses, and it is thought that St Stephen's Chapter, Retford, Nottinghamshire, possesses headdresses which, however, have not been worn for many years. In some chapters both Z. and H. wore a crown, and J. a mitre, and it is thought that there are still one or two chapters where the headdresses are worn at installations. In the early Grand Chapter in London the three principals, known apparently as the 'Most Excellent Grands,' were robed and wore caps. In American chapters, the King, as he is called, wears a crown.

The Royal Arch Ritual

The Royal Arch ritual was growing all through the second half of the eighteenth century. We suspect there were considerable variations, especially as between those of the 'Moderns' and those of the 'Antients.' At the time of the union of the Grand Chapters in 1817 it must have been necessary to reconcile various workings, but we believe that the chief revision took place in 1834–36, the work being done by a committee appointed by the Supreme Grand Chapter, with the object of providing a uniform and agreed ritual. Even so, there still continued to be considerable variations as between chapter and chapter; for example, the ceremony of the veils was observed in some, and ceased to be observed in others. Of the printed rituals, the oldest is believed to be the 'Oxford,' produced in 1854–60, but not printed until 1870.

The custom of working a catechism at table after dinner is a return to (possibly a continuation of) a practice which long obtained in the early Craft lodges.

The Attachment of English Chapters to Lodges

An English R.A. chapter must be attached to an existing Craft lodge under the control of the United Grand Lodge, and this is so whether or not its warrant was originally issued or authorized by the Grand Master, but it does not apply if the original lodge becomes extinct. The precedence of a chapter is determined not by its own date of constitution but by that of the lodge to which it is attached. Whereas petitioners for a new Craft lodge must have been Master Masons for a minimum period of three years, any Companion, however newly exalted, may join in petitioning for a new chapter. The Committee of General Purposes, if it so pleases, makes a recommendation of the grant and the Supreme Grand Chapter accepts it.

Threshing-floor as a Symbol

The reference in the Royal Arch ritual to the threshing-floor points to a familiar symbol. H. W. Wethered in his book, *The Mind of the Ancient World,* tells us that the circular shape of the threshing-floor

when the corn was trodden out by oxen or mules in endless rotation obviously suggests the universe, with the sun, moon and stars carried round from day to day. But another interpretation of the floor is even more relevant when the corn is beaten out with sticks, as appears in Habakkuk iii, 12, where God is spoken of as marching through the land in indignation and threshing the heathen in anger.

Royal Arch Toasts

There is much individuality in the toasts used by the Companions of the Royal Arch. In Browne's ritual, written in cipher (1798), we get this toast: "To the pious memory of the two Saint John's, those two great parallels in Masonry; we follow their precepts and profit by their example." The place of the two saints has been taken in the modern ritual by 'Those Grand Originals.' Late in the 1700's there must have been considerable diversity in all such matters.

J. R. Rylands rescues from the minutes of Wakefield Royal Arch Lodge of 1769 an extraordinary collection of toasts, from which the following are taken:

> All tha's gone thro' y^e. seven.
> To him that grop'd in y^e. dark.
> The first man that enter'd y^e. Arch.
> To him that first shak'd his cable.
> To the memory of him that first moved his stones in the dark.
> Harmony among all those who have rec'd the cord of love.
> As the Jewish High Priests put off their shoes when they enter'd the Sanctum Sanctorum, so may every Mason divest himself of every vice when he enters this Lodge.

Royal Arch Masonry : the Quintessence of Masonic Philosophy

The Degree of Royal Arch as practised under the English rite, says W. Redfern Kelly, in an eloquent passage in his paper printed in *A.Q.C.* xxx (here somewhat abbreviated), contains

> the quintessence of orthodox masonic philosophy. Its symbolism is of the most exalted and sublime type, and its beautiful ritual is expressive of the highest ideals associated with the intimate search for, and the ultimate discovery of, Divine Light and Truth. Without the Royal Arch Degree, the several degrees which precede it would be incomplete and inconsistent. W. J. Chetwode Crawley has well said that "all the so-called higher degrees might be swept away, and the fabric of Freemasonry would be left untouched, none the less perfect for their removal. But, if the Royal Arch fell into desuetude, the copestone would be removed, and the building be obviously incomplete." The 'Golden Legend of the Craft' is to be found only in the Royal Arch Degree, the Alpha and the Omega, the Centre and the Circumference of the ancient masonic symbolic system.

Chapter Thirty-five

MARK MASONRY

THE marks of the operative masons have been found on stone buildings all over the world and the marks themselves date back a few hundred, even a few thousand, years. But we cannot claim that the ceremonies of Mark masonry as practised to-day go back further than some time in the eighteenth century. Actually, there is no clear indication as to when speculative Mark masonry came into being. There are certain hard dates on which we can say that Brethren of the Craft were made Mark masons, but the fact that Mark masonry was practised in the eighteenth-century Fellow Craft lodges for some time before we hear of it in lodge minutes and other records makes it quite impossible to say when it was introduced. Probably, and almost certainly, Mark masonry came in on the heels of Royal Arch masonry. We find the two closely related in the second half of the eighteenth century, and there is even a relationship to-day which will be explained as this chapter develops.[1]

Operative Masons' Marks and their Registration

Although we find masons' marks in the buildings of all civilized countries, and although they are quite common in many of the old English churches, abbeys, etc., it is only in at most two countries—Scotland and Germany—that we know those marks to have been registered and organized. To Scotland we turn for much of the early history of the operative mark.

The oft-quoted Schaw Statutes of 1598 afford clear evidence of the system of registration. Article 13, which provides a foundation on which has been erected the edifice of Mark masonry, recites that no Master or Fellow Craft is to be received or admitted except in the presence of six Masters (who must include the Warden of the lodge) and two Entered Apprentices. The date of the admission must be entered in the book, and the Candidate's name and mark inserted in that book, together with the names of the Masters and Apprentices present, as well as that of the

[1] For further information on the history of English Mark masonry see J. A. Grantham's *Introduction to Mark Masonry*, based on a paper read before the Manchester Association for Masonic Research in November 1933. The present chapter is greatly indebted to that paper.

Intender (whom we may suppose to be the Candidate's guide and instructor). No Candidate must be admitted without submitting an "assay, and sufficient tryall of his skill and worthynes in his vocatioun and craft." This assay was an essay-piece or proof-piece, of which more later. So here, in 1598, we have clear evidence that the Scottish operative mason apprentice on becoming a Fellow Craft had to register his mark.

In that very same year we learn from the minutes of the Lodge of Aitchison's Haven (an operative lodge acting as the head lodge of registration) that the marks adopted by new brethren were recorded. An entrant paid his 'buiking silver' (admission fee or registration fee).

Themark books of the lodges at Edinburgh and Aberdeen contain the registration of masons' marks, not only the marks of operatives, but also the marks accorded to or chosen by gentlemen masons (a class mentioned in the chapter devoted to early Scottish history). The Laird of Auchinleck attested the minutes of a meeting of the Lodge of Edinburgh in 1600 by means of his mark. The mark book of the lodge of Aberdeen in 1670 bears the names of forty-nine members, all but two of whom have inserted their marks opposite their names; among these members were merchants, ministers, and card-makers.

Later in this chapter it will be shown that marks were common to a great many trades, even in some cases including bakers, whose products perished within a day or so of making, whereas the marks of the mason have been preserved for hundreds and thousands of years.

Speculative Mark Masonry

So far so good. The difficulty comes in when we try to discover when the mason's mark began to form the motif of a masonic and esoteric symbolic ceremony. Mark masonry was undoubtedly practised in Fellow Craft lodges, which indeed worked a diversity of ceremonies at times throughout the eighteenth century. But, maybe as early as 1758 the lodge Doric Kilwinning, No. 68, of Port Glasgow, was actually working a speculative ceremony, for the twelfth article of its bylaws in that year ordered that any member admitted to the lodge was to pay "one shilling and a pinie half pinie for being made Mark Master."

Pride of place in Mark history is generally given to the great Thomas Dunckerley. The Chapter of Friendship, Portsmouth, working under the 'Moderns,' kept their minute-book in cipher, as did some other masonic bodies in the eighteenth century. The very first entry (1769) reads: "At a Royal Arch Chapter held at the George Tavern in Portsmouth ... the Pro Grand Master Thomas Dunckerley bro't the Warrant of the Chapter, and having lately rec'd the 'Mark' he made the Bre'n

'Mark Masons' and 'Mark Masters,' and each chose their 'Mark.'"
Then follow six names and marks.

The chapter had only been warranted on the 11th of August, and the
meeting referred to was held on the 1st of September of the same year. It
should be specially noted that the very first mark here recorded is the six-
pointed star, otherwise the hexalpha. The minute clearly indicates that
Mark masonry of those days consisted of two degrees, which we may
assume to have been Mark Man and Mark Master. English Mark masonry
now more or less combines them, but elsewhere they are still worked as
separate degrees, which however differ from those of 1769.

The Mark Man Degree was for Fellow Crafts, the Mark Master
exclusively for Master Masons. We are told that "no Brother received
the Royal Arch in this chapter, down to at least 1844, without also
receiving the Mark." What was long thought to be the first record of
Mark masonry in Scotland is in the minutes of the Journeyman Lodge of
Dumfries, which in 1770 recorded a certificate issued in the following
form:

> In the beginning was the Word. . . . we . . . hereby certify . . . that the
> said worshipful brother, after having been examined and found duly quali-
> fied as an Entered Apprentice, Fellow Craft, Master, and Mark Master
> Mason, was by us elected Master of the Chair, and then by us elevated to
> the Sublime Degree of Excellent, Super Excellent, and Royal Arch Mason.

Here was a craft lodge legitimately working both Mark and Royal Arch
masonry, and apparently working the 'constructive' chair Degree.

The Marquis of Granby Lodge, Durham, now No. 124 (dating back
to 1738, although not constituted until 1763), was regularly working
Mark masonry in 1773. Knight Templars of Kinsale, Ireland, appear to
have made a Mark mason in 1775. St Thomas's Lodge, London, now
No. 142, was constituted in 1775 and two years later was working Mark
masonry. St John's Operative Lodge, Banff, made Mark masons in 1778,
and Knight Templars of Tyrone made them in 1790.

It is evident that Mark masonry between the 1780's and the Act of
Union 1813 must have made great progress, but the second article of that
Act was a disappointment to the Mark Masons of the day, for it declared
that pure ancient masonry consists of the three Craft degrees, the Royal
Arch, and no more. It went on to recite that "this article is not intended
to prevent any Lodge or Chapter from holding a Meeting in any of the
degrees of the Orders of Chivalry, according to the constitutions of the

said Orders." (The words here given within inverted commas are no longer included in the English *Constitutions*.) J. A. Grantham tells us that many lodges believed that this article conceded the legality of Mark masonry, but they believed in vain. The Mark ceremonies continued to be worked during the first half of the nineteenth century, but "without any actual authority or authorisation other than that of old custom," except that one lodge conferred the degree under an old constitution derived from the Grand Lodge of York. This was Lodge of Hope, Bradford, actually warranted by the 'Moderns' in 1794, its present number being 302.

At that time some Mark lodges were meeting on Sunday evenings. Many years later the Travelling Mark Lodge of Ashton-under-Lyne met on Sunday afternoons at various Craft lodges in Cheshire, Lancashire, and Yorkshire, when, the lodge having been opened in all three degrees, the Mark Master entered and took the chair, Candidates were balloted for, and the lodge then opened as a Mark lodge.

The lack of any organization was a great hindrance to Mark masonry in the first half of the nineteenth century. Six Brethren who had been advanced in the Bon-Accord Royal Arch Chapter of Aberdeen wished to start a Mark lodge in London, and, in their desire that it should be regular, they obtained from that chapter a charter or warrant to bring into existence the Bon-Accord Lodge of Mark Masters. The Charter was granted on September 17, 1851, and the Lodge had its first meeting two days later. Although the charter stipulated that the allegiance of the Mark lodge was due primarily to the Supreme Grand Chapter of Scotland, the Bon-Accord Chapter was considered by that Grand Chapter to have acted illegally in chartering a subordinate body. Failing in its attempts to make the chapter recall the warrant, the Scottish Grand Lodge suspended the chapter in 1855, but by this time the daughter Mark lodge in London had a membership of more than 120.

The Bon-Accord Mark lodge was so successful that in 1856 seven members of the United Grand Lodge of England met seven members of the Supreme Grand Chapter of England in a joint committee (not consisting wholly of Mark Masons). That same year the Committee reported to Grand Lodge that the Mark Masons' Degree, so called, did not form a portion of the Royal Arch Degree and was not essential to Craft masonry, but that there was nothing objectionable in it, or anything which militated against the universality of masonry, and that it might be considered as forming a graceful addition to the Fellow Craft's degree. This was well received by Grand Lodge, which unanimously resolved

That the degree of Mark Mason or Mark Master is not at variance with the ancient landmarks of the Order, and that the degree be an addition to and form part of Craft Masonry; and consequently may be conferred by all regular Warranted Lodges, under such regulations as shall be prepared by the Board of General Purposes, approved and sanctioned by the Grand Master.

But in June of that year Grand Lodge refused to confirm the minute, and with the refusal disappeared any reasonable hope of the recognition of Mark masonry by Grand Lodge.

Within a month, however, a Mark Grand Lodge had been brought into existence by the energetic action of four Mark lodges—the Northumberland and Berwick, Newcastle-on-Tyne; Royal Cumberland, Bath; the Old Kent, London; and the Bon-Accord, London, the last-named being the leader. The new Grand Lodge naturally met with some opposition. In a small way it was 1717 all over again, some Mark lodges coming under the banner of the new Grand Lodge, others holding that they were working by inherent right and needed no Grand Lodge to make them 'regular,' ánd still others believing that Article II of the Act of Union gave them all the authority they needed, while some actually deemed the new Grand Lodge to be itself illegal, inasmuch as its chief begetter, the Bon-Accord Mark Lodge of London, had received its warrant from a subordinate chapter. Mark lodges began to apply to the Supreme Grand Royal Arch Chapter of Scotland for warrants, and within a year or two there were about fifty Mark lodges spread over England, Wales, and the Colonies, all owning allegiance to the Scots Grand Chapter, as did also two Provincial (Australian) Grand Mark Lodges, those of Victoria and New South Wales. The Scottish Grand Chapter regarded the English Mark Grand Lodge as having been illegally constituted, and that in consequence England was a non-man's-land in respect to the Mark Degree.

In spite of all this the English Mark Grand Lodge prospered, and in spite also of the very awkward position in which it found itself in regard to the Scottish Grand Lodge, which continued to warrant new Mark lodges and which in 1870 created Lancashire a Provincial Grand Mark District with its own Provincial Grand Master. Fortunately, in 1878, peace came with the formation of the present "Grand Lodge of Mark Master Masons of England and Wales and the Dominions and Dependencies of the British Crown."

The Travelling Mark Lodge of Ashton-under-Lyne already referred to (and whose story as traced by F. L. Pick in *Miscellanea Latomorum* for 1932–33 is one of the most interesting in the history of Mark masonry) attempted in 1857 to form a Grand Lodge of Mark Master Masons for England. In 1899 the Honourable United Grand Lodge of Mark Masons of the Ashton-under-Lyne District wound itself up and applied to the

Mark Grand Lodge of England for a warrant to meet under the name of
the Ashton District TI Mark Lodge, under which name it operates to-day.

The Origin of Mark Masonry

One of the soundest of our masonic writers has said that the Mark
Degree, although not recognized as part of the Craft system of freemasonry, "should be supported and practised for its antiquity as well as
for the beauty and teaching of its ritual." It is the system of allotting,
using, and, to a certain extent, registering the individual mark that
possesses the undeniable antiquity. We have no evidence from which to
judge whether the admission of a mason's mark involved any special
ceremony, but it must be frankly acknowledged that any such ceremony
could hardly have been any of the many ceremonies worked either in
English Mark masonry or in the supernumerary Mark degrees.

The early association of Royal Arch and Mark masonry cannot be
doubted. One of the early ceremonies going by the name of Mark
Master made no mention of the stone that was rejected, but it referred to
the 'Ineffable Name.' We can safely assume that in the late 1700's the
Mark and the Royal Arch degrees were mutually reminiscent. In the
Lodge of Unanimity, Dukinfield, No. 89, four Brethren "received Mark
Masonry" on one evening in 1807, and five months later in the same lodge
five Brethren were admitted to "Royal Ark Masonry."

Evidence is lacking to support the theory that the 'Antients' found in
the freemasonry of the early 1700's the early prototype of Mark masonry,
and that in their undoubted keenness for Royal Arch masonry they were
responsible, in the teeth of the 'Moderns' opposition, for the development of the Mark degrees. Indeed, Irish masons, who were of strong
'Antient' sympathies and had a high regard for Royal Arch masonry,
knew nothing of Mark masonry, so far as is known, until late in the
century, although they had been working the Royal Arch from the
1740's. J. Heron Lepper says that as late as 1870 certain outlying chapters
in Ireland had difficulty in finding a Brother able to confer the Mark
Degree. So we can dismiss from our minds any alleged neglect by the
'Moderns' in this matter.

Then how did Mark masonry find its way into the English system?
Are we not compelled to assume that it came from much the same source
as the Royal Arch, with which it was closely associated in its first half-
century and in some masonic jurisdictions still is? Both the Mark Man
and the Mark Master degrees of early days adhered fairly closely to
Biblical accounts of the building of King Solomon's Temple, and made
their appeal particularly in Scotland, which was not only a deeply religious

country but one in which the idea of the masons' mark was a common-place. The conclusion seems forced upon us that, while the underlying idea of the Mark degrees takes us back thousands of years, the degrees themselves were devised in the eighteenth century, and probably re-modelled again and again until they arrived at the form in which they are worked in England and other countries to-day under the name of Mark masonry.

It is possible that the Mark Man Degree is the earliest version of Mark masonry, although so far as recorded history goes we learn of it at exactly the same date as the Mark Master Degree—that is, in the year 1769.

Of the Mark Man Degree as practised in the 1820's we learn much from an irregular manual then published. The degree was opened as the Fellow Craft's. The apron worn by the Brethren carried ten mathe-matical characters, the signature of Hiram Abif, and the Mark of the degree. The Candidate in his Initiation made a valuable discovery, was introduced to certain secrets, and learned of the trumpet signal given to denote the approach of danger at the time of the erection of the first Temple in the City of Jerusalem.

The degree of Mark Man at one time recited a curious legend, which is known in more than one form. On the morning that the foundation-stone of the Temple was laid, King Solomon attended, and from the royal crown there fell accidentally a precious stone, which was picked up by the Senior Master of the Order of Mark Man and returned to the King. The stone was set into the sacred name of God which "is thus assumed to have been depicted upon the Royal diadem, even as it was upon the High Priest's mitre." "And thou shalt make a plate of pure gold, and grave upon it, like the engravings of a signet, Holiness to the Lord" (Exodus xxviii, 36).

The Candidate in the old Mark Man Degree learned that there were two thousand mark men at the building of the King Solomon's Temple, twenty lodges with a hundred masons in each, and the duty of the mark man was

> to mark the materials, as they came out of the hands of the workmen, to enable them to put them together with greater facility and precision, when brought from the quarries of Tyre, the Forests of Lebanon and the clay ground of the Jordan, between the Succoth and Zarthan, to the holy city of Jerusalem.

The keystone of King Solomon's arch, and the circle and letters it bore, are described, and we learn that there were employed in the quarries of Tyre one thousand four hundred Mark Men in fourteen lodges with a hundred masons in each. The legend is recited that the curious keystone containing many valuable coins "and the ten letters in precious stone work" was lost, and that an ingenious Entered Apprentice made a keystone to fit, which the Fellow Crafts in their jealousy threw away. The Candidate finds this keystone and is suitably rewarded. This is a bare outline of the Mark Man Degree as practised in all probability in the second half of the eighteenth century and in the early years of the nineteenth. The 'rejection' motif is not developed in the way the present Mark mason knows it. The degree was conferred on Fellow Crafts, the following degree—that of Mark Master—being conferred on Mark masons who are also Master Masons.

In the Mark Master Degree, a century or more ago, the Candidate was informed of the lighthouse which stood on the highest part of Mount Lebanon to guide and direct the ancient mariners employed in fetching gold, ivory, and precious stones from Ophir for the decoration of the Temple. The ritual introduces a reference to the 'link,' an idea which went through a number of the early Mark ceremonies and gave its name to some of them. In the degree, presumably as worked in the early 1800's, the 'link' referred to one of the names of the Creator, "a grand ineffable name." The Mark Masters at the building of the Temple were said to be a thousand in number, fifty to each of the twenty lodges, their duty being to re-examine the materials after they were brought to Jerusalem, that every part might duly correspond; they added their additional marks, to prove and pass the work previously examined by the Mark Men. The Mark mason of to-day will recognize certain features of these two old degrees, but he should know that there were a number of Mark degrees between which was considerable confusion, and that, as already pointed out, there is no exact correspondence between any of them and the degree as worked to-day.

The ceremonies of Mark masonry as practised in the eighteenth and early nineteenth centuries were not always based on the 'rejection' motif. The Mark Degree to-day centres upon the rejection of a worked stone which is afterwards found to be essential in the erection of a building— an elaborate paraphrase, as it were, of Matthew xxi, 42: "The stone which the builders rejected, the same is become the head of the corner," a text which in slightly varying forms can be found in Psalms, Mark, Luke, and elsewhere in the New Testament. This motif was absent from the Mark Degree long worked in the Lodge of Hope at Bradford, but there is mention of the keystone in many Mark ceremonies early in the nineteenth century. The name Mark has been applied to a great many degrees, and does not necessarily indicate the content of the degree. It is thought that some of the material for these degrees has been separated from old Fellow Craft workings, into which presumably the material had been interpolated some time after the middle of the eighteenth century. It can be readily understood, therefore, how considerable diversity in the various Mark degrees came into being. We learn, for example, that in Bristol a significant part of the Mark working was given in the course of the Fellow Craft ceremonies, and did not arrive at a separate existence until after the union of 1813.

In connexion with the old Mark degrees we learn of such curious titles as the "Passing of the Bridge," "the Mark and Link," the "Mark or Link," the "Link and Wrestle," "Link or Wrestle," etc. There are many workings to-day in which some part or other of these old degrees survives. The North Country lodges early in the last century worked a ceremony or degree known as the "Passing of the Bridge." The American Royal Arch chapters to-day have a dramatic working under exactly the same name, and in it is introduced an actual passing of a real bridge as a preliminary to exaltation in the Royal Arch. It is difficult to see any connexion whatever between the operative mark and some to these old degrees, although with regard to the word 'link' there does seem some ground for supposing that the link masons united in a link to heave aside the discarded stone that was too large for one man to lift. There appears to be a reflection of this in the Mark ceremonies of to-day.

In many cases the Royal Arch chapters conferred these curious degrees, and we can well imagine the confusion to which such a practice led—the admixture and the interlarding which was the almost inevitable result of degrees being worked in the same lodges through one or two generations at a time when printed rituals were taboo.

The 'Wrestle' degree seems to have made much of the story told in Genesis xxxii, of Jacob wrestling with the angel until the breaking of the day. The Rock Lodge at Gibraltar, working under the Irish constitution, early in the nineteenth century was working two or more of these curious 'link' and 'wrestle' degrees, including what was known as the 'Ark and Link,' which bears some resemblance to one of the additional degrees worked to-day.

The Mark Tracing-board

The Mark tracing-board is capable of a very useful interpretation. On the first, fifth, and ninth rungs of a ladder are certain Hebrew letters. Ignoring the possibility of their possessing some cabalistic meaning based on their numerical values (which might have meant something in superstitious days, but now is completely valueless), these initials appear to represent the moral virtues. On the first rung is 'Aleph,' meaning 'faith' or 'faithfulness and truth,' possibly 'steadiness'; on the fifth rung is the letter 'Tau,' indicating 'hope,' 'expectation,' 'eager and ardent desire'; and on the ninth rung is the letter 'Tzadde,' which means 'charity,' 'liberality,' 'beneficence,' and, in another connexion, 'justice.'

The Mark Regalia

Symbolically much is to be learned from the regalia of the Mark Degree, in which the emblem of office is surrounded by a wreath of rose leaves and hyssop. We associate grace, simplicity, beauty, happiness, with the rose; but the hyssop is a symbol of a very different kind, to which reference is frequently made in old Biblical texts, of which the most apt is Psalm li, 7: "Purge me with hyssop, and I shall be clean: wash me, and I shall be whiter than snow." Hyssop was a rock-growing plant, probably a moss which was used as a cleansing agent; but there were probably two hyssops, both of them rock-plants, one of them being the caper plant, *Capparis spinosa.* In Jewish ceremonies hyssop has uses in connexion with burnt sacrifices and with the sprinkling of the unclean with water into which the hyssop had been dipped.

The Mark Pledge

The Mark mason is under an obligation to receive a Brother's Mark when presented to him and grant his request if in his power to do so; but he is not bound to relieve him a second time until the Brother shall have redeemed his pledge.

This is a matter made much more of in American Mark masonry, and we learn from Mackey that Marks or pledges were in frequent use among the ancients, and are referred to in the literature of mythology. Thus Jason (of Golden Fleece fame) promises Medea, on her parting from him, to send her the symbols of hospitality, which shall ensure for her a kind reception in foreign countries. There was once a custom, when a guest had been entertained, of breaking a die in two parts, one of which was kept by the guest, so that at any future time he could match up his broken piece with his host's and renew the friendship, a friendship which apparently extended to the descendants of the contracting parties. These dies, or pledges, were known by the Romans as *tessaræ,* and were then small pieces of bone, ivory, or stone, suitably inscribed and broken into two.

Mackey says that the Christians carried *tessaræ* as a means of introduction to fellow Christians, and even relates this custom to the text in Revelation ii, 17: "To him that overcometh will I give . . . a white stone, and in the stone a new name written, which no man knoweth saving he that receiveth it."

It is a possibility that a certain custom once commonly followed in England is a survival of that ancient practice, for it is well known that in Lancashire, in the last century, a betrothed couple would break "'t lucky sixpence and vow they'd never part," each of them retaining half. Often there was much virtue in the coin being a bent or crooked one. We learn from Brand's *Antiquities* that in ancient days it was customary among the ordinary run of people to break a piece of gold or silver in token of a verbal contract of marriage, one half being kept by the woman and the other by the man. John Gay (1685–1732), the author of *The Beggar's Opera,* has some lines in one of his plays which are much to the purpose:

> KITTY. Yet, Justices, permit us ere we part
>   To break this ninepence, as you've broke our heart.
> FILBERT (*breaking the ninepence*). As this divides, thus are we torn in twain.
> KITTY (*joining the pieces*). And as this meets, thus may we meet again.

Masons' Marks and their Registration

Let us consider the mason's mark itself, the *operative* mason's mark found on the stonework of buildings of the Egyptians, Assyrians, Babylonians, Greeks, etc., as far back as 1500 B.C., and which, of course, is to be seen on the stonework of the Gothic buildings of England and other countries.

There has long been much discussion as to the reason for, and meaning of, these marks. Countless writers have associated them with magical or esoteric matters, and there are still some authors who incline towards that idea; but the generality of students now conclude that the marks were of a severely practical nature, probably to identify the man who shaped the stone, or to indicate the position in which the stone should be laid. Even if we take the purely practical view much is to be learned from them.

If we concede that every skilled mason working on an important building had his individual mark, it is difficult to avoid the conclusion that there must have been some organization and registration of marks; but in only two countries do we know of anything of the kind, and then only in recent centuries. We have already seen that in Scotland, in 1598, instructions were issued that every mason on admission to the fraternity should enter his name and mark in the register in the presence of six Masters, two Entered Apprentices, and an Intender. In German mason usage fellows of the *Steinmetzen* were required to swear they would not vary their distinctive marks. And later in this chapter, when dealing with the marks of other trades, it is made clear that, at any rate in one instance, there was registration of marks more than five hundred years ago. Curiously, that too was in Scotland.

In a speculative Mark lodge every Brother selects the mark by which he is afterwards to be known, and this mark is enrolled and registered in the books of his own lodge, and also in the General Register Books of Marks in the Mark Grand Lodge. It is usual for such marks to have a geometrical character, and to consist for the most part of straight lines and angles.

The rise of the craft guilds in England and other countries appears to have intensified the need of craft marks, not only the masons'. There was great industrial activity of every kind in early medieval days; the various countries were exchanging goods, merchants were growing rich, their wealth was finding its way into the coffers of King and Church and noble, buildings were being erected—churches, abbeys, castles, bridges —and the number of men employed as masons must have steadily and quickly increased generation by generation. In all probability the only masons on any building who could read and write were the Master Mason and perhaps an overseer or two. The rest could indicate their identity only by means of a simple mark, easy of invention, still easier to adapt from an earlier one. There are certain marks that a man with a mason' saxe or hammer and chisel will instinctively make, and such are the marks that we find repeated again and again over thousands of years.

The study of any comprehensive lists of marks, such as those, for example, to be found in *A.Q.C.*, vol. lviii, and in these pages, will reveal that over and over again the marks are such as can be extremely easily executed—in fact, made in a few seconds by the application of very simple tools. We find the same marks or types of mark used in many places, with of course infinite variations to please the fancy of the individual mason. Curves are comparatively rare, neither ·the tools of the mason nor the material on which he worked favouring the easy or natural production of a curved mark. There are probably a hundred straight marks for one curved one. Most of the marks are extremely obvious and many of them originated with two lines forming a cross, so: + or ×, from which basis can be built easily and simply all sorts of figures.

Such an authority as Wyatt Papworth considers, with many other writers, that mason marks "often took the place of a proper sign manual to a document; they designated the stone which each man worked and pointed out instantly who was responsible for defect or mistake." The marks were generally put on the face of the stone near one of the edges, so that they remained exposed when the stone was built into the wall;

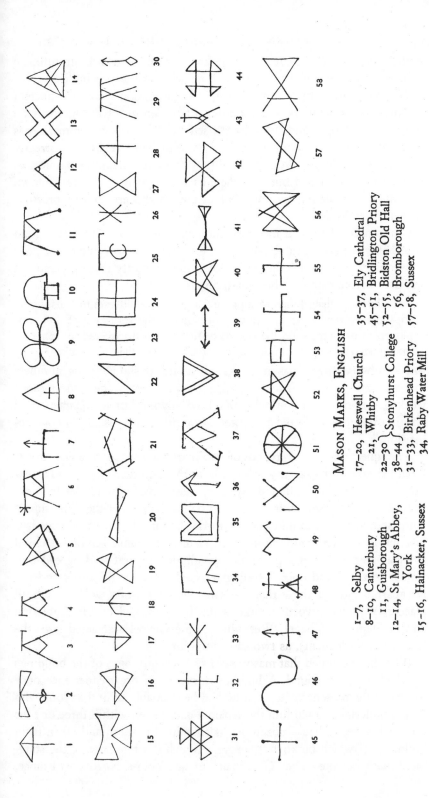

MASON MARKS, ENGLISH

1-7, Selby
8-10, Canterbury
11, Guisborough
12-14, St Mary's Abbey, York
15-16, Halnacker, Sussex
17-20, Heswell Church
21, Whitby
22-30, Stonyhurst College
38-44, Stonyhurst College
31-33, Birkenhead Priory
34, Raby Water Mill
35-37, Ely Cathedral
45-51, Bridlington Priory
52-55, Bidston Old Hall
56, Bromborough
57-58, Sussex

in the stoneyard to-day masons' marks are applied to indicate ultimate position and consequently are covered up when the wall is built.

We may reasonably assume, then, that the mason's mark in ancient and medieval stonework was a guide to the identity of the mason who prepared the stone, and was either itself a tally, or another mark was added as a tally, to ensure that the man who laid the stones correctly interpreted the Master Mason's wishes. The overwhelming opinion of architects and technical building men, as well as that of the best-known students of speculative masonry, is that the marks were entirely practical in their intention.

Gould notes that "our medieval ancestors were superstitious and fond of alchemy, believing in certain signs, etc., and that workmen may have occasionally chosen such figures for their marks, partly from superstition and partly from caprice," but what, he asks,

> could be more absurd than to suppose that poor and illiterate masons should copy the signs of magical lore on stones under the very eyes of their employers—the clergy—on the chance of their being discovered by some remote generation which would have lost all sense of their symbolism?

But he observes that mason marks are useful as showing the numbers that worked on any particular building, and whether the same masons worked on any other building, but how anyone but a dreamer could imagine that they referred to esoteric doctrines "surpasses his comprehension."

The question of the repetition of marks must be touched upon. Gould speaks of the same simple marks as the triangle or the broad arrow existing all over England, and says they must have existed independently in thousands of cases. But it seems to be inevitable that the same simple mark should be found all over the world, because in so many cases it is just the instinctive production of an elementary mind guiding a chisel and hammer. This is a point already alluded to, but it is agreed that similar marks found upon buildings erected one after the other and not far apart do go to show that the same set of masons worked at both places. Wyatt Papworth mentions the Lady Chapel of Ely Cathedral and St Stephen's Chapel, Westminster (the Chapel associated with the Houses of Parliament), as two cases in point.

It has been claimed that mason marks indicate the ages of the buildings in which they are found. A building surveyor of great experience once informed the present writer that he had been unable to find anyone who would undertake to tell him the separate dates, even within three or four hundred years, of half a dozen marks submitted by him, and taken from buildings of which he knew the ages. Which is a reminder of the statement that when the Abbey Church at Vézelay, Yonne, North-east France,

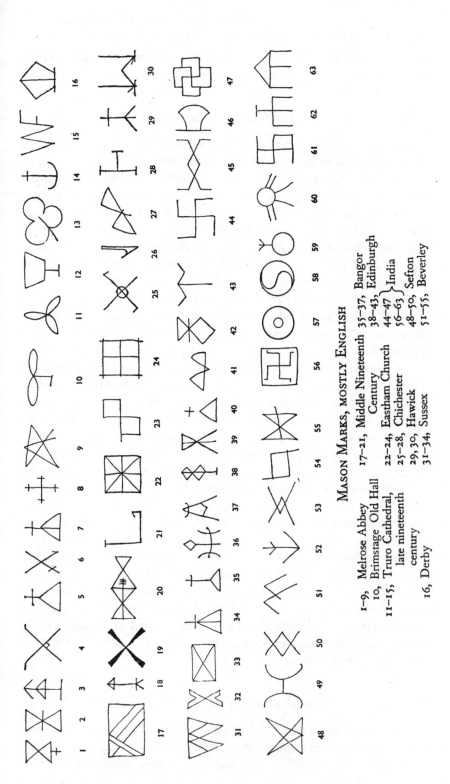

MASON MARKS, MOSTLY ENGLISH

1–9, Melrose Abbey
10, Brimstage Old Hall
11–15, Truro Cathedral, late nineteenth century
16, Derby
17–21, Middle Nineteenth Century
22–24, Eastham Church
25–28, Chichester
29, 30, Hawick
31–34, Sussex
35–37, Bangor
38–43, Edinburgh
44–47, } India
56–63, }
48–50, Sefton
51–55, Beverley

was restored about 1840, and many of the old decayed stones were replaced by new ones, the masons were instructed to reproduce the old mason marks!

The Marks of Other Trades

Many other trades marked their products, but the idea, even in medieval days, was far from novel. Ancient fabrics bore the weaver's mark. In ancient China, Persia, Egypt, and Rome makers' marks as evidence of genuineness were affixed to articles of merchandise, and the Romans introduced the idea to Britain, where ancient pottery has been found carrying such marks. One of the most notable instances is that of the goldsmiths and silversmiths, who marked their work in medieval days to indicate both maker and quality of the precious article. The custom has survived, as everybody knows, and these marks are now affixed in accordance with Acts of Parliament. Carpenters and joiners marked their work up to the end of the sixteenth century, and to-day, although they do not usually apply marks of identity, they still mark their work to indicate what will be the finished face of the woodwork when erected. The Coopers' Company had very clear and most distinctive marks, of which the circle, representing the barrel or cask, was invariably a part.

In past centuries in France nearly every type of craftsman was required to mark his work, and according to a French author goldsmiths, clothworkers, potters, coopers, etc., each possessed a stamp or private mark.

In Scotland not only masons marked their work but also the bakers! At any rate, that was so in Aberdeen, where in 1398 the magistrates ordered every baker to mark his loaves so that any sample of adulterated bread could be traced to its maker. These marks consist usually of a rough circle containing a varying number of dots, somewhat suggestive of a Bath bun, and illustrations of many of them are still in existence.

Not only the makers of goods, but merchants also, were required in England and elsewhere to mark their goods. The idea of the mark of origin grew in strength in the eighteenth and nineteenth centuries, so much so that to-day we find countless thousands of manufactured articles in every country bearing the maker's mark, applied in conformity with special and complicated trade-mark laws, and most carefully registered and indexed by a Government office.

Masons' Marks of Unusual Character

Many of the old masons' marks strike us nowadays as unusual. Two Roman architects two thousand years ago, working together, carved a lizard and a frog on their temple building to reveal their identity to any informed person, as they had been forbidden to associate their names with the building. At York a Master Mason, named Hyndeley, carved on his work the device of a *hind ly*ing down.

A most curious mark, assumed to be a mason's mark, has been disclosed on the walls of temples at Yucatan, the 'Egypt' of America. These temples were built thousands of years ago, had arched ceilings and very thick walls, the latter finished with plaster. The scaling off of this plaster in course of time has revealed what appears to be a mason's mark on a stone near the main entrance—not the usual hieroglyph, but the imprint of a hand in red dye. Some words, however, in William Crooke's *Religion and Folklore of Northern India* suggest a very different interpretation of this mark, even though India and Yucatan be thousands of miles apart. The author is speaking of an officer performing the sacrifice at a marriage in Madras, who dips his hands in the blood of a slaughtered goat and imprints his palms on the wall of the room, and he says that the practice of impressing the mark of the hand and spread fingers on a house near the door, as a protection from evil influences, is common throughout India. Of many instances given by him, here are two. At a Brahmin wedding in Gujarät the bride and bridegroom dip their hands in vermilion and mark both doorposts of the house, while pilgrims at a certain temple, as they offer prayer, make a similar impression, fingers upward, and if the prayer is fulfilled they return and make a second mark, this time with the fingers downward.

There may survive on stonework here and there a mark quite distinct in its purpose from any yet mentioned, for we learn from a letter book of the City of London (1580) containing orders "for yee compayne of Fremasons" that Purbeck stone had usually been marked to declare the full content whereby the Queen's subjects had not found it necessary to measure the stone, but had bought it according to the mark, but that "of late yeares the bryngers of such stone have falselye and deceiptfullye marked their stone, whereby the buyers trustinge vppon the former good and true vsage, have bene and be daylye deceaved." It was ordered that stones found falsely overmarked should be forfeited, and that no freeman of the City should buy Purbeck stone to sell again until it had been "vewed searched and measured," the Wardens of the Freemasons Company to be paid one per cent. of the purchase price for their "travaile in viewinge, searchinge, and measuringe of the said stone."

Chapter Thirty-six

THE ADDITIONAL DEGREES

ORGANIZED speculative masonry had not long emerged into the dim light of the early eighteenth century and begun to see itself as a system of three Craft degrees before Brethren were tempted to add ceremonies which sought to explain and extend those they already had. The lively, fertile mind of the French mason, who had received speculative masonry from England and was to return it with many elaborations, was soon at work devising rites, which, when introduced to the freemasons of Great Britain (as degrees of allegedly Scottish origin, it is thought) were welcomed in many quarters as amplifications of the ancient ceremonies with which they were now familiar.

It may help to restate very briefly the suggested explanation (see p. 502) of how it came about that the earlier and more important of these innovations came to be widely accepted. Some of the innovations were of considerable interest, told an attractive story, exemplified a highly developed symbolism, or reintroduced a definitely Christian motif. Curiously, they were given the warmes t encouragement by those who one might have thought would have been the most obstinate in refusing to have anything to do with them, for whereas the Premier Grand Lodge officially looked askance at this particular kind of innovation and continued to do so all through the eighteenth century, the 'Antients,' who derided their opponents as being 'Moderns,' were—paradoxically enough —the chief agents in the spread of the invented degrees. Such authorities as W. J. Songhurst and J. Heron Lepper agree on this point. "I see in every British Knight Templar or Chevalier Rose Croix," says the second of these writers, "a probable scion of 'Antient' craft masonry."

The additional degrees are often called the 'higher degrees,' but the term seems hardly fair to "pure, ancient masonry." The 'highest' degrees must always remain those which authentic masonic history proves to be the oldest. They are the three Craft degrees. Other degrees may be designated by higher numbers, but in no sense other than, in some cases, that of a more highly developed symbolism, can they be said to be higher—a statement which does not in any way detract from their value or beauty. The Grand Lodges of England and of all English-speaking countries acknowledge the Craft degrees and, to a varying extent, Royal Arch masonry and Mark masonry. All other degrees are 'additional' or 'side' degrees, and among them the Rose Croix and the Knights Templar occupy honoured and exceptional places.

It would be unfair to conceal that there have been masonic students of great merit who would not agree with this judgment. For example, J. E. S. Tuckett contributed to *A.Q.C.*, vol. xxxii, a learned paper inquiring into the development of the separate exclusive degrees, and in the course of it he expounded the theory that these degrees were founded on freemasonry's pre-1717 "store of legend, tradition and symbolism of wide extent," of which from 1717 the Grand Lodge, selecting only a portion of this store, gradually evolved the three Craft degrees and the Royal Arch. His views, highly controversial, received little support.

Experienced Brethren, whose opinions matter, agree that the better-known and more important of the additional degrees possess special and peculiar value, and that in them is much that serves to throw a revealing light upon the symbolic content of the fundamental Craft degrees. But the words of W. J. Hughan in his small but valued work *The English Rite* should not be forgotten. He says:

> It is much to be regretted that after a lapse of over a hundred and fifty years [he was writing in, say, 1884] the inordinate craving to amplify, distort, and sometimes misrepresent the beautiful ceremonies of the Craft, which were, doubtless, in part adapted and continued from the older organization, has not yet exhausted itself.

It will be understood that it is no part of the purpose of this chapter to enter into detailed explanation or discussion of the additional degrees. Instead is appended a list (by no means exhaustive) based upon one in C. Walton Rippon's paper in the *Transactions of the Merseyside Association for Masonic Research* (vol. viii (1930)). Following the three Craft degrees and the Royal Arch and the Mark degrees come:

Royal Ark Mariner.
Allied Degrees.
   Knight of St Lawrence the Martyr
   Knight of Constantinople
   Knight of the Red Cross of Babylon
   Grand Tyler of King Solomon
   Secret Monitor
   Grand High Priest
Thirty-seven or more Degrees and Orders under the jurisdiction of the Grand Council of the Allied Masonic Degrees.
The Knights Templar and Malta Orders—the 'Chivalric' orders—essentially Christian and confined to R.A. Companions.

Three Other 'Chivalric' Orders.
Knight of the Red Cross of Constantine
Knight of St John
Knight of the Holy Sepulchre

Four 'Cryptic' Degrees.
Most Excellent Master
Royal Master
Select Master
Super Excellent Master

The Ancient and Accepted Rite: the Rose Croix.
Thirty-three degrees referring to the thirty-three years of our Lord's life on earth.

The Supreme Council of England and Wales, dating back to 1845, controls all except the first three, following which are:
Secret Master
Perfect Master
Intimate Secretary
Provost and Judge
Intendant of the Buildings
Elect of Nine
Elect of Fifteen
Sublime Elect, etc., etc.

The thirty-third degree is Sovereign Grand Inspector General, with thirty-three members only and a few hon. members; it leads the quest from the "Lost Word" to Mount Calvary.

Royal Order of Scotland (claimed to have been working from the middle of the eighteenth century). Its two degrees are:
The Harodim
The Rosy Cross

Order of the Secret Monitor. Two Degrees and a Chair degree, attached to it being the Order of the Scarlet Cord.

The Societas Rosicruciana in Anglia (S.R.I.A.), whose 'Fratres' are distributed in nine grades, arranged in three orders, each having its own distinctive name.

Ancient and Primitive Rite and the

Rites of Memphis and Miẓraim, each consisting of a multiplicity of degrees.

Some others, as to which, and all those here mentioned, the reader may consult J. S. M. Ward's *The Higher Degrees Handbook.*

Appendix

THE ARMS OF
THE THREE SISTER GRAND LODGES

T HE Arms of the United Grand Lodge of England, illustrated in Plate XXXI, are exclusively for Grand Lodge use and may not be used by Provincial or District Grand Lodges or by private lodges.

Arms were in use a very long time before occasion was taken to apply to the College of Heralds for a proper grant, for not until 1919 were they officially granted, an addition being made fourteen years later.

In the Arms two cherubim stand one each side of a large shield whose border has lions on it. The 'quarterings' on the shield itself are (*a*) on the left, three castles and a chevron, (/\); on the chevron is a pair of open compasses: (*b*) on the right are the four quarterings of a lion, an ox, a man, and an eagle. Above the shield is the Ark of the Covenant with cherubim, and over the Ark is Hebrew lettering. At the foot of the whole device is a scroll bearing a Latin motto: In explaining the features of the Arms any difficult heraldic terms will be avoided.

Let us take the shield first. Its quarterings are derived partly from the Arms of the Premier Grand Lodge, that of the 'Moderns,' and partly from the Arms of the Grand Lodge of the 'Antients.' The castles, chevron, and compasses are taken, with some amount of adaptation, from the original Arms that were granted to the London Company of Free-masons in 1472. The castle is a device commonly found in heraldry, and it is said that the three castles signify the Trinity. There is much doubt about that, however, for we find *four* castles in an engraving of the London Company's Arms in 1677. Originally in the Company's Arms the castles were much more obvious castles complete with iron gates, but in course of time they became the simple towers we now see on the shield. In the Company's Arms the chevron which is now quite plain was originally 'engrailed'—that is, it had indented or serrated edges. Originally, too, the Company's Arms carried the motto "God is our Guide," altered by the time the engraving of 1677 was made to "In the Lord is all our Trust"; this, however, was altered back again to the original motto late in the nineteenth century. Both of these mottos carry a great significance for the Initiate, who quite early in his career is required to affirm that he puts his trust in God.

After the union of 1813 the Arms of the two Grand Lodges were combined, but the castles, chevron, and compasses represent all that survived of the Arms of the Premier Grand Lodge. It was the 'Antients' who had adopted, years before, the device of the lion to represent strength;

the ox, patience and assiduity; the man, intelligence and understanding; and the eagle, promptness and celerity—four emblems which reveal to us that to the 'Antients' the Royal Arch was an integral part of the Order. In the year 1675 a Spanish Jew, Jacob Jehudah Leon, had exhibited in London a model of King Solomon's Temple which attracted considerable notice. Laurence Dermott, the alert Secretary of the 'Antients' Grand Lodge, examined this model about ninety years after its first exhibition, and in connexion with it he saw at the same time a strange coat-of-arms, of which he promptly availed himself in settling the Arms of his Grand Lodge.

Around the shield is a wide border carrying eight lions. This was added in 1919 to commemorate the long association of King Edward VII and other members of the Royal family with the Grand Lodge.

The Hebrew lettering over the Ark of the Covenant is "Kodes la Adonai"—that is, "Holiness to the Lord," the full significance of which we learn in Exodus xxviii, 36.

The scroll at the bottom of the Arms carries three Latin words, *Audi, Vide, Tace* which may be translated, "Hear, See, be Silent," and is part of a leonine or rhyming motto of a type fashionable some hundreds of years ago, *Audi, vide, tace, si vis vivere in pace,* translatable as "Hear, see, be silent, if you would live in peace."

The castles, cherubim, and compasses have been repeated many times in the Arms of operative and speculative masonic bodies, and we find the cherubim and Ark in the Arms of other Grand Lodges. For example, the Irish Grand Lodge retains the cherubim and Ark, includes the national harp in the scroll underneath, but its shield does not preserve the castles and chevron; whereas in the arms of the Scottish Grand Lodge the shield carries the familiar castles and chevron in addition to the cross of St Andrew, but there is no place for the cherubim and Ark. In the Scottish arms illustrated in Plate XXXI prominence is given in the surrounding ornament to the Scots thistle.

BIBLIOGRAPHY

OF the hundreds of books, papers, and other sources consulted and drawn upon for information, the following short list represents those which the author has found particularly helpful.

ABBREVIATIONS

"*A.Q.C.*," *Ars Quatuor Coronatorum*—the "Transactions" of the Quatuor Coronati Lodge, No. 2076, London.
"*Misc. Lat.*"—*Miscellanea Latomorum.*
"*Merseyside*"—*Transactions of the Merseyside Association for Masonic Research.*

Constitutions of the Ancient Fraternity of Free and Accepted Masons under the United Grand Lodge of England. Published under the authority of the United Grand Lodge (London, 1940).

The Book of Constitutions comprising the Laws and Regulations of the Grand Lodge of Free and Accepted Masons of Ireland. Published by authority of the Grand Lodge of Ireland (Dublin, 1947).

The Constitution and Laws of the Grand Lodge of Ancient Free and Accepted Masons of Scotland. Published by authority of Grand Lodge (Edinburgh, 1944).

Masonic Year Book. Published annually under the authority of the United Grand Lodge of England (London).

ADAMS, CECIL C.: "Ahiman Rezon, the Book of Constitutions," in *A.Q.C.*, vol. xlvi.

BALL, REV. CHARLES JAMES: "The Proper Names of Masonic Tradition," in *A.Q.C.*, vol. v.

BAXTER, RODERICK HILDEGAR: "The Masonic Poem of the 1390 *circa*; a Modernized Transcript of the Regius MS.," in *Merseyside*, vol. iv.

BRAND, JOHN: *Popular Antiquities of Great Britain.* With corrections and additions by W. Carew Hazlitt (three volumes, London, 1870).

BRIGGS, MARTIN S.: *The Architect in History* (London, 1927).

BULLAMORE, GEORGE W.: "The Beehive and Freemasonry," in *A.Q.C.*, vol. xxxvi.

CALVERT, ALBERT F.: "Lodge Nights in the Olden Days," in *Merseyside*, vol. iv.

CONDER, EDWARD: "The Masons' Company and the Lodge of Accepted Masons," in *A.Q.C.*, vol. ix.

   Records of the Hole Crafte and Fellowship of Masons, with a Chronicle of the History of the Worshipful Company of Masons of the City of London (London, 1894).

CRAWLEY, W. J. CHETWODE: "Masonic Blue," in *A.Q.C.*, vol. xxiii.

CROWE, FREDERICK JOSEPH WILLIAM: "Colours in Freemasonry," in *A.Q.C.*, vol. xvii.

"Masonic Clothing," in *A.Q.C.*, vols. v and vi.

COVEY CRUMP, REV. WALTER WILLIAM: *The Hiramic Tradition: A Survey of Hypotheses concerning it.* Masonic Record, Ltd, London; "The Orientation of Masonic Lodges," in *A.Q.C.*, vol. xxxv; "Quasi-Biblical Accretions in the Masonic Ceremonies" (address), in *A.Q.C.*, vol. xxxix; "Scriptural Evidence Concerning Hiram," in *A.Q.C.*, vol. xliii.

DASHWOOD, J. R.: "First Minute Book of the Excellent Grand and Royal Chapter," in *A.Q.C.*, vol. lxii; "Falsification of the Charter of Compact," in *A.Q.C.*, vol. lxiv.

DAYNES, GILBERT W.: *The Birth and Growth of the Grand Lodge of England, 1717–1926.* Masonic Record, Ltd, London.

DRING, EDMUND HUNT: "The Evolution and Development of the Tracing or Lodge Board," in *A.Q.C.*, vol. xxix.

EDWARDS, LEWIS: "Anderson's Book of Constitutions of 1738," in *A.Q.C.*, vol. xlvi; "The Colours in a Royal Arch Chapter" (address), in *Misc. Lat.*, vol. xxii; "Freemasonry; Ritual and Ceremony" (Prestonian Lecture), in *4.Q.C.*, vol. xlix.

FLATHEK, DAVID: "The Foundation-stone," in *A.Q.C.*, vol. xlviii.

GOULD, ROBERT FREKE: *A Concise History of Freemasonry* (London, 1903).

"The Degrees of Pure and Ancient Freemasonry," in *A.Q.C.*, vol. xvi.

The History of Freemasonry (three volumes, London, 1884–87).

GRANTHAM, JOHN A.: *An Introduction to Mark Masonry* (based on a paper read before the Manchester Association for Masonic Research, November, 1933).

GRANTHAM, W. IVOR: "The Attempted Incorporation of the Moderns," in *A.Q C.*, vol. xlvi.

HALLETT, H. HIRAM: "Four Historical Lodges—Promulgation, Reconciliation, Stability and Emulation," in *Merseyside*, vol. ix.

HALLIDAY, R. T.: "The Landmarks of the Order," in *Merseyside*, vol. x.

HALL-JOHNSON, A. S.: "Castles and Cherubim: Notes on the Origin, History and Significance of the Arms of the Grand Lodge of England," in *Misc. Lat.*, vol. xxv.

HAZLITT, W. CAREW: *The Livery Companies of the City of London* (London, 1892).

HEIRON, ARTHUR: "Masters' Lodges," in *A.Q.C.*, vol. xxxix.

HERBERT, WILLIAM: *History of the Twelve Great Livery Companies of London* (London, 1836–37).

HEXTALL, WILLIAM B.: "Old Landmarks of the Craft," in *A.Q.C.*, vol. xxv.
" The Special Lodge of Promulgation (1809–11)," in *A.Q.C.*, vol. xxiii.
HILLS, GORDON P. G.: "Patron Saints and Masonry," in *A.Q.C.*, vol. xxxi.
HOBBS, J. WALTER: "Notes on the Mark Degree," in *Merseyside*, vol. ii.
"The Travelling Masons and Cathedral Builders," in *A.Q.C.*, vol. xl.
HORSLEY, CANON JOHN WILLIAM: "Masonic Symbolism," in *A.Q.C.*, vol. x.
"Solomon's Seal and the Shield of David Traced to their Origin," in *A.Q.C.*, vol. xv.
HUGHAN, WILLIAM J.: *The Masonic 'Old Charges,'* a pamphlet (1906).
Origin of the English Rite of Freemasonry, edited by John T. Thorp (1909).
JAMES, P. R.: "The Bear Lodge at Bath (1732–85), in *A.Q.C.*, vol. lix."
JOHNSON, G. Y.: "The York Grand Chapter, or Grand Chapter of ALL England," in *A.Q.C.*, vol. lvii.
JONES, BERNARD E.: " 'Free' in 'Freemason' and the Idea of Freedom through Six Centuries"(Prestonian Lecture for 1952); in *Transactions* of Manchester Association for Masonic Research, vol. xlii, and elsewhere.
KELLY, W. REDFERN: "Advent of Royal Arch Masonry," in *A.Q.C.*, vol. xxx.
KNOOP, DOUGLAS: "The Connection between Operative and Speculative Masonry" (address), in *A.Q.C.*, vol. xlviii.
"The Mason Word" (Prestonian Lecture), in *A.Q.C.*, vol. li.
"Pure Ancient Masonry," in *A.Q.C.*, vol. liii.
KNOOP, DOUGLAS and JONES, G. P.: "A Dialogue between Simon and Peter," in *A.Q.C.*, vol. lvii.
The Genesis of Freemasonry (Manchester, 1947).
A Handlist of Masonic Documents (Manchester, 1942).
An Introduction to Freemasonry (Manchester, 1937).
The Mediæval Mason (Manchester, 1933).
"Prolegomena to the Mason Word," in *A.Q.C.*, vol. lii.
The Scottish Mason and the Mason Word (Manchester, 1939).
A Short History of Freemasonry to 1730 (Manchester, 1940).
"The Sixteenth Century Mason," in *A.Q.C.*, vol. l.
KNOOP, DOUGLAS, JONES, G. P., and HAMER, DOUGLAS: *The Early Masonic Catechisms* (Manchester, 1943).
LANE, JOHN: *Masonic Records (1717–1894)*. With an Introduction by William James Hughan (1895).
LEPPER, JOHN HERON: "The Evolution of Masonic Ritual in England in the Eighteenth Century" (Prestonian Lecture for 1932), manuscript.
"The Traditioners," in *A.Q.C.*, vol. lvi.
LEPPER, JOHN HERON, and CROSSLÉ, PHILIP: *History of the Grand Lodge of Free and Accepted Masons of Ireland*, vol. i (Dublin, 1925).
LYON, DAVID MURRAY: *History of the Lodge at Edinburgh (Mary's Chapel)*, No. 1 (Edinburgh, 1873).
MACKEY, ALBERT GALLATIN: *An Encyclopædia of Freemasonry*. New and revised edition prepared under the direction of William James Hughan by Edward L. Hawkins (two volumes, Chicago, 1924).

MEEKREN, R. J.: "The Aitchison's Haven Minutes and Early Scottish Free Masonry," in *A.Q.C.*, vol. liii.

MURRAY, ALFRED A. ARBUTHNOT: "Freeman and Cowan," in *A.Q.C.*, vol. xxi.

OLIVER, BRUCE W.: "A Tale of Two Lodges," in *A.Q.C.*, vol. lvii.

PARKER, JOHN HENRY: *An Introduction to Gothic Architecture* (twelfth edition, London, 1898).

PICK, FRED L.: "Preston—the Gild and the Craft," in *A.Q.C.*, vol. lix.

POIGNANT, AXEL J. A.: "The Landmarks," in *A.Q.C.*, vol. xxiv.

POOLE, REV. HERBERT: "The Antiquity of the Craft," in *A.Q.C.*, vol. li.
"The Graham Manuscript," in *A.Q.C.*, vol. l.
"Masonic Ritual and Secrets before 1717," in *A.Q.C.*, vol. xxxvii.
The Old Charges. Masonic Record, Ltd, London.

POWELL, ARTHUR CECIL: "Freemasonry in Bristol," in *A.Q.C.*, vol. xlix.
"French Rituals in Manuscript" (address), in *A.Q.C.*, vol. xxx.

ROGERS, NORMAN: "200 Years of Freemasonry in Bury," in *A.Q.C.*, vol. lviii; "The Lodge of Elias Ashmole," in *A.Q.C.*, vol. lxv.

ROSENBAUM, REV. MORRIS: "Ahiman Rezon—Faithful Brother Secretary," in *A.Q.C.*, vol. xxiii; "Masonic Words and Proper Names," in *Transactions of the Installed Masters' Association*, Leeds, vol. vi.

RYLANDS. J. R.: "Early Freemasonry in Wakefield," in *A.Q.C.*, vols. lvi and lxv.

RYLANDS, WILLIAM HARRY: "The Masonic Apron," in *A.Q.C.*, vol. v.
"Masonic Symbols," in *A.Q.C.*, vol. viii.

SADLER, HENRY: *Masonic Facts and Fictions* (London, 1887).

SALZMAN, L. F.: *Building in England down to* 1540 (Oxford, 1952).

SAUNDERS, JAMES W.: "William Schaw, Master of Works to King James VI," in *A.Q.C.*, vol. l.

SIMPSON, F. M.: *A History of Architectural Development* (three volumes, London, 1910).

SPETH, G. W.: "The Foundation of Modern Freemasonry," in *A.Q.C.*, vol. ii.
"The Steinmetz Theory Critically Examined," in *A.Q.C.*, vol. i.

THORP, JOHN T.: "The Origin and Meaning of the Letter 'G' in Free-masonry," in *Merseyside*, vol. iii.
"The Two Pillars at the Porchway-entrance of King Solomon's Temple," in *Merseyside*, vol. ii.

TREVELYAN, GEORGE MACAULAY: *English Social History* (London, 1944).

TUCKETT, JAMES EDWARD SHUM: "The Origin of Additional Degrees," in *A.Q.C.*, vol. xxxii.

UNWIN, GEORGE: *Gilds and Companies of London* (London, 1908).

VIBERT, LIONEL: "Anderson's Constitutions of 1723," in *A.Q.C.*, vol. xxxvi.
"The Early Freemasonry of England and Scotland," in *A.Q.C.*, vol. xliii.
"The Evolution of the Second Degree" (Prestonian Lecture), in *Merseyside*, vol. iv.
"The Interlaced Triangles of the Royal Arch," in *Misc. Lat.*, vol. xxi.
"The Second Degree: a Theory," in *A.Q.C.*, vol. xxxix.

WESTCOTT, WILLIAM WYNN: "Rosicrucians, Their History and Aims," in
A.Q.C., vol. vii.

WILLIAMS, W. J.: "The King's Master Masons," in *A.Q.C.*, vol. xliii.

WOODFORD, REV. ADOLPHUS FREDERICK ARTHUR: *Kenning's Masonic Cyclo-
pædia* (London, 1878).

A Note on the Prestonian Lecture

The foregoing Bibliography includes mention of certain Prestonian Lectures, and it needs to be explained that in the year 1818 William Preston (his name is mentioned in earlier pages) bequeathed £300 in 3 per cent. Consolidated Bank Annuities, the interest of which was to be applied "to some well-informed Mason to deliver annually a Lecture on the First, Second, or Third Degree of the Order of Masonry according to the system practised in the Lodge of Antiquity during his Mastership." For a long time the terms of his bequest were acted upon, but certain difficulties became apparent, and no Prestonian Lecture was delivered for many years prior to 1923, in which year Grand Lodge approved a scheme under which the Board of General Purposes nominated each autumn "two Brethren of learning and responsibility" from whom the Trustees appoint the Prestonian Lecturer for the following year. In the choice of subject he is wisely allowed a scope extending rather beyond the founder's original intention. Generally he gives three official deliveries of the lecture, one to a London lodge (Preston's old lodge, Antiquity, No. 2, having a prior right but seldom exerting it), and two to provincial lodges, receiving for each a small fee from the fund, while his travelling expenses and accommodation are mostly provided by the lodges concerned; in addition, he may give any number of unofficial deliveries at the invitation of any lodges throughout the country, his travelling and accommodation being at their expense. Applications for the official delivery are made by London lodges through the Grand Secretary and by provincial lodges in the first place through the Provincial Grand Secretaries. Copies of certain of the lectures may be consulted in the library at Freemasons Hall, London, and elsewhere.

INDEX

Cross, on the,' colloquial term, 301
Crow of a cock,' 348
Crowe, F. J. W., on masonic colours, 470
Crowland—see Croyland
Crown Ale-house, lodge at, 169
Crown of martyrdom, 342
Crown worn in American Royal Arch, 528
Croyland Abbey, 324, 328, 423
Cruciform lodges, 354
Cruden, Alexander, and the veils or vails, 523
Crump, W. W. Covey, quoted and referred to, 298, 308, 311, 319, 320, 332, 526
Crusades and Crusaders, 29, 49, 319, 340
Crypt and cryptic, the words defined, 291
Crypt, vaulted, and its symbolism, 514
Crypt, York Minster, chapter opened in, 508
Cryptic degrees, 550
Cumberland, Henry Frederick, Duke of, 175
Cumberland, William Augustus, Duke of, 209
Cunnigar Hill, Aberdeen masons' meeting at, 348
Cunningham, Rev. Dr, on the word 'free,' 148
Cursing, fines for, 365, 366
Custom, ceremony, and rite, 256, 257
Customs officer's wand, 382
Cutlers Guild apprentices, 261
Cyclops, wall-builders, 20
Cylinders, Babylonian terracotta, 325
Cypress, symbol of mourning, 491
Cyrus and King Solomon's Temple, 512, 513

DALCHO, DR, 211
Dalmietta mosque, apprentice minaret at, 321
Dalvalle, Daniel, Jewish freemason, 186
d'Alviella, Count Goblet, quoted and referred to, 121, 326, 499
Damascus tessellated pavements, 399
Dan, tribe of, 307
Danger, candles thought to avert, 360; slipshod shoe possibly to avert, 268
Daniel, Glyn, on Ancient Britons, 26
Danish: altar, lamb buried under, 327; Initiate's trowel jewel, 448, lodges, pillars in, 357, 376, 377; swearing of oath, 275; voters standing on stones, 412
Darius and Solomon's Temple, 513
Darkness, emblems and significance of, 267, 268, 290
Darnley, Edward Bligh, second Earl of, Grand Master, 368
Dassigny, Dr Fifield, and early Royal Arch, 199, 496
Daughter of a freemason ('Lewisa'), 419
David, the Biblical, 122, 358, 512; shield of, 519
Davies, Widow, 147
Day: high, 322; "to see in," 322; well-spent, 24-in. gauge the emblem of, 430
Day, H. F., drawing by, 31
Day, J. W.: The Banner Song, 471
De Soto's expedition, 115
Deacon of Tailors' Fraternity, 67
Deacons: in 'Antient' lodges, 202, 378; apprentices as, 137, 138; badges, Plates XII, XXVIII; black rods, 352; Church, 357, 379; crossed wands, 383, 384; derivation of word, 378; Grand, 176; investing, with wand, 249, 380; in Irish lodges, 202, 379; jewels, 379,

467; Junior, admit Brethren in American lodges, 392; as messengers, 379; in 'Modern' lodges, 219, 378, 379; presidents of operative lodges, 376; regular officers, 364; a Scots term, 128, 129, 376, 378; Stewards as, 380; in Swalwell Lodge (1734), 379; Taster's, 379; their wands—see Wand: Wardens closely related to, 376, 378, 379
Dead, hour-glass buried with the, 357
Deal lodge officers' wands, 384
Death: colour emblem, 472, 473; the great leveller, 442; its contemplation and the Hiramic legend, 319; violent, emblem of, 430
Death benefit, 486
Decanters, 482
Decorated period or style, 28
Defeat, emblem of, 270
Defoe, Daniel, 102
Degree (the word): definitions and meanings, 232, 233; lodge opened 'in' a, 232; occurrence of word in medieval manuscripts, etc., 232; used in modern sense in 1730, 232
Degrees—see also Rite: ancient, providing foundations of present degrees, 238–242; aprons with emblems of many, 456; 'Antients' controversy affects, 193, 219, 224; ashlar so suspended as to indicate, 412; Chair (installation ceremony), 251; charity test in relation to, 240; comparison of pre-1717 with to-day's, 238–242; Craft or symbolic, 428; Degree, Fourth (early Royal Arch), 495, 507; elaboration of, by learned speculatives?, 233; Fellow Craft qualification for Master's Chair in relation to, 235, 236, 241, 242; five, in one evening, 245; 'Five Points' and relationship between, 241; Hebraic phrases but Christian teaching, 121; how early lodges may have adapted themselves to rearrangement of, 239; 'in the making,' 240; Installation ceremony and relationship between, 241; Installed Master only may confer, 377, 378; intervals between conferring, 246; Lodge of Reconciliation revises, 223, 224; 'lost secret restored in higher degrees,' 121; minutes read in each, 232; one-degree theory, Findel's, 233; one comprehensive, possible before 1717?, 231; one or two in Ashmole's day, 233; proposal, etc., separate to each, 266; rapid progress through, 244–246; Regulation XIII (1723) in relation to, 234–238; square in blazing star to indicate, 300; symbolic, 294; Third Degree not everywhere known till middle eighteenth century, 231; three, mentioned in 1711–30 period, 231, 233, 242 243; three, in Paris, Scotland, and Sweden (1731–37), 244; three, possible before 1717, 231; three lights to indicate, 220; tracing-board for both First and Second, 241; how two became three, 231; two in 1717–23 period or earlier, 231, 233; two, only, worked in places long after 1717, 243; two or more, in one evening, 244, 245; Warden may not confer, 377
Deity—see God
De la Mare, Walter, on John Peel's funeral, 491
Delarant, Bro.: his 'lewisa,' 419
Delorme, Charles, French physician, 520
Delvalle, Daniel, Jewish freemason, 186